MW01378542

CAMBRIDGE
SPECTRUM
MATHS 9

Carol Osborne and J. Goodman   5.3

CAMBRIDGE
UNIVERSITY PRESS

PUBLISHED BY THE PRESS SYNDICATE OF THE UNIVERSITY OF CAMBRIDGE
The Pitt Building, Trumpington Street, Cambridge, United Kingdom

CAMBRIDGE UNIVERSITY PRESS
The Edinburgh Building, Cambridge CB2 2RU, UK
40 West 20th Street, New York, NY 10011–4211, USA
477 Williamstown Road, Port Melbourne, VIC 3207, Australia
Ruiz de Alarcón 13, 28014 Madrid, Spain
Dock House, The Waterfront, Cape Town 8001, South Africa

http://www.cambridge.edu.au

First published in 2004

Printed in Singapore by Craft Print International Ltd

Typeface New Aster 9.5/12 pt
System Adobe Framemaker® [PH]

National Library of Australia Cataloguing in Publication data
  Osborne, Carol, 1962– .
  Spectrum mathematics. 5.3 Year 9 advanced.
  For secondary school students.
  ISBN 0 521 53043 1.
  1. Mathematics – Juvenile literature. 2. Mathematics –
  Problems, exercises, etc. I. Priddle, A. G. (Anthony
  George). II. Goodman, Jennifer. III. Title.
510.76

ISBN 0 521 53043 1

Contents

Introduction : Spectrum 9 5.3

While the content changes in the 2004 Mathematics Syllabus are small, Cambridge has taken the opportunity to fully revise the original successful *Spectrum Mathematics Year 9 Advanced* to comprehensively address the requirements of Year 9 students aiming to complete Stage 5.3 when they are in Year 10. The material in *Cambridge Spectrum Maths 9 5.3* covers all of the Syllabus Outcomes for Stages 5.1, 5.2 and 5.3. Extensive reviews were conducted with teachers from a wide range of schools in order to improve on the original text.

As a result, this new edition is able to cater for a wider range of abilities. Revisions were made to the chapter sequence and the level of development within a chapter, and the exercises have been given three levels. Initial questions are straightforward in style, and are closely tied to the Worked Examples to ensure early success. Level 2 questions are designed to develop the rules and concepts of the section and may incorporate more than one step, explanations, applications involving the new concepts and links to previous sections. Where appropriate, more challenging Level 3 questions have been included in exercises to broaden and extend understanding. These questions require students to apply concepts to unfamiliar situations, or demonstrate superior problem solving skills.

Central to the new Syllabus is the idea of continuity—'take the student from where they are at'. *Cambridge Spectrum Maths 9 5.3* links prior learning to the new work in each chapter through an introductory MathsCheck. Related Stage 4 Outcomes are listed alongside Stage 5 Outcomes at the start of each chapter and are directly linked to syllabus requirements. Additional course material covering prior (Year 8) and further (Year 10) learning is provided on the Teacher CD-ROM to allow teachers the flexibility to cater for students at different levels in different content areas.

In the *Cambridge Spectrum Maths* series, Working Mathematically is treated as an approach rather than a topic and throughout the text students are asked to apply strategies, communicate their solutions, display questioning and reasoning skills as well as reflect on their chosen methods and solutions. Theory explanations use colour extensively to highlight new ideas and to demonstrate important steps in the solutions to the Worked Examples. Frequent hint boxes coach the student on anticipated common misunderstandings.

The material has been written to meet the requirements of both a classroom lesson and homework. The enhanced CD-ROM version of the text (*E-Book Plus*) can be taken home, weighty school bags can be avoided and the student has access to a large range of interactive resources that aid understanding. The work in the student text and *E-Book Plus* CD-ROM can be supplemented by the wealth of additional planning, extension, revision and assessment tasks that can be printed from the Teacher CD-ROM. Teachers are permitted to make copies of these files for use within their school.

We are confident we have published a text that will enhance the learning of mathematics and appeal to both students and teachers. We welcome any feedback, which may be sent to:

Education Commissioning Editor, Mathematics
Cambridge University Press
477 Williamstown Road
Port Melbourne 3207
Email: educationpublishing@cambridge.edu.au

At each level Spectrum offers ...

The full colour text book

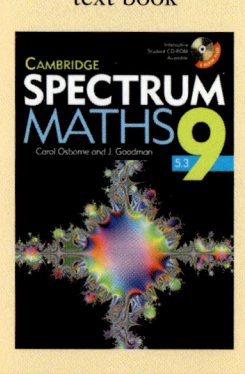

A Resource CD-ROM for your teacher

Book and student CD-ROM package

The Student CD-ROM offers the full text PLUS additional interactive study resources

In each chapter you will find ...

Keeping Mathematically Fit exercises to refresh maths fundamentals

Chapter Review Exercises

Maths Check Revision of existing maths skills required for success in this chapter

In-depth study of the topic

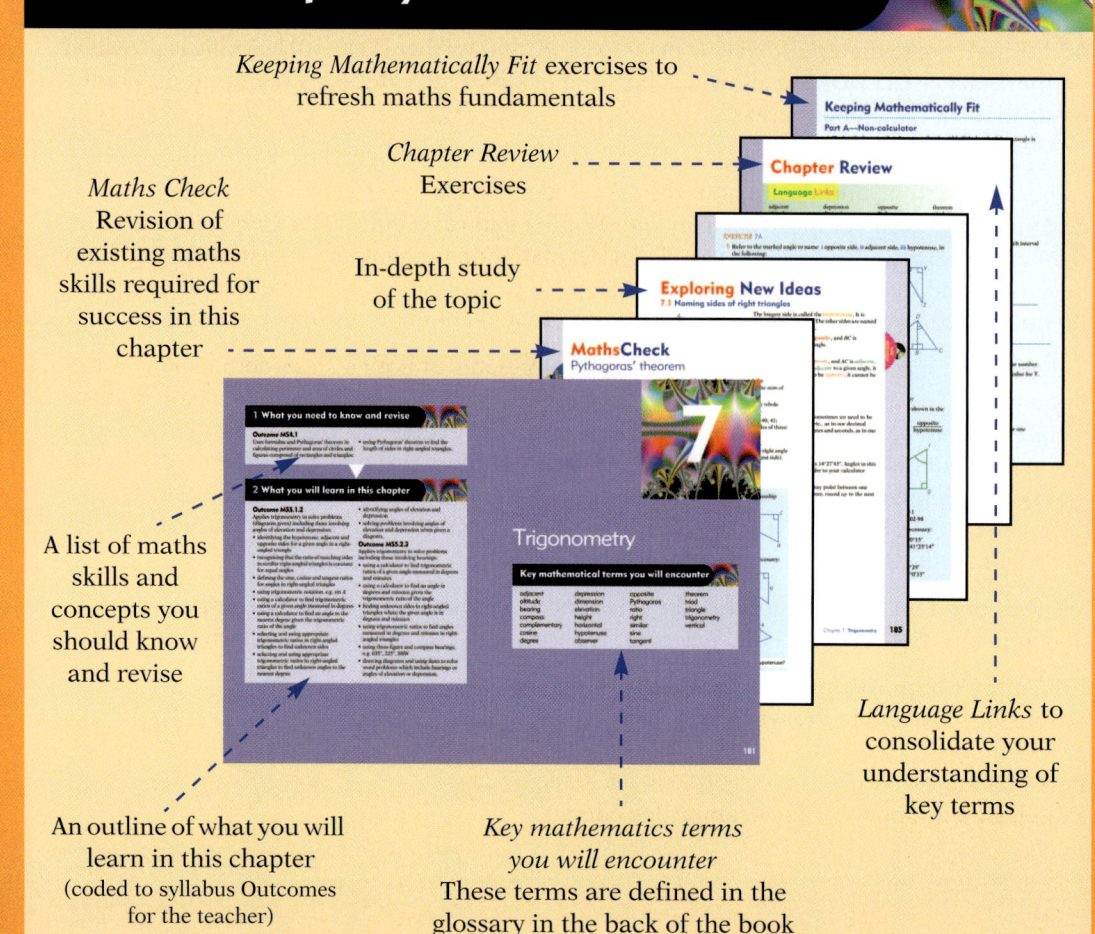

Language Links to consolidate your understanding of key terms

A list of maths skills and concepts you should know and revise

An outline of what you will learn in this chapter (coded to syllabus Outcomes for the teacher)

Key mathematics terms you will encounter These terms are defined in the glossary in the back of the book

How to use our navigation tools ...

Theory explanations introduce each new idea with clear and concise explanations that make every topic immediately understandable.

Worked examples demonstrate how to set out your work. Effective use of colour highlights mathematical steps.

Colour-coded links to the student CD-ROM help you to confidently select the appropriate additional interactive resources provided on the CD-ROM.

Links to support material on Teacher CD-ROM.

Key facts are summarised throughout the text.

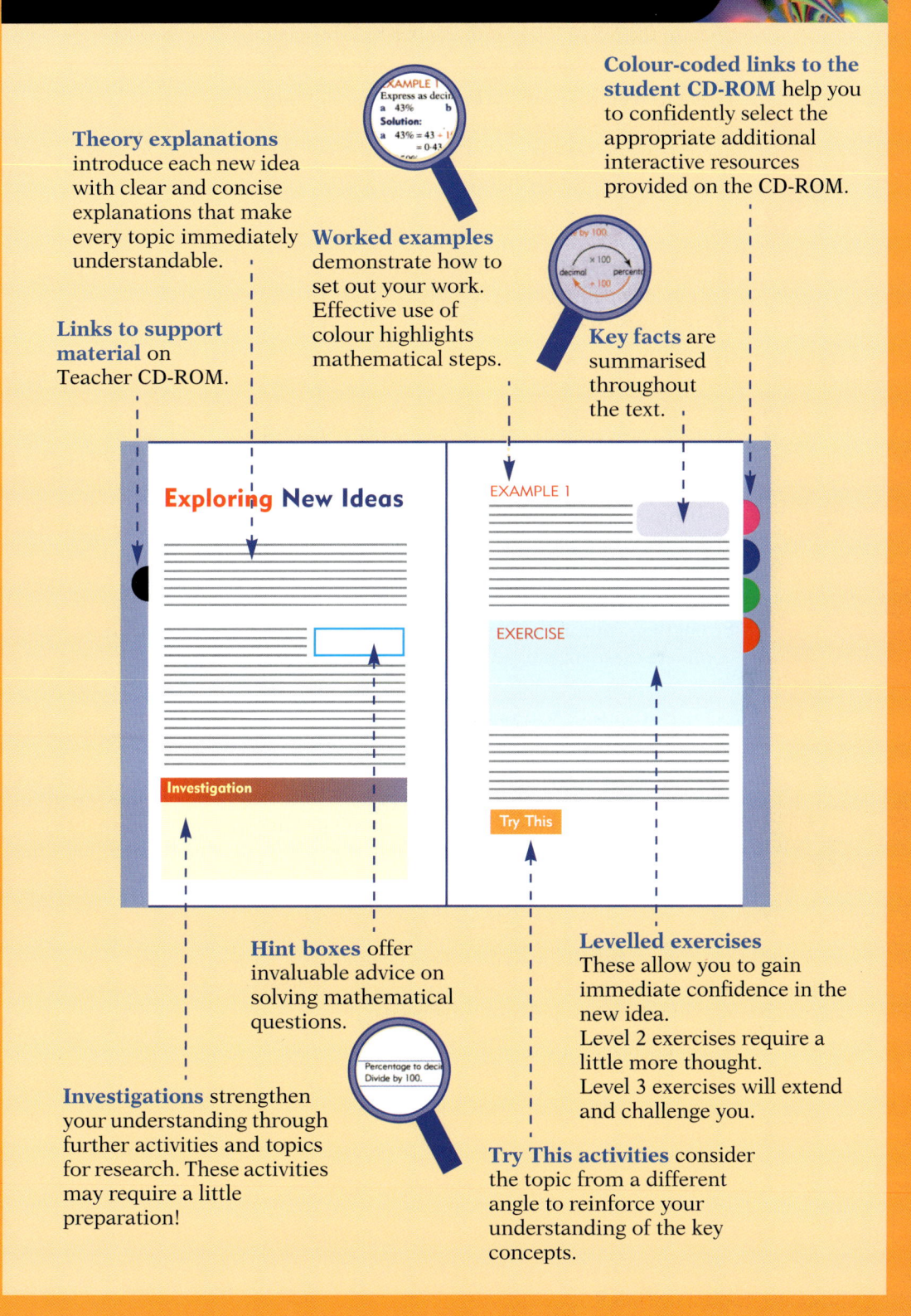

Hint boxes offer invaluable advice on solving mathematical questions.

Levelled exercises
These allow you to gain immediate confidence in the new idea.
Level 2 exercises require a little more thought.
Level 3 exercises will extend and challenge you.

Investigations strengthen your understanding through further activities and topics for research. These activities may require a little preparation!

Try This activities consider the topic from a different angle to reinforce your understanding of the key concepts.

Using the CD-ROMs

The *Cambridge Spectrum Maths 9 5.3 E-Book Plus* provides students with an enhanced electronic copy of the textbook, *Cambridge Spectrum Maths 9 5.3*. Appropriate additional resources, written to the NSW 2004 Mathematics Syllabus, can be launched directly from icons on the page of the electronic text.

Links to web research activities on the *E-Book Plus*
Research various aspects of mathematics – including concepts, personalities and the history of mathematical ideas – using the web. Links to particularly useful websites are included.

Links to interactive geometry activities on the *E-Book Plus*
Explore geometric concepts independently using current technology applications. Activities for both Cabri Geometry and Geometer's Sketchpad are offered.

Links to spreadsheet activities on the *E-Book Plus*
Enhance your understanding of mathematical concepts using dynamic Excel activities. Many activities are linked to HELP files offering hints for solving the problems.

Links to investigative activities on the *E-Book Plus*
Strengthen your understanding of key concepts using a variety of resources to complete these investigations.

Links to graphic calculator activities on the *E-Book Plus*
Use your graphic calculator to gain greater understanding of mathematical concepts with boxplots, histograms, graph plotting and area and volume calculations. Instructions are given for both the Texas Instruments TI-83 and the Casio-FX-7400G.

There is also a Teacher CD-ROM in the *Cambridge Spectrum 9 5.3 Maths* series. This Teacher CD-ROM provides a rich resource of planning, testing, challenging and assessing activities that can be tailored to meet specific learning needs.

These icons indicate to your teacher that there are additional resources on the *Spectrum Maths 9 Teacher CD-ROM*.

Contents list for *E-Book Plus* and Teacher CD-ROM

Chapter	Teacher CD Resources		E-Book Plus Resources	
6	MathsCheck	MathsCheck	Web research	Plotted?
6	Additional activities	Practical graphs and answers	Spreadsheet activity	Airmail
6	Additional activities	Investigation – Maximum/minimum room temperatures	Spreadsheet activity	Day trip
6	Chapter review material	Tests and answers	Spreadsheet activity	Handling costs
6	Chapter review material	Analysis Q & A	Spreadsheet activity	Hot water
6	KMF	Keeping fit Q & A	Spreadsheet activity	Misleading profits
6			Spreadsheet activity	Metric paper sizes
6			Spreadsheet activity	Runner's progress
6			Spreadsheet activity	Growing twins
6			Graphic calculator activities	Growing twins
6			Graphic calculator activities	Hot water
6			Graphic calculator activities	Runner's progress
6			Graphic calculator activities	Day trip
7	MathsCheck	MathsCheck	Web research	Hipparchus
7	Additional activities	Trigonometry puzzle	Web research	Shadow measurement
7	Additional activities	What's the bearing? and answers	Spreadsheet activity	Triads – subtraction process
7	Additional activities	Two triangle trigonometry and answers	Interactive geometry	Investigation goal A (GSP/CAB)
7	Chapter review material	Tests and answers	Interactive geometry	Investigation goal B (GSP/CAB)
7	Chapter review material	Analysis Q & A	Interactive geometry	Measuring inaccessible distances A (GSP/CAB)
7	KMF	Keeping fit Q & A	Interactive geometry	Measuring inaccessible distances B (GAP/CAB)
7			Interactive geometry	Trigonometric ratios and angles (GSP/CAB)
8	MathsCheck	MathsCheck	Web research	Coordinate geometry
8	Additional activities	Graphing straight lines and answers	Spreadsheet activity	Baby weight
8	Additional activities	Graphing using intercepts and answers	Spreadsheet activity	Calf weight
8	Additional activities	Investigation – Celsius and Fahrenheit	Spreadsheet activity	Paydays
8	Additional activities	Co-ordinate geometry review	Spreadsheet activity	Car rental
8	Chapter review material	Tests and answers	Spreadsheet activity	Finding the rule
8	Chapter review material	Analysis Q & A	Interactive geometry	Distance between two ports (GSP/CAB)
8	KMF	Keeping fit Q & A	Interactive geometry	Gradient (GSP/CAB)
8			Interactive geometry	Characteristics of linear graphs (GSP/CAB)
8			Interactive geometry	Midpoint of an interval (GSP/CAB)
8			Interactive geometry	Problems (GSP/CAB)
8			Graphic calculator activities	Baby weight predictions
8			Graphic calculator activities	Calf weight predictions
8			Graphic calculator activities	Car rental predictions
8			Graphic calculator activities	Function analysis
8			Graphic calculator activities	Characteristics of linear graphs
8			Graphic calculator activities	Plot and match

Symbols and abbreviations

$=$	is equal to
$\neq$	is not equal to
$\approx$ or $\doteq$	is approximately equal to
$<$	is less than
$>$	is more than
$+$	addition operation (plus)
$-$	subtraction (minus)
$\times$	multiplication (times)
$\div$	division (divided by)
$\sqrt{\ }$	square root
$\sqrt[3]{\ }$	cube root
2^3	two to the third power $(2 \times 2 \times 2)$ index notation
HCF	highest common factor
LCM	lowest common multiple
$0.\dot{8}$	a decimal in which the 8 recurs forever
$0.\dot{2}3\dot{6}$	a decimal in which the 236 repeats forever
$\frac{3}{4}$	the common fraction three fourths, or $3 \div 4$
LCD	lowest common denominator
$\angle ABC$	angle A, B, C; B is the vertex of $A\hat{B}C$ or turning point
ㄴ	right angle; 90°
$72°$	72 degrees; angle measurement
A B	interval AB
A B	line AB
A B	ray AB
$\perp$	is perpendicular to
$\parallel$	is parallel to
	parallel lines

	lines equal in length
km	kilometre
m	metre
cm	centimetre
mm	millimetre
kg	kilogram
g	gram
mg	milligram
ML	megalitre
kL	kilolitre (capacity; liquids)
L	litre
mL	millilitre
ha	hectare
m^2	square metre (area)
m^3	cubic metre (volume)
$6t$	$6 \times t$, where t is an algebraic symbol or pronumeral whose value may vary
$\%$	percentage; hundredths
$P = 2(l + b)$	perimeter of a rectangle equals 2 times the sum of length and breadth
$P = 4s$	perimeter of a square equals 4 times the side
$A = lb$	area of a rectangle equals length times breadth
$A = s^2$	area of a square equals side squared
$A = \dfrac{bh}{2}$	area of a triangle equals base times perpendicular height divided by 2
$V = lbh$	volume of a rectangular prism equals length times breadth times height
3:45	digital clock display for forty-five minutes past three **am** or **pm**
0345 h	24-hour system of expression for the same time **am**
1545 h	24-hour time for 3:45 **pm**

Reviewer details

Dr Irene Abbott, formerly Mathematics Coordinator at Mt St Benedict College, Pennant Hills, is currently teaching part time at Normanhurst Boys' High School.

Cindy Berwick, Mathematics Head Teacher, Marrickville High School.

Ann Commens has been a mathematics teacher for over 20 years, and is a member of the NSW Maths Association.

Colin Robinson, Moorebank High School.

Desley Williams, Tara Anglican School for Girls.

Tony Priddle, a key author for the first edition of Spectrum Maths 9, provided encouragement and support in the development of this new edition.

Acknowledgments

The author and publisher would like to thank the following for permission to reproduce material:

Page 7 Neil Templeman, Vale Royal Athletic Club, Cheshire, England; 12, 118, 349 Photolibrary.com; 16 Courtesy Images SI Inc.; 20 © Nick Benjaminsz; 33, 45, 82, 104 (bottom), 188, 203, 235, 284, 286 (bottom), Tourism Queensland; 36 © David Bamber; 37, 97, 166, 288, 304, 365, 406 (top) Photodisc Australia; 39 NASA; 40 Courtesy James Evarts; 43, 162, 355 © Tim Gulick; 46, 393 Carlos Gustavo Curado; 58 (top) © Emmanuel Wuyts (bottom) Photo by Emily W courtesy: the charger.com; 59 © David E. Henderson; 63 © Jan De Bondt; 65 NY State Fair; 67 Martin Stieglmayer, Vienna, Austria; 68 MDBC; 71, 106, 143 imageafter.com; 76 Photo by Martin Kessel; 78 spaceimaging; 89 © Balazs Dudas ; 93 © Anthony Crowley; 104 (top), 105, 120, 205, 283, 377, 382, 408, 417 Courtesy Tourism New South Wales, 109 Library of Congress; 115 © Stella Reese; 131, 299, 309, 371 freeimages.com; 142 Nick Winchester; 152 © Giuseppe Costanza; 164 © Katje Borba; 172 © Graeme Rainsbury; 191, 247, 286 (top) USDA; 193 Courtesy Mi-Tek; 208 © Wout J Reinders; 209 © Boldizsar Csernak; 211 Courtesy St Joseph's College: www.terrace.qld.edu.au; 215 © Boris Kukec; 217 Courtesy Reserve Bank of Australia; 220 www.bigfoto.com; 248 © Adam Fowler; 260 © Didier Faucher; 279 © Ryan Thomas; 280 red zone laboratories, san jose, California; 281 © Ren Schroeder; 289 Courtesy Di Jones Real Estate; 302 Texas Instruments; 306, 313 Courtesy St.George Bank; 352 Roy Morgan Research; 361 © Erika Thorpe; 363 © Randall Hop; 366 © Atena Kasper; 385© Simon George; 400 © Andras Deak; 403 © Leslie Fay Richards; 405 © Sasha Davas, 406 (bottom) Hale Indian River Groves; 413 © Ryan Scott Waxberg; 421 © Euan McInnes.

Every effort has been made to trace and acknowledge copyright but there may be instances where this has not been possible. Cambridge University Press would welcome any information that would redress this situation.

1 What you need to know and revise

Outcome PAS 4.2:
Creates, records, analyses and generalises number patterns using words and algebraic symbols in a variety of ways:
- building and describing geometric patterns, in words and algebraic symbols and representing the relationship on a number grid
- identifying and describing a number pattern, in words and algebraic symbols and representing the relationship on a number grid.

2 What you will learn in this chapter

Outcome PAS 5.1.1:
Applies the index laws to simplify algebraic expressions:
- identifying and using the laws relating to positive integer indices
- establishing and using the index law for a power of zero
- simplifying algebraic expressions that include index notation.

Outcome PAS 5.2.1:
Simplifies, expands and factorises algebraic expressions involving fractions and negative and fractional indices:
- writing and using the index laws including fractional and negative indices
- expanding and simplifying expressions involving grouping symbols
- factorising by determining common factors.

Outcome PAS 5.3.1:
Uses algebraic techniques to simplify expressions, expand binomial products and factorise quadratic expressions:
- simplifying algebraic expressions
- expanding binomial products
- the difference of two squares
- perfect squares
- factorising using the HCF.

Working Mathematically outcomes WMS 5.1, 5.2, 5.3
Students will be required to *question*, *apply strategies*, *communicate*, *reason* and *reflect* in the sections of this chapter.

Algebra so far

MathsCheck
Algebra so far

1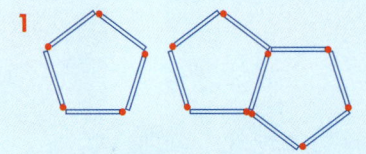

No. of pentagons (n)	1	2	3	4	5	...
No. of matches (m)	5	...				

  a How are the numbers of pentagons and matches related? Use algebra to show it.
  b How many matches would build 18 pentagons?
  c How many pentagons can be built from exactly 37 matches?
  d Build a similar sequence of *hexagons*.
  e Compile a table and find the rule in algebra.
  f Develop a *general* rule for all such number polygon type sequences.

2 a If $y = x + 2$, copy and complete the table of values below.

x	$^-2$	$^-1$	0	1	2
y					

  b If $y = 2 - 2x$, copy and complete the table of values below.

x	$^-2$	$^-1$	0	1	2
y					

  c On a number plane, sketch the relationships from parts **a** and **b** above. Where do the two lines cross?

3 Write a rule for the nth term in each of the following:

  a 1, 2, 3, 4, ...   **b** 0, 3, 8, ...   **c** $1, \frac{1}{2}, \frac{1}{3}, ...$

4 Find the value of the fifteenth term in each of the patterns in question **2**.

5 Find the value of the $(n + 1)$th term for each of the patterns in question **2**.

6 If $a = 3$, $b = 1$, $c = 4$ and $d = 0$, find the value of:

  a $c^3 + \dfrac{d}{b}$ **b** $\dfrac{ac - d}{b^2}$ **c** $\dfrac{d + bc}{^-ac}$

7 If $a = 7$, $b = ^-6$, $c = ^-4$, find the value of:

  a $b^2 - c^2$ **b** $\dfrac{^-bc}{2}$ **c** ab^2c

8 Evaluate, using replacements given:

  a $\dfrac{1}{2}xy; x = 20, y = 5$ **b** $x^2 + 5x + 6; x = ^-2$ **c** $^-3a^2 + 5a - 7; a = ^-3$

9 Give the value of the constant term (the term with no pronumeral) in:

  a $x^2 + 3x + 4$ **b** $x^3 - x^2 + x$ **c** $x^2 + 3$

  d $\dfrac{x^2 + x + 1}{2}$ **e** $7x$

10 Give the coefficient of x in each of the expressions in question **9**.

In $x^2 - 6x + 1$
constant term $= 1$
coefficient of $x = {}^-6$

11 Write expressions for the following:

    a the sum of $3x$ and $4ab$
    b the difference between $6t$ and $2ab$
    c the product of $4g$ and $(a + b)$
    d $6ab$ divided into $2m$ equal shares.

12 Write an expression for each of the following:

    a the cost of x CDs at $\$(4 + p)$ each
    b the average of $3x$ and $5x$
    c the age of 14 year old in x years' time
    d the counting number coming 3 before n
    e the next odd number after $5t$ (given $5t$ is odd)
    f the distance travelled in $2x$ hours at y km/h
    g the length remaining when four pieces of carpet, each $(x + 2)$ metres long, are cut from a $10x$ metre roll
    h the perimeter of a rectangle of length $(a + 6)$ metres, width $(a + 2)$ metres
    i area of a triangle of base t metres, altitude $(t + 2)$ metres.

13 Simplify where possible:

    a $8h + 5 + 3h - 2$
    b $9a - a + 4 + 3c$
    c $7p - 12p$
    d ${}^-5x^2 + 3x - 7x - 2x^2$

14 Simplify:

    a $4 \times a \times 3 \times 6$
    b $a \times a \times b$
    c ${}^-3a \times 4b$
    d $16xy \div 8x$
    e $x \div x$
    f $0 \div a$
    g $(4x + 6x) \div 20x$
    h $7x \times 6x \div 3x^2$

15 Simplify each algebraic expression:

    a $4p \times \dfrac{1}{2}t$
    b $3d \times {}^-2t \times {}^-4d$
    c $\dfrac{18a}{12b}$
    d $25pt \div 15pt^2$
    e $4cd^2 \div 2c$
    f ${}^-24x^2y \div 36xy^2$

16 The measures of the sides in the following figures are given in terms of a and b. Find a simplified expression for perimeter:

    a

    b

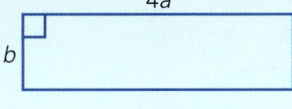

    c

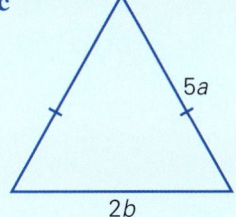

    d

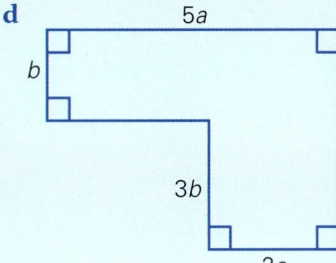

17 For each expression, simplify first, then evaluate if $x = 4$, $y = 3$ and $a = {}^-2$:

   a $5a - 3a - a + x^y$ **b** $x^2 + 2x - 5x + a^y$

18 Write the simplest expression for the area of each figure:

   a 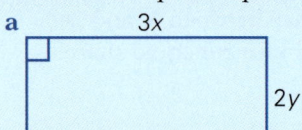   **b** 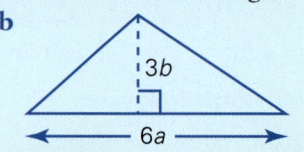   **c**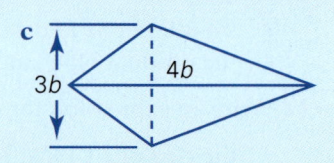

19 Write the simplest expression for the shaded area in each figure:

   a 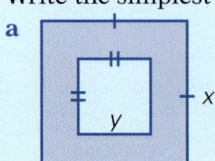   **b** 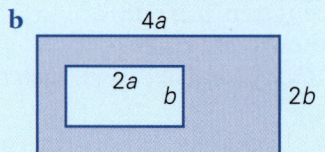   **c**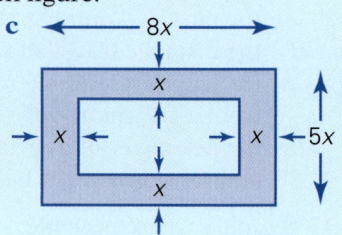

20 Expand:

   a $(a + 5)x$ **b** $(3p - t)t$ **c** $7a(2a - 5b)$ **d** $^-3(x + 5)$ **e** $^-(4x - 5a)$

21 Expand and simplify:

   a $6 + 4(2x + 1)$ **b** $x + 3(x - 1) - 6$ **c** $x + 8(5 - x)$ **d** $8(x - 4) + 10x + 3$

22 Expand and simplify:

   a $8x - 2(x + 3)$ **b** $x^2 - x(x + 3)$ **c** $12 - (3x + 5)$
   d $2x^2 - x(x - 3)$ **e** $a^2 + b - (a^2 - b)$ **f** $x + 7 - 3(x - 4)$

23 Expand and simplify:

   a $5(x + 1) + 2(x - 1)$ **b** $x(x + 2) + 5(x + 2)$ **c** $5(x + 1) - 2(x - 1)$
   d $3(2 - x) + 2(x + 2)$ **e** $x(x + 7) - 3(x + 7)$ **f** $x(3 - x) - 5(x + 1)$

24 If $f(x) = x^2 + 4x - 1$, evaluate:

   a $f(0)$ **b** $f(2)$ **c** $f(^-1)$ **d** $f(\frac{1}{2})$ **e** $f(^-x)$ **f** $f(2p)$

25 $f(A) = 4 - A^2$. Find:

   a $f(^-1)$ **b** $f(6)$ **c** $f(3A)$ **d** $f(^-B)$ **e** $f(^-A)$

26 If $f(x) = 3x - 4$ find $f(x + h)$

27 $f(p) = p^2 + p$. Find:

   a $f(0)$ **b** $f(^-1)$ **c** $f(\frac{1}{2})$ **d** $f(^-p)$

28 A row of n tables is placed between two parallel walls; each table is w metres wide. The tables are placed so that there is 1 m between each table and 1 m to the walls. What is the width of the room?

29 How many times must the number a be subtracted from a^2 to give a result of zero?

30 If a is the smallest of three consecutive odd numbers, what is their sum?

TEACHER

4

Exploring New Ideas

1.1 General binomial expansions

Francois Viete (1591) of France did much of the development of symbolic algebra, using vowels to represent unknown quantities and consonants for known ones.

We have inherited a system that uses letters and symbols, known as pronumerals. A pronumeral may stand for a single number or a variable (many different values).

Last year we saw that algebraic expressions could be simplified. In this section we will look at how expressions involving two factors in brackets can be simplified by expanding.

EXAMPLE 1

Expand:

$(a + 4)(a + 3)$

$$(a + b)(c + d)$$
$$= a(c + d) + b(c + d)$$

Solution

$(a + 4)(a + 3)$
$= a(a + 3) + 4(a + 3)$
$= a^2 + 3a + 4a + 12$
$= a^2 + 7a + 12$

	a	4
a	a^2	$4a$
3	$3a$	12

$= a^2 + 3a + 4a + 12$
$= a^2 + 7a + 12$

You can consider these binomial products by finding the area of the rectangle.

$a \times a = a^2$
$a \times a^2 = a^3$
$a^2 \times a^2 = a^4$

Do you remember the rule?

EXAMPLE 2

Expand:

$(x - 2)(2x + 3)$

Solution

$(x - 2)(2x + 3)$
$= x(2x + 3) - 2(2x + 3)$
$= 2x^2 + 3x - 4x - 6$
$= 2x^2 - x - 6$

EXAMPLE 3

Expand:

$(x^2 + x - 3)(x^2 - x + 1)$

We will take a closer look at indices later in the chapter.

Solution

$(x^2 + x - 3)(x^2 - x + 1)$
$= x^2(x^2 - x + 1) + x(x^2 - x + 1) - 3(x^2 - x + 1)$
$= x^4 - x^3 + x^2 + x^3 - x^2 + x - 3x^2 + 3x - 3$
$= x^4 + 4x - 3$

EXERCISE 1A

1 Copy and complete:

a $(a + 3)(m + 5)$
$= (a + 3) \ldots + (a + 3) \ldots$
$= am + \ldots + 5a + \ldots$

b $(x + 3)(x + 6)$
$= (x + 3) \ldots + (x + 3) \ldots$
$= x^2 + \ldots + 6x + \ldots$
$= x^2 + \ldots + 18$

c $(a + 2)(a - 3)$
$= (a + 2) \ldots + (a + 2) \ldots$
$= a^2 + \ldots + \ldots + \ldots$
$= a^2 + \ldots + \ldots$

d

	m	4
m	m^2	$4m$
6	$6m$	$\ldots$

e

	x	$^-6$
x		
8		$^-48$

f

	a	$^-7$
a		
$^-1$		

2 Expand and simplify where possible:

a	$(b+2)(b+4)$	**b**	$(d+4)(d+1)$	**c**	$(a+3)(b+5)$
d	$(x+3)(x+3)$	**e**	$(a+4)(a+4)$	**f**	$(c+6)(c-2)$
g	$(x-1)(x+7)$	**h**	$(a+5)(a-5)$	**i**	$(x+4)(x-4)$
j	$(c-6)(c+6)$	**k**	$(d-4)(d-2)$	**l**	$(k-7)(k-7)$
m	$(a+3)(b-4)$	**n**	$(2x+7)(x-4)$	**o**	$(x-6)(3x+5)$
p	$(8t-6)(2t-3)$	**q**	$(2k-5)(4k-3)$	**r**	$(4n-3)^2$
s	$(2+x)(3-x)$	**t**	$(2x+4)(x-1)$	**u**	$2(x+2)(x-1)$

>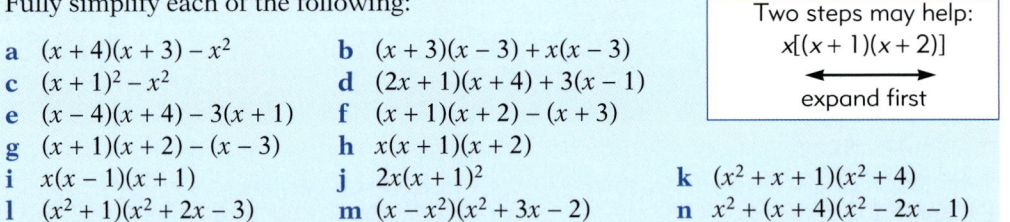
> $(b+2)(b+4)$
> First outer, inner last.
> It's foiled!

3 Expand and simplify:

a	$(x+1)(x-1)$	**b**	$(a+4)(a-4)$	**c**	$(x+y)(x-y)$
d	$(x-2)(x+2)$	**e**	$(2x+1)(2x-1)$	**f**	$(2x+y)(2x-y)$
g	$(x+3)(x-3)$	**h**	$(3x+4)(3x-4)$	**i**	$(5-x)(5+x)$
j	$(a-4)(a+4)$	**k**	$(y+6)(y-6)$	**l**	$(5y-x)(5y+x)$

4 Expand and simplify:

a	$(x+4)^2$	**b**	$(x-4)^2$	**c**	$(2x+3)^2$	**d**	$(2x-3)^2$
e	$(5+x)^2$	**f**	$(5-x)^2$	**g**	$(3x+2y)^2$		

5 Fully simplify each of the following:

a	$(x+4)(x+3)-x^2$	**b**	$(x+3)(x-3)+x(x-3)$		
c	$(x+1)^2-x^2$	**d**	$(2x+1)(x+4)+3(x-1)$		
e	$(x-4)(x+4)-3(x+1)$	**f**	$(x+1)(x+2)-(x+3)$		
g	$(x+1)(x+2)-(x-3)$	**h**	$x(x+1)(x+2)$		
i	$x(x-1)(x+1)$	**j**	$2x(x+1)^2$	**k**	$(x^2+x+1)(x^2+4)$
l	$(x^2+1)(x^2+2x-3)$	**m**	$(x-x^2)(x^2+3x-2)$	**n**	$x^2+(x+4)(x^2-2x-1)$

> Two steps may help:
> $x[(x+1)(x+2)]$
> expand first

1.2 Special expansion patterns

When expanding the binomial products in the previous exercise you may have noticed in question 3 and question 4 that the answers formed a pattern for each question. We can use these patterns to quickly expand perfect squares $(a \pm b)^2$ and the difference of the two squares $(a+b)(a-b)$.

Did you notice something special about question 3 and question 4 in the previous exercise?

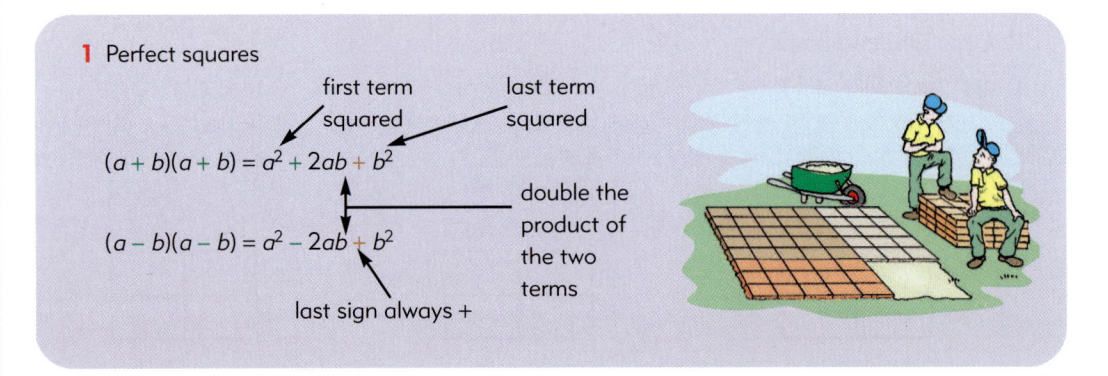

1 Perfect squares

first term squared — last term squared

$$(a+b)(a+b) = a^2 + 2ab + b^2$$

$$(a-b)(a-b) = a^2 - 2ab + b^2$$

double the product of the two terms

last sign always +

2 Difference of two squares

$$(a + b)(a - b) = a^2 - b^2$$

Square of the first term *minus* the square of the second term.

EXAMPLE 1

Expand:

a　$(x - 5)^2$　　　　**b**　$(3d + 4)^2$

Solution

a　$(x - 5)^2$
$= x^2 - (2 \times x \times 5) + (^-5)^2$
$= x^2 - 10x + 25$

b　$(3d + 4)^2$
$= (3d)^2 + (2 \times 3d \times 4) + (4)^2$
$= 9d^2 + 24d + 16$

EXAMPLE 2

Expand:

a　$(x + 3)(x - 3)$　　　　**b**　$(2m - 7)(2m + 7)$

Solution

a　$(x + 3)(x - 3)$
$= x^2 - 3^2$
$= x^2 - 9$

b　$(2m - 7)(2m + 7)$
$= (2m)^2 - (7)^2$
$= 4m^2 - 49$

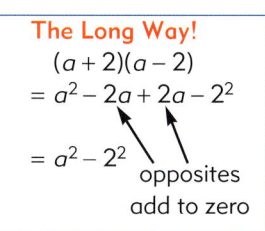

The height reached by a javelin is given by
$h = \dfrac{^-r}{16}(d - 10)^2 + 9$

EXERCISE 1B

1 Expand and simplify:

a　$(a + 2)^2$　　　**b**　$(a - 2)^2$　　　**c**　$(x + 3)^2$　　　**d**　$(x - 3)^2$
e　$(c + 8)^2$　　　**f**　$(d + 10)^2$　　**g**　$(b - 4)^2$　　　**h**　$(c - 5)^2$
i　$(d + 1)^2$　　　**j**　$(x - 1)^2$　　　**k**　$(2k + 1)^2$　　**l**　$(2k - 1)^2$
m　$(2n + 3)^2$　　**n**　$(3x + 4)^2$　　**o**　$(5a + 7)^2$　　**p**　$(5 + 3f)^2$

q　$(5x - 4)^2$　　**r**　$(2a + \frac{1}{2})^2$　　**s**　$(8 - 2p)^2$　　**t**　$\left(^-6x - \dfrac{3}{4}\right)^2$

2 Expand and simplify:

a　$(a + 4)(a - 4)$　　　**b**　$(a - 4)(a + 4)$　　　**c**　$(x + 5)(x - 5)$
d　$(c - 7)(c + 7)$　　　**e**　$(d - 8)(d + 8)$　　　**f**　$(10 + h)(10 - h)$
g　$(9 - t)(9 + t)$　　　**h**　$(x + y)(x - y)$　　　**i**　$(h - k)(h + k)$
j　$(2a + 1)(2a - 1)$　　**k**　$(3x + 5)(3x - 5)$　　**l**　$(5p - 3)(5p + 3)$
m　$(9n - 8)(9n + 8)$　　**n**　$(11 - 6k)(11 + 6k)$　**o**　$(2x + y)(2x - y)$

p　$(3a + 2b)(3a - 2b)$　**q**　$(4n - 5p)(4n + 5p)$　**r**　$\left(\dfrac{1}{2}x - \dfrac{3}{4}y\right)\left(\dfrac{1}{2}x + \dfrac{3}{4}y\right)$

3 Verify the following using replacements $a = 3$, $b = 2$:

a　$a^2 + b^2 \neq (a + b)^2$　　　　　　　**b**　$a^2 + b^2 \neq (a + b)(a - b)$

4 Complete:

a $(2a + ...)^2 = 4a^2 + ... + 9$ b $(4 + ...)(4 - ...) = ... - a^2$
c $y^2 + ... + 36 = (y + ...)^2$ d $w^2 - 2w + 1 = (w - ...)^2$
e $(... + 16)^2 = ... + 96x + ...$

5 Expand and simplify:

a $(x + \frac{1}{x})(x - \frac{1}{x})$ b $(m^2 - 1)(m^2 + 1)$ c $(7 - x^2)(7 + x^2)$ d $(x + \frac{1}{x})^2$

e $(x - \frac{1}{x})^2$ f $(x^2 - y^2)^2$ g $(xy + 2)^2$

Level 3

6 Expand and simplify:

a $(x - 4)^2 - 4$ b $(x + 1)(x - 1) + x^2$ c $(x + 1)(x - 1) - x^2$
d $(a + 2)^2 + 3a - 1$ e $(a - 3)^2 - (a - 3)$ f $(a + 2)^2 + (a + 1)^2$
g $(7 - a)^2 + (7 + a)^2$ h $(7 - a)^2 - (7 + a)^2$ i $2x + 3 + (x + 1)^2$
j $2x + 3 - (x + 1)^2$ k $^-8(x + 7)(x + 6)$ l $(x + 3)(x - 4) - (x - 5)$
m $(x + 7)^2 - (x - 7)(x + 7)$ n $(2x + 3)(3x - 4) - (2x - 3)$

7 a If $x^2 - 18x + A = (x - B)^2$, find the value of A and B.
b If $x^2 - Ax + 9 = (x - B)^2$, find the value of A and B.
c If $(a + b)^2 = a^2 + b^2 + 2$, give all possible values for a and b.
d Find P and A if $4y^2 - 12y + P = (2y + A)^2$.

Try these: Can you reverse the process?

1 $x^2 - 9 = ($ $)($ $)$

2 $x^2 - 16 = ($ $)($ $)$

3 $A^2 - B^2 = ($ $)($ $)$

4 $x^2 + 2x + 1 = ($ $)^2$

5 $x^2 - 2x + 1 = ($ $)^2$

6 $x^2 + 6x + 9 = ($ $)^2$

If you can't do these now, don't worry.
We will look at them again in Chapter 11.

Investigation Difference of two squares

Using the first 21 whole numbers, write as many as possible as a difference of two squares.

For example, $0 = 0^2 - 0^2$, $8 = 3^2 - 1^2$.

Which cannot be expressed in this way? Make a generalisation about the results.

1.3 Factorising linear expressions

Factorising is the reverse of expanding and you had some experience of this last year. In this section we will revisit factorising linear expressions. Factorising binomial expressions will be dealt with in Chapter 11.

To *factorise* an expression (sum or difference) means to select the *highest common factor* of the terms, then *insert brackets* to make it a product.

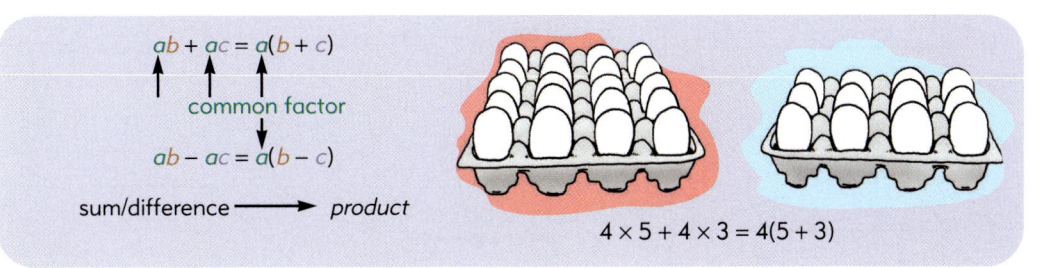

$$ab + ac = a(b + c)$$

common factor

$$ab - ac = a(b - c)$$

sum/difference $\longrightarrow$ product

$$4 \times 5 + 4 \times 3 = 4(5 + 3)$$

Factorise is the reverse process of *expand*.

EXAMPLE
Factorise:

a $8x - 12$ **b** $6d^2 - 9dt$ **c** $^-x^2 - xy$

Solutions

a $8x - 12$
$= 4 \times 2x - 4 \times 3$
$= 4(2x - 3)$

b $6d^2 - 9dt$
$= 3d \times 2d - 3d \times 3t$
$= 3d(2d - 3t)$

c $^-x^2 - xy$
$= ^-x(x + y)$

> Watch the signs!
> $-ve \times +ve = -ve$
> $-ve \times -ve = +ve$

EXERCISE 1C

1 Fill in the missing parts:

> If **all** terms are negative, use the **negative HCF** to **fully** factorise.

a $5x + 5y = 5(\ldots + y)$ **b** $^-2a + {}^-2b = ^-2(a + \ldots)$
c $ax + ay = a(\ldots + \ldots)$ **d** $p + pq = p(\ldots + \ldots)$
e $12k + 18kp = 6k(\ldots \ldots \ldots)$ **f** $^-18a^2 + 27a = ^-9a(\ldots \ldots \ldots)$

2 Factorise, then check by *expanding*:

a $8x + 8y$ **b** $ap - at$ **c** $4k + 8$ **d** $8x - 3x$ **e** $xy + 4y$
f $15 + 12t$ **g** $7b - 7$ **h** $kp + p$ **i** $14d - 7dp$

Level 2

3 Factorise:

a $3x + 12xt$ **b** $5y - y^2$ **c** $6xy + 8x^2$
d $16gh - 36pg$ **e** $^-5x + 15$ **f** $4p^2 - 6p$
g $21a^2 - 14at$ **h** $^-25a + 10$ **i** $^-3y - 12$
j $^-16x^2 - 24x$ **k** $28t^2p + 14tp - 21p^2t$ **l** $^-6x^2y - 12xy$
m $^-9a^2 - 12a$ **n** $5x + 20y - 15$ **o** $p^2q - pq^2 + pq$

4 Expand, simplify, then factorise:

a $3(x + 2) + 9$ **b** $7(a + 3) - 14$ **c** $5(y - 4) + 3y$
d $2(m + 5) + 3m + 5$ **e** $^-4(x - 3) - 2x$ **f** $^-2a(a - 8) - (a^2 + a)$

5 Express the area of each figure as the product of factors. Expand where possible.

a 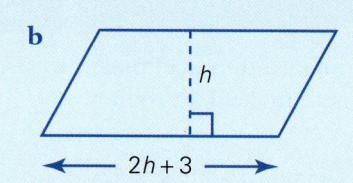 $x+5$, 4

b 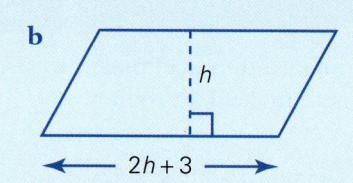 h, $2h+3$

c 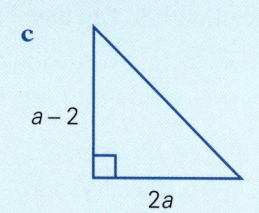 $a-2$, $2a$

d 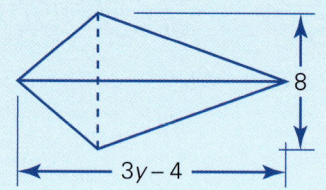 8, $3y-4$

e 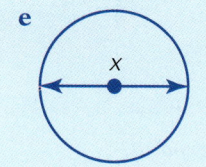 x

f 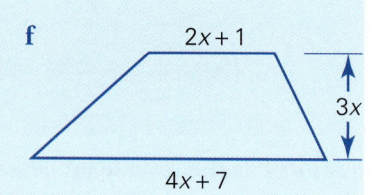 $2x+1$, $3x$, $4x+7$

6 Factorise each of the following:

a $4(x+1) + x(x+1)$

b $x(a+7) - y(a+7)$

c $\dfrac{x^2}{4} + \dfrac{x}{2}$

d $a(x+y) + b(x+y)$

e $\dfrac{xy}{2} + \dfrac{x^2}{2}$

f $A(x+1) + A^2(x+1)$

g $a(x+y) - b(x+y)$

h $\pi r^2 + \pi r$

i $p(p-2) + p$

j $5(x+y) + 5$

k $x(x-2) - 4(x-2)$

l $\dfrac{1}{2}\pi r^2 - \dfrac{1}{2}\pi R^2$

Investigation Library research—development of mathematics

WEB RESEARCH

The development of mathematics is the history of humankind. It has involved men and women from many races and cultures, living in many different situations.

Use your library to investigate the following:

1 The computer language **ADA** was named after **Ada Lovelace**, the daughter of a famous English poet. Which poet? What outstanding contribution to mathematics did she make, for her to be honoured in this way?

2 The author of the children's book *Alice in Wonderland* was an excellent mathematician. Who was he, and under what pseudonym did he write?

3 The **Mayans** of Central and South America invented a highly developed number system. What was the *base* of the system, and how did their *system of numeration* work?

1.4 The first four index laws

You may already be familiar with the index laws listed below. You might have seen them last year. The index laws can be used when the factor repeating is a number or an algebraic term. The following section will look at the uses of the index laws below for both integer factors and algebraic ones.

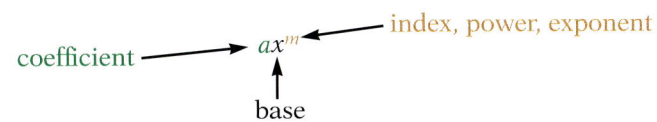

coefficient $\longrightarrow$ ax^m $\longleftarrow$ index, power, exponent

base

$x^m \times x^n = x^{m+n}$	When multiplying indices of the same base, the powers can be added: $5^3 \times 5^4 = 5^7$
$x^m \div x^n = x^{m-n}$	When dividing index expressions of the same base, the powers may be subtracted: $8^{10} \div 8^3 = 8^7$
$(ax^m)^n = a^n . x^{m \times n}$	A power raised to a power means the two indices can be multiplied: $(5^3)^4 = 5^{3 \times 4} = 5^{12}$ $(2a^3)^3 = 8a^9$
$x^0 = 1$	Anything raised to the power of zero equals one: $x^0 = 1$ $6 \div 6 = 6^{1-1}$ but $6 \div 6 = 1$ $\qquad = 6^0$ $\therefore 6^0 = 1$ Generally, $x^0 = 1$

EXAMPLE 1

Simplify:

a $2a^3 \times 3a^4$ **b** $4x^7y^6 \div 6x^9y^3$ **c** $(x^7)^3$

d $(4x^7)^3$ **e** $6x^0 + (7x)^0$ **f** $5^6 \times 5^4 \div 5^2$

Solutions

a $2a^3 \times 3a^4$
$= 6a^7$

b $4x^7y^6 \div 6x^9y^3$
$= \dfrac{4x^7y^6}{6x^9y^3}$
$= \dfrac{2y^3}{3x^2}$

c $(x^7)^3$
$= x^{21}$

d $(4x^7)^3$
$= 4^3(x^7)^3$
$= 64x^{21}$

e $6x^0 + (7x)^0$
$= 6 \times 1 + 1$
$= 6 + 1$
$= 7$

f $5^6 \times 5^4 \div 5^2$
$= 5^{10} \div 5^2$
$= 5^8$

EXAMPLE 2

Simplify $10^m \div 5^m$.

Solution

$$10^m \div 5^m$$
$$= (5 \times 2)^m \div 5^m$$
$$= \frac{5^m \times 2^m}{5^m}$$
$$= 2^m$$

Express 10 as a product of its factors.

EXAMPLE 3

If $8^x = 16$, find x.

Solution

$$8^x = 16$$
$$(2^3)^x = 2^4$$
$$2^{3x} = 2^4$$
$$3x = 4$$
$$x = \frac{4}{3}$$

Express each term as a common base.

Equate the powers.

From a single bacteria, the number after n divisions is $(2)^n$. Under ideal conditions divisions can occur every fifteen minutes.

EXERCISE 1D

1 Complete the following:

a $5^3 \times 5^4 = 5^?$ **b** $9^2 \times 9^4 = 9^?$ **c** $7^8 \times 7^3 = 7^?$

d $4^9 \div 4^5 = 4^?$ **e** $6^4 \div 6 = 6^?$ **f** $8^9 \div 8^2 = 8^?$

2 Write the following as products of identical factors, then simplify to a single power:

a $3^2 \times 3^4$ **b** 5×5^3 **c** $8^5 \div 8^3$ **d** $t^4 \div t^3$ **e** $a^2 \times a^3 \div a$

3 Write the value of each of the following:

a 8^0 **b** $(^-3)^0$ **c** $\left(\frac{3}{5}\right)^0$ **d** $(0.4)^0$ **e** k^0

f $4^0 + 5^0$ **g** $4a^0$ **h** $(a+b)^0$ **i** $3a^0 \times 2b^0$ **j** cd^0

k $(3x)^0$ **l** $(xy)^0$ **m** $(n^0)^0$ **n** $(x^2y^3)^0$ **o** $(x^5)^0$

4 Simplify the following expressions to a single power, where possible:

a $2^8 \times 2^3$ **b** $3^5 \times 3^2$ **c** 8×8^9

d $5^4 \times 5^4$ **e** $4^6 \times 3^6$ **f** $6^2 \times 5^3$

g $m \times m^5$ **h** $10^3 \times 10^2 \times 10$ **i** $p^4 p^2$

j $a^2 \times b^3$ **k** $x^3 \times x^3$ **l** $x^5 + x^3$

m $9^5 - 9^2$ **n** $(2a)^2 \times (2a)^3$ **o** $\left(\frac{2}{3}\right)^4 \times \left(\frac{2}{3}\right)^3$

p $(0.8)^5 \times 0.8 \times (0.8)^3$ **q** $3a^5 \times 2a^4$ **r** $8p^4 \times 3p^6$

s $7x^6 \times x$ **t** $14a^2 \times \frac{1}{7}a^7$ **u** $2.5k^2 \times 4k^2$

v $^-6c^5 \times 3c$ **w** $x^2y^3 \times xy$ **x** $2c^3 \times \frac{1}{2}c \times {}^-4c^4$

5 Find the value for x in the following:

a $4^x = 1$ **b** $d^x = 1$ **c** $(2.4)^x = 1$ **d** $1 = \left(\frac{n}{2}\right)^x$

6 Simplify:

a $6^5 \div 6^5$ **b** $a^4 \div a^4$ **c** $15c^7 \div 5c^7$ **d** $a^3 \times a^2 \div a^5$

e $x^{10} \div x^3 \div x^7$ **f** $3^4 \times 3^0$ **g** $5^0 \times 5^{10}$ **h** $1 \times a^0$

i 0×4^0 **j** $a^0 - 6$ **k** $2p^4 \times 8p^0$ **l** $7^5 \div 7^0$

m $2^8 \div 2^5$ **n** $3^5 \div 3^2$ **o** $8^4 \div 8$ **p** $4^6 \div 3^3$

q $a^5 \div a^3$ **r** $c^7 \div c$ **s** $10^8 \div 10^4 \div 10^2$ **t** $\dfrac{a^7}{a^3}$

u $a^3 \div b^3$ **v** $x^3 \div x^2$ **w** $x^4 - x^4$ **x** $x^7 - x^4$

y $\dfrac{x^8}{y^8}$ **z** $\left(\dfrac{1}{2}\right)^6 \div \left(\dfrac{1}{2}\right)^3$

7 Complete:

a $(x^3)^2 = x^{\square}$ **b** $(3x^2)^3 = 27x^{\square}$ **c** $(4x^3)^2 = \square x^6$

d $(x^7y^2)^3 = x^{\square}y^6$ **e** $(9x^7)^2 = \square x^{14}$

8 Apply the power of a power rule where possible:

a $(3^2)^5$ **b** $(2^3)^4$ **c** $(5^2)^3$ **d** $(4^2)^2$ **e** $(3^3)^3$

f $[(^-2)^3]^2$ **g** $\left[\left(\dfrac{3}{4}\right)^2\right]^4$ **h** $[(2 \cdot 5)^3]^2$ **i** $(a^2)^4$ **j** $(c^5)^3$

k $(x^4)^4$ **l** $(p^{10})^2$ **m** $(k^5)^7$ **n** $(2x)^2$ **o** $(3x^2)^3$

p $(2a^3)^3$ **q** $(4n^4)^2$ **r** $(5c^5)^5$ **s** $(2^3x^4)^2$ **t** $(a^3x^4)^5$

9 Simplify:

a $2 - 3x^0$ **b** $(2x)^0 + 2p^0$ **c** $4 + 6w^0$ **d** $4 + (6w)^0$ **e** $5(x + y)^0$

Level 2

10 a $\dfrac{3^5 \times 3^2}{3^4}$ **b** $\dfrac{x^7 \times x^3}{x^8}$ **c** $\dfrac{5^{15}}{5^3 \times 5^4}$ **d** $\dfrac{a^{10}}{a \times a^6}$

e $\dfrac{6a^2}{3a}$ **f** $\dfrac{15a^5}{5a^2}$ **g** $\dfrac{18x^8}{9x^7}$ **h** $\dfrac{a^2b^3}{b^2}$

i $\dfrac{a^3b^9}{ab^5}$ **j** $\dfrac{12x^4y^3}{8x^2y}$ **k** $\dfrac{4^7x^9}{4^3x^8}$ **l** $\dfrac{3 \times 4^5c^3}{2 \times 4^3c^2}$

m $\dfrac{a^2b^6c^8}{ab^5c^7}$ **n** $\dfrac{8x^8y^2}{24yx^6}$ **o** $\dfrac{^-16a^3b^7}{^-12a^2b^8}$ **p** $x^7y^4 \div x^7y^5$

11 Simplify:

a $9^0 \div 9^0$ **b** $^-3t^2 \times {}^-t^0$ **c** $\dfrac{^-18x^3x^5}{24x^8 + 3x^8}$ **d** $\dfrac{0 \cdot 5c^2 - 1 \cdot 5c^2}{(^-c^2)^0}$

12 True or false?

a $5a^0 - 4a^0 = 1$ **b** $a^0 \div a^0 = 0$ **c** $\dfrac{0}{4^0} = 1$ **d** $\dfrac{5^0}{0} = 0$

13 Simplify:

a $3 \times 10^4 \times 2 \times 10^5$ **b** $7 \times 10 \times 2 \times 10^4$ **c** $1 \cdot 5 \times 10^2 \times 4 \times 10^5$

d $1.8 \times 10^3 \times 3 \times 10^3$ **e** $\dfrac{8 \times 10^5}{4 \times 10^3}$ **f** $\dfrac{7 \times 10^3}{10}$

g $\dfrac{3.2 \times 10^7}{8 \times 10^5}$ **h** $\dfrac{4.8 \times 10^8}{3.6 \times 10^2}$ **i** $\dfrac{3 \times 10^6 \times 4 \times 10^4}{6 \times 10^8}$

14 Use the distributive law to expand the following:

a $3x(2x^3 - 5x^2)$ b $^-5a(2a^2 + 3a)$ c $^-2n(5n^4 - n^2)$ d $\dfrac{^-2}{3}x^2(3x^3 - 4x - 6)$

15 Copy and complete:

a $8a^3 = 4a \times \ldots$ b $12x^5 = 4x \times \ldots$
c $15a^4 = 3a^3 \times \ldots$ d $^-56x^4y^3 = 7xy^2 \times \ldots$

16 Simplify, then evaluate if $x =$ **i** 3   **ii** $^-2$ **iii** $\dfrac{2}{3}$

a $2x \times 3x^2$ b $6x^9 \div 2x^7$ c $x(x^2 + 3x^2)$ d $\dfrac{4x^5 \times 6x^2}{8x^4}$

Level 3

17 Find n:

a $a^4 \times a^n = a^{12}$ b $2^n = 256$ c $59\,049 = 9^n$ d $n^7 = 16\,384$

18 Find the value of x and y in:

a $6^4 = 2^x \times 3^y$ b $10^5 = x^5 \times 5^y$ c $3^x \times y^4 = 5625$

19 Simplify:

a $\dfrac{2^{n+1}}{2^{n-1}}$ b $\dfrac{6^x}{3^x}$ c $\dfrac{4^x}{2^x}$ d $\dfrac{3^{2x+1}}{3^x}$ e $\dfrac{x^m}{x^{-m}}$

20 Simplify each of the following expressions:

a $\dfrac{(2x^7y^4)^2 \times 3xy}{10x^4y^6}$ b $\dfrac{3x^4y^3}{(x^4y^6)^3}$ c $\dfrac{x^7y^4z^2 \times xy}{(xyz^2)^3}$ d $8a^6 \div 4a^2 \times 3a$

e $(n^4)^3 \div (n^2)^4$ f $\dfrac{(a^5)^2 \times a^8}{(a^2)^3}$ g $\dfrac{(2m^3)^2 \times 4m^3}{8m^8}$ h $\dfrac{(6^2a^3)^3 \times 6a^5}{30a^4 + 6a^4}$

21 Simplify:

a $\dfrac{5^m \times 2^m}{10^m}$ b $\dfrac{15^m}{5 \times 3^m}$ c $\dfrac{6^m - 10^m}{2^m}$ d $\dfrac{6^m - 2 \times 6^m}{6^m}$

e $\dfrac{x^{2m}}{x^m}$ f $\dfrac{10^{x+1}}{10}$ g $\dfrac{x^m}{x^{3-m}}$ h $\dfrac{5^m - 15^m}{1 - 3^m}$

22 Find the value of x in:

a $2^x = 512$ b $16^x = 64$ c $2^{x+1} = 128$
d $7^{2x} = 49$ e $5^x = 125$ f $8^x = 128$

Investigation A pattern with powers

1 a Evaluate the terms of the sequence: $1^5, 2^5, 3^5, 4^5, 5^5 \ldots$
  b Write any pattern you find.
  c Investigate further.
  d Develop other sequences of powers and investigate

2 Which is larger, 2^3 or 3^2? 3^5 or 5^3?
  a Describe in words the index notation pattern of each pair of expressions.
  b Investigate other such pairs. Report on your findings.

3 a Evaluate 2^3 and 4^3; 2^4 and 4^4. Look for a pattern.
  b Investigate the relationship between 2^n and 4^n. Be systematic!
  c Widen your investigation by asking, 'What if …?'.

1 Continue the pattern of dividing by 10 with each move to the right.

10^3	10^2	10^1	10^0	$10^?$	$?^?$
1000	100	…	…	$\dfrac{1}{10}$	$\dfrac{1}{10^2}$

2 Make up a similar table of powers of 2. Compare the pattern of signs for the indices.

3 Generalise your findings into a word statement and an algebraic statement.

4 Simplify $4^2 \div 4^3$ using the index law for division.

5 Simplify $\dfrac{4^2}{4^3}$ by cancelling common factors.

6 Repeat questions 4 and 5 for $a^2 \div a^3$ and $\dfrac{a^2}{a^3}$. Compare results with those of the table above.

7 Simplify $3^2 \times 3^{-2}$, $a^3 \times a^{-3}$, and $a^x \times a^{-x}$, using the index rule for multiplication. Compare results with those of **multiplying reciprocals** for fractions. Write your conclusions about a^x and a^{-x} in words.

1.5 The negative index

An expression raised to a negative index indicates the **reciprocal** of the expression is required, i.e. $10^{-2} = \dfrac{1}{10^2}$, $5^{-3} = \dfrac{1}{5^3}$.

$$x^{-m} = \frac{1}{x^m}$$

EXAMPLE 1
Write with positive indices:

a $\quad 6^{-3}$
b $\quad 5x^{-4}$
c $\quad \dfrac{1}{2^{-3}}$
d $\quad \left(\dfrac{4}{5}\right)^{-2}$

Solutions

a $\quad 6^{-3}$

$= \dfrac{1}{6^3}$ $\quad$ Evaluate if necessary.

$= \dfrac{1}{216}$

b $\quad 5x^{-4}$

$= 5 \times x^{-4}$

$= 5 \times \dfrac{1}{x^4}$

$= \dfrac{5}{x^4}$

c $\quad \dfrac{1}{2^{-3}}$

$= 1 \div 2^{-3}$

$= 1 \div \dfrac{1}{2^3}$

$= 1 \times 2^3$

$= 2^3$

A negative index in the denominator moves the term to the numerator.

d $\quad \left(\dfrac{4}{5}\right)^{-2}$ $\quad$ Take the reciprocal.

$= \left(\dfrac{5}{4}\right)^2$

$= \dfrac{5^2}{4^2}$

$= \dfrac{25}{16}$

EXAMPLE 2
Change from fractions to negative index form:

a $\quad \dfrac{1}{5}$
b $\quad \dfrac{1}{6^4}$
c $\quad \dfrac{4}{x^7}$
d $\quad \dfrac{3}{4x^2}$

Solutions

a $\dfrac{1}{5}$
= 5^{-1}

b $\dfrac{1}{6^4}$
= 6^{-4}

c $\dfrac{4}{x^7}$
= $4x^{-7}$

d $\dfrac{3}{4x^2}$
= $\dfrac{3}{4} \times \dfrac{1}{x^2}$
= $\dfrac{3}{4} \times x^{-2}$
= $\dfrac{3x^{-2}}{4}$

Levels of radioactivity can be received by a Geiger Counter. Radioactive substances decay according to the formulae $\left(\dfrac{1}{2}\right)^n M$, where M is the original mass and n the number of half lives

EXERCISE 1E

1 Complete:

a $\dfrac{1}{6} = 6^{\square}$

b $\dfrac{1}{x^2} = x^{\square}$

c $5^{\square} = \dfrac{1}{125}$

d $x^{-3} = \dfrac{\square}{x^3}$

e $4^{-2} = \dfrac{1}{\square}$

f $2a^{-3} = \dfrac{\square}{a^3}$

g $p^2 q^{-1} = \dfrac{\square}{q}$

h $p^{-2}q = \dfrac{q}{\square}$

i $\dfrac{1}{2a^4} = \square a^{-4}$

j $\dfrac{x^2}{y^3} = x^2 y^{\square}$

2 Write with positive indices:

a 3^{-4}
b 7^{-1}
c 4^{-2}
d 2^{-5}
e x^{-3}

f n^{-6}
g 10^{-8}
h $8x^{-7}$
i $3t^{-2}$
j $(2p)^{-3}$

k $(-9)^{-4}$
l $(-3\cdot6)^{-2}$
m $\dfrac{1}{3^{-4}}$
n $\dfrac{1}{x^{-2}}$
o $\dfrac{1}{a^{-x}}$

3 Without the use of a calculator, find the value of:

a 5^{-2}
b 10^{-4}
c $(4^{-1})^2$
d $(-3)^{-3}$
e $\left(\dfrac{1}{2}\right)^{-4}$

4 Answer the following as either true or false:

a $1^{-1} = 1$

b $(-5)^3 = 5^{-3}$

c $\dfrac{4}{3x} = \dfrac{4}{3}x^{-1}$

d $\dfrac{1}{5a^3} = \dfrac{a^{-3}}{5}$

e $4a^{-2} = \dfrac{1}{4a^2}$

f $\left(\dfrac{a}{b}\right)^{-1} = \dfrac{b}{a}$

Level 2

5 Write using negative indices:

a $\dfrac{1}{3}$
b $\dfrac{1}{10}$
c $\dfrac{1}{2^3}$
d $\dfrac{1}{x^2}$
e $\dfrac{1}{a}$

f $\dfrac{3}{a^3}$
g $\dfrac{4}{x^2}$
h $\dfrac{1}{5p}$
i $\dfrac{1}{3x^2}$
j $\dfrac{2}{5a^3}$

k $\dfrac{3x}{y^4}$
l $\dfrac{-7}{x^2 y^5}$
m $\dfrac{-8a}{5(bc)^6}$

6 True or false?

  a $6^3 \times 6^{-3} = 6$ **b** $3^{-5} \div 3^4 = 3^{-1}$ **c** $8^0 \div 8^{-3} = 8^3$ **d** $(4^2)^{-2} = 4^0$

  e $\left(\frac{2}{3}\right)^{-1} = \frac{2}{3}$ **f** $\left(\frac{2}{3}\right)^{-1} = 1\frac{1}{2}$

7 Find the value of x in each of the following:

  a $4^x = \frac{1}{16}$ **b** $2^x = \frac{1}{16}$ **c** $x^{-3} = \frac{1}{27}$ **d** $x^{-3} = \frac{1}{-8}$

Level 3

8 Using only the numbers 2, 3 and 4 once each, what is the number of *greatest* value you can make?

9 If you are allowed to use operation symbols ($+$, $-$, $\times$, $\div$), write the number of *least* possible value, with the same digits as in question **8**.

10 Simplify:

  a $\frac{6x^4y^6}{12x^4y^8}$ **b** $(ab^{-2})^2$ **c** $(a^2b^{-3})^2$ **d** $\frac{x^{-2m}}{x^{-m}}$

  e $x^{-\frac{1}{2}} \times x^{-\frac{1}{2}}$ **f** $(4^{-1}x^{-2})^3$

Investigation Fractional indices

1 Solve for x:

  a $2^x \times 2^x = 2^6$ **b** $3^x \times 3^x = 3^2$ **c** $6^x \times 6^x = 6$
  d $(3^x)^2 = 3^4$ **e** $(2^x)^2 = 2^2$ **f** $(4^x)^2 = 4$
  What is new about the index value in **c** and **f**?

2 Copy and complete the following:

  a If $3^2 = 9$, then $\sqrt{9} = \square$ **b** If $2^2 = 4$, then $\square = 2$

  c If $(5^{\frac{1}{2}})^2 = 5$, then $\sqrt{5} = \square$ **d** If $(8^{\frac{1}{2}})^2 = 8$, then $\square = \square$

  e If $(a^{\frac{1}{2}})^2 = a$, then $\square = \square$ **f** $\sqrt{a} \times \sqrt{a} = \square$

  g $\sqrt{a \times a} = \sqrt{a^2} = \square$ **h** $a^{\frac{1}{2}} \times a^{\frac{1}{2}} = \square$

3 Solve for x:

  a $2^x \times 2^x \times 2^x = 2^9$ **b** $5^x \times 5^x \times 5^x = 5^3$
  c $4^x \times 4^x \times 4^x = 4$ **d** $a^x \times a^x \times a^x = a$

4 Copy and complete the following:

  a If $2^3 = 8$, then $\sqrt[3]{8} = \square$ **b** If $4^3 = 64$, then $\square = 4$

  c If $(3^{\frac{1}{3}})^3 = 3$, then $\sqrt[3]{3} = \square$ **d** If $(6^{\frac{1}{3}})^3 = 6$, then $\square = \square$

  e If $(a^{\frac{1}{3}})^3 = a$, then $\square = \square$

5 Write a summary of your findings about square and cube roots.

1.6 Fractional indices

> The **index** $\frac{1}{2}$ means the **square root** of the base: $x^{\frac{1}{2}} = \sqrt{x}$.
>
> The **index** $\frac{1}{3}$ means the **cube root** of the base: $x^{\frac{1}{3}} = \sqrt[3]{x}$.

EXAMPLE 1
Evaluate:

a $8^{\frac{1}{3}}$ **b** $\left(\frac{1}{4}\right)^{\frac{1}{2}}$ **c** $0\cdot027^{-\frac{1}{3}}$

Solutions

a $8^{\frac{1}{3}}$

$= \sqrt[3]{8}$

$= 2$

b $\left(\frac{1}{4}\right)^{\frac{1}{2}}$

$= \sqrt{\frac{1}{4}}$

$= \frac{\sqrt{1}}{\sqrt{4}}$

$= \frac{1}{2}$

c $(0\cdot027)^{-\frac{1}{3}}$

$= \dfrac{1}{(0\cdot027)^{\frac{1}{3}}}$

$= \dfrac{1}{\sqrt[3]{0\cdot027}}$

$= \dfrac{1}{0\cdot3}$

$= \dfrac{10}{3}$

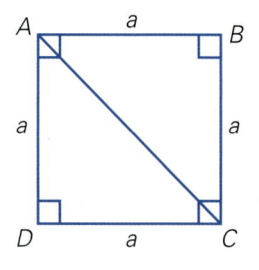

The length of the diagonal of this square is

$$(2a^2)^{\frac{1}{2}} = \sqrt{2}\,a.$$

EXERCISE 1F

1 Complete:

   a $\sqrt{x} = x^{\square}$ **b** $\sqrt{36} = 36^{\square}$ **c** $\sqrt[3]{a} = a^{\square}$ **d** $4^{\square} = 2$ **e** $\sqrt[3]{x} = x^{\square}$

   f $a^{\frac{1}{2}} = \sqrt{\square}$ **g** $5a^{\frac{1}{2}} = 5^{\square}$ **h** $6p^{\frac{1}{3}} = \square \times \sqrt[3]{p}$

2 Evaluate without using a calculator:

   a $4^{\frac{1}{2}}$ **b** $100^{\frac{1}{2}}$ **c** $27^{\frac{1}{3}}$ **d** $125^{\frac{1}{3}}$ **e** $^{-}(36^{\frac{1}{2}})$

   f $^{-}(216^{\frac{1}{3}})$ **g** $\left(\frac{1}{9}\right)^{\frac{1}{2}}$ **h** $(0\cdot04)^{\frac{1}{2}}$ **i** $\left(\frac{4}{25}\right)^{\frac{1}{2}}$ **j** $\left(\frac{8}{27}\right)^{\frac{1}{3}}$

   k $(0\cdot064)^{\frac{1}{3}}$ **l** $1000^{\frac{1}{3}}$ **m** $25^{\frac{1}{2}}$ **n** $\left(\frac{1}{64}\right)^{\frac{1}{3}}$

   o $(1 \times 10^{-4})^{\frac{1}{2}}$ **p** $\left(\frac{8}{125}\right)^{\frac{1}{3}}$

3 Simplify where possible, without using a calculator:

   a $4^{\frac{1}{2}} \times 4^{\frac{1}{2}}$ **b** $8^{\frac{1}{3}} \times 8^{\frac{1}{3}} \times 8^{\frac{1}{3}}$ **c** $5^2 \times 5^{\frac{1}{2}}$ **d** $7^{\frac{1}{2}} \times 7^{\frac{3}{2}}$

   e $6^{\frac{1}{3}} \times 6^{\frac{2}{3}}$ **f** $a^{\frac{1}{2}} \times a^2 \times a^{\frac{1}{2}}$ **g** $9 \div 9^{\frac{1}{2}}$ **h** $10^2 \div 10^{\frac{1}{2}}$

i $a^{\frac{1}{2}} \times a^{\frac{1}{3}}$ **j** $a^{\frac{1}{2}} \div a^{\frac{1}{3}}$ **k** $a^{\frac{1}{2}} \times b^{\frac{1}{3}}$ **l** $6a^{\frac{1}{2}} + 3a^{\frac{1}{2}}$

m $5a + 2a^{\frac{1}{3}} - 3a$ **n** $7a^{\frac{1}{3}} - 4a^{\frac{1}{3}}$ **o** $a \times a^{\frac{1}{3}}$

4 Evaluate without the use of a calculator:

a $49^{\frac{-1}{2}}$ **b** $64^{\frac{-1}{3}}$ **c** $\left(\frac{1}{36}\right)^{\frac{-1}{2}}$ **d** $\left(\frac{1}{125}\right)^{\frac{-1}{3}}$ **e** $(0 \cdot 64)^{\frac{-1}{2}}$

f $(1000)^{\frac{-1}{3}}$ **g** $\left(\frac{8}{125}\right)^{\frac{-1}{3}}$ **h** $\left(\frac{4}{9}\right)^{\frac{-1}{2}}$

5 Simplify each of the following:

a $a^3 \times a^{\frac{1}{3}}$ **b** $a^{-2} \times a^{\frac{1}{2}}$ **c** $a^{-4} \div a^{\frac{1}{2}}$ **d** $a^0 \div a^{\frac{1}{3}}$ **e** $(x^{\frac{1}{3}})^3$

f $(x^{\frac{1}{2}})^4$ **g** $(x^{\frac{1}{2}})^{-4}$ **h** $(x^{\frac{-1}{3}})^6$ **i** $\sqrt{\dfrac{18a^9b^4}{2b^{-2}a^5}}$

6 If $x^{\frac{2}{3}} = \sqrt[3]{x^2}$ or $(\sqrt[3]{x})^2$, without using a calculator, evaluate:

a $8^{\frac{2}{3}}$ **b** $64^{\frac{2}{3}}$ **c** $125^{\frac{2}{3}}$ **d** $\left(-1\right)^{\frac{2}{3}}$ **e** $\left(\frac{1}{8}\right)^{\frac{2}{3}}$

f $\left(\frac{1}{8}\right)^{\frac{-2}{3}}$ **g** $\left(\frac{64}{125}\right)^{\frac{2}{3}}$ **h** $\left(\frac{64}{125}\right)^{\frac{-2}{3}}$

7 If $x^{\frac{3}{2}} = \sqrt{x^3}$ or $(\sqrt{x})^3$, evaluate without the use of a calculator each of the following:

a $4^{\frac{3}{2}}$ **b** $25^{\frac{3}{2}}$ **c** $49^{\frac{3}{2}}$ **d** $1^{\frac{3}{2}}$ **e** $\left(\frac{1}{16}\right)^{\frac{3}{2}}$

f $4^{\frac{-3}{2}}$ **g** $25^{\frac{-3}{2}}$ **h** $\left(\frac{4}{25}\right)^{\frac{-3}{2}}$

8 Rewrite each of the following in full index notation:

a $\sqrt{x}$ **b** $\sqrt[3]{x}$ **c** $\sqrt[3]{x^2}$ **d** $5\sqrt[3]{x}$ **e** $\dfrac{1}{\sqrt[3]{x^2}}$

f $\dfrac{5}{\sqrt[3]{w^2}}$ **g** $\dfrac{5}{\sqrt{w^3}}$ **h** $\dfrac{\sqrt{x}}{\sqrt[3]{y}}$

1.7 The *n*th root

> In general, the **nth root** of any number is equal to the number raised to the corresponding **fractional power**.
>
> $$\sqrt[n]{x} = x^{\frac{1}{n}}$$

Consider:

$$a^{\frac{1}{2}} \times a^{\frac{1}{2}} = a^{\frac{1}{2}+\frac{1}{2}} = a^1, \text{ so } \sqrt[2]{a^1} = a^{\frac{1}{2}}$$

$$a^{\frac{1}{3}} \times a^{\frac{1}{3}} \times a^{\frac{1}{3}} = a^{\frac{1}{3}+\frac{1}{3}+\frac{1}{3}} = a^1, \text{ so } \sqrt[3]{a^1} = a^{\frac{1}{3}}$$

$$\underbrace{a^{\frac{1}{n}} \times a^{\frac{1}{n}} \times \ldots \times a^{\frac{1}{n}}}_{n \text{ factors}} = a^{\overbrace{\frac{1}{n}+\frac{1}{n}+\ldots+\frac{1}{n}}^{n \text{ terms}}} = a^1, \text{ so } \sqrt[n]{a^1} = a^{\frac{1}{n}}$$

EXAMPLE 1

Rewrite without the use of surds: $\sqrt[5]{\dfrac{x}{y}}$

Solution

$$\sqrt[5]{\frac{x}{y}}$$

$$= \left(\frac{x}{y}\right)^{\frac{1}{5}}$$

EXAMPLE 2

Rewrite without negative indices: $a^{-\frac{2}{3}}$

Solution

$$a^{-\frac{2}{3}}$$

$$= (a^{-2})^{\frac{1}{3}}$$

$$= \left(\frac{1}{a^2}\right)^{\frac{1}{3}}$$

$$= \sqrt[3]{\frac{1}{a^2}}$$

$$= \frac{1}{\sqrt[3]{a^2}}$$

The value of money invested doubles every six year period. Value = investment $\times 2$ (to the power of n) where n = number of periods.

EXERCISE 1G

1 Complete:

a $a^{\frac{1}{3}} = \sqrt[\square]{a}$

b $a^{\frac{1}{4}} = \sqrt[\square]{a}$

c $a^{\frac{2}{3}} = \sqrt[\square]{a^2}$

d $\sqrt[5]{x} = x^{\square}$

e $5x^{\frac{3}{4}} = 5\sqrt[4]{\square}$

f $x^{-\frac{3}{4}} = \dfrac{1}{\sqrt[4]{\square}}$

2 Use a calculator to evaluate each of the following:

a 4^8

b 5^7

c 6^5

d 12^4

e 3^{-4}

f 128^{-3}

g $196^{\frac{1}{2}}$

h $256^{\frac{1}{8}}$

i $1000^{-\frac{1}{3}}$

j $72^{-\frac{1}{4}}$

Level 2

3 Express each of the following in root form:

a $16^{\frac{1}{2}}$

b $8^{\frac{1}{3}}$

c $12^{\frac{1}{4}}$

d $59^{\frac{1}{6}}$

e $x^{\frac{1}{6}}$

f $p^{\frac{1}{7}}$ **g** $10^{\frac{1}{c}}$ **h** $t^{\frac{1}{x}}$ **i** $4 \times 9^{\frac{1}{2}}$ **j** $6 \div 9^{\frac{1}{9}}$

k $x^{\frac{4}{7}}$ **l** $6p^{\frac{2}{5}}$

4 Express each of the following in index form:

a $\sqrt{2}$ **b** $\sqrt[3]{5}$ **c** $\sqrt[4]{12}$ **d** $\sqrt[9]{28}$ **e** $\sqrt[10]{184}$

f $\sqrt{8}$ **g** $\sqrt[x]{10}$ **h** $\sqrt[p]{t}$ **i** $\dfrac{1}{\sqrt{6}}$ **j** $\dfrac{1}{\sqrt[3]{20}}$

k $\dfrac{1}{\sqrt[6]{x}}$ **l** $\dfrac{1}{\sqrt[n]{a}}$

5 Evaluate each of the following without a calculator:

a $64^{\frac{1}{2}}$ **b** $64^{\frac{1}{3}}$ **c** $16^{\frac{1}{4}}$ **d** $32^{\frac{1}{5}}$ **e** $81^{\frac{1}{4}}$

f $3125^{\frac{1}{5}}$ **g** $8^{\frac{-1}{3}}$ **h** $49^{\frac{-1}{2}}$ **i** $256^{\frac{-1}{4}}$ **j** $1^{\frac{-1}{8}}$

6 Simplify each of the following, without using a calculator. Some answers may need to be left in index form.

a $9^{\frac{1}{2}} \times 3 \times 9^{\frac{1}{2}}$ **b** $4^0 \times 4^1 \times 4^{\frac{1}{2}} \times 4^{\frac{1}{2}}$ **c** $(6^{\frac{1}{3}})^3$ **d** $(5^2)^{\frac{1}{2}} \times 27^{\frac{1}{3}}$

e $(\sqrt{5})^4$ **f** $(\sqrt{6})^6$ **g** $(\sqrt[3]{7})^6$ **h** $\left(\dfrac{1}{\sqrt[3]{8}}\right)^{-9}$

i $\left(\dfrac{1}{\sqrt[5]{25}}\right)^{-10}$ **j** $\left(\dfrac{9}{16}\right)^{\frac{1}{2}} \times \left(\dfrac{8}{27}\right)^{\frac{1}{3}}$ **k** $\dfrac{\sqrt{3}}{3}$ **l** $\dfrac{\sqrt[3]{7}}{\sqrt{7}}$

Level 3

7 Simplify:

a $a^{\frac{1}{3}} \times a^{\frac{1}{3}}$ **b** $x^{\frac{1}{2}} \times x^{\frac{1}{3}}$ **c** $p^{\frac{1}{2}} \div p^{\frac{1}{4}}$ **d** $n^{\frac{1}{5}} \div n^{\frac{1}{2}}$

e $(x^{\frac{1}{2}})^{\frac{1}{2}}$ **f** $(25a^4)^{\frac{1}{2}}$ **g** $(27xy^3)^{\frac{1}{3}}$ **h** $\sqrt{x^4 m}$

i $\left(\dfrac{a^4}{x^8}\right)^{\frac{1}{2}}$ **j** $t^{\frac{-1}{3}} \times t^{\frac{-1}{4}}$ **k** $\left(\dfrac{m^4}{x^8}\right)^{\frac{-1}{2}}$

8 If $x^{\frac{1}{n}} = \sqrt[n]{x}$, then $x^{\frac{m}{n}} = \sqrt[n]{x^m}$ or $(\sqrt[n]{x})^m$.
Evaluate without the use of a calculator:

a $81^{\frac{1}{4}}$ **b** $81^{\frac{3}{4}}$ **c** $81^{\frac{5}{4}}$ **d** $81^{\frac{5}{2}}$

e $1^{\frac{5}{2}}$ **f** $27^{\frac{4}{3}}$ **g** $27^{\frac{-4}{3}}$ **h** $\left(\dfrac{1}{125}\right)^{\frac{4}{3}}$

9 Rewrite each of the following in full index notation:

a $\sqrt[4]{x^3}$ **b** $(\sqrt[4]{x})^3$ **c** $\sqrt[5]{x}$ **d** $\sqrt[5]{x^2}$

e $\dfrac{1}{\sqrt{x^7}}$ **f** $\dfrac{3}{\sqrt[3]{x^5}}$ **g** $\sqrt{\dfrac{x^5}{y^3}}$ **h** $\dfrac{1}{\sqrt[4]{x^3 y^3}}$

1.8 The index laws together

We have now had some experience with the index laws. The full list of the index laws, which you should now know, is given below.

1 $x^m \times x^n = x^{m+n}$

2 $x^m \div x^n = x^{m-n}$

3 $(ax^m)^n = a^n.x^{mn}$

4 $x^0 = 1 \ (x \neq 0)$

5 $\left(\dfrac{x}{y}\right)^n = \dfrac{x^n}{y^n}$

6 $x^{-m} = \dfrac{1}{x^m}$

7 $x^{\frac{1}{n}} = \sqrt[n]{x}$

8 $x^{\frac{m}{n}} = \sqrt[n]{x^m}$

EXAMPLE 1

Simplify $\sqrt{\dfrac{x^{10}}{4x^6}}$

Solution

$\sqrt{\dfrac{x^{10}}{4x^6}}$

Perhaps a better use of our index laws would be …

$\sqrt{\dfrac{x^{10}}{4x^6}}$

$= \dfrac{\sqrt{x^{10}}}{\sqrt{4x^6}}$

$= \sqrt{\dfrac{x^4}{4}}$

$= \dfrac{(x^{10})^{\frac{1}{2}}}{(4x^6)^{\frac{1}{2}}}$

$= \left(\dfrac{x^4}{4}\right)^{\frac{1}{2}}$

$= \dfrac{x^5}{2x^3}$

$= \dfrac{x^2}{2}$

$= \dfrac{x^2}{2}$

By choosing the best combination of index laws questions can be simplified easily.

EXERCISE 1H

1 Simplify:

a $36^{\frac{-1}{2}}$

b $(4x^6)^3 \div 16x^{10}$

c $(-125)^{\frac{1}{3}}$

d $\sqrt{\dfrac{49a^{10}}{b^4}}$

e $49^{\frac{-1}{2}}$

f $ab^{-2} \div (ab)^{-2}$

g $(3x^{-2})^{-3}$

h $3 - 4x^0$

i $16^{\frac{3}{4}}$

j $2^{5-p} \div 2^p$

k $\left(\dfrac{4}{5}\right)^{-2}$

l $6x^4y^6 \times {}^-4x^{-2}y$

m $^-16^{\frac{-3}{4}}$

n $5^{3-2p} \div 5^2$

o $\left(\dfrac{5x}{2}\right)^3$

p $6x^7y^4 \div 2x^7y^3$

q $\sqrt{x^8}$

r $(16^{\frac{1}{2}})^{\frac{1}{2}}$

s $\sqrt{49a^{10}}$

t $(3x^7)^4$

Level 2

2 Simplify each of the following:

a $(16)^{-\frac{1}{2}}$ **b** $\sqrt{\dfrac{36x^4}{y^6}}$ **c** $576^{\frac{1}{2}}$ **d** $(9x^{-4}y^2)^{-2}$

e $\sqrt{\dfrac{16}{25}}$ **f** $\dfrac{3x^{-3}}{x^4}$ **g** $(m^{-2})^{-1}$ **h** $\sqrt{x^{-6}y^4}$

i $(m^{-1})^{-2}$ **j** $a^{-\frac{1}{2}} \times \sqrt{a}$ **k** $\sqrt{36x^8y^4}$ **l** $\dfrac{(4x^7y^6)^2 \times 3x}{\sqrt{16x^2y^2}}$

m $\sqrt[3]{8x^9y^3}$ **n** $\left(\dfrac{x^2}{y}\right)^{-3}$ **o** $\left(\dfrac{x}{y}\right)^{-1}$ **p** $\sqrt[3]{x^4} \times \sqrt[4]{x^3}$

Level 3

3 Simplify:

a $\dfrac{4x^7 \times (3x^2)^3}{x^4}$ **b** $\sqrt{x^2} \times \sqrt[3]{8x^9}$ **c** $(9a^3)^{-\frac{1}{3}}$ **d** $(16a^3)^{\frac{5}{4}}$

e $\dfrac{8x^3y^{-2} \times 10x^2y^4}{(2x^2)^2}$

4 If $24 = 2^a \times 3^b$, then find $2^b \times 3^a$.

5 If $\dfrac{2^{3n+1}}{2^{n-1}} = 2^b$, find b.

6 If $\sqrt{\dfrac{y^{m+n}}{y^{2n}}} = y^a$, find a.

7 If $2^x \times 4^{x-1} \times 8^{-1} = 2^a$, find a.

8 If $\dfrac{1}{4x^4} = bx^c$, find the values of b and c.

9 If $2^4 \times 3^y = 6^x$, find the values of x and y.

10 $\dfrac{5^{x+1} \times 5^{-3}}{5^{1-2x}} = 5^a$. Find a.

Chapter Review

algebra	evaluate	formula	substitute
base	expand	index	symbol
coefficient	exponent	power	variable
constant	expression	pronumeral	
distributive	factorise	sequence	

1 Write pairs of sentences to demonstrate the difference between everyday and mathematical usage of these words: expand, expression, power.

2 Copy and complete:
To **simplify** an expression is to ...
To **expand** an expression is to ...
To **evaluate** an expression is to ...
A **sequence** in mathematics is ...

3 Write in index notation a power in which the base is rational, and the exponent is integral and less than zero, with a decimal fraction coefficient.

4 Write the *plural* of: index, sequence, formula.

5 Match *word* with correct *meaning*:
algebra   insert brackets by selecting common factors
constant   a symbol standing for one or more numbers
factorise   a pattern governing expansion and factorisation
pronumeral   generalised arithmetic: symbols in place of numerals
distributive   a number whose value does not vary

Chapter Review Exercises

MC

1 Give algebraic expressions for the following:

   a The even number just before $3x + 2$, itself an even number.
   b P dollars and 50 cents converted to cents.
   c Develop a formula for this sequence and find term 15: 5, 8, 11, ...

1.4

2 Express in index form:

   a $3 \times 3 \times 3 \times 3$ **b** $p \times p \times p$ **c** 1 (use base 2)   **d** $^-3a \times {^-3a} \times {^-3a}$

1.4

3 Referring to $8x^5$, write the:

   a power   **b** exponent   **c** base   **d** coefficient

1.8

4 Evaluate each expression:

   a 4^3 **b** $(-2)^4$ **c** $\left(\dfrac{3}{5}\right)^3$ **d** $(0.6)^2$ **e** 4×3^2

   f 7^0 **g** 10^{-4} **h** $100^{\frac{1}{2}}$ **i** 0^{-5} **j** $1000^{-\frac{1}{3}}$

k $(2^3)^2$ **l** $\left[\left(\dfrac{-2}{3}\right)^2\right]^2$ **m** $-9x^0$ **n** $-4 \times 9^{\frac{1}{2}}$ **o** $(-8)^{\frac{1}{3}} \times 16^{-\frac{1}{2}}$

p $64^{\frac{1}{6}}$ **q** $243^{-\frac{1}{5}}$ **r** $\dfrac{1}{\sqrt[4]{2401}}$ (use a calculator)

5 Simplify where possible:

a $a^2 \times a^3$ **b** $4p^5 \times 3p^5$ **c** $x^5 \div x^2$ **d** $g^3f^4 \times gf^2$

e $12c^6 \div 3c^3$ **f** $\dfrac{a^4b^3}{ab^2}$ **g** $7t^0$ **h** $-27x^3 \div 18x^3$

i $(a^4)^5$ **j** $(8x^4)^{\frac{1}{2}}$ **k** c^{-3} **l** $\left(\dfrac{a}{4}\right)^{-1}$

m $8a^2 - 6a^3$ **n** $k^3 + k^0$ **o** $\dfrac{-7w^5}{w^0}$ **p** $\left(\dfrac{1}{8}\right)^0 \div \dfrac{1}{8}$

q $-5k^{\frac{1}{2}} + 3k^{\frac{1}{2}}$ **r** $\dfrac{-4a^6 \times 3a^{-2}}{2a^4 - a^4}$ **s** $(64a^3b^6)^{\frac{1}{3}}$ **t** $\sqrt[5]{m^{10}t}$

6 Simplify $6p^3 - 3p^2 + 4p^3 - p^2 + 5p$, then evaluate if $p = 2$.

7 Expand, simplifying where possible:

a $6(3x - 4)$ **b** $-3(2a^2 - 5a)$ **c** $\dfrac{2}{3}(6x - 2)$ **d** $-5x(2x^3 - 3x)$

e $4(2a - 5) - 3a$ **f** $-3c^2(c^3 + 2c) + c^5$ **g** $(2m - 1)(m - 6)$ **h** $(3x - 5)^2$

8 Factorise:

a $7x - 7a$ **b** $6k + 12$ **c** $xp - 7p$ **d** $-16x + 24$

e $6ap - 3p^2$ **f** $x^2 - 100$ **g** $-6a^3 + 9a^2x$ **h** $\dfrac{1}{2}x^5y^3 - \dfrac{1}{4}xy^2$

9 What numeral goes in each box?

a $(\square x^3)^2 = 25x^{\square}$ **b** $\dfrac{\square(4x^2)^2}{12x^{\square}} = 4x$

10 Consider the equation $ax^2 = (ax)^2$.

a Is this true for *all* values of a? Give a reason for your answer.
b Is it true for *any* values of a? Show why or why not.

11 Simplify:

a $\dfrac{4x^7y^6}{\sqrt{9x^4y^6}}$ **b** $\left(\dfrac{4}{9}\right)^{-\frac{1}{2}}$ **c** $\sqrt{\dfrac{x^m}{x^{-m}}}$ **d** $\dfrac{w^{3m+1}}{w^2}$

12 Find the value of x in each of the following:

a $5^x = 125$ **b** $5^x = \dfrac{1}{125}$ **c** $\sqrt[3]{x^4} = 256$ **d** $8^x = \dfrac{1}{16}$

13 Rewrite without the use of any radical signs (i.e. $\sqrt{\ }$, $\sqrt[3]{\ }$, etc.):

a $\sqrt{x}$ **b** $\sqrt[3]{w}$ **c** $\sqrt[4]{p}$ **d** $\sqrt[3]{x^2}$

e $\sqrt[3]{x}$ **f** $\sqrt{a}$ **g** $\sqrt{16x}$ **h** $\sqrt[3]{xy^3}$

14 Rewrite using full index notation:

a $\sqrt[5]{x^4}$ **b** $\dfrac{1}{\sqrt[5]{x^4}}$ **c** $\dfrac{\sqrt{x}}{\sqrt[3]{y}}$ **d** $\dfrac{3}{\sqrt[3]{x^2y}}$

1.8

MC

1.1
1.2

1.3

1.4

1.4

1.8

1.7

1.7

1.7

TEACHER

Keeping Mathematically Fit

Part A—Non-calculator

1 Evaluate 0.3×0.2.

2 Write a fraction that is between $\frac{1}{3}$ and $\frac{1}{2}$.

3 This step graph shows the parking costs at a shopping centre car park.

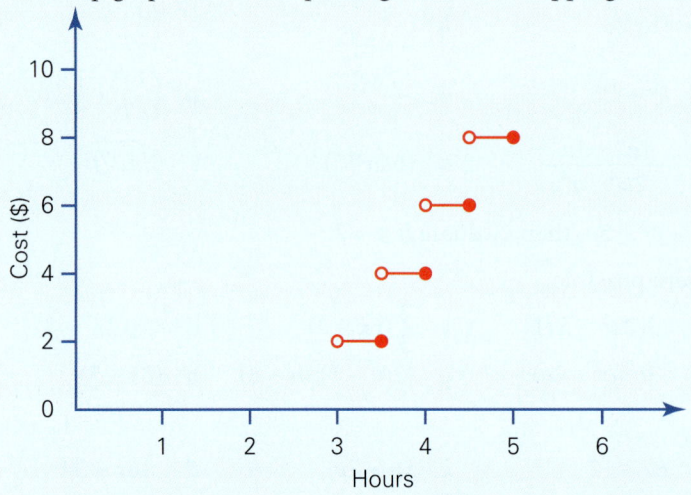

  a How many hours of free parking can shoppers have?
  b Bill's ticket shows he entered the car park at 10:37 am. If he leaves at 2:15 pm how much will he have to pay?

4 Estimate the value of $\dfrac{16.7 + 12.1}{4.8}$. Give your answer as a whole number.

5 The point $(9, y)$ lies on the line shown. What is the value of y?

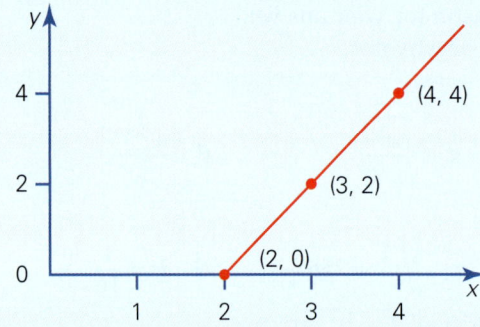

6 Between which two consecutive whole numbers does $\sqrt{71}$ lie?

7 Given $62.4 \times 1.9 = 118.56$, what is the value of 0.624×19?

8 A menu has two different entrees, four main meals and three desserts. How many different three-course meal combinations are possible?

9 Write the next two terms in this sequence: 21, 15, 9, …, …

10 Write $\frac{1}{3}$ as a repeating decimal.

Part B—Calculator

1 An airfare changed from \$368 to \$398. What percentage increase was this, to the nearest tenth?

2 The largest square possible is to be cut from a circle of card of diameter 30 cm.

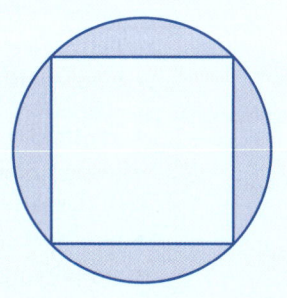

    a What size is the square?
    b What area of card is wasted?

3 Eight times a certain number gives an answer between 0 and 1. Between which two values must this number lie?

4 Reuben's recipe requires $\frac{3}{4}$ tspn nutmeg, $\frac{2}{3}$ tspn ground ginger and $\frac{1}{2}$ tspn cinnamon.

What total quantity of spices is required?

5 Evaluate $\sqrt{13\cdot6 - 1\cdot4^2}$ correct to 2 decimal places.

6 Using the digits 2, 4, 5, 7 and 9 with just one multiplication sign,

    a What is the largest possible answer you can obtain?
       For example, 4295×7 gives 30 065. Can you do better?
    b How many different answers are possible?

1 What you need to know and revise

Outcome PAS 4.3:
Operates with fractions, decimals, percentages, ratios and rates:
- rounding decimals to a given number of decimal places
- converting fractions to decimals and percentages
- converting terminating decimals to fractions and percentages
- converting percentages to fractions and decimals
- calculating percentages of a quantity
- increasing and decreasing a quantity by a given percentage
- ordering fractions, decimals and percentages
- expressing one quantity as a percentage of another
- another
- using ratios to compare various quantities of the same type
- writing ratios in various forms
- simplifying ratios
- using ratios, unitary method and dividing a quantity into a given ratio.

2 What you will learn in this chapter

Outcome PAS 5.1.1:
Applies index laws to simplify and evaluate arithmetic expressions and uses scientific notation to write large and small numbers:
- recognising the need for a notation to express very large or very small numbers
- expressing numbers in scientific notation
- entering and reading scientific notation using a calculator
- using index laws to make order of magnitude checks for numbers in scientific notation, e.g. $(3 \cdot 12 \times 10^4) \times (4.2 \times 10^6)$ $12 \times 10^{10} = 1 \cdot 2 \times 10^{11}$
- converting numbers expressed in scientific notation to decimal form
- ordering numbers expressed in scientific notation.

Outcome NS 5.2.1:
Rounds decimals to a specified number of significant figures, expresses recurring decimals in fraction form and converts rates from one set of units to another:
- identifying significant figures
- rounding numbers to a specified number of significant figures
- using the language of estimation appropriately, including:
  – rounding
  – approximate
  – exact
  – level of accuracy
- using the symbols for approximation, e.g. determining the effect of truncating or rounding during calculations on the accuracy of the results.
- converting rates from one set of units to another.

Working Mathematically outcomes WMS 5.1, 5.2, 5.3
Students will be required to *question*, *apply strategies*, *communicate*, *reason* and *reflect* in the sections of this chapter.

2

Rational numbers

MathsCheck
Rational numbers

1 Round off the following numbers to complete the table:

	Number	Nearest 10	Nearest 100	Nearest 1000
a	2643			
b	7068			
c	16 435			
d	8904			
e	12 305			
f	10 512			
g	8007			
h	6999			

2 Round off to the nearest *tenth*:
  a 0·83 **b** 2·6 **c** 0·85 **d** 7·382

3 Round to the nearest *hundredth*:
  a 0·764 **b** 0·857 **c** 6·175 **d** 8·998

4 Round correct to *3 decimal places*:
  a 0·6712 **b** 0·1585 **c** 8·0406 **d** 4·0055

5 In 1995, the estimated population of Australia was 17 875 906. Approximate this to the nearest:
  a 10 **b** 100 **c** 1000 **d** 10 000
  e 100 000 **f** million **g** 10 million

6 Which of **5a–g** above would be most appropriate rounding for the following purposes?
  a Comparing Australia's population with that of another country.
  b Dividing the population into age groups for a road accident survey.
  c Treasury Department calculating projected income tax collected by the government from all the workers in Australia.
  d Using a sample of 1000 people as a way of finding out what the whole of Australia thinks about a certain issue.
  e Finding the percentage of the population receiving social security benefits.
  f When might the *exact* number be necessary?

7 Approximate each decimal to suit the situation:
  a I'd like 2·483 76 kilograms of sausages, please.
  b Boil my egg for 2·806 minutes, please
  c Australia exported 254 602·87 t of sugar to China.
  d The state champion sprinted 100 m in 10·2804 s.
  e The shopper paid the bill when the supermarket register showed $112·43.
  f Today's exchange rate is A$1 = US$0·75263.

8 3·78☐ was correctly rounded to 3·79. What could ☐ have been?

9 A rounded number was given as 3400. What could the original number have been if it had been rounded to the nearest:

   a 10?   **b** 100?

10 Change to common fractions or mixed numbers:

a	0·75	**b**	0·18	**c**	0·60	**d**	1·50	**e**	0·09
f	2·58	**g**	0·01	**h**	0·008	**i**	12·07	**j**	0·000 014

11 Change to decimal fractions:

  a $\dfrac{7}{100}$ **b** $\dfrac{4}{10}$ **c** $\dfrac{3}{50}$ **d** $\dfrac{3}{2}$ **e** $\dfrac{4}{5}$

  f $\dfrac{7}{4}$ **g** $\dfrac{4}{9}$ **h** $\dfrac{5}{6}$ **i** $\dfrac{4}{15}$ **j** $\dfrac{2}{7}$

12 Replace ☐ with >, < or =:

  a 0·325 ☐ 0·326   **b** 9·003 ☐ 9·01   **c** 00·47 ☐ 0·470

13 Write in *descending order*:

  a 8·31, 8·302, 8·132   **b** 0·404, 0·4, 0·44   **c** 0·05, 0·47, $\dfrac{3}{8}$

14 These are library catalogue numbers for books. In what order would they appear on the shelves?
310·16, 258·34, 103·61, 258·41, 258·35, 103·9

15 Express as a basic fraction:

a	80%	**b**	58%	**c**	15%	**d**	8%	**e**	150%
f	2%	**g**	235%	**h**	300%	**i**	$17\frac{1}{2}\%$	**j**	$5\frac{1}{4}\%$

16 Express as a decimal fraction:

a	27%	**b**	45%	**c**	6%	**d**	9%	**e**	13%
f	120%	**g**	240%	**h**	108%	**i**	$3\frac{1}{2}\%$	**j**	$11\frac{3}{4}\%$
k	72·8%	**l**	117·9%	**m**	1·5%	**n**	6·45%	**o**	321·4%

17 Change each fraction to a percentage:

  a $\dfrac{7}{100}$ **b** $\dfrac{65}{100}$ **c** $\dfrac{9}{50}$ **d** $\dfrac{13}{20}$ **e** $\dfrac{7}{10}$

  f $\dfrac{3}{25}$ **g** $\dfrac{3}{2}$ **h** $\dfrac{3}{4}$ **i** $\dfrac{3}{5}$ **j** $\dfrac{5}{8}$

  k $\dfrac{2}{3}$ **l** $\dfrac{1}{6}$ **m** $\dfrac{5}{9}$ **n** $1\frac{3}{4}$ **o** $2\frac{4}{5}$

18 Change each decimal to a percentage:

a	0·58	**b**	0·7	**c**	0·25	**d**	0·09	**e**	0·02
f	1·4	**g**	2·6	**h**	0·925	**i**	0·855	**j**	0·035
k	1·275	**l**	0·1825	**m**	0·008	**n**	0·6	**o**	0·16

19 a Express the test results, 17 out of 20, as a percentage.

  b 23 out of every 25 students do mathematics in Year 11. What percent do *not* study maths?

c Ludwig won seven out of eight chess matches.

    i What percent did he win?

    ii What percent did he lose?

d Janet scored 13 of her netball team's 40 points.

    i What percent of the total points did she score?

    ii What percent did her goal attack partner score?

20 Calculate:

a 10% of 80	**b** 50% of 300	**c** 25% of 400	**d** $33\frac{1}{3}$% of 60
e 20% of $40	**f** 75% of $80	**g** 5% of 200 m	**h** $12\frac{1}{2}$% of $800
i 110% of 200 kg	**j** 150% of $70	**k** 30% of 80 km	**l** 90% of 50 mL
m 2% of $5000	**n** $2\frac{1}{2}$% of $80	**o** $66\frac{2}{3}$% of $90	**p** 225% of 400 g

21 If necessary, convert the measurement to a smaller unit to find:

a 6% of 2 m	**b** 18% of 3·8 km	**c** 86% of 1·4 cm	**d** 156% of 1·5 t

22 Calculate to the nearest 5 cents:

a 70% of $46·40   **b** 29% of $58·20

c 3·55% of $112·36   **d** 209·75% of $3·25

23 Find the value of:

a $7\frac{1}{2}$% of $200   **b** $6\frac{1}{4}$% of $90   **c** $11\frac{3}{4}$% of $72·84

d $16\frac{2}{3}$% of $120   **e** $\frac{1}{2}$% of $2000   **f** 0·155% of $130 000

g $8\frac{1}{3}$% of $743   **h** 0·95% of $120 000

24 a Increase $600 by 20%.   **b** Increase 2000 revs by 15%.

    c Decrease $750 by 35%.   **d** Decrease 93 kg by 8%.

    e Increase 45 s by 67%.   **f** Decrease 850 m^2 by $7\frac{1}{2}$%.

    g Increase 5·3 m by 125%.   **h** Decrease $4200 by $13\frac{1}{4}$%.

25 a Shoes formerly $89 were *reduced* by 30% in a sale. Find the sale price.

    b A car worth $26 000 new *depreciates* by $22\frac{1}{2}$% in the first year. What is it worth at the end of the year?

    c Ford Falcon production, normally 450 vehicles per day, was *stepped up* by $12\frac{1}{2}$% to meet demand. What is the new production rate?

26 Find the **percentage increase** if the price *rises* from:

a $20 to $25	**b** $15 to $20	**c** 40¢ to 45¢
d $2·50 to $2·80	**e** $180 to $200	**f** 43¢ to 45¢
g $3·60 to $8·50	**h** 62·5¢/L to 68·9¢/L	

27 Find the **percentage decrease** if the price *falls* from:

a $80 to $60	**b** $50 to $40	**c** 75¢ to 70¢
d $1·60/min to $1·50/min	**e** $89 to $69	**f** $210 to $197
g $39·95 to $29·95	**h** $27·78 to $23·45	

28 Movie tickets are reduced from the usual $10·80 for a night session to $7 for a daytime session. What percent reduction is this?

29 A worker on $398·50/wk was offered a new wage of $406·95/wk. What percentage rise was this?

30 To negotiate a corner in a motor race, engine revolutions were reduced from 8500 to 6800. What percent reduction was this?

31 A house *appreciates* in value from $154 000 to $178 000 over 3 years. What was the average percentage increase per year in that time?

32 Simplify each ratio:

  a $5 : 10$ **b** $0·12 : 6$ **c** $1\frac{1}{2} : 3\frac{1}{2}$

  d $1 \text{ h } 30 \text{ min} : 45 \text{ min}$ **e** $450 \text{ g} : 1·5 \text{ kg}$ **f** $2\frac{1}{2} \text{ min} : 40 \text{ s}$

33 Express as a **unit ratio** in the form X : 1 (round to 1 decimal place if necessary):

  a $30 : 10$ **b** $24 : 8$ **c** $3·5 : 0·5$ **d** $2·4 : 1·6$

34 Express in the form 1 : Y (round to 1 decimal place if necessary):

  a $4 : 5$ **b** $2 : 7$ **c** $100 : 368$ **d** $24 : 36$

35 Divide:

  a $50 in the ratio 2 : 3   **b** $800 in the ratio 3 : 5
  c 420 m in the ratio 4 : 3   **d** 360 kg in the ratio 11 : 7
  e 7·2 km in the ratio 4 : 5   **f** 60 kg in the ratio 1 : 2 : 3

36 A syndicate of three people enters Lotto each week, contributing in the ratio 3 : 4 : 5. If a prize of $1 200 000 is won, how much should each person receive?

37 A jewellery manufacturer makes an alloy of 3 parts copper to 22 parts gold.

  a What weight of each metal is in an 85 g ring?
  b What is the percentage composition of the alloy?

38 A 650 g jar of curry paste consists of chillies, garlic and nutmeg in the proportions 5 : 6 : 2. How much of each ingredient is in the mixture?

39 Find the *greater* of each pair of ratios.

  a $2 : 5, 1 : 4$ **b** $7 : 10, 2 : 3$ **c** $\frac{3}{5}, \frac{5}{8}$ **d** $\frac{7}{8}, \frac{5}{6}$

  e $0·3 : 4, 0·4 : 5$ **f** $\frac{4·8}{3·7}, \frac{2·3}{1·8}$ **g** $\frac{x}{6}, \frac{3x}{12}$ **h** $\frac{4}{m}, \frac{11}{3m}$

40 If $A : B = 2 : 3$ and $B : C = 4 : 7$ find the ratio of A to C.

41 Pineapple juice and orange juice are mixed in the ratio of 2 : 3. This juice mixture is then diluted with water in the ratio of 5 : 12. Find the ratio of:

  a pineapple juice to water   **b** orange juice to final mixture.

TEACHER

Exploring New Ideas

2.1 Rational numbers

THE REAL NUMBER SYSTEM

Rational numbers can be written in fraction notation — that is, as a/b where a and b are integers. The term **rational** comes from the word '*ratio*' and a fraction is the ratio of two integers.

Fractions are rational: $0 \cdot \dot{6} = \frac{2}{3}$; $0 \cdot 8 = \frac{8}{10}$; $^-0 \cdot 75 = \frac{^-3}{4}$, $3\frac{1}{2} = \frac{7}{2}$

Integers are rational: $8 = \frac{8}{1}$; $^-4 = \frac{^-4}{1}$; $1 = \frac{1}{1}$

Numbers that are **not** rational include π, $\sqrt{2}$, $\sqrt{3}$, ... They cannot be written as the ratio of two integers.

The rational numbers form part of the real number system:

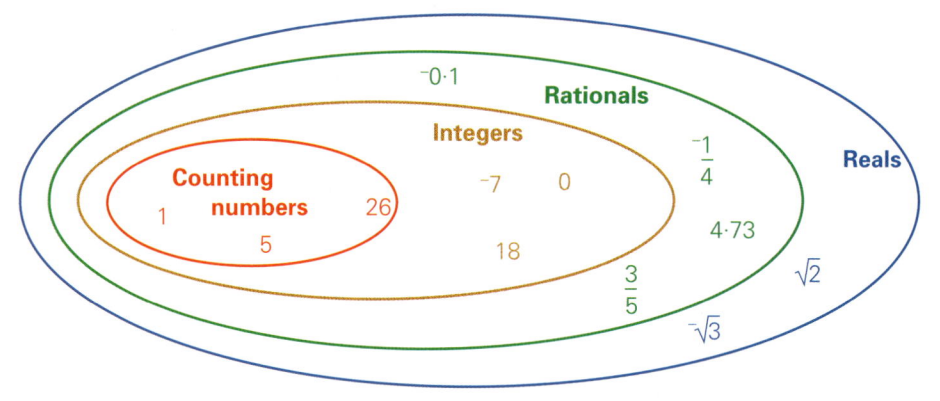

Real numbers can be located on the number line:

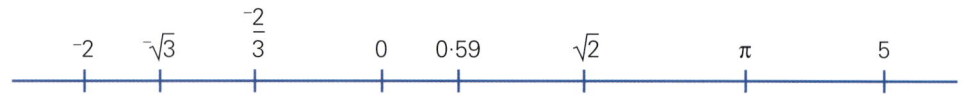

There are numbers that are **not** in the real number system, and cannot be placed on this line.

An example is $\sqrt{^-1}$. You will encounter these numbers later.

ESTIMATING

Estimating an answer before doing calculations gives us an idea of what answer to expect. It helps us to check whether our answer is reasonable.

For all calculations, whether pen-and-paper or by calculator, it is essential to:

1 **Estimate** *first*, as a guide to a *reasonable* answer. Rounding appropriately is the key.

2 **Calculate exactly**, checking your answer against the estimate. Does your answer *make sense?*

3 If appropriate, do a **final approximation** of the answer.

EXAMPLE 1

Estimate the result in each of the following:

a 3609×7105 **b** $8{\cdot}56 \times 4{\cdot}173$ **c** $0{\cdot}0316 \div 0{\cdot}35$

Solutions

a 3609×7105
$\approx 4000 \times 7000$
$\approx 28\,000\,000$

b $8{\cdot}56 \times 4{\cdot}173$
$\approx 9 \times 4$
≈ 36

c $0{\cdot}0316 \div 0{\cdot}35$
$= 3{\cdot}16 \div 35$
$\approx 3 \div 35$
$\approx \dfrac{1}{10} \text{ or } 0{\cdot}1$

EXAMPLE 2

Give an upper and lower boundary estimate for the answer to $\dfrac{329 + 566}{7{\cdot}4}$.

Solution

Lower boundary: $\dfrac{329 + 566}{7{\cdot}4} \approx \dfrac{300 + 500}{8}$

$\approx \dfrac{800}{8}$

≈ 100

> Round **down** the numerator.
> Round **up** the denominator.

Upper boundary: $\dfrac{329 + 566}{7{\cdot}4} \approx \dfrac{350 + 600}{7}$

$\approx \dfrac{950}{7}$

≈ 140

> Round **up** the numerator.
> Round **down** the denominator.

> $980 \div 7 = 140$

Helpful hints

- Look for links with **numbers easy to work with**, such as wholes, tens, hundreds, thousands: $38{\cdot}4 \times 94{\cdot}86 \approx 38 \times 100$

- **Fractional equivalents of decimals** can simplify operations:

  $0{\cdot}518 \approx \dfrac{1}{2}$, $1{\cdot}23 \approx 1\frac{1}{4}$, and so on.

- If one factor or term rounds **up** conveniently, look for another that rounds **down**, to keep the approximation closer to the actual answer:

  3814×7132
  $\approx (\uparrow)\, 4000 \times (\downarrow)\, 7000$

  $27{\cdot}64 + 32{\cdot}51$
  $\approx (\uparrow)\, 28 \times (\downarrow)\, 32$

  > How have we bent the rules here? Why?

- For fractional expressions, round to numbers that **cancel easily**:

  $\dfrac{19{\cdot}32 \times 5{\cdot}27}{1{\cdot}86} \approx \dfrac{\overset{10}{\cancel{20}} \times 5}{\underset{1}{\cancel{2}}}$

  ≈ 50

EXERCISE 2A

1 Which of the following are rational numbers?

    a 0·1   **b** 15%   **c** 5   **d** $6\frac{1}{4}$ **e** $0.\dot{3}$

    f $\sqrt{12}$ **g** π **h** $\sqrt{9}$ **i** $^-7$ **j** $\frac{2}{9}$

2 Express the following in rational form (a/b):

    a 0·25   **b** 8   **c** $^-6$ **d** $3\frac{1}{4}$ **e** 2·4

    f 20%   **g** $^-1\cdot\dot{3}$ **h** $\sqrt{144}$

Level 2

3 Show how you estimate the result in each of the following, *then* use a calculator to find the *exact* answer:

    a $538 + 797$ **b** $71\cdot8 + 43\cdot2$ **c** 497×212

    d $0\cdot49 \div 0\cdot8$ **e** $70\,483 - 38\,795$ **f** $7\cdot6 \div 1\cdot9 \times 2\cdot75$

    g $31\cdot6 \times 9\cdot81$ **h** $9\cdot003 \div 5\cdot7$ **i** $3\cdot25 \times 0\cdot12$

    j $0\cdot54 \times 4\cdot236$ **k** $9\cdot3 \times 1\cdot7 \div 2\cdot54$ **l** $\dfrac{\sqrt{67\cdot32}}{6\cdot8 - 5\cdot17}$

    m $(2\cdot74)^3 \div \sqrt{8\cdot65}$ **n** $\dfrac{12\cdot47 \times 3\cdot04}{3\cdot806 + 1\cdot48}$

4 Are the following calculator answers **reasonable**? Explain.

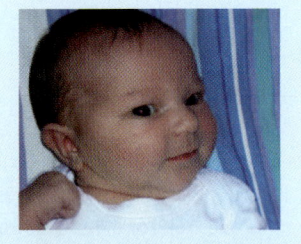

    a 9·4 kg for the weight of a newborn baby.

    b 32·8 s for the 1 km running race.

    c 6·7 m² for the area of a room measuring 2·7 m × 4·1 m.

    d 7258·4 for the product of 84·4 and 8·6. Suggest how this answer was obtained.

    e 9 for the quotient of 8·7 ÷ 0·94.

5 Suggest the *most suitable level of rounding* for the following situations. Give a reason for your selection.

    a Various sections of a crowd at a football match contained 2761, 3907, 1803, 2370, 3124 and 5076 people. You are a sports journalist reporting on the match.

    b A $186·45 restaurant bill is to be shared equally among six diners.

    c 2·81 m × 4·12 m are the exact measurements of a room to be tiled. *Area* needs to be calculated.

    d Perimeter 56·357 m, height of walls 2·815 m. You are a house painter needing to find the area of the walls to calculate the quantity of paint necessary.

    e You are a cabinetmaker producing kitchen cupboards to fit snugly into a space measuring 2835 mm long by 608 mm deep.

6 Give appropriate *upper and lower boundaries* for the estimated answers to these calculations, *then* find the **accurate** answer with a calculator.

    a $3609 + 7105$ **b** $4763 - 2316$ **c** 2604×5020

    d $7\cdot6 \times 85\cdot34$ **e** $18\cdot35 \div 3\cdot52$ **f** $7\cdot92 + 0\cdot81 \times 0\cdot263$

7 **Estimate** high/low boundaries first, **then calculate** using exact figures given. **Finally, round** to the nearest tenth.

    a $9\cdot647 + 3\cdot538$ **b** $32\cdot56 - 18\cdot49$ **c** $8\cdot64 - (3\cdot44 + 0\cdot98)$

    d $15\cdot31 \times 5\cdot97$ **e** $61\cdot07 \div 9\cdot64$ **f** $\pi \times 8\cdot239$

g	$12{\cdot}036 + 2{\cdot}195 \times \pi$	**h**	$(4{\cdot}137)^2 - 5{\cdot}83$	**i**	$\sqrt{28{\cdot}07}$
j	$\dfrac{8{\cdot}291 + 3{\cdot}876}{2{\cdot}4 \times 5{\cdot}85}$	**k**	$\dfrac{(2{\cdot}1)^3}{4{\cdot}037}$	**l**	$\dfrac{198{\cdot}7 - 47{\cdot}86}{\sqrt{104{\cdot}081}}$

8 Explain how you would make a reasonable estimate of the following:

    a the size of the crowd at a football game in Sydney Stadium
    b the number of students at your school
    c the number of people in a movie theatre
    d the thickness of a single sheet of paper
    e the number of grains of sand in a handful.

9 To calculate the circumference of a circle of diameter 6·248 m, to 1 decimal place, we use the formula $C = \pi d$.

    a Round off π and d to 1 decimal place, then calculate C and round to 1 decimal place.
    b Calculate C using unrounded values, then round C to 1 decimal place.
    c What is the difference between the answers in parts **a** and **b**?
    d Which of the answers in **a** and **b** is more accurate?

2.2 Scientific notation

VERY LARGE NUMBERS

Whether it be the **gross national product** (total value of all goods and services) of an entire country, or the phenomenal **distances in the universe**, very large numbers are needed to describe the situation.

The international system has a special name for *every third place* of whole numbers after 1000.

> You will use this in science.

Name	Amount	Numeral	Power of 10
million	a thousand thousand	1 000 000	10^6
billion	a thousand million	1 000 000 000	10^9
trillion	a thousand billion	1 000 000 000 000	10^{12}
quadrillion	a thousand trillion	…	…
quintillion	…	…	…

Can you complete and extend the list?

> The names are used differently in the UK.

Writing names or numerals for such huge (but real) numbers becomes very tedious: 3 846 750 600 000 is three trillion, eight hundred and forty-six billion, seven hundred and fifty million, six hundred thousand!

Because science must deal with such numbers all the time, a special system was devised to abbreviate the numerals.

> A numeral in **scientific notation** or **standard form** is written as the *product* of a *number from 1 to (but not including) 10* and a power of 10:
>
> $3\,650\,000 = 3{\cdot}65 \times 1\,000\,000$
> $\qquad\qquad = 3{\cdot}65 \times 10^6$

To key this into a calculator:

Either   3·65 $\boxed{\text{EXP}}$ 6   *Note*: there is no need to press $\boxed{\text{X}}$ 10. The $\boxed{\text{EXP}}$ key does this for you.

Or   3·65 $\boxed{\text{X}}$ 10 $\boxed{y^x}$ 6

Note: most calculators will display this as $3{\cdot}65^{06}$. Remember this means $3{\cdot}65 \times 10^6$ (not $3{\cdot}65$ to the power of 6).

EXAMPLE 1
Express $4\,800\,000\,000$ in scientific notation.

Solution
$4\,800\,000\,000{\cdot}$
$= 4{\cdot}8 \times 10^9$

EXAMPLE 2
Write the basic numeral for $7{\cdot}2 \times 10^5$.

Solution
$7{\cdot}2 \times 10^5$ | Move the decimal point five places to the right.
$= 720\,000$

EXAMPLE 3
Estimate the answer to $(2{\cdot}8 \times 10^4) \times (5{\cdot}13 \times 10^7)$.

Solution
$(2{\cdot}8 \times 10^4) \times (5{\cdot}13 \times 10^7)$
$\approx 15 \times 10^{11}$
$= 1{\cdot}5 \times 10^{12}$

EXERCISE 2B

1 Write in words:

   a 650 000 000   **b** 7 804 900 000

2 Write in digits: Five hundred and thirty trillion, one hundred and ninety-four billion and seventy million.

3 Which of these are in correct scientific notation?

   a $3{\cdot}8 \times 10^5$ **b** $1{\cdot}7 \times 10^{15}$ **c** $10{\cdot}34 \times 10^6$ **d** $36{\cdot}5 \times 10^4$
   e $0{\cdot}98 \times 10^7$ **f** $4{\cdot}0 \times 10^8$ **g** 8×10^9 **h** $9{\cdot}999 \times 10^9$

4 Copy and complete:

   a $1800 = 1{\cdot}8 \times 1000 = 1{\cdot}8 \times 10^{\square}$ **b** $2\,400\,000 = 2{\cdot}4 \times \square = 2{\cdot}4 \times 10^{\square}$

c $120\ 000 = \boxed{} \times 100\ 000 = \boxed{} \times 10^5$ **d** $508\ 000 = \boxed{} \times \boxed{} = \boxed{} \times 10^5$

5 Write in scientific notation:

a 7400	**b** 850	**c** 90 000	**d** 34 000
e 108 000	**f** 4 300 000	**g** 2 070 000	**h** 5 634 000 000
i 678·4	**j** 34·08	**k** 4·28	**l** 876×10^5

6 Write the basic numeral for:

a $3·9 \times 10^2$	**b** 2×10^5	**c** $7·08 \times 10^6$	**d** $2·06 \times 10^4$
e $8·0 \times 10^7$	**f** $3·024 \times 10^5$	**g** $7·0 \times 10$	**h** $2·983 \times 10^2$
i $5·0769 \times 10^3$	**j** $4·0 \times 10^1$	**k** $6·805 \times 10^8$	**l** $\boxed{5·07^{09}}$

Level 2 $\boxed{\text{Calculator readout}}$

7 Write the basic numeral and scientific notation for:

    a $125\ 000 \times 40\ 000$ **b** $678\ 000 \times 347\ 000$ **c** $2\ 000\ 000 \times 8\ 000\ 000$

8 Estimate each answer:

    a $(4·1 \times 10^5) \times (2·1 \times 10^3)$ **b** $(1·9 \times 10^7) \times (3·1 \times 10^2)$

    c $(5·85 \times 10^6) \times (5·02 \times 10^9)$ **d** $(3·2 \times 10^3) \times (6·92 \times 10^8)$

    e $(7·07 \times 10^2) \times (9·16 \times 10^{12})$

9 Rewrite each scientific fact in scientific notation:

    a The human brain contains 10 000 000 000 neurons.

    b Saturn is 1 430 000 000 km from the sun.

    c The moon's average distance from the earth is 384 400 km.

10 Translate each statement into basic numeral form:

    a The area of all the oceans on earth is $3·617 \times 10^8$ km².

    b $1·67 \times 10^{21}$ protons have a mass of 1 mg.

    c $2·2 \times 10^7$ people live in Australia and New Zealand.

11 Use the distributive law to simplify the following.
(Answer in scientific notation.)

    Distributive law:

    $ab + ac = a(b + c)$

a $5 \times 10^4 + 3 \times 10^4$	**b** $8 \times 10^6 - 5 \times 10^6$
c $3·7 \times 10^5 + 2·3 \times 10^5$	**d** $9·0 \times 10^8 - 4·2 \times 10^8$
e $8·6 \times 10^7 + 5·4 \times 10^7$	**f** $2·8 \times 10^7 + 3·6 \times 10^8$

12 Check each result above on your calculator.

13 Use your calculator to find the following:

    a $6 \times 10^5 \times 3 \times 10^4$ **b** $3·8 \times 10^6 \times 2·1 \times 10^5$ **c** $1·82 \times 10^4 \times 1·2 \times 10^4$

    d How many times greater than $3·5 \times 10^4$ is $3·5 \times 10^7$?

    e What must I take from $8·2 \times 10^5$ to get $3·5 \times 10^5$?

    f What must I multiply $1·4 \times 10^4$ by to get $4·2 \times 10^4$?

    g Our planet has total land area of 1 480 000 000 km², with a population of $5·2 \times 10^9$. If all land were shared equally, how much would each person get?

    h Einstein developed the famous formula $E = mc^2$, where the amount of energy contained in matter is equal to its mass times the speed of light squared (the speed of light $= 3 \times 10^8$ m/s). Restate the formula using a numeral in scientific notation in place of c^2.

VERY SMALL NUMBERS (LESS THAN 1)

We can use scientific notation to simplify the writing of very small numbers, for example:

$$0{\cdot}000\,035 = \frac{3{\cdot}5}{100\,000} = \frac{3{\cdot}5}{10^5} = 3{\cdot}5 \times \frac{1}{10^5} = 3{\cdot}5 \times 10^{-5}$$

We use a **negative index** to show **division** by a power of 10.

Here, the decimal point must be moved five places **to the left** to restore it to its original position. The power of 10 is $^-5$.

EXAMPLE 1

Express $0{\cdot}0071$ in scientific notation.

Solution

$0{\cdot}0071 = 7{\cdot}1 \times 10^{-3}$

> Decimal point must be moved three places to the **left**, so power is $^-3$.

EXAMPLE 2

Change $4{\cdot}028 \times 10^{-6}$ to its basic numeral.

Solution

$4{\cdot}028 \times 10^{-6}$

$= 0{\cdot}000\,004\,028$

> Move the decimal point **six places left**.

EXERCISE 2C

1 Which of these are in correct scientific notation?

  a $6{\cdot}8 \times 10^{-3}$ **b** $0{\cdot}8 \times 10^{-4}$ **c** $0{\cdot}36 \times 10^{-2}$ **d** $2{\cdot}05 \times 10^{-5}$

  e $4{\cdot}0 \times 10^{-6}$ **f** 8×10^{-7} **g** $^-6{\cdot}0 \times 10^{-5}$ **h** $\frac{3}{4} \times 10^{-3}$

2 Write in scientific notation:

  a $0{\cdot}0047$ **b** $0{\cdot}003$ **c** $0{\cdot}000\,07$ **d** $0{\cdot}000\,102$

  e $0{\cdot}06$ **f** $0{\cdot}19$ **g** $0{\cdot}000\,080\,5$ **h** $0{\cdot}000\,200\,6$

  i $0{\cdot}509$ **j** $0{\cdot}000\,000\,001$ **k** 3 **l** 34×10^{-4}

3 Write the basic numeral for:

  a $5{\cdot}2 \times 10^{-3}$ **b** $2{\cdot}54 \times 10^{-5}$ **c** $1{\cdot}3 \times 10^{-1}$ **d** $6{\cdot}044 \times 10^{-4}$

  e 5×10^{-6} **f** $2{\cdot}0 \times 10^{-2}$ **g** $3{\cdot}707 \times 10^{-5}$ **h** 1×10^{-1}

  i $3{\cdot}045 \times 10^{-7}$ **j** $8{\cdot}076 \times 10^{-8}$ **k** $1{\cdot}02 \times 10^{0}$ **l** 37×10^{-4}

4 Use a calculator, and write the scientific notation and basic numeral for:

  a $0{\cdot}0036 \times 0{\cdot}000\,51$ **b** $0{\cdot}008 \times 0{\cdot}000\,109$ **c** $0{\cdot}000\,080\,9 \times 0{\cdot}0104$

5 Rewrite each fact in scientific notation:

  a The single-celled *paramecium* has a length of $0{\cdot}002$ mm.
  b A large *molecule* has a diameter of $0{\cdot}000\,001\,2$ mm.
  c The mass of one *proton* is $0{\cdot}000\,000\,000\,000\,000\,000\,001\,67$ mg.

6 Rewrite each fact in its base numeral.

  a The *density* of hydrogen gas is $8{\cdot}0 \times 10^{-5}$ g/cm^3.
  b *Animal cells* average $1{\cdot}5 \times 10^{-5}$ cm in diameter.
  c A *micrometre* (μm) is $1{\cdot}0 \times 10^{-6}$ m.

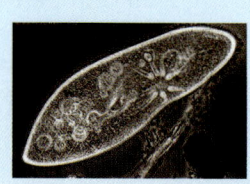

7 Arrange the following in ascending order:

    a $2.73 \times 10^7, 5.2 \times 10^{-2}, 8.33 \times 10^1$ **b** $6.1 \times 10^{-1}, 2.04 \times 10^3, 6.71 \times 10^{-7}$

    c $4.5 \times 10^5, 5.907 \times 10^{-3}, 6 \times 10^{-5}$ **d** $2.05 \times 10^{-2}, 7.6 \times 10^3, 2.2 \times 10^{-2}$

8 Express answers in scientific notation—try first without using your calculator.

    a $6.7 \times 10^{-4} + 2.5 \times 10^{-4}$ **b** $4.3 \times 10^{-8} - 2.4 \times 10^{-8}$ **c** $7 \times 10^{-5} + 5 \times 10^{-5}$

    d $3 \times 10^{-8} \times 8 \times 10^{-9}$ **e** $5 \times 10^{-3} \times 9 \times 10^{-7}$ **f** $2 \times 10^{-4} \times 1.8 \times 10^9$

Investigation Speed of light

1 a Find the **speed of light** in metres per second. If a **light year** is the standard astronomical measure of distance, find out how far light travels in 1 year, in kilometres.

  b The closest star (other than our sun) to earth is **Proxima Centauri**. It is 4·3 light years from earth. How far away in kilometres is it?

  c The **Andromeda** galaxy is 1.9×10^{22} km from earth. How long (in years) does its light take to reach us? Does this mean astronomers can see into the past? Explain.

2 What is the **total mass of earth's entire population**? Show any assumptions, estimates or calculations you make.

3 How many times will your **heart beat during your lifetime**? Again, show assumptions, estimates and calculations.

2.3 Significant figures

The degree of accuracy required in measurement varies according to the situation. *3·2 tonnes* is just as accurate as 3200 kg but *more accurate than 3 tonnes*. In general, the **more** *digits of significance* in the measurement number, the **more accurate** it is.

The digits that show the degree of accuracy of the measurement are called **significant figures**. 3·2 t and 3200 kg are both accurate to 2 significant figures.

> The *significant figures* make up *the number from one to (but not including) ten in scientific notation*. The number of significant figures in a measurement is an important indicator of its *degree of accuracy* in science.
>
>   7 036 000 m = **7·036** $\times 10^6$ m, with **4 significant figures**.
>
>   0·000 080 2 g = **8·02** $\times 10^{-5}$ g, with **3 significant figures**.

It is not necessary for a number to be in scientific notation for us to round to a certain number of significant figures. To round a number to 3 significant figures, the first three digits are determined, then zeros must be inserted to maintain the correct place values.

So,   50 762, correct to 3 significant figures, is 50 800
and   0·002 831, correct to 2 significant figures is 0·002 8.

Note that zeros are sometimes significant and sometimes not.
For example above in 50 800:

This zero is one of the three significant figures.

These zeros are not significant—they are place-holders.

EXAMPLES
Round to 2 significant figures:

a 305 800 km **b** 0·000 007 01 mm

Solutions

a $305\ 800$ **b** $0{\cdot}000\ 007\ 01$
$= 3{\cdot}058 \times 10^5$ $= 7{\cdot}01 \times 10^{-6}$
$\approx 3{\cdot}1 \times 10^5$ $\approx 7{\cdot}0 \times 10^{-6}$ mm
$= 310\ 000$ km $= 0{\cdot}000\ 007\ 0$ mm

EXERCISE 2D

1 i Write each number in scientific notation.
ii State the number of significant figures in the measurement.

a 350 000 km	**b** 6 780 000	**c** 408 000 000	**d** 0·000 920 4
e 0·000 750	**f** 0·002 007	**g** 90 000	**h** 0·000 000 2

2 Round off to 2 significant figures:

a 4 936 000	**b** 307 000	**c** 0·000 067 5	**d** 0·005 09
e 0·000 320	**f** 603 000 000	**g** 0·163 087	**h** 8·937 64
i 2 437 984	**j** 16·902	**k** 299 000	**l** 999·976

3 a Round off 304 to 1 significant figure.
  b Round off 304 to 2 significant figures.
  c What did you notice?
  d If a measurement is given as 2000 kg, how many significant figures could this have been rounded to?

Level 2

4 Electronic scales showed the weight of some bacon rashers as 1·037 02 kg. Explain your choice for the number of significant figures the weighing machines should be set to display and use in calculating costs.

2.4 Rates

Rates compare quantities of different units in a definite order.

A common rate is speed.

45 km/h means 45 km (each) hour.

If the speed an object is travelling doesn't change it is known as a *uniform* rate.

As rates use units it is possible to convert rates from one set of units to another.

EXAMPLE 1

Tasha runs a 100 m race in 15 s.

a Express her speed as a rate in m/s. **b** Convert her speed to km/h.

Solutions

a $\dfrac{100 \text{ m}}{15 \text{ s}}$

$= \dfrac{100}{15}$ m/s

$= 6 \cdot \dot{6}$ m/s

b $6 \cdot \dot{6}$ m/s

$\boxed{\div 1000}$

$= 0 \cdot 006\dot{6}$ km/s

$\boxed{\times 60}$

$= 0 \cdot 4$ km/min

$\boxed{\times 60}$

$= 24$ km/h

> Remember you can travel further in 1 hour than in 1 second.

Alternative solution

$$\dfrac{6 \cdot \dot{6} \text{ m}}{1 \text{ s}} = \dfrac{0 \cdot 006\dot{6} \text{ km}}{\frac{1}{3600} \text{ h}}$$

$$= \dfrac{3600 \times 0 \cdot 006\dot{6} \text{ km}}{1 \text{ h}}$$

$$= 24 \text{ km/h}$$

EXAMPLE 2

Convert 108 km/h to m/s.

Solution

108 km/h

$\boxed{\div 1000}$

$= 108\ 000$ m/h

$\boxed{\div 60}$

$= 1800$ m/min

$\boxed{\div 60}$

$= 30$ m/s

Alternative solution

$$\dfrac{108 \text{ km}}{\text{h}} = \dfrac{108\ 000 \text{ m}}{3600 \text{ s}}$$

$$= \dfrac{108\ 000}{3600} \text{ m/s}$$

$$= 30 \text{ m/s}$$

EXAMPLE 3

A dripping tap loses 5 mL of water per second. Express this as a rate in litres per year.

Solution

5 mL/s

$\boxed{\div 1000}$

$= 0 \cdot 005$ L/s

$\boxed{\times 60}$

$= 0 \cdot 3$ L/min

$\boxed{\times 60}$

$= 18$ L/h

$\boxed{\times 24}$

$= 432$ L/d

$\boxed{\times 365}$

$= 157\ 680$ L/yr

EXERCISE 2E

1 For each of the rates given below, choose quantity names from the list to write which ones are being compared:

- mass   • time   • length   • money   • area   • distance   • capacity

  a 100 km/h   **b** \$60/h   **c** \$5/m   **d** 4 kg/wk
  e \$2·65/kg   **f** \$10 000/ha   **g** 800 L/min   **h** 4·8 g/m²

2 Express each rate in its simplest form:

  a \$40 in 5 h   **b** \$3·60 for 3 cans   **c** 4500 revs in 2 min
  d 4·5° rise in 3 h   **e** 9·8 L in 100 km   **f** 200 m in 21·8 s

  g 250 mL for 5000 cm²   **h** 245 runs for 8 wickets   **i** 80 km in $\frac{1}{2}$ h

  j \$110 000 for 720 m²   **k** 30 students in 120 m³   **l** \$360 for 32·8 g

3 This ready-reckoner is used to mix weed-killer in proper proportions:

Weed-killer (mL)	Water (L)
5	4
10	8
15	12
20	16
25	20

  a Graph the data, labelling horizontal axis *Water* and vertical axis *Weed-killer*. From the graph, answer the following questions.
  b How much weed-killer should be mixed with:
     i 2 L of water?   **ii** 14 L of water?
  c How much water should be mixed with:
     i 23 mL of weed-killer?
     ii 14 mL of weed-killer?
  d Find an equation that describes this relationship.

4 A car is stolen every 4·7 s in Australia. How many cars are stolen in a year?

5 A telemarketer makes 15 calls in the first hour of her shift, 18 in the second and 16 in the third. What is her *average* rate in:

  a calls per hour?   **b** minutes per call?

6 1·2 t of fertiliser must be spread *uniformly* over 8 ha of farming land. At what rate in kilograms per hectare must it be spread?

7 On the first 350 km leg of a driving tour, a car used 38 L of fuel; on the next 480 km it used 42 L; and on the final 310 km it consumed 29 L. At what *average rate* did it consume fuel?

8 Find the average speed, in kilometres per hour, when a car travels:

  a 180 km in 2 h   **b** 260 km in 1·2 h   **c** 428 km in 2 h 45 min

9 A vehicle travelling at 100 km/h will take how long to travel:

  a 75 km?   **b** 125 km?   **c** 280 km?   **d** 100 m?

10 At 60 km/h, how far does a car travel in:

  a 3 h?   **b** $4\frac{1}{2}$ h?   **c** 2 h 15 min?

> **Remember:**
>
> $\frac{D}{S \mid T}$

11 If the speed of sound is 330 m/s, how far does sound travel in:

   a 5 s?   **b** 12 s?   **c** $\frac{3}{4}$ min?

12 What is the flow rate per minute if 3750 L flow through a pipe in 0·2 of an hour?

13 Electricity rates are 10·25¢/kWh. A refrigerator used 710 kWh of electricity in a year. How much does it cost to run?

14 Allan can type at the rate of 65 words per minute. How long should it take him to type a four-page document containing an average of 450 words per page?

15 Compare the rates in each of the following:

   a Runner X covers 200 m in 22 s, while runner Y races at 9 m/s.
      i Who is faster?
      ii By how much would the faster runner win the race:
         I in time?   **II** in distance?
   b One 350 g jar of marmalade sells for $1·85, while a competing brand is packaged in 450 g jars for $2·69. Which is the better buy?
   c Jim pays $3000 tax on $22 000 income, while Jennifer pays $2800 tax on $20 000.
      i Using *percentages* ($ tax/$100 income), find who pays the *greater rate* of taxation.
      ii Explain the difference between 'greater rate' and 'more' in tax.
   d Curtain material normally sells at $7·95/m. With only $4\frac{1}{2}$ m left on the roll, the store owner decides to unload it at the *bargain* price of $30. Show whether or not it is really a bargain.
   e 2 L bottles of one brand of soft drink sell for $1·95, while 750 mL bottles of a rival brand sell for 79¢.
      i Which is the better value for money? (Use ¢/250 mL as your basis of comparison.)
      ii What other factors might influence your decision about which is the better buy?
   f A 1·5 L motor car uses 85 L of petrol in driving from Sydney to Brisbane, a distance of 960 km. A 2·5 L car uses 70 L to cover 680 km along the same route. Which car is more economical on fuel? (Use L/100 km as the basis of comparison.)

16 Cycling journeys

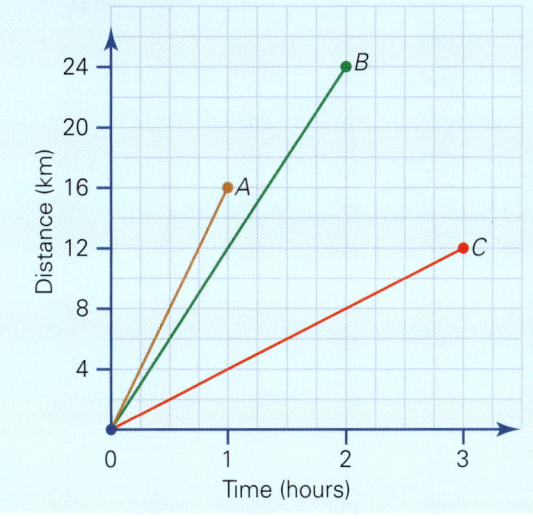

a Which cyclist covered the most distance?
b Which cyclist rode for the longest time?
c Which cyclist had the fastest speed? Explain.
d Find the average speed of each cyclist (to 2 decimal places) in:
    i km/h   **ii** m/h   **iii** m/s

17 Convert the units for each of the following rates:

a 5 m/s = ☐ m/min   **b** 60 km/h = ☐ km/min   **c** 0·05 kg/s = ☐ g/s
d 57 ¢/s = ☐ $/s   **e** 57¢/s = ☐ $/min   **f** 57¢/s = ☐ $/h
g $942/d = ☐ $/h   **h** $942/d = ☐ $/min   **i** 120 km/h = ☐ m/min

Level 2

18 Convert each of the following rates to m/s:

a 60 km/min   **b** 80 km/h   **c** 100 km/h   **d** 198 km/h

19 Convert each of the following rates to km/h:

a 4 km/min   **b** 300 m/min   **c** 6 m/s   **d** 0·6 m/s

20 A speed skater travels 4000 m in 5 minutes. What is the average speed in kilometres per hour?

Level 3

21 A car travels around a 4500 m track in 25·4 seconds. Find its average speed in kilometres per hour.

22 It takes 15 seconds to fill a 10 litre bucket with water. What is the rate of flow in litres per hour?

23 A leaking tap loses 4 drops of water every 30 seconds. If each drop contains on average 3 mL of water, express this as a rate in:

a mL/s
b L/h
c kL/year

24 Complete the equivalent rates.

a 9 kg/h = ☐ g/s   **b** 1·5 g/s = ☐ kg/h   **c** 5 c/s = ☐ $/yr

25 The space shuttle zooms at 12 km/s. How far does it travel in:

a 5 s?   **b** $\frac{3}{4}$ min?   **c** $2\frac{1}{2}$ h?   **d** 1 day?

26 A car travelling at 100 km/h is now 5 km behind a truck travelling in the same direction at 90 km/h. In how many minutes will the car overtake the truck?

27 How long does it take an RAAF F-18 jet to travel east to west across Australia at Mach 1·9, in hours and minutes? (You will need to research the speed, *Mach 1*, and the distance across Australia.)

28 The speed of sound at sea level is around 340 m/s.

   a Write this in kilometres per hour.

   b For people living 10 km from a lightning strike, how long before they hear its thunder?

   c The speed of light is approximately 300 000 km/s. How long does it take light to travel 10 km?

   d What is the *time difference* between *seeing* the lightning and *hearing* the thunder, over 10 km?

   e Develop a simple equivalence table showing time in seconds and distance in kilometres, as a way of counting the time from when you see lightning to the time when you hear its thunder. Produce the simplest system you can that enables you to determine how far away the lightning is.

   f How long does it take voice communication to travel at the speed of light along a fibre-optic cable from Sydney to Perth, a distance of around 3600 km?

Investigation World records—athletics

Male

Running	Time (min:s)	Name and country	Date
100 m	0:9·86	Carl Lewis, USA	1991
200 m	0:19·32	Michael Johnson, USA	1996
400 m	0:43·18	Michael Johnson, USA	1999
800 m	1:41·11	Wilson Kipketer, Denmark	1997
1500 m	3:26·00	Hicham El Guerrouj, Morocco	1998
10 000 m	26:22·75	Haile Gebreselassie, Ethiopia	1998
20 000 m	56:55·6	Arturo Barrios, Mexico	1991
30 000 m	89:18·8	T. Seko, Japan	1981
400 m hurdles	0:46·78	Kevin Young, USA	1992

Source: 2000 Guinness Book of Records, Guinness Publishing, UK.

Female

Running	Time (min:s)	Name and country	Date
100 m	0:10·49	Griffith-Joyner, USA	1988
200 m	0:21·34	Griffith-Joyner, USA	1988
400 m	0:47·6	Marita Koch, GDR	1985
800 m	1:53·28	J. Kratochivilova, Czech	1983
1500 m	3:50·46	Qu Yunxia, China	1993
10 000 m	29:31·78	Wang Junxia, China	1993
400 m hurdles	0:52·61	Kim Batten, USA	1995

Source: 2000 Guinness Book of Records, Guinness Publishing, UK.

1 Calculate the record sprint speeds in metres per second for:

   a men's 100 m   **b** women's 100 m   **c** men's 800 m   **d** women's 800 m

2 How much under 'even time' of 10 s is Carl Lewis's 100 m record?

3 Round each 10 000 m time to the nearest second.

4 Calculate the average speed of each 10 000 m champion in metres per second.

5 How much slower (in m/s) is the male 10 000 m record speed than the male 400 m speed? (Round to the nearest tenth of a second.)

6 Compare the women's 400 m sprint speed with the 400 m hurdles speed. What is the difference, in metres per second?

7 If Hicham El Guerrouj of Morocco could maintain his 1500 m pace, how long would it take him to run 2 km?

8 How fast did Wang Junxia of China run, in kilometres per hour, to set the record for the 10 000 m race?

Investigation Using rates

Property/council rates

Many services are provided by local government (councils). List as many as you can, suggested by the illustrations at left. Through group discussion list two that may not be pictured.

One main way of paying for these services is through charging property owners a certain amount *for every dollar of the unimproved value of their land*.

Find out what this means. Who decides this value? How often? How is the owner told? Can he/she object to the valuation?

Some councils charge for every kilolitre of water used, for every garbage bin collection, for every toilet pedestal in the house, and so on. All these charges are collectively known as '**rates**'.

RATE ASSESSMENT NOTICE (ANNUAL)		**SUNNYVALE**
		Local Council
Property location: 7 NEWTON ST DEE WHY NOT	Rateable value: $85 000	
GENERAL RATES	0·8208 cents in the dollar (residential; owner occupied)	
WATER RATES	0·5012 cents in the dollar (minimum charge $251·68)	
SEWERAGE CHARGE	$166·68	
CLEANSING CHARGE	$169·08 for each refuse service	
(A **5% discount** on the total account is allowed if paid by the due date.)		

1 Find **i** the general rates, **ii** the water rates, **iii** the total annual rates (no discount), for residential owner-occupied homes with one refuse service on land valued at:

  a $60 000   **b** $82 000   **c** $98 500   **d** $125 800   **e** $50 200

2 What land valuation would merit the minimum charge for water rates?

3 Property valued at $85 000 three years ago is revalued at $102 000 today. By how much does the annual rates bill increase if the discount applied at both times?

Telephone rates

The table below explains the cost per minute or part of a minute, from your own phone.

Distance (km) / Category	50–85	85–165*	165–745*	>745	
DAY—8 am–6 pm Mon to Sat	24¢	34¢	34¢	50¢	*Costs in these two categories are actually slightly different, but have been rounded to the nearest cent.
NIGHT—6 pm–10 pm Mon to Fri	16¢	23¢	23¢	34¢	
ECONOMY—10 pm–8 am 6 pm Sat–8 am Mon	10¢	14¢	14¢	18¢	

1 Calculate the cost of each of the following STD calls:

	Length of call	Distance	Time and day
a	5 min	70 km	11 am Wed
b	12 min	200 km	3 pm Sat
c	8 min 10 s	900 km	8:30 pm Mon
d	15 min 50 s	125 km	5 pm Sun
e	6 min 30 s	730 km	6:30 pm Sat
f	30 min 1 s	750 km	4:30 pm Fri

2 How much would Luke in Newcastle save by ringing Rachael in Cairns (over 745 km away) at 7 pm Saturday instead of 5 pm Saturday, if the call lasts 15 min 45 s?

3 A mobile phone carrier charges 42¢ for the first 10 minutes or part thereof and then 18¢ per 30 s for phone calls made between 7 pm and 7 am. The normal rate is 15¢ per 30 s. Find the cost of:

  a 7 min phone call made at 6:10 pm   **b** 9 min phone call made at 8:30 pm
  c 6 min 45 s phone call made at 7:10 am **d** 12 in 15 s call made at midnight.

4 If a phone call using the carrier in **3** is to be made between 7 pm and 7 am, what is the minimum length of time the call needs to be to obtain the cost saving suggested by the flat 10 minute rate?

Pulse rate and exercise

Work in groups of three: 'patient', 'doctor' and recorder. The doctor should practise taking the pulse of the patient, either at the wrist or neck.

You need: stopwatch, results table, graph paper

Time (min)	Pulse rate (beats/min)
0 (stationary	
2 (exercise)	
3 (recovery phase)	
4 "	
5 "	
6 "	

1 Take the patient's pulse for 20 s. Calculate the pulse rate in beats per minute. The recorder enters the result in the table.

2 The patient runs on the spot vigorously for 2 min. The doctor then takes the pulse and the recorder enters it.

3 The pulse is taken after each successive minute for the next 4 min, and recorded.

4 Graph the data from the table.

5 Describe any relationship that seems to exist between pulse rate and recovery time.

6 Repeat the experiment, swapping jobs. Use the same table and axes to record and graph results. Compare trends and comment on similarities or differences.

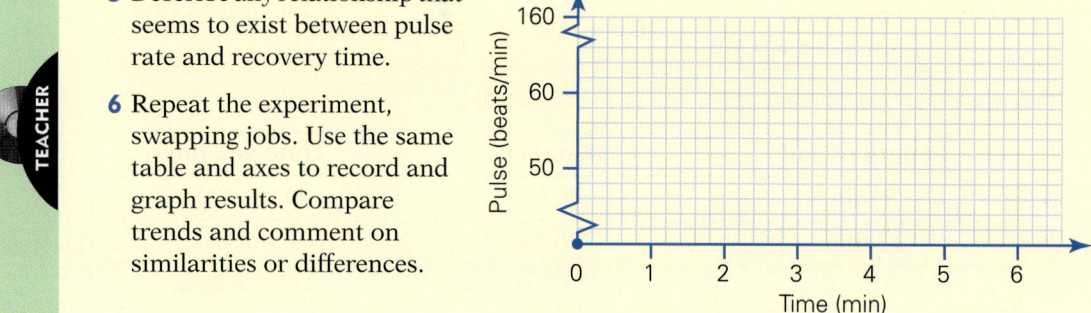

Chapter Review

average	estimate	ratio	significant
approximate	fraction	rational	uniform
constant	integer	rounding	
equivalent	rate	scientific	

1 a What is a rational number?
   b Give an example of a rational number.
   c Give an example of a number that is not rational.

2 What is an integer? Give two examples.

3 a Give an example of a question where it is more appropriate to round off to a certain number of significant figures rather than a certain number of decimal places.
   b Give an example where it is more appropriate to ask for an answer to be given to a certain number of decimal places rather than significant figures.

4 Explain the difference between a ratio and a rate.

5 List three everyday uses of rates. In which subjects have you encountered rates at school?

Chapter Review Exercises

1 Round 4705·0396:

   a to the nearest tenth   **b** to the nearest thousandth
   c to 1 decimal place   **d** to 2 decimal places
   e to 3 decimal places.

2 a Give appropriate upper and lower limits for estimating the value of $7{\cdot}6 \times 74{\cdot}4$.
   b Show how you estimate the result of $56{\cdot}3 - 2{\cdot}7 \times 0{\cdot}18$.

3 Write in scientific notation:

   a 0·000 082 6   **b** 302 000

4 Write the basic numeral for:

   a 7×10^6 **b** $3{\cdot}8 \times 10^{-4}$
   c $3{\cdot}02 \times 10^8 \times 1{\cdot}703 \times 10^{-3}$.

5 Write 55 074 000:
   a rounded to the nearest hundred thousand
   b in scientific notation
   c correct to 3 significant figures.

6 Round to 2 significant figures:

   a 4325   **b** 63 824   **c** 7·691   **d** 0·003 98

7 Round to 3 significant figures:

   a 53 290   **b** 0·000 392 499   **c** 43·952   **d** 0·7997

8 A number is rounded to 2150. What could the integer have been?

9 a Express each ratio in simplest form:
     i 1800 : 120   **ii** $3\frac{1}{2}$: 5   **iii** 0·12 : 4·2   **iv** 300 m to 6 km
  b Express 3 : 8 as a unit ratio in the form X : 1 (to 2 decimal places).
  c Show which ratio is the smaller: 6 : 7 or 13 : 15.
  d Share $2400 in the ratio 1 : 2 : 5.

10 Find x in the following proportions:

   a $\dfrac{7}{8} = \dfrac{21}{x}$ **b** 7 : 5 = x : 8

11 Notebooks are on sale at four for $2·60. How much would nine cost?

12 If it takes 176 palings to complete a 22 m fence:

   a how many palings will be needed for a 30 m fence?
   b how long a fence could be erected with 124 palings?

13 Alistair and Penny invested $5000 and $12 500 respectively to start a small business. In a year when the business made a net profit of $84 000, what should Penny's share be if profits are shared in the same ratio as investments?

14 Express the following as rate:

   a 240 km in 3 hours 20 minutes   **b** 200 grams in $\frac{1}{2}$ hour

15 Convert to m/s:

   a 1600 m/h   **b** 90 km/h   **c** 240 km/h

16 Convert to km/h:

   a 5 km/min   **b** 600 m/min   **c** 9 m/s

17 A Qantas jumbo jet flies the 3200 km from Sydney to Darwin in 4 h 45 min. Find its average speed in:

   a kilometres per hour   **b** kilometres per minute   **c** metres per second.

18 The average reaction time for a driver in an emergency is $2\frac{1}{2}$ s. How far will a car travel in this time at a speed of 100 km/h?

19 Which is the better buy: a 1 kg box of dishwashing detergent for $3·85, or a 750 g box for $2·98?

20 How much less time does it take for Craig, who types at 60 words per minute, to type a 1500-word document, than it does for Naseema, who types at 45 wpm?

21 Two airliners are 300 km apart. If they are flying straight towards each other, one at 650 km/h, the other at 580 km/h, how far apart are they 2 min before impact?

22 From the following data, estimate the number of fish in a dam: 85 tagged fish were released in to the dam known to contain fish. From a sample of 53 fish netted later, two were found to be tagged. The netted fish were then released.

23 The fuel bill for a certain trip was $285 when the car averaged 12 km/L. What difference in fuel costs would it make if the trip had been done in a car averaging 9·8 km/L?

Keeping Mathematically Fit

Part A—Non-calculator

1 A portion of fish and chips costs $6. If the fish cost three times as much as the chips, how much does it cost?

2 Give an approximate value for 103×98.

3 Write $\frac{2}{3}$ as a recurring decimal.

4 In its birthday sale, a shop offers all items at 30% discount. How much will you save if you buy two pairs of shorts which usually cost $15 a pair?

5 Which time/distance graph could represent the following journey?
Walk to the bus stop, catch the bus to school, travel home by car.

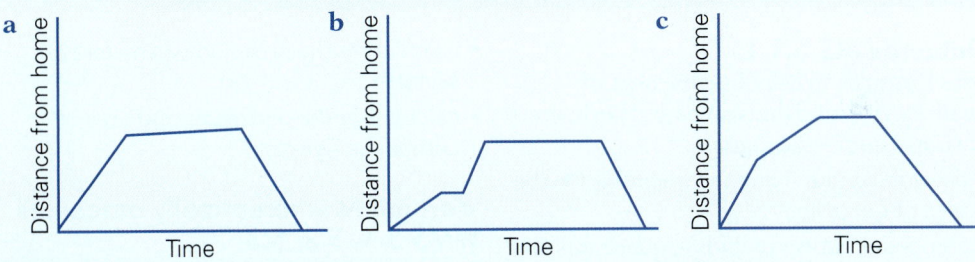

6 The maximum temperature in New York in January was 2°C with a minimum of ⁻15°C. What was the range?

7 A bus leaves the terminus every 15 minutes, with the first one leaving at 5:52 am. If a traveller arrives at the terminus at 8:15 am, which bus will he catch and how long will he have to wait for it?

8 Evaluate $\sqrt{10^2 - 8^2}$.

9 The fraction $\frac{\Delta}{4}$ has a value between 3 and 4. Give a possible value for Δ.

10 Find the area of the parallelogram with base 10 cm and height 4 cm.

Part B—Calculator

1 A square with sides of 20 cm is inscribed in a circle. What is the area of the circle?

2 Telephone poles along a roadside are 50 m apart. A car passenger notices she passes a pole every 3 seconds. How fast is the car travelling in kilometres per hour?

3 Evaluate $300^{\frac{1}{3}}$ to 2 significant figures.

4 Pepe's Pizzeria sells large pizzas (30 cm diameter) for $12 and family pizzas (40 cm diameter) for $18.

  a Which gives the best value for money?

  b Pepe introduces a small pizza (20 cm diameter) and has a special offer of two for the price of one. What price should this be to make it the same value for money as the large pizza?

5 A cube frame is made from 84 cm of wire.

  a What is the volume of the cube?

  b How long would a diagonal brace be that stretches from one corner to another through the centre of the cube?

1 What you need to know and revise

Outcome MS 4.1:
Uses formulas and Pythagoras's theorem in calculating the perimeter and the area of circles and figures composed of rectangles and triangles:

- units of measurement and their accuracy
- converting units of length
- using Pythagoras's theorem.

2 What you will learn in this chapter

Outcome MS 5.1.1:
Uses formulas to calculate the area of quadrilaterals and finds areas and perimeters of simple composite figures:

- developing and using the formulas for the area of quadrilaterals
- composite figures including quadrants and semicircles.

Outcome MS 5.2.1:
Finds areas and perimeters of composite figures:

- calculating the area and perimeters of sectors
- calculating the perimeter and area of composite figures.

Working Mathematically outcomes WMS 5.1, 5.2, 5.3
Students will be required to *question*, *apply strategies*, *communicate*, *reason* and *reflect* in the sections of this chapter.

Measurement

Key mathematical terms you will encounter

accuracy	diameter	milli	rectangular
area	estimate	octagon	rhombus
centi	hexagon	parallel	scale
circle	kilo	pentagon	side
circular	kite	perimeter	trapezium
circumference	length	perpendicular	trapezoidal
conversion	measurement	pi	triangular
diagonals	mega	radius	

MathsCheck
Measurement

1 Why can't you be sure of the reading on this scale?

   a Give two readings that could be correct.

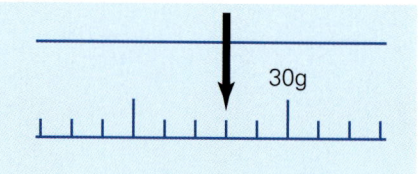

   b Give the reading suggested by this scale.

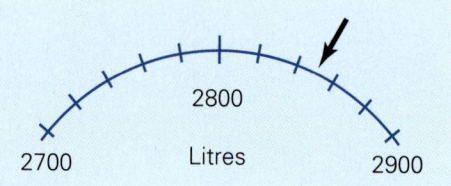

2 Draw four different scales that show a reading of 58 km/h. Make two of the readings exact and two approximate. Remember that each scale must have different divisions.

Logarithmic scales

Sounds are measured by means of amplitude, which represents the size of the sound wave. The amplitude of a sound that causes pain is one trillion times louder than the quietest sound that can be heard by the human ear. As you can imagine, a standard scaled number line used to measure amplitude would be either enormous or very inaccurate.

To overcome this problem a **logarithmic scale** is used, with **decibels** (dB) as the units. Every time you go up 10 dB on the scale, sound becomes **10 times** louder. The scale starts at 0 decibels, which represents the faintest sound detectable.

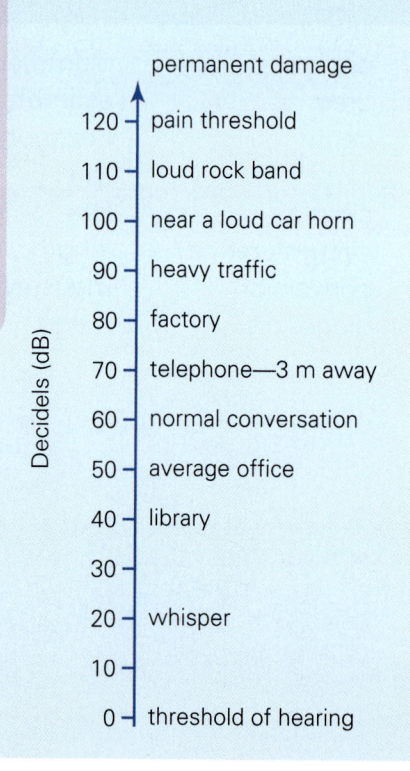

3 Answer the following questions using the decibel scale:

   a How much louder than a normal conversation is a rock band?

   b Heavy traffic is 100 times louder than a vacuum cleaner. How many decibels is the vacuum cleaner noise?

   c Give a different example from the one on the scale of a noise that is 1/10 000 as loud as a car horn.

4 The Richter scale is a logarithmic scale used for measuring earthquake intensity. The scale goes from 0 to 9, with a scale 2 earthquake having 10 times the strength of a scale 1 earthquake.

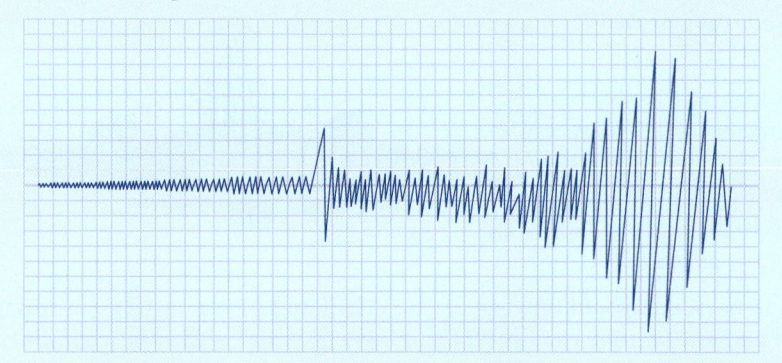

    a How many times more powerful than scale 1 would an earthquake of scale 6 be?
    b How would you describe the intensity of a scale 3 earthquake compared with one of scale 5?

5 Convert the following masses to the units given:

    a 2 kg to g   **b** 4·5 t to kg   **c** 7·02 kg to g
    d 0.06 kg to g   **e** 7000 g to kg   **f** 10 000 mg to g
    g 54 200 kg to t   **h** 900 g to kg   **i** 2·5 t to g
    j 0·032 kg to mg   **k** 130 g to t   **l** 65 000 mg to t

6 Vitamin C tablets contain 250 mg of ascorbic acid. If you took one tablet each day for 3 weeks, how many grams of ascorbic acid would you have consumed?

7 A recipe for pumpkin soup requires 800 g of pumpkin. How many kilograms of pumpkin would be needed to make four times the quantity of soup shown in the recipe?

8 A carton containing 18 cans of soft drink has a mass of 8 kg. What is the mass of each can, to the nearest gram? (Ignore the small mass of the carton.)

9 James buys oats for his horse in 12 kg sacks. If he feeds his horse 650 g of oats each day, what mass of oats would be left in the sack after 1 week?

The **mass** of an object is the amount of matter in the object.

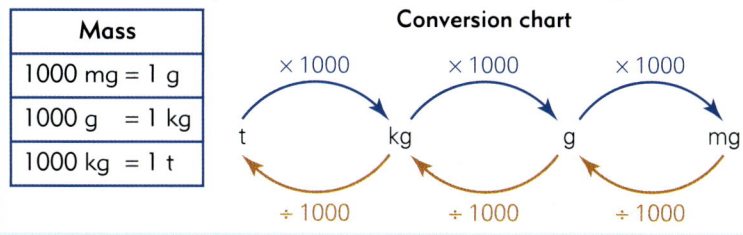

Mass
1000 mg = 1 g
1000 g = 1 kg
1000 kg = 1 t

10 When Jahinda was born her mass was 3·84 kg. At 6 weeks her mass was recorded as 5·07 kg. By how many grams has her mass increased?

11 A bridge has a weight limit of 3 t. An unladen truck weighs 1·6 t, and it is carrying 15 palettes that each weigh 90 kg. Should the truck cross the bridge? Explain your answer.

12 The recommended daily intake of calcium for teenagers is 1·2 g per day. If reduced fat milk contains 128 mg of calcium per 100 mL, how much milk would you need to drink if that was your only source of calcium?

13 The total mass of passengers and luggage on flight QF8 to London is 42 t. Assuming each of the 450 passengers took exactly 20 kg of luggage, what is the average mass of the passengers, to the nearest kilogram?

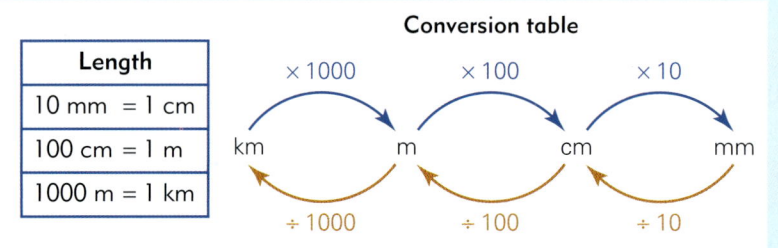

Conversion table

Length	
10 mm	= 1 cm
100 cm	= 1 m
1000 m	= 1 km

km → m → cm → mm
× 1000 × 100 × 10
÷ 1000 ÷ 100 ÷ 10

14 Convert the following:

a 7 cm to mm	**b** 6 m to cm	**c** 29 cm to mm	**d** 5·1 m to mm
e 0·43 km to m	**f** 0·206 m to cm	**g** 68 mm to cm	**h** 34 000 m to km
i 450 cm to m	**j** 812 mm to cm	**k** 7025 m to km	**l** 8 cm to m
m 284 mm to m	**n** 60·5 m to km	**o** 3 mm to m	**p** $\frac{1}{2}$ m to mm
q $2\frac{1}{4}$ km to m	**r** $5\frac{1}{5}$ cm to m		

15 Complete the following conversions:

a 3 km = … cm   **b** 6 512 000 cm = … km
c 0·04 km = … mm   **d** 673 mm = … km

> You may need to do more than one calculation.

16 How many boxes, each 28 cm high, can fit under a shelf that is 1·5 m above the floor?

17 Pierre ran 13 laps of a 400 m running track. How many kilometres did he run?

18 Jenny jumped half a metre more than her previous jump of 2·94 m. Claire was aiming for a 4 m jump, but was 62 cm short of her target. Who jumped further, and by how much?

19 Yumi had a piece of wooden dowelling 1·5 m long. After cutting off four pieces, each of length 135 mm, how much of the dowelling would be left?

20 How many 45 cm pieces of ribbon can be cut from a 5 m roll? How much would be left over?

21 Cameron's wife drives him the 2·8 km to the station. He takes the train a distance of 14 km, and then walks the remaining 150 m to his office. What total distance does he travel?

22 Dawn's roof rack is 1·68 m off the ground. Her bicycle extends another 87 cm above the rack. Could she safely drive under a 2·5 m barrier?

23 If all the pages in this book were laid end to end, how far would they stretch? How many book pages would be needed to stretch from Sydney to Canberra? (This distance is approximately 300 km.)

24 Find the length of the hypotenuse by using Pythagoras's theorem for the following right-angled triangles.

a
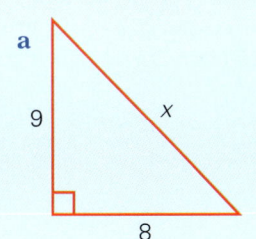

b
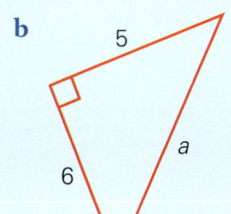

c
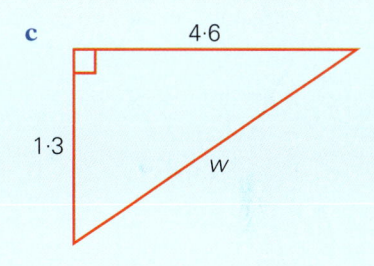

The limits of accuracy tell you the lower and upper boundaries for the actual measurement.

They are stated to one place of decimals *beyond* that of the given measurement, i.e. $\pm \dfrac{1}{2}$ the smallest unit of measure.

25 Give the limits of accuracy for the following measurements:

  a 34 cm   **b** 45·9 m
  c 13·55 mm   **d** 24°
  e 0·89 km

26 Give the dimensions of three rectangles whose perimeter is 30 cm

27 Find the perimeter of each shape.

a

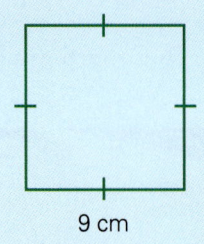

9 cm

b

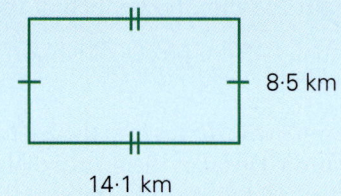

8·5 km

14·1 km

c

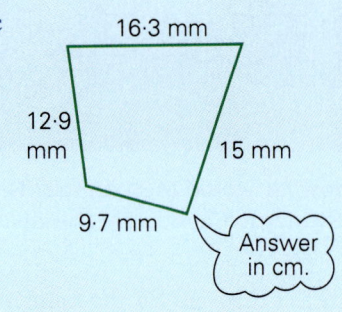

16·3 mm

12·9 mm

15 mm

9·7 mm

Answer in cm.

d

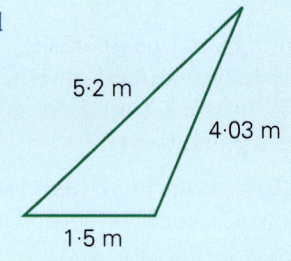

5·2 m

4·03 m

1·5 m

e

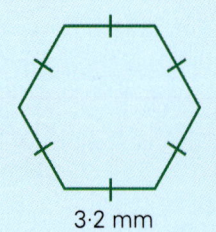

3·2 mm

f

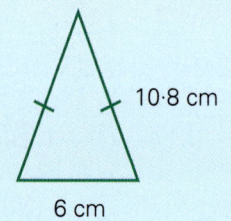

10·8 cm

6 cm

g

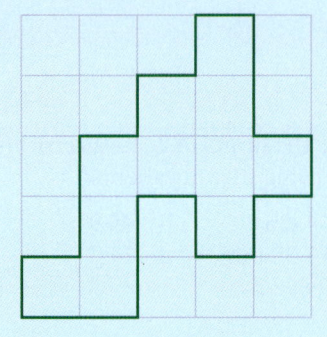

h

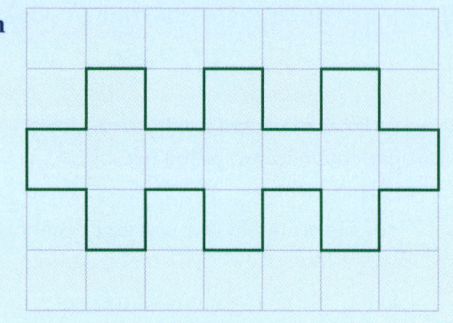

i

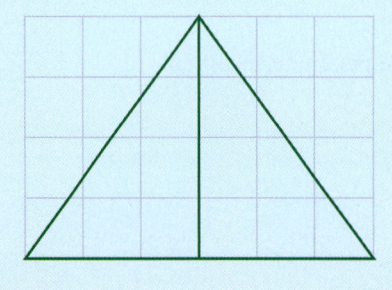

Exploring New Ideas

3.1 Perimeter

The **perimeter** of a shape is the total distance around the edge of the shape.

EXAMPLE 1

Calculate the perimeters of the following figures:

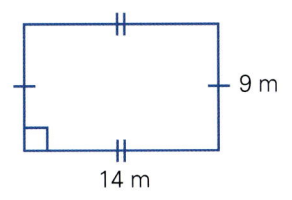

9 m

14 m

Solution

Perimeter = $2l + 2b$
$= 2 \times 14 + 2 \times 9$
$= 28 + 18$
$= 46$ m

EXAMPLE 2

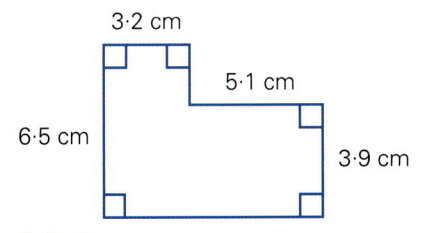

3·2 cm

5·1 cm

6·5 cm

3·9 cm

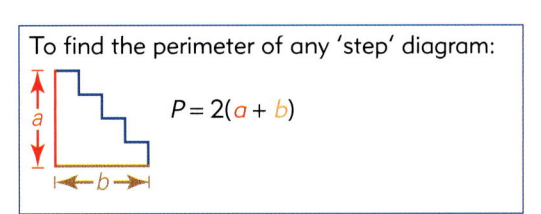

To find the perimeter of any 'step' diagram:

$P = 2(a + b)$

Solution

$6·5 - 3·9 = 2·6$
$32 + 5·1 = 8·3$
Perimeter $= 6·5 + 3·2 + 2·6 + 5·1 + 3·9 + 8·3$ or $2(6·5 + 8·3)$
           $= 29·6$ cm $= 29·6$ cm

EXERCISE 3A

1 Calculate the perimeter of these shapes.

| Look at the units. |

a   9·1 m   **b**   **c**

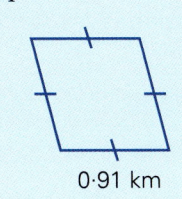

8·75 m

16·8 m

0·91 km

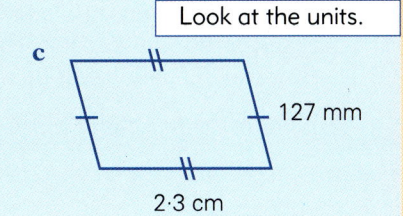

127 mm

2·3 cm

2 What is the perimeter of each of these shapes?

  a   A 7 cm square.
  b   A rectangle that measures 15·5 cm by 27·9 cm. (Give answer in m.)
  c   An equilateral triangle with side length 19·4 cm.
  d   The perimeter of a square is 29·2 m. What is the side length of the square?

e An equilateral triangle has a perimeter of 51·75 mm. What is the length of one of the sides of the triangle?

f The width of a rectangle is 6·6 cm. If the perimeter of the rectangle is 39 cm, what is the length of the rectangle?

Level 2

3 Find the perimeter of each shape. (All angles are right angles.)

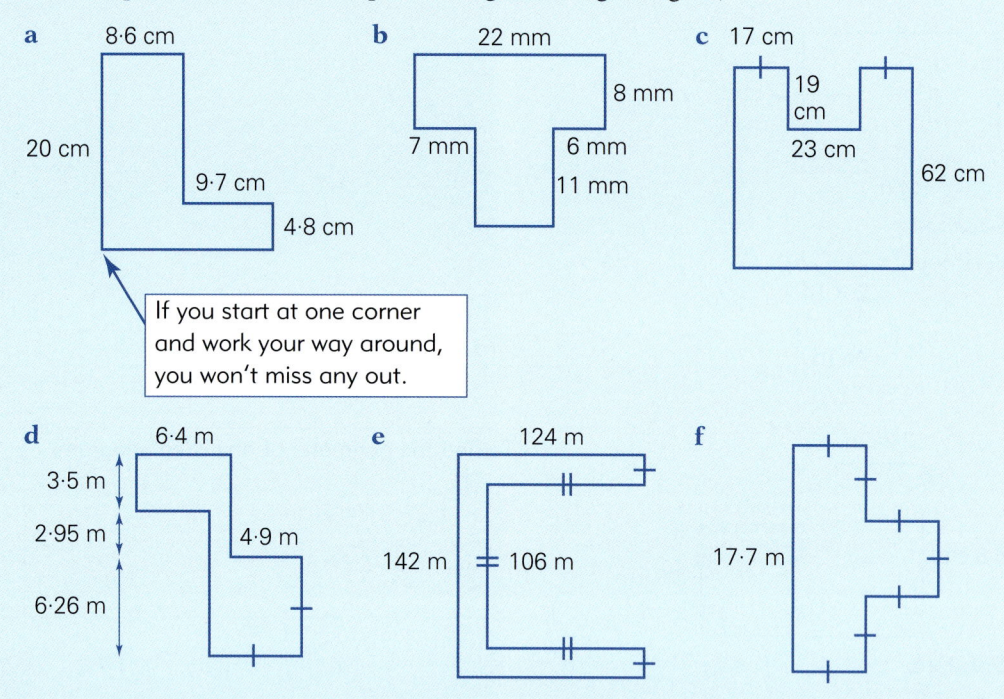

If you start at one corner and work your way around, you won't miss any out.

4 Jock does his running training around the edge of a rectangular paddock measuring 180 m by 255 m.

   a If he normally does eight laps of the paddock, how far does he run?

   b How many complete laps should he do if he wants to run at least 10 km?

Level 3

5 Don wishes to put up a small fence along both sides of the path in his garden. The path is 1·5 m wide. How much fencing will he need?

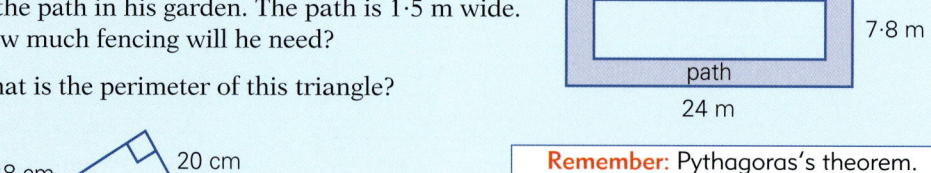

6 What is the perimeter of this triangle?

48 cm   20 cm

Remember: Pythagoras's theorem.

7 Find the perimeter of *ABCD*.

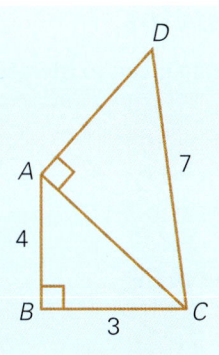

8 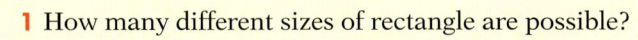 Find the perimeter of field *ABCDE* (all lengths are in metres).

Surveyors use diagrams similar to this to find the perimeter and area of land. It is called an offset or transverse survey.

9 The length of a square is given as 10 cm. Find:

a the upper and lower limits of the square's side length

b the upper and lower limits of the square's perimeter.

Remember: the limits of accuracy
$= \pm \frac{1}{2}$ the smaller unit of measure.

10 Repeat question **9** if the square had a side length measured to be 7·5 cm.

11 The length of a rectangle was measured as 5 cm, and its width 6 cm. Find the lower limit of its perimeter.

Investigation Maximum area

Sahar wants to make a rectangular enclosure to keep her chickens in at night. She has 20 sections of fencing, each 1 m long.

1 How many different sizes of rectangle are possible?

2 What is the area enclosed by each rectangle?

3 Which arrangement should Sahar choose? Why?

Note: Be systematic when investigating, and present your findings clearly. Tables are often useful in these situations.

3.2 Circumference of circles

The **circumference** is the special name given to the perimeter of a circle. We use the formula:

$$C = \pi d$$
$$\text{or } C = 2\pi r$$

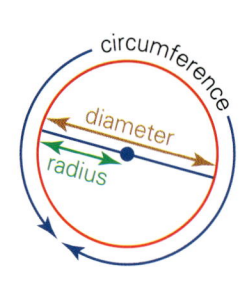
circumference
diameter
radius

C stands for the circumference of the circle.
d is the diameter of the circle.
r is the radius of the circle.

> π (pi) is the ratio of the length of the circumference of a circle to its diameter, i.e. $C : D$.
>
> $\pi = 3.141\ 59...$

To find the **arc length** of a sector: whatever *fraction* the sector is of a whole circle, the arc length is the *same fraction* of the circumference.

This is half of a circle.

$$C = \frac{\pi d}{2}$$

This is a quarter of a circle.

$$C = \frac{\pi d}{4}$$

ARC LENGTH

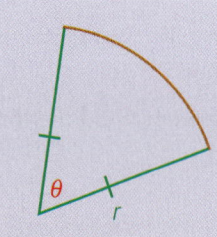

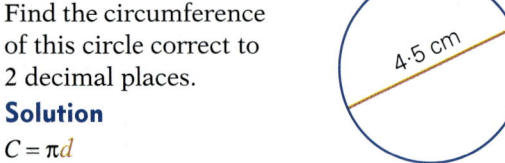

$$\text{arc length} = \frac{\theta}{360} \times 2\pi r$$

EXAMPLE 1

Find the circumference of this circle correct to 2 decimal places.

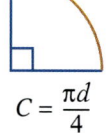
4·5 cm

Solution

$C = \pi d$
$\quad = \pi \times 4.5$
$\quad = 14\cdot137\ 166...$
$\quad = 14\cdot14$ cm (to 2 decimal places)

EXAMPLE 2

Find the circumference of a circle with radius 6 mm, correct to the nearest millimetre.

Solution

$C = 2\pi r$
$\quad = 2 \times \pi \times 6$
$\quad = 37\cdot699\ 111...$
$\quad = 38$ mm (to the nearest mm)

EXAMPLE 3

Calculate the perimeter of this shape correct to 1 decimal place.

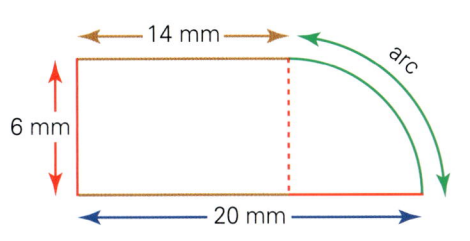

This is a quarter of a circle.

Solution

Arc length = $2\pi r \div 4$
$= 2 \times \pi \times 6 \div 4$
$= 9\cdot424...$

Perimeter $= 9\cdot424... + 14 + 6 + 20$
$= 49\cdot4$ m (to 1 decimal place)

EXAMPLE 4

A circle has a radius of 7 cm and an arc length of 9·6 cm. Find the angle at the centre of the circle (to the nearest degree).

Solution

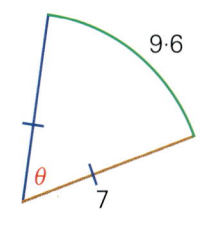

$$\text{Arc length} = \frac{\theta}{360} \times 2\pi r$$

$$9\cdot6 = \frac{\theta}{360} \times 2 \times \pi \times 7$$

$$3456 = 14\pi\theta$$

$$\theta = \frac{3456}{14\pi}$$

$$= 78\cdot577...$$

$$\therefore \text{angle} = 79°$$

EXERCISE 3B

1 Give all answers in this exercise correct to 3 significant figures. Find the circumference of the following circles:

   a $d = 12\cdot5$ cm   **b** $r = 3\cdot6$ mm   **c** $d = 0\cdot85$ m   **d** $d = 120$ km

   e $r = 0\cdot5$ cm   **f** $r = 87$ mm   **g** $d = \frac{1}{2}$ m   **h** $r = 1\frac{3}{4}$ cm

   i $r = 12\frac{4}{5}$ km

2 A circular cake tin has a diameter of 25 cm. How much ribbon would be needed to go around the edge of the cake?

3 If you set your compasses to a radius of 3·5 cm and use them to draw a circle, how long is the curve you have drawn?

4 The second hand on a clock is 7 cm long. How far does the tip of the second hand travel:

   a in 1 min?   **b** in 1 h? (answer in m)   **c** in 10 s?

5 A bicycle wheel has a diameter of 55 cm.

   a How far would the bicycle travel in one complete revolution of the wheel?
   b How many revolutions would be needed for the bicycle to travel 100 m?

6 The distance around a circular running track is 200 m. What is the diameter of the track?

7 How many complete circles of diameter 19 cm could be made from 5 m of string?

8 The circumference of a pizza is 1 m. What size would the base of a box need to be if a 1 cm gap was required between the pizza and the edge of the box?

Level 2

9 Work out **i** the arc lengths and **ii** the perimeter of each figure:

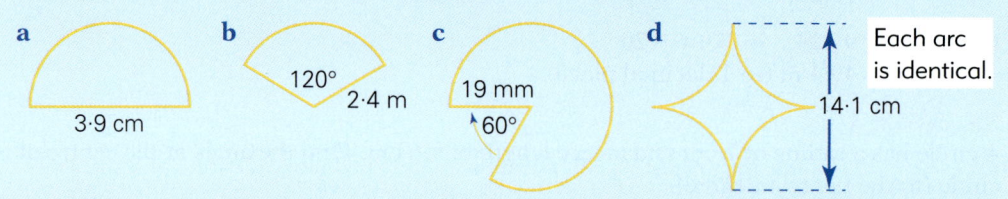

10 A circular tablecloth is made for a circular table of diameter 85 cm and height 65 cm. If the tablecloth just reaches the floor, how much lace would be required to trim around its edge? (Answer in m to the nearest cm.)

11 Find the perimeter of:

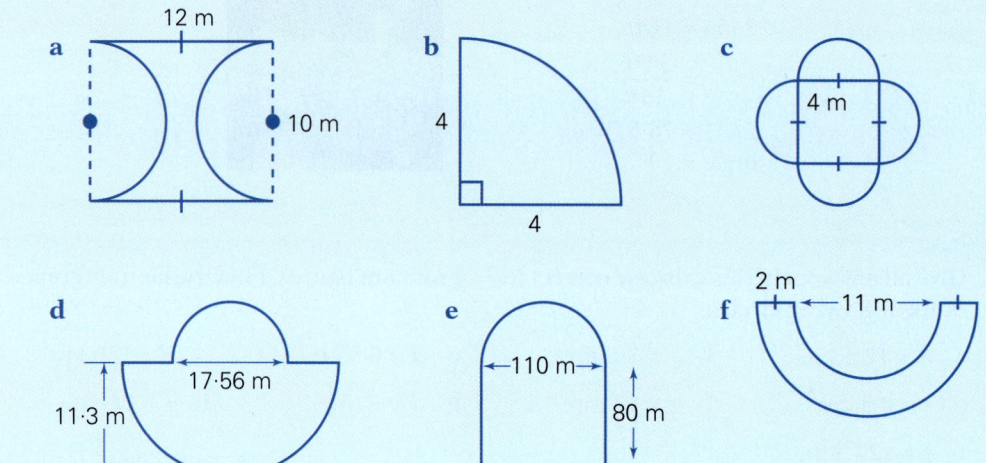

12 If the area of the square is 64 cm², calculate the circle's circumference.

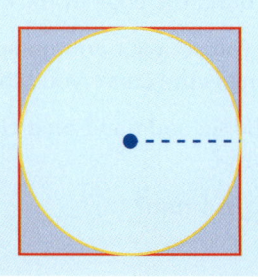

13 What length of tape would be needed to mark out all of the lines on this netball court? (Answer to the nearest cm.)

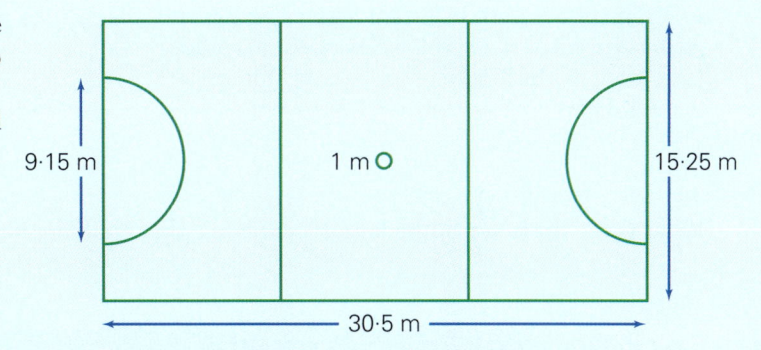

9·15 m   1 m ○   15·25 m

30·5 m

14 Construct formulas that will give the perimeter (*P*) of the following:

a
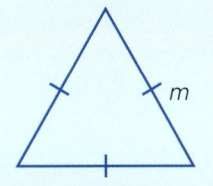
m

b
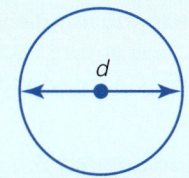
d

c
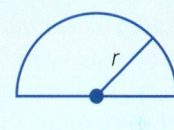
r

d

r

e
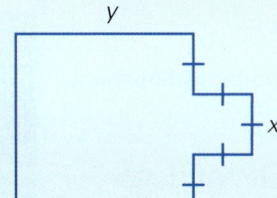
y
x

f
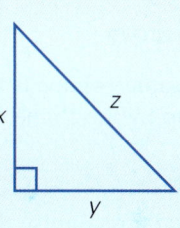
z
x
y

g
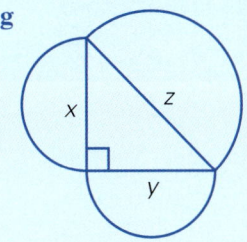
x
z
y

15 Find the perimeter of the shaded region.

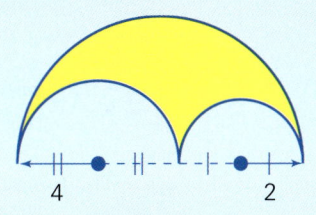

4   2

16 If the circumference of the smaller circle is 30π, calculate the circumference of the larger circle.

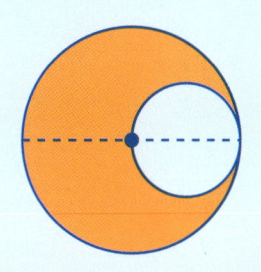

17 The diagram shows two alternative paths from X to Y. The upper path is a semicircle. The lower path comprises of 3 semicircles of equal radius (r). Calculate the length of each path. Which path is the longest?

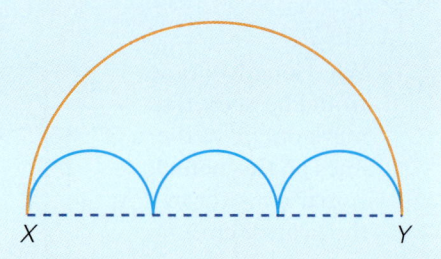

18 What is the diameter of the largest *semicircle* that could be made from 1 m of wire?

Investigation History of π

Find out all you can about the history of the number π. Many people have spent a lot of their time trying to find more and more accurate values for π. They include Archimedes of Syracuse, Ptolemy, and more recently Gottfried Wilhelm Leibniz and William Shanks, but there were many others.

For approximation purposes, π is approximately 3.

3.3 Area

The **area** of a shape is the amount of flat space taken up by the shape.

REVIEW OF AREA FORMULAS

You should recognise the formulas for the area of each of these shapes. Remember that the units for area are always **square** units, for example cm^2, mm^2, m^2.

Square	Rectangle	Circle	Triangle

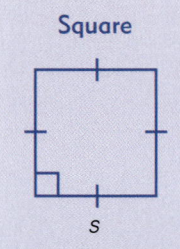 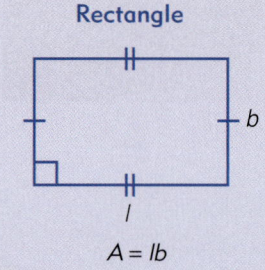 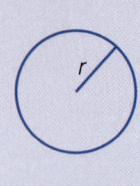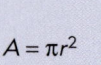 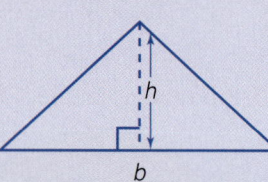

Square: s, $A = s^2$

Rectangle: l, b, $A = lb$

Circle: r, $A = \pi r^2$

Triangle: b, h, $A = \dfrac{1}{2} bh$ or $A = \dfrac{bh}{2}$

Remember: The height must be at right angles to the base.

UNIT CONVERSIONS

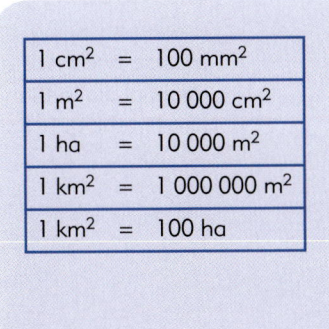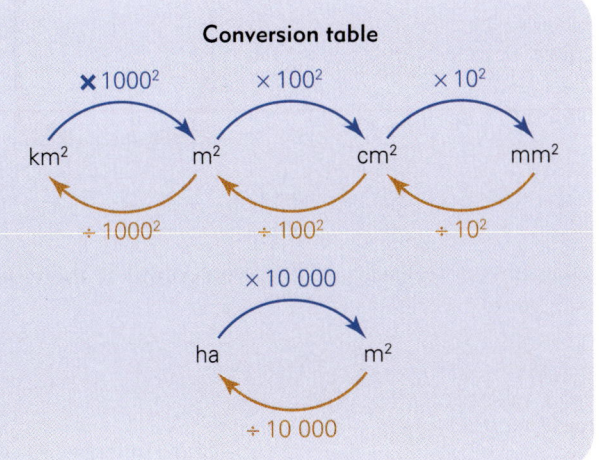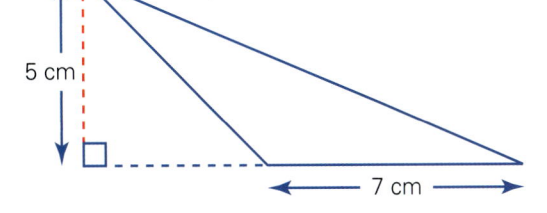

Conversion table

1 cm²	=	100 mm²
1 m²	=	10 000 cm²
1 ha	=	10 000 m²
1 km²	=	1 000 000 m²
1 km²	=	100 ha

EXAMPLE 1
Convert an area of 362 000 m² to hectares.

Solution

$362\ 000 \div 10\ 000 = 36 \cdot 2$ ha

EXAMPLE 2
What is the area of a circle with radius 26 m, to the nearest square metre?

Solution

$$\text{Area} = \pi r^2$$
$$= \pi \times 26^2$$
$$= 2123 \cdot 716\ 634 \text{ m}^2$$
$$= 2124 \text{ m}^2 \text{ (to the nearest m}^2\text{)}$$

EXAMPLE 3
Find the area of this triangle.

Solution

$$\text{Area} = \frac{bh}{2}$$
$$= \frac{7 \times 5}{2}$$
$$= 17 \cdot 5 \text{ cm}^2$$

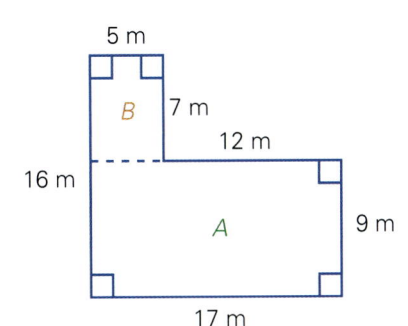

EXAMPLE 4
Calculate the area of this figure.

Solution

$$\text{Area of section } A = lb$$
$$= 17 \times 9$$
$$= 153 \text{ m}^2$$
$$\text{Area of section } B = lb$$
$$= 7 \times 5$$
$$= 35 \text{ m}^2$$
$$\text{So total area} = 153 + 35$$
$$= 188 \text{ m}^2$$

EXAMPLE 5

Calculate the area of the shaded region.

Solution

A = square − circle
$= 12 \times 12 - \pi \times 6^2$
Area = 30·9 cm² (1 decimal place)

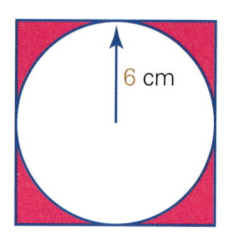

6 cm

> When rounding an answer it is usual to choose one more decimal place than used in the question.

EXERCISE 3C

1 Draw diagrams if necessary to help you complete the following list:
1 cm² = ... mm²
1 m² = ... cm²
1 ha = ... m²
1 km² = ... m²
1 km² = ... ha

2 Find the area of each figure:

> Show at least *two different* ways to calculate this area—make sure your answers match.

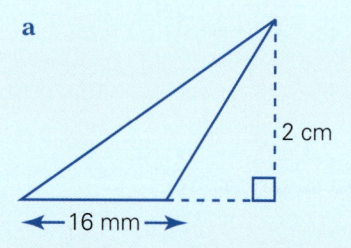

a 2 cm, 16 mm

b 42 cm

c 22 m, 28 m, 47 m, 36 m

Level 2

3 Calculate the shaded area:

a 3 cm, 5·2 cm, 8·7 cm, 9·6 cm

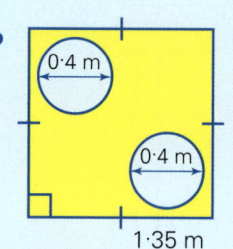

b 0·4 m, 0·4 m, 1·35 m

c 12 cm

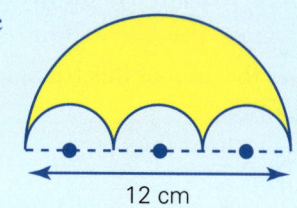

4 Find the area of each figure, correct to 2 decimal places where necessary:

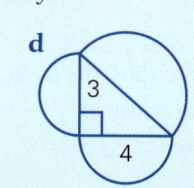

a 3·1 mm, 12·9 mm, 7·8 mm, 4·2 mm, 3·6 mm

> Think: can you use less than four triangles?

b 35 m, 14 m

c 6·8 cm, 1·6 cm, 7·9 cm

d 3, 4

5 What area of card would be needed to make a closed rectangular box measuring 28 cm by 30 cm by 57 cm?

6 Ngoc measures the circumference of her circular swimming pool to be 27·5 m. There is a 1 m wide path around the edge of the pool. What is the area of the path, to the nearest square metre?

7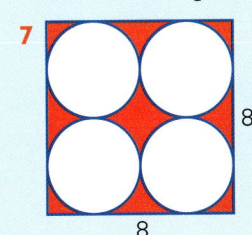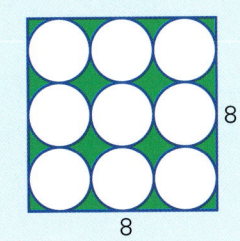

a Find the shaded area ($A1$) in the figure on the far left.
b Find the area ($A2$) in the figure to its right.
c Find the ratio $A1 : A2$.

8 If $AB = 15$ cm, calculate the shaded area.

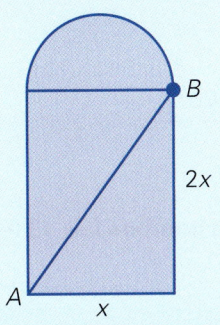

9 A goat is tethered to a post in one corner of a rectangular paddock 15 m by 7 m. If the rope used is 5 m in length, calculate the percentage of the paddock that the goat can eat.

10 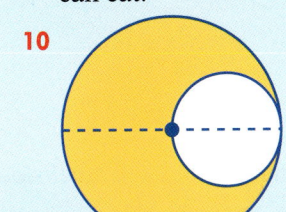 The circumference of the smaller circle is 30π.

a Calculate the shaded area.
b Find the ratio of the white area to the shaded area.

11 a A rectangular paddock is to be fenced using 50 m of fencing. Find the dimensions of the rectangular paddock that encloses the maximum area.
b If the paddock in part **a** is to be constructed against an existing wall so that only three sides of the paddock need to be fenced with the 50 m of fencing, what are the dimensions that enclose the maximum area now?

> A graph or graphics calculator may help.

12 The radius of a circle was measured as 4 cm. Write down the upper and lower limits for its circumference and area.

Try this

Which is the better fit: a square peg in a round hole or a round peg in a square hole?

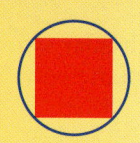 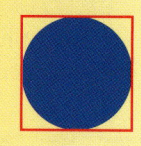

3.4 Areas of parallelograms, kites and trapeziums

Commonly occurring quadrilaterals with special properties are parallelograms, kites and trapeziums.

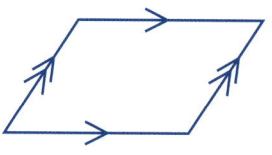

A **parallelogram** is a quadrilateral that has two pairs of parallel sides.

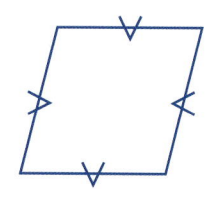

A **rhombus** has all four sides equal.

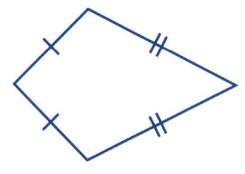

A **kite** has two pairs of equal adjacent sides.

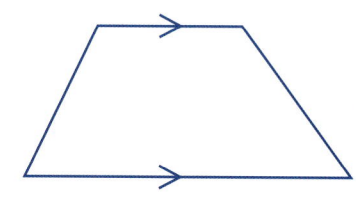

A **trapezium** is a quadrilateral with one pair of parallel sides

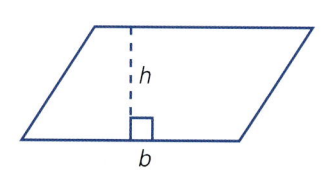

PARALLELOGRAM

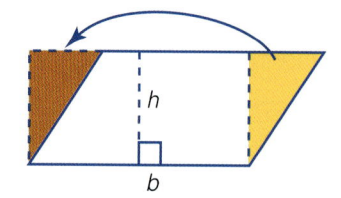

Area:
$A = hb$

KITE

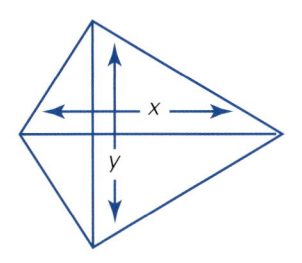 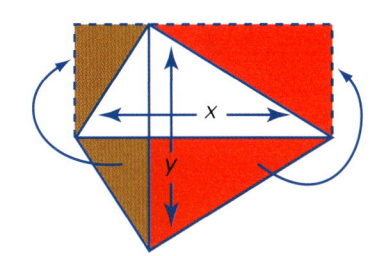

Area:
$$A = \frac{x \times y}{2}$$

TRAPEZIUM

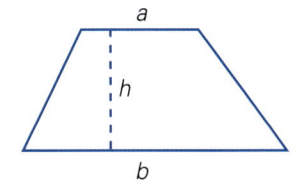 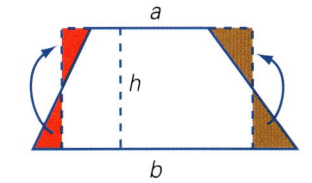

Area:
$$A = \frac{(a + b)h}{2} \text{ or } \frac{h}{2}(a + b)$$

RHOMBUS

A rhombus can be considered:

a a special parallelogram **or** **b** a special kite

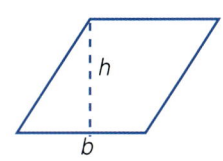 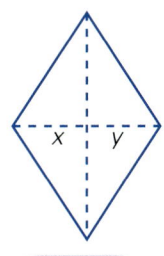

Area:
$A = bh$

Area:
$$A = \frac{xy}{2}$$

EXAMPLE 1
Calculate the area of this parallelogram.
Solution

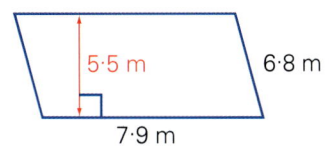

Area $= bh$
$\quad = 7{\cdot}9 \times 5{\cdot}5$
Area is $43{\cdot}45$ m^2.

EXAMPLE 2

Calculate the area of rhombus *ABCD* to the nearest square centimetre.
AC = 34·5 cm and *BD* = 21·7 cm

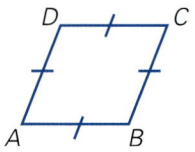

Solution

Area = $\frac{1}{2}xy$

$= \frac{1}{2} \times 21\cdot7 \times 34\cdot5$

$= 374\cdot325$

Area is 374 cm² (to the nearest cm²).

EXAMPLE 3

Find the area of this trapezium.

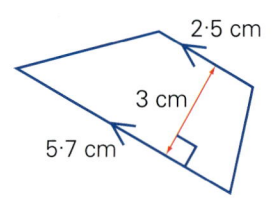

Solution

Area = $\frac{(a+b)}{2}h$

$= \frac{(2\cdot5+5\cdot7)}{2} \times 3$

Area is 12·3 cm².

EXAMPLE 4

Find the area of the kite *ABCD*, given the diagonals have lengths 4 and 6 metres.

Solution

Draw a diagram (is this the only possibility?)

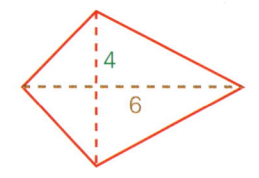

Area = $\frac{1}{2}xy$

$= \frac{1}{2} \times 4 \times 6$

Area is 12 m².

EXERCISE 3D

1 Calculate the area of these parallelograms. Make a note of any measurements that are unnecessary.

a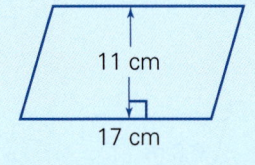

b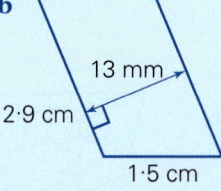

c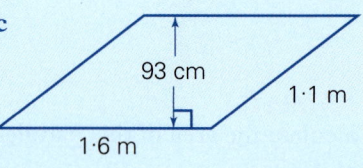

2 Make the necessary measurements to calculate the area of this parallelogram:

a using *JK* as the base
b using *KL* as the base

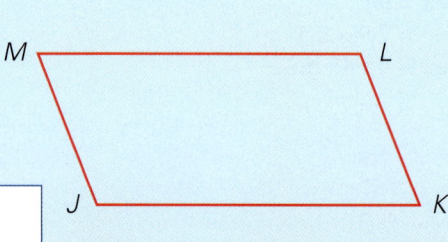

> A set square may be useful for measuring the perpendicular height.

3 Divide this kite into two identical triangles.

  a What is the area of each triangle?
  b What is the area of the whole kite?

  c Use the formula $A = \frac{1}{2}xy$ to find the area.
    Is this the same as your answer to **b**?

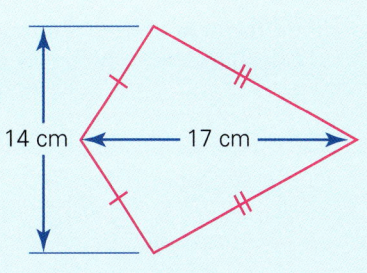

4 Calculate the area of each rhombus or kite:

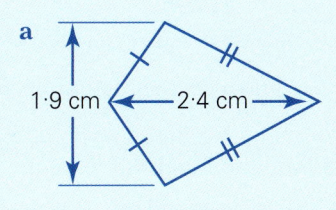
        a

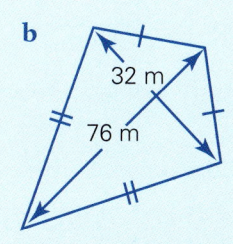
b

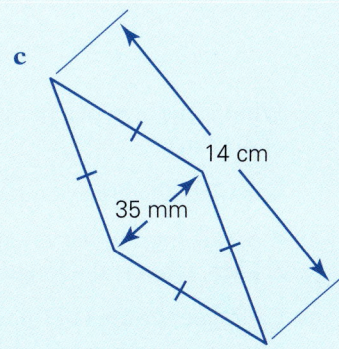
c

5 Give answers to the following areas in square centimetres:

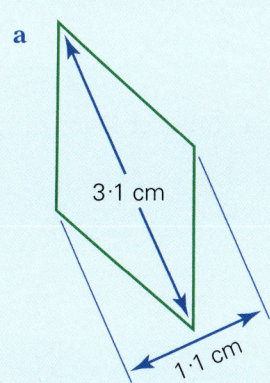
a

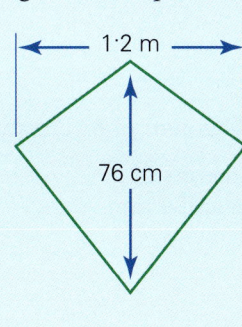
b

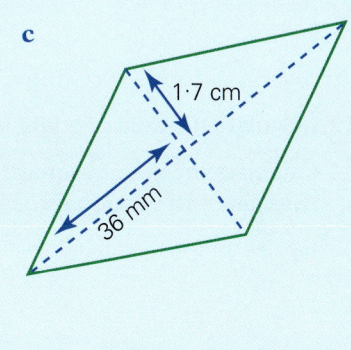
c

6 Make the necessary measurements to find
the area of this trapezium in square
centimetres, correct to 1 decimal place.

> Make sure you measure
> the height ⌐ to the base.

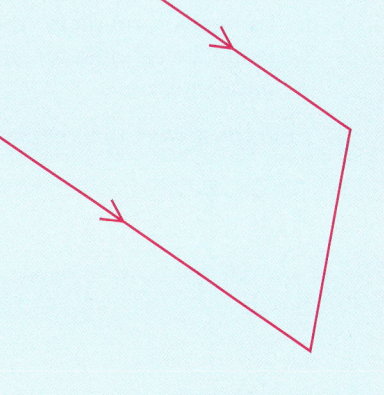

7 Find the area of each shape, correct to 3 significant figures. Show the subdivisions of those shapes for which it is necessary:

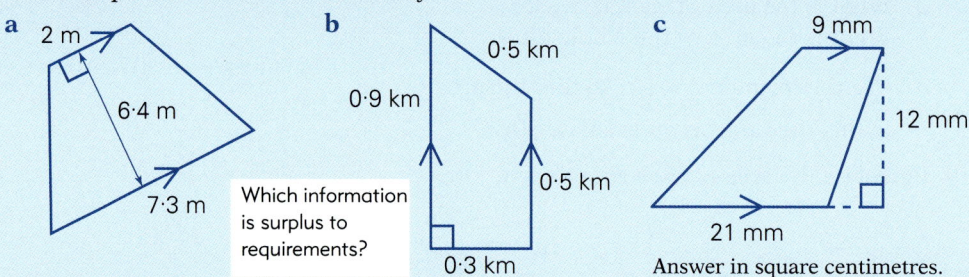

a 2 m, 6·4 m, 7·3 m

Which information is surplus to requirements?

b 0·5 km, 0·9 km, 0·5 km, 0·3 km

c 9 mm, 12 mm, 21 mm

Answer in square centimetres.

8 What is the area of a parallelogram that has a base of 6·5 m and a perpendicular height of 4·13 m?

9 Calculate the area of a parallelogram with a base of 45 mm and height of 7·2 cm.

10 A parallelogram has an area of 45 km². If the perpendicular height is known to be 6·1 km, what is the length of the base? (Correct to the nearest m.)

11 Calculate the area of this shape, giving your answer in square centimetres.

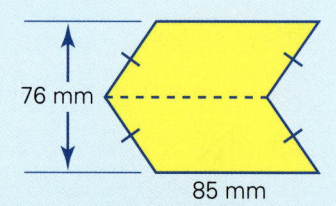

76 mm

85 mm

12 Calculate the area of a kite with diagonals of 85 cm and $2\frac{3}{4}$ m. (Answer in m².)

13 Calculate the area in square centimetres of a rhombus with diagonals of 2·4 cm and 9 mm.

14 Make the necessary measurements and calculate the area of this rhombus:

a using the formula for the area of a kite
b using the formula for the area of a parallelogram

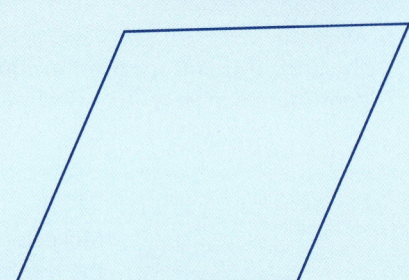

15 Find the area of this regular hexagon:

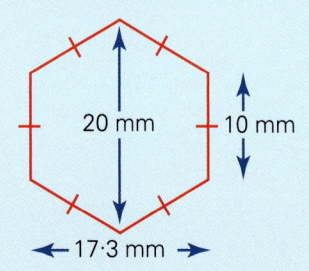

20 mm   10 mm

17·3 mm

16 Calculate the area of the figure shown.

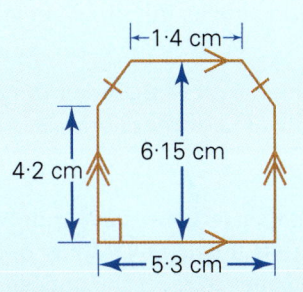

Level 2

17 Brahmagupta, an Indian mathematician and astronomer (c. 598–c. 665 AD) used the formula $A = \sqrt{(s-a)(s-b)(s-c)(s-d)}$, where a, b, c and d are the lengths of the sides of the quadrilateral and s is equal to half the perimeter, to calculate the area of any quadrilateral. Using this formula find the area of the following quadrilaterals:

a

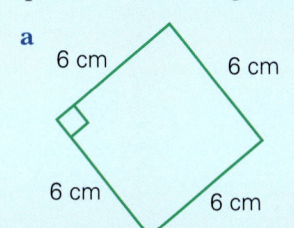

b

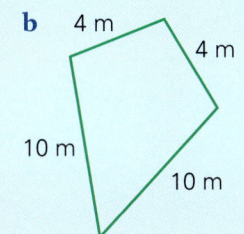

c

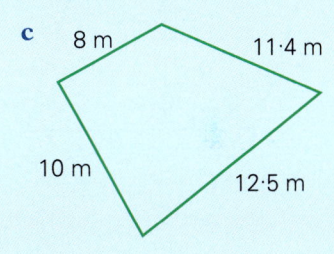

18

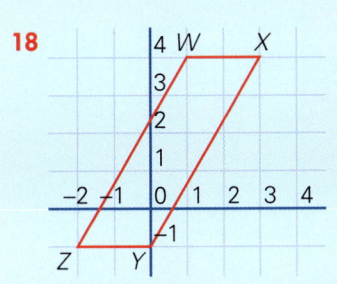

Calculate the area of parallelogram $WXYZ$.
(Answer in square units.)

19 Calculate the area of a parallelogram that has corners at $(^-1, ^-2)$, $(4, 3)$, $(4, 6)$ and $(^-1, 1)$.

20 A parallelogram has three of its corners at $(^-2, 1)$, $(0, 4)$, $(5, 1)$. What are the coordinates of the other corner?

21 What is the area of the parallelogram in question **20**?

22 a What is the area of parallelogram $EFGH$?
   b What is the length of side GH, correct to 2 decimal places?
   c What is the perpendicular height to base GH, correct to 2 decimal places?

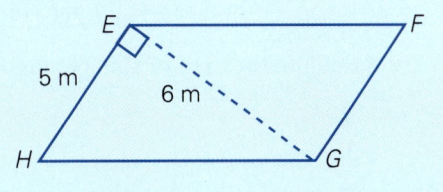

23 The area of a rhombus is 230 cm² and the length of one diagonal is 32 cm.

   a Calculate the length of the other diagonal.
   b Calculate the perimeter of the rhombus.

24 A rhombus has a side length of 26 cm and the length of one diagonal is known to be 20 cm.

    a Calculate the length of the other diagonal.
    b Calculate the area of the rhombus.

Level 3

25 A piece of A4 paper measures 298 mm by 211 mm. A parallelogram is formed by folding opposite corners of the paper to meet the opposite side. What is the area of the parallelogram?

26 Find the value of x.

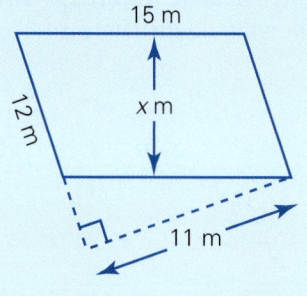

27 Find the area of this figure:

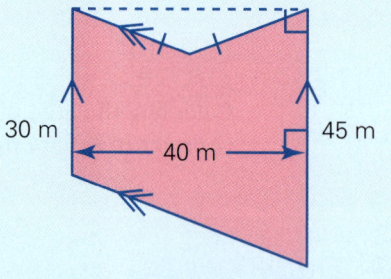

28 Find the area of:

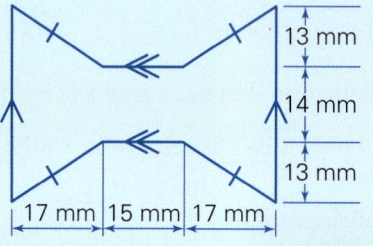

29 Calculate the area of this pentagon:

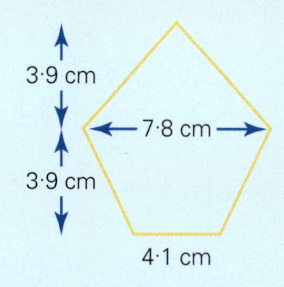

30 Find the shaded area of each shape:

a
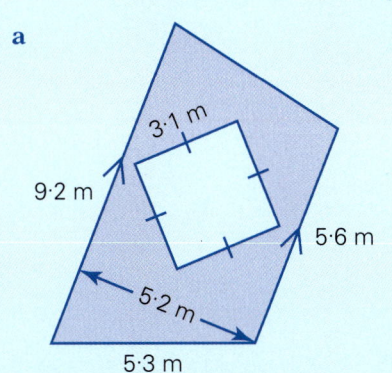

b
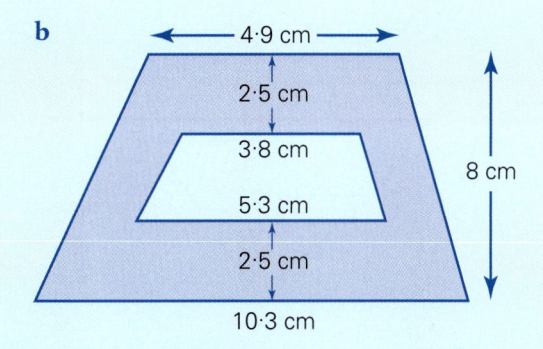

31 This diagram shows the end wall of a warehouse.

    a Calculate the area of the wall.

    b If 1 L of paint covers an area of 12 m² how much paint will be needed to cover the wall with three coats of paint?

    c Paint costs $23·26 for a 5 L can. How much will it cost to buy the paint for the wall?

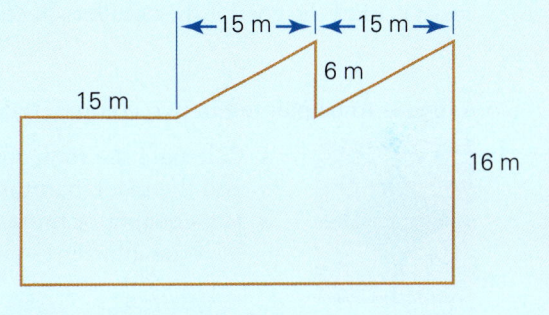

32 The coloured triangle is equilateral. What percentage of the square is coloured?

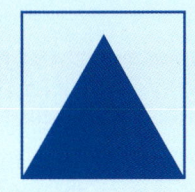

Use Pythagoras to find the ⌐ height.

33
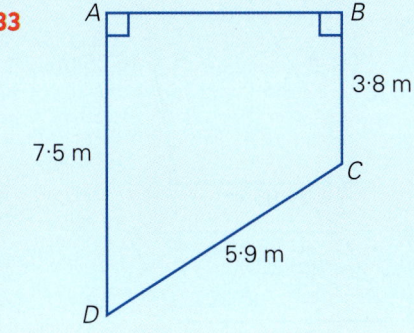

Joanna is planning to buy some carpet for her dining room. She sketches a plan as shown, and marks on the measurements, forgetting to measure the length *AB*.

    a Explain how length *AB* can be calculated from the measurements she already has.

    b Calculate the floor area, to 2 significant figures.

    c If the carpet Joanna chooses costs $45 per square metre, what will it cost (to the nearest $5) to carpet the room?

34 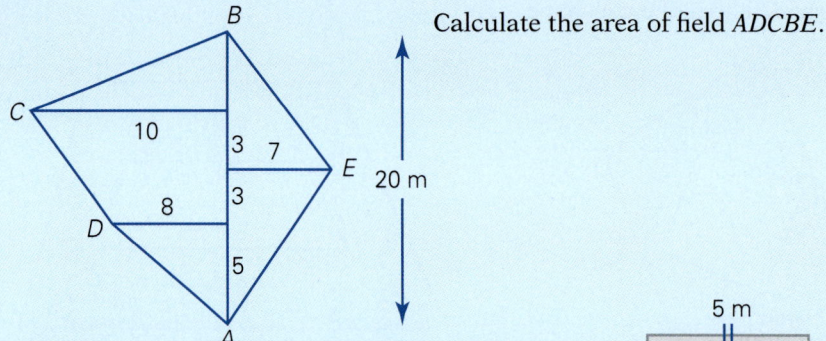 Calculate the area of field *ADCBE*.

35 These diagrams represent two sheets of the same metal, both of equal thickness. The larger sheet cost $x. Find the cost of the smaller sheet.

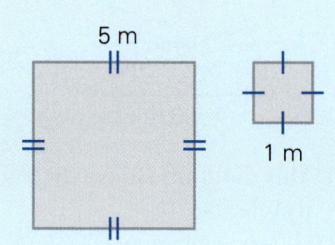

36 A logo is to be painted in two colours, red and black.

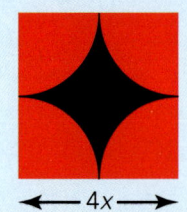

 a Calculate the total cost if red paint costs $18 per square metre and the black paint is half the price of the red.
 b Is it cheaper or more expensive if the colours are swapped—that is, if the quarter circles become black and the centre red?

Investigation Area and perimeter

1 A new airline is designing a logo for the tails of its planes. Their marketing manager insists that the logo should cover at least 60% of the area of the tail. The designer has come up with three ideas as shown.

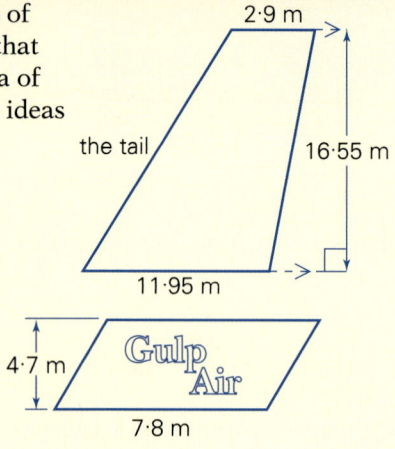

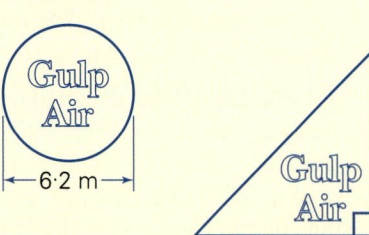

 a Which of these would satisfy the marketing manager?
 b Which design would you select? Why?
 c Create another design based on geometrical shapes, and show that it would satisfy the marketing manager.

TEACHER
TEACHER

2 a What is the perimeter of this square?

b What is its area?

c If the **perimeter** of the square is **doubled** what is the new area?

d Try the same thing with squares of different sizes, and record your results in a table.

e Complete this sentence: When you double the perimeter of a square, the area …

f Now explore what happens to the *perimeter* of a square if you double its *area*. Write a similar sentence.

g Are these relationships true for other shapes, for example rectangles and circles?

> 'Integral' comes from *integer*, meaning 'whole number'.

3 A trapezium is drawn with its parallel sides 5 cm apart. If you are told that the area of a trapezium is 30 cm and that the lengths of the parallel sides are integral numbers of centimetres, what possible lengths could the parallel sides be?

4 The area of a rectangle is 36 cm^2, and the perimeter of the rectangle is 30 cm.

a What is the size of the rectangle?

b Is this the only possible answer?

5 Peter has a theory that there is just one rectangle that has the same perimeter in centimetres as it has area in square centimetres. Which of the following is true? Justify your selection.

a Peter's theory is correct. (What size is the rectangle?)

b Peter's theory is wrong because there are no such rectangles.

c Peter's theory is wrong because there is more than one rectangle for which this is true. (Give the sizes of the rectangles.)

Investigation The carpet puzzle

Mark's games room is 10 m long and 10 m wide.

While out shopping he sees a bargain carpet, which is reduced in price because it is a rather unusual shape: 12 m long, 9 m wide, but with a hole 8 m by 1 m exactly in the middle.

He buys the carpet, and cuts it into two pieces. He sews the pieces together with just one seam, producing a carpet exactly the right shape and size for his room.

How did he do it?

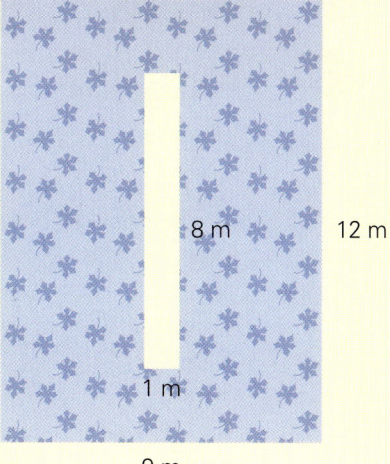

3.5 Area of irregular figures

In reality, many of the areas we are required to find are not geometrical shapes for which a formula can be used.

If this is the case, an estimate can be made using one of several methods:

- A centimetre square grid, or a collection of plastic centimetre squares, can be placed over the shape, and the squares counted. (This is useful only with small shapes.)

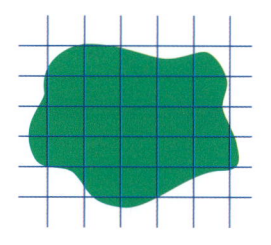

- The shape can be divided into areas that roughly resemble geometrical shapes, and their formulas can be used to calculate the area.

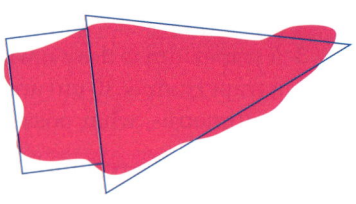

- An estimate can be made based on an area that is already known.

EXAMPLE

Find the area of this figure:

Solution

The shape has roughly the same area as a trapezium and a rectangle.

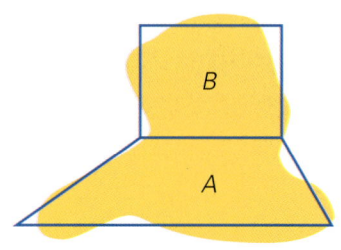

$$\text{Area of } A \quad = \frac{(a+b)}{2}h$$

$$= \frac{(4 \cdot 5 + 2)}{2} \times 1 \cdot 2$$

$$= 3 \cdot 9 \text{ cm}^2$$

$$\text{Area of } B \quad = lb$$

$$= 2 \times 1 \cdot 5$$

$$= 3 \text{ cm}^2$$

$$\text{Total area} \quad \approx 3 \cdot 9 + 3$$

$$\approx 6 \cdot 9 \text{ cm}^2$$

EXERCISE 3E

1 Trace each of the following figures into your book, then use combinations of geometrical shapes to estimate their areas. Draw the geometrical shapes onto your figures.

a 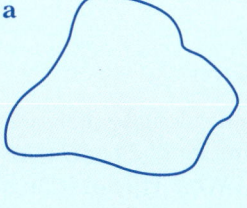   **b**    **c**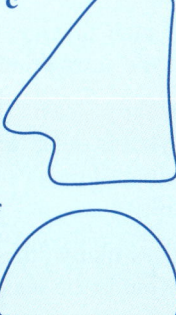

d 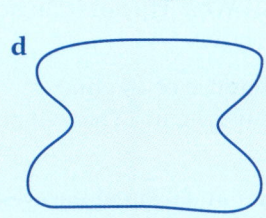   **e**   **f**

Level 2

2 The area of New South Wales is 802 000 km².

   a Estimate the area of Western Australia.
   b Estimate the area of the whole of Australia.

Level 3

3 Estimate the area covered by the palm of your hand using two different methods. Describe the steps taken and include diagrams. Which do you think is the best estimate? Explain why.

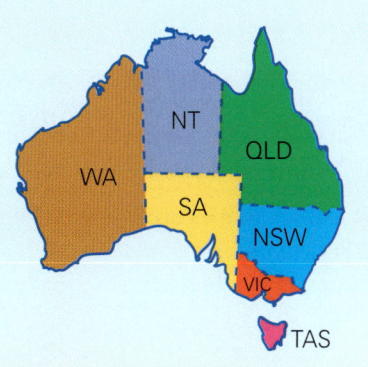

Try this

Draw the figure on the left onto squared paper. Cut out the pieces and arrange them as shown on the right. Where has the extra square come from?

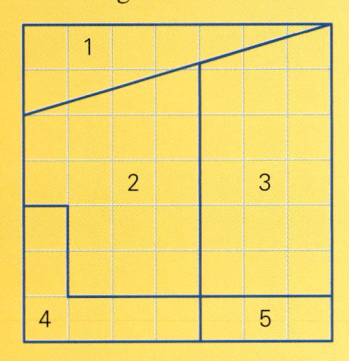   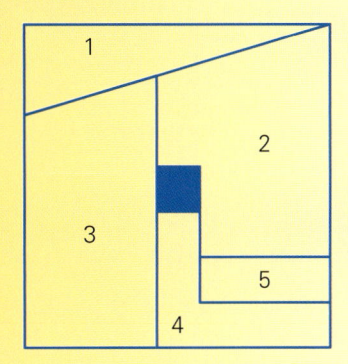

Investigation String figures

You need: a piece of string 24 cm long, and some centimetre square paper for estimating areas. A geoboard may also be useful.

1 What is the largest area for a rectangle with a perimeter of 24 cm:

   a if each side has to be an integral number of centimetres?
   b if the sides do not have to be integral numbers of centimetres?

2 a Make at least three different triangles using the string, and calculate their areas.
   b What is the largest possible area for a triangle with a perimeter of 24 cm? (Use the squared paper to estimate any necessary measurements.) What type of triangle is this?

3 a How many different circles can be made with a circumference of 24 cm?
   b What is the maximum area for a circle with a perimeter of 24 cm? (You will need to use the formulas for perimeter and area.)

4 a What shape would you choose if you had a fixed perimeter and wanted the area to be as large as possible?
   b Give some examples of how this fact could be used in a practical situation.

Investigation Pick's theorem

You need: square dot paper

Closed shapes are made by joining dots together with straight lines. The dots need not be adjacent.

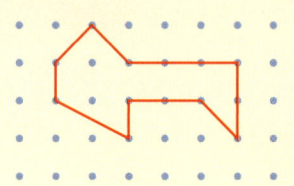

The aim is to find a relationship between the number of dots on the *perimeter* of the shape (p), the number of dots *within* the shape (d) and the *area* of the shape (a).

Shape	p	d	a
Example	13	2	7·5
1			
2			

Record your results in a table as shown. The data for the shape in the example are included.

Be systematic when looking for relationships. It may help to keep one variable constant while you look at the other two.

For example, start off by looking at shapes that have no dots inside, and try to find a relationship between p and a.

Then you can see what happens as you increase the number of dots inside the shape.

Make sure you record your information carefully. When you find a relationship, write it in words first, then write it as a mathematical sentence if you can.

Chapter Review

Language Links

accuracy	diameter	milli	rectangular
area	estimate	octagon	rhombus
centi	hexagon	parallel	scale
circle	kilo	pentagon	side
circular	kite	perimeter	trapezium
circumference	length	perpendicular	trapezoidal
conversion	measurement	pi	triangular
diagonals	mega	radius	

1 To fill each space, select the best word from the list above. (No word is used more than once, and some words will not be used at all.)

The tools used to measure quantities determine the _____ of the measurement. Sometimes it is more appropriate to _____ a measurement.

Knowing the meaning of certain prefixes can help with unit conversions, for example _____ means 'one thousandth', and _____ means 'one thousand'.

The _____ of a shape is how much flat space it takes up, and the _____ of a shape is the distance around the edge. The formula for the perimeter of a regular _____ is $P = 6s$ (where s represents the _____ of one _____). The formula $A = xy$ is used to calculate the area of both a _____ and a _____, where x and y represent the lengths of the _____.

The _____ of a shape is how much flat space it takes up, and the _____ of a shape is the distance around the edge. The formula for the perimeter of a regular _____ is $P = 6s$ (where s represents the _____ of one _____). The formula $A = xy$ is used to calculate the area of both a _____ and a _____, where x and y represent the lengths of the _____.

The special name given to the perimeter of a circle is the _____, and this is calculated by multiplying the _____ by _____.

When calculating the area of a parallelogram, _____ or triangle, the height must be measured _____ to the base.

2 Describe *in words* the measurements and calculations that are necessary to find the area of a parallelogram. Be as precise as possible.

3 Describe the similarities and differences between:

a a kite and a rhombus

b a rhombus and a parallelogram

Chapter Review Exercises

MC

1 What reading is shown on each of these scales?

a 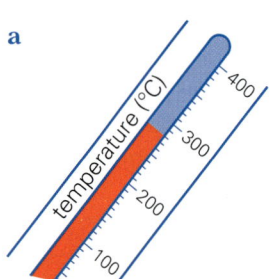 **b** volts (V)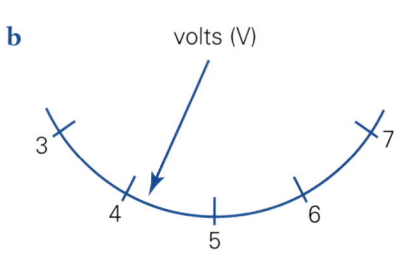

MC

2 Where on the Richter scale would an earthquake be if it was 1000 times more powerful than one measured at 4 on the scale?

MC

3 Name two possible measuring tools that could be used to measure the length of a car. For each tool give:

    a how accurate the measurement would be
    b a situation for which the use of the tool would be appropriate

MC

4 Give the limits of accuracy for the following measurements:

    a 4 m   **b** 23·8 min   **c** 5·40 kg

MC

5 Convert the following:

    a $2\frac{3}{4}$ h to min   **b** 495 s to min, s   **c** 1·2 h to h, min
    d 19·5 cm to m   **e** 59 200 cm to km   **f** 0·06 km to mm
    g 17 650 g to kg   **h** 450 kg to t   **i** 0·34 kg to mg

MC

6 If a locust has a mass of 3·5 g, what would be the combined mass of a plague of half a million locusts?

MC

7 What time is it $4\frac{1}{4}$ hours before 2:08 pm?

MC

8 How many pavers, each 18 mm thick, would there be in a stack 2 m high?

MC

9 Estimate the following:

    a The height of the door into the classroom.
    b The mass of this book.
    c The distance from one edge of the school grounds to the other.
    d The time it would take you to walk 5 km.

10 Calculate the perimeter of each shape:

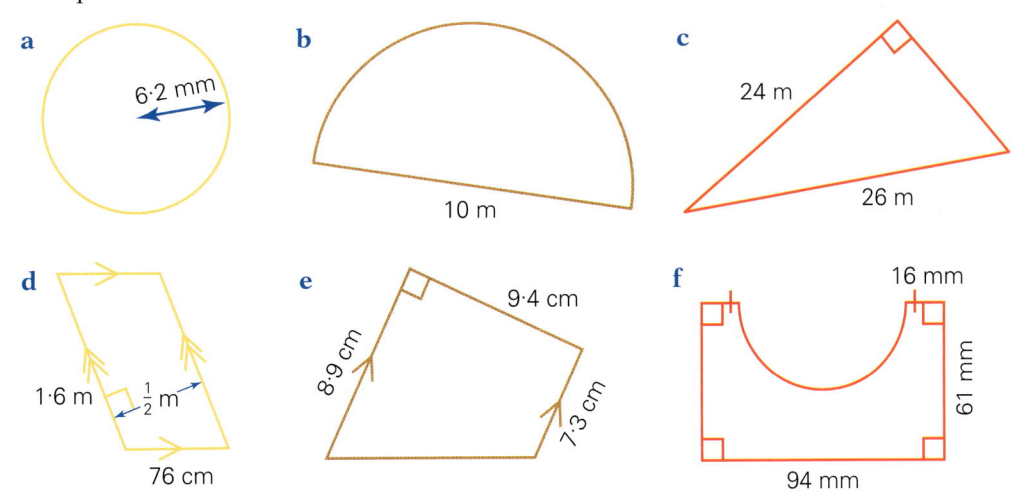

a 13 cm 14·5 cm 22 cm 15 cm

b 2·9 mm

c 1·7 m 40 cm 50 cm 2·9 m 3·5 m 60 cm

11 The perimeter of a rectangle is 56 cm. If two of the sides are 22 cm long, what is the length of the other sides?

12 The distance around the earth at the equator is approximately 40 000 km. What is the radius of the earth, correct to 2 significant figures?

13 For each of these shapes find:
i the perimeter   ii the area

a 6·2 mm

b 10 m

c 24 m 26 m

d 1·6 m $\frac{1}{2}$ m 76 cm

e 8·9 cm 9·4 cm 7·3 cm

f 16 mm 94 mm 61 mm

14 Estimate the area of this shape, and comment on the accuracy of your answer.d

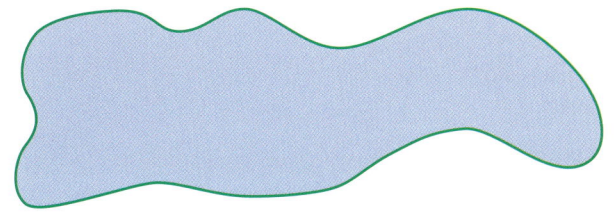

15 Trish has a piece of paper that measures 29·7 cm by 21·1 cm. She folds the paper in half longways, then in half crossways, and then cuts across from one corner to the other to make a triangle.

a What shape would be produced when the paper is unfolded? Explain how you came to this conclusion.

b What is the area of the shape, to the nearest square centimetre?

central point of paper

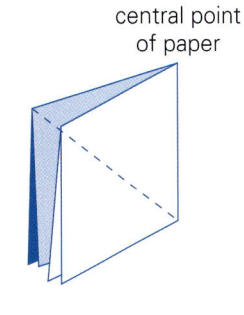

Keeping Mathematically Fit

Part A—Non-calculator

1 It takes $\frac{3}{5}$ of a can of drink to fill a glass. How many glasses can be filled from 15 cans?

2 The sum of two numbers is $a + b$. One of the numbers is $a - b$. What is the other number?

3 Find the relationship between and x and y.

4 Estimate the height of the building.

x	1	2	3	4	5
y	5	8	11	14	17

5 One of these clocks is 10 minutes fast, the other is 5 minutes slow. What is the correct time?

6 A fuel tank can hold 60 litres. The gauge shows the amount of fuel in the tank.

  a What fraction of the fuel has been used?
  b How much fuel is left in the tank?

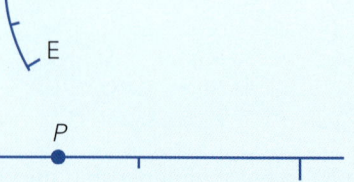

7 Write the decimal represented by point P.

4.0   4.1

8 In a tennis tournament, players need to win their matches to progress to the next round. If 32 players enter, how many matches will the winner play?

9 Evaluate 0.2^3.

10 $3 \text{ cm}^3 = \dots \text{ mm}^3$

Part B—Calculator

1 Write the answer to 7621×4396 in scientific notation, correct to 3 significant figures.

2 The amount of usable timber in a tree is calculated using the formula $V = 0.5\, hd^2 + 10$ where:

d = the diameter of the tree trunk
h = height of the first branch
v = amount of usable timber in cubic metres.

Calculate the amount of usable timber in a tree with a circumference of 92 cm if the first branch is 2.3 m high.

3 Every day Jock arrives 5 minutes late to school. How many hours late is he over the 40-week school year?

4 Find the area of the rhombus.

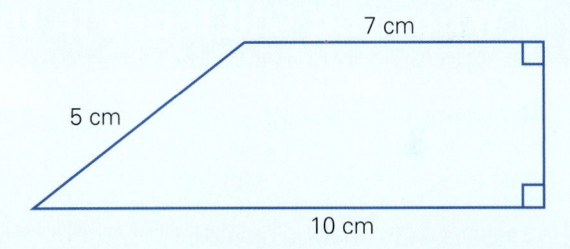

5 In a 1 km race, Jan finishes 50 m ahead of Leanne, who leads Emma by 20 m. If Leanne and Emma continue on at their same rates, how far is Emma behind Leanne when Leanne finishes?

1 What you need to know and revise

Outcome PAS 4.4:

Uses algebraic techniques to solve linear equations and simple inequalities:

- solving simple linear equations using a variety of strategies

- solving equations using algebraic methods that involve up to and involving three steps
- checking solutions by substitution
- solving equations arising from substitution into formulas.

2 What you will learn in this chapter

Outcome §PAS 5.2.2:

Solves linear and simple quadratic equations, solves linear inequalities and solves simultaneous equations using graphical and analytical methods:

- solving linear equations
- solving word problems that result in equations
- simple quadratic equations, i.e. $x^2 = c$
- solving equations arising from substitution into formulas
- solving inequalities.

Outcome PAS 5.3.2:

Solves linear, quadratic and simultaneous equations, solves and graphs inequalities, and rearranges literal equations:

- solving a range of linear equations including ones that involve brackets and fractions
- solving problems involving linear equations
- using $<$, $\leq$, $>$, $\geq$ to generate linear equalities from problems
- solving a variety of inequalities and problems involving inequalities
- changing the subject of a formula
- conditional equations.

Working Mathematically outcomes WMS 5.1, 5.2, 5.3

Students will be required to *question*, *apply strategies*, *communicate*, *reason* and *reflect* in the sections of this chapter.

Equations

MathsCheck
Equations

1 If $A = LB$, find the value of A given:

    a $L = 6, B = 4$ **b** $L = 4, B = 4$ **c** $L = 7\cdot8, B = 6\cdot07$

2 If $a = 7, b = 4, c = {}^-3$, evaluate:

    a $a^2 + b^2 + c^2$ **b** $2(a + b + c)$ **c** $3(a + b)^2$

    d ${}^-c$ **e** $\sqrt{bc^2}$ **f** $\dfrac{ab + c}{5}$

3 If $A = \dfrac{m + n}{2}$, find A given:

    a $m = 8\cdot1, n = 9\cdot6$ **b** $m = 3\frac{3}{4}, n = 1\frac{1}{2}$ **c** $m = 0\cdot96, n = 1\cdot2$

4 If $C = \dfrac{nA}{n + 12}$, evaluate C given:

    a $n = {}^-2, A = 6$ **b** $n = 0\cdot4, A = 3\cdot6$ **c** $n = {}^-2, A = {}^-12$

5 A formula for calculating the area of a trapezium is written as $A = h\left(\dfrac{a + b}{2}\right)$. Find the value of A for each of the following:

    a $a = 5\cdot6, b = 3\cdot4, h = 8$ **b** $a = 45, b = 58, h = 12$
    c $a = 23\cdot4, b = 17\cdot09, h = 16\cdot2$

6 A straight line has an equation of the form $y = mx + b$, where m represents the gradient and b represents the y-intercept. For a line with gradient $\dfrac{1}{2}$ and y-intercept of ${}^-3$ find the value of y when x is:

    a 0 **b** 1 **c** 4

7 If a line has a gradient of ${}^-2$ and a y-intercept of ${}^-3$, find the value of y for each of the values given in question **6**.

8 If a line has a gradient of 1 and a y-intercept of 0, find the value of y for each of the values given in question **6**.

9 To convert degrees Fahrenheit to degrees Celsius we use $C = \dfrac{5}{9}(F - 32)$.

    To convert degrees Celsius to degrees Fahrenheit we use $F = 32 + \dfrac{9}{5}C$.
    Use the appropriate formula for each of the following:

    a $C = ?$ when $F = 10°$ **b** $F = ?$ when $C = 0°$ **c** $F = 0°$ when $C = ?$

Level 2

10 Write the following as a formula:

    a   The circumference (c) of a circle is double the product of the radius (r) and pi.
    b   Distance (D) equals speed (S) multiplied by time (T).
    c   Interest (I) equals the principal (P) multiplied by the interest rate (R) and by the time period n.

d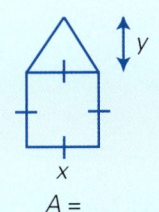

$A =$

e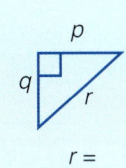

$r =$

f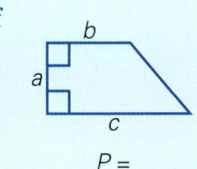

$P =$

g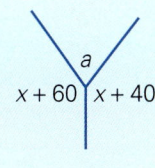

$x + 60$ $x + 40$

Angle sum $=$

11 Solve:

a $x + 3 = 8$ **b** $x - 5 = 9$ **c** $5x = 30$ **d** $\dfrac{x}{6} = 3$

e $12 = n + 5$ **f** $x + (^-2) = ^-6$ **g** $7 - x = 4$

12 Find the value of the pronumeral in each of the following:

a $2x + 1 = 9$ **b** $\dfrac{x}{2} - 1 = 6$ **c** $5 - x = 9$ **d** $2x - 7 = 7$ **e** $\dfrac{a}{4} - 1 = 3$

13 In which of the following is $x = 2$ a solution? What is the answer for the others?

a $4x = 8$ **b** $\dfrac{16}{x} = 4$ **c** $2(x + 1) = 2$ **d** $\dfrac{x + 4}{2} = 2$

e $\dfrac{16}{2x} = 4$ **f** $2x + 6 = x + 8$ **g** $\dfrac{x - 4}{2} = 2$ **h** $2x + 4 = x + 6$

14 Solve each of the following:

a $\dfrac{x + 1}{6} = 4$ **b** $\dfrac{3x - 1}{4} = 0$ **c** $\dfrac{2x}{3} = 9$ **d** $\dfrac{2x}{3} - 1 = 6$ **e** $\dfrac{5 - x}{^-3} = 4$

15 The initial cost of hiring a wedding car is $850 plus a charge of $156 per hour.

  a Write an equation for the cost (C) of hiring a car for h hours.

  b If the bride and groom have budgeted for the cars to cost a maximum of $2000, find the maximum of hours they can hire the car.

  c If the car picks the bride up at 1:15 pm, at what time must the event finish if the cost is to remain in budget?

- Write an equation/formula.
- Substitute the values given.
- Solve the equation.
- Make sure you answer the question fully, in words.

16 A tax agent charges $350 for an 8-hour working day. The agent uses the formula

$F = \dfrac{350x}{8}$ to calculate a fee to a client in dollars.

  a What does the x represent?

  b If the fee charged to a client came to $328·13, how many hours were spent by the agent working on the client's behalf?

17 a 5 was subtracted from a certain number, then the result was multiplied by 3. If the answer obtained was 3, what was the original number?

b 4 was added to a number, then the result was doubled. If 15 was obtained, find the original number.

18 Solve:

   a $7x = 12 + 3x$ **b** $5n = 12 - n$ **c** $^-x = x + 6$

19 Find the value of the pronumeral in each of the following equations:

   a $4 + 3d = 28 - d$ **b** $5 - 2x = x - 6$ **c** $3m + 5 = 30 - 3m$ **d** $x + 7 = 7 - x$

20 In which of the following is $x = 3$ a solution?

   a $x + 7 = 13 - x$ **b** $6 - x = x$ **c** $4x + 1 = 6x$

   d $^-6 + x = x$ **e** $3x + 1 = x + 2$ **f** $4x + 2 = x + 2$

21 Find the value of x in each of the following:

   a

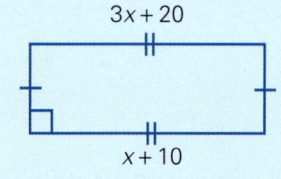

   b The product of a number (x) and 3 is equal to 5 less than twice the number.

   c   **d**

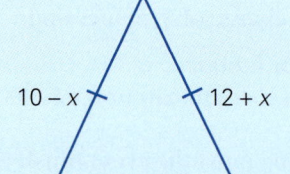 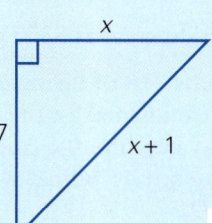

> **d** requires Pythagoras's theorem.

   e

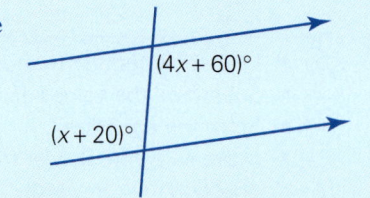

22 Write an equation with pronumerals on both sides whose solution is $m = ^-3$.

23 If $2p + 7 = w$, write an expression for w in terms of p so that the solution to $2p + 7 = w$ is $p = \dfrac{1}{2}$.

TEACHER

Exploring New Ideas

4.1 Equations involving grouping symbols

Mohammed ibn Musa al-Khowarizmi worked at the 'House of Wisdom' in the court of Caliph Al-Mamun in Baghdad around 825 AD. His book, *Hisab-al-jabr w'al muquabalah*, was about solving equations.

The need to solve equations exists in many fields today, science and economics to name but two. A linear equation is an algebraic statement where one of the numbers is unknown and represented by a pronumeral of index 1.

$x + 5 = 6$, $3x - 7 = 2x$, $4(2x - 3) + 5x = 0$ and $\dfrac{x}{3} - 4 = {}^-7$ are all **linear** equations.

Let us look at solving equations involving grouping symbols.

EXAMPLE 1

Find the value of the pronumeral:

a $2(x - 6) = 8$ **b** $12 - (b - 6) = 10$ **c** $3(2x - 1) = 5(2x - 6)$

$-ve \times -ve = +ve$

Solutions

a
$$2(x - 6) = 8$$
$$2x - 12 = 8$$
$$+12 \quad +12$$
$$\frac{2x}{2} = \frac{20}{2}$$
$$x = 10$$

b
$$12 - (b - 6) = 10$$
$$12 - b + 6 = 10$$
$$18 - b = 10$$
$$-18 \qquad -18$$
$$\frac{{}^-b}{{}^-1} = \frac{{}^-8}{{}^-1}$$
$$b = 8$$

c
$$3(2x - 1) = 5(2x - 6)$$
$$6x - 3 = 10x - 30$$
$$+3 \qquad +3$$
$$6x = 10x - 27$$
$$-10x \quad -10x$$
$$\frac{{}^-4x}{{}^-4} = \frac{{}^-27}{{}^-4}$$
$$x = \frac{27}{4}$$

Don't forget to check your solutions.

EXERCISE 4A

1 Solve the following equations by removing grouping symbols:

a $3(x + 2) = 18$ **b** $7(n + 3) = 49$ **c** $2(3 + p) = 10$
d $4(a - 1) = 16$ **e** $25 = 5(x + 4)$ **f** $3(2n + 4) = 18$
g $6(3 + 2t) = 30$ **h** $10 = 5(2b - 6)$ **i** $3(2 - x) = 9$

Level 2

2 Find the value of each pronumeral:

a ${}^-3(2 - x) = 0$ **b** $\dfrac{1}{2}(2x - 4) = 6$ **c** $4(5 - 3x) = 4$ **d** $15 = 5(x - \dfrac{1}{2})$

3 Solve:

a $7(5 - c) = 14$ **b** $4(3 - 2d) = 4$ **c** $6 - (x + 5) = 3$
d $8 = 22 - (h - 3)$ **e** $4 + 2(k + 1) = 12$ **f** $5(2m - 4) + 5 = 15$

4 Solve each of the following equations:

a $3(n + 4) = 2(n + 8)$ **b** $4(2p - 4) = 5(p + 4)$ **c** $2(q + 4) + 3(2q + 1) = 43$
d $r - (2r - 3) = 4$ **e** $2t - 3(1 - t) = 22$ **f** $4w - 3(2w + 5) = 3(w - 2)$

5 Translate the following into algebraic equations, then solve:

   a 6 is added to an unknown number, then the result is multiplied by 5. If 40 is obtained, find the number.

   b 5 was subtracted from a certain number, then the result was multiplied by 3. If the answer obtained was 3, what was the original number?

   c 4 was added to a number, then the result was doubled. If 15 was obtained, find the unknown number.

   d One-third of the result of adding 6 to a number is 8. What is the number?

   e Three-quarters of the difference between double a number and 4 is 6. Find the number. **f** Make up two 'unknown number' descriptions of your own and give them to your partner to solve.

6 Solve the following equations:

   a $2p + 3(p - 2) = p - 8$ **b** $x + 8 - 3(x - 2) = 2x$ **c** $3(p - 4) - (p + 2) = {}^-3p$

   d $5(a - 2) - 3(7 - 2a) = 2$ **e** $4d - 3(2d + 6) = 2(d + 3)$ **f** $7 - (z - 8) = {}^-2(2z - 7)$

4.2 Equations with algebraic fractions

Equations do not always involve integers. In the following section we look at solving equations involving fractions.

EXAMPLE 1

Solve:

   a $\dfrac{p}{3} - 4 = 2$ **b** $\dfrac{3m + 4}{2} = 5$

   c $\dfrac{n}{3} + \dfrac{n}{2} = 5$ **d** $\dfrac{n}{n - 3} = 6$

Solutions

a $\dfrac{p}{3} - 4 = 2$

      $\dfrac{p}{3} = 6$

      $p = 18$

b $\dfrac{3m + 4}{2} = 5$ $\boxed{\times \text{ by } 2}$

    $3m + 4 = 10$

       $3m = 6$

        $m = 2$

c $\dfrac{n}{3} + \dfrac{n}{2} = 5$

   $\dfrac{2n}{6} + \dfrac{3n}{6} = 5$ $\boxed{\begin{array}{c}\text{Common}\\ \text{denominator}\\ = 6\end{array}}$

     $\dfrac{5n}{6} = 5$

    $5n = 30$

     $n = 6$

d $\dfrac{n}{n - 3} = 6$ $\boxed{\times \text{ by } (n - 3)}$

    $n = 6(n - 3)$

    $n = 6n - 18$

  $n + 18 = 6n$

     $18 = 5n$

      $n = \dfrac{18}{5}$

EXAMPLE 2

Find the value of the pronumeral in each of the following equations:

a $\dfrac{7}{n+1} = \dfrac{8}{2n-1}$ b $\dfrac{x+1}{3} - \dfrac{2x-1}{4} = \dfrac{1}{2}$

> Multiply each term by the LCM of the denominators.

Solutions

a
$$(2n-1)(n+1) \times \dfrac{7}{n+1} = \dfrac{8}{2n-1} \times (2n-1)(n+1)$$
$$7(2n-1) = 8(n+1)$$
$$14n - 7 = 8n + 8$$
$$6n = 15$$
$$n = \dfrac{15}{6}$$
$$n = \dfrac{5}{2}$$

An equation to find the escape velocity for Earth is given by $V = \sqrt{2gr}$

b
$$12 \times \dfrac{(x+1)}{3} - 12 \times \dfrac{(2x+1)}{4} = \dfrac{1}{2} \times 12$$
$$4(x+1) - 3(2x-1) = 6$$
$$4x + 4 - 6x + 3 = 6$$
$$^-2x + 7 = 6$$
$$^-2x = ^-1$$
$$2x = 1$$
$$x = \dfrac{1}{2}$$

Alternative solution
$$\dfrac{4(x+1) - 3(2x-1)}{12} = \dfrac{1}{2}$$
$$^-2x + 7 = \dfrac{1}{2} \times 12$$
$$^-2x + 7 = 6$$
$$\dfrac{^-2x}{^-2} = \dfrac{^-1}{^-2}$$
$$x = \dfrac{1}{2}$$

EXERCISE 4B

1 Solve the following equations:

a $\dfrac{x}{4} + 2 = 9$ b $\dfrac{n}{3} - 6 = 4$ c $7 + \dfrac{x}{6} = 6$ d $8 = \dfrac{x}{5} + 2$

e $3 = \dfrac{c}{6} - 1$ f $10 = 4 + \dfrac{m}{5}$ g $10 - \dfrac{x}{4} = 3$ h $13 - \dfrac{e}{7} = 2$

i $\dfrac{5x}{2} = 20$ j $\dfrac{4a}{3} = 8$ k $\dfrac{3c}{4} = 9$ l $15 = \dfrac{5d}{3}$

m $\dfrac{4}{5x} = ^-3$ n $\dfrac{x+3}{5} = 2$ o $\dfrac{x-2}{8} = 4$ p $\dfrac{7+z}{4} = 2$

q $7 = \dfrac{a+3}{2}$ r $\dfrac{4t+3}{5} = 3$ s $\dfrac{12d-6}{5} = 6$ t $4 = \dfrac{18-3h}{3}$

u $^-8 = \dfrac{2-3k}{5}$ v $\dfrac{20+11l}{7} = \dfrac{^-2}{7}$ w $t - \dfrac{2t}{3} = 5$

2 Find the errors, if any, in the following solutions of equations. Lines are numbered for reference.

a $4p - 3 = 5$
$$p - 3 = \frac{5}{4} \qquad ①$$
$$p = 1\tfrac{1}{4} + 3 \qquad ②$$
$$p = 4\tfrac{1}{4} \qquad ③$$

b $3(s - 4) = 8$
$$3s - 4 = 8 \qquad ①$$
$$3s = 12 \qquad ②$$
$$s = 4 \qquad ③$$

c $6 + 3k - k = {}^-2$
$$6 + 2k = {}^-2 \qquad ①$$
$$8k = {}^-2 \qquad ②$$
$$k = \tfrac{{}^-1}{4} \qquad ③$$

d $8 - (x + 4) = {}^-7$
$$8 - x + 4 = {}^-7 \qquad ①$$
$$12 - x = {}^-7 \qquad ②$$
$$19 = x \qquad ③$$

e ${}^-5(3x - 4) = 3(6 + 5x)$
$${}^-15x + 20 = 18 + 15x \qquad ①$$
$$20 = 18 + 30x \qquad ②$$
$$20 = 48x \qquad ③$$
$$\frac{5}{12} = x \qquad ④$$

f $\dfrac{x + 5}{5} = 6$
$$x = 6 \qquad ①$$

g $\dfrac{m}{7} - 1 = 4$
$$\frac{7 \times m}{7} - 1 = 4 \times 7 \qquad ①$$
$$m - 1 = 28 \qquad ②$$
$$m = 29 \qquad ③$$

h $\dfrac{2n + 1}{3} = 5$
$$\frac{2n + 1}{3} \times 3 = 5 \qquad ①$$
$$2n + 1 = 5 \qquad ②$$
$$2n = 6 \qquad ③$$
$$n = 3 \qquad ④$$

i $\dfrac{3t}{5} - \dfrac{1}{5} = 7$
$$5 \times \frac{3t}{5} - 5 \times \frac{1}{5} = 5 \times 7 \qquad ①$$
$$3t - 1 = 35 \qquad ②$$
$$3t = 36 \qquad ③$$
$$t = 12 \qquad ④$$

3 Solve the equations given in question **2**, correctly stating each solution.

4 Solve:

a $4 - \dfrac{x}{2} = 6$

b $\dfrac{x}{3} - \dfrac{x}{4} = {}^-3$

c $\dfrac{x + 4}{3} = \dfrac{x - 2}{2}$

d $\dfrac{a}{2} + \dfrac{a}{3} = 10$

e $\dfrac{w}{4} - 3 = \dfrac{w}{3}$

f $\dfrac{a}{3} - \dfrac{a}{6} = 1$

g $\dfrac{3x}{7} - \dfrac{x}{4} = 3$

h $\dfrac{x}{7} - \dfrac{x}{2} = {}^-3$

i $\dfrac{a}{6} - \dfrac{a}{3} = 4$

j $\dfrac{n}{5} - n = \dfrac{1}{2}$

k $\dfrac{5a}{4} - \dfrac{a}{3} = {}^-1$

l $\dfrac{x}{6} + 4 = \dfrac{x}{2}$

Level 2

5 Solve the following equations:

a $\dfrac{a}{a - 5} = 7$

b $\dfrac{w}{w + 4} = \dfrac{1}{2}$

c $\dfrac{x + 1}{x - 3} = 3$

d $\dfrac{x - 6}{x} = 8$

e $\dfrac{x}{x + 5} = 7$

f $\dfrac{2x + 1}{x} = {}^-2$

g $\dfrac{6 - y}{y} = 2$

h $\dfrac{5 + 2k}{3k} = {}^-1$

6 Solve:

a $\dfrac{m - 3}{4} + \dfrac{m - 1}{3} = 2$

b $\dfrac{3}{x} - \dfrac{1}{x - 2} = 0$

c $\dfrac{1}{a} - \dfrac{2}{3a} = 4$

d $\dfrac{2x+3}{2} - \dfrac{x-2}{3} = \dfrac{x-1}{4}$ 　　**e** $\dfrac{4}{x} - \dfrac{2}{3x} = {}^-1$ 　　**f** $\dfrac{2n-3}{4} = n+1$

g $\dfrac{4x-3}{2} = x-3$ 　　**h** $\dfrac{6}{x+3} = \dfrac{2}{2x-7}$ 　　**i** $\dfrac{x+7}{3} - \dfrac{4(x+1)}{5} = 0$

j $\dfrac{a}{1-2a} - 3 = \dfrac{1}{2}$

7 Answer the following as true or false. If the answer is false, solve.

a $x = 3$ is a solution to $\dfrac{2x+1}{2} = \dfrac{21}{2x}$ 　　**b** $x = 0$ is a solution to $4x + 7 = 3x - 7$

c $a = \dfrac{1}{2}$ is a solution to $\dfrac{3a-1}{2} = 2a$ 　　**d** $a = \dfrac{1}{2}$ is a solution to $4a - 1 = 2a$

e $w = {}^-4$ is a solution to $\dfrac{w}{w-6} = \dfrac{2}{5}$

Level 3

8 Find the value of x if the area of the first figure is the same as the area of the second.

a

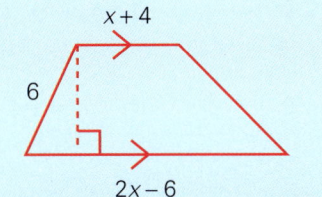 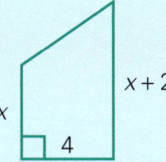

b Given that $\dfrac{1}{f} = \dfrac{1}{v} + \dfrac{1}{u}$, solve for f.

c If $S = \dfrac{a}{1-r}$, find the value of r given 　**i** $S = 40, a = 40$ 　**ii** $S = 40, a = 50$.

9 Write an equation with pronumerals on both sides, containing algebraic fractions, for which the solution is $t = 3$.

4.3 More complex equations

Throughout your study of mathematics you will systematically develop skills to solve different sets of equations.

Here we consider equations involving x to a whole power (x^2, x^3, x^4, etc.) and equations that contain $\sqrt{x}$, $\sqrt[3]{x}$, $\sqrt[5]{x}$, etc.

> To solve equations involving powers you will use the property:
>
> $$(\sqrt{x})^2 = x \qquad (\sqrt[3]{x})^3 = x \qquad (\sqrt[4]{x})^4 = x \qquad (\sqrt[5]{x})^5 = x, \text{ etc.}$$
>
> and conversely:
>
> $$\sqrt[3]{x^3} = x \qquad \sqrt[5]{x^5} = x \qquad \sqrt[7]{x^7} = x \qquad \sqrt[9]{x^9} = x, \text{ etc.}$$
>
> Note:
>
> $$\sqrt{x^2} = \pm x \qquad \sqrt[4]{x^4} = \pm x \qquad \sqrt[6]{x^6} = \pm x \qquad \sqrt[8]{x^8} = \pm x$$

Solve these equations:

a $\sqrt{x} = 6$ **b** $x^2 = 16$ **c** $(x - 1)^2 = 9$ **d** $\sqrt[3]{x + 1} = 3$

Solutions

a $\quad \sqrt{x} = 6$

$\quad (\sqrt{x})^2 = 6^2$

$\quad x = 36$

b $\quad x^2 = 16$

$\quad \sqrt{x^2} = \pm\sqrt{16}$ $\boxed{\begin{array}{l} 4^2 = 16 \\ (^-4)^2 = 16 \end{array}}$

$\quad x = \pm 4$

c $\quad (x - 1)^2 = 9$

$\quad \sqrt{(x - 1)^2} = \pm\sqrt{9}$

$\quad x - 1 = \pm 3$

$\quad x - 1 = 3, \ x - 1 = ^-3$

$\quad \therefore x = 4, \ x = ^-2$

d $\quad (\sqrt[3]{x + 1})^3 = 3^3$

$\quad x + 1 = 27$

$\quad x = 26$

$\boxed{\begin{array}{r} \text{as } 3^2 = 9 \text{ and } \sqrt{9} = 3 \\ \text{but } (^-3)^2 = 9 \\ \therefore x^2 = 9 \text{ has two solutions, } x = \pm 3. \end{array}}$

EXERCISE 4C

1 Solve:

a $\sqrt{a} = 2$ **b** $\sqrt{w} = 4$ **c** $\sqrt{p} = 7$ **d** $\sqrt{x} = 0$

2 Solve:

a $\sqrt[3]{x} = 1$ **b** $\sqrt[3]{p} = 2$ **c** $\sqrt[3]{x} = 6$ **d** $\sqrt[3]{a} = 1{\cdot}4$

3 Find the two solutions to:

a $x^2 = 1$ **b** $x^2 = 100$ **c** $x^2 = 1{\cdot}44$ **d** $x^2 = 0{\cdot}6$

4 Find the value of the pronumeral in:

a $x^3 = 8$ **b** $x^3 = ^-8$ **c** $x^3 = 1000$ **d** $x^3 = 0$

Level 2

5 Solve:

a $4x^2 = 100$ **b** $3\sqrt{x} = 9$ **c** $4\sqrt{x} = 1$ **d** $5x^2 = 10$

e $x^2 + 7 = 57$ **f** $x^3 - 1 = 63$ **g** $\dfrac{\sqrt[3]{x}}{2} = ^-1$ **h** $\dfrac{x^2 + 1}{2} = 3$

6 Solve:

a $\sqrt{x + 1} = 3$ **b** $\sqrt{x - 1} = 3$ **c** $\sqrt[3]{x + 1} = 3$ **d** $\sqrt{2x} = 5$

e $2\sqrt{x} = 5$ **f** $\sqrt[3]{5 - x} = 1$ **g** $\sqrt{4 - x} = 7$ **h** $\sqrt{\dfrac{x}{3}} = \dfrac{11}{2}$

Level 3

7 Solve each of the following (given answers in exact/surd form if necessary):

a $\dfrac{x^2}{3} + 1 = 7$ **b** $\dfrac{x^3}{4} - 1 = 0$ **c** $3x^2 + 4 = 10$ **d** $7x^3 + 1 = 57$

e $\dfrac{3x^2}{4} + 3 = 7\frac{11}{16}$ **f** $3 - \dfrac{x^3}{2} = 2{\cdot}5$ **g** $(x + 1)^2 = 25$ **h** $(x - 1)^2 = 25$

i $(2x + 1)^3 = 4$ **j** $(3x - 4)^2 = 1$ **k** $(4x + 1)^3 = ^-6$ **l** $(5 - x)^2 = 16$

8 Solve:

    a $4x^2 + 7 = x^2 + 10$ **b** $x^3 + 7 = {}^-1 - x^3$ **c** $\sqrt{x+1} = \sqrt{1-x}$

4.4 Solving indicial equations

Indicial equations involve powers of pronumerals. To solve these equations we use the index laws learnt in year 8 and revised earlier in Chapter 1.

    First Index Law: $x^n \times x^m = x^{n+m}$

    Second Index Law: $x^n \div x^m = \dfrac{x^n}{x^m} = x^{n-m}$

    Third Index Law: $(x^n)^m = x^{n \times m}$

> The critical ideas we use to solve indicial equations are:
>
> If $(A)^x = (A)^y$, then $x = y$
>
> and if $(A)^x = (B)^x$, then $A = B$.

EXAMPLE

Solve these equations:

a $3^y = 27$ **b** $25 = 5^x$ **c** $4^{x+1} = 16$ **d** $4^x = \sqrt{8}$

Solutions

a $3^y = 27$
$3^y = 3^3$
$y = 3$

b $25 = 5^x$
$(5)^2 = 5^x$
$x = 2$

c $4^{x+1} = 16$
$(2^2)^{x+1} = 2^4$
$2^{2x+2} = 2^4$
$2x + 2 = 4$
$x = 1$

> You could have used a base of 4 here. Why?

d $4^x = \sqrt{8}$
$(2^2)^x = 8^{\frac{1}{2}}$
$2^{2x} = (2^3)^{\frac{1}{2}}$
$2^{2x} = 2^{\frac{3}{2}}$
$\therefore 2x = \dfrac{3}{2}$
$x = \dfrac{3}{4}$

EXERCISE 4D

1 Find the value of x in each of the following equations:

    a $5^x = 5^2$ **b** $2^x = 4$ **c** $0{\cdot}1^x = 0{\cdot}1$
    d $3^x = 9$ **e** $7^x = 49$ **f** $0.7^x = 0.49$

2 Solve:

    a $2^{2x} = 2^3$ **b** $2^{3x} = 16$ **c** $3^{x+1} = 27$
    d $4^{x-1} = 16$ **e** $5^{x+1} = 125$ **f** $10^{2x} = 100\,000$

Level 2

3 By expressing both sides with a base of 2, solve:

    a $2^x = 32$ **b** $4^x = 32$ **c** $4^{x-1} = 128$
    d $4^{x+1} = 8$ **e** $8^x = 4$ **f** $16^x = 8$

4 Solve the following indicial equations:

a $3 = 27^x$

b $9^{x+1} = 27$

c $5^x = \dfrac{1}{125}$

d $10^{x+1} = \dfrac{1}{1000}$

e $25^x = \dfrac{1}{125}$

f $2^x = \sqrt{8}$

g $5^x = \sqrt{125}$

h $4^x = \dfrac{1}{8}$

i $8^{-x} = \dfrac{1}{64}$

j $16^x = \sqrt[3]{32}$

k $\dfrac{1}{2^x} = 128$

l $5^x = \dfrac{1}{\sqrt[3]{625}}$

4.5 Mixed equations

You now know how to solve a variety of equations, so let's try them when they are all mixed up.

EXERCISE 4E

1 Solve:

a $4x = x + 3$

b $\dfrac{x-7}{3} = 4$

c $3(2x - 1) = 9$

d $x^2 = 0$

e $\dfrac{x}{3} = 0$

f $5 - x = 0$

g $k^2 = 16$

h $x^2 = 9$

i $x^2 - 9 = 0$

j $\sqrt{x} = 7$

k $p^2 = 25$

l $p^2 = 1$

m $w^3 = 8$

n $2a^2 = \dfrac{1}{8}$

o $\sqrt{w} = 3$

Level 2

2 Find the value of x:

a $(x - 1)^2 = 16$

b $(x + 1)^2 = 16$

c $\dfrac{2x^2}{3} = 1$

d $\dfrac{x}{x+1} = 6$

e $\dfrac{x+1}{4} - \dfrac{x}{3} = 1$

f $\dfrac{x}{x+1} = \dfrac{1}{6}$

g $\sqrt{x-1} = 4$

h $\sqrt[3]{x} = 4$

i $x^2 = \dfrac{4}{9}$

j $\dfrac{x-1}{3} - \dfrac{2x+1}{2} = 1$

k $4x - 3(2x - 1) = 3(x + 1)$

l $\dfrac{4x}{5-x} = -2$

m $\dfrac{x+1}{3} = \dfrac{x-4}{4}$

n $x^2 + 3(x - 4) = x^2$

o $\dfrac{3}{x+1} + \dfrac{x}{x+1} = 3$

Level 3

3 Solve for x:

a $x^{-1} = 3$

b $2^x = 4$

c $5^x = 125$

d $4^x = 8$

e $5^x = 1$

f $x^{-2} = \dfrac{4}{9}$

g $16^x = 2$

h $5^x = \dfrac{1}{5}$

i $p^3 - 1 = 7$

j $x^3 = 64$

k $6x^2 = 0$

l $\dfrac{1}{16} = 4^x$

m $4^x = 5^x$

n $\sqrt{x} = -3$

o $5^x = -2$

4.6 Translating word problems into equations

Most equations come from our everyday need to relate events often described in words or as a diagram.

To solve these problems we must follow the procedure below.

> **1** Read the problem description once through to get an overview of the situation.
>
> **2** Re-read, underlying key-points as you go. Look for:
>
>   **a** what has to be found
>
>   **b** all relevant data
>
>   **c** key words suggesting operation
>
> **3** Translate the problem into a symbolic equation, using a pronumeral to represent the unknown number.
>
> **4** Solve the equation.
>
> **5** Relate the solution to the situation.

EXAMPLE 1

Holly earns *$5·20 an hour* working for *5 hours each week* at a fast-food store after school. In *how many weeks* will she have earned $156?

Solution

Let *number of weeks* be x.

$$5{\cdot}2 \times 5 \times x = 156$$
$$26x = 156$$
$$x = 6$$

In 6 weeks, she will earn $156.

EXAMPLE 2

A *rectangle* is *6 cm longer* than it is wide. If the *perimeter* is *44* cm, what are its dimensions?

Solution

Let *width* be w cm.

$$P = 2L + 2W$$
$$44 = 2(w + 6) + 2w$$
$$44 = 2w + 12 + 2w$$
$$44 = 4w + 12$$
$$32 = 4w$$
$$8 = w$$

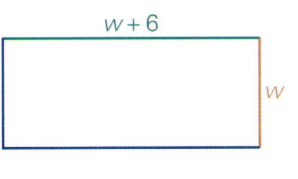

Width is 8 cm, length 14 cm.

Translate into an algebraic equation and solve.

1 Helga walked a certain distance, then another 6 km. If she covered 25 km altogether, what was that first distance she walked?

2 If in his build-up for weightlifting Mark doubled his weight and then put on another 3 kg, he would move into the heavyweight 117 kg division. What is his present weight?

3 Kurt the jockey must shed one-tenth of his body weight to meet the weight requirements for his ride next Saturday. If he meets his goal of losing 6 kg, how much did he originally weigh?

4 12 is subtracted from a certain number, and the result is divided by 5. If the answer is 14, what is the number?

5 The sum of three consecutive integers is 165. Find the numbers.

6 The sum of two consecutive odd integers is 76. Find the larger.

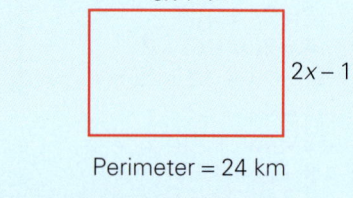

7 Julie is paid a retainer of $350 a week as a car salesperson, with $180 per car sold profitably for the dealership. How many cars must she sell in a week to make $1250 gross?

8 Adding 16 to a number is the same as trebling it. Find the number.

9 Double a number and 7 more gives the same result as three times the number plus 1. Find the number.

10 a
$5n$

$2n$

Perimeter = 42 cm

Find length.

b

$x + 3$

Perimeter = 52 m

Find the side length.

c
$3x + 4$

$2x - 1$

Perimeter = 24 km

Find the dimensions.

11 A rectangle is twice as long as it is wide. If its perimeter is 72 cm, find its dimensions.

12 An equilateral triangle has a side of $(5x - 2)$ centimetres. Find the side length if the perimeter is 219 cm.

13 Find the value of the pronumeral in each of the following:

a
$(x - 2)$ cm
7 cm
$(3x + 4)$ cm
Area = 49 cm²

b
$4y - 1$
$3y + 4$

c
$4x + 16$
$5x + 4$
$3y$

14 In a crowd of 32 000 spectators, there were 6000 more men than women. How many women were in the crowd?

Level 3

15 Justine is 15 years older than Emily now, but in 6 years time will be twice as old as Emily. What are their present ages?

16 A storage tank is two-thirds full. After 500 L are drained out it is still two-fifths full. What is the capacity of the tank?

17 A blended wine is made up of 600 L of an inferior red and 300 L of a quality red costing $3 a litre more. The total cost of all the wine is $5400. What is the price of the ingredients?

18 Pump A delivers water at one-and-a-half times the rate of pump B. Both operating together can fill a 15 000 L tank in 20 minutes. Find the delivery rate of each pump in litres per minute.

19 Increasing average speed from 80 km/h to 100 km/h saves 10 minutes on a certain trip. How far is the trip?

20

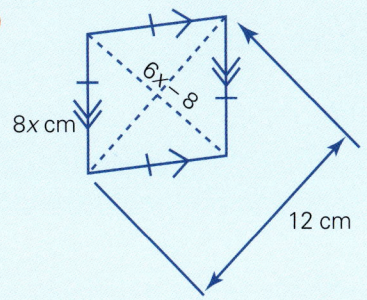

$6x - 8$
$8x$ cm
12 cm

Find the area of the rhombus *ABCD* if the area = perimeter.

4.7 Formulas

An important application of algebra is in **formulas**. A **formula** (or **rule**) is an equation connecting two or more variables. The value of one of the variables can be determined if you are given the values of the other unknowns.

Common formulas often contain squares, cubes, square roots and cube roots. Examples of formulas include those for area, time and strength.

$$A = \frac{(a+b)h}{2}$$

Area, A, of a trapezium
with lengths and heights shown.

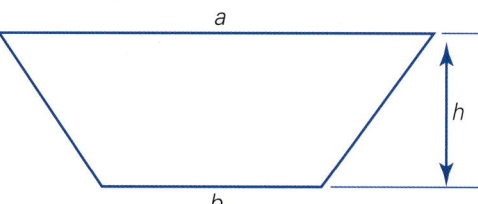

$$T = \sqrt{\frac{2\pi}{L}}$$

The time, T, for one complete swing of a pendulum (called the **period**) of length L.

$$S = \frac{KHW}{L^2}$$

The strength of a beam of thickness, H, width, W, and length, L, of a beam. The value of K depends on the material the beam is made from. A steel beam would have a larger value than a wooden beam of the same dimensions.

A, S and T are the **subjects** of these formulas. If you need to find the value of a pronumeral that is not the subject, you can still substitute the values of the pronumerals known and solve the resultant equation using the steps discussed in the preceding sections

EXAMPLES

If $v = u + at$:

a find v when $u = 4$, $a = 3$, $t = 5$ **b** find t when $v = 50$, $u = 8$ and $a = 10$

Solutions

a $v = u + at$
$v = 4 + 3 \times 5$
$v = 19$

b $v = u + at$
$50 = 8 + 10t$
$42 = 10t$
$t = 4·2$

> Copy.
> Substitute.
> Calculate.

1 In each of the following, use the given replacements to find the value of the pronumeral stated.

How many of these formulas do you recognise?

	Formula	Replacements	
a	$B = 2l - 7$	**i** Find B if $l = 10$.	**ii** Find l if $B = 83$.
b	$E = IR$	**i** Find E if $I = 3\cdot2$, $R = 20$.	**ii** Find R if $E = 36$, $I = 12$.
c	$s = \dfrac{d}{t}$	**i** Find s if $d = 24\cdot5$, $t = 0\cdot5$.	**ii** Find t if $s = 100$, $d = 75$.
d	$A = \dfrac{bh}{2}$	**i** Find A if $b = 10$, $h = \dfrac{3}{5}$.	**ii** Find h if $A = 40$, $b = \dfrac{4}{3}$.
e	$l = \dfrac{PRT}{100}$	**i** Find l if $P = 1000$, $R = 4$, $T = 2$.	**ii** Find R if $P = 250$, $l = 25$, $T = 5$.
f	$P = 2(l + w)$	**i** Find P if $l = 10$, $w = 6$.	**ii** Find l if $P = 84$, $w = 14$.
g	$C = 2\pi r$	**i** Find C if $r = 2\frac{1}{2}$, $\pi = 3\cdot14$.	**ii** Find r if $C = 628$, $\pi = 3\cdot14$.
h	$F = \dfrac{9}{5}C + 32$	**i** Find F if $C = 35$.	**ii** Find C if $F = 32$.
i	$A = \dfrac{1}{2}(a + b)h$	**i** Find A if $h = 10$, $a = 6$, $b = 5$.	**ii** Find b if $A = 86$, $h = 4$, $a = 15$.
j	$T = a + (n - 1)d$	**i** Find T if $n = 9$, $a = {}^-4$, $d = \dfrac{3}{4}$.	**ii** Find n if $T = 11\cdot8$, $d = \dfrac{{}^-2}{3}$, $a = 4\cdot2$.

Level 2

2 If $v = \sqrt{u^2 + 2at}$, find v when $u = 3\cdot5$, $a = 6\cdot8$, $t = 0\cdot8$. Answer correct to 3 significant figures.

3 If $s = \dfrac{a(r^n - 1)}{r - 1}$, find s correct to 1 decimal place when $a = 4\cdot8$, $r = 1\cdot2$ and $n = 3$.

4 If $s = \dfrac{a}{1 - r}$, **a** find s when $a = 6\cdot5$, $r = 0\cdot75$ **b** find r when $s = 10$, $a = 1\cdot5$.

5 If $s = ut + \dfrac{1}{2}at^2$, find a when $s = 30$, $u = 4$ and $t = 10$.

Level 3

6 Give answers for the following, to 2 significant figures where necessary:

a If $R = \dfrac{1}{R_1} + \dfrac{1}{R_2}$, find R_1 when $R = 10$ and $R_2 = 0\cdot8$.

b If $T = 2n\sqrt{\dfrac{L}{G}}$, find L when $T = 5\cdot4$, $n = 0\cdot3$ and $G = 0\cdot2$.

c If $R = \dfrac{S}{2\pi(L + P)}$, find P when $R = 14\cdot4$, $S = 1200$, $\pi = 3\cdot14$ and $L = 21\cdot2$.

d If $P = \dfrac{3n + 2}{6n - 1}$, find n when $P = 0\cdot6$.

4.8 Transposition—changing the subject of an equation

As we saw in the previous exercise, it is still possible to find the value of a pronumeral in a given formula, even when it is not the subject of the formula. However, a formula can be rearranged to make the required pronumeral the subject, before substitution. This process is called transposition. The rules for transposing formulas are the same as those you have already used to solve equations.

EXAMPLE 1
Make t the subject in:
$$v = u + at$$

Solution
$$v = u + at$$
$$v - u = at$$
$$\frac{v - u}{a} = t$$
$$\therefore t = \frac{v - u}{a}$$

EXAMPLE 2
Make b the subject of the formula $c^2 = a^2 + b^2$.

Solution
$$c^2 = a^2 + b^2$$
$$c^2 - a^2 = b^2$$
$$b^2 = c^2 - a^2$$
$$\therefore b = \pm\sqrt{c^2 - a^2}$$

> We often need to choose if the appropriate value is + or − or both.

EXAMPLE 3
Find a formula for A from $r = \sqrt{\dfrac{A}{\pi}}$.

Solution

$$r = \sqrt{\frac{A}{\pi}}$$

$$r^2 = \frac{A}{\pi}$$

$$\pi r^2 = A$$
$$\therefore A = \pi r^2$$

> Here we only have positive values because a negative value for the radius r is meaningless.

> Square both sides.

EXAMPLE 4
Make x the subject in $y = \dfrac{x}{2 - x}$.

Solution

$$y = \frac{x}{2 - x}$$
$$y(2 - x) = x$$
$$2y - yx = x$$
$$2y = x + xy$$
$$x + xy = 2y$$
$$x(1 + y) = 2y$$
$$x = \frac{2y}{1 + y}$$

> It is necessary to factorise in this expression to ensure that only the pronumeral, x, is the subject of the equation and is written only once on the LHS.

EXERCISE 4H

1 Make n the subject of each formula:

a $p = n + ab$ **b** $x = a + nb$

c $L = x - n$ **d** $s = \dfrac{d}{n}$

e $p^2 n = a + b$

f $p = 2l + 2n$

g $P = 2(l + n)$

h $E = nc^2$

i $F = ac + nt$ **j** $X = 2p(3 - n)$

k $A = \dfrac{1}{2}(a + b)n$ **l** $A = \dfrac{1}{2}(a + n)b$

> The most famous equation of modern times is $E = mc^2$. It was stated by Albert Einstein. E stands for energy, m for mass and c for the speed of light. This formula led to the production of atomic energy.

Level 2

2 Change the subject of each equation to the pronumeral indicated in the brackets:

a $C = 2\pi r$ (r) **b** $A = \pi r^2$ (r)

c $I = PRT$ (T) **d** $v = u + at$ (a)

e $y = mx + b$ (m) **f** $\dfrac{5}{n + 2} = 4p$ (n)

g $\dfrac{6}{n - 2} = 8p$ (n) **h** $ax + by + c = 0$ (y)

i $ax + by + c = 0$ (x)

3 Make n the subject of each formula:

a $A = P(1 + nt)$ **b** $T = a + (n - 1)d$ **c** $S = \dfrac{a(n^r - 1)}{t - 1}$ **d** $x = \sqrt{an}$

e $p = \sqrt{a - n}$ **f** $p = \sqrt{a} - n$ **g** $an^2 = x$ **h** $t = m - n^2$

i $\dfrac{x}{3} = \dfrac{n}{4} - 1$ **j** $\dfrac{n + t}{3} = \dfrac{n - u}{4}$ **k** $p = \dfrac{n}{n + 2}$ **l** $m = \dfrac{n^2}{2} + \dfrac{t}{3}$

m $q = 6 - \dfrac{5}{n}$ **n** $t = \sqrt{\dfrac{a + b}{3n}}$ **o** $a^2 = \sqrt{p^2 - 3nt}$ **p** $\dfrac{n}{t} = \dfrac{n - t}{r}$

> You may have encountered $E = \dfrac{1}{2}mv^2$ in science.
> Many formulas are not only used in this subject.

4 Change the subject of each formula to the pronumeral indicated in the brackets:

a $T = a + (n - 1)d$ (n) **b** $S = \dfrac{n}{2}(a + l)$ (a) **c** $C = \dfrac{5}{9}(F - 32)$ (F)

d $E = \dfrac{1}{2}mv^2$ (v) **e** $V = \sqrt{u^2 + 2as}$ (u) **f** $V = \sqrt{u^2 + 2as}$ (s)

g $V = \dfrac{4}{3}\pi r^3$ (r) **h** $x = \sqrt{b^2 - 4ac}$ (b) **i** $S = \pi rl + \pi r^2$ (l)

j $\dfrac{1}{x} = \dfrac{1}{r} + \dfrac{1}{s}$ (r)

5 Make x the subject of:

   a $A = \dfrac{x+4}{3}$ **b** $M = \dfrac{3x}{x-4}$ **c** $4a - x = n(x+6)$ **d** $A = \dfrac{x+4}{x}$

   e $\dfrac{a}{x+1} = \dfrac{b}{x}$ **f** $\sqrt{2x-1} = A$ **g** $4x^2 + A = x^2 + 9$ **h** $\sqrt[3]{5-x} = A$

6 Answer to 2 decimal places where necessary in the following:

   a Find the diameter of a circle of area 1256 cm².

   b The formula for the volume of a cone is $V = \dfrac{1}{3}\pi r^2 h$ where h is the height and r the radius of the cone. By first rearranging the formula, find the radius of a cone whose height is 10 cm and volume is 1000 cm³.

7 a If the surface area of a sphere is found using the formula $A = 4\pi r^2$ what are the restrictions on the values of r? What effect do these restrictions have for the value/s of A?

   b Make r the subject of the formula for the surface area of a sphere. What value/s of A can be substituted into the formula?

8 a Given $Z = 3x^2$, write the values of x that may be substituted into this formula as it is written.

   b What additional restrictions exist on the variables if the formula is rearranged to give $x = \sqrt{\dfrac{Z}{3}}$?

9 $x^2 + y = 4$. Make t the subject if $x = 2at$.

Try this

If $x = 2at$ and $y = at^2$ write an equation relating x and y by eliminating the ts.

4.9 Inequations and the number line

A business may decide that its turnover must be greater than $100 000 for the business to be profitable. This could be expressed as $T > \$100\,000$.

> $>$ greater than
>
> $<$ less than
>
> $\geq$ greater than or equal to
>
> $\leq$ less than or equal to

The exact amount of the turnover is not specified, just that it is greater than $100 000. On a number line this is shown as:

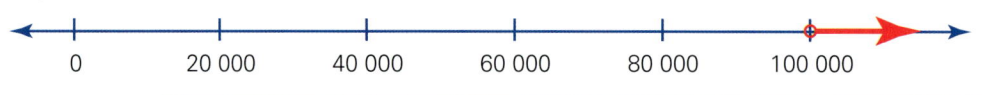

| 0 | 20 000 | 40 000 | 60 000 | 80 000 | 100 000 |

The open circle is used to show that 100 000 is not included in the solution set.

An 'open' circle on a number line indicates that the number *is not* included in the solution set. A 'closed' circle indicates the number *is* included.

EXAMPLE 1

Show the following equations on individual number lines:

  a $x = 4$ **b** $x > 4$ **c** $x \geq 4$ **d** $0 < x \leq 4$ **e** $x < 0$

Solutions

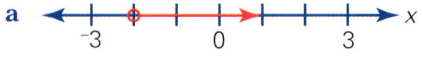

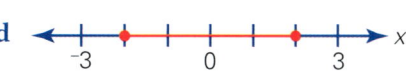

EXAMPLE 2

Write what is meant by the inequations given in example 1.

Solutions

a x has the value of 4 only.

b x is greater than but not equal to 4.

c x is greater than or equal to 4.

d x is between 0 and 4: x is greater than 0 but less than or equal to 4.

e x is less than 0; x is the set of negative numbers.

EXAMPLE 3

Write the inequality suggested by:

Solutions

  a $x > {}^-2$ **b** $x \geq 0$ **c** $x = {}^-2$ **d** $x \geq {}^-2, x \leq 2$ or ${}^-2 \leq x \leq 2$

> We say 'x is between ${}^-2$ and 2'.

EXERCISE 4I

1 Express the following inequalities in words:

  a $x = 3$ **b** $x \leq 3$ **c** $x \geq {}^-2$ **d** $0 < x < 3$
  e $x = {}^-3$ **f** $x > 2$ **g** $x = \pm 6$ **h** $0 \leq x \leq 3$
  i $x > 3$ **j** $x > {}^-2$ **k** $x < 5, x > 4$ **l** $x < 0, x > 3$

2 Show the inequalities in question **1** on separate number lines.

3 Match the inequalities to each of the following number lines.

  A $x < 4$

  1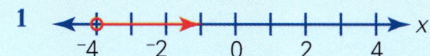

  B $x > {}^-4$

  2

  C $x \geq 4$

  3

  D $x < 0, x > 4$

  4

  E $0 < x < 4$

  5

4 Give the inequalities for each of the following number lines.

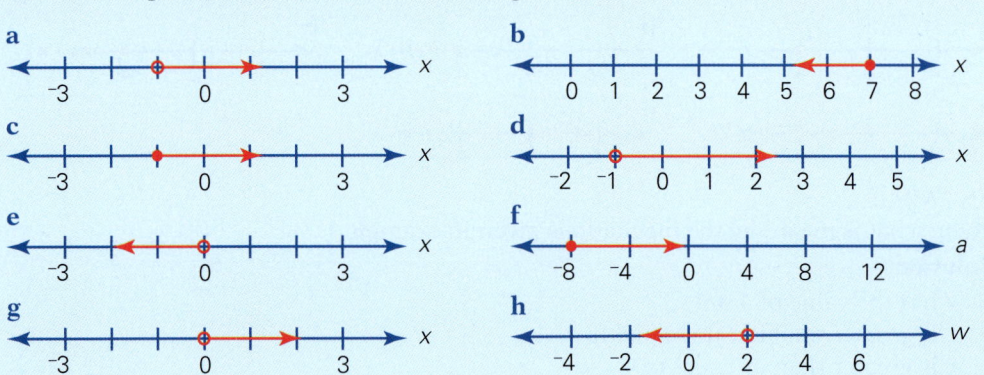

a

b

c

d

e

f

g

h

i

j

Level 3

5 Write the inequalities suggested by:

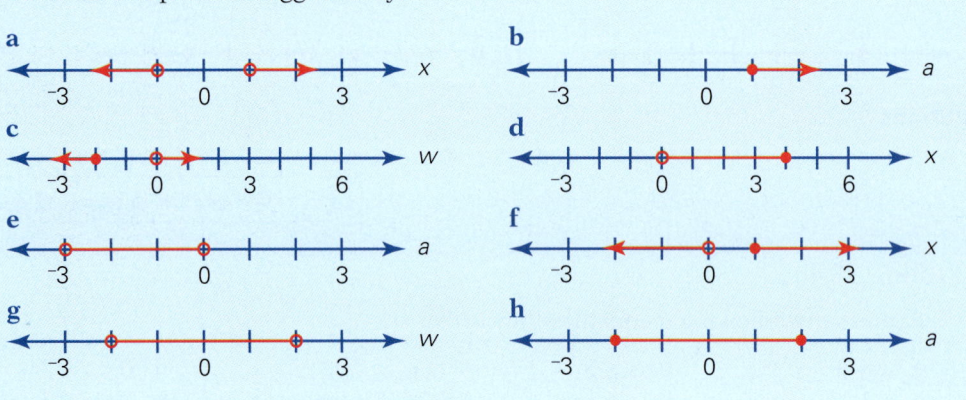

a

b

c

d

e

f

g

h

6 Show each of the following on separate number lines:

a $x > 5, x < 1$

b $x \leq 0, x > 3$

c $0 \leq x \leq 4\frac{1}{2}$

d $0 < x < 4\frac{1}{2}$

e $x \geq {}^{-}1, x < 4$

Investigation Solving inequations

Consider the inequation $n + 5 > 7$.
Picture the LHE, $n + 5$, on the left tray
of a set of scales, and the RHE, 7,
on the right tray.

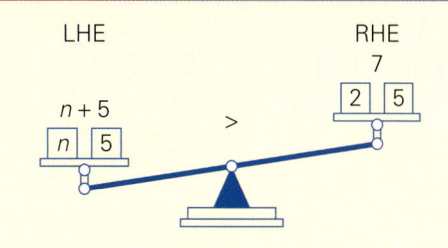

1 Why are the scales shown as unbalanced?

2 Is the balance tipped in the correct manner?
Explain.

3 Draw a diagram of the scales' appearance after the operation − 5 has been performed
on *both sides*.

4 Write a simple inequation that shows the solution to the original sentence. Graph the
integral values for n on a number line.

5 Using real scales or by making a new set of drawings, picture the process of solving
these inequations: $n - 4 < 3$, $2n > 10$, $\frac{n}{3} < 5$.

6 Write a sentence comparing the process of solving **inequations** with that of solving
equations.

Investigation Negative numbers and solving inequations

1 Take the inequality, $3 > 2$, which we know is a true statement.

- Add a positive number to both sides. Does the statement remain true?
- Subtract a positive number from both sides of the original inequality. Does the
  statement remain true?
- Multiply both sides of the original inequality by a positive number. Does the
  statement remain true?
- Multiply both sides of the original inequality by a negative number. Does the
  statement remain true?
- Divide both sides of the original inequality by a negative number. Does the
  statement remain true?
- Divide both sides of the original inequality by a positive number. Does the statement
  remain true?

2 Complete:
If an inequality is multiplied or divided by a _____ number,
the inequality sign must be _____ for the statement to remain true.

4.10 Solving inequations

The rules for solving equations and for solving inequations are the same, except when multiplying or dividing an inequation by a negative number.

Linear inequations

- Any number can be added or subtracted from both sides without changing the value of the expression.
- Both sides can be multiplied or divided by any non-zero positive number without changing the value of the expression.
- If both sides are multiplied or divided by a negative number, the inequality sign is reversed.

EXAMPLE

Solve and display the solution for each of the following on a number line:

a $6 + 3n > 10$ **b** $-3n \geq 6$ **c** $\dfrac{5 - 3n}{2} < 6$ **d** $5 + 2x < 7x - 5$

Solutions

a $6 + 3n > 10$
$3n > 4$
$n > \dfrac{4}{3}$

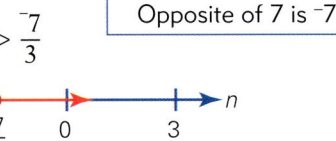

b $-3n \geq 6$
$3n \leq -6$
$n \leq -2$

> Take the opposite of each term:
> Opposite of $-3n$ is $3n$
> Opposite of $\geq$ is $\leq$
> Opposite of 6 is -6

c $\dfrac{5 - 3n}{2} < 6$
$5 - 3n < 12$
$-3n < 7$
$3n > -7$
$n > \dfrac{-7}{3}$

> Opposite of $-3n$ is $3n$
> Opposite of $<$ is $>$
> Opposite of 7 is -7

d $5 + 2x < 7x - 5$
$5 < 5x - 5$
$10 < 5x$
$5x > 10$
$x > 2$

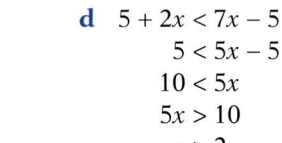

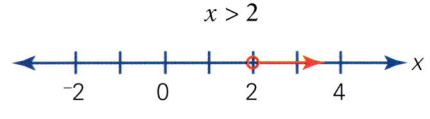

> If you multiply or divide by a negative number the inequality sign changes.

EXERCISE 4J

1 Solve and display the solution on a number line:

a $6n \geq 12$ **b** $^{-}x > 7$ **c** $7 - p \geq 6$ **d** $n - 7 < 5$ **e** $5 - x \geq 2$

f $\dfrac{^{-}x}{2} < 6$ **g** $n - 7 \leq 0$ **h** $\dfrac{x}{^{-}3} < 4$ **i** $5 - x \geq 0$ **j** $\dfrac{n}{3} > 4$

k $4x \leq 0$ **l** $a + 7 < 0$ **m** $^{-}n < 6$

2 Solve:

a $n + 3 > 5$ **b** $n - 6 < 2$ **c** $7n < 35$ **d** $\dfrac{n}{3} \geq 4$

e $\dfrac{1}{5}x > 2$ **f** $\dfrac{t}{4} \leq 0$ **g** $3 + p \geq ^{-}2$ **h** $15 < a - 2$

i $^{-}12 > 3h$ **j** $^{-}1 \leq c - 1$ **k** $^{-}4y < 36$ **l** $^{-}3z \geq ^{-}21$

m $\dfrac{2n}{3} \geq 8$ **n** $^{-}14 < \dfrac{7d}{5}$ **o** $^{-}x \leq \dfrac{^{-}4}{5}$ **p** $2n + 3 < 7$

q $3p - 1 \geq 11$ **r** $2 < 5t - 3$ **s** $5 - 7c > 3$ **t** $20 \leq 2 - 6d$

u $\dfrac{w}{3} - 2 > 5$ **v** $7 \leq 3 + \dfrac{a}{5}$ **w** $2(b + 3) < 14$ **x** $12 \geq (c - 1)4$

Level 2

3 Solve:

a $4(3 - 2y) \leq ^{-}12$ **b** $2(3p - 4) - 8p \geq 0$ **c** $2 - f < ^{-}4$

d $\dfrac{4 - 3n}{5} \geq \dfrac{1}{2}$ **e** $7k + 3 > 4k - 2$ **f** $4 - 2(x + 1) < 0$

g $3n - 5 < 5n + 6$ **h** $\dfrac{3 - 4n}{8} > \dfrac{^{-}2(1 - n)}{6}$

Level 3

4 Translate into symbols, then solve:

a Three times a certain number is always smaller than 8.
b 6 more than double a number is greater than 12.
c 4 less than six times a number is less than or equal to 14.
d Eight times the sum of a certain number and 3 is larger than 23·5.
e Decreasing a certain number by 7, then dividing the result by 4, gives a value more than or equal to five-eighths.

5 Translate into algebraic inequations, by choosing a pronumeral to stand for the unknown variable:

a A planned bridge must be able to bear a load of *at most* 8000 tonnes. (Perhaps use *l* for load.)
b To receive 4·8% interest on your savings, you must have *at least* $1000 in your account. (Perhaps use *s* for savings.)
c Having *below* $500 in your account means that you are charged a monthly account-keeping fee.
d *No more than* 76 people may ride in this bus at one time.
e The carrying capacity of this truck is *at most* 4·5 tonnes.
f *Any number* of people from two to eight can play this game.
g The *maximum* number of adults allowed in this lift is 10.
h To qualify for this special mobile phone offer, you must spend a *minimum* of $85 each month on calls.

4.11 Conditional inequations

Restricted values of pronumerals may be necessary to fit a real-life situation. For example, if x stands for the number of people who can fit into a bus, obviously solutions for an inequation involving x must be restricted to whole numbers.

The restrictions, if any, are written after the inequation.

Solve the inequation, then select only those values that obey the conditions given.

EXAMPLE 1
Solve $5x - 3 > {}^{-}13$ if x is a positive integer less than 5 and display on a number line.

Solution

$5x - 3 > {}^{-}13$

$\quad 5x > {}^{-}10$

$\quad\ \ x > {}^{-}2$

$\therefore x = 1, 2, 3$ and 4 as x is a +ve integer less than 5

EXAMPLE 2
Solve $8 - 3x < 4$ if $x \leq 3$ and display on a number line.

Solution

$8 - 3x < 4$

$\quad\ \ 4 < 3x$

$\quad\ \ \dfrac{4}{3} < x$

$\quad\ \ x > 1\dfrac{1}{3}$ but $x \leq 3$

$\therefore x > 1\dfrac{1}{3}$ and $x \leq 3$ $\left(1\dfrac{1}{3} < x \leq 3\right)$

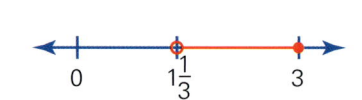

EXERCISE 4K

1 Solve each inequation, observing the restrictions mentioned:

   a $2n - 3 < 5$, n is a positive integer

   b $3n + 20 > 8$, n is a negative integer

   c $4(n + 3) > 18$, $n < 5$

   d ${}^{-}3(4 - 2n) \leq 3$, n is positive

Level 2

2 a $\dfrac{4n - 3}{2} < 7.5$, $n > {}^{-}3$ and integral

   b $\dfrac{3n}{4} - \dfrac{2n}{5} \leq {}^{-}2$, $n > {}^{-}65$ and integral

   c $\dfrac{6}{3n} - 2 > \dfrac{4}{6n} + 1$, n is a negative integer

Level 3

3 What negative numbers less than ${}^{-}3$ fulfil the condition that three times the sum of the number and 2 must be greater than ${}^{-}15$?

4 If two-thirds of a number less three-fifths of the same number must always be less than or equal to 45, which integers of at least ${}^{-}3$ in value satisfy the conditions?

Try these

1 Edita has $3 in 20-cent and 10-cent coins. There are twice as many 20-cent pieces as there are 10-cent pieces. How many of each does she have?

2 The product of three numbers is 336. They are all less than 10 and consecutive. Find the numbers.

3 A square and an equilateral triangle have equal perimeters. The side of the triangle is 3 cm longer than the side of the square. Find the area of the triangle.

4 Fatima is 10 years older than Yuri. In 3 years time, she will be twice as old as Yuri. How old are they now?

5 The pages of a book needed 414 digits to form the page numbers 1, 2, 3, … How many pages are in the book?

6 The Greek mathematician Diophantus lived in Alexandria in the third centry AD. The age at which he died is hidden in the following problem that was inscribed on his tombstone.

Diophantus' boyhood lasted $\frac{1}{6}$ of his life, after the next $\frac{1}{12}$ of this life he grew a beard, and after another $\frac{1}{7}$ he married. Five years later his son was born. The son's life was only half as long as his father's, and Diophantus died four years after his son.

At what age did Diophantus die?

Chapter Review

Language Links

algebra	graph	linear	solve
backtrack	inequality	operation	substitute
distributive	inequation	pronumeral	symbol
equation	integer	rational	translate
expression	inverse	replacement	unknown
formula	isolate	solution	variable

1 Write the *plurals* of: equation, pronumeral, formula, inequality.

2 Write *adjectives* from: algebra, graph, line, ratio, symbol, vary.

3 Form *nouns* from: isolate, replace, solve, substitute, translate.

4 Use each word in a sentence to show its *mathematical* meaning: backtrack, expression, inverse, rational, inequation.

5 Use each *group* of words in a single sentence:

  a solve—isolate—pronumeral—inverse—operation.
  b translate—equation—unknown—pronumeral—variable.

6 Find from the list above words that mean:

  a spreading across   **b** put in place of
  c words $\rightleftarrows$ symbols   **d** two expressions that are not equal

Chapter Review Exercises

MC

1 Express each of the following in words:

  a $3 + 5x$ **b** $^-4(p - 7)$ **c** $8 + \dfrac{3a}{2}$ **d** $\dfrac{(6 - 4t)5}{7}$

MC

2 If $x = 7$ and $y = {}^-4$ evaluate:

  a $x + y$ **b** xy^2 **c** $x^3 - x^2$ **d** $y^3 - y^2$ **e** $\dfrac{x + y}{x}$

4.1

3 Solve the following equations, checking all solutions:

  a $3n + 7 = 22$ **b** $\dfrac{2a}{3} = 5$ **c** $2(m + 5) - 3m = 0$

  d $3x - 1 = 5 + x$ **e** $\dfrac{2x - 1}{4} = 2$

4.3

4 Solve:

  a $\dfrac{3x}{5} + 2 = 3$ **b** $6x - (x - 9) = {}^-3x$ **c** $^-3(2x - 5) = 2(x + 5)$

  d $\dfrac{7x - 3}{4} = {}^-2(x + 1)$ **e** $\dfrac{2n}{3} - \dfrac{4n}{9} = {}^-1$ **f** $\dfrac{3n - 5}{7} = 2 - n$

g $\dfrac{2}{n} + \dfrac{1}{n-1} = {}^{-}3$ **h** $x^2 - 6 = 30$ **i** $\sqrt[3]{\dfrac{x+1}{4}} = 2$

j $5^x = 3125$

5 If $E = \dfrac{1}{2}mv^2$, find:

  a E if $v = {}^{-}7$, $m = \dfrac{4}{7}$ **b** v if $E = 64$, $m = \dfrac{1}{2}$

6 Write symbolic sentences, then solve:

  a A certain number, when halved and then increased by three, gives 31. What is the number?

  b Seven more than a number is double that number. Find the unknown number.

  c Three times a number is always smaller than $^{-}8$. Find the set of numbers that satisfies this condition.

  d The area of a triangle is 42 cm² and the base length is 14 cm. What is the height of the triangle?

  e A student earns $10 for the first hour of babysitting and $6 for each hour after that. If she earned $34 for one evening's work, for how many hours did she work?

  f A deposit of $500, together with seven equal instalments, must amount to at least $3000.

7 Make A the subject of $P = \dfrac{h}{2}(A + B)$.

8 Make r the subject in:

  a $A = 2\pi rh$ **b** $A = 4\pi r^2$

9 Make x the subject in $\dfrac{x}{x+1} = P$.

10 List three integers that would satisfy each inequation:

  a $x < 11$ **b** $x \leq {}^{-}2$ **c** $5 < x \leq 10$

11 Give an inequality for:

  a    **b** 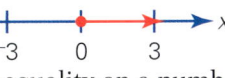   **c**

12 Graph the rational solution to each inequality on a number line:

  a $2n - 7 > 10$ **b** $^{-}5n \leq 45$ **c** $3 > 5 - 7p$ **d** $2x - 5 \geq 5x + 3$

13 Solve:

  a $8(3r - 4) \leq \dfrac{^{-}2}{3}(6r - 9)$ **b** $\dfrac{^{-}2x - 5}{14} \geq \dfrac{x + 3}{21}$, $x > {}^{-}6$ and integral

4.6

4.5

4.7

4.7

4.7

4.8

4.8

4.9

4.10

TEACHER

Keeping Mathematically Fit

Part A—Non-calculator

1 Calculate $(^-0{\cdot}1)^3$.

2 Kylie watches a movie that lasts for 105 minutes. If it finishes at 9:30 pm, at what time does it start?

3 Find 5% of 8 kg.

4 A rectangular box has a volume of 60 cm^3. If all dimensions have integer values, give two possible sizes for the box.

5 John eats $\frac{1}{3}$ of a pizza, Elaine has $\frac{1}{3}$ of the remainder, and the left-over piece is shared equally between Shireen and Abdul. What fraction of the pizza does Abdul eat?

6 Between which two consecutive integers does $\sqrt{53}$ lie?

7 Given $\frac{4}{5} < \ldots < \frac{8}{9}$, give a possible value to complete the expression.

8 Write 26·4391 to the nearest hundredth.

9 The colour burnt orange is made by mixing red and yellow paint in the ratio 3 : 1. How much red paint is used to make 2 litres of burnt orange paint?

10 In his pocket David has two 50-cent coins, five 20-cent coins and five 10-cent coins.

    a In how many different ways can he make up 1 dollar?
    b What is the probability that a coin taken from his pocket will be a 20-cent piece?

Part B—Calculator

1 The cost of a taxi ride is calculated using the formula below:
    $2 flagfall (hire fee)
    plus
    $1.80 per km.

    a How much would a 6 km journey cost?
    b How far did Paula travel if she paid $23.60?

2 There are 8·3 million employees in Australia. If the number increases by 250 thousand every year for 10 years:

    a How many employees will there be after 10 years?
    b What is the percentage increase in the number of employees?

3 Solve $\dfrac{3x - 6}{5} = 6$.

4 For the data 6, 0, 3, 10, 4, 1, 7, 5, 2, 3, calculate:

    a the mean   **b** the median   **c** the mode.

5 A farmer has 2 m lengths of fence using 80 sections to surround some grazing land. Find the largest area of land that he can fence off.

Cumulative Review 1

1 Simplify the following expressions:

   a $5 + 3t - 3 + t$ **b** $4k - 5k^2 + k + 3k^2$ **c** $17a - 2 + 5b + 6 - a$

   d $9 + 6e - 4e^2 + 4e - 1 + e$ **e** $^-3v \times 4vw$ **f** $25rd^2 \div 35r^2d$

2 An expresson for the perimeter of this figure is:

   A $11s + 9t$ **B** $47st$

   C $30s^2 + 14t^2$ **D** $22s + 14t$

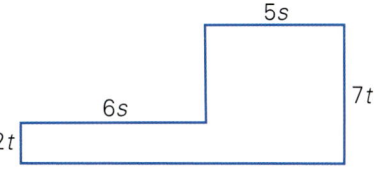

3 Which of the following is equal to $4p\,(2p - 1) - 5\,(3p - 2)$?

   A $8p^2 - 15p - 3$ **B** $8p^2 + 11p - 10$ **C** $8p^2 - 19p - 10$ **D** $8p^2 - 19p + 10$

4 $36f^2g - 24fg + 30fg^2$ when *fully* factorised gives:

   A $2(18f^2g - 12fg + 15fg^2)$ **B** $12f^2(3g - 2g + g^2)$

   C $6fg(6f - 4 + 5g)$ **D** $6(6f^2g - 4fg + 5fg^2)$

5 An expression for the area of this figure is:

   A $7h + 4$ **B** $3h^2 + 2h$

   C $h(6h + 4)$ **D** $\dfrac{6h + 4}{2h}$

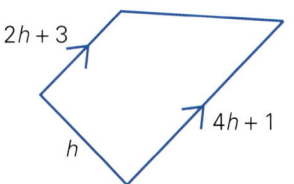

6 $(6t^2)^3 =$

   A $6t^5$ **B** $6t^6$ **C** $216t^6$ **D** $36t^6$

7 $p^0 \div p^0 =$

   A 0 **B** 1 **C** infinity   **D** you can't tell without knowing the value of p

8 $\left(\dfrac{1}{3}\right)^{-4} =$

   A $\dfrac{1}{12}$ **B** $\dfrac{^-1}{81}$ **C** 81 **D** $\sqrt[4]{3}$

9 $4d^{\frac{1}{2}} \times 3d^{\frac{1}{2}} =$

   A $12d^{\frac{1}{4}}$ **B** $12d$ **C** $7d$ **D** $12d^2$

10 The length of a rectangle is 5 cm more than its width. If the width of the rectangle is y, an expression for the area of the rectangle is:

   A $y^2 + 5$ **B** $y^2 + 5y$ **C** $4y + 10$ **D** $5y^2$

11 Expand and simplify $(2x - 7)(4x + 3)$.

12 Express the following in root form, and then simplify if possible:

   a $27^{\frac{1}{3}}$ **b** $f^{\frac{-1}{4}}$ **c** $36^{\frac{-1}{2}}$ **d** $t^{\frac{-3}{2}}$

13 Evaluate $200^{\frac{1}{4}}$ to 3 significant figures.

14 Express in rational form 3·8.

15 Estimate the answer to $382 \times 1·9$, then check with your calculator.

16 Round off as instructed:
    a 3561 to the nearest 100
    b 12·745 to 1 decimal place
    c 2·995 to 2 decimal places
    d 10 356 to 3 significant figures

17 Write three and a half million in scientific notation.

18 Write the basic numeral for:
    a $1·09 \times 10^2$ **b** $7·9 \times 10^4$ **c** $2·314 \times 10^{-3}$

19 If the population of NSW is $6·5 \times 10^6$ and the population of Queensland is $3·4 \times 10^6$, write the difference in population **a** in scientific notation and **b** as a basic numeral.

20 In 4 h I walk x km. My speed is:
    A $4x$ km/h   **B** $\dfrac{x}{4}$ km/h   **C** $\dfrac{4}{x}$ km/h   **D** x^4 km/h   **E** x km/h

21 $45 is divided among X, Y and Z. X and Y each get the same amount, and Z gets $9 more than Y. How much does X get?
    A $12   **B** $15   **C** $9   **D** $(Y + 9)$ **E** $45 - (Y - Z)$

22 The ratio of 2 h 24 min to 3 h in simplest form is:
    A $2·24 : 3$ **B** $224 : 300$ **C** $56 : 75$ **D** $4 : 5$ **E** $144 : 180$

23 I spend 80% of my income and save the rest. The ratio of savings to spendings is:
    A $4 : 1$ **B** $1 : 5$ **C** $2 : 8$ **D** $8 : 10$ **E** none of these

For each figure calculate **a** the perimeter   **b** the area:

24

2 m
4·5 m

25
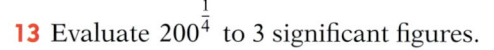
4 cm
6 cm   5 cm   5·4 cm
8 cm

26
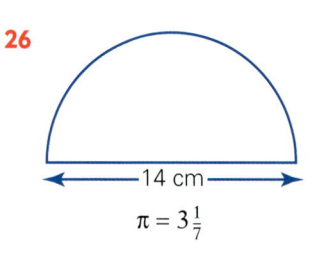
14 cm
$\pi = 3\frac{1}{7}$

27 A wire 36 cm long is shaped to form a rectangle in which the length is twice the breadth. The *area* of this rectangle is:
    A 72 cm^2 **B** 36 cm^2 **C** 48 cm^2 **D** 18 cm^2 **E** 96 cm^2

28 1·04 kg is equal to:

  A 10·4 g **B** 0·0104 t **C** 1040 g **D** 1040 mg **E** 104 g

29 How many bags of sugar weighing 250 g could be taken from a bin containing 50 kg if at least $12\frac{1}{2}$ kg is to be left in the bin?

30 'Three times a number plus six less than that number' is represented by which expression if the number referred to is x?

  A $3x - 6$ **B** $3x + 6 - x$ **C** $3(x + 6) - x$ **D** $3x + x - 6$

31 If $v = u + 10t$ find:

  a v when $u = 6$ and $t = 2\frac{1}{2}$ **b** t when $v = 36$ and $u = 7$

32 Solve the following:

  a $20 - 4p = 6$ **b** $8(t + 7) = 36$ **c** $7y + 32 = 11$

  d $2d + 6 = 5d - 3$ **e** $\dfrac{5a}{3} - 2 = 8$ **f** $\dfrac{3t + 8}{4} = t + 1$

33 I think of a number, multiply it by 3, then add 6, and the answer is 33. What number am I thinking of?

34 Solve the following equations:

  a $\dfrac{x}{3} + \dfrac{x}{4} = 7$ **b** $\dfrac{f + 12}{f} = 19$ **c** $\dfrac{n}{2} - 1 = \dfrac{3n - 2}{3}$

35 Make t the subject of each formula.

  a $P = \dfrac{y}{t}$ **b** $V = u + at$ **c** $A = \dfrac{1}{2}(t + b)h$

36 Which of the following is one possible solution to $8 - 3t < 5$?

  A $t = {}^-2$ **B** $t = 0$ **C** $t = 1$ **D** $t = 5$

37 Graph the solution to each inequality on a number line:

  a $3f - 5 > 7$ **b** $3 \geq 7 - 2x$ **c** $4(n - 1) < 3(6 - n)$

1 What you need to know and revise

Outcome SGS 4.2:
Identifies and names angles formed by the intersection of straight lines, including those related to transversals on sets of parallel lines, and makes use of the relationships between them:

- identifying right angles, straight angles and angles of complete revolution
- establishing and using the equality of vertically opposite angles
- recognising the equal and supplementary angles formed when a pair of parallel lines are cut by a transversal
- using angle properties to identify parallel lines
- using angle relationships to find unknown angles in diagrams.

Outcome SGS 4.3:
Classifies, constructs and determines the properties of triangles and quadrilaterals:

- recognising and naming types of triangles
- constructing various types of triangles using geometrical instruments

constructing triangles given different information, e.g. the length of each side only, two sides and the included angle, two angles and one side.

2 What you will learn in this chapter

Outcome SGS 5.2.1:
Develops and applies results related to the angle sum of interior and exterior angles for any convex polygon:

- extending the result for the interior angle sum of a triangle to finding the interior angle sum of any polygon
- defining the exterior angle of a convex polygon
- establishing that the sum of the exterior angles of any convex polygon is 360°
- applying angle sum results to find unknown angles.

Outcome §SGS 5.3.2:
Determines properties of triangles and quadrilaterals using deductive reasoning:

- Stating a definition as the minimum amount of information needed to identify a particular figure.

Working Mathematically outcomes WMS 5.1, 5.2, 5.3
Students will be required to *question*, *apply strategies*, *communicate*, *reason* and *reflect* in the sections of this chapter.

Geometry

Key mathematical terms you will encounter

acute	diagonal	parallel	rhombus
adjacent	diameter	parallelogram	scalene
alternate	equilateral	perpendicular	sector
bisect	exterior	polygon	segment
circumference	geometric	properties	square
co-interior	horizontal	quadrilateral	supplementary
compasses	interval	radius	triangle
complementary	isosceles	rectangle	transversal
concentric	kite	reflex	trapezium
construction	line	revolution	vertex
corresponding	obtuse	right	vertical

MathsCheck
Angle relationships

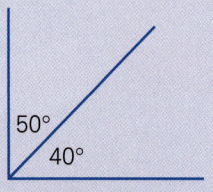

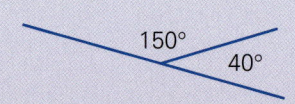

Angles on a straight line sum to 180°.
They are *adjacent* **supplementary** angles.

Angles in a right angle sum to 90°.
They are *adjacent* **complementary** angles.

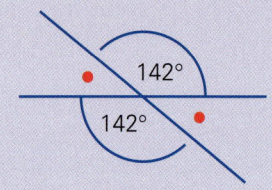

Vertically opposite angles are equal.

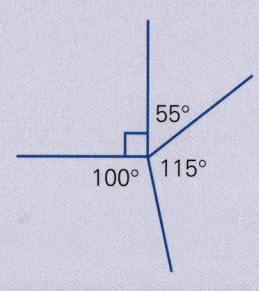

Angles at a point sum to 360°.

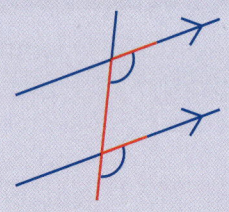

Corresponding angles are *equal.*
(Characteristic F shape.)

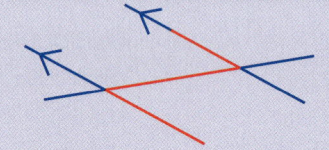

Alternate angles are *equal.*
(Characteristic Z shape.)

Note: These angles
are *not* equal.

Co-interior angles are *supplementary.*
(Characteristic ⌐ shape.)

You need: sharp pencil, ruler, protractor, compasses, set square. It is preferable to do constructions onto blank paper.

1 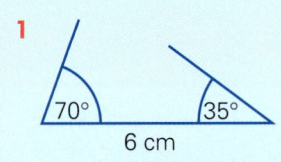 Construct a triangle with a base of 6 cm, and angles of 35° and 70° at the ends of the base.

    a What is the size of the other angle?

    b What are the lengths of the other two sides?

2 Construct a triangle with side lengths of 3 cm, 4 cm and 6 cm.

3 Using the same centre for each, construct circles with radii of 2 cm, 3·5 cm and 5 cm. (Circles with the same centre are called **concentric** circles.)

> **Radii** is the plural of *radius*.

4 Find the value of the pronumerals in each of these diagrams, giving reasons for your answers:

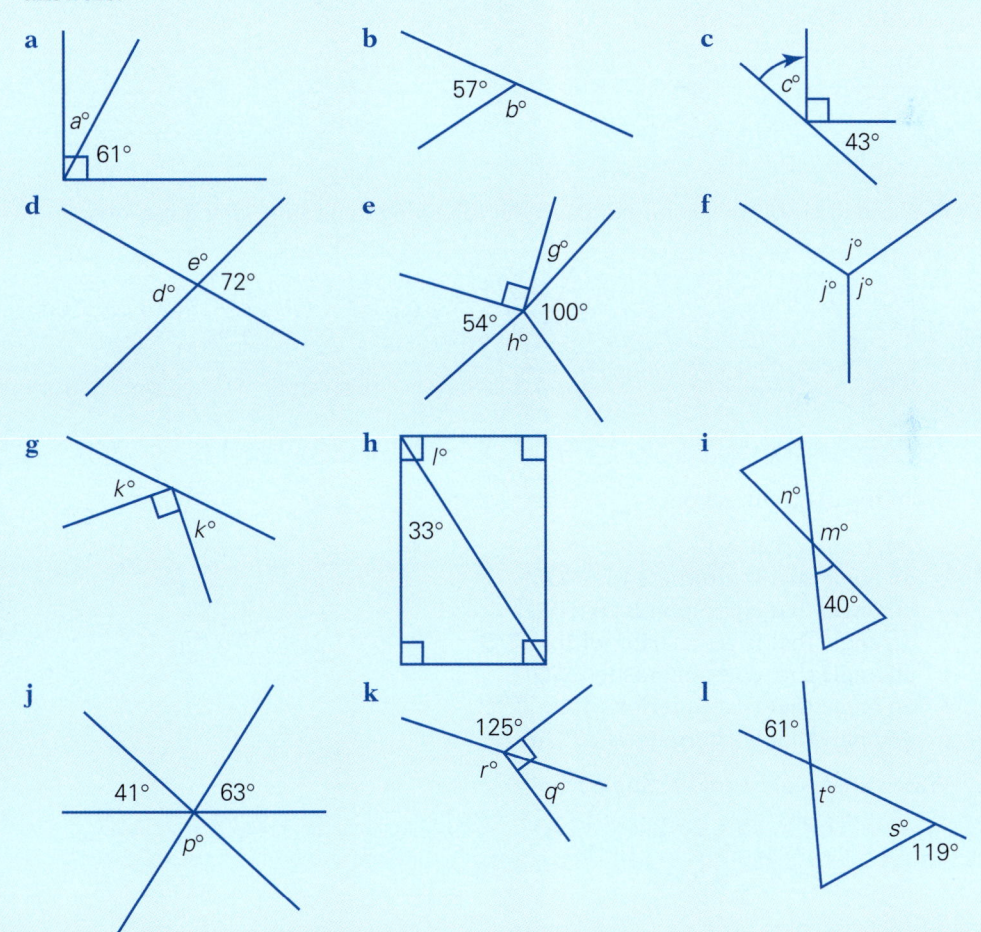

m What can you deduce about the triangle in part **l**?

5 In which of the following *must DEF* be a straight line? (Explain how you know in each case.)

a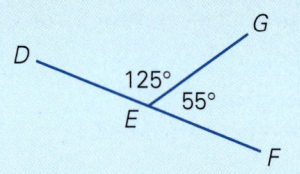

b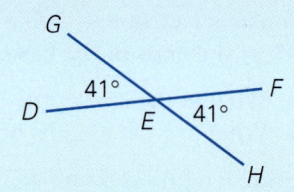

c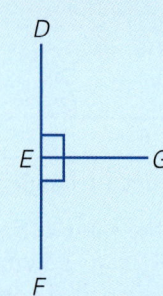

d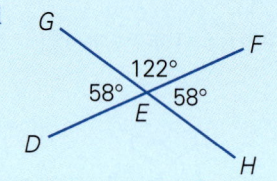

e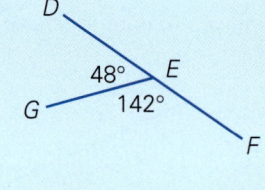

f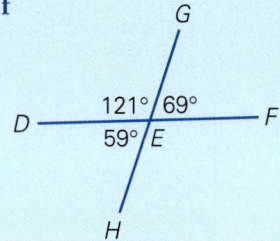

6 Find the value of the pronumerals in the following diagrams, giving reasons:

a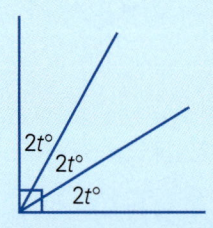

b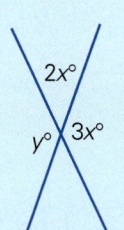

c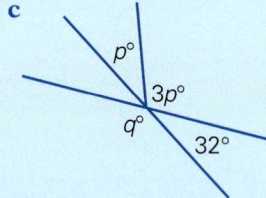

7 From the diagram, name:

  a the transversal
  b an angle that is alternate to $\angle SQU$
  c an angle that corresponds to $\angle WUV$
  d an angle that is co-interior with $\angle TUQ$
  e an angle that corresponds to $\angle SQU$
  f an angle that is co-interior with $\angle PQU$
  g an angle that is alternate to $\angle PQU$.

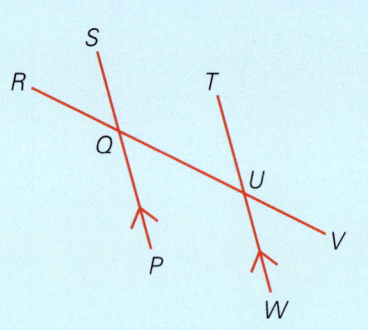

8 Which angles are equal to angle *r*?

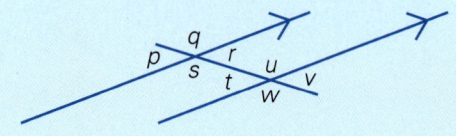

9 Find the value of the pronumerals, giving a reason for each:

a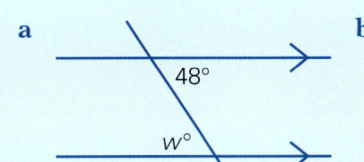

48°

w°

b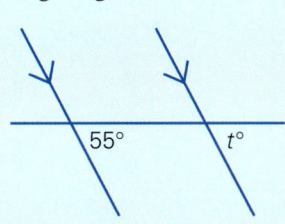

55°   t°

c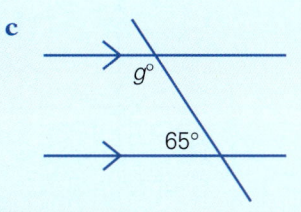

g°

65°

d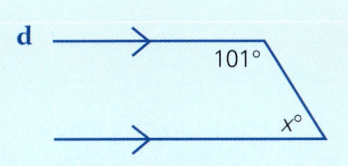

101°

x°

e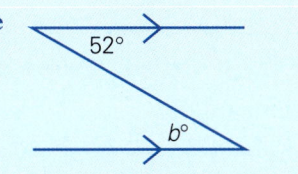

52°

b°

f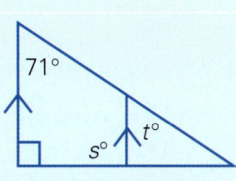

71°

s° t°

g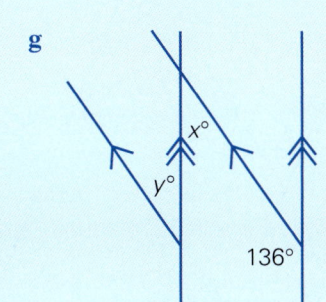

x°

y°

136°

h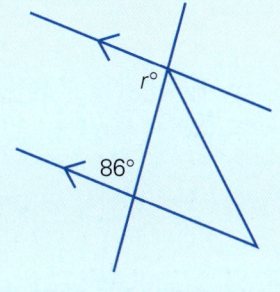

r°

86°

i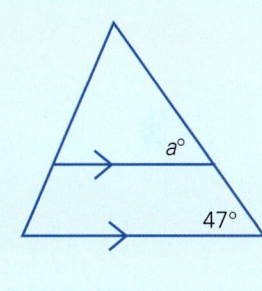

a°

47°

j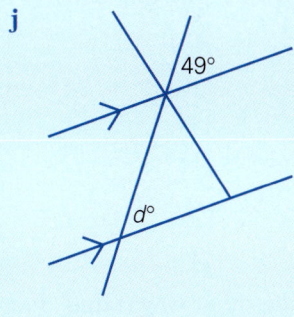

49°

d°

k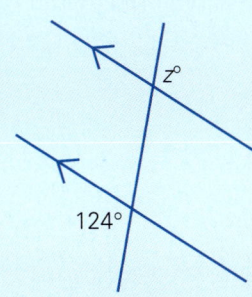

z°

124°

l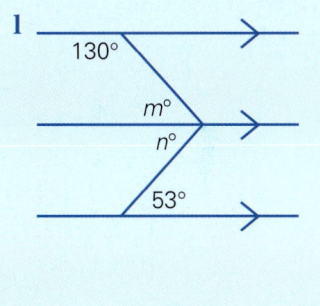

130°

m°

n°

53°

m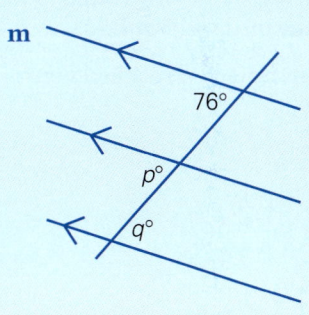

76°

p°

q°

n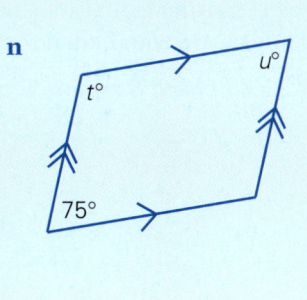

t°   u°

75°

o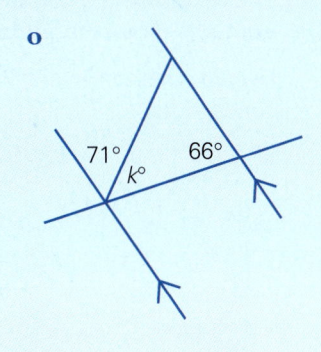

71° 66°

k°

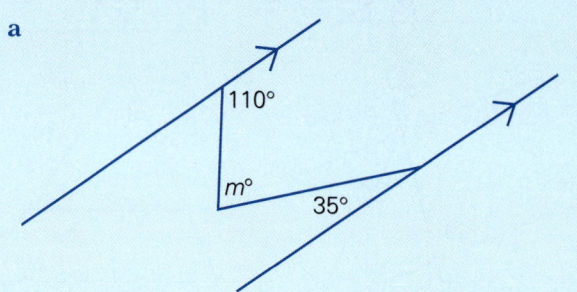
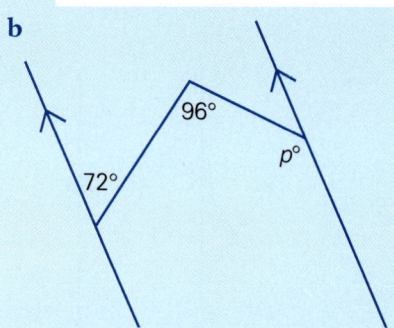

10 Which information in question **9** parts **p**, **q** and **r** is not needed?

11 Find the value of the pronumeral.

> Draw in another parallel line.

a

b

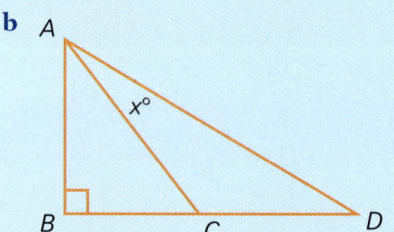

12 What additional information is required to find the value of x in the following?

a

b

13 The relationships you have been using can also be used 'the other way round'. For example, *if* corresponding angles are equal, then the lines *must be parallel*.

Decide whether or not $WX \parallel YZ$ in each diagram. Explain how you reached your conclusions.

a   **b**   **c**

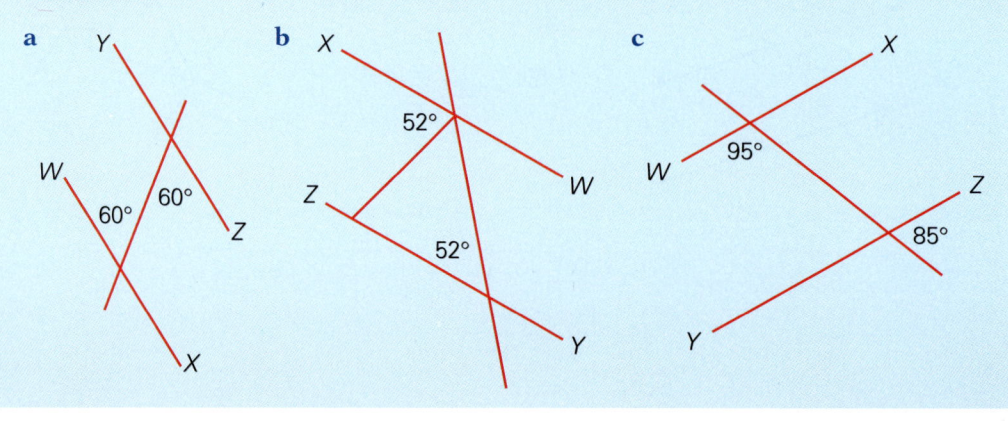

Exploring New Ideas

5.1 Triangles

Triangles can be classified according to their **side lengths** or their **angles**.

CLASSIFICATION ACCORDING TO SIDE LENGTHS

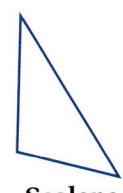

Scalene
All sides are
different lengths.

Isosceles
Two sides are the *same* length
(and the angles opposite those
sides are equal).

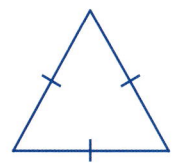

Equilateral
All *three* sides are the
same length (and all
angles are 60°).

CLASSIFICATION ACCORDING TO ANGLES

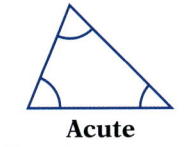

Acute
All angles are *acute*.

Right-angled (or Right)
One angle is *90°*.

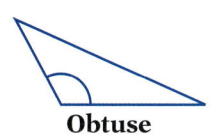

Obtuse
One angle is *obtuse*.

TRIANGLE RELATIONSHIPS

The angle sum of a triangle is 180°.

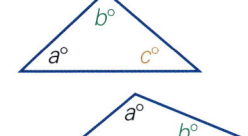

$$a + b + c = 180$$

An **exterior** angle of a triangle is
equal to the *sum* of the two
opposite interior angles.

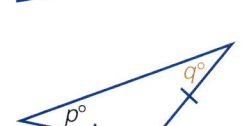

$$c = a + b$$

An **isosceles triangle** has two
equal angles opposite the two
equal sides.

$$p = q$$

DANGER
Electric
shock risk

An **equilateral triangle** has three
equal sides, and three equal
angles of 60°.

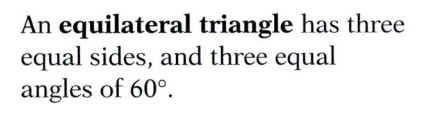

$$k = l = m = 60$$

EXERCISE 5A

1 The angle marked '*b*' is called an **exterior angle**
of the triangle.

Draw an accurate copy of this triangle.
You need: sharp pencil, protractor, ruler

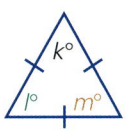

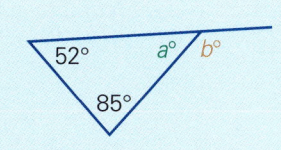

a **i** Calculate what the angle marked '*a*' must be. Check it with your protractor.
  ii Calculate what the angle marked '*b*' must be. Check it with your protractor.
  iii What is the connection between angle *b* and the two given angles?

b **i** Using the pronumerals shown in this triangle, write an expression for the size of angle *z*, and explain why this must always be true.

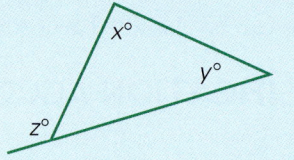

  ii Write a sentence in words that clearly states the result you have found.

c Draw another triangle, and mark on **all** the possible exterior angles. How many are there?

2 Classify each triangle according to: **i** its angles, and **ii** its side lengths.

a 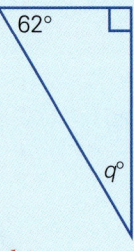 **b** 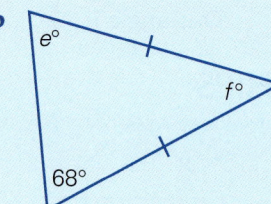 **c**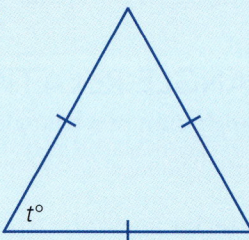

3 Find the value of the pronumerals, giving reasons for your answers.

a   **b**  **c**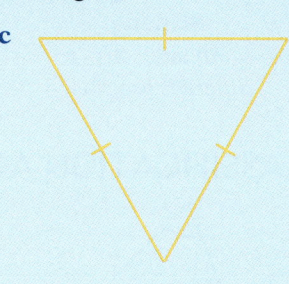

Level 2

d 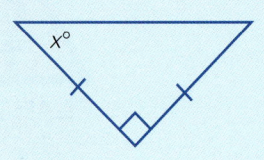 **e** 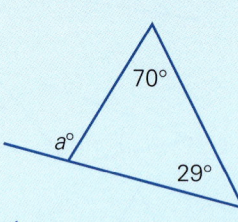 **f**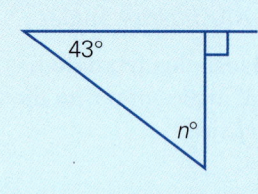

g 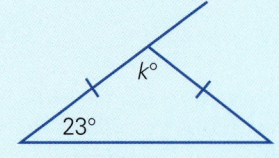 **h** 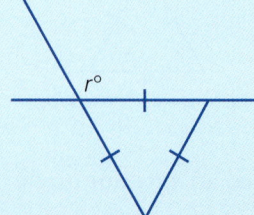 **i**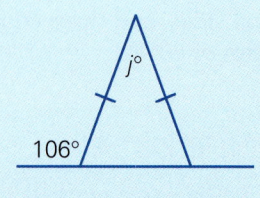

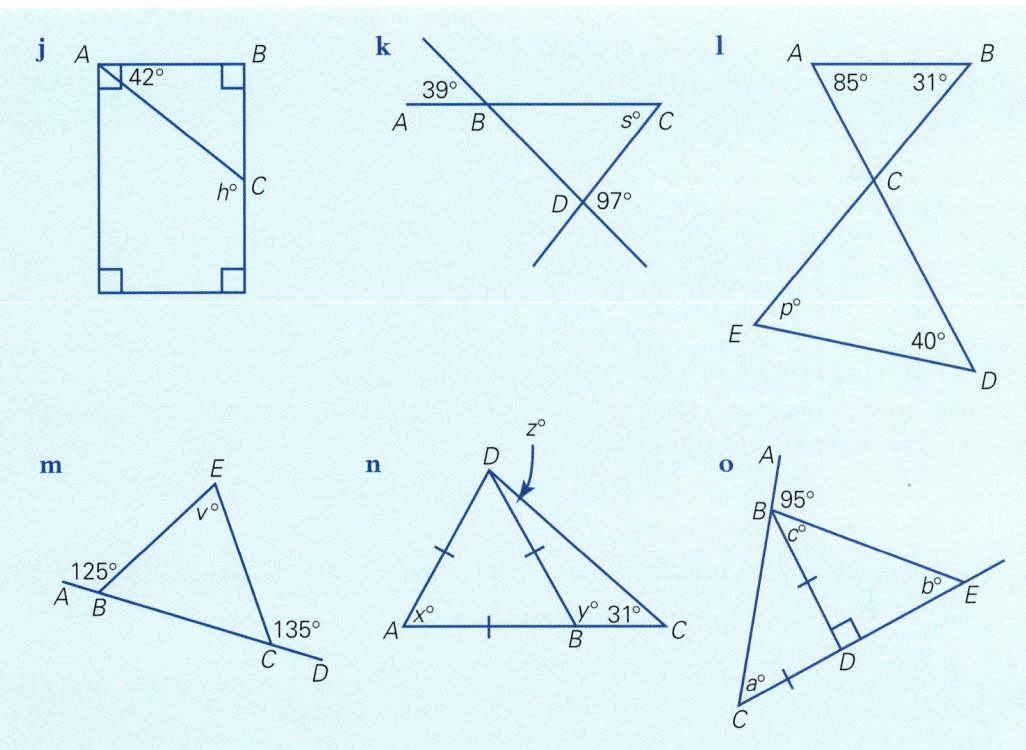

4 Use your knowledge of triangles and parallel lines to find the value of x in the following (giving reasons):

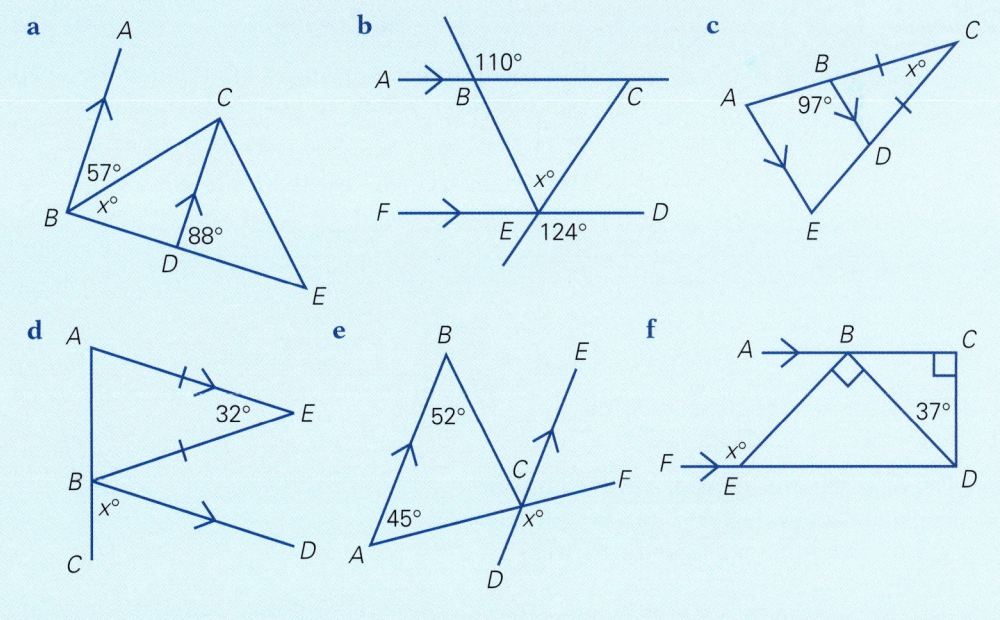

5 PQR is a scalene triangle with each side produced in both directions. How many pairs of equal angles are there? Draw diagrams!

6 $\angle RST = 310°$. SV bisects $\angle RST$. What is the size of $\angle VST$?

7 $\angle ABC = 32°$. Point D is marked so that $\angle ABD = 164°$. What are the possible values for $\angle CBD$?

8 PQR is an isosceles triangle with $PQ = QR$ and $\angle QPR = 42°$. Find the sizes of the other two angles.

9 **a** If possible, draw triangles with the following side lengths:

      i 4 cm, 5 cm and 6 cm
     ii 5 cm, 4 cm and 11 cm
   iii 6 cm, 4 cm and 10 cm.

  b Use your results from part **a** to write a statement that explains how you can tell if it is possible to draw a triangle from a set of side lengths.

  c Investigate the conditions necessary for it to be possible to draw a *quadrilateral* from a given set of side lengths.

10 Is it possible to draw a triangle with more than one obtuse angle? If it is possible, draw an example. If not, explain why not.

11 Is it possible to draw a scalene triangle that is:

  a acute?   **b** right angled?   **c** obtuse?

If it is possible, draw an example. If not, explain why not.

12 Repeat question **11** for both isosceles and equilateral triangles.

Try this

1

How many *different* triangles are there in this shape (i.e. *completely* different, not just in a different position)?

How many triangles are there *altogether*?

2 ABC is an isosceles triangle with $\angle A = \angle C = 36°$ and $\angle B = 108°$.

Draw an accurate copy of $\triangle ABC$ into your book, and show how ABC can be split into *two* triangles that are *both themselves isosceles*.

Can you find another isosceles triangle, different from $\triangle ABC$, that can also be split into two isosceles triangles?

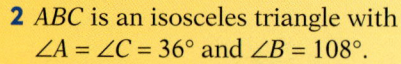

How many *different* isosceles triangles are there that can be split in this way?

Investigation Angle in a semicircle

You need: sharp pencil, compasses, protractor

1 Draw a semicircle with radius 5 cm.

2 Form a triangle with vertices at each end of the diameter, and one vertex on the semicircle.

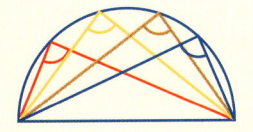

3 Measure the angle of the vertex on the semicircle.

4 Draw three more triangles as in question **2**, but with the vertex at different places on the semicircle. Measure the angle of each of the vertices on the semicircle.

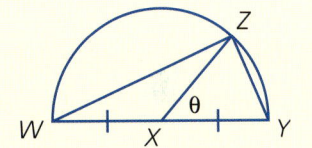

5 Comment on your findings.

Now try proving the result is true for any triangle in any semicircle:

6 Consider this diagram in which $\angle ZXY$ is labelled θ.

7 Write an expression for $\angle WXZ$ in terms of θ.

8 Which other angle is equal to $\angle XZY$? Why? Label these angles 'a'.

9 Which other angle is equal to $\angle XZW$? Why? Label these angles 'b'.

10 Write expressions for angles a and b in terms of θ.

11 Express $\angle WZY$ in terms of $\angle a$ and $\angle b$, then substitute the expressions from question **10**.

5.2 Quadrilaterals

A quadrilateral is a plane figure with four straight sides.

ANGLE SUM OF A QUADRILATERAL

If we split a quadrilateral into two triangles as shown, we can calculate the angle sum:

$$\text{Angle sum} = a + b + c + d + e + f$$

but $a + b + c = 180$
and $d + e + f = 180$
So the angle sum $= 180 + 180 = 360°$

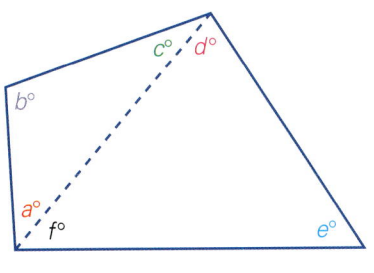

> Angle sum of a quadrilateral $= 360°$

EXAMPLE

Find the value of the pronumerals, giving reasons.

Solutions

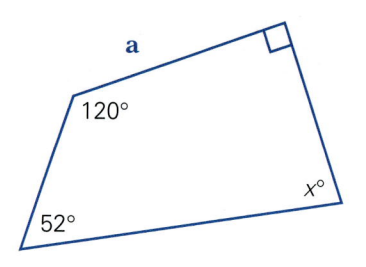

a $x + 120 + 90 + 52 = 360$ (angle sum of a quadrilateral)

$$x + 262 = 360$$
$$x = 98$$

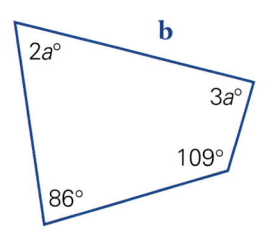

b $3a + 2a + 86 + 109 = 360$ (angle sum of a quadrilateral)

$$5a + 195 = 360$$
$$5a = 165$$
$$a = 33$$

EXERCISE 5B

1 Find the value of the pronumeral, giving reasons.

a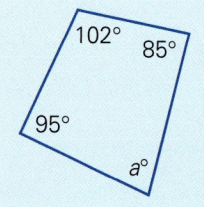

b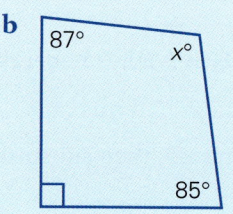

c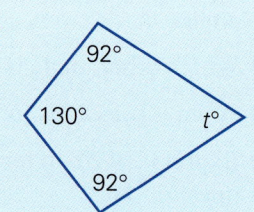

d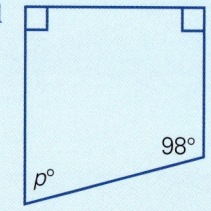

e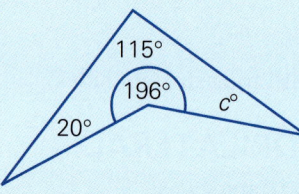

f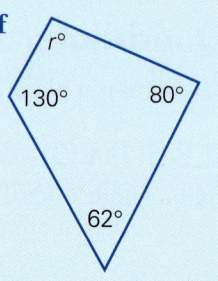

Level 2

g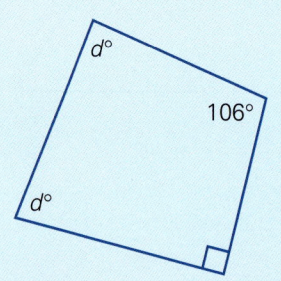

h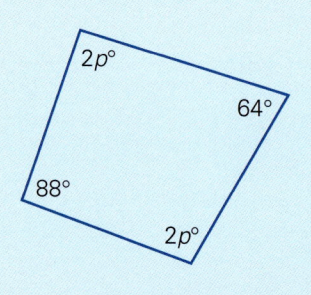

i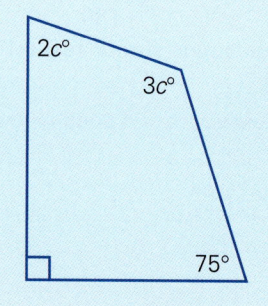

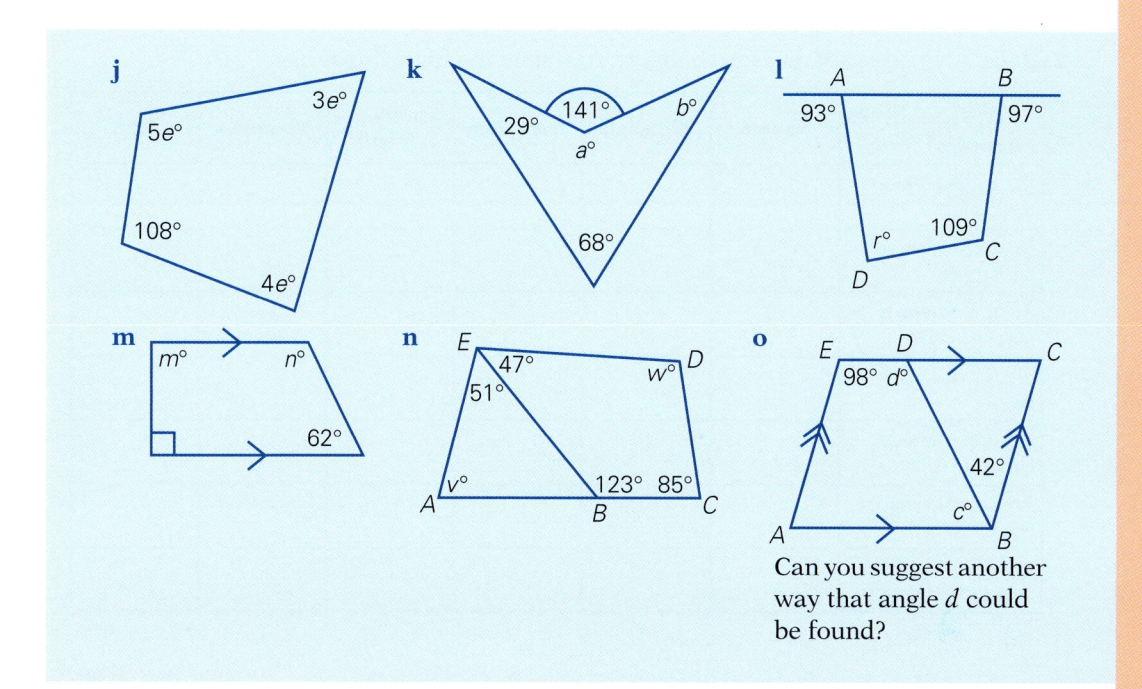

o Can you suggest another way that angle d could be found?

Investigation Properties of quadrilaterals

1 Construct each of these quadrilaterals using any necessary instruments:

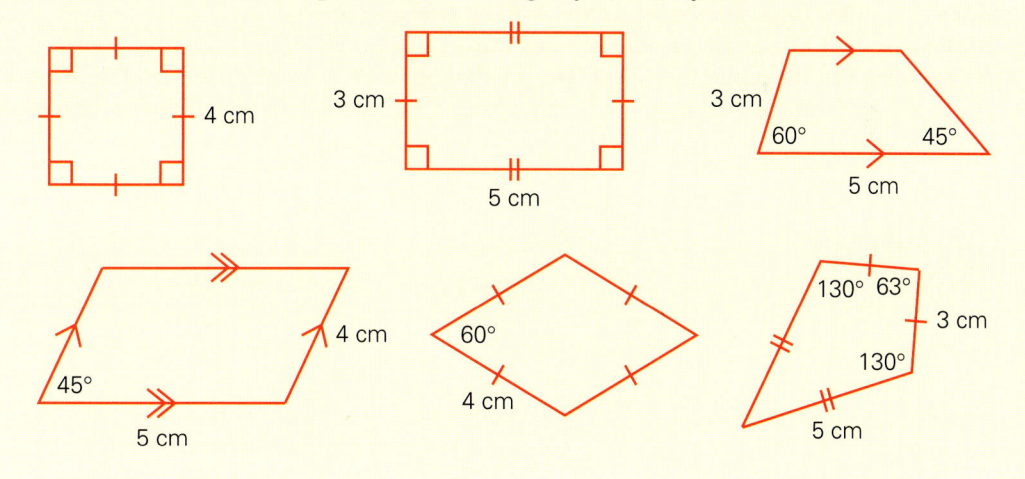

2 Make any necessary measurements to complete the following table:

Properties \ Shape	Square	Rectangle	Trapezium	Parallelogram	Rhombus	Kite
Do diagonals bisect the angles?						
Do diagonals bisect each other?						
Are the diagonals perpendicular?						
Are the diagonals equal?						
Are opposite sides equal?						
Are opposite angles equal?						
How many lines of symmetry?						

5.3 Tests for quadrilaterals

The **properties** of a quadrilateral are the *features* that are characteristic of that shape. They can include any of the following:

Sides: Are the side lengths *equal*? Are the sides *parallel*?

Angles: Are any angles *equal*? Are any angles *right angles?*

Diagonals: Are the diagonals *equal*? Do the diagonals *bisect each other*? Do the diagonals *bisect the angles* through which they pass? Do the diagonals cut at *right angles*?

The *combination* of properties is different for each quadrilateral.

Quadrilateral		Properties
Trapezium		One pair of opposite sides *parallel*.
Kite		Two pairs of *adjacent* sides equal. One axis of symmetry (one diagonal).
Parallelogram		Two pairs of *parallel* sides. Opposite *sides* are *equal*. Opposite *angles* are *equal*. Diagonals *bisect* each other.

Quadrilateral		Properties
Rhombus		All properties of a parallelogram plus: • *All* sides are equal. • Diagonals bisect at *right angles*. • Diagonals bisect the angles through which they pass. • Two axes of symmetry (both diagonals).
Rectangle		All properties of a parallelogram plus: • All angles are *right angles*. • Diagonals are *equal*. • Two axes of symmetry (perpendicular to sides).
Square		All properties of a rectangle plus: • All properties of a rhombus. • Four axes of symmetry.

Each of the quadrilaterals have several properties, but it is not necessary to check *all* of the properties when trying to identify a shape.

TESTS FOR A PARALLELOGRAM

Satisfying **any one** of these conditions is sufficient to identify the shape as a parallelogram:

1 Both pairs of opposite sides are parallel *or* equal.
2 Both pairs of opposite angles are equal.
3 One pair of opposite sides is equal and parallel.
4 Diagonals bisect each other.

TESTS FOR A RHOMBUS

Satisfying **any one** of these conditions is sufficient to identify the shape as a rhombus:

1 All sides are equal.
2 Diagonals bisect at right angles.

EXAMPLE
Name all the quadrilaterals that have opposite sides equal, and name the properties that can be deduced from the one given.

Solution
Parallelogram, rhombus, rectangle, square all have opposite sides equal.
The properties that can be deduced from the one given are:
• diagonals bisect each other
• opposite angles are equal.

> These are the properties that the named quadrilaterals all have in common.

EXERCISE 5C

1 For each of the properties listed, name all the quadrilaterals that have the property.

    a All sides are equal.
    b Diagonals are equal.
    c Opposite angles are equal.
    d Adjacent sides are equal.
    e Diagonals do *not* bisect each other.

2 Describe the possible quadrilaterals that could be formed if two identical isosceles triangles are joined together. Draw sketches to illustrate your explanations.

3 Name two properties of a rhombus that are not properties of a parallelogram.

4 Name two properties of a rectangle that are not properties of a parallelogram.

5 Choose from 'always', 'sometimes', or 'never' to complete these sentences:

    a A square is _____ a rectangle.
    b A parallelogram is _____ a rhombus.
    c A rectangle is _____ a square.
    d A parallelogram is _____ a trapezium.
    e A rectangle is _____ a parallelogram.
    f A square is _____ a rhombus.
    g A kite is _____ a rhombus.
    h A trapezium is _____ a kite.

Level 2

6 Use the tests for a parallelogram to decide which of these figures are parallelograms. Write down the number of the test used from the previous page.

    a 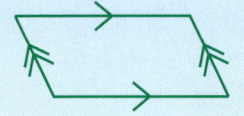   **b** 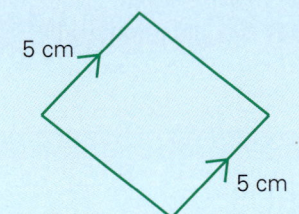   **c**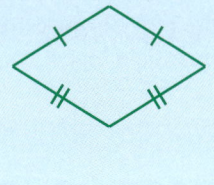

Remember: Diagrams are not always drawn to scale!

    d 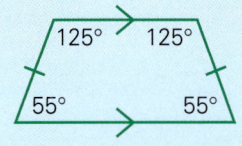   **e** 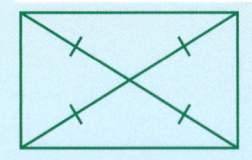   **f**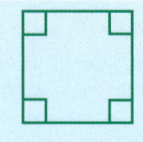

7 Use the tests for a rhombus to determine which of the following are rhombuses. Write down the number of the test used.

    a 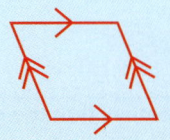   **b** 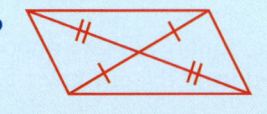   **c**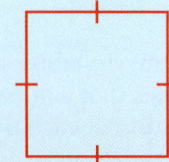

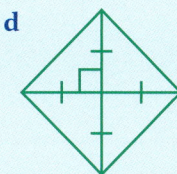 d

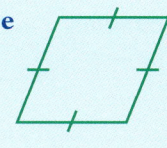 e

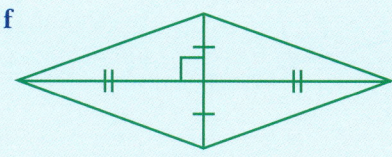 f

8 Each of these figures is a parallelogram. Find the value of the pronumerals.

a  $a°$ $125°$ $c°$ $b°$

b 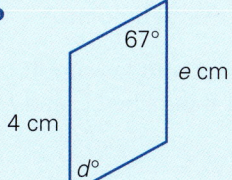 $67°$ e cm 4 cm $d°$

c 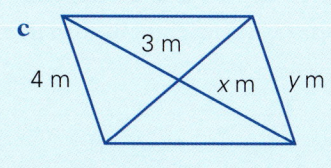 3 m 4 m x m y m

5.4 Geometric constructions

Constructions should be done using only a straight edge and a pair of compasses. You need to be familiar with the properties of a rhombus, a kite and a square.

PERPENDICULAR FROM A POINT TO A LINE

To draw a perpendicular from point D to line PQ.

Remember that the diagonals of a rhombus are perpendicular. So if a rhombus is constructed with vertices at D, X, Y and Z then the diagonals DZ and XY will be perpendicular.

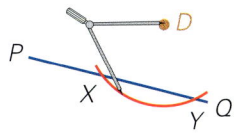

1 Place the compass point on D. Draw an arc to cross PQ twice.

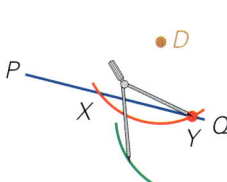

2 Keeping the radius the same, place the compass point on one intersection. Draw an arc on the opposite side of line PQ to point D.

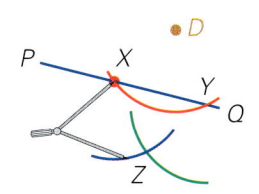

3 Keeping the radius the same, repeat step 2 for the other intersection.

INTERACTIVE GEOMETRY

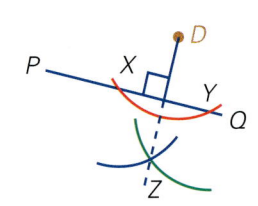

4 Place the ruler on the line joining D to the intersection of the arcs. Draw in the required interval.

PERPENDICULAR TO A LINE FROM A POINT ON THE LINE

To draw a perpendicular to line AB through point P.

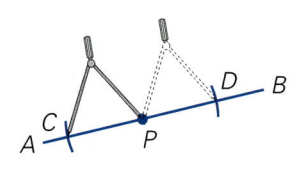

1 Place the compass point on P. Mark off equal distances each side of P (labelled C and D).

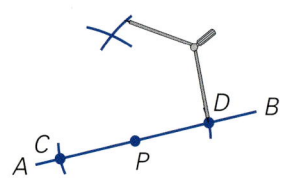

2 Reset the radius larger. Draw equal arcs from C and D.

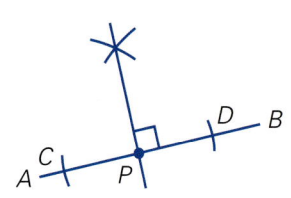

3 Join the intersection of the arcs to point P.

BISECTING AN INTERVAL

To **bisect** an interval AB, we construct a line that is *equidistant* from A and B.

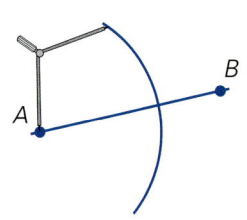

1 Place the compass point on A and set the radius greater than half the distance AB. Draw an arc that crosses the line.

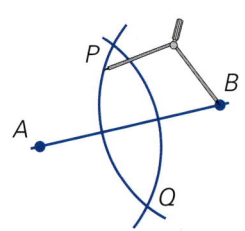

2 Keeping the radius the same, place the compass point on B and draw an arc that intersects the first one above and below the line AB. Label the points of intersection P and Q.

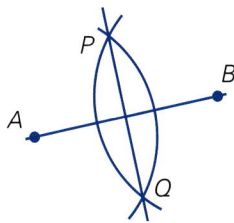

3 Draw a straight line through P and Q.

BISECTING AN ANGLE

1 Copy acute $\angle ABC$ into your book.

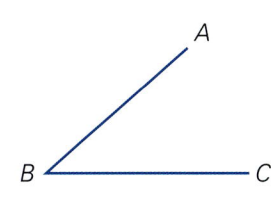

2 Place the compass point on B and mark equal distances on each arm. Label these points D and E.

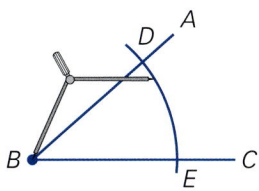

3 Keeping the radius the same, place the compass point on D. Draw an arc between the arms. Repeat for E. Label the intersection F.

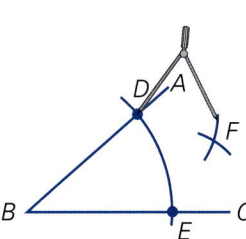

4 Draw a line from the vertex to point F.

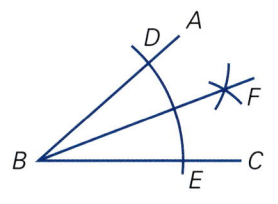

2 Draw an interval *XY* in your book, and mark point *Z* as shown. Construct a perpendicular to *XY* that goes through *Z*.

3 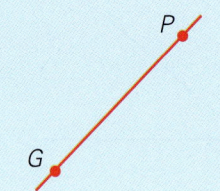 Copy this diagram into your book, and construct a line through *D* perpendicular to line *GH*.

Check that the line you have drawn is perpendicular to *GH*.

4 Copy interval *PG* into your book, and bisect it to find the mid-point. Label the mid-point *T*.

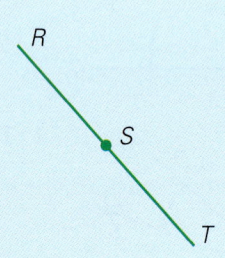

5 a Draw an interval *AB* and find the mid-point. Label this point *M*.
  b Check by measuring that *M* is the mid-point.
  c Describe how you could check by folding that *M* is the mid-point.

6 a Draw an acute angle and bisect it.
  b Check your construction using a protractor.
  c Describe how you could have checked your construction by folding.

7 Draw an obtuse angle and bisect it. Check your construction.

Level 2

8 Draw *two* copies of line *RST* as shown.

  a On one copy, bisect ∠*RST*.
  b On the other copy, construct a line through *S* that is perpendicular to *RT*.
  c What do you notice? Explain why this is the case.

9 a Construct an equilateral triangle, and label the vertices *DEF*.
  b Check that each angle is 60°.
  c Using this information, construct an angle of 30°.

10 Construct the following angles using compasses, giving a brief description of your method for each:

  a 45°   **b** 270°   **c** 120°
  d 15°   **e** 150°   **f** 225°

11 Two neighbours, Mrs P and Mr Q, wish to erect a fence that is the same distance from each of their houses. Copy this plan showing their houses, and construct the line that the fence should follow.

12 Construct a square of side length 3·5 cm.

13 Construct the following figures using only compasses and a ruler:

a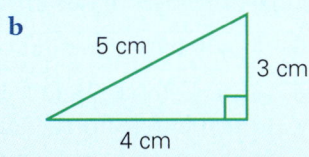

b

c

d

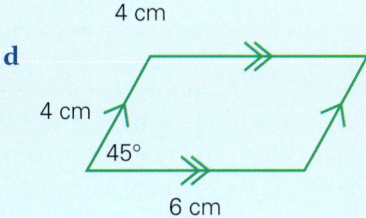

14 a Construct triangle *PQR* such that *PQ* = 6 cm, *QR* = 4 cm and *PR* = 5 cm.
  b Construct the perpendicular bisector of each side.
  c Where the bisectors meet is the **circumcentre**. Label this point *C*, and measure the *CP*, *CQ* and *CR*. What do you notice?
  d Draw a circle with centre *C* passing through *P*, *Q* and *R*. This is called the **circumcircle**.

15 Mark three points *J*, *K* and *L* in your book as shown. Draw a circle that passes through *J*, *K* and *L*.

K
•

J
•

Look at the method in question **14**.

L
•

16 a Construct a triangle with sides 7 cm, 4 cm and 6 cm.
  b Bisect each angle of the triangle.
  c Where the angle bisectors meet is called the **incentre**. Label this point *N*.
  d Using *N* as the centre, draw a circle that just touches the three sides of the triangle. This is called the **incircle**.

17 Copy triangle *FGH* into your book, and draw the largest circle that will fit completely within it.

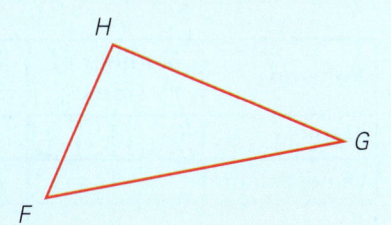

For questions **18–21** refer to the constructions on pages 144–146.

18 Perpendicular from a point to a line:

  a Explain why this construction produces a **rhombus** *DXYZ*.
  b What shape would be formed if the compass radius was changed at step 2?

c Would the resulting construction still produce a perpendicular from point *D* to line *PQ*?

d What if the radius was changed at step 3?

19 Perpendicular to a line from a point on the line:

   a If at step 2 the arcs from *C* and *D* had been continued below the line, what shape would be formed by joining the intersections of the arcs to points *C* and *D*?

   b Why was it not necessary to construct the lower half of the shape?

20 Bisecting an interval:

   a What shape is quadrilateral *AQBP* in the construction?

   b Explain how you know this to be the case.

   c What property of quadrilateral *AQBP* relates to the fact that the construction was to bisect interval *AB*?

21 Bisecting an angle:

   a What shape is quadrilateral *BDFE*?

   b What property of this shape indicates that the construction bisects $\angle ABC$?

   c What shape would be produced if the compass radius was changed prior to step 3?

   d Would the resulting construction still bisect $\angle ABC$?

   e What shape would be produced if the radius was changed between drawing the arcs from *D* and *E*?

   f Would the resulting construction still bisect $\angle ABC$?

5.5 Angle sum of polygons

A 'vertex' is a corner.

To find the angle sum of a quadrilateral (see section 5.2) the figure was divided into triangles.

Investigate the angle sum of other polygons (pentagon, hexagon, heptagon, octagon) using the same method (make sure that all the triangles meet at one vertex).

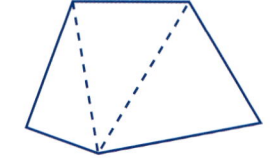

By recording the results in a table we can see a pattern.

Regular polygons have all sides and angles equal.

Polygon	Number of sides	Number of triangles	Angle sum	
Triangle	3	1	180	1×180
Quadrilateral	4	2	360	2×180
Pentagon	5	3	540	3×180
Hexagon	6	4	720	4×180

USING THE PATTERN

The angle **sum** of a polygon with n sides is equal to $(n-2) \times 180°$.
The size of **each** interior angle of a regular polygon with n sides is
$$\frac{(n-2) \times 180°}{n} \text{ (divide the angle sum by } n\text{)}$$
The sum of the exterior angles of any polygon is 360.

EXERCISE 5E

1 Find the angle sum of the following polygons:

a 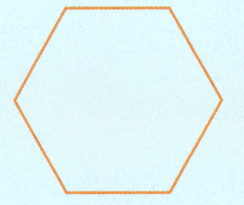 **b** 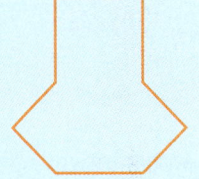 **c**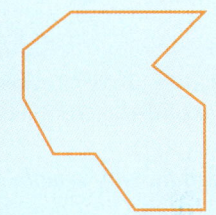

2 Calculate the angle sum and the interior angle of each of these regular polygons:

a 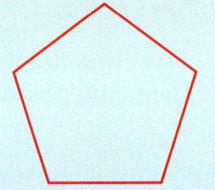 **b** 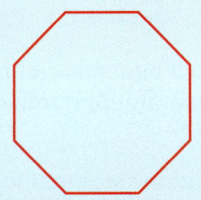 **c**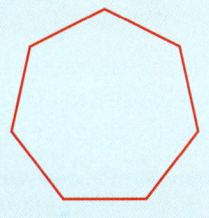

d A nonagon (9 sides) **e** A dodecagon (12 sides)

Level 2

3 Find the value of the pronumeral in each of these regular polygons:

a 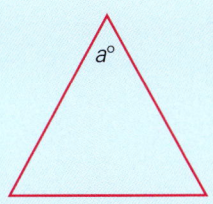 **b** 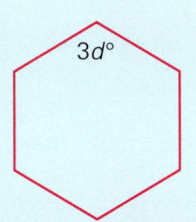 **c**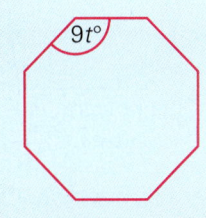

4 a What is the size of each *exterior* angle of a regular octagon?
b What is the *sum* of the exterior angles?
c Explain why this must always be the case for any regular polygon.

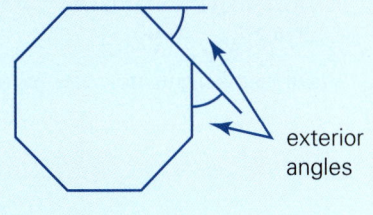

exterior angles

5 a How many sides would a regular polygon have if the exterior angle was 20°?
b Explain why a regular polygon cannot have an interior angle of 100°.

6 a What is the exterior angle of a regular polygon with 15 sides?
b What would be the interior angle of this polygon?

Level 3

7 a What would be the exterior angle of a polygon with n sides?
b What would be the interior angle of this polygon?
c Show that your expression for the interior angle in part **b** is equivalent to the one given on the previous page.

Try these

1 Draw a circle of radius 3 cm.
Keeping the compass radius the same, mark off equal chords around the circle.
Explain why *exactly* six chords can be drawn.

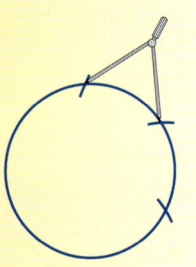

2 You are shown four points marked on a piece of paper and told that they are the corners of a square. What is the minimum number of measurements you would need to make to prove that this is true?

3 A polygon is **convex** if the straight line segment joining *any* two points on its edge lies entirely within the polygon.

 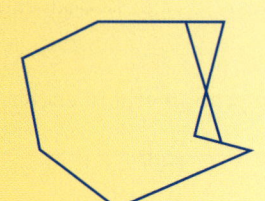

This polygon *is* convex.

This polygon is *not* convex.

Joey suggested an alternative definition:

'Any polygon is convex if no vertex lies inside the triangle formed by any three other vertices.'

Is Joey's definition really equivalent to the first one?

Chapter Review

Language Links

acute	diagonal	parallel	rhombus
adjacent	diameter	parallelogram	scalene
alternate	equilateral	perpendicular	sector
bisect	exterior	polygon	segment
circumference	geometric	properties	square
co-interior	horizontal	quadrilateral	supplementary
compasses	interval	radius	triangle
complementary	isosceles	rectangle	transversal
concentric	kite	reflex	trapezium
construction	line	revolution	vertex
corresponding	obtuse	right	vertical

- Copy the grid into your book.
- Write the words suggested by the clues into the grid.
- Rearrange the letters in the coloured boxes to spell out a word associated with this chapter.
- Write the word and explain what it means.

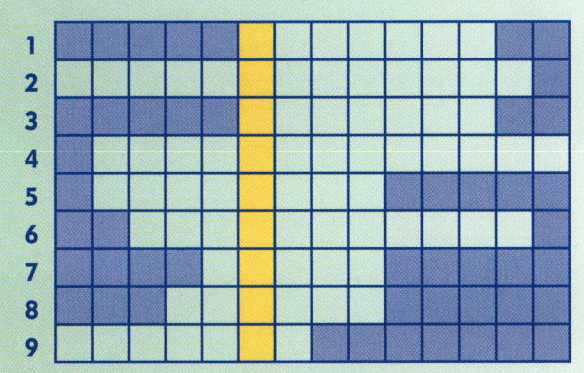

1 Triangle with all sides different.

2 Angles that sum to 90°.

3 The area cut off by a chord in a circle.

4 At right angles to.

5 Lines that never meet.

6 A triangle with all sides the same length.

7 An angle between 0° and 90°.

8 Cut into 2 equal parts.

9 A many-sided plane shape.

Write two *different* meanings for each word:

10 obtuse   **11** revolution   **12** exterior

What word is used for the *plural* of:

13 radius?   **14** vertex?

Chapter Review Exercises

You need: sharp pencil, ruler, protractor, compasses

1 Construct a triangle with side lengths 5 cm, 6·5 cm and 8 cm.

2 Explain why it is impossible to construct a triangle with side lengths 9 cm, 4 cm and 4·5 cm.

3 An isosceles triangle *PQR* has *PQ* = *QR* = 5 cm and ∠*QPR* = 70°. Draw triangle *PQR*.

4 Give the necessary instructions for a person to draw an accurate copy of this figure. (It is not necessary to make any measurements.)

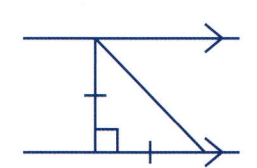

5 Find the value of the pronumerals, giving reasons:

a
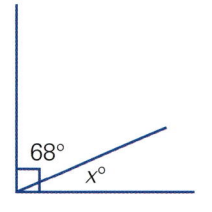

b
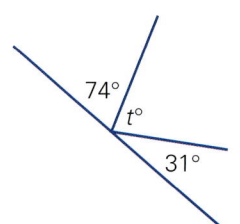

c
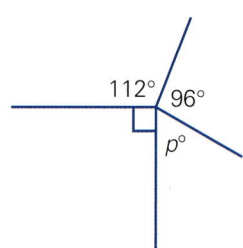

d
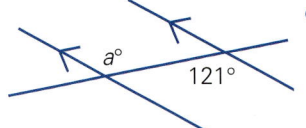

e
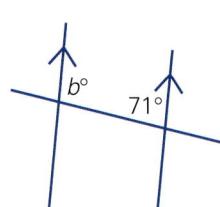

f
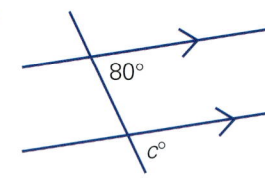

g
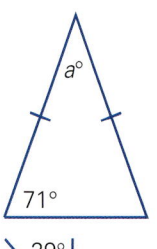

h
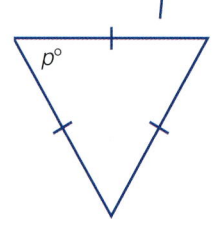

i
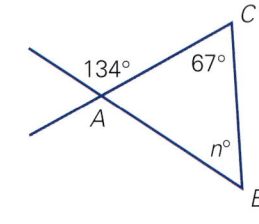

j
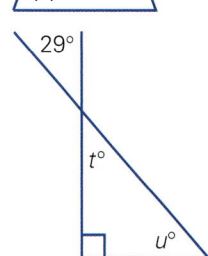

k
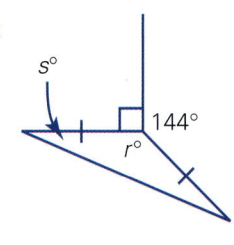

l
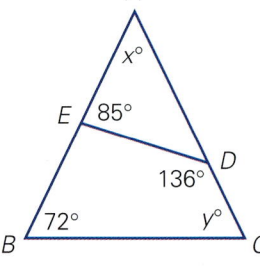

m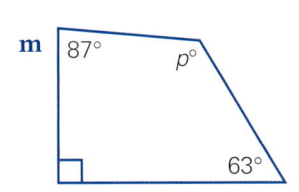
n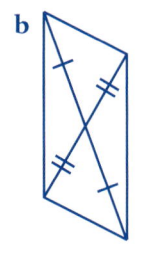
o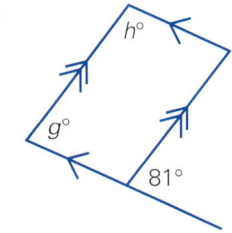

6 A quadrilateral has one pair of parallel sides. Its diagonals are equal, but do not bisect each other. Name the shape and draw a sketch showing its features.

7 State which test is used to prove that each of these figures is a parallelogram:

a 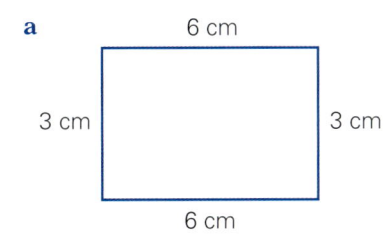   **b**   **c**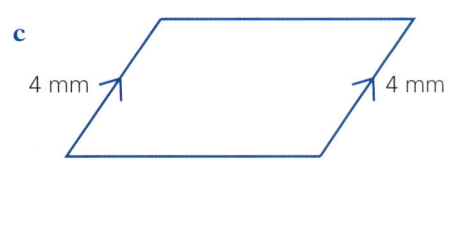

8 Which quadrilaterals have:

  a all sides equal?   **b** diagonals that bisect at right angles?

9 a Is *every* rectangle also a rhombus?
  b Is it *possible* to have a rectangle that is a rhombus? Explain.

10 Copy this diagram and construct a perpendicular to *DE* through *J*.

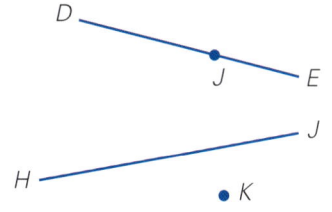

11 Copy this diagram into your book, and construct a perpendicular from point *K* to the line *HJ*.

12 Draw an interval in your book and construct its perpendicular bisector.

13 Draw an acute angle and bisect it.

14 a Construct an angle of 45° using only compasses and a straight edge.
  b Name the quadrilateral produced by the construction in part **a** and explain the connection.

15 Construct an angle of 30° using only a straight edge and compasses.

16 Draw two intervals that are equal and bisect each other, then join up the end points. What types of quadrilaterals *could* be formed this way?

17 Draw two intervals that are not equal, but that bisect each other. What types of quadrilaterals could be formed by joining up the endpoints?

18 What is the angle sum of:

  a a pentagon?   **b** a 15-sided polygon?

19 What is the size of each interior angle of a regular hexagon?

20 A regular polygon has an interior angle of 162°. How many sides has the polygon?

Keeping Mathematically Fit

Part A—Non-calculator

1 A proper fraction has a positive numerator and denominator. If 3 is added to both parts, the new value is:

    A unchanged   **B** increased by 1   **C** decreased   **D** closer to 1

2 a Find the lowest common multiple of 6 and 9.
   b Find the lowest common factor of $4a^2$ and $6ab$.

3 The mass of a truck is 6·8 t. Four pipe sections each with a mass of 450 kg are to be loaded onto the truck. What is the combined mass of the truck and pipe sections?

4 A bag contains 14 counters coloured white, black and red. If one counter is selected at random:

   a it is least likely to be black
   b it is twice as likely to be red than black.

What would the contents of the bag be? Is there only one possible answer?

5 Write a number between 8·9 and 9.

6 The length of a piece of wood is given as 1·3 m. What is the shortest actual length the wood could have been?

7 Evaluate 99×17.

8 Find the area of a rhombus with sides of 5 cm and one diagonal of 8 cm.

9 This number machine performs the operation 'add 1, then multiply by 3' on numbers that are fed into the machine.

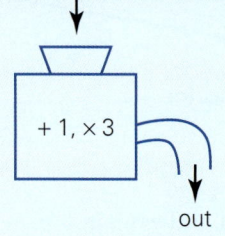

   a What number comes out if 5 is fed in?
   b What number was fed into the machine if 48 came out?

10 Andrew buys 2 ice creams and 1 can of soft drink, and pays $4·70. Sally buys 1 ice cream and 2 cans of soft drink, and pays $4·90. What is the cost of an ice cream?

Part B—Calculator

1 The angles of a quadrilateral are shown. Find the size of the largest angle.

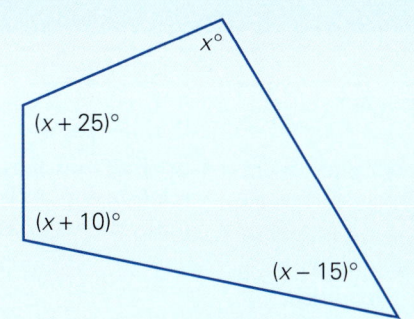

2 A cylinder is to be sculptured from this square prism.
Find the volume of the cylinder correct to 3 significant figures.

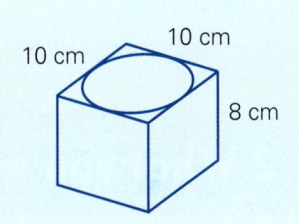

3 When a certain number is divided by 0·6, the answer is 12. What is the number?

4 This table shows the percentage composition of the audience at a play.

Adult	Child	Pensioner
65%	28%	7%

If 35 pensioners attended, how many children were there?

5 The volume of a cube is 125 cm³ Find its surface area.

1 What you need to know and revise

Outcome PAS4.5:
Graphs and interprets linear relationships on the number plane:

- graphing points on the number plane from a table of values using an appropriate scale
- extending the line joining a set of points to show that there is an infinite number of ordered pairs that satisfy a given linear relationship
- interpreting the meaning of the continuous line joining the points that satisfy a given number pattern
- reading values from the graph of a linear relationship to demonstrate that there are many points on the line.

2 What you will learn in this chapter

Outcome PAS5.2.5:
Draws and interprets graphs of physical phenomena:

- interpreting and drawing distance/time graphs
- determining which variable should be placed on the horizontal axis
- telling a story shown by a graph
- sketching informal graphs to model familiar events
- using the relative positions of two points on a graph to interpret information.

Outcome DS4.1:
Constructs, reads and interprets graphs, tables, charts and statistical information:

- drawing and interpreting a variety of types of graphs
- drawing and interpreting travel graphs, choosing appropriate scales.

Working Mathematically outcomes WMS 5.1, 5.2, 5.3
Students will be required to *question*, *apply strategies*, *communicate*, *reason* and *reflect* in the sections of this chapter.

Graphs

MathsCheck
Scales

When choosing scales for the axes, consider how big you want the graph to be. For example, if your vertical scale needs to go from $0 to $1500, choosing a scale of 1 cm to $100 would make the graph 15 cm tall. Choosing 1 cm to $200 would make it 7·5 cm tall.

Choosing a simple scale makes plotting the graph easier—if you chose 1 cm to $150 it would be more difficult to plot a value of, say, $385.

1 a Complete this table of values for the rule $y = 2x + 1$.

x	0	1	2

b Draw a number plane with the x-axis from $^-4$ to 5 and the y-axis from $^-8$ to 10. Plot the points from the table in part **a** onto the number plane.

c From the graph, find:
  i the y-value of a point whose x-value is 2
  ii the x-value of a point whose y-value is 9
  iii the x-value of a point whose y-value is 6.

2 This graph shows Rachel's distance from home when she went to visit a friend.

a How long did it take Rachel to reach her friend's house?
b How far is the journey to her friend's house?
c How long did she stay at her friend's house?
d How long did her journey home take?
e When was Rachel travelling the fastest?

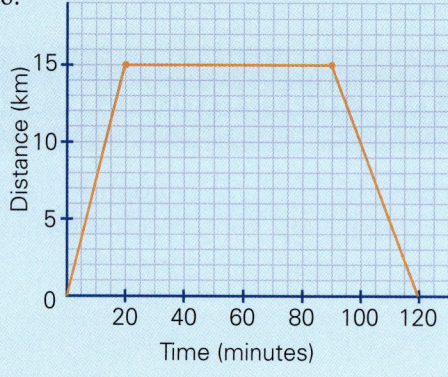

3 The following temperatures were recorded in a greenhouse one day:

Time	8 am	9 am	10 am	11 am	12 noon	1 pm
Temperature °C	16	21	25	28	30	31

a What type of graph is most appropriate to represent this information?
b Draw a graph to show the variation in temperature.
c Estimate the temperature at 10:15 am.
d At what time is the temperature 20°C?
e What would you expect the temperature to be at 2 pm?

4 Choose an appropriate type of graph and appropriate scales for the axes for the following questions:

a Draw a graph to show this information on the population distribution of Australia.

b What is the total population of Australia?

State or Territory	Population
NSW	6 068 900
Vic.	4 482 100
Qld	3 216 500
SA	1 471 000
WA	1 710 000
Tas.	472 600
NT	171 400
ACT	301 000

5 a Draw a graph to show these temperatures recorded at Thredbo one day during the winter ski season.

Time	9 am	10 am	11 am	12 pm	1 pm	2 pm	3 pm	4 pm	5 pm	6 pm
Temp (°C)	-8	-4	-2	0	1	1	-1	-2	-4	-5

b Estimate the temperature at 11:30 am.

c At what times was the temperature -3°C?

Exploring New Ideas
6.1 Everyday graphs

Graphs can be used to show the changes that happen during everyday events.

Consider the activity of blowing up a balloon:

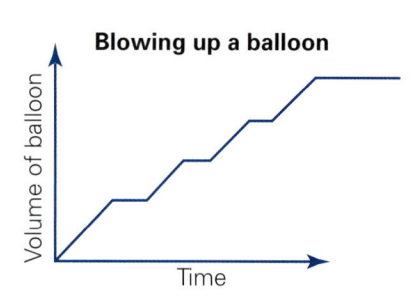

The sloping parts of the graph represent air being blown into the balloon; the flat parts are when the person blowing up the balloon takes another breath. There are no scales on the axes, but the **shape** of the graph tells the story.

AXES

We sometimes choose to show only the part of the vertical axis that is required to plot the values for the graph; that is, we don't start the scale at zero. This allows us to choose a scale that shows changes more clearly.

For example, these two graphs show the same information: Jill's time to run 200 m in six races. The second graph shows the information more clearly. The ⚡ symbol indicates that the axis has been truncated; that is, part of the axis has been left out.

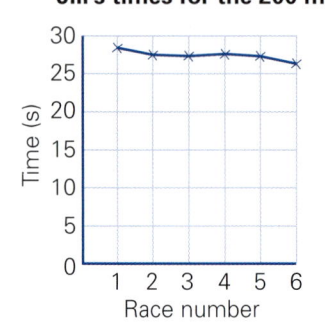

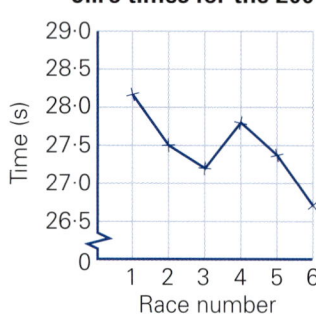

When we draw a graph we are showing the relationship between two **variables**, one of which is *dependent* on the other. The **horizontal** axis is always used for the **independent** variable—that is, the one that is not dependent on the other. The **vertical** axis is used for the **dependent** variable.

If we were to draw a graph showing the distance travelled over a period of time, the **distance** is the *dependent* variable (it *depends* on the time) and so it is shown on the *vertical* axis. The **time** taken is the *independent* variable; the time ticks away, and is not affected by the distance travelled. The time taken is therefore shown on the *horizontal* axis.

EXAMPLE

Sue goes to a hockey game to support her team. Sketch a graph showing her happiness during the afternoon, labelling the significant points.

Sue's team are the favourites to win, and they score a goal soon after the start of the match. Just before half time the other team score, and 5 minutes into the second half they score again. A few minutes later Sue's team equalise, then 2 minutes before full time her team score again and win the match.

Solution

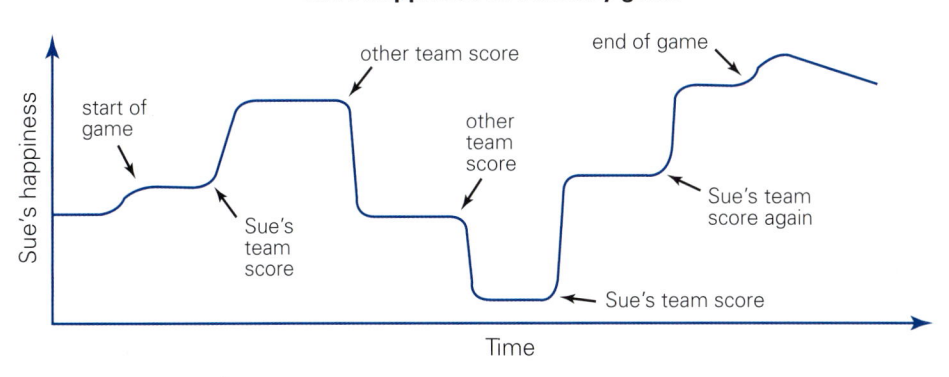

Sue's happiness at a hockey game

EXERCISE 6A

1 Select one of the following situations and draw a 'happiness graph' for yourself, with time on the horizontal axis. Label the important points with letters, and provide a key explaining what caused the changes in the graph at those points.

- Competing in a sporting event yourself.
- Watching a sporting event involving your favourite team or sportsperson.
- Playing a computer adventure game, board game or card game.
- A normal school day.

2 Sandra draws a graph of the amount of money in her wallet over a period of a week. Create a story to fit the graph, describing the possible events leading to the changes in the graph.reasons.

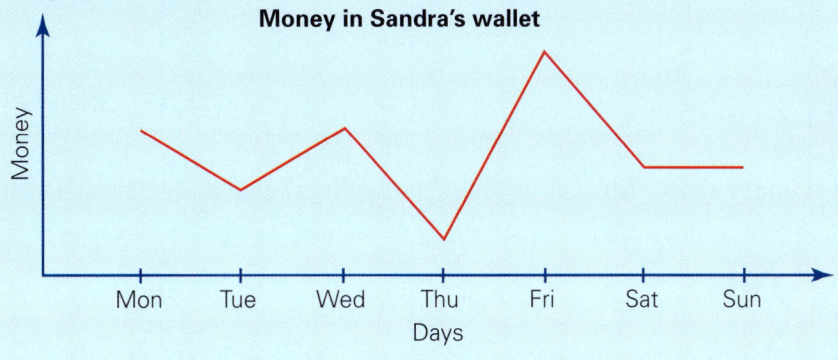

Money in Sandra's wallet

3 Leon has a bath, and draws this graph showing the depth of water in the bath. Tell the story of events represented by this graph.

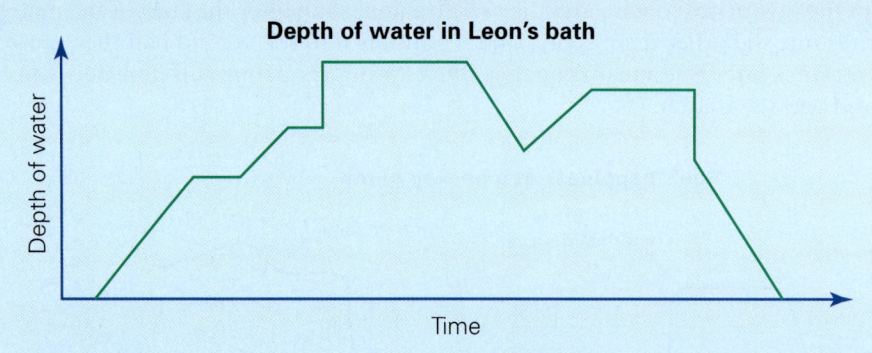

Depth of water in Leon's bath

4 This graph shows the noise level in a classroom during a lesson. Describe what could be happening at each of the points indicated, giving suggestions as to the possible reasons.

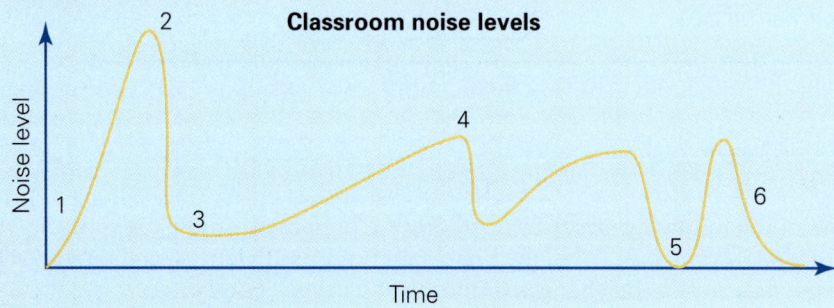

Classroom noise levels

Level 2

5 Select the graph that best represents each of the following circumstances:

a The height of water in a cylindrical bucket being filled from a tap.

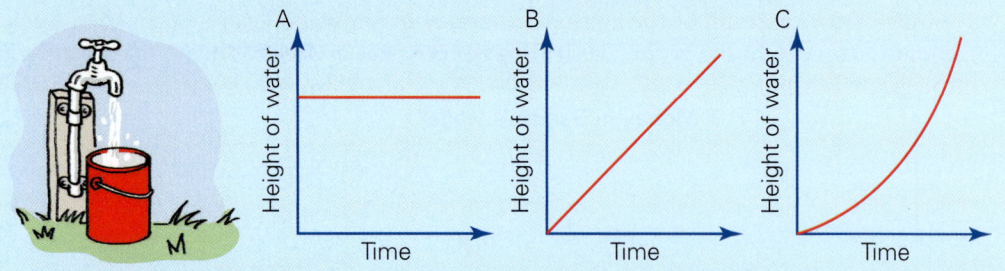

b The volume of sports drink left in a bottle while it is being drunk through a straw.

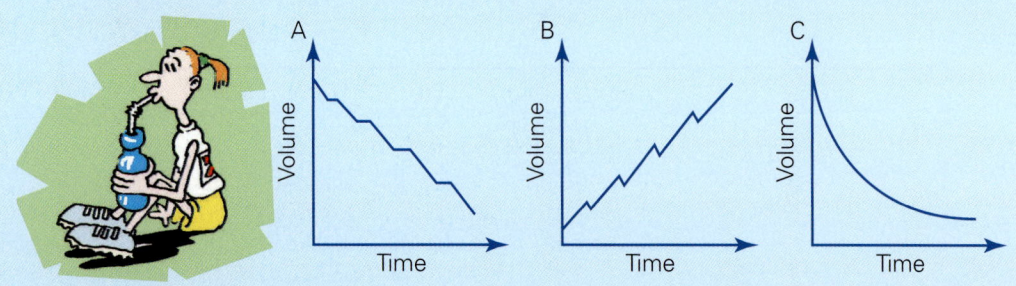

c The speed of a car as it is driven around a sharp bend in the road.

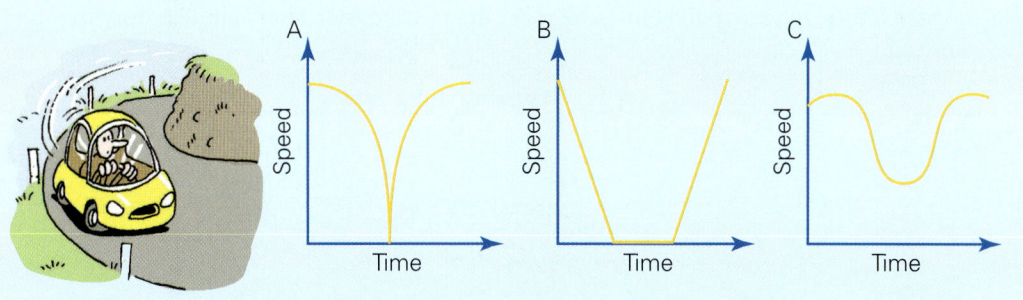

d The height of water in this bottle as it is being filled from a tap.

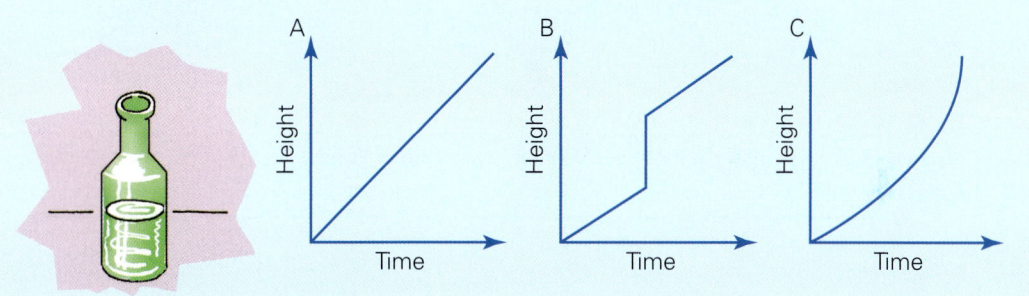

e The speed of a girl walking up a hill then running back down.

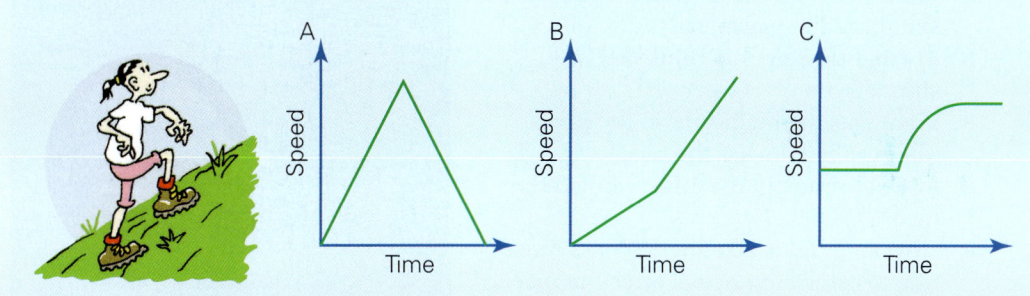

6 This graph shows the pulse rate of an athlete before, during and after a race. She jogged a little to warm up before the race, then rested for a short while before the race started.

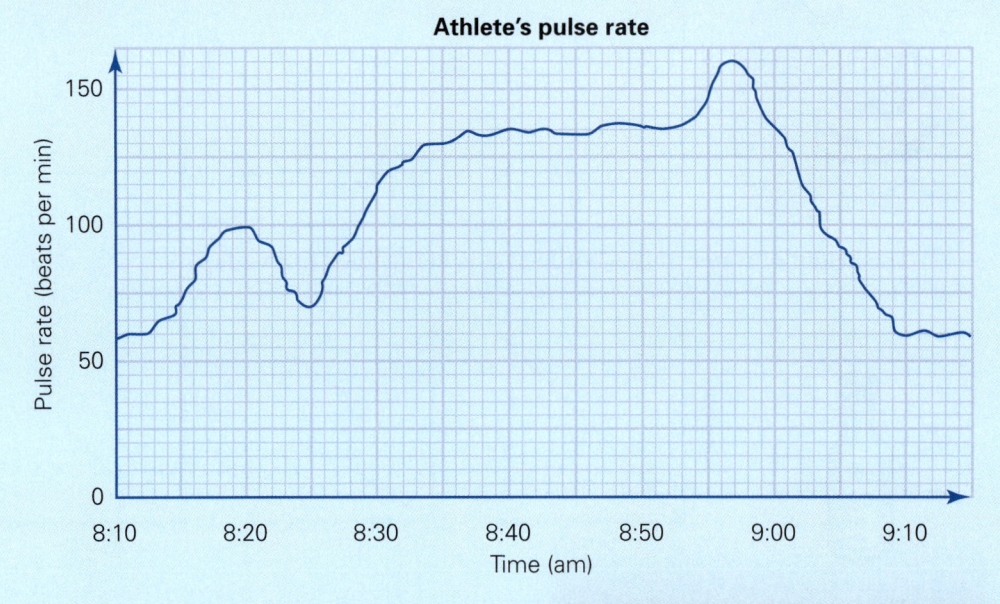

Athlete's pulse rate

a What was the athlete's pulse rate before she started to warm up?

b At what time do you think the race started?

c What was the highest level the pulse rate reached during the race?

d At what time did the athlete finish the race?

e How long did it take the athlete's pulse rate to return to normal after the race?

f If the athlete ran at an average speed of 15 km/h, how far was the race?

7 This graph shows the distances walked by Beryl and Cheryl.

   a Who walks faster?
   b How far has Beryl gone in 10 minutes?
   c How far has she gone in 20 minutes?
   d What is her speed in metres/minute?
   e How far has Cheryl gone in 30 minutes?
   f How far behind Beryl is she after 30 minutes?

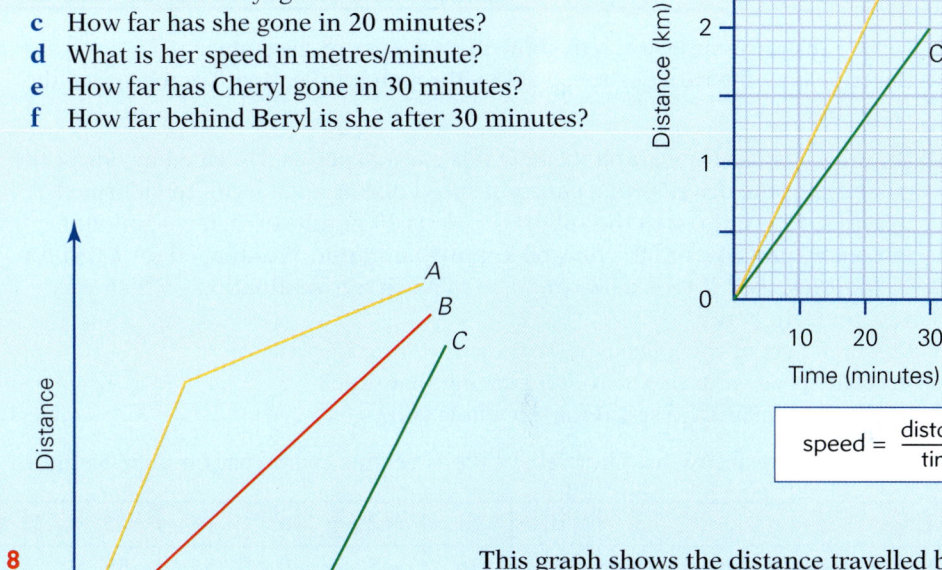

$$\text{speed} = \frac{\text{distance}}{\text{time}}$$

8 This graph shows the distance travelled by three cyclists. Give a description of the speed of the journey for each cyclist (for example, started off slowly, then speeded up).

9 This graph shows the journeys of two trains, **A** and **B**, from Central to Normsby.

   a How many stations did train A stop at?
   b How many minutes went past between train A and B leaving Central?
   c At what time did train B pass train A?
   d What was the average speed of each train over the journey?

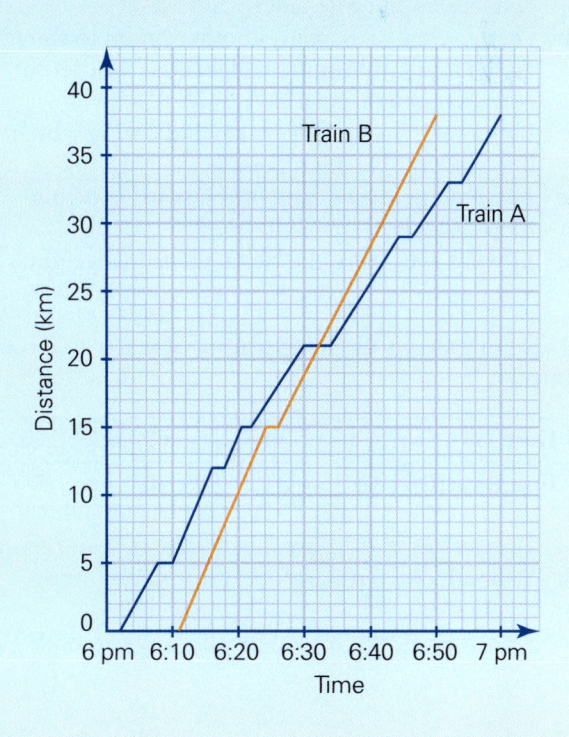

SPREADSHEET ACTIVITY

GRAPHIC CALCULATOR

GRAPHIC CALCULATOR

SPREADSHEET ACTIVITY

GRAPHIC CALCULATOR

SPREADSHEET ACTIVITY

SPREADSHEET ACTIVITY

GRAPHIC CALCULATOR

10 The following times were recorded as a runner competed in a 400 m race:

Distance (m)	0	50	100	150	200	250	300	350	400
Time (s)	0	8·5	17·5	26·5	37	46·5	56·5	65·5	74

a Draw a distance–time graph to show the progress of the runner.
b Describe how the runner's speed varies throughout the race. Try to explain the variation.

11 a Draw a distance–time graph to show this car journey as described by one of the passengers (the driver kept a constant speed during each leg of the journey):
'The first 15 km through the suburbs took us 20 minutes. Then we got on the motorway and covered the next 60 km in 40 minutes. We stopped for a rest for 15 minutes, then it took us 25 minutes to reach our destination—which was 120 km from home.'
b In which part of the journey were they travelling the fastest?
c At what speed were they travelling during that time?
d What was the average speed for the whole trip?

12 Neeta and Sunny are twins. They record their weights every year on their birthday.

Age	9	10	11	12	13	14	15	16
Neeta's weight (kg)	25	30	36	43	50	54	55	56
Sunny's weight (kg)	26	29	32	36	44	52	63	68

a Draw a line graph to show how Neeta's weight changes as she gets older.
b On the same axes, draw another graph to show the changes in Sunny's weight. Use a different coloured pen or pencil.
c Label each line, or give a key indicating which line represents which person.
d At what ages were each of the twins growing most quickly?
e At what ages were the twins the same weight?

13 This table shows the temperature of water in a beaker being heated over a Bunsen burner.

Time (s)	30	60	90	120	150	180
Temperature (°C)	23	40	56	69	81	92

a Draw a graph to show the change in water temperature against time.
b Estimate the temperature of the water after:
    i 45 s   **ii** 130 s
c How long would it take for the water to boil? (Water boils at 100°C.)

14 a Record the following information in a table.

b Draw a graph showing the variation in Athena's temperature.

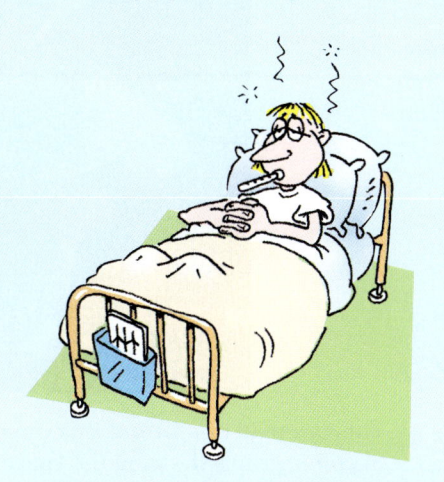

Athena was not feeling well when she woke up. When her mother took her temperature at 7 am the reading was 39·1°C. At 11 am her temperature had risen to 39·3°C, and 4 hours later it had risen by another 0·5°C. The doctor was called, and she recommended Athena be taken to hospital to receive treatment. She was admitted to hospital at 7 pm, with a temperature of 39·9°C, and by 11 pm it had dropped by half a degree. By 3 am it had fallen to 38·1°C, and at 7 am it was recorded at 37·6°C. Three more readings were taken at 4-hourly intervals, all recording a normal temperature of 37°C.

c How many degrees above normal was Athena's temperature when she was admitted to hospital?

d Estimate Athena's temperature at 2 pm on the first day.

e How long did it take for Athena's temperature to return to normal from its maximum?

15 Graham cycles to school most mornings. This graph shows his **speed** one morning:

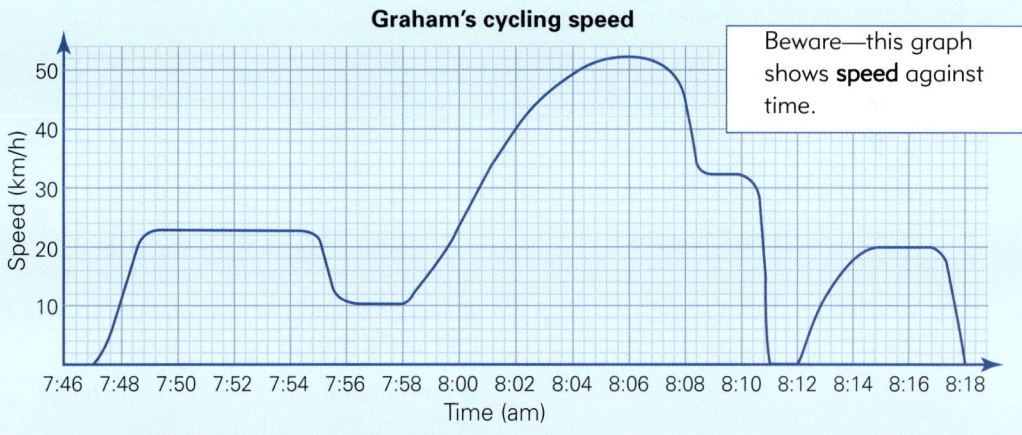

a At what time did Graham leave for school?

b After leaving home Graham cycled at a steady speed for a while. What speed was this?

c When did Graham stop at traffic lights?

d How long did he have to wait at the lights?

e Graham has to cycle up one steep hill. At what speed did he go up the hill?

f What was the fastest speed he reaching during the cycle?

g How long did it take Graham to cycle to school?

16 Sketch a graph showing the emotions of Mike and Connie during the following tennis game, labelling the significant features.

They win the first two games, then their opponents win the next four games. Mike and Connie fight back to win the next three, then lose one more before winning the next two to win the set 7–5.

Level 3

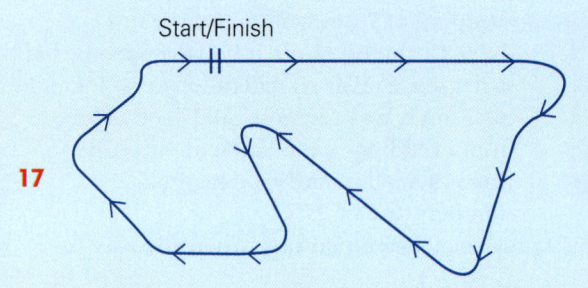

Start/Finish

17 This is a plan of a Grand Prix circuit. Sketch a graph showing the speed of a car as it completes one lap of the circuit.

6.2 Step graphs

A step graph is a type of line graph that does not have a continuous line. Instead it has a series of horizontal intervals or steps, hence its name.

This table shows the cost of sending a large letter (larger than 122 mm by 237 mm) from Sydney to Perth.

The graph looks like this:

Mass	Charge
Up to 50 g	75¢
Over 50 g, up to 125 g	95¢
Over 125 g, up to 250 g	$1·50
Over 250 g, up to 500 g	$2·65

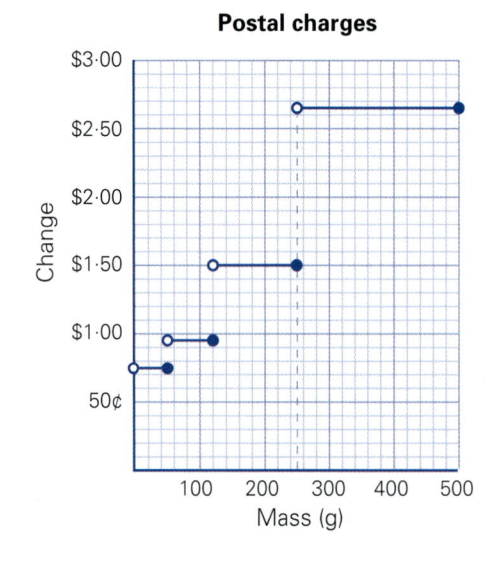

Postal charges

The end of one step is on the same vertical line as the beginning of the next step.

● A **coloured** circle means that charge applies to the 'borderline' mass.

○ An **open** circle means that charge does *not* apply to the 'borderline' mass.

So the charge for 250 g is $1·50.

EXERCISE 6B

Parking charges

1 This graph shows parking charges in a city parking station.

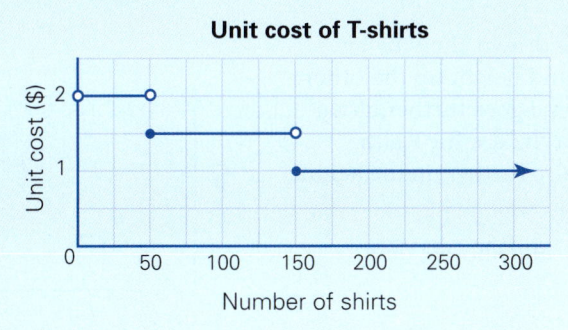

a What is the minimum charge for parking?

b What is the maximum charge for parking?

c How much does it cost to park for 3 h 47 min?

d What is the maximum length of time you can park for $6?

e Marie is leaving the parking station at 5:12 pm. If the time of entry is shown on the ticket as 3:35 pm how much will she need to pay?

f According to the graph, how much should you pay if you stay for 2 h 1 min? Would this happen in reality? Discuss.

2 Michael buys T-shirts from a wholesaler and sells them at his local market. The unit cost of the shirts reduces if Michael buys large quantities, as shown by this graph.

Unit cost of T-shirts

a What is the unit cost of shirts if Michael buys 15 shirts?

b What is the minimum number of shirts Michael must buy to get them at a cost of $1 each?

c How much would Michael pay *in total* if he bought 70 shirts?

Level 2

3 The table shows the cost of sending a letter by air mail to China.

Weight	Charge
Up to 20 g	$1·20
Over 20 g, up to 50 g	$1·30
Over 50 g, up to 125 g	$2·30
Over 125 g, up to 250 g	$4·00
Over 250 g, up to 500 g	$7·50

a Draw a graph to show the information in the table.

b What is the minimum charge for sending a letter to China?

c How much does it cost to send a letter weighing 100 g?

d What is the heaviest letter that can be sent for $4·00?

e What is the difference in cost for two letters weighing 21 g and 125 g?

f What is the difference in cost for two letters weighing 50 g and 51 g?

g Nigel has a letter weighing 180 g. What extra weight can he include in the letter without increasing the cost?

SPREADSHEET ACTIVITY

4 The postage and handling costs when ordering wine by mail order are shown in the table:

Number of bottles	Cost per bottle
Up to 12	15¢
13–24	12¢
25–36	10¢
37 and over	8¢

a Draw a graph to show this information.
b What would be the total cost of postage and handling on an order of 20 bottles?
c How many bottles were ordered if the total postage and handling cost was $2·90?

6.3 Scattergraphs

Each point on a scattergraph represents a separate item—for example a person, a place or an object—and shows how **two** quantities relate to the item. It is not necessary to have scales on the axes, since we are concerned mainly with **comparing** the items.

Jerome   Keith

For example, Jerome and Keith are brothers. Jerome is 14 and Keith is 11.

A scattergraph is drawn showing age along one axis, and height up the other. The dot for Jerome goes further along the age axis than the dot for Keith. Jerome's dot is also further up the height axis than Keith's.

Keith is younger and shorter than Jerome.

EXAMPLE
a Which bunch of flowers is the cheapest?
b Which two bunches cost the same?

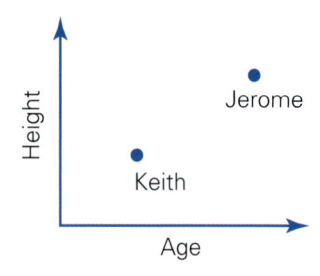

carnations   roses

gladioli   freesias

Count the flowers!
A: carnations
B: roses (least flowers)
C: freesias (most flowers)
D: gladioli

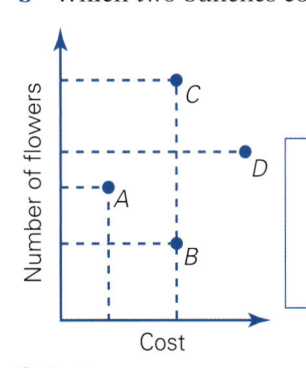

Solution
a The cheapest flowers are the carnations.
b The roses and the freesias cost the same.

Bunch A is first along 'cost' axis.

Bunch B and C are at the same position on the 'cost' axis.

EXERCISE 6C

1 Who is represented by each point on the scattergraph?

2 Which box of chocolates contains more chocolates?

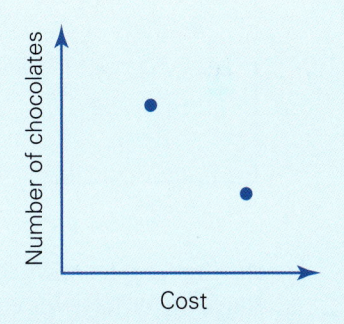

3 Which bird has the loudest song?

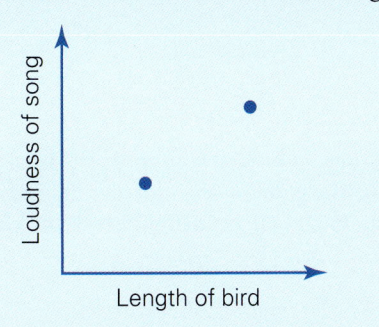

4 Which necklace costs the most?

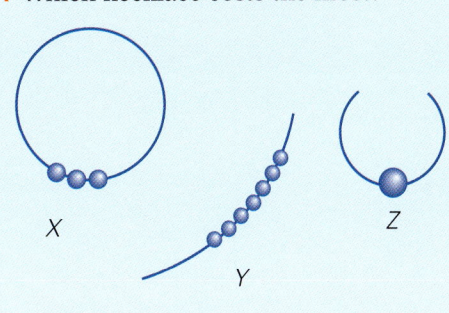
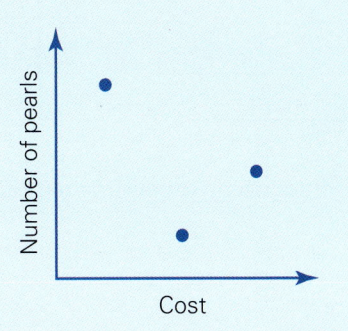

5 This scattergraph shows the heights and ages of Alex (*A*), Bree (*B*), Cecil (*C*) and Dorothy (*D*).

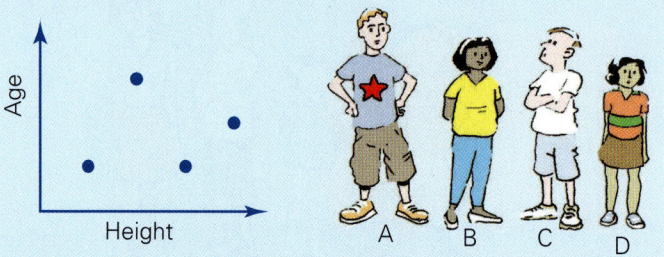

a Who is the oldest?
b Which two are the same age?

6 The following scattergraphs describe two cars, *A* and *B*.

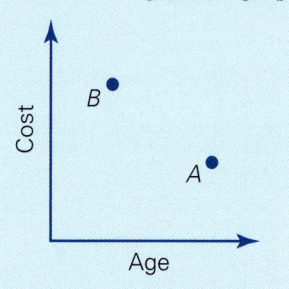 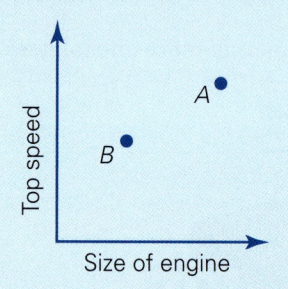 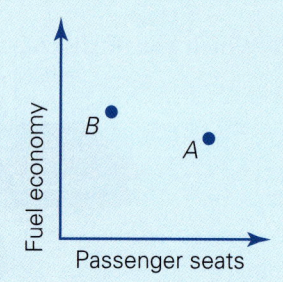

a The first graph shows that car *A* is older than car *B*. What else does it show? State true or false for each of the following:

   i The older car is cheaper.
  ii The faster car has the smaller engine.
 iii The more economical car has more seats.
  iv The car with the larger engine is older.
   v The cheaper car has fewer passenger seats.
  vi The dearer car is more economical.

b Summarise the features of car *A* in comparison to car *B*.
c Copy the graphs below, and mark two points on each representing cars *A* and *B*.

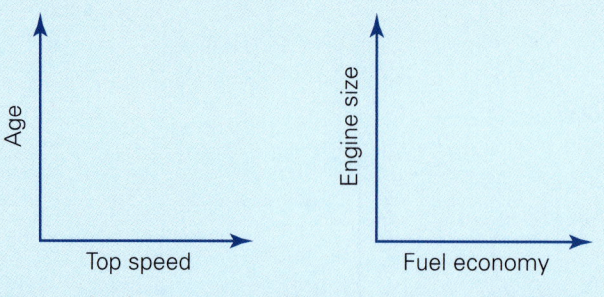

7 Draw cylinders corresponding to points *A*, *B* and *C*.

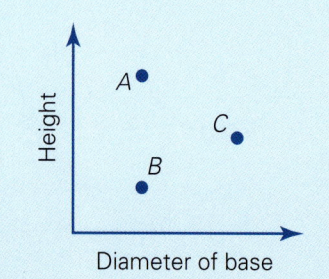

8 At a school basketball game, Nila scored the most baskets. Who had the next highest score?

Sam Bob Ann Nila

Level 3

9 Claude made four telephone calls one evening, as shown on the scattergraph. Decide which calls fit each category, and explain your reasons:

a International calls
b Local calls
c Long distance within Australia.

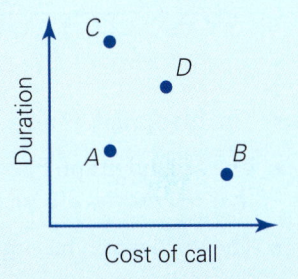

10 These four shapes each have an area of 36 square units.

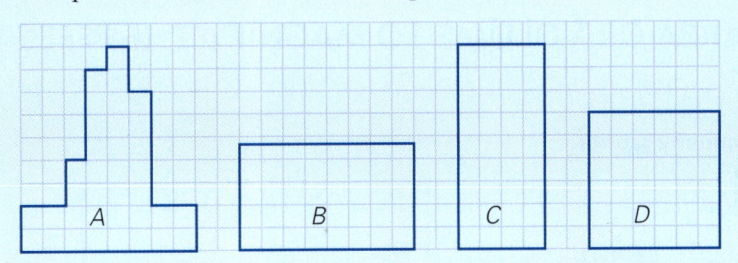

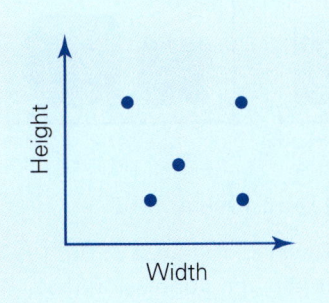

a Label four of the points on the scattergraph with the letters A, B, C and D corresponding to the four shapes.
b Can a fifth shape corresponding to the other point on the graph be drawn with an area of 36 square units? Explain.
c What shape would be produced by the dots if a scattergraph were drawn showing *all* rectangles with an area of 36 square units?

6.4 Misuse of graphs

Graphs are drawn to give a visual impressions of data. However, the impression can be misleading if the graphs are drawn in certain ways.

SCALES MISSING, IRREGULAR OR NOT STARTED AT ZERO

For example these graphs show the monthly company profits of 'Out of nowhere solutions'.

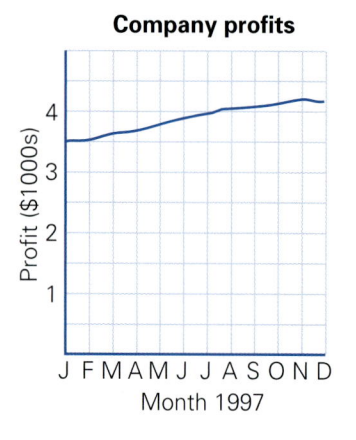

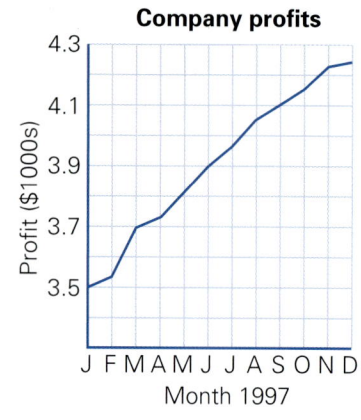

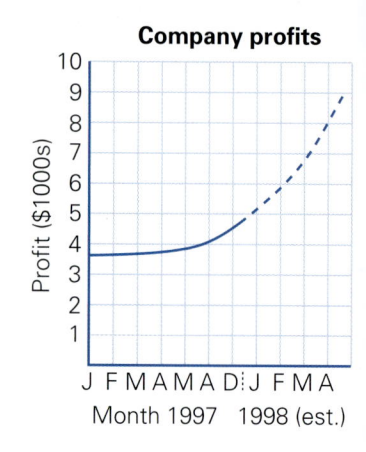

- The first graph is an accurate representation of the data.

- The second graph has a vertical scale that does not start at zero, so gives an impression that the profits are increasing at a greater rate than they really are.

- The third graph has an irregular horizontal scale that distorts the line, and this distortion has then been used as a basis for a prediction of the next year's profits.

USING AREA OR VOLUME TO MAGNIFY THE EFFECT OF HEIGHT

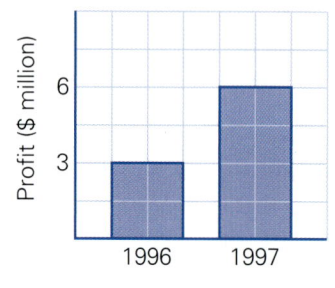

- The first graph accurately shows that profits have doubled from 1996 to 1997.

- The second graph shows a $20 note that doubles in size. However, the **area** of the 1997 note is *four times the area* of the one for 1996, so the reader gets the impression that profits have multiplied by four.

- The third graph shows a money box that is twice as tall. However, since the impression is of a 3-dimensional shape, the 1997 box will be twice as *tall*, twice as *wide* and twice as *deep* as the one for 1996. In other words, the **volume** of the 1997 box is *eight times the volume* of the 1996 box, so the reader gets the impression that profits have multiplied by eight.

1 For each of the following graphs, comment on why they are misleading, and where possible draw an alternative that gives a more accurate picture.

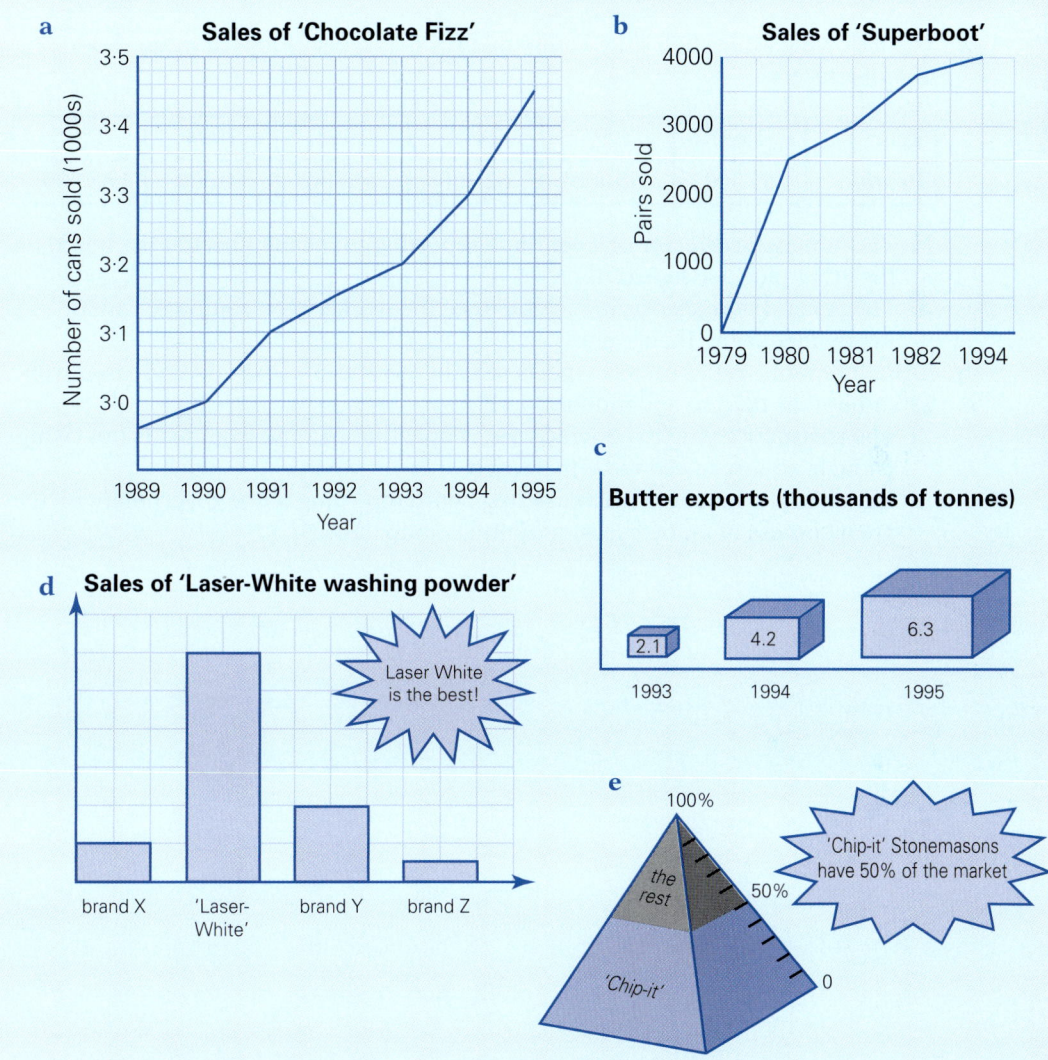

a **Sales of 'Chocolate Fizz'**

b **Sales of 'Superboot'**

c **Butter exports (thousands of tonnes)**

d **Sales of 'Laser-White washing powder'**

Laser White is the best!

e 'Chip-it' Stonemasons have 50% of the market

Investigation Research

Collect any examples of misleading graphs you can find, perhaps from newspapers and magazines. Stick them into your book, comment on why they are misleading, and draw an alternative graph for each that accurately represents the data.

Investigation Misleading graphs

1 Draw a graph to support each position stated below. Any misrepresentation techniques may be used.

a The following table shows the company profits for 'Feet First' running shoe manufacturers.

Year	1990	1991	1992	1993	1994	1995
Profit	63 500	65 000	62 000	66 500	60 000	68 500

   i The managing director of 'Feet First' reporting to the members of the board on the great increase in profits.

   ii The general manager trying to convince the workers the company cannot justify increasing their wages.

b A small republic relies on tea exports to gain income. Tea exports increased from $20 million in 1975 to $30 million in 1995.

   i The treasurer trying to convince the people that income from tea is not rising enough, so taxes need to be increased.

   ii The chairperson of the tea marketing board reporting to the government on the great success of an overseas marketing campaign.

Chapter Review

Language Links

axis	graph	misrepresent	sketch
column	horizontal	quantity	step graph
continuous	irregular	point	title
data	label	scale	vertical
discrete	line	scattergraph	

1 Select the word from the list that matches each definition:

    a A type of graph most suitable for non-numeric or discrete data.
    b A graph that is a series of horizontal line segments.
    c The axis that is parallel to the longer side of the page.
    d A graph consisting of a series of points each representing a separate person, place or object.
    e Every graph needs one to state what the graph is about.
    f Describes a graph drawn roughly, with no scales on the axes.

2 Rearrange these anagrams to produce words from the list:

    a laces   **b** neil   **c** a ruler rig   **d** reprint seems

Chapter Review Exercises

1 Select the graph that represents the depth of water in this container as it is filled from a tap.

6.1

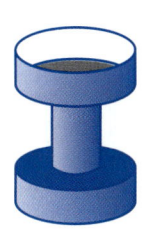 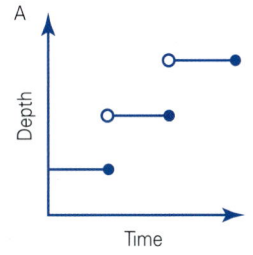 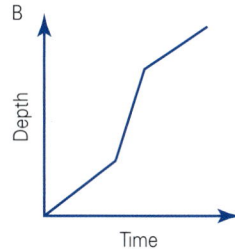 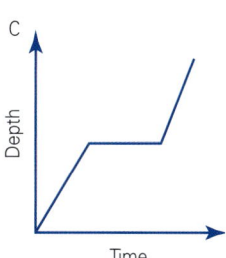

2 **a** Draw a graph to show the speed of the big dipper following this track. Put time on the horizontal axis and speed on the vertical axis. Label points R to X on your graph.

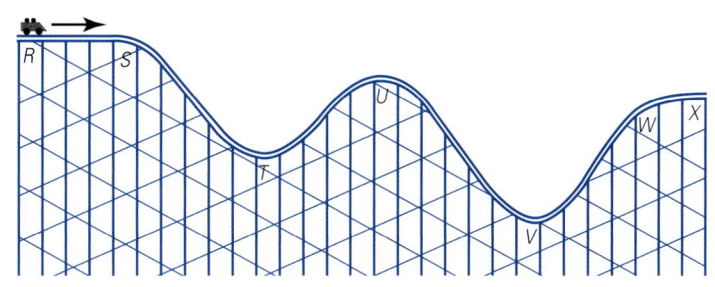

    b Describe the relationship between the shape of the graph and the shape of the track.

3 This graph shows the cost of taking a vehicle on the car ferry from Melbourne to Launceston (one way).

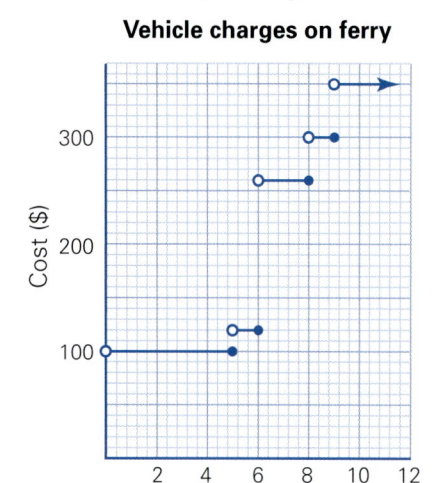

Vehicle charges on ferry

Cost ($) vs Vehicle length (m)

a How much does it cost to take a car that is 4·1 m long?
b Anthony and Nicky's car is 3·5 m long, and it is towing a 3·9 m caravan. How much will they have to pay if the car and caravan together are considered as a single vehicle?
c What is the maximum length of vehicle that can be transported for $300?
d What is the difference in *length* between a 5·9 m vehicle and a 6·1 m vehicle?
e What would be the difference in *price* of transporting the two vehicles in part **d**?

4 A cup of tea is left to cool, and the temperature is taken every 2 minutes.

Time (min)	0	2	4	6	8	10	12
Temperature °C	88	82	78	75	72	70	68

a Draw a graph to show this information.
b After how long is the tea at 76°C?
c Estimate the time it would take for the tea to reach a temperature of 65°C?

5 Which tree is represented by each dot on this scattergraph?

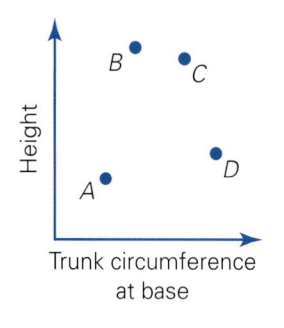

Height vs Trunk circumference at base

bluegum   she-oak   poplar   fig

6 Draw this scattergraph into your book, and mark on points for shapes *A*, *B*, *C* and *D*.

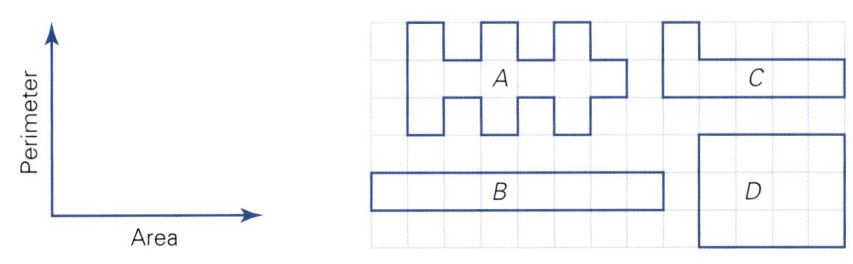

7 Comment on *two* features of this graph that could mislead readers.

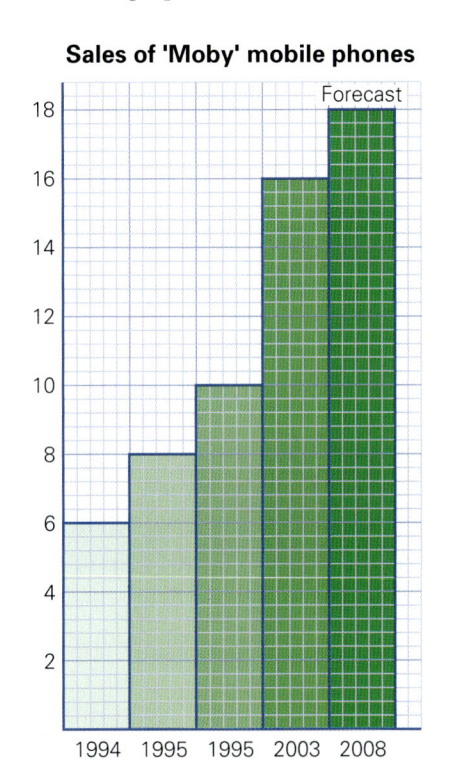

Keeping Mathematically Fit

Part A—Non-calculator

1 Each day Amanda goes to work in a jacket, a blouse and a skirt. She owns 2 jackets, 5 blouses and 3 shirts. How many different outfit combinations can she choose from?

2 A travel company advertises 2 package tours to a resort:

   a   5 nights' accommodation plus return airfare: $1400
   b   7 nights' accommodation plus return airfare: $1700.
   What is the cost of the return airfare?

3 Which decimal is closest to 4·36?

   A   4·364   B   4·354   C   4·4   D   4·37

4 Write the sum of $\frac{4}{1000}$ and $\frac{2}{10}$ as a decimal.

5 Find the cost of a $40 cycle helmet bought in a store offering 20% discount off all items.

6 A craft project needs 6 pieces of wood each 300 mm long and 5 pieces each 400 mm long. If the wood comes in 1 m lengths, what is the minimum number of lengths that must be bought?

7 Evaluate $0·3 \times 0·2$.

8 Michael's friends are arriving for dinner at 7:30 pm. He knows that the main dish takes 75 minutes to cook and needs to stand for 10 minutes before serving. If he wants to serve dinner 15 minutes after his friends arrive, at what time should he put the dish in the oven?

9 Ann aged 6, Bettina aged 9, and Soureya aged 10 share $200 in the ratio of their ages. How much does each child receive?

10 Find the area of the smallest circle that can surround a 6 cm square.

Part B—Calculator

1 This table shows information about Year 9 students:

	Wear glasses	Do not wear glasses
Girls	19	52
Boys	27	48

   a   What percentage of the girls wear glasses?
   b   What percentage of the children are boys?

2 Express $\frac{7}{11}$ as a decimal.

3 The speed limit on freeways is 110 km/h. What is this in metres per second?

4 Shane scored 68% and 75% in his last two tests. What does he need to score in his next test to make his average for the three tests be 76%?

5 In addition crosses, the left-hand number plus the middle number gives the right-hand number, and the top number plus the middle number gives the bottom number. An example is shown below.

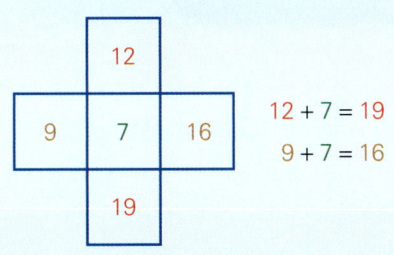

$12 + 7 = 19$

$9 + 7 = 16$

Find the missing numbers in this cross, given that the left-hand number is three times the top number.

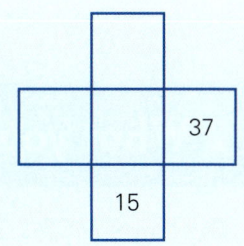

1 What you need to know and revise

Outcome MS4.1
Uses formulas and Pythagoras' theorem in calculating perimeter and area of circles and figures composed of rectangles and triangles:

- using Pythagoras' theorem to find the length of sides in right-angled triangles.

2 What you will learn in this chapter

Outcome MS5.1.2
Applies trigonometry to solve problems (diagrams given) including those involving angles of elevation and depression:

- identifying the hypotenuse, adjacent and opposite sides for a given angle in a right-angled triangle
- recognising that the ratio of matching sides in similar right-angled triangles is constant for equal angles
- defining the sine, cosine and tangent ratios for angles in right-angled triangles
- using trigonometric notation, e.g. sin A
- using a calculator to find trigonometric ratios of a given angle measured in degrees
- using a calculator to find an angle to the nearest degree given the trigonometric ratio of the angle
- selecting and using appropriate trigonometric ratios in right-angled triangles to find unknown sides
- selecting and using appropriate trigonometric ratios in right-angled triangles to find unknown angles to the nearest degree
- identifying angles of elevation and depression
- solving problems involving angles of elevation and depression when given a diagram.

Outcome MS5.2.3
Applies trigonometry to solve problems including those involving bearings:

- using a calculator to find trigonometric ratios of a given angle measured in degrees and minutes
- using a calculator to find an angle in degrees and minutes given the trigonometric ratio of the angle
- finding unknown sides in right-angled triangles where the given angle is in degrees and minutes
- using trigonometric ratios to find angles measured in degrees and minutes in right-angled triangles
- using three-figure and compass bearings, e.g. 035°, 225°, SSW
- drawing diagrams and using them to solve word problems which include bearings or angles of elevation or depression.

Working Mathematically outcomes WMS 5.1, 5.2, 5.3
Students will be required to *question*, *apply strategies*, *communicate*, *reason* and *reflect* in the sections of this chapter.

Trigonometry

Key mathematical terms you will encounter

adjacent	depression	opposite	theorem
altitude	dimension	Pythagoras	triad
bearing	elevation	ratio	triangle
compass	height	right	trigonometry
complementary	horizontal	similar	vertical
cosine	hypotenuse	sine	
degree	observer	tangent	

MathsCheck
Pythagoras' theorem

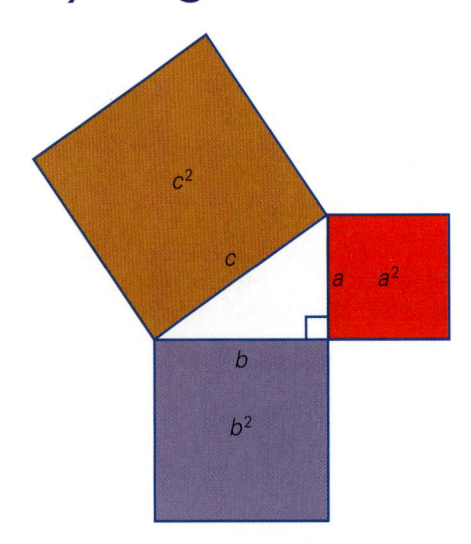

In every right triangle, the square of the **hypotenuse** (longest side) is equal to the sum of the squares on the other two sides.

A **Pythagorean triad** is any set of three whole numbers that fit the pattern $a^2 + b^2 = c^2$.

Common triads are 3, 4, 5; 7, 24, 25; 9, 40, 41; 5, 12, 13; 8, 15, 17; 11, 60, 61 and multiples of these: 6, 8, 10, and so on.

Any triangle whose sides fit the pattern $c^2 = a^2 + b^2$ must be right-angled and the right angle will be located opposite side c (the longest side).

1 First identify the hypotenuse, then use Pythagoras' theorem to write a relationship between the sides of the following triangles:

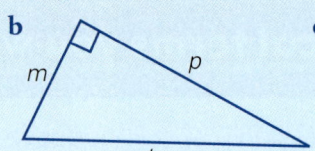

2 Find x in each of the following, giving answers to 2 decimal places where necessary:

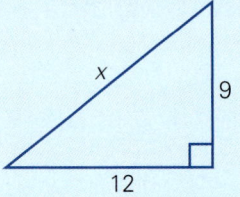

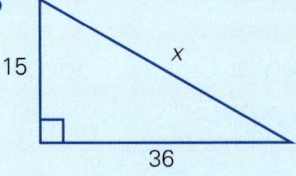

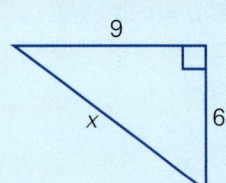

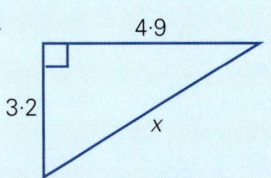

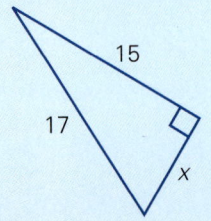

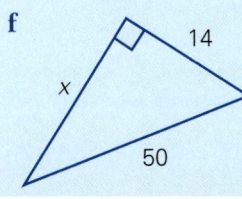

Careful—is x the hypotenuse?

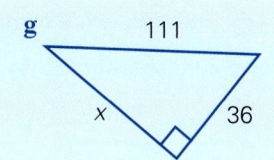

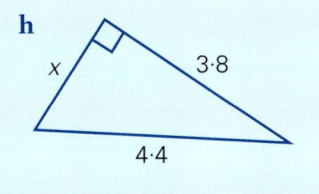

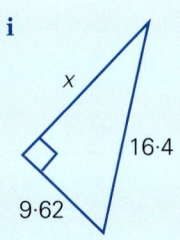

3 Use calculation to test whether the following are right triangles:

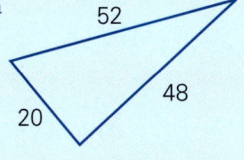

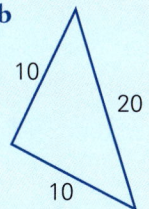

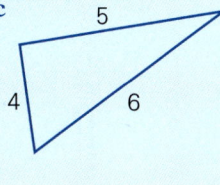

4 Test to see if the following are Pythagorean triads:

   a 6, 8, 10   **b** 12, 35, 37   **c** 9, 27, 28   **d** 8, 12, 16

5 The hypotenuse of a right triangle is 28 m long and its shortest side measures 7·5 m. Find the length of the third side to the nearest centimetre.

6 a   **b**   **c**

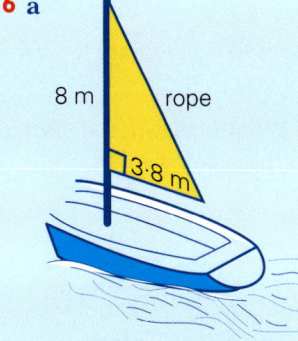

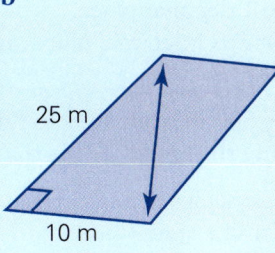

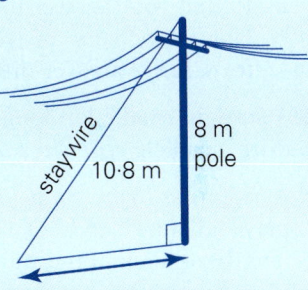

Sail rope length?   Length of pool diagonal?   How far?
(2 decimal places)   (1 decimal place)   (1 decimal place)

7 Could a right triangle be constructed with the measurements 5·5 cm, 30 cm, 30·5 cm? Explain.

8 In $\triangle MPQ$, $MP = 10$, $PQ = 24$, $QM = 26$. Show that $\triangle MPQ$ is a right triangle. Identify the right angle, giving a reason for your choice.

9 A rectangular gate measuring 1·5 m wide and 1·8 m high needs a piece of timber placed diagonally to brace against warping. How long should the timber be cut, to the nearest millimetre?

10 A catamaran sails 2 km north, then tacks 1·8 km west. How far is it from the starting point?

11 Calculate x, then y in the following, leaving answers to part **a**, **b** and **c** in exact form.

Exact form means you leave your answer as a surd, i.e. with a $\sqrt{}$ sign.

a
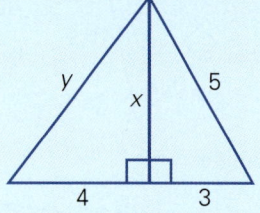

b
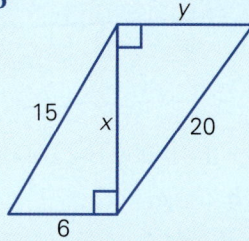

c
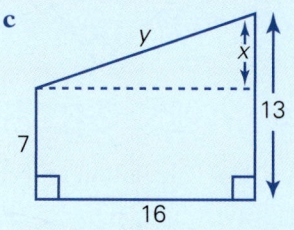

d
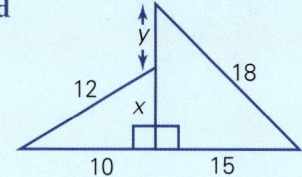

e
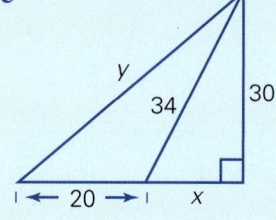

f
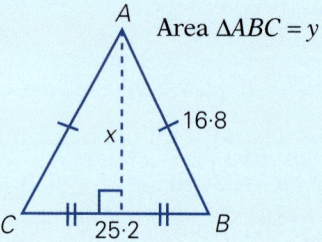

Area $\triangle ABC = y$

12 Consider question **11**, part **b**:

a Round your answer for y to 1 decimal place.

b Now round your answer for x to 1 decimal place and use it to recalculate the value for y. Is the answer different?

13 A straight road 8 km long rises 500 m from start to finish. What horizontal distance does a vehicle cover in travelling the length of the road (to the nearest m)?

14 A roof truss in the shape of an isosceles triangle has a perpendicular height of 1·5 m and a span (base length) of 6·3 m. Find the length of its sloping edges.

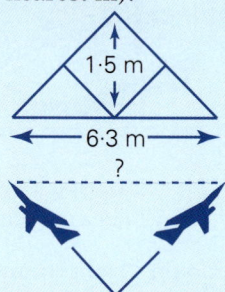

15 Two jets took off from Sydney airport. Jet A moved north-east at 600 km/h, jet B north-west at 500 km/h. How far apart were they after $1\frac{1}{2}$ hours, to the nearest 100 m?

16 A rectangular prism box measures 6 cm wide, 20 cm long and 5 cm high. Find the length of the longest pencil that can fit into the box, to the nearest millimetre.

TEACHER

Exploring New Ideas

7.1 Naming sides of right triangles

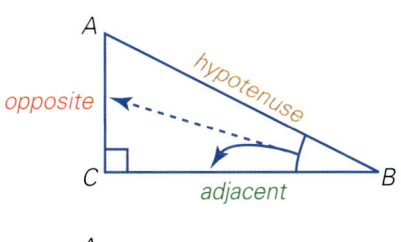

The longest side is called the **hypotenuse**. It is opposite the right angle C. The other sides are named in relation to angle A or B.

Judged from $\angle B$, AC is **opposite**, and BC is **adjacent**, or *next to*, the angle.

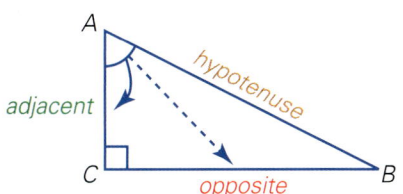

Judged from $\angle A$, BC is *opposite*, and AC is *adjacent*. Note that for a side to be *adjacent* to a given angle, it forms part of the angle. To be *opposite*, it cannot be a side of the angle.

ANGLE MEASUREMENT

Previously we have used only degrees for measuring angles but sometimes we need to be more accurate. Degrees can be divided into tenths, hundredths, etc., as in our decimal number system. However, they are more usually divided into minutes and seconds, as in our time measurement system. Why do you think that is?

$$1 \text{ degree} = 60 \text{ minutes—60'}$$
$$1 \text{ minute} = 60 \text{ seconds—60''}$$

So an angle of 14 degrees, 27 minutes and 43 seconds is written as 14°27'43''. Angles in this form may be entered into your calculator using the $\boxed{\circ \,'\,''}$ key. Refer to your calculator manual if necessary.

To round off angles written in this way, remember that the half-way point between one degree and the next is 30 minutes. So, if the minutes are 30 or more, round *up* to the next degree. The same applies to rounding seconds.

EXAMPLE 1
Round 27°41' to the nearest degree.

Solution

27°41' is 28° to the nearest degree.

EXAMPLE 2
Round 1°52'29'' to the nearest degree.

Solution

1°52'29'' is 1°52' to the nearest minute.

EXERCISE 7A

1 Refer to the marked angle to name **i** opposite side, **ii** adjacent side, **iii** hypotenuse, in the following:

a 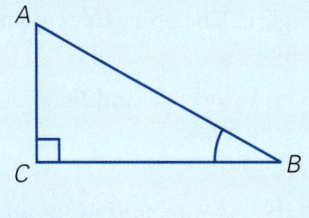 **b** 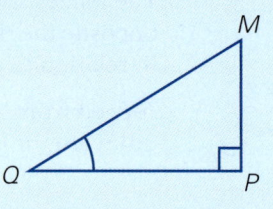 **c**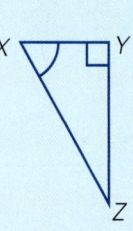

d 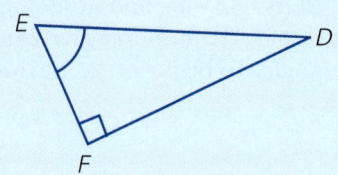 **e**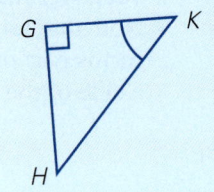

f ∠BAD
g ∠BCD
h ∠BDC

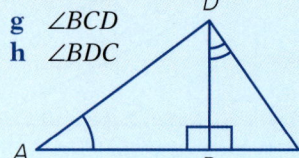

2 a Judged from ∠T, name
   i the opposite side
   ii the adjacent side.
  b Judged from ∠R, name
   i the opposite side
   ii the adjacent side.

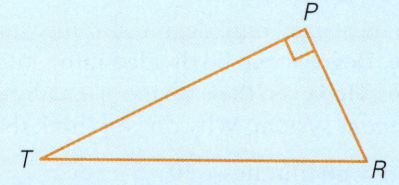

3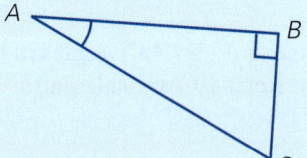

With respect to angle A, name the sides shown in the following ratios:

a $\dfrac{\text{opposite}}{\text{adjacent}}$ **b** $\dfrac{\text{adjacent}}{\text{hypotenuse}}$ **c** $\dfrac{\text{opposite}}{\text{hypotenuse}}$

4 Rewrite each ratio using the words 'opposite', 'adjacent' or 'hypotenuse'.

a $\dfrac{RS}{RT}$

b $\dfrac{RS}{TS}$

c $\dfrac{TS}{RT}$

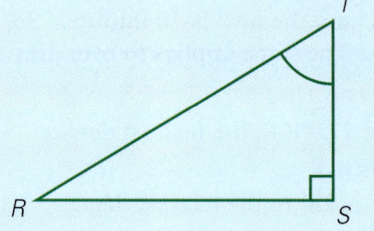

5 Write these angles in degrees, minutes, seconds form:

  a 42·5   **b** 16·4   **c** 243·6   **d** 0·1
  e 3·29   **f** 180·8   **g** $3\frac{1}{4}$ **h** 302·98

6 Write these angles in decimal form correct to 2 decimal places where necessary:

  a 23°30′   **b** 8°6′   **c** 8°0′6″   **d** 90°15′
  e 123°45′   **f** 1°1′1″   **g** 5°16′3″   **h** 241°25′14″

7 Round to the nearest degree:

  a 13°22′   **b** 63°52′   **c** 132°38′   **d** 4°29′
  e 9°30′   **f** 48°42′51″   **g** 3°29′31″   **h** 5°0′35″

8 Round to the nearest minute:

a 7°14′15″   b 93°57′34″   c 136°21′5″   d 2°39′29″
e 305°29′56″   f 19°42′30″   g 3°3′3″   h 253°59′48″

Level 2

9 In the following, calculate the value of

i $\dfrac{\text{opposite}}{\text{adjacent}}$ ii $\dfrac{\text{opposite}}{\text{hypotenuse}}$ iii $\dfrac{\text{adjacent}}{\text{hypotenuse}}$

to 2 decimal places where necessary:

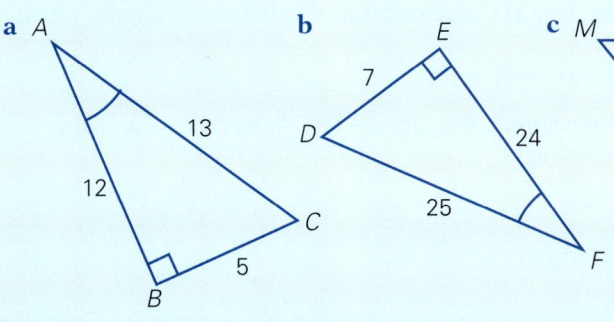

10 Find the complement of each of the following:

a 15°   b 20°40′   c 52°13′   d 39°4′

> **Remember:**
> complementary
> angles add to 90.

Investigation The tangent ratio

1

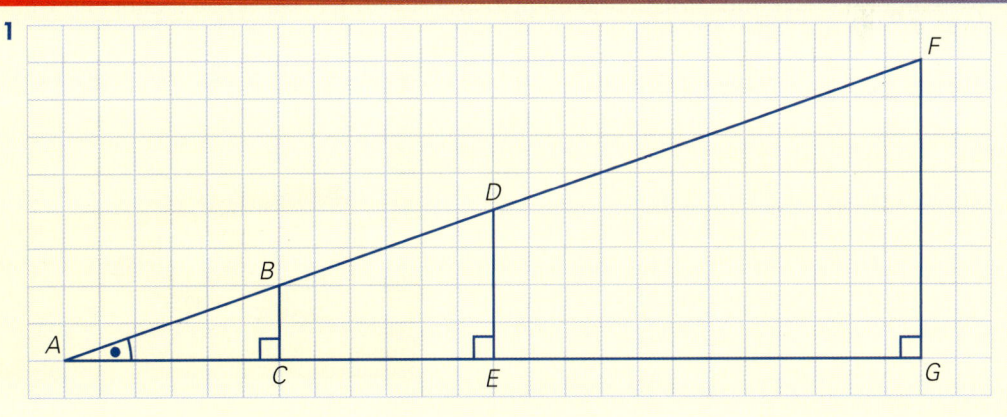

Check the diagram above to answer the following:

a What do the angles of $\triangle ABC$, $\triangle ADE$ and $\triangle AFG$ have in common?

b Measure the lengths of the sides of $\triangle ABC$, $\triangle ADE$ and $\triangle AFG$. What do you notice?

c By counting squares, calculate $\dfrac{\text{opposite}}{\text{adjacent}}$ (height : base) ratio with respect to $\angle A$ for each triangle. Are the ratios equal?

2

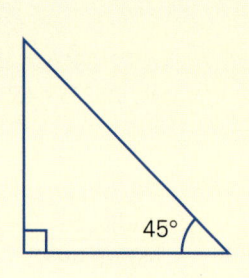 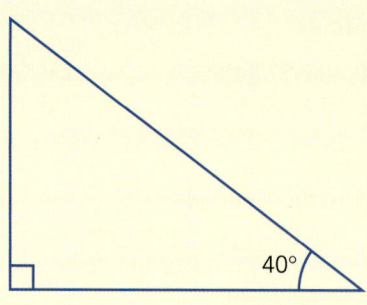 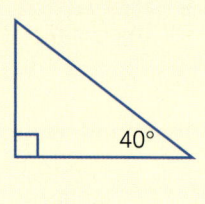

    a Compare by measuring the height : base ratios of these three triangles. Calculate to 2 decimal places.

    b What do you notice about the three ratios?

3 True or false? For any particular angle, the ratio $\dfrac{\text{opposite}}{\text{adjacent}}$ has the same value whatever the size of the right triangle.

7.2 Calculating tangents

For every acute angle in a right triangle, there is a particular value for its $\dfrac{\text{opposite}}{\text{adjacent}}$ ratio that always stays the same (constant).

This ratio is called the tangent ratio: $\tan = \dfrac{\text{opposite}}{\text{adjacent}}$.

For example, $\tan 30°$ means the tangent ratio for a $30°$ angle.

Note: it is essential that your calculator is in the degrees mode for all trigonometry calculations. Check your instruction manual or ask your teacher if you do not know how to do this.

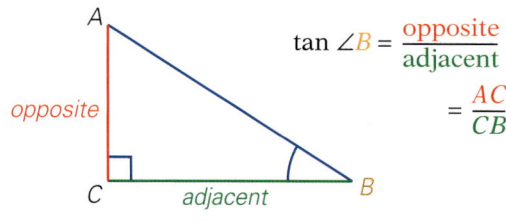

$$\tan \angle B = \frac{\text{opposite}}{\text{adjacent}}$$
$$= \frac{AC}{CB}$$

EXAMPLE
Find $\tan A$ to 3 decimal places.

Solution

$$\tan A = \frac{\text{opposite}}{\text{adjacent}}$$
$$= \frac{5}{12}$$
$$= 0{\cdot}417 \text{ (3 dec. pl.)}$$

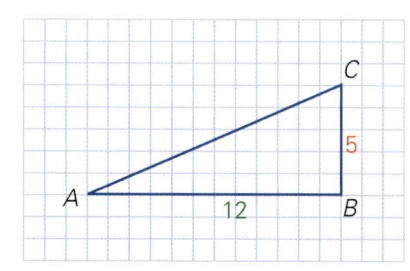

EXERCISE 7B

1 Follow the pattern $\dfrac{\text{opposite}}{\text{adjacent}}$ to name the tangent ratio sides for each of the angles shown:

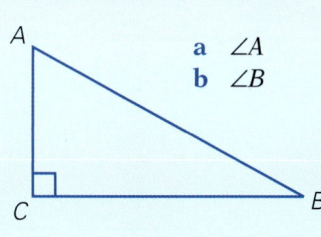

a ∠A
b ∠B

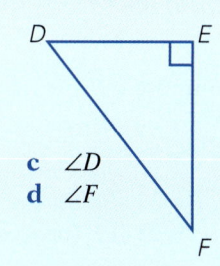

c ∠D
d ∠F

e ∠H
f ∠K
g ∠KGJ

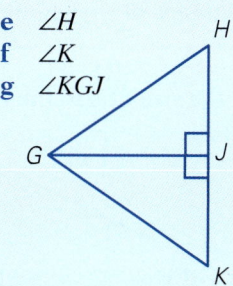

2 For each of the following, write an equation like $\tan 20° = \dfrac{AB}{BC}$ for the angle indicated:

a 30°
b 60°

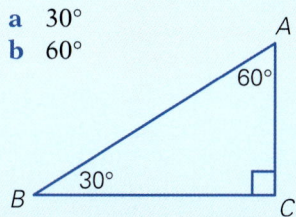

c 45°
d 58°

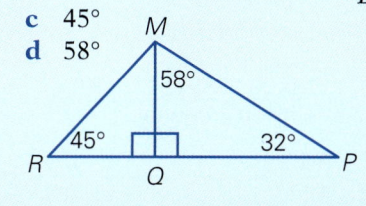

e 40°
f 27°
g $x°$

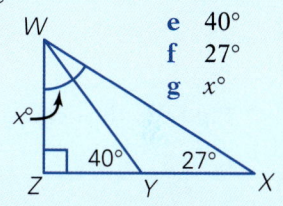

3 Calculate the tangent ratio of the marked angles, rounding to 4 decimal places as necessary:

a

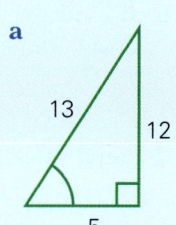

b

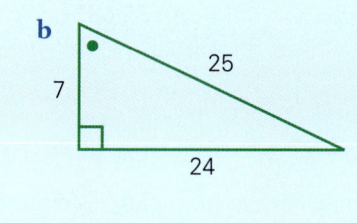

c

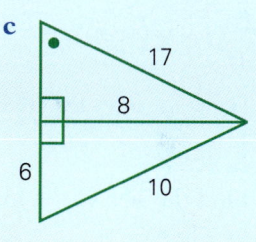

4 Use a calculator to evaluate the tangent (to 4 decimal places) of:

a 4°   **b** 8°   **c** 16°   **d** 32°   **e** 64°
f 80°   **g** 89°   **h** 0°   **i** 90°   **j** 45°
k 10°   **l** 20°   **m** 30°   **n** 40°   **o** 50°

Level 2

5 *Estimate*, to 1 decimal place, the tangent ratio of the following (use your answers to question **4** as a guide):

a 44°   **b** 48°   **c** 2°   **d** 75°   **e** 30°

6 Find, with a calculator, to 4 decimal places:

a tan 45°30′   **b** tan 73°15′   **c** tan 16°45′   **d** tan 61°2′
e tan 8°12′   **f** tan 27°40′   **g** tan 50°50′   **h** tan 34°17′

7 **a** Choose any angle (x). Find the tangent, then double your answer ($2 \tan x$).
   b For the same angle, first double then find the tangent ($\tan 2x$).
   c Are your results for parts **a** and **b** the same?

7.3 Calculating angle sizes

If we know the tangent ratio for an angle, we can determine the size of the angle. If $\tan B = \frac{3}{4}$, to find the size of the angle B use the inverse or 2nd function key before the Tan key: 36·869 89 …, which is 36° 52' to the nearest minute.

EXAMPLE
Find the size of θ to the nearest minute.

Solution

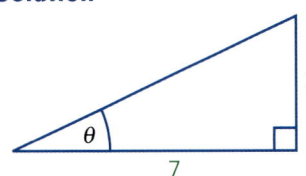

$\tan \theta = \frac{3}{7}$

$\theta = 23·198\ 59$

$= 23°\ 12'$ (nearest minute)

23° 11'54·9 rounds *up*.

EXERCISE 7C

1 Find x to the nearest degree if $\tan x$ equals:

a 0·5	**b** 3·2	**c** 0·42	**d** 2·011
e 10	**f** 4	**g** 0·4	**h** 0·04

2 Find the size of angle θ, to the nearest minute, if $\tan \theta$ equals:

a 0·075	**b** 0·528	**c** 4·9	**d** 2·4007
e 1·6	**f** 0·2908	**g** 35·6821	**h** 0·7358

Level 2

3 Solve for θ, to the nearest minute:

a $\tan \theta = 1$	**b** $\tan \theta = 2·7$	**c** $\tan \theta = 8·144$	**d** $\tan \theta = 0·952$

4 Find the size of the marked angles in the following, to the nearest minute where necessary:

a   **b**   **c**

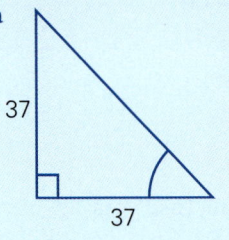
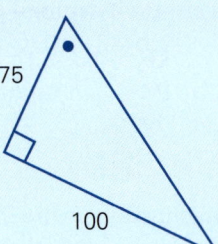

Greek:
α = alpha
β = beta
θ = theta

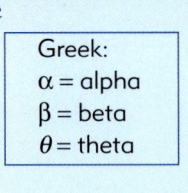

d   **e**   **f**

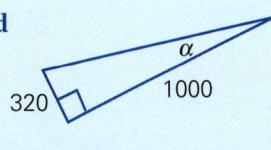
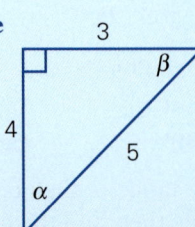
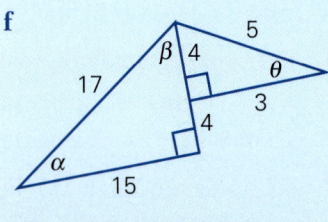

7.4 Finding unknown sides

We can use the tangent ratio to calculate unknown sides of right-angled triangles. Surveyors use this technique to calculate lengths or heights that are not accessible.

EXAMPLE 1

Find MP, to the nearest metre, if $\angle Q$ is $38°$.

Solution

$$\tan 38° = \frac{\text{opp}}{\text{adj}}$$

$$\tan 38° = \frac{x}{80}$$

$$x = \tan 38° \times 80$$
$$x = 62{\cdot}502\,85\ \ldots$$
$$MP = 63 \text{ m (to the nearest m)}$$

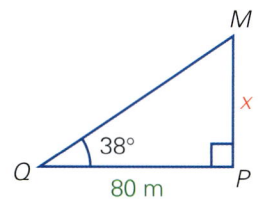

EXAMPLE 2

Find AC, to the nearest kilometre.

Solution

$$\tan 67°23' = \frac{42}{x}$$

$$\tan 67°23' \times x = 42$$

$$x = \frac{42}{\tan 67°23'}$$

$$x = 17{\cdot}4972\ \ldots$$

AC (to the nearest km) $= 17$ km

> Can you see an easier method using A and B as complementary angles?

> Can you see an alternative method using reciprocals?

EXERCISE 7D

1 Find x in the following, correct to 2 decimal places:

a $\dfrac{x}{60} = \tan 16°$

b $\dfrac{x}{6.7} = \tan 39°$

c $\dfrac{x}{15.8} = \tan 52°$

d $\dfrac{50}{\tan 20°} = x$

e $\dfrac{78}{\tan 78°} = x$

f $\dfrac{1{\cdot}42}{\tan 36°} = x$

g $\dfrac{50}{x} = \tan 20°$

h $\dfrac{28}{x} = \tan 11°$

i $\dfrac{18{\cdot}7}{x} = \tan 2°$

j $x = \tan 20°10' \times 50$

k $x = 37 \times \tan 35°7'$

l $x = 16{\cdot}5 \times \tan 3°48'$

m $\dfrac{x}{30} = \tan 45°28'$

n $\dfrac{x}{2{\cdot}8} = \tan 74°20'$

o $\dfrac{x}{0.04} = \tan 62°51'$

p $\dfrac{200}{x} = \tan 4°5'$

q $\dfrac{13{\cdot}7}{x} = \tan 58°30'$

r $\dfrac{0{\cdot}083}{x} = \tan 81°20'$

2 Find x correct to 1 decimal place in the following:

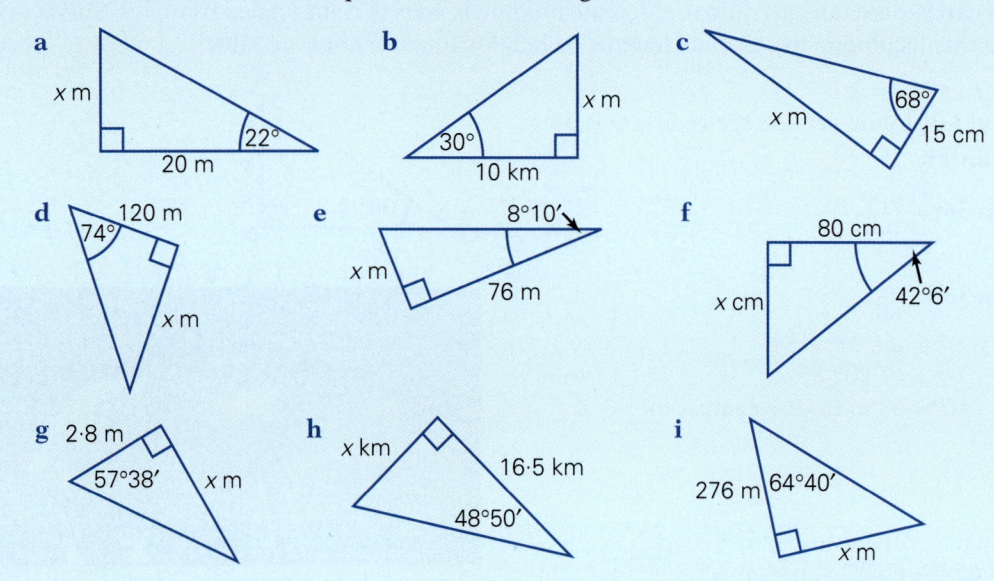

a x m, 20 m, 22°

b x m, 30°, 10 km

c 68°, x m, 15 cm

d 120 m, 74°, x m

e 8°10′, x m, 76 m

f 80 cm, x cm, 42°6′

g 2·8 m, 57°38′, x m

h x km, 16·5 km, 48°50′

i 276 m, 64°40′, x m

Level 2

3 Calculate θ in the following, then find x, using $\tan \theta$ (round to 2 decimal places):

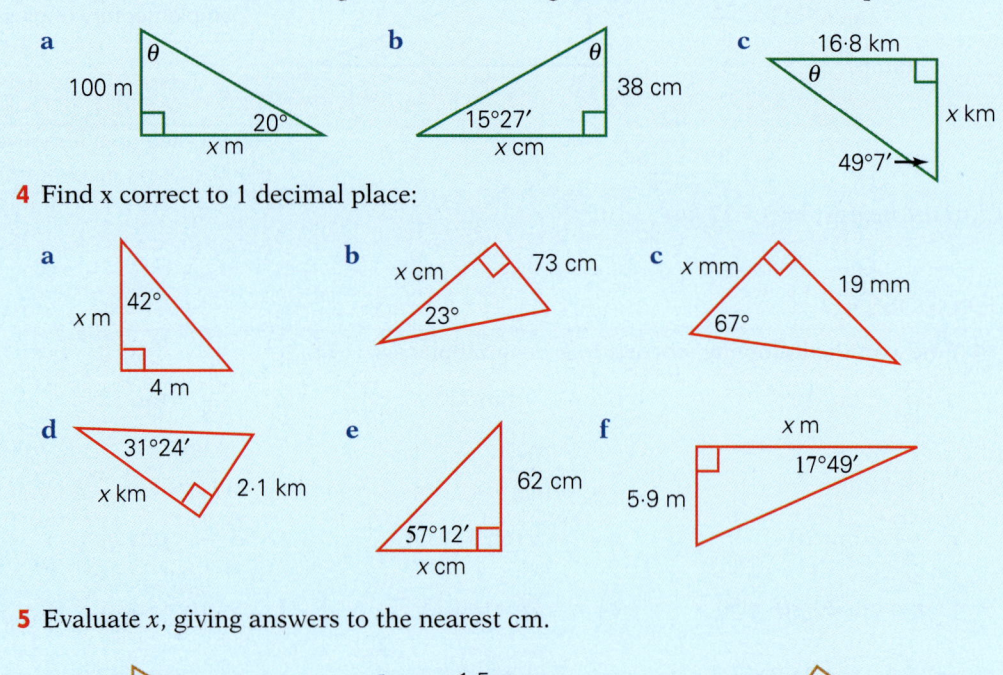

a θ, 100 m, 20°, x m

b θ, 38 cm, 15°27′, x cm

c 16·8 km, θ, x km, 49°7′

4 Find x correct to 1 decimal place:

a x m, 42°, 4 m

b x cm, 73 cm, 23°

c x mm, 19 mm, 67°

d 31°24′, x km, 2·1 km

e 62 cm, 57°12′, x cm

f x m, 17°49′, 5·9 m

5 Evaluate x, giving answers to the nearest cm.

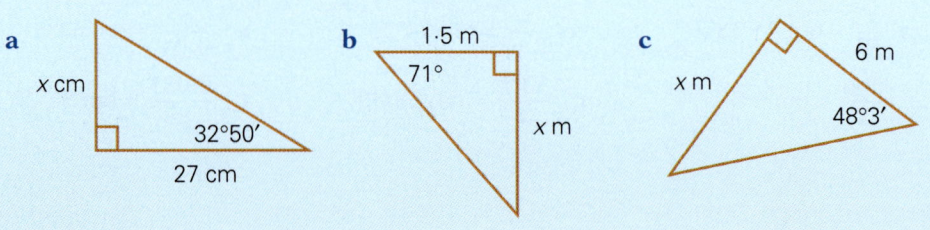

a x cm, 32°50′, 27 cm

b 1·5 m, 71°, x m

c 6 m, x m, 48°3′

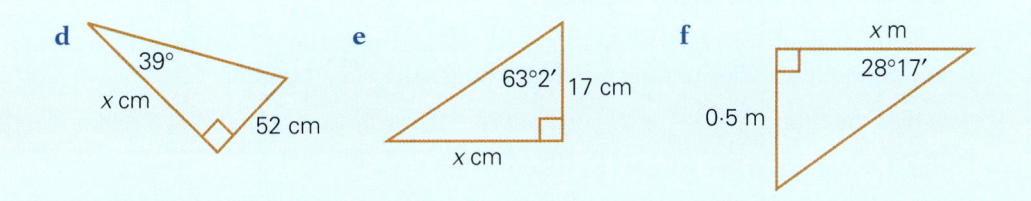

d 39° x cm 52 cm

e 63°2′ 17 cm x cm

f x m 28°17′ 0·5 m

6 Use Pythagoras or tangent ratio to find the named side in the following (round to 2 decimal places):

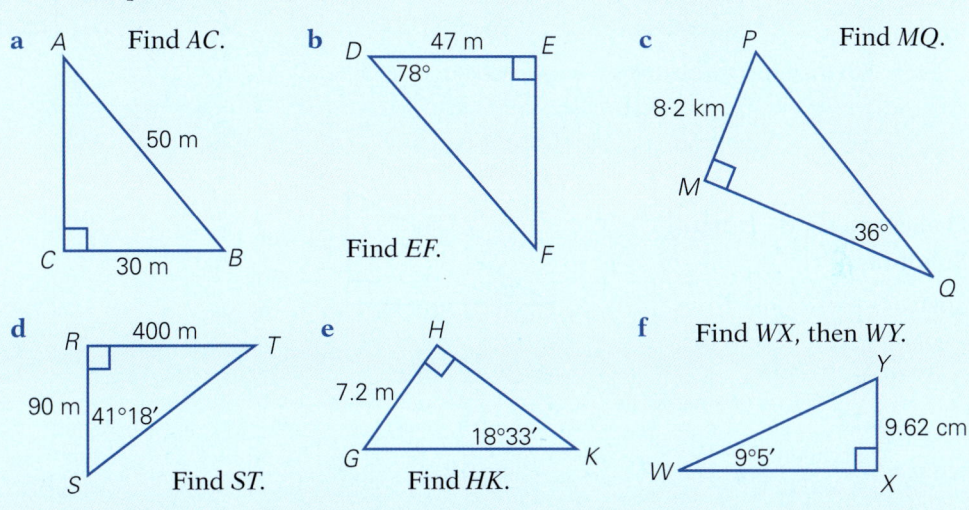

a A — Find AC. 50 m C 30 m B

b D 47 m E 78° Find EF. F

c P — Find MQ. 8·2 km M 36° Q

d R 400 m T 90 m 41°18′ S — Find ST.

e H 7.2 m 18°33′ G K — Find HK.

f Find WX, then WY. Y 9.62 cm W 9°5′ X

Level 3

7

pitch 62° 28 cm (span)

Find the height of this isosceles triangle similar to a roof truss.

8 An isosceles triangle roof truss has a perpendicular height of 2·5 m, and a pitch of 15°. Find the span, to the nearest centimetre.

9 In $\triangle MPQ$, $\angle P = 90°$, $\angle M = 51°$, and $MP = 24$ cm. Find PQ, to the nearest millimetre.

10 In $\triangle ABC$, $\angle A = 6°41′$, $\angle C = 90°$, and $BC = 20·62$ m. Find AC and AB, to the nearest centimetre.

11 A power pole's staywire joins the top to the ground, forming an angle of 62°30′ with the ground, and fixed 3·7 m from the base of the pole. How high is the pole?

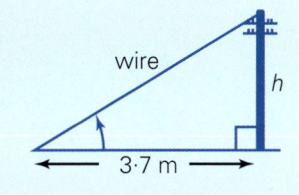

wire h 3·7 m

7.5 Sine and cosine ratios

Earlier in the chapter we established that, because all right triangles containing a certain angle are *similar*, the ratios of their corresponding sides stay the same.

We saw that the ratio $\dfrac{\text{opposite}}{\text{adjacent}}$ was constant for right triangles containing a certain angle.

Two other special ratios are formed as follows:

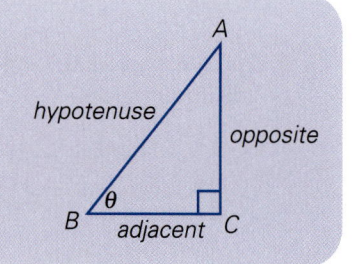

The sine ratio $= \dfrac{\text{opposite}}{\text{hypotenuse}}$, $\sin \theta = \dfrac{AC}{AB}$

The cosine ratio $= \dfrac{\text{adjacent}}{\text{hypotenuse}}$, $\cos \theta = \dfrac{BC}{BA}$

Note that the *hypotenuse* forms the denominator of each ratio.

EXAMPLE
Evaluate: **a** $\sin \alpha$　**b** $\cos \alpha$.

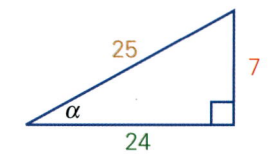

Solution

$\sin \alpha = \dfrac{\text{opposite}}{\text{hypotenuse}}$

$\quad = \dfrac{7}{25}$

$\quad = 0{\cdot}28$

$\cos \alpha = \dfrac{\text{adjacent}}{\text{hypotenuse}}$

$\quad = \dfrac{24}{25}$

$\quad = 0{\cdot}96$

EXERCISE 7E

1 Name **i** the sine ratio sides, **ii** the cosine ratio sides, **iii** the tangent ratio sides, for each of the following marked angles:

a 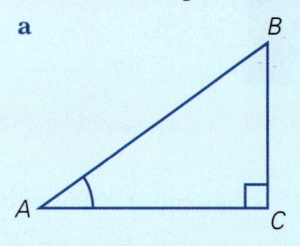　**b** 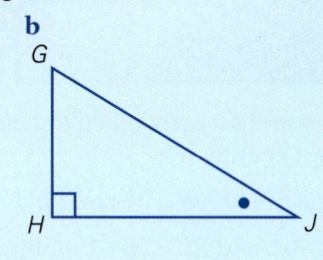　**c**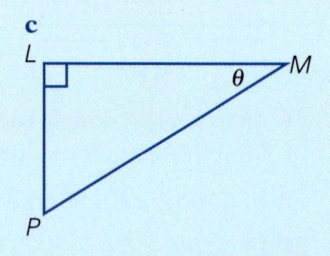

d 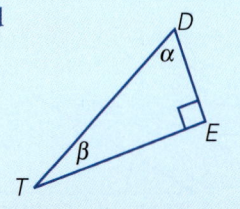　**e** 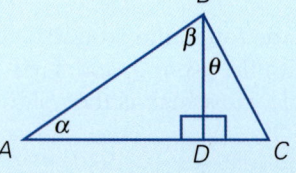　**f**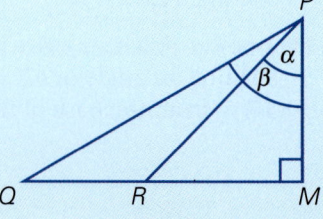

2 Calculate (to 4 decimal places) **i** sin α, **ii** cos α, **iii** tan α in the following:

a 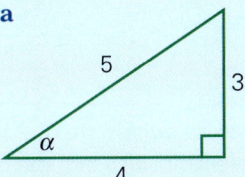 **b** 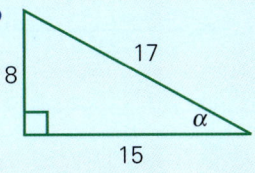 **c**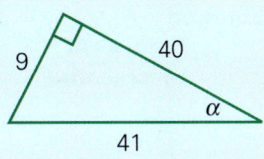

3 Find the value of φ to the nearest minute:

a $\sin \phi = 0\cdot8$ **b** $\sin \phi = 0\cdot88$ **c** $\sin \phi = 0\cdot8888$

d $\cos \phi = 0\cdot5$ **e** $\cos \phi = 0\cdot55$ **f** $\cos \phi = 0\cdot555\ 55$

g $\tan \phi = 0\cdot2$ **h** $\tan \phi = 0\cdot222\ 222\ 22$

4 Find a value for the **i** sin, **ii** cos and **iii** tan ratios for the angles α and β.

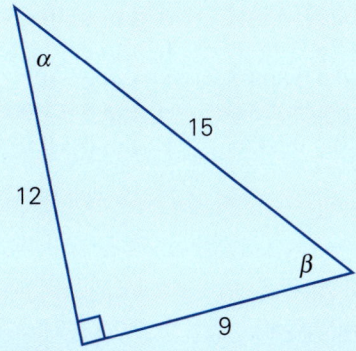

Level 2

5 Using your answer to question **4b** above, explain why:

a $\cos \alpha = \sin \beta$ **b** $\cos \beta = \sin \alpha$ **c** $\tan \alpha = \dfrac{1}{\tan \beta}$

6 Find (to 4 decimal places) the value of **i** sin, **ii** cos and **iii** tan in each of the following:

a 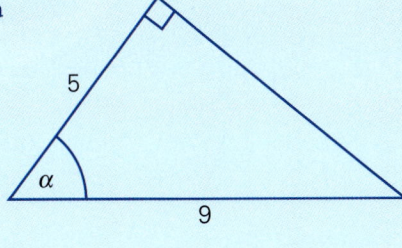 **b**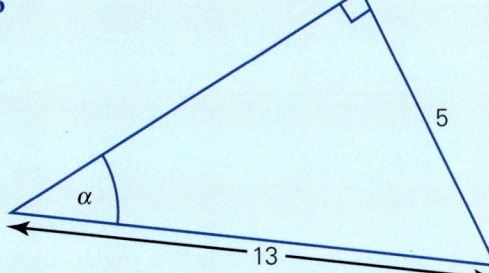

7.6 Calculating angles

If we know the lengths of the two sides of a right-angled triangle, we can calculate the sizes of the other angles.

EXAMPLE

Find θ, to the nearest minute.

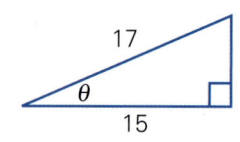

Solution

$\cos \theta = \dfrac{\text{adjacent}}{\text{hypotenuse}}$

$\cos \theta = \dfrac{15}{17}$

$\qquad = 0{\cdot}882\,352\,9$

So $\theta = 28°4'20{\cdot}9$

$\qquad = 28°4'$ (to the nearest minute)

> The three quantities are the adjacent and hypotenuse sides and the angle θ. These are connected by the cosine ratio
> $\cos \theta = \dfrac{\text{adjacent}}{\text{hypotenuse}}$.

EXERCISE 7F

1 Find from a calculator the size of angle θ to the nearest degree, given that:

a $\sin \theta = 0{\cdot}5$	**b** $\sin \theta = 0{\cdot}682$	**c** $\sin \theta = 0{\cdot}454$	**d** $\tan \phi = 0{\cdot}654$
e $\cos \theta = 0{\cdot}225$	**f** $\cos \theta = 0{\cdot}766$	**g** $\cos \theta = 0{\cdot}4848$	**h** $\tan \phi = 1{\cdot}519$
i $\sin \theta = 1{\cdot}0$	**j** $\cos \theta = 0$	**k** $\sin \theta = 0{\cdot}809$	**l** $\tan \phi = 0$
m $\sin \beta = 0{\cdot}3748$	**n** $\cos \beta = 0{\cdot}8749$	**o** $\sin \beta = 0{\cdot}5732$	**p** $\tan \beta = 1{\cdot}000$
q $\cos \beta = 0{\cdot}669$	**r** $\sin \beta = 0{\cdot}8915$	**s** $\cos \beta = 0{\cdot}5426$	**t** $\tan \beta = 0{\cdot}099$

2 Use your calculator to find α to the nearest degree:

a **i** $\sin \alpha = 0{\cdot}9703$ **ii** $\cos \alpha = 0{\cdot}9703$
b **i** $\sin \alpha = 0{\cdot}2756$ **ii** $\cos \alpha = 0{\cdot}2756$
c **i** $\sin \alpha = 0{\cdot}788$ **ii** $\cos \alpha = 0{\cdot}788$

What do you notice about the pairs of angles in parts **a–c**?

3 Find the size of angle θ to the nearest minute in the following:

a 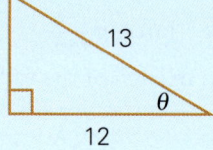 **b** 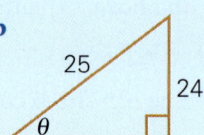 **c**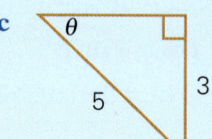

d 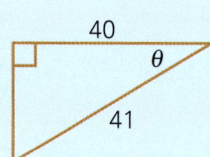 **e** 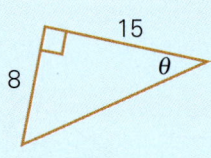 **f**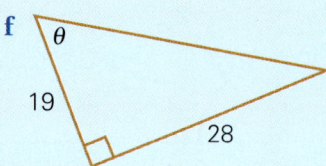

4 Find the size of the marked angles in each of the following:

a **b** 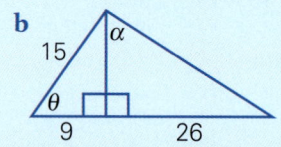 **c** **d**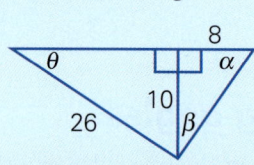

5

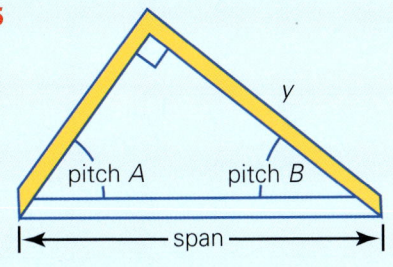

A roof is pitched so that the angle at its peak is 90°. If each roof truss spans 10·5 m and distance y is 7·2 m, find pitch angles A and B.

6

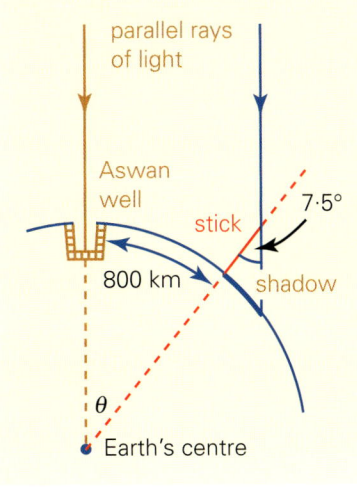

A rock fall has trapped miners at the work face of an existing shaft 1·5 km long, located at a vertical distance of 0·8 km below the entrance.

a At what angle from the vertical must a rescue shaft from the entrance be drilled?

b What will be the length of the rescue shaft?

Investigation Strange but true

1 See if you can find the method Eratosthenes used, based on geometric properties of angles formed by a transversal cutting parallel lines, to calculate the angle at the centre of the earth (θ).

2 Then go on to retrace his steps to find the circumference of the earth.

3 What value did Eratosthenes calculate? Was he far out, by modern measurements?

4 Report on your findings.

Eratosthenes, a Greek who lived around 200 BC, used trigonometric principles to measure the exact size of the earth!

He found that at the city of Aswan, 800 km due south of Alexandria in Egypt, there was a well where the sides cast no shadow at a certain time of day.

This meant that the sun was vertically overhead.

He arranged for a simultaneous measurement of the angle of elevation of the sun at Alexandria, using a shadow stick.

This led to the $7\frac{1}{2}°$ discovery as shown in the diagram.

7.7 Finding unknown sides

If an angle and the length of one side of a triangle are known, the value of other sides can be calculated by using one of sine, cosine or tangent.

EXAMPLE 1
Find: **a** JK **b** KL
correct to 2 decimal places.

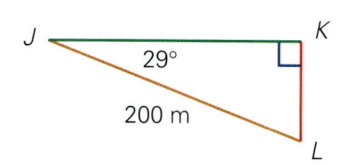

Solution
a $\cos 29° = \dfrac{\text{adjacent}}{\text{hypotenuse}}$

$\qquad = \dfrac{JK}{200}$

$\qquad JK = \cos 29° \times 200$

$\qquad JK = 174\cdot923\,94$

$\qquad JK = 174\cdot92$ m (to 2 decimal places)

> We need to find the side adjacent to the angle. We know the hypotenuse, so use cos!

b $\sin 29° = \dfrac{\text{opposite}}{\text{hypotenuse}}$

$\qquad \sin 29° = \dfrac{KL}{200}$

$\qquad KL = \sin 29° \times 200$

$\qquad KL = 96\cdot961924$

$\qquad KL = 96\cdot96$ m (to 2 decimal places)

or $\quad \tan 29° = \dfrac{KL}{KJ}$

$\qquad \tan 29° = \dfrac{KL}{174.92}$

$\qquad KL = 174\cdot92 \times \tan 29$

$\qquad KL = 96\cdot96$ m (to 2 decimal places)

> How could you have used Pythagoras's theorem?

EXAMPLE 2
Find AB, to the nearest tenth.

Solution
$\cos 34° = \dfrac{\text{adjacent}}{\text{hypotenuse}}$

$\qquad = \dfrac{15}{AB}$

$AB = \dfrac{15}{\cos 34°}$

$AB = 18\cdot093\,269$

$AB = 18\cdot1$ cm (to nearest tenth)

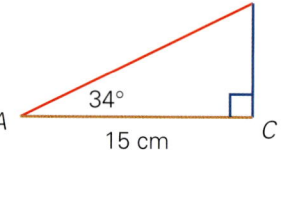

EXAMPLE 3
Sketch a right triangle ABC, given $\sin A = \dfrac{5}{8}$. Then calculate $\cos A$, to 3 decimal places.

Solution

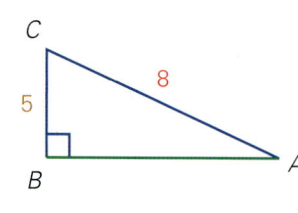

$8^2 = 5^2 + AB^2$

$8^2 - 5^2 = AB^2$

$\quad AB = \sqrt{39}$

$\cos A = \dfrac{\text{adjacent}}{\text{hypotenuse}}$

$\cos A = \dfrac{\sqrt{39}}{8}$

$\qquad = 0\cdot780\,624\,7$

$\qquad = 0\cdot781$ (to 3 decimal places)

> Leave in exact form to retain accuracy.

EXERCISE 7G

1 Find x in the following, correct to 2 decimal places.

a $x = \sin 58° \times 100$ **b** $x = \cos 31° \times 18$ **c** $x = \sin 79° \times 2{\cdot}5$ **d** $\dfrac{x}{50} = \cos 10°$

e $\dfrac{x}{13{\cdot}8} = \sin 2°$ **f** $x = \tan 50 \times 10$ **g** $\dfrac{x}{20} = \tan 29$ **h** $\dfrac{20}{x} = \tan 29$

i $\dfrac{27}{\tan 42} = x$ **j** $\dfrac{20}{\sin 15°} = x$ **k** $\dfrac{6{\cdot}2}{\cos 21°} = x$ **l** $\dfrac{2{\cdot}04}{\sin 82°} = x$

m $\dfrac{30}{x} = \cos 75°$ **n** $\dfrac{48{\cdot}2}{x} = \sin 18°$ **o** $\dfrac{20{\cdot}2}{x} = \cos 84°$ **p** $\dfrac{x}{0{\cdot}05} = \cos 63°$

2 Use the *sine* ratio to find x in each of the following, rounding to 2 decimal places:

a 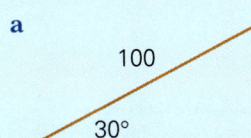   **b** 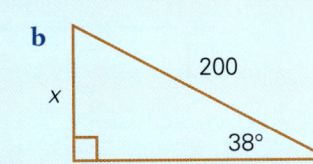   **c**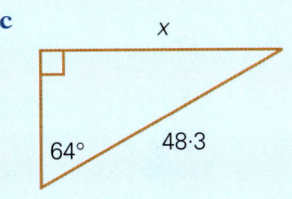

Think complementary angles.

d 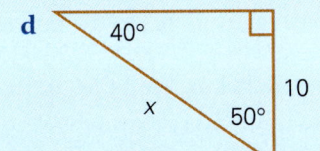   **e** 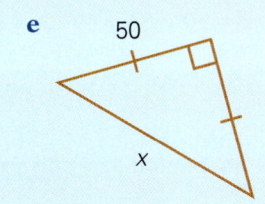   **f**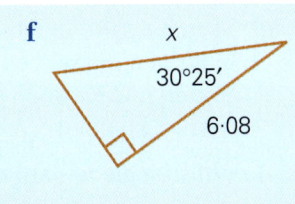

3 Use the *cosine* ratio to find AB in each of the following, to 1 decimal place:

a 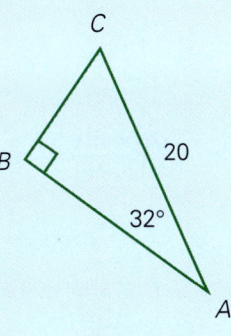   **b** 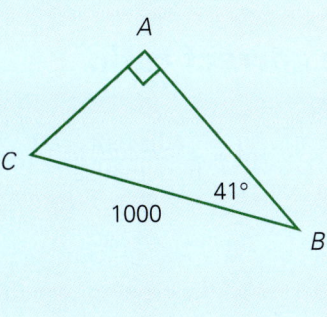   **c**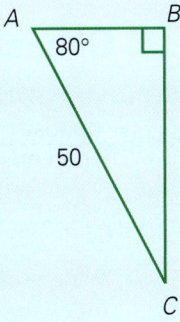

d 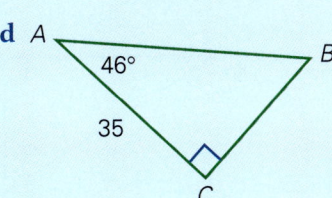   **e** 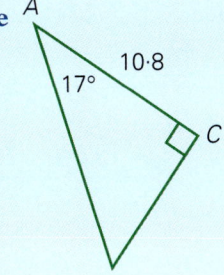   **f**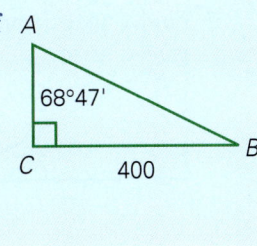

Level 2

4 In the following, all answers involving angle sizes should be rounded to the nearest *minute*:

a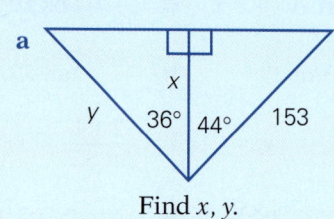

Find x, y.

b Find x.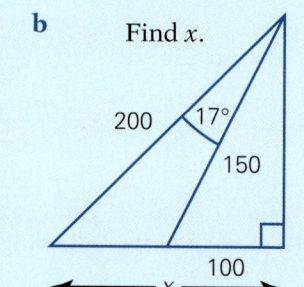

c Find x.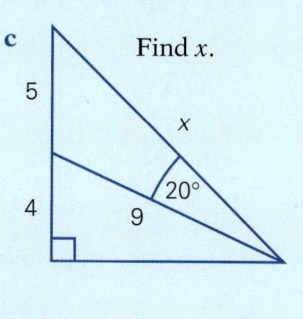

5 Use Pythagoras and/or the sine or cosine ratios for the following:

   a Sketch a right triangle PQR, given that $\sin P = \dfrac{4}{5}$. Then calculate $\cos P$.

   b Sketch a right triangle ABC, given that $\cos C = \dfrac{5}{13}$.
   i Find $\sin C$, to 1 decimal place.
   ii Find angle C.

   c Sketch $\triangle ABC$, in which $\angle B = 90°$, $\angle A = 49°$ and $BC = 10$ m. Find AC, to the nearest tenth of a metre.

   d Sketch $\triangle MPQ$, such that $\angle M = 76°$, $\angle P = 90°$ and $MP = 6\cdot08$ km. Find QM, to the nearest kilometre.

6 A right triangle has $\sin A = 0\cdot28$. Sketch an appropriate triangle AXT, finding:

   a $\cos A$ **b** $\angle A$ **c** the other acute angle

7.8 Choosing the correct ratio

Remember SOH CAH TOA:

$$\sin = \frac{\text{opposite}}{\text{hypotenuse}} \qquad \cos = \frac{\text{adjacent}}{\text{hypotenuse}} \qquad \tan = \frac{\text{opposite}}{\text{adjacent}}$$

EXERCISE 7H

1 **i** Which relationship best suits the given information in order to find x in each of the following?
   ii Find x, to 1 decimal place.

a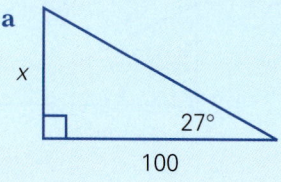

b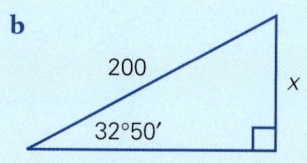

c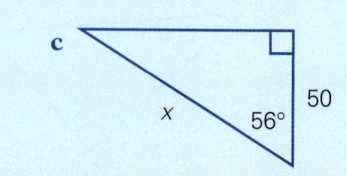

200   **Cambridge Spectrum Maths 9 5.3**

d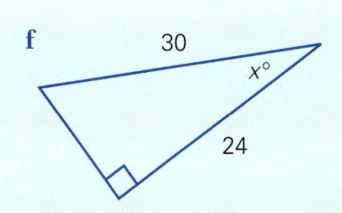

30

15°2′

x

e 9, x, 41

f 30, x°, 24

Level 2

2 An oil and gas pipeline must traverse a downward slope at an angle of depression of 47°. If the point at which it starts the downward slope is 86 m above the base level:

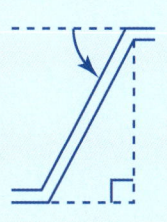

a What length of pipe lies along the slope?
b What is the horizontal distance from the foot of the slope to a point vertically below the start of the slope?

Level 3

3 a

S

12, 8, 10

X, V, T

Find $\angle XST$.

b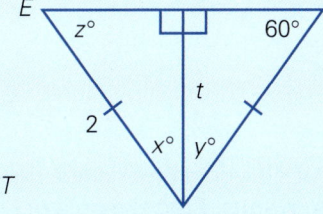

E, F, G

z°, 60°

t

2

x°, y°

H

Find x, y, z, t.
Classify $\triangle EGH$.

c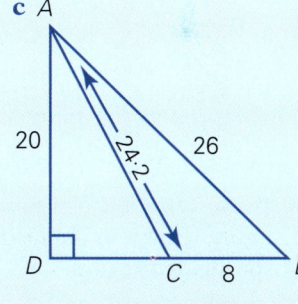

A

20, 24·2, 26

D, C, 8, B

Find $\angle CAB$.

4 a A square field has a diagonal length of 212 m. How long is each side, to the nearest centimetre?
b Describe another method that could be used to solve this question.

5 Rhombus $MPQR$ has diagonals intersecting at X, sides 32 cm in length, and $\angle R = 40°$.

a Find the lengths of the diagonals.
b Find the area.

6 The hypotenuse of a right triangle is three times as long as the shortest side. What is the size of each acute angle of the triangle?

7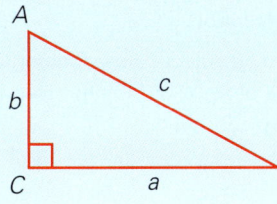

A, b, c, C, a, B

In $\triangle ABC$, show that:

a $a = c \sin A$
b $b = c \cos A$
c $\tan A = \dfrac{\sin A}{\cos A}$
d $\sin^2 A + \cos^2 A = 1$
$[\sin^2 A$ means $(\sin A)^2]$

8 Find:

    a the length of *BD*   **b** ∠*DBC*

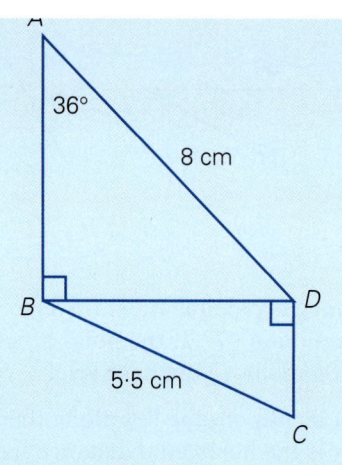

9   Find the length of *BC*.

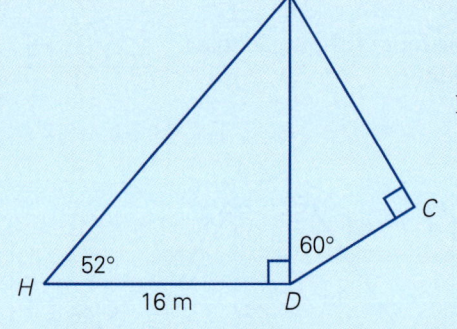

10 If a vertex angle of a square of side 4 cm is trisected, the figure shown in the diagram results. Find the area of the shaded region.

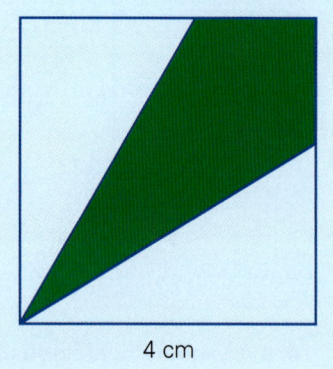

7.9 Angles of elevation and depression

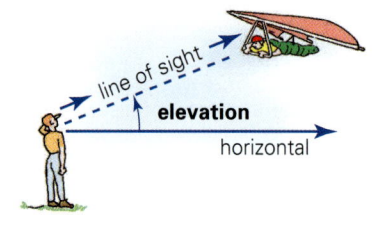

Looking *up* to an object *above*, the angle between the line of sight and the horizontal is an angle of **elevation**.

Looking *down* to an object *below*, the angle between the line of sight and the horizontal is an angle of **depression**.

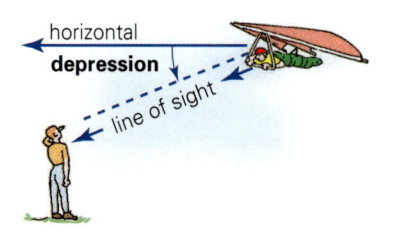

EXAMPLE 1

From the observation room of Centrepoint Tower, height 160 m, the angle of depression of a boat moored at Circular Quay is observed to be 7°. How far from the foot of the tower is the boat?

Solution

$$\tan 7° = \frac{\text{opposite}}{\text{adjacent}}$$

$$\tan 7° = \frac{160}{x}$$

$$x = \frac{160°}{\tan 7°}$$

$$x = 1303 \cdot 095 \ldots$$

Distance = 1303 m

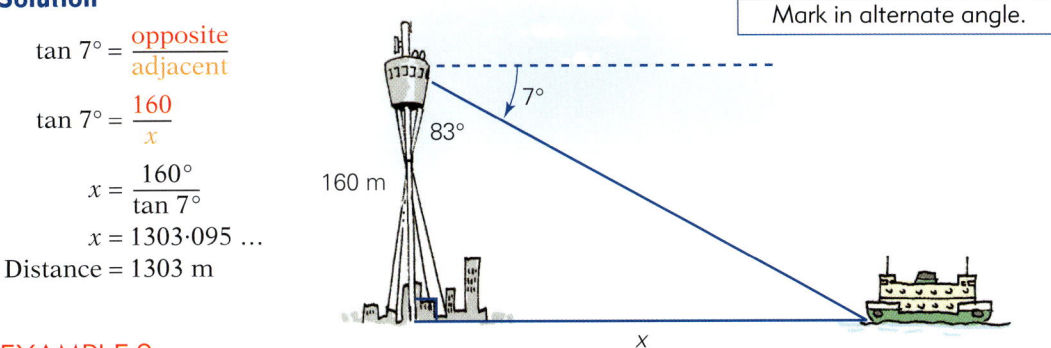

Mark in alternate angle.

EXAMPLE 2

An observer walks 100 m from his home to see a hang-glider at an angle of elevation of 28° directly above the home. What is the glider's altitude?

Solution

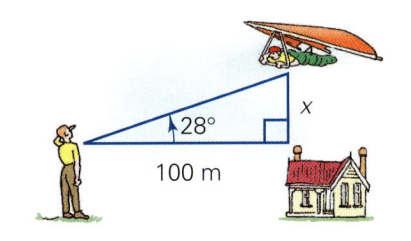

$$\tan 28° = \frac{\text{opposite}}{\text{adjacent}}$$

$$\tan 28° = \frac{x}{100}$$

$$x = \tan 28° \times 100$$

$$x = 53 \cdot 170 \ 194$$

Altitude = 53 m

EXERCISE 7I

1 An observer on top of a 50 m high cliff sights a vessel at sea at an angle of depression of 12°, as shown in the diagram below. How far out to sea is the ship?

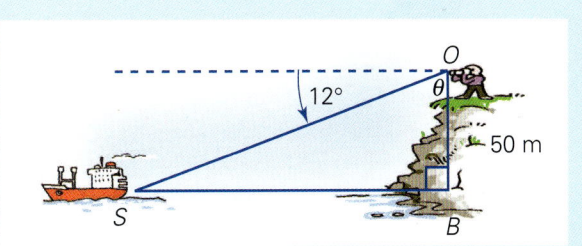

a Copy the diagram.
b Label SB, the distance from ship to shore, as x.
c Use $\tan \theta$ to find x.

2 The angle of elevation of the sun is 26°.

   a Find the shadow length of a tower 48·5 m tall.

   b What is the height of a tower that casts a shadow 142 m long?

Level 2

3

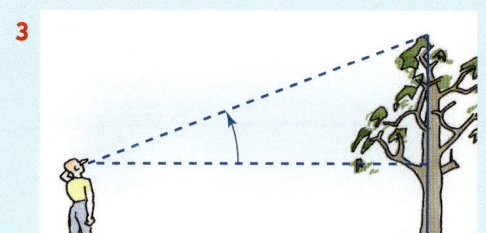

A person stands 15 m from the trunk of a tree and measures the angle of elevation of the top of the tree to be 22°. If the observer's eye-level is 1·6 m, find the height of the tree.

4 A fishing boat detects a school of fish at a depth of 12 m, and at a distance of 0·4 km away.

   a At what angle of depression was the detecting sonar beam, to the nearest minute?

   b At what depth was a school of fish when detected 500 m away at an angle of depression of 2·1°?

5

A forestry worker in a lookout tower sees a fire at an angle of depression of 4°. The tower is sited on a hill, making the observation platform a total of 50 m above the plain of the forest.

   a How far from a point vertically below the tower is the fire?

   b What would be the angle of depression of a fire detected 2 km away, to the nearest minute?

6 A staircase of height 3 m must have an angle of depression of 40°. How far out from the wall will the bottom step finish? (Draw a diagram that shows the staircase as the hypotenuse of a right triangle.)

7 To accommodate the disabled, a ramp to a footbridge 6 m high must be at an angle of elevation of 9°. What is the length of the ramp?

8 The top of a 120 m hill is seen from two positions *A* and *C* in line with, but on opposite sides of, the hill. The angle of elevation from *A* is 21° and from *C* is 37°. How far is *A* from *C*, to the nearest metre?

9 An awning is needed to shade a shop window from 9:00 am onward, when the sun is at an angle of elevation of 42°. For a window height of 2·1 m, will a 2 m wide awning accomplish the task? Support your answer with calculation.

10 Two searchlights spaced 500 m apart both focus on the same point on the underside of a cloudmass. If one is aimed vertically while the other is at an angle of elevation of 63°45′:

  a What is the height of the cloudmass?
  b How long is the beam of the inclined searchlight?

11 From a helicopter hovering 500 m up, the angles of depression of a farmhouse and a rocky outcrop directly in front of it are 34°10′ and 45°21′ respectively. Both objects are in line with a point directly below the helicopter. How far from the farmhouse is the rocky outcrop, to the nearest metre?

12 A missile was launched at an angle of elevation of 32°.

  a How far had it travelled along its straight flight path when it was at an altitude of 3·5 km? Answer to the nearest metre.
  b What horizontal (ground) distance had it come?

13 A hot-air balloon at an altitude of 520 m is sighted by an onlooker at an angle of elevation of 42°24′. Four minutes later, it has drifted in a straight line towards her, at the same altitude, so that now its angle of elevation is 67°10′.

  a How far had it drifted?
  b At what speed must it be travelling?
  c How long before it drifts directly over the onlooker?

You will need: measuring tape, clinometer.

Select a building or other structure (e.g. statue, flagpole) to calculate the height of. You must be able to measure right up to the base of the structure.

1 Choose a position from which you can see the top of your structure, and measure the angle of elevation (θ) from your eye-level. (Hold the clinometer close to your eye.)

2 Measure the distance along the ground (d) from your location to the base of the structure.

3 Calculate the height of the structure. Remember to make an adjustment for the height of your eye-level from the ground.

4 Move to another position and repeat the measurements. Calculate the height using your new measurements.

5 Was there much difference between the two calculated heights? Suggest reasons for any inaccuracies.

7.10 Bearings and navigation

An important application of trigonometry occurs in navigation, with the use of compass bearings.

You have previously used the compass directions of north, south, east and west, and should also know about the directions between these four points, namely NE, SE, SW and NW.

The mariners compass shown here shows 16 directions. The direction between E and SE is known as ESE and so on. The angle between each of the points is 22°30'.

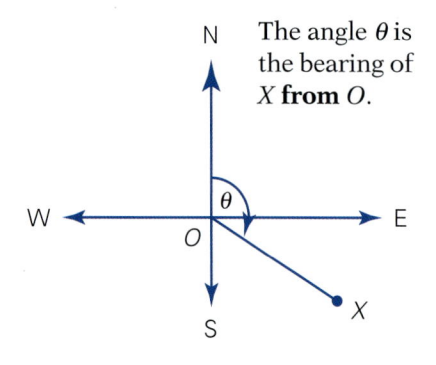

The angle θ is the bearing of X **from** O.

When sailors needed a more accurate way to measure their direction, they adopted the use of compass bearings. The angle of the bearing is measured from the north line in a clockwise direction. These are also known as true bearings, and three digits are always given. A bearing of 23° would be given as 023°.

Early explorers calculated their position and set their course using basic navigational aids and their skills at charting, observing moon and sun, and performing mathematical calculations. Gradually things began to improve, and engravers were able to produce equipment that enabled angles to be read to minutes rather than whole degrees.

EXAMPLE 1

What is the compass bearing of point A from point B?

Solution

Bearing $= 360° - 58°$
$\qquad = 302°$

The bearing of A from B is $302°$.

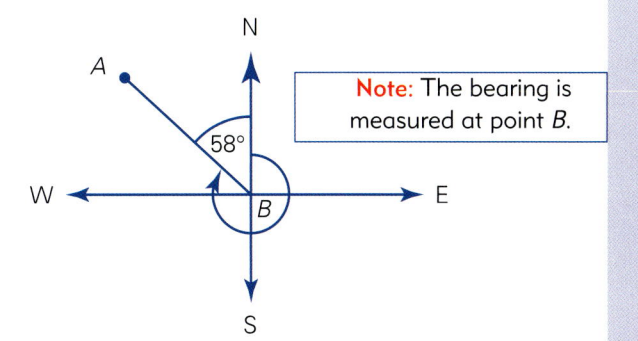

Note: The bearing is measured at point B.

EXAMPLE 2

A ship sails **ESE** from a port. On what bearing has it sailed?

Solution

Bearing $= 90° + 22°30'$
$\qquad = 112°31'$

The ship has sailed on a bearing of $112°30'$.

EXAMPLE 3

An aircraft flies 150 km from Sydney along a bearing of $320°$.

a How far north of Sydney has it flown?
b How far west has it flown?

Solution

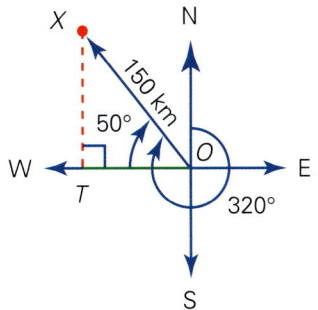

Bearings are used in orienteering, which you may do in PDHPE. Bearings are also used in geography.

$$\angle XOT = 320° - 270°$$
$$\qquad\qquad = 50°$$

a $\dfrac{TX}{150} = \sin 50°$

$\qquad TX = \sin 50 \times 150$
$\qquad\quad\ = 114{\cdot}9066 \dots$
$\qquad TX = 115$ km (to the nearest km)

It has flown 115 km.

b $\dfrac{OT}{150} = \cos 50°$, etc.

$\qquad OT = \cos 50 \times 150$
$\qquad\quad\ = 96{\cdot}418$

It has flown 96 km (to the nearest km).

EXAMPLE 4

An off-road vehicle drives 300 m due north, then 400 m due east.

a What is the bearing *of* the vehicle *from* the starting point?
b What is the bearing *of* the starting point *from* the vehicle?

Solution

> O is the starting point.
> X is the vehicle.

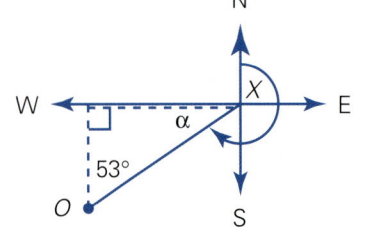

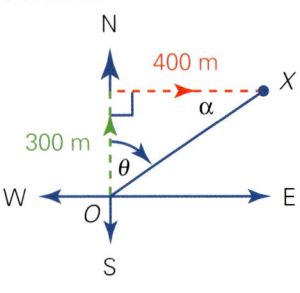

$$\tan \theta = \frac{\text{opposite}}{\text{adjacent}}$$

a $\tan \theta = \dfrac{400}{300}$

$ = 51{\cdot}131 \ldots$

$\theta = 53°$ (to the nearest degree)

Bearing of the vehicle from the starting point is 035°.

b

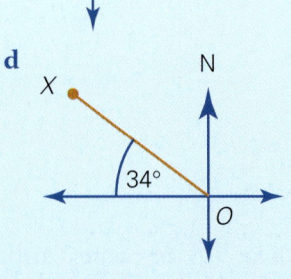

$\alpha = 90 - 53 = 37°$

Bearing of the starting point from the vehicle is

$270 - 37$

$ = 233°$

EXERCISE 7J

1 State the true bearing of X from O in each of the following diagrams.

a

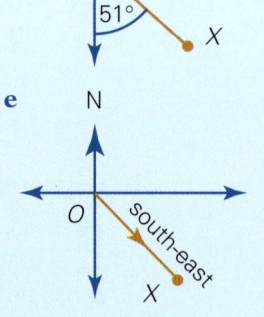

b

c

d

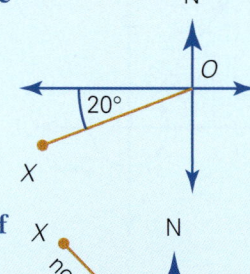

e

f

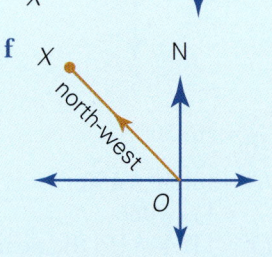

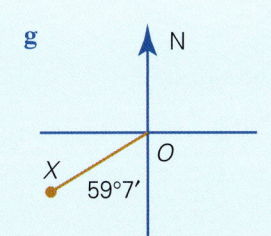
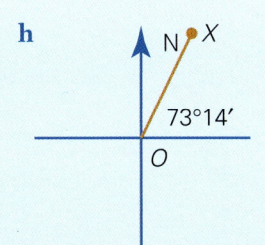
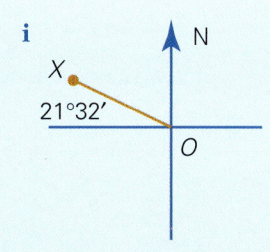

2 Draw a diagram showing an acute angle for each bearing of X from O (like those shown for question 1).

   a 009   **b** 212   **c** 127   **d** 335   **e** 241   **f** 286

3 Write each of the following directions as a bearing:

   a NNE   **b** WSW   **c** SSE   **d** WNW   **e** ENE

Level 2

4 A ship sails in 100 km in the direction SSW.

   a How far due east of its starting point has it come?
   b How far north has it come?

5 An off-road vehicle drives 8 km from its campsite along a bearing of 130°.

   a How far south of the campsite is it?   **b** How far east is it?

6 An aircraft flies 100 km due west, then 80 km due south.

   a What is the bearing of the aircraft from its starting point?
   b How far in a direct line has it come?

7 Three towns A, B, C are located such that A is 8 km north-east of B, while C is 17 km south-east of B.

   a How far is A from C?   **b** What is the bearing of B from C?

8 Having sailed south, then west, a ship is situated 350 km on bearing 202° from where it started.

   a How far had it sailed
      i southward? **ii** westward?
   b What is the bearing of the starting point from the ship?

9 A plane flies at a speed of 680 km/h. After passing over town A, it flies on a bearing of 162° for $2\frac{1}{2}$ hours. How far is it then:

   a south of A?   **b** east of A?

10 a What is the bearing of B from A?
    b What is the size of $\angle\alpha$?
    c What is the bearing of A from B?

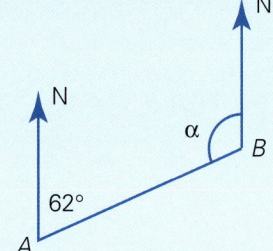

11 For each pair of points, give:

   i the bearing of B from A   **ii** the bearing of A from B.

a 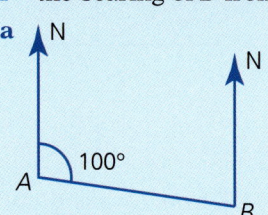   **b** 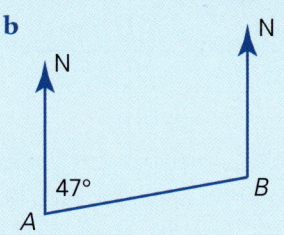   **c**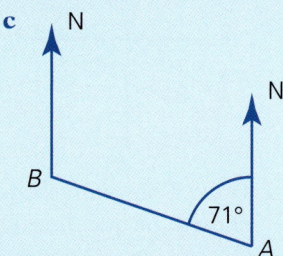

  d Calculate the *difference* between your answers to parts **i** and **ii** for each of **a**, **b** and **c**. What do you notice?

  e If the bearing of x from y is 210°, what is the bearing of y from x?

12 Find the bearing of:

  a B from A   **b** A from C   **c** C from B.

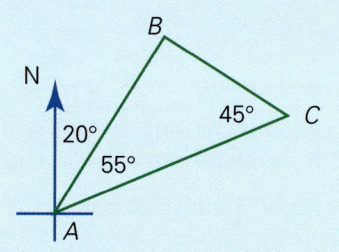

Level 3

13

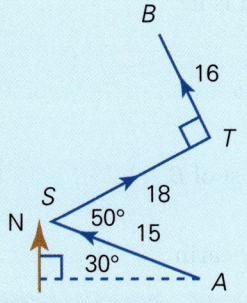

  a Describe the paths shown in the diagram at left.

  b How far from S is B?

  c What is the bearing of S from B?

14 Two aircraft take off simultaneously from an airport. One flies 60 km on a bearing of 035°, while the other flies along a bearing of 305°. The first pilot then observes that the second plane is due west of him.

  a How far is the second plane from the airport?

  b How far apart are the planes?

15 A ship is 7 nautical miles N42°W from a port, while a lighthouse is 12·5 nautical miles S48°W from the port. Find the bearing of the ship from the lighthouse.

16 A whale is seen moving due north while it was 200 m east of a spotter boat. Assuming it continues on this course, what is the closest it will come to a whale-watching boat 400 m N8°W from the spotter boat?

Investigation Goal!

The try has been scored—now for the conversion! (Or perhaps a penalty.)

Why does the kicker mostly bring the ball back to the 22 m line, if the rules allow the kick to be taken anywhere along the coloured line?

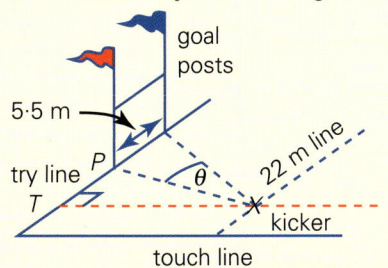

1 Set up a 2D model adapted from this diagram. Discuss why angle θ should be as large as possible. Draw to scale a right triangle diagram in which TX is: **a** 10 m **b** 15 m. Find θ each time by measuring.

2 Which trigonometric ratio fits this situation?

3 Vary the try locations (TP) and make a report.

4 Investigate the effect on θ when the ball is taken closer to the try line, or further out from it. What other factors affect the decision on how far out to take the ball?

Investigation Measuring inaccessible distances

In the days before sophisticated surveying instruments, trigonometry was used to calculate distances that could not be measured directly. For example, an army general may have needed to know the distance from the cannon to the castle across the river.

Using only a quadrant, which measured angles from 0 to 90, and using pacing to measure out 100 yards, enough information was gathered to enable the distance to the castle to be measured.

Can you calculate the distance from the cannon to the castle?

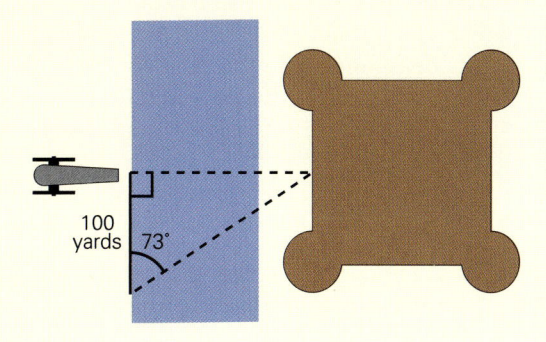

Chapter Review

Language Links

adjacent	depression	opposite	theorem
altitude	dimension	Pythagoras	triad
bearing	elevation	ratio	triangle
compass	height	right	trigonometry
complementary	horizontal	similar	vertical
cosine	hypotenuse	sine	
degree	observer	tangent	

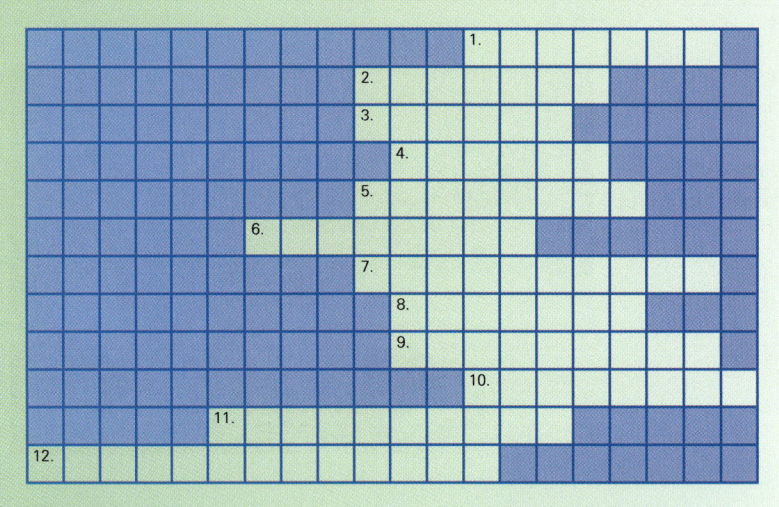

CLUES

Across

1. The ratio involving opposite and adjacent sides of a right triangle.
2. A word meaning 'direction' with respect to a compass.
3. The ratio involving adjacent and hypotenuse.
4. The unit for measuring angles.
5. The numerator in the sine ratio.
6. The denominator in the tangent ratio.
7. The denominator in the cosine ratio.
8. An instrument for finding direction.
9. The angle between the horizontal and the line of sight, looking up.
10. A figure containing three angles.
11. The developer of the $c^2 = a^2 + b^2$ relationship for right triangles.
12. An adjective describing angles whose sum is 90°.

Down

1. Literally means 'triangle measurement'.

Chapter Review Exercises

1 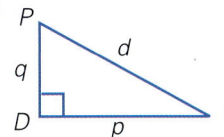 In $\triangle PQD$, which one of the following must be true?

   a $p^2 + d^2 = q^2$ **b** $q^2 = p^2 - d^2$
   c $p^2 = q^2 + d^2$ **d** $p^2 + q^2 = d^2$

MC

2 Which of the following are right triangles? Show your reasoning:

  a 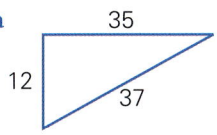   **b** 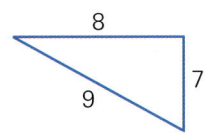   **c**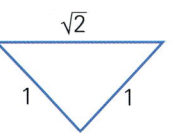

MC

3 If $a^2 + b^2 = c^2$, complete the following: **a** $c = \ldots$ **b** $b = \ldots$

MC

4 Complete the Pythagorean triad: 15, 36, ...

MC

5 Find x in the following, correct to 1 decimal place where necessary:

  a 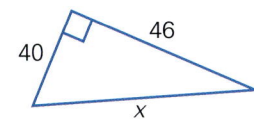   **b**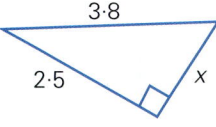

M

6 Calculate the value of the tangent ratio for angle θ in each of these figures:

  a 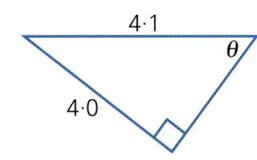   **b**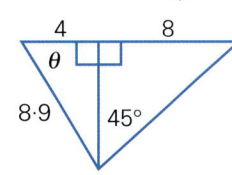

7.2

7 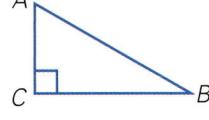 BC equals: **a** $AB \times \tan C$ **b** $AB \times \tan A$
  c $\tan A \times AC$ **d** $\tan C \times CA$
  e none of these

7.4

8 Using $\triangle ABC$, complete the following:
  a $\tan C = \frac{\cdots}{\cdots}$ **b** $\sin A = \frac{\cdots}{\cdots}$

  c $\cos C = \frac{\cdots}{\cdots}$ **d** $AB^2 = \ldots \ldots$

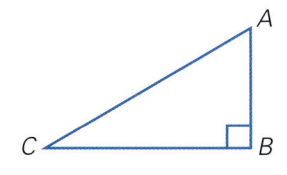

7.5

9 Find, to 3 places of decimals:

  a $\cos 68°$ **b** $\sin 82°$ **c** $\tan 44°$

10 Find, to the nearest minute, the angle for which the ...

  a cosine is $0\cdot65$ **b** tangent is $2\cdot58$ **c** sine is $0\cdot996$

7.6

11 a Express to 2 places of decimals:
  i $\tan \theta$ **ii** $\cos \beta$ **iii** $\sin \theta$
  b $\sin \beta = \ldots$
    A $\frac{12}{13}$ **B** $\frac{13}{12}$ **C** $\frac{5}{13}$ **D** $\frac{13}{5}$ **E** none of these
  e Find θ and β to the nearest degree.

12 Find x in the following, correct to 2 decimal places:

  a $\frac{x}{4\cdot8} = \cos 25°$ **b** $\frac{5\cdot7}{\sin 61°} = x$ **c** $\frac{12}{x} = \tan 40°$

7.8

13 Find t in each of the following, to the nearest hundredth:

a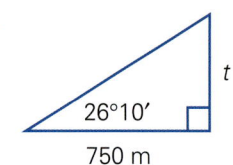

b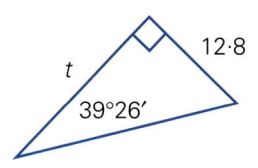

c Find also
   i y
   ii α
   iii β

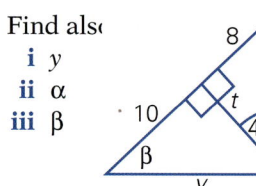

7.9

14 With the sun at an angle of elevation of 48°6′, the shadow of a building is 30 m long. How tall is the building?

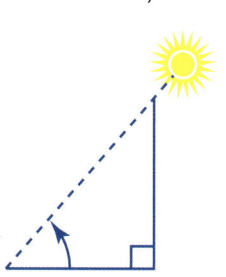

7.10

15 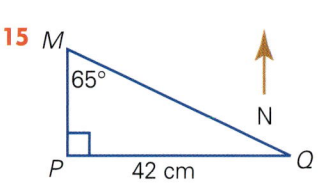 Calculate:

   a MP to the nearest centimetre
   b MQ to the nearest centimetre
   c the bearing of Q from M
   d the bearing of M from Q.

16 Given $\angle B = 90°$, $\angle A = 40°$ and $BC = 30$ cm, give as much additional information about $\triangle ABC$ as you can.

7.9

17 An owl at the top of a 4 m lamp post sees a mouse at an angle of depression of 23°41′. How far is the owl from the mouse?

7.9

18 Draw a right triangle DEF, such that $\cos F = \dfrac{15}{17}$. Then find $\sin F$, to 2 decimal places.

7.9

19 A hot-air balloon is tethered by 200 m of line at an angle of depression of 73°. How high is it?

7.8

20 The diagonal of a rectangle makes an angle of 38° with the longer side, which is 12·6 cm long. Find (correct to 2 places of decimals):

   a the length of the diagonal
   b the width of the rectangle.

MC

21 An allotment of land in the shape of a right triangle has a hypotenuse of 46 m and another side of 40 m. It was sold for $210 per square metre. Find the selling price.

7.9

22 The altimeter of a coastguard plane shows 4000 m as it flies over a trawler illegally fishing. At that instant, its radar detects a naval patrol boat at an angle of depression of 12°.

   a How far is the patrol boat from the trawler?
   b How long will it take the naval boat to reach the stationary trawler at its top speed of 45 km/h?

7.8

23

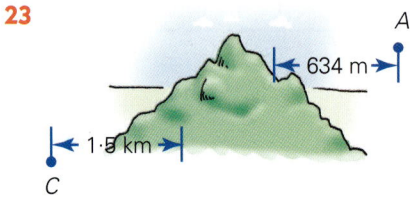

A **A** tunnel is needed through this mountain. A surveyor locates three reference points to form a triangle as shown. $\angle A$ is 90°, $\angle B$ is 65°, AB is 4·23 km.

   a What angle should she measure at C to ensure proper completion of the triangle?
   b If the distances from A to the mountain and C to the mountain are 634 m and 1·5 km respectively, how long will the tunnel be?

• B

24 Find x, y.

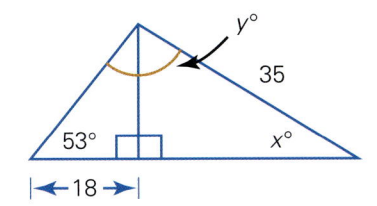

25 Find PQ.

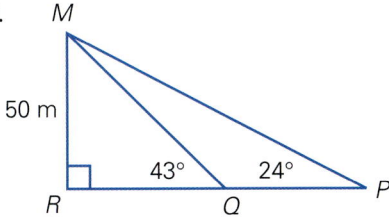

26 A pilot intended to fly due north, but strong winds pushed her plane onto bearing $352°$.

7.10

   a After flying for 100 km on this wrong course, how far off course was she? (To the nearest km.)
   b How far north had she flown?
   c Along what bearing must she fly to reach a location 300 km north of her starting point?

27

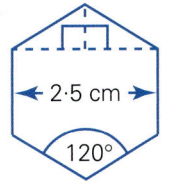

This nut has the shape of a regular hexagon. Find the length of each edge, to 3 significant figures.

7.8

28 AD is an altitude of an equilateral $\triangle ABC$. If $AB = 2x$, show that $AD = \sqrt{3}\,x$, and hence find the area of $\triangle ABC$.

29 Two observers simultaneously sight a UFO at an estimated height of 300 m. The first determines its angle of elevation to be $15°$, with the UFO due north of him. The second finds the angle of elevation to be $10°$, with her position due east of the other observer.

7.9

   a Find the line of sight distance from each observer to the UFO.
   b Find the ground distance from the second observer to the UFO.
   c How far apart were the two observers?
   d What is the bearing of the UFO from the second observer?

30 a Find AC.   **b** Find QR.

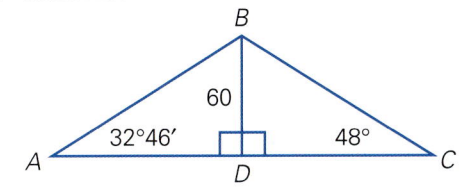 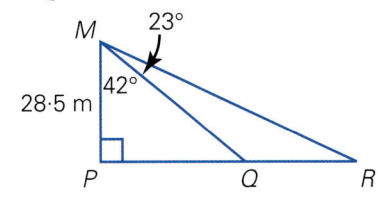

7.8

Keeping Mathematically Fit

Part A—Non-calculator

1 The length of a rectangle is 5 cm more than its width. If the length of the rectangle is y cm, write an expression for the area of the rectangle.

2 Find n if $\dfrac{1}{y} = y^n$.

3 Find three consecutive even numbers the sum of which is 132.

4 Write $\tan \theta$ as a fraction.

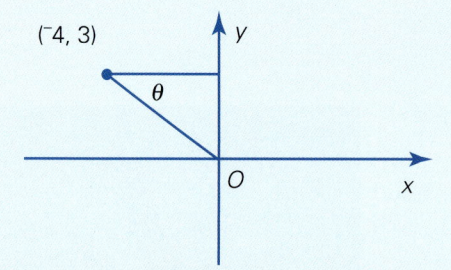

5 The disc, centre c, is rolled along the page for one complete revolution. Which interval best shows the distance c has travelled?

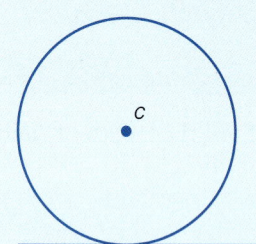

A _____

B _____

C _____

D _____

6 Make x the subject of the formula $y = \dfrac{3x - 1}{5}$.

7 The sum of one-third of a number and twice the same number is 28. Find the number.

8 The fraction $\dfrac{\nabla}{5}$ has a value between 6 and 7. Give a possible whole number value for ∇.

9 $^-20p^2 = 4p \times \square$. Find the missing factor.

10 $65 \text{ mm}^2 = \ldots \text{ cm}^2$

Part B—Calculator

1 Calculate $\dfrac{3 \cdot 6}{15 \cdot 3 + 21 \cdot 9}$ correct to 2 significant figures.

2 Map printing costs are $45 set-up fee plus $1·20 per map. If the total cost for one customer was $225, how many maps were ordered?

3 When this tank is 3/5 full, it contains 12 000 L. What is the capacity of the tank?

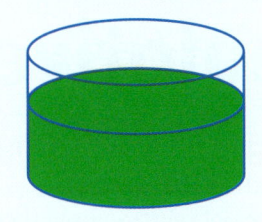

4 Biscuits are packed in rectangular prism-shaped packets measuring 5 cm × 4 cm × 25 cm. How many packets of biscuits could be packed into a box measuring 60 cm × 50 cm × 30 cm?

5 An amount of $160 was paid to a bank teller in $20 and $5 notes. If there were 14 notes altogether, how many of each were there?

Cumulative Review 2

1 Write algebraic expressions for the following:

   a four less than one-third of d.
   b the number of metres altogether in p metres and q centimetres.

2 Express in index form:

   a $7 \times 7 \times 7$ **b** $t \times t \times t \times t \times t$ **c** $^-2b \times {}^-2b \times {}^-2b \times {}^-2b$

3 Simplify:

   a $12p^2q \div 3pq^2$ **b** $(w^3)^2$ **c** $a^0 + 3b^0$

4 Expand and simplify where possible:

   a $3(x + 4) - 5$ **b** $4p(p + 1) - 3p$ **c** $(c + 6)(c - 6)$ **d** $(3p - 5)^2$

5 Factorise fully:

   a $5x + 10$ **b** $12t^2 - 3t$

6 Express answers to the following in scientific notation:

   a $3 \times 10^4 \times 2 \cdot 7 \times 10^3$ **b** $3 \cdot 78 \times 10^2 \times 7 \cdot 9 \times 10^1$

7 Write the basic numeral, rounded to 2 decimal places, for:

   a $2 \cdot 04 \times 10^4 \times 9 \cdot 01 \times 10^{-3}$ **b** $4 \cdot 206 \times 10^5 \div 6 \cdot 04 \times 10^3$

8 A distance is given as 5000 km. What could the exact distance have been if the given distance is correct to:

   a 1 significant figure?   **b** 3 significant figures?

9 Estimate the answers to the following—check your answers with a calculator!

   a $78 \cdot 9 + 163 \cdot 2$ **b** $3884 - 1218$ **c** $3 \cdot 7 \times 22$
   d $3992 \div 4 \cdot 1$ **e** $432 \cdot 8 \div 16 \cdot 87$ **f** $6243 + 989 \times 2 \cdot 2$

10 Write as a simplified fraction:

   a 25%   **b** 95%   **c** 250%   **d** 2%

11 Karen measured a length of fabric. What could its actual length have been if she recorded the measurement as: **a** 75 cm? **b** 75·0 cm?

12 Convert the following measurements as indicated:

   a 2·75 kg to g   **b** 155 min to h, min   **c** 2700 mm to m

13 If $1\frac{1}{2}$ m of material cost \$9·60, what is the cost per metre?

14 Anton pays income tax at the rate of 20¢ in the dollar. What tax would he pay on a taxable income of \$24 000?

15

Wheel **a** has 12 teeth and wheel **b** has 16 teeth. When **b** turns through 40 revolutions, how many revolutions does **a** turn through?

16 Find **i** perimeter, **ii** area of each figure:

a
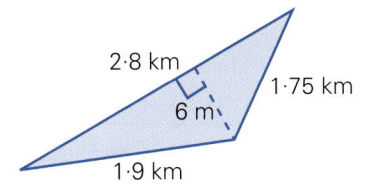
2·8 km, 6 m, 1·75 km, 1·9 km

b
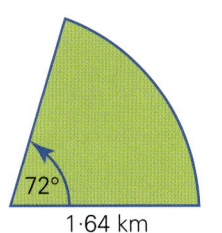
72°, 1·64 km

17 Solve the following equations:

  a $4x - 2 = 10$ **b** $2d - 10 = 2 - d$ **c** $\dfrac{4}{x-2} = \dfrac{5}{x}$

18 Solve the following, and graph the solutions on the number line:

  a $6x - 12 < 0$ **b** $4x + 1 \le x - 5$

19 If $v = u + at$, find:

  a v when $u = 100$, $a = {}^-6$, $t = 2 \cdot 5$ **b** u when $v = 100$, $a = 15$, $t = 5 \cdot 2$

20 Rearrange to make x the subject: $y = p - rx$.

21 The area of a trapezium is 36 cm². If the two parallel sides measure 8·2 cm and 9·7 cm, what is the distance between them?

22 Construct a triangle with side lengths 4 cm, 5·5 cm and 7 cm.

23 Construct an accurate copy of this figure in your book:

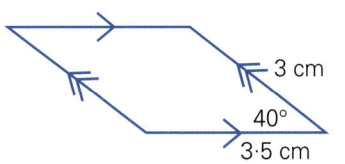
3 cm, 40°, 3·5 cm

24 Using only compasses and a ruler, construct angles of:

  a 60°   **b** 45°

25 Calculate the value of each pronumeral, giving reasons:

a
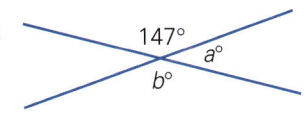
147°, $a°$, $b°$

b
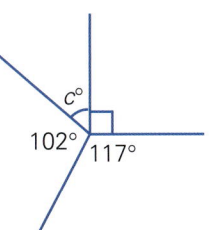
$c°$, 102°, 117°

c
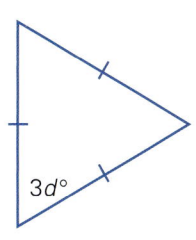
$3d°$

d
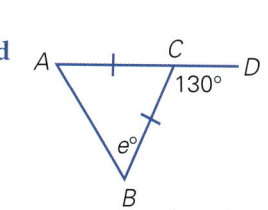
A, C, D, 130°, $e°$, B

e
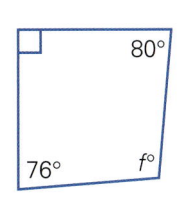
80°, 76°, $f°$

f
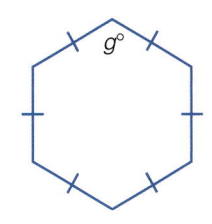
$g°$

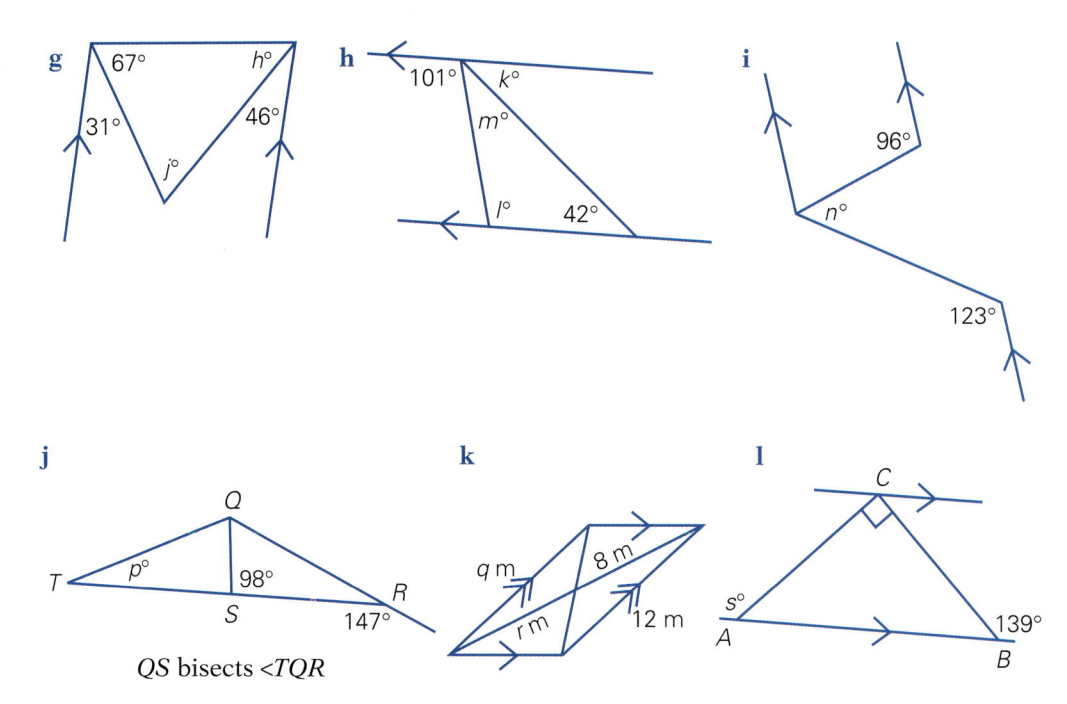

g 67° h° | **h** 101° k° m° l° 42° | **i** 96° n° 123°

j Q T p° 98° S R 147° — QS bisects <TQR

k q m 8 m r m 12 m

l C s° A 139° B

26 Which quadrilaterals have equal diagonals?

27 What is the size of each interior angle of a regular octagon?

28 A quadrilateral with diagonals intersecting at right angles is:

  A a rectangle   **B** a parallelogram   **C** a kite   **D** all of these

29 Draw a graph of the height of water in this bottle as it is being filled from a tap flowing at a constant rate.

30

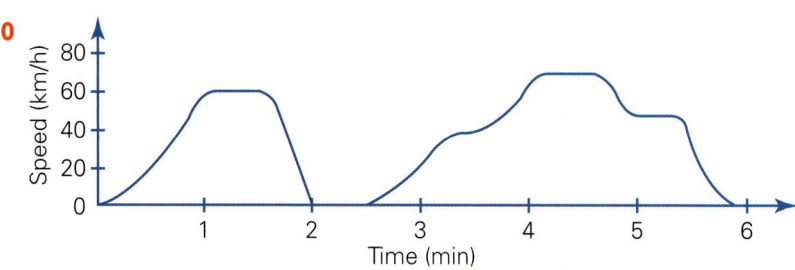

Christina is having her first driving lesson. The first 6 minutes' movements of her car are recorded on the graph above. Write a story to describe what was happening at each stage shown.

31 A step graph showing 'special' STD phone rates is displayed at right.

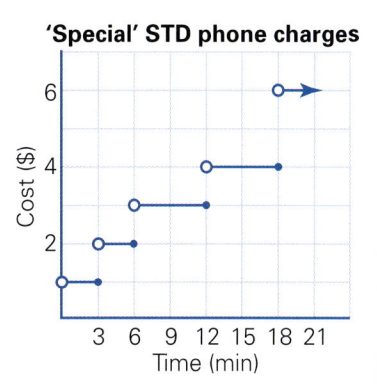

'Special' STD phone charges

  a What are the minimum and maximum charges for an STD call?

  b How much does a 6 min call cost?

  c What is the maximum time you can speak for $4?

  d How much does a $9\frac{1}{2}$ min call cost?

  e How much extra does a 3 min 1 s call cost compared with a 3 min call?

32 Use the diet chart to answer the following:

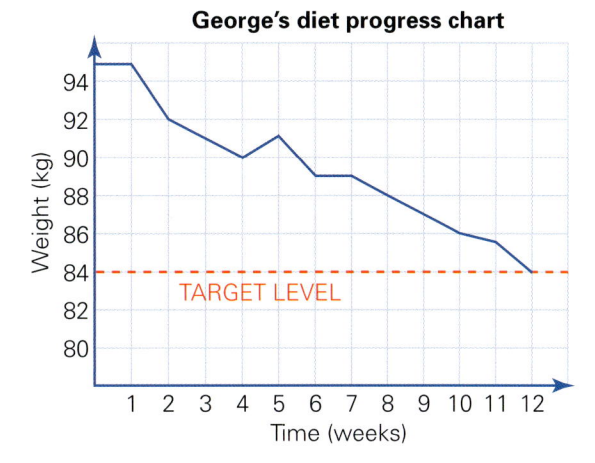

George's diet progress chart

  a How much weight did George lose over the whole time?

  b What was his *average* weight loss per week?

  c In which week did he lose most weight? How can you tell from the graph without looking up the numbers?

  d During which week/s did his weight remain constant? How does this show up on the graph?

  e In which week did he 'pig out'? How does the graph show this?

  f Compare the *rate* of weight loss for weeks 3 and 4 with weeks 8, 9 and 10. Relate your answer to the slope of the graph.

  g If George had maintained the rate of weight loss achieved during the second week, when would he have reached the target level?

33

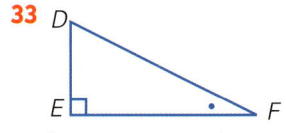

  a In $\triangle DEF$, judged from $\angle F$, name the side that is the:
    i adjacent   **ii** hypotenuse   **iii** opposite   **iv** numerator
    of the tangent ratio.

  b Complete the following: $\dfrac{FE}{DE} = \ldots \angle D$

  c What relationship exists between $\angle D$ and $\angle F$?

  d What relationship exists between $\tan \angle D$ and $\tan \angle F$?

34 Find from your calculator, to 3 decimal places where necessary:

  a $\tan 2°$ **b** $\tan 45°$ **c** $\tan 80°$ **d** $\tan 88°$

35 What does your calculator show for: **a** $\tan 0°$?   **b** $\tan 90°$? Use diagrams to explain your answers.

36 Find, to the nearest hundredth of a degree, the angle whose tangent is:

  a $3·7$ **b** $25·372$ **c** $0·985$

37 Solve these equations:

   a $\tan x° = 1$ **b** $\tan x° = 0\cdot5$ **c** $\tan x° = 2\cdot891$

38 Find x, to 2 decimal places:

  a 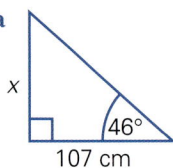   **b** 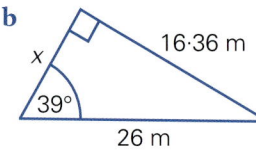   **c**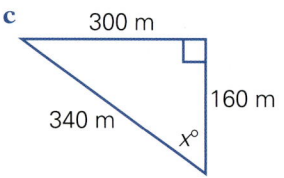

39 One mine shaft is sunk at an angle of depression of $61\cdot9°$ until it is $1\cdot7$ km long. Starting from the same location, a second is sunk vertically to a depth of 1500 m. What is the length of the horizontal shaft that connects the lower ends of both shafts?

40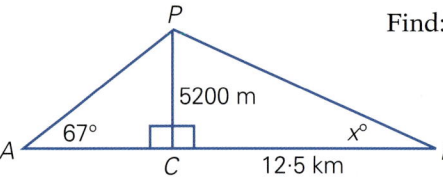

Find: **a** x (to nearest min)
       b PB (to 3 significant figures)
       c AC (to 3 significant figures)

41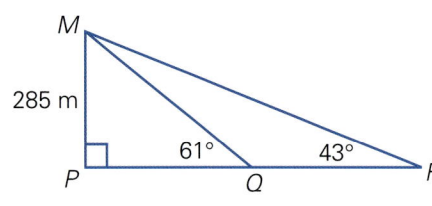

Find: **a** PQ **b** PR **c** QR **d** MR
to the nearest metre.

Show all appropriate working for questions **42** to **48**.

42 In $\triangle ABC$, right angled at B, $AB = 3$ cm, $BC = 4$ cm and M is the mid-point of AC. Find:

  a AC **b** MC **c** $\angle ACB$ **d** $\dfrac{\sin C \times \sin A}{\cos A}$

43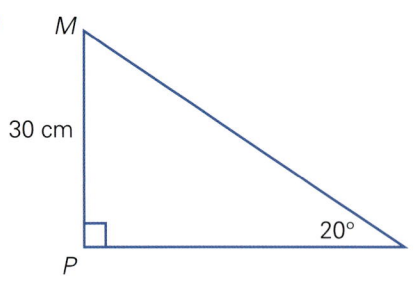

  a Find MQ, to 2 decimal places.
  b Find PQ, using Pythagoras's theorem.

44 Draw a right triangle ABC with right angle at C and $\cos B = 0\cdot6$. Calculate $\tan A$.

45 An aeroplane leaves Newcastle and flies for $1\frac{1}{2}$ hours at 320 km/h on a bearing of 304°.

  a How far has it travelled?   **b** How far north of Newcastle is it?

46 A road rises 75 m in a road length of 2 km. Find the angle of elevation of the road (also known as the *angle of slope*).

47 The equal sides of an isosceles triangle are 15 cm and the angle between them is 70°. Calculate, using trigonometry, the length of the third side.

48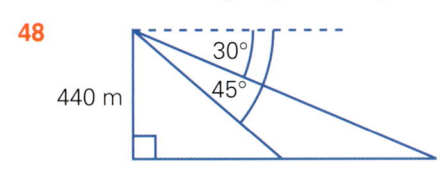

From the top of a 440 m high cliff, the angles of depression of two boats due south of the cliff are 45° and 30°. How far apart are the boats?

1 What you need to know and revise

Outcome PAS 4.5:

Graphs and interprets linear relationships on the number plane:

- interpreting the number plane formed from the intersection of a horizontal x-axis and vertical y-axis
- reading, plotting and naming ordered pairs on the number plane including those with values that are not whole numbers
- graphing points on the number plane from a table of values using an appropriate scale
- deriving a rule for a set of points that have been graphed on a number plane by forming a table of values or otherwise
- forming a table of values for a linear relationship by substituting a set of appropriate values for either of the letters and graphing them on a number plane.

2 What you will learn in this chapter

Outcome PAS 5.1.2:

Determines the mid-point, length and gradient of an interval joining two points on the number plane and graphs linear and simple non-linear relationships from equations:

- constructing tables of values and using coordinates to graph vertical and horizontal lines
- identifying the x- and y-intercepts of graphs
- identifying the x-axis as the line $y = 0$
- identifying the y-axis as the line $x = 0$
- graphing a variety of linear relationships on a number plane by constructing a table of values and plotting coordinates using an appropriate scale
- determining whether a point lies on a line by substituting into the equation of the line
- determining the mid-point of an interval by finding the point halfway between the x-value and the y-value
- using Pythagoras's theorem to determine the length of the interval joining the two points
- using the relationship $\text{gradient} = \dfrac{\text{rise}}{\text{run}}$ to find the gradient of the interval joining two points
- defining positive gradients for lines that slope to the right and defining negative gradients for lines that slope to the left
- finding the gradient of a straight line from the graph by drawing a right-angled triangle joining two points on the line.

Outcome PAS 5.2.3:

Develops and uses formulas to find mid-point, distance and gradient and applies the gradient/intercept form to interpret and graph straight lines:

- $M(x, y) = \left(\dfrac{x_1 + x_2}{2}, \dfrac{y_1 + y_2}{2} \right)$
- $d = \sqrt{(x_2 - x_1)^2 + (y_2 - y_1)^2}$
- $m = \dfrac{y_2 - y_1}{x_2 - x_1}$
- constructing tables of values and using coordinates to graph straight lines of the form $y = mx + b$
- recognising and graphing equations of the form $y = mx + b$, interpreting the x-coefficient (m) as the gradient and the constant (b) as the y-intercep.
- rearranging an equation in general form ($ax + by + c = 0$) to the gradient–intercept form
- determining that two lines are parallel if their gradients are equal
- finding the gradient and the y-intercept of a straight line from the graph and using them to determine the equation of the line.

Working Mathematically outcomes WMS 5.1, 5.2, 5.3

Students will be required to *question*, *apply strategies*, *communicate*, *reason* and *reflect* in the sections of this chapter.

8

Coordinate geometry and linear functions

Key mathematical terms you will encounter

axis (axes)	graph	ordered	solution
coordinates	horizontal	origin	substitution
dependent	hypotenuse	parallel	variable
distance	intercept	Pythagoras	vertical
equation	interval	rise	vertices
function	linear	run	
gradient	mid-point	slope	

MathsCheck
Coordinate geometry and linear functions

1 Give the coordinates for each of the following points:

   a S **b** E **c** T **d** N

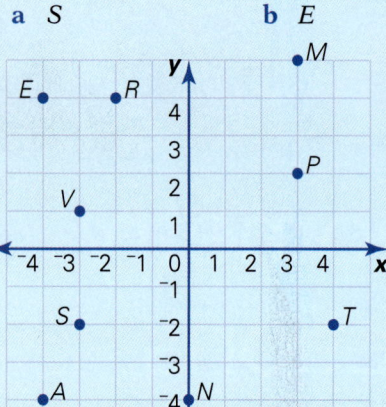

2 Find the distance between:

   a M and P **b** E and R

   c S and T **d** V and S

   e A and N **f** N and origin

3 a Write the y-coordinates of M and P.

   b Find their difference.

   c Compare your result with that for question 2 part **a**. Comment.

4 Write the x-coordinates of R and E. Find their difference. Compare the result with that for question 2 part **b**. Comment.

5 Find the distance between:

   a $(4, 2)$ and $(4, 5)$ **b** $(^-2, 0)$ and $(^-2, 4)$ **c** $(3, ^-1)$ and $(3, ^-5)$

   d $(^-1, 2)$ and $(^-1, ^-3)$ **e** $(4, 3)$ and $(1, 3)$ **f** $(4, ^-2)$ and $(2, ^-2)$

   g $(^-1, 4)$ and $(^-5, 4)$ **h** $(^-2, ^-5)$ and $(^-5, ^-5)$ **i** $(3, 0)$ and $(^-2, 0)$

6 Graph the points from each table on a separate number plane.

a

x	0	2	⁻3
y	3	5	0

b

x	0	3	⁻2
y	⁻1	5	⁻5

c

x	0	4	⁻3
y	3	⁻1	6

7 Copy and complete the following tables:

a

$y = x - 2$			
x	0	2	⁻2
y			

b

$y = 3x + 2$			
x	0	3	⁻1
y			

c

$y = ^-2x + 3$			
x	0	1	⁻1	3
y				

d

$y = 2(x - 3)$			
x	0	4	⁻2
y			

e

$y = ^-3x - 2$			
x	0	2	⁻2
y			

f

$x + y = 0$			
x	⁻3	0	4
y			

8 Try to find the rule for each set of points.

A table of values might help.

a

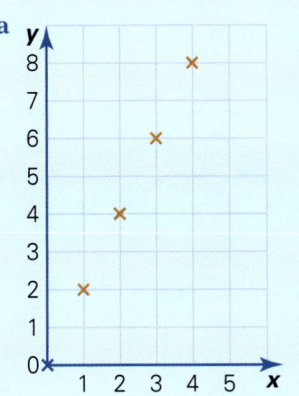

b

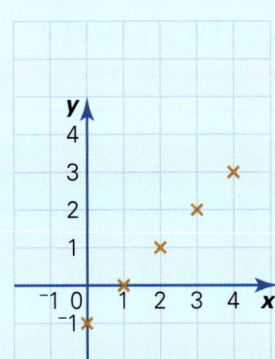

c

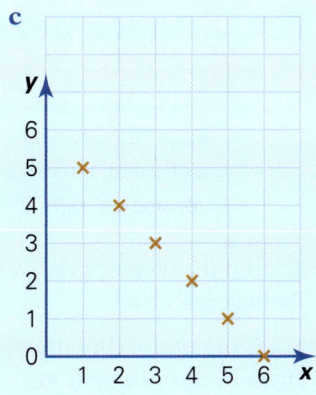

Exploring New Ideas

8.1 Distance between two points

The number plane we use for plotting points is called the Cartesian number plane after Rene Descartes, the French philosopher and mathematician. Descartes, along with Pierre de Fermat, developed analytical geometry on the number plane in the mid-1600s. They are considered to be the first of the modern mathematicians.

To find the distance between two points A and B we use Pythagoras's rule.

Mark in point C directly below B and to the right of A. Draw in lines BC and AC.

We now have a right-angled triangle where the distance we are trying to find is the hypotenuse.

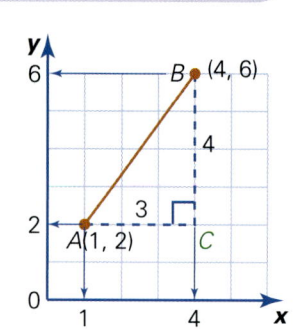

$AC = 4 - 1$ (x-coordinate of B minus x-coordinate of A)
  $= 3$ units

$BC = 6 - 2$ (y-coordinate of B minus y-coordinate of A)
  $= 4$ units

Now use Pythagoras's rule:
$AB^2 = AC^2 + BC^2$
$AB^2 = 3^2 + 4^2$
$AB = \sqrt{3^2 + 4^2}$
$AB = \sqrt{25}$
$AB = 5$ units

From Pythagoras's rule a formula can be developed to find the distance between any two points without needing to plot the points.

We use subscripts to distinguish between points on the number plane. Thus (x_1, y_1) and (x_2, y_2) are any two points on the number plane.

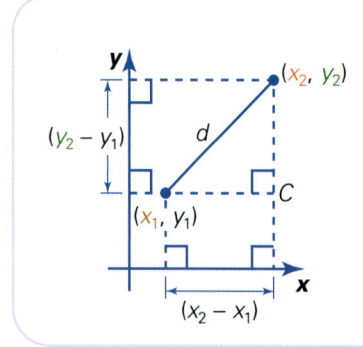

The distance d between two points (x_1, y_1) and (x_2, y_2) is found using the formula:

$$d = \sqrt{(x_2 - x_1)^2 + (y_2 - y_1)^2}$$

Find the difference between x-coordinates (right−left), then square it. Similarly, find the difference between the y-coordinates and square it. Finally, calculate the square root of the sum.

EXAMPLE 1

Find the distance between the points $(2, 3)$ and $(7, 15)$.

Solution

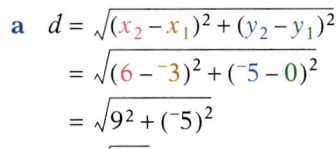

$$d = \sqrt{(x_2 - x_1)^2 + (y_2 - y_1)^2}$$
$$= \sqrt{(7 - 2)^2 + (15 - 3)^2}$$
$$= \sqrt{5^2 + 12^2}$$
$$= \sqrt{169}$$

Distance = 13 units

EXAMPLE 2

Find the distance from $(^-3, 0)$ to $(6, ^-5)$:

a as an exact length

b to 1 decimal place.

Solutions

a $d = \sqrt{(x_2 - x_1)^2 + (y_2 - y_1)^2}$
$= \sqrt{(6 - ^-3)^2 + (^-5 - 0)^2}$
$= \sqrt{9^2 + (^-5)^2}$
$= \sqrt{106}$ This is the exact distance.

b $\sqrt{106} \approx 10{\cdot}295\,63$
Distance = 10·3 units (to 1 decimal place)

EXAMPLE 3

Show that the points $(^-2, 0)$, $(1, ^-4)$ and $(2, 3)$ form the vertices of an isosceles triangle.

Solution

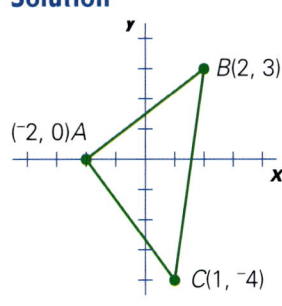

$$AB = \sqrt{(x_2 - x_1)^2 + (y_2 - y_1)^2}$$
$$= \sqrt{(2 - ^-2)^2 + (3 - 0)^2}$$
$$= \sqrt{4^2 + 3^2}$$
$$= 5$$
$$AC = (1 - ^-2)^2 + (^-4 - 0)^2$$
$$= 3 + (^-4)^2$$
$$= 5$$
$$AB = AC$$
The triangle is isosceles.

> Sketch suggests we find lengths of AB and AC.

> Discussion point:
> Is it necessary to find BC?

EXERCISE 8A

1 Use Pythagoras's rule to find the length of each interval in the following number plane. (Leave answers in square root form.)

a AB **b** CD
c EF **d** GH

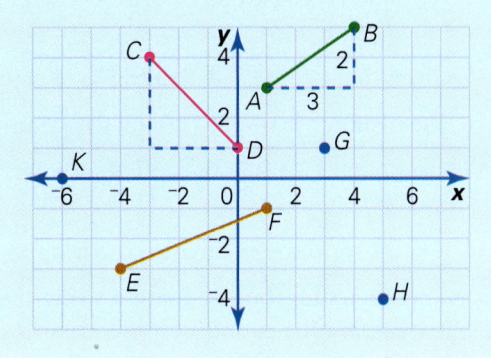

2 Use the formula $d = \sqrt{(x_2 - x_1)^2 + (y_2 - y_1)^2}$ to find the distance between the following points correct to 1 decimal place:

a (2, 3) and (5, 7) b (0, 1) and (6, 9) c (0, 0) and (5, 12)
d ($^-$4, 8) and (2, 0) e ($^-$3, 0) and (0, 4) f (0, $^-$1) and (2, $^-$4)
g (2, 5) and (1, $^-$3) h (4, 9) and ($^-$1, $^-$3) i (5, $^-$3) and ($^-$2, $^-$7)
j (2, $^-$3) and ($^-$2, 3) k (0, 0) and ($^-$2$\frac{1}{2}$, 6) l ($^-$4·5, 4·5) and ($^-$3·5, 3·5)

3 Find the exact distance between these pairs of points:

Exact distance means leave the $\sqrt{}$ sign in.

a (1, 3) and (2, 2) b (4, 1) and (7, 3)
c ($^-$3, $^-$1) and (0, 4) d ($^-$2, $^-$3) and (3, 5)
e ($^-$1, 0) and ($^-$6, 1) f (1, $^-$3) and (4, $^-$2)

Level 2

4 Calculate the distance from the origin to ($^-$4, $^-$7).

5 Which of the points (3, 5) and ($^-$4, $^-$4) is closer to the origin?

6 Show that the points (3, 6) and ($^-$1, 4) are equidistant from (2, 3).

7 a Show that the points (0, $^-$5) and (6, 1) are equidistant from (3, $^-$2).

b Find another point that is the same distance from (3, $^-$2).

8 a Find the distance of (5, 2) from (2, $^-$2).

b Find two more points that are the same distance from (3, $^-$2).

9 A triangle has vertices ($^-$4, 0), (0, 3) and (0, $^-$3). Show that it must be isosceles.

Level 3

10 The vertices of a triangle are $P(4, 5)$, $Q(8, 8)$ and $R(10, ^-3)$.

Draw a diagram.

a Show that ΔPQR is right angled. **b** Find its area.

11 A quadrilateral has vertices ($^-$1, $^-$1), (3, 1), (1, $^-$3) and ($^-$3, $^-$5).

a Find the lengths of its sides.
b Find the lengths of its diagonals. What sort of quadrilateral is it?

You could use a property of the diagonals.

12 Prove that a circle can be drawn with centre ($^-$2, 1) passing through the points ($^-$5, 3), ($^-$4, $^-$2) and (1, 3).

13 Given that ($^-$6, $^-$1), ($^-$4, 3) and ($^-$2, $^-$1) are vertices of a rhombus, find the fourth vertex.

14 The distance from (5, 7) to (3, a) is 6 units. Find a.

15 The point (3, 1) is at the end of an interval that is 5 units long. Where could the other end be?

16 If (x, y) are the coordinates of *any* point on the number plane 4 units from the origin:

a form an algebraic equation using the distance formula
b simplify the equation by eliminating square root signs
c what shape is represented by the equation?

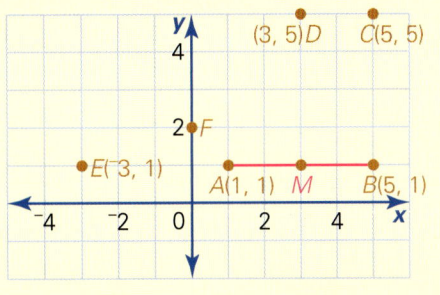

The **mid-point** of an interval is the *halfway* point. Is there a pattern for calculating the coordinates of the mid-point of *any* interval, so that we don't need to draw diagrams each time? Let's see.

1 Find from the diagram the coordinates of the mid-point of the interval:

   a AB **b** BC **c** AC
   d AD **e** AE

2 For each interval in question **1**, list the coordinates of the end-points, then those of the mid-point. Look for a number pattern in the x-coordinates, then in the y-coordinates, remembering that we are investigating *halfway* points.

3 Use your discovery to *predict* the coordinates of the mid-point of:

   a DC **b** BD **c** CE

4 If one end of an interval is at E, and F is the mid-point, where is the other endpoint?

5 Develop a formula for x_M, the x-coordinate of any mid-point, and another for y_M, the y-coordinate of any mid-point. Write verbal instructions as to how to use your formula.

8.2 Mid-point of an interval

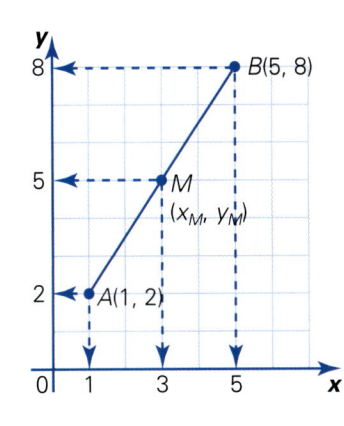

If M is the **mid-point** of AB, it is the *halfway* point between A and B.

The x-coordinate of M, (x_M), is halfway between 1 and 5;

that is, the **average** of 1 and 5: $\dfrac{1+5}{2} = 3$

So $x_M = \dfrac{x_A + x_B}{2}$

Similarly, the y-coordinate of M, (y_M), is halfway between 2 and 8;

that is, the **average** of 2 and 8: $\dfrac{2+8}{2} = 5$

So $y_M = \dfrac{y_A + y_B}{2}$

The mid-point formula

For the mid-point, coordinates are: $x_M = \dfrac{x_1 + x_2}{2}, \quad y_M = \dfrac{y_1 + y_2}{2}$

EXAMPLE 1

Find the mid-point of the interval joining $A(2, 3)$ to $B(5, 7)$.

Solution

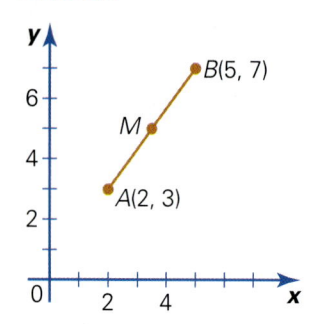

$$x_M = \frac{x_1 + x_2}{2} \qquad\qquad y_M = \frac{y_1 + y_2}{2}$$

$$= \frac{2 + 5}{2} \qquad\qquad = \frac{3 + 7}{2}$$

$$= 3{\cdot}5 \qquad\qquad = 5$$

$$M = (3{\cdot}5,\ 5)$$

EXAMPLE 2

$(1, {}^-2{\cdot}5)$ is the mid-point of the interval from $(t, {}^-4)$ to $(4, {}^-1)$. Find t.

Solution

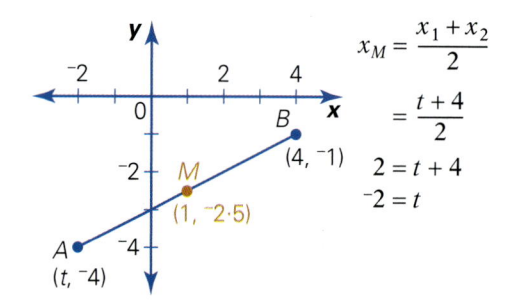

$$x_M = \frac{x_1 + x_2}{2}$$

$$= \frac{t + 4}{2}$$

$$2 = t + 4$$

$${}^-2 = t$$

EXERCISE 8B

1 Find the mid-point of the interval, joining the points:

a	$(1, 4)$ and $(3, 6)$	**b**	$(3, 7)$ and $(5, 9)$	**c**	$(0, 4)$ and $(6, 6)$
d	$(2, 4)$ and $(3, 5)$	**e**	$(7, 2)$ and $(5, 3)$	**f**	$(1, 6)$ and $(4, 2)$
g	$(0, 0)$ and $({}^-2, {}^-4)$	**h**	$({}^-2, {}^-3)$ and $({}^-4, {}^-5)$	**i**	$({}^-3, {}^-1)$ and $({}^-5, {}^-5)$
j	$({}^-3, {}^-4)$ and $(5, 6)$	**k**	$(0, {}^-8)$ and $({}^-6, 0)$	**l**	$(3, {}^-4)$ and $({}^-3, 4)$

Level 2

2 a Show that the mid-point of the interval joining $({}^-4, {}^-4)$ and $(4, 0)$ lies on the y-axis.
  b How far from the origin is this mid-point?

3 Show that the x-axis bisects the interval joining $({}^-6, 3)$ to $({}^-8, {}^-3)$.

4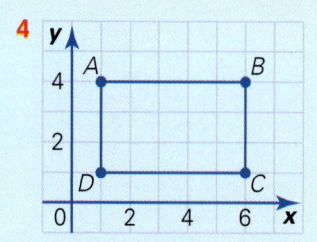

  a Find the mid-point of AC.
  b Find the mid-point of BD.
  c Are both **a** and **b** the same point?
  d What property of the diagonals of a rectangle does this show?

5 a Plot the four corner points of any square in the first quadrant.
  b Use the coordinates of the points to show that the diagonals of your square bisect each other, and that the diagonals are equal.

6 In each of the following, M is the mid-point of AB. Find the unknown coordinate:

a $M(3, 5), A(0, 4), B(6, t)$
b $M(1, 5\frac{1}{2}), A(^-4, 6), B(p, 5)$
c $M(1, 3), A(^-1, 1), B(p, t)$
d $M(8, 5), A(a, b), B(10, 2)$
e $M(1, 4), A(^-2, a), B(b, 1)$
f $M(^-2\cdot5, 4), A(3\cdot5, ^-6), B(m, t)$

7 The diameter of a circle, centre C, stretches from $A(1, 1)$ to $B(5, 7)$.

a Find the coordinates of C.
b Find the radius of the circle.
c Show that $D(5, 1)$ lies on the circle.

8 Find the point of bisection of AB:

a $A(^-3, ^-4), B(^-8, ^-3)$
b $A(3a, 2t), B(5a, 4t)$
c $A(4p, ^-2n), B(2p, 6n)$

d $A(a, 3b), B(^-a, ^-3b)$
e $A\left(\frac{1}{3}, \frac{1}{4}\right), B\left(\frac{1}{2}, \frac{2}{3}\right)$
f $A(2n^2, ^-3p), B(n^2, ^-p)$

9 If the mid-point of an interval is $(1, 4)$, what could the end-points be?

Level 3

10 A triangle has vertices $A(^-1, ^-1), B(5, ^-2)$ and $C(0, ^-7)$. AN is an axis of symmetry. Find:

a the coordinates of N
b the mid-point of AN
c the distance from A to N.

11 Three vertices of a parallelogram are $(10, 2), (2, 6)$ and the origin. Use the property of diagonals of a parallelogram bisecting each other to find the fourth vertex. Is there more than one possible answer?

12 If B is the mid-point of AC, what is the ratio of:

a $AB : BC$?
b $AB : AC$?

8.3 Gradient

Engineers involved in road or rail construction must consider **gradient** or **slope** of the track.

As a way of describing it mathematically, the distance moved **vertically** is compared to the distance moved **horizontally**.

RISING SLOPES

For the rockclimber, the **rise** is 5 units (up) and the **run** is 1 unit (left to right). Gradient $= \frac{5}{1}$ or 5.

For the car, the **rise** is 1 unit (up) and the **run** is 5 units (left to right). Gradient $= \frac{1}{5}$.

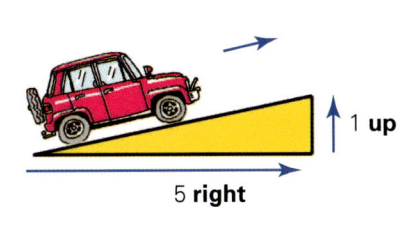

1 **up**

5 **right**

5 **up**

1 **right**

$$\text{Gradient} = \frac{\text{rise}}{\text{run}} = \frac{\text{vertical movement}}{\text{horizontal movement}} = \frac{\text{change in } y\text{-value}}{\text{change in } x\text{-value}} \quad \text{moving from left to right}$$

FALLING SLOPES

For the skier, there is a **fall** of 5 units (down).

$\text{Gradient} = \dfrac{^-5}{2}$ or $^-2{\cdot}5$.

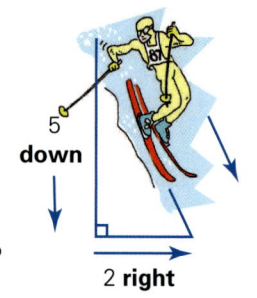

For the car, the fall is 2 units, so the rise is $^-2$. The run is 5 units (left to right).

Gradient is $\dfrac{^-2}{5}$ or $^-0{\cdot}4$.

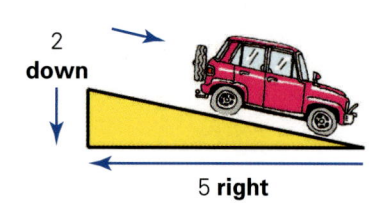

The gradient is **positive** for slopes that **rise** from left to right.
The gradient is **negative** for slopes that **fall** from left to right.

Note that the larger the value of the gradient number (ignoring the +/− signs), the steeper the slope.

EXAMPLE 1

Find the gradient of:

a AB

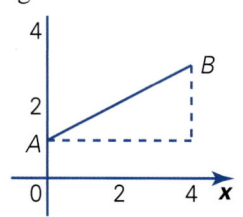

b CD

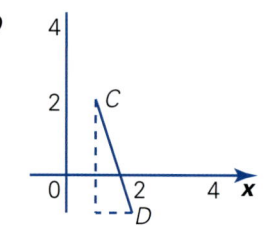

Solution

a Gradient $AB = \dfrac{2}{4}$

$\qquad = \dfrac{1}{2}$

b Gradient $CD = {}^-3$

$\qquad = {}^-3$

EXAMPLE 2

Draw a line MT, with $M(1, 2)$, gradient $\dfrac{2}{3}$. Give one possible set of coordinates for T.

Solution

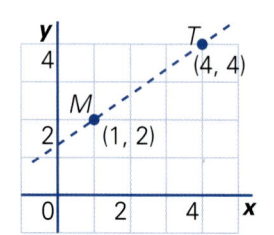

Go from M **up** 2, **right** 3.

EXERCISE 8C

Remember the **run** goes from left to right.

1 For the figures below, determine the **rise** and **run** to calculate the gradient of each slope.

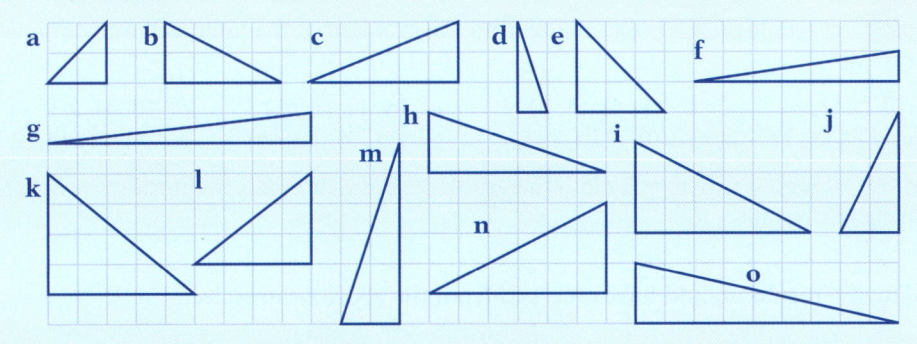

2 Find the gradient of each line in the number plane.

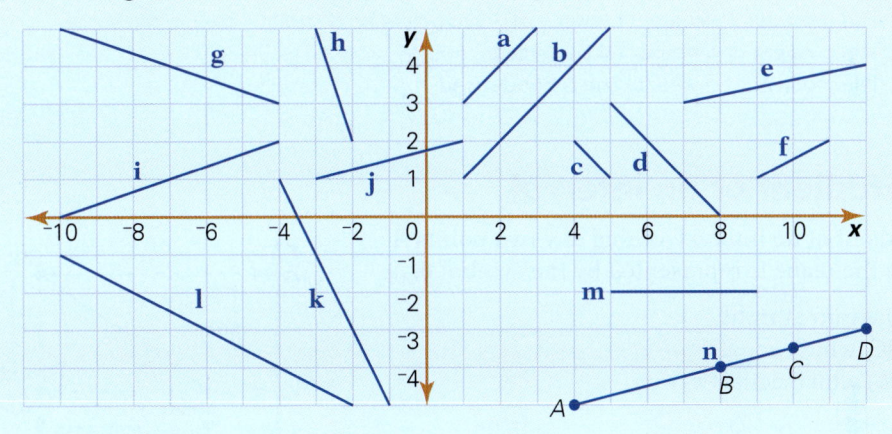

Level 2

3 a What special geometrical relationship exists between the lines in parts **a** and **b** of question **2**?
  b What do you notice about the gradients of these two lines?
  c For which other pairs of lines in question **2** is this the case?

4 Consider the line in question **2** part **n**. Calculate the gradient of:

  a AB
  b AD
  c BC
  d CD

  e Comment on your findings from parts **a–d**.

5 Draw up a set of axes on a grid such as the one in question **2**. Construct line intervals with beginning points and gradients as follows:

  a $A(2, 3)$, gradient $\frac{1}{4}$
  b $C(2, 0)$, gradient 2
  c $E(1, 7)$, gradient $\frac{-2}{3}$

  d $G(-6, 4)$, gradient $\frac{-1}{5}$
  e $J(-5, -2)$, gradient -3
  f $L(0, -4)$, gradient $\frac{4}{5}$

  g $N(0, -2)$, gradient $\frac{1}{4}$
  h $Q(-6, 0)$, gradient 0.4

Chapter 8: **Coordinate geometry and linear functions** **235**

6 What is the gradient of a horizontal line?

7 a What problem is encountered when you try to find the gradient of a vertical line?
 b What is the best answer to give for the gradient of a vertical line?

8 By plotting points on a number plane, find the gradient of the interval connecting the following:

a $(2, 3), (3, 6)$	**b** $(1, 4), (4, 0)$	**c** $(5, 1), (1, {}^-1)$	**d** $(0, 4), ({}^-3, 3)$
e $({}^-1, 7), (3, 7)$	**f** $(0, {}^-1), ({}^-2, 5)$	**g** $({}^-3, {}^-4), (2, {}^-4)$	**h** $({}^-1, {}^-3), (8, {}^-0.5)$

9 Can you suggest a way to calculate the gradient of the intervals in question **8** *without* plotting the points?

The following results should have emerged from the previous exercise:

> The gradients of parallel lines are equal.
> The gradients calculated between any two points on a straight line are the same.
> The gradient of a horizontal line is zero.
> The gradient of a vertical line is not defined.

8.4 Gradient of an interval

The gradient of an interval joining any two points A and B in the plane is represented by the symbol m_{AB}.

In the diagram at right,
rise is BC, which equals $y_2 - y_1$
run is AC, which equals $x_2 - x_1$

So $m_{AB} = \dfrac{\text{rise}}{\text{run}} = \dfrac{y_2 - y_1}{x_2 - x_1}$

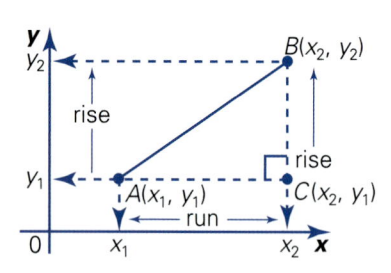

> The gradient of any interval $= \dfrac{\text{rise}}{\text{run}} = \dfrac{\text{change in } y}{\text{change in } x} = \dfrac{\text{difference of } y\text{-coordinates}}{\text{difference of } x\text{-coordinates}}$
>
> $m = \dfrac{y_2 - y_1}{x_2 - x_1}$

EXAMPLE
Find the gradient of the line joining $P({}^-2, 3)$ to $Q(3, {}^-5)$.

Solution

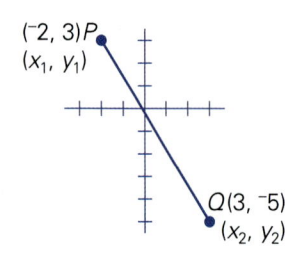

$m_{PQ} = \dfrac{y_2 - y_1}{x_2 - x_1}$

$= \dfrac{{}^-5 - 3}{3 - {}^-2} = \dfrac{{}^-8}{5}$

Is m_{QP} the same?

1 Use the formula to find the gradient of the interval joining these points:

- **a** (2, 3) and (3, 5)
- **b** (2, 2) and (4, 3)
- **c** (3, 5) and (6, 7)
- **d** (0, 0) and (4, 6)
- **e** (1, 2) and (9, 8)
- **f** (1, 7) and (5, 2)
- **g** (6, 1) and (2, ⁻1)
- **h** (0, 3) and (⁻3, 2)
- **i** (⁻1, ⁻1) and (⁻4, ⁻1)
- **j** (⁻5, ⁻3) and (⁻2, ⁻5)
- **k** (0, ⁻2) and $(3, \frac{-1}{2})$
- **l** (7·5, 4) and (⁻4·5, 1·5)

2 What is the gradient of the line passing through the origin and (⁻3, 2)?

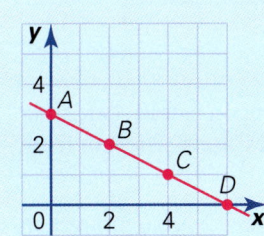

3 Refer to the diagram at left to find the gradient of:

- **a** AB
- **b** BC
- **c** CD
- **d** AC
- **e** BD
- **f** AD

Level 2

4 Consider the results of question **3** to decide true or false for the following:

- **a** *Any* two points on a straight line can be used to find its gradient.
- **b** The gradient of a line remains the same for its entire length.
- **c** If A, B and C are three points such that $m_{AB} = m_{BC}$, then the points must be **collinear**. (Note that a common point B is used in both gradients.)

5 Find the gradient of the interval joining these points:

- **a** (t, t) and $(3t, 5t)$
- **b** $(n, ⁻n)$ and $(4n, 0)$
- **c** $(t, 2t)$ and $(5t, 0)$

6 The gradient of the line going through the points $(3, p)$ and $(4, 7)$ is 5. Find p.

7 Find:

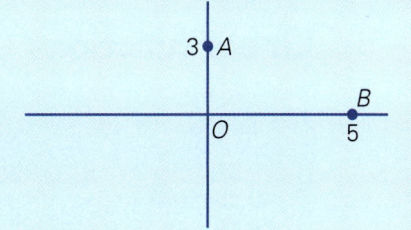

- **a** the gradient AB
- **b** the distance AB
- **c** the midpoint, M, of AB
- **d** the distance from the origin O to M
- **e** the area of triangle OAB.

GRAPHIC CALCULATOR

Consider a common type of function similar to those discussed on the previous pages:
$y = x + 2$

1 Construct a table of ordered pairs in which the input (x) values are $^-3, ^-1, 0, 1, 3$.

$y = x + 2$					
x					
y					

2 Draw up a number plane with values on the axes large enough to handle the x- and y-coordinates from the table. Use the same scale on both axes.

3 Plot the ordered pairs from the function table.

4 What shape do the five points form? To see if this shape remains consistent, calculate y when x is $^-6, ^-1\frac{1}{2}, 0\cdot5, 2\cdot8$, or any other 'in-between' or extended values different from those in the table. Do all new points maintain their shape?

5 Imagine: if *all possible* ordered pairs that satisfy the function $y = x + 2$ were plotted on the graph, would you expect them to maintain this path? Explain.

6 Select any new point with integral coordinates that appears to lie on the path or shape formed by $y = x + 2$. Substitute the coordinates into the equation. Do they *satisfy* it?

7 Select a point in each quadrant so that it appears *not* to lie on the defined path. Go for integral coordinates again. Substitute each set of coordinates into the function. Do they *satisfy* it?

8 Write a statement to summarise your findings in questions **6** and **7**.

9 If it seems that the shape you have discovered is consistently maintained *for all values of x*, what is the **minimum number of points** you could plot in future to graph such a function? Explain your decision.

8.5 Linear functions

GRAPHIC CALCULATOR

> A **function** is a *rule* that relates one number to another.
>
> It is generally written as an *equation* using the *variables* x and y. For each value of x there is just one value of y.

The equation of a line is the relationship between the x- and y- coordinates for any point on the line.

Where the rule is known, we simply **input** a value for x (*substitute* in the expression) and the **output** (*value* of the expression) is labelled y. The value of y *depends* upon the value of x, so y is often called the **dependent variable**.

An ordered pair satisfies the function if it makes the equation true when the values are substituted.

FINDING THE FUNCTION

To find the function from a table of values where consecutive values of x are taken, look at the **differences** between consecutive y-values. This tells you what to multiply x by. Then look at any of the (x, y) pairs to see what must be added or subtracted to make the rule correct.

For example, consider the table:

x	0	1	2	3
y	$^-1$	1	3	5

For a unit increase in x, the y-values increase by 2. This tells us that the rule is $y = 2x + \square$

Substitute $x = 0$, $y = {}^-1$:

$$^-1 = 2 \times 0 + \square$$
$$^-1 = 0 + \square$$
$$\square = {}^-1$$

So the rule is $y = 2x + {}^-1$ or $y = 2x - 1$

> How could you adapt this method if the x-values were not consecutive?

> **Linear functions** produce *straight line* graphs.
> They fit the pattern $y = mx + b$
> A point lies on a line if its coordinates satisfy the equation of the line.

Note:
1. Both x and y are variables to the *power of one* and only one.
2. m and b may have *any constant values*:

These are all variations of the **linear function** pattern.

$$y = mx + b$$
$$y = 2x + 3$$
$$y = {}^-4x + 0 \quad (y = {}^-4x)$$
$$y = \frac{1}{2}x + {}^-1$$
$$y = 0{\cdot}8x + \frac{3}{4}$$

EXAMPLES

a. Graph $y = 2x - 1$.
b. Does the point $(^-2, {}^-5)$ lie on the graph?
c. From your graph, find y when x is $^-1$; x when y is 6.

Solutions

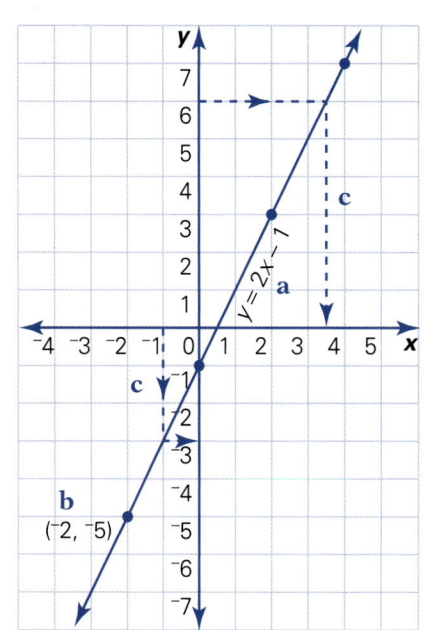

x	0	2	4
y	⁻1	⁻3	7

$y = 2x - 1$

Choose three simple values for x, then calculate y.

b (⁻2, ⁻5) lies on the line.
c When $x = ^-1$:
$$y = 2x - 1 - 1$$
$$= ^-3$$
When $y = 6$:
$$6 = 2 \times x - 1$$
$$7 = 2x$$
$$x = 3{\cdot}5$$

Plot the point on the graph.

EXERCISE 8E

1 Which of the following are linear functions?

  a $y = 3x + 2$ **b** $y = x^2 - 3$ **c** $y = ^-2x - 1$ **d** $y = \frac{1}{3}x + 4$

  e $y = 5x$ **f** $y = \frac{1}{x}$ **g** $y = 3 - 2x$ **h** $x + y = 4$

2 For the following linear equations, give the replacement for
i m, **ii** b, from the pattern $y = mx + b$:

  a $y = 5x + 8$ **b** $y = \frac{1}{2}x - 3$ **c** $y = ^-3x$

  d $y = x - 4$ **e** $y = 6 - x$ **f** $y = ^-x$

  g $y = 0{\cdot}9 - 4x$

Remember: each equation must be in the exact pattern $y = mx + b$. Rearrange if necessary.

3 Complete the following tables, then graph each pair on the same axes.

a   **i**

$y = x + 2$			
x	0	2	4
y			

  ii

$y = ^-x + 2$			
x	0	2	4
y			

Cambridge Spectrum Maths 9 5.3

b i

$y = x - 4$			
x	0	4	6
y			

ii

$y = 4 - x$			
x	0	1	2
y			

c i

$y = 2 + 3x$			
x	⁻3	0	3
y			

ii

$y = 3x - 4$			
x	⁻3	0	3
y			

4 Choose your own x-values to draw the graphs of $x + y = 3$ and $x + y = 6$ on the same axes.

5 Find which of the given ordered pairs *satisfies* (makes true) the equation:

a $y = x$ (0, 0) (2, 2) (⁻3, 3)   **b** $y = 2 + 3x$ (0, 5) (1, 5) (⁻2, ⁻4)
c $y = ⁻2x - 3$ (0, ⁻3) (1, ⁻5) (⁻1, ⁻1)

6 If $y = x + 3$, find the value of x if y equals:

a 6   **b** 0   **c** ⁻1   **d** ⁻2·6   **e** $⁻3\frac{3}{4}$

7 How many ordered pairs satisfy the equation $y = 3x - 2$?

8 Without graphing, test to see which of the following points lie on the line $y = 2x - 1$:

a (3, 5)   **b** (0, ⁻1)   **c** (⁻1, ⁻1)   **d** $\left(\frac{1}{2}, 0\right)$

9 Does the line $y = 2 - 3x$ pass through the point (⁻2·5, ⁻5·5)?

Level 2

10 Find a function rule for each of the following tables:

a

x	0	1	2	3
y	4	5	6	7

b

x	0	1	2	3
y	⁻1	0	1	2

c

x	1	2	3	4
y	3	6	9	12

d

x	⁻2	0	4	6
y	⁻1	0	2	3

e

x	⁻2	0	2	4
y	⁻3	1	5	9

f

x	⁻3	0	2	4
y	3	0	⁻2	⁻4

Investigation Linear functions of the form $y = mx + b$

Gradients

1 Draw these graphs:

a $y = x$ **b** $y = 2x$ **c** $y = 4x$ **d** $y = \frac{1}{2}x$

e $y = ⁻x$ **f** $y = ⁻2x$ **g** $y = ⁻3x$ **h** $y = \frac{⁻1}{3}x$

2 Calculate the gradient of each graph in question **1**.

3 What is the connection between the coefficient of the x-value in the equation and the gradient of the line? Write a sentence summarising your observations.

SPREADSHEET ACTIVITY

INTERACTIVE GEOMETRY

GRAPHIC CALCULATOR

4 What would you expect the gradient of these lines to be?

  a $y = 10x$ **b** $y = \frac{2}{5}x$ **c** $y = \frac{^-1}{2}x$ **d** $y = \frac{x}{3}$ **e** $y = \frac{^-3x}{4}$

Intercepts

1 Draw these graphs:

  a $y = x$ **b** $y = x + 2$ **c** $y = x + 5$ **d** $y = x - 3$ **e** $y = x + \frac{1}{2}$

2 The y-intercept of a graph is the point where the graph crosses the y-axis. What is the y-intercept of each of the graphs in question 1?

3 What is the connection between the equation of the graph and its y-intercept?

4 Where would you expect the y-intercept to be for these graphs?

  a $y = x - 1$ **b** $y = x + 3 \cdot 4$ **c** $y = 2 + x$

5 a Draw the graph of $y = 2x + 3$.
  b What would you expect the gradient and y-intercept to be? Check that you are correct.

6 Give the gradient and y-intercept for these graphs:

  a $y = 6x$ **b** $y = {}^-2x + 1$ **c** $y = 2x - 3$ **d** $y = \frac{2}{3}x + 5$

  e $y = {}^-4x + 7$ **f** $y = 5 + 4x$ **g** $y = 6 - x$ **h** $y = \frac{x}{4} - 5$

7 Which functions would produce these graphs?

8.6 Gradient–intercept form of a linear function

An equation in the form $y = mx + b$ graphs as a straight line in which m tells the **gradient** and b the **y-intercept**.

$$y = mx + b$$
$$\text{gradient} \uparrow \quad \uparrow \ y\text{-intercept}$$

Note: The y-intercept is the point where the graph cuts the y-axis.

EXAMPLE 1

For each linear function, find: **i** gradient, **ii** y-intercept.

  a $y = {}^-2x + 3$ **b** $y = \frac{3x}{2}$ **c** $y - x = 4$ **d** $2x + 3y = 6$

Solutions

a **i** $m = {}^-2$

  ii $b = 3$

b **i** $m = \frac{3}{2}$

  ii $b = 0$

c $y - x = 4$ | Make y the subject. |
   $y = x + 4$

   i $m = 1$ **ii** $b = 4$

d $2x + 3y = 6$ | Rearrange to make y the subject. |
   $3y = {}^-2x + 6$

   $y = \frac{^-2}{3}x + 2$

   i $m = \frac{^-2}{3}$ **ii** $b = 2$

EXAMPLE 2

From the graph, find:

a gradient   **b** intercept   **c** equation

of the line.

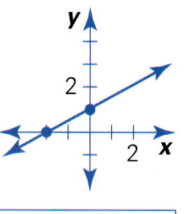

Solutions

a $m = \dfrac{1}{2}$ **b** $b = 1$ **c** $y = \dfrac{1}{2}x + 1$

$$y = mx + b$$

EXERCISE 8F

1 State **i** gradient, **ii** y-intercept, for each of the following lines:

a $y = 2x + 5$ **b** $y = 3x - 2$ **c** $y = 1x + 1$ **d** $y = x - 3$

e $y = {}^-2x + 4$ **f** $y = {}^-5x - 6$ **g** $y = 4x + 0$ **h** $y = 3x$

i $y = x$ **j** $y = {}^-2x$ **k** $y = \dfrac{1}{2}x + 4$ **l** $y = \dfrac{2x}{3}$

m $y = \dfrac{{}^-3}{5}x$ **n** $y = {}^-x$ **o** $y = {}^-x - \dfrac{1}{2}$ **p** $y = 1{\cdot}8x - 0{\cdot}4$

q $y = \dfrac{x}{5} - 7$ **r** $y = 3 - x$ **s** $y = \dfrac{1}{2} - 3x$ **t** $y = 8 - \dfrac{2x}{5}$

u $y - x = 5$ **v** $y - 2x = 4$ **w** $y = 4$ **x** $2y - 4x = 6$

Level 2

2 a   Write the equation of the line that has gradient and y-intercept of:

   i $m = 3, b = 2$ **ii** $m = 1, b = 6$ **iii** $m = 2, b = 0$

   iv $m = {}^-4, b = 3$ **v** $m = \dfrac{1}{2}, b = 4$ **vi** $m = \dfrac{{}^-3}{4}, b = \dfrac{1}{2}$

   vii $m = 0, b = 2$ **viii** $m = 0, b = {}^-3$ **ix** $m = 0, b = 0$

b   What special line in the number plane is part **a, ix**?

3 Find the gradient and y-intercept of each line from its graph, and hence write its equation:

a 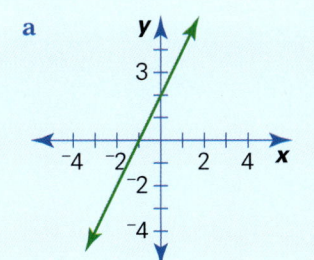   **b** 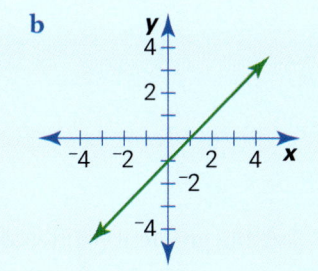   **c**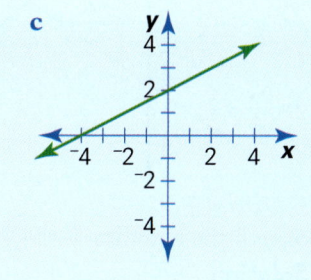

d 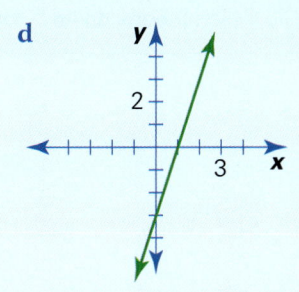   **e** 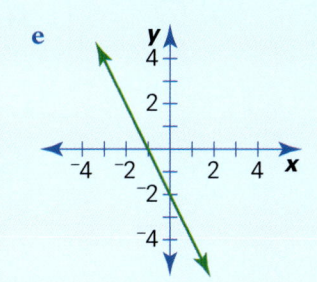   **f**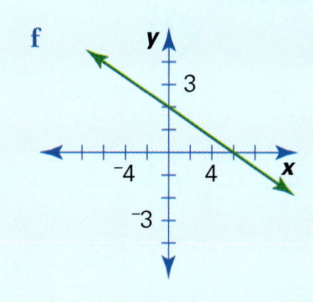

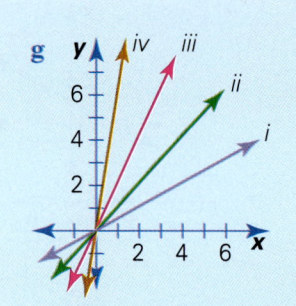
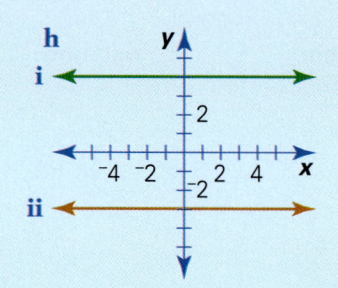
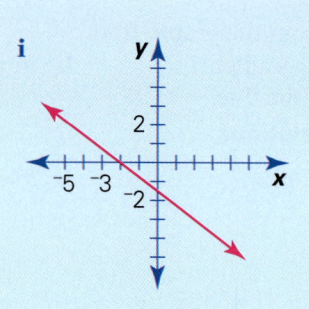

4 a List four points that lie on line A.
  b Write the equation of the line A.
  c Write the equation of line B.
  d What is the equation of the y-axis?

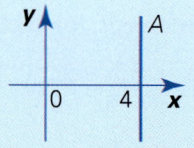
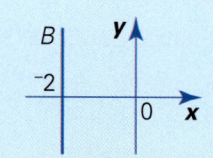

5 Why is it not possible to use the $y = mx + b$ pattern for the lines in question **4**?

8.7 Graphing lines

GRAPHING LINES USING GRADIENT AND Y-INTERCEPT

Given the gradient and y-intercept of a line, which can be determined from its equation, we can draw its graph.

EXAMPLE 1
Sketch the function $y = \dfrac{2x}{3} - 2$, using gradient, y-intercept.

Solution

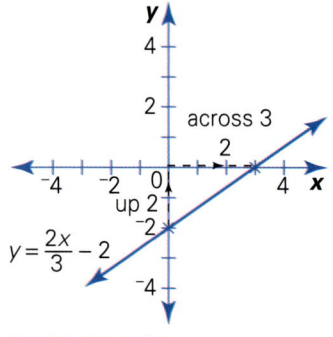

> Mark the y-intercept at $y = {}^-2$.

> Gradient $= \dfrac{2}{3}$ so rise = 2, run = 3.

EXAMPLE 2
Sketch the equation $y = \dfrac{{}^-5x}{4} + 3$, using gradient, y-intercept.

Solution

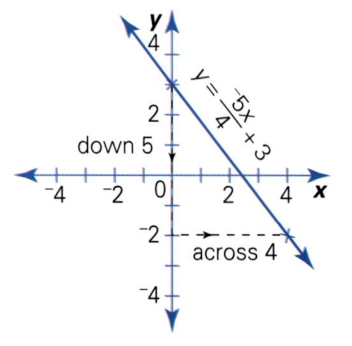

> $M = \dfrac{{}^-5}{4}$, which means **down** 5, **right** 4.

EXERCISE 8G

1 Graph each linear function using the data given:

   a gradient 2, y-intercept 3   **b** gradient 1, y-intercept $^-2$

   c gradient $\frac{1}{2}$, y-intercept 1   **d** gradient $\frac{3}{4}$, y-intercept 0

   e $m = {}^-3, b = 4$ **f** $m = {}^-2, b = 1$ **g** $m = \frac{^-2}{3}, b = {}^-1$

   h $m = 0, b = 2{\cdot}5$ **i** $m = \frac{1}{5}, b = {}^-2$ **j** $m = \frac{^-3}{2}, b = 2\frac{1}{2},$

   k $y = 2x + 1$ **l** $y = 3x - 2$ **m** $y = x + 2$

Level 2

   n $y = {}^-4x$ **o** $y = \frac{1}{3}x$ **p** $y = \frac{x}{4} - 3$

   q $y = \frac{^-1}{2}x + 4$ **r** $y = \frac{^-2x}{5} + 3$ **s** $y = 4 - \frac{6x}{5}$

2   **i** Change each equation into the form $y = mx + b$.

    ii Find gradient and y-intercept.

    iii Draw the function.

   a $3y = 6x - 9$ **b** $2y = 8x - 4$ **c** $4y = 6x$ **d** $^-2y = 3x$

   e $5y = 10 - 4x$ **f** $3y = 12$ **g** $y + 2 = x$ **h** $y - 3 = 2x$

   i $\frac{y}{2} = x + 3$ **j** $\frac{1}{3}y = x - 1$ **k** $2y - 4 = 4x$ **l** $3y + 6 = 3x$

   m $y - 2x = 5$ **n** $2y - x = 4$ **o** $x + y = 2$ **p** $x - y = 5$

   q $x + 3y = 12$ **r** $5y + 2x = 10$ **s** $2x + 3y - 6 = 0$ **t** $4x + 8y - 12 = 0$

3

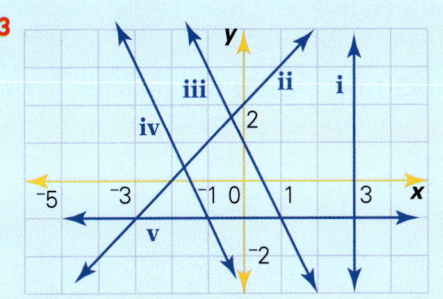

Match each line in the graph with its equation:

   a $2y = 2x + 4$ **b** $3y = {}^-3$

   c $y + 2x = 1$ **d** $4x = 12$

   e $x + \frac{y}{2} + 1\frac{1}{2} = 0$ **f** $^-3y = 0$

4 Which of the following lines are parallel to the line $y = 3x + 4$?

   a $y = 5x + 4$ **b** $y = 3x + 8$ **c** $y = 4x + 3$

   d $y = 3x$ **e** $3x - y + 7 = 0$ **f** $6x - 2y + 3 = 0$

5 Write the equations of two lines that are parallel to:

   a $y = 5x - 1$ **b** $y = \frac{x}{2} + 7$ **c** $x + 2y + 3 = 0$

6 Determine whether $AB \parallel CD$ for the following points:

   a $A(1, 3), B(5, 5), C(3, 2), D(7, 4)$ **b** $A(2, 0), B(8, 2), C(4, 2), D(2, ^-4)$

   c $A(4, 8), B(7, 2), C(^-3, ^-4), D(0, 2)$ **d** $A(^-5, 5), B(3, ^-7), C(^-4, ^-5), D(5, 1)$

7

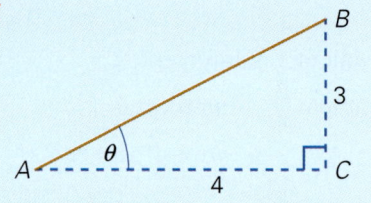

a What is the gradient of *AB*?
b What is tan θ?
c From parts **a** and **b**, what is the relationship between the gradient of a line and the angle the line makes with the horizontal? (In the positive direction of the *x*-axis.)

Use your findings from question **7** to answer questions **8** and **9**.

8 Find the gradients of the lines that make these angles with the positive direction of the *x*-axis.

a 45°	**b** 11°	**c** 76°	**d** 63°	**e** 31°
f 42°	**g** 58°	**h** 87°	**i** 22°	**j** 39°

9 Find the angle made with the positive direction of the *x*-axis by lines with these gradients.

a $\frac{1}{2}$	**b** $\frac{3}{4}$	**c** 2	**d** $\frac{6}{5}$	**e** $\frac{1}{10}$
f $\frac{13}{5}$	**g** 20	**h** $\frac{2}{3}$	**i** 3	**j** $\frac{3}{2}$

PRACTICAL APPLICATIONS

Linear relations occur on many occasions in everyday life. Often a graph of a formula or rule enables easy calculation of new data or display of trends.

EXAMPLE

Scales for weighing fruit and vegetables can be made from a spring that stretches according to the rule $E = 3w$, where E means the extension of the spring in centimetres and w stands for the weight placed on the scales, in kilograms.

Graph the relationship, and from your graph find:

a the extension produced by a weight of 4·5 kg
b the weight causing an extension of 20 cm.

Solutions

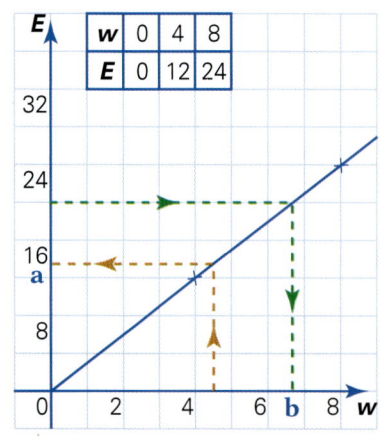

w	0	4	8
E	0	12	24

> The rule is of the pattern $y = mx + b$,
>
> $E = 3w + 0$

a $E \approx 14$ cm
b $w \approx 6.6$ kg

TEACHER

TEACHER

EXERCISE 8H

Explore each of the following situations by graphing.

1 In an experiment, the distance travelled (in cm) by a moving part in a machine and the time taken (in seconds) are found to fit the formula $d = \frac{t}{2}$. For times up to 40 seconds find:

  a how far the part travels in 12 seconds
  b how long the part takes to move 12·5 cm.

2 A salesperson is paid a retainer of $200/week plus 20% commission on the value of sales. The formula is $P = 0{\cdot}2S + 200$, where P means pay in dollars, S means sales in dollars. Find:

  a the pay when sales are $2000 for the week
  b the sales needed to earn a weekly pay of $1000.

Level 2

3 Researchers in the beef industry have found that the relationship between the weight (w) of a calf in kilograms and the time (t) in weeks after its birth is $w = 10t + 40$. Examine the first 6 weeks of calf life to find:

  a the weight of a calf at birth
  b the weight when $2\frac{1}{2}$ weeks old
  c the age of a 95 kg calf.

4 A car rental agency formulates a rule to cover the cost of running a car as $C = 0{\cdot}3d + 10$, where C = cost in dollars and d is distance travelled, in kilometres.

  a For distances up to 600 km, find:
     i how much it costs to run a car for 360 km in a day
     ii how far in a day a car can be driven for $106
     ii the weekly cost of travelling to work if it is a 40 km trip each way each day. Assume a 5-day working week.
  b What is the meaning of the constant term, 10?

5 Average baby birth weight is 3·2 kg, with weight gain at the average rate of one-quarter of a kilogram per week for the first 15 weeks.

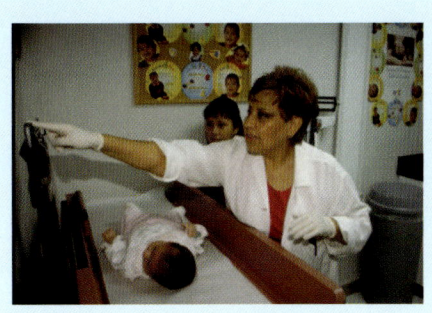

  a Write a formula for baby weight (W) in kilograms connected with time (t) in weeks.
  b What will an 8-week-old baby weigh?
  c How long will it take a baby to reach a weight of 5 kg?
  d How long will it take a baby to double its birth weight?
  e How much lighter than average is a 9-week-old baby that weighs 4850 grams?

6 A plane is now 9 km east (x) and 2 km north (y) of its destination airstrip (the origin). Strong winds blow it on to a course mapped as $x = 2y + 5$. If it continues on this course

a how far from the airstrip will it be:
   i when it is due east of the airstrip?
   ii when it is due south of the airstrip?
   iii when it is at the closest point to the airstrip? (Use scale measurement.)
b how are the intercepts on the axes related to **i** and **ii** of part **a**?

7 On a navigation map in which the N–S line is designated as y, E–W as x, a ship is currently located at coordinates (4, ⁻3·5). If it sails along a course described by the relationship $3x + 4y + 2 = 0$ and all scaled units represent kilometres:

a how far north of rocks located at (0, ⁻1) will it pass?
b how far east of a reef located at (⁻2, 0) will it pass?
c is it on the correct course to rendezvous with a tugboat waiting at coordinates (⁻6, 4)?

Chapter Review

Language Links

axis (axes)	graph	ordered	slope
coordinates	horizontal	origin	solution
dependent	hypotenuse	parallel	substitution
distance	intercept	Pythagoras	variable
equation	interval	rise	vertical
function	linear	run	vertices
gradient	mid-point		

Fill in the missing words in the following passage by referring to the list above. (Some words may need adapting to fit the context.)

The number plane is divided into four _____ by two _____, labelled x and y. Each point is identified by two _____, arranged as an _____ pair (x, y). Each rule relating _____ x and y, if it fits the pattern $y = mx + b$, is called a _____ _____, since its _____ is a straight line.

The _____ of each line is defined as $\frac{\text{rise}}{\text{run}}$. _____ lines have the same slope.

The _____ $y = mx + b$ reveals two key features to enable quick sketching of the corresponding line. m stands for _____, b stands for y-_____.

If $b = 0$, the line must pass through the _____.

If $m = 0$, the line must be _____ to the x-_____.

CLUES

Across

5 Part of a line (joining two points).
6 A trigonometry ration: opposite/hypotenuse.
7 A source of great sound.
8 The point halfway along an interval.
11 The longest side of a right triangle.
12 Calculated in the same way as gradient.
14 Something put on wildlife to keep track of them.
15 Running in the same direction without meeting.
16 Measured between two points using Pythagoras's Theorem.

Down

1 Trig. ratio: adjacent/hypotenuse, abbreviated.
2 The number of intersection points when two straight lines cross.
3 $\dfrac{y_2 - y_1}{x_2 - x_1}$ for two points, minus the last one-eighth.
4 The degree of steepness of a line, minus the last 20%.
5 The size of the gradient of a line parallel to the y-axis (first four letters only).
7 The prefix meaning 'with or together' in the word, 'coordinates'.
8 The first word when asking permission.
9 The developer of the rule $c^2 = a^2 + b^2$ for right triangles.
10 Describes a line with infinitely large gradient, less the seventh letter.
11 Where earth meets sky, the slope is zero.
12 Thank you (abbreviation).
13 What our international rugby team always need more of.
14 A hint.

Chapter Review Exercises

MC

1

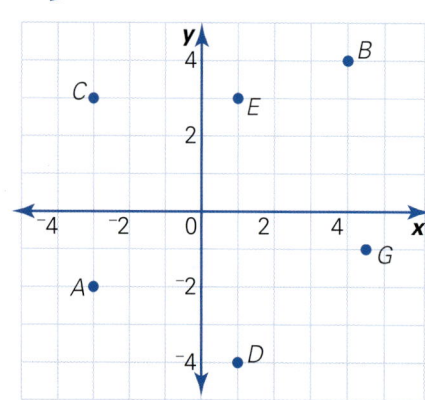

a Use the diagram to find these gradients:
  i AB **ii** AC **iii** CE
  iv CD **v** DG **vi** EG
b Name a pair of parallel lines, stating why they must be so.
c Find the length of AB.
d Find the mid-point of CD.
e Show which of the lines CD and EG has the steeper slope.

2 Use the gradient formula to find the slope of the interval joining:

a $(-2, -3)$ and $(5, -4)$ **b** $(-4, -7)$ and $(3, -7)$ **c** $(4, -3)$ and $(4, 5)$
d Show that $A(-5, -11)$, $B(0, -1)$ and $C(4, 7)$ must be collinear.

8.4

3 $M(3, -2)$ is the mid-point of the interval joining $P(-3, 4)$ and T. Find T.

8.2

4 a Find out if the interval from $(-4, 3)$ to $(3, -1)$ is parallel to the interval joining $(4, -8)$ and $(-3, -4)$.
b Determine whether or not the lines $3x - 4y + 2 = 0$ and $8x + 6y = 0$ are parallel.

8.3

5 $A(-3, -1)$, $B(1, 2)$, $C(4, 0\cdot5)$ and $D(-2, -4)$ form the vertices of a quadrilateral.

a Investigate gradients to classify the figure.
b Find out if diagonals are equal.

8.3

6 A quadrilateral is formed with $(-4, 1)$, $(0, 3)$, $(5, -2)$ and $(-2, -3)$ as vertices. Using the methods of coordinate geometry, find:

a what type of quadrilateral it is
b whether or not its diagonals bisect each other
c its area.

7 Use the number plane below to find the following:

a the y-intercept of function a
b the y-intercept of function b
c the gradient of b
d the equation of a.

8.6

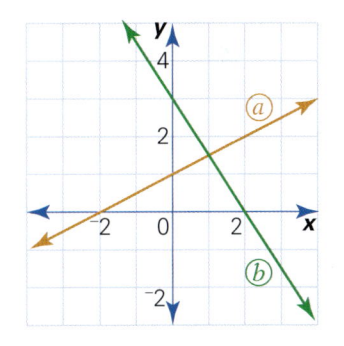

8 For the following functions, give **i** the gradient, **ii** the y-intercept:

a $y = 4x - 8$ **b** $2y = x - 8$ **c** $3x - 2y = 12$

8.6

9 Write the equation of:

a the x-axis   **b** the y-axis.

8.7

10 Find the equation of each line, given the following values:

a $m = -3, b = 0$ **b** $m = \dfrac{2}{3}, \; b = -2$

8.6

11 Which of the following are parallel to $y = 2x + 5$? Show why.

a $y = -2x$ **b** $y = 2x - 3$ **c** $y + 2x = 5$ **d** $2y = 4x + 6$

8.3

12 Sketch each function using gradient and y-intercept:

a $y = 4x - 2$ **b** $y = 2 - \dfrac{3x}{4}$ **c** $4x - 6y = 12$

8.7

13 Find the equation of a line that:

a is parallel to the x-axis, with a y-intercept of 3
b is parallel to $y = -2x + 1$, with a y-intercept of -3
c is parallel to the y-axis, with an x-intercept of -4.

TEACHER

Keeping Mathematically Fit

Part A—Non-calculator

1 Write an expression for the product of m and one-half of n.

2 Mrs McDonald used her handspan to measure the width of a window. She measured it as 8 handspans. The width of the window has approximately:

    A 1·6 m   **B** 3·5 m   **C** 8 m   **D** 16 m

3

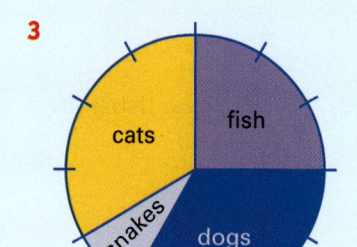

600 people were surveyed to find the most popular pet. How many preferred dogs?

4 A driver on her way from Canberra to Sydney wants to stop for a rest at the halfway point. How much further should she travel after she sees this sign?

Sydney 220 km   Canberra 80 km

5 The length of a rectangle is three times its width. The perimeter of the rectangle is:

    A 6 times the length   **B** 8 times the length
    C 6 times the width   **D** 8 times the width

6 $\frac{3}{5}$ of an amount is $30. What is the amount?

7 If $S = \frac{a}{l-r}$, find S when $r = \frac{1}{2}$ and $a = 6$.

8 Write a simplified expression for the perimeter of this square.

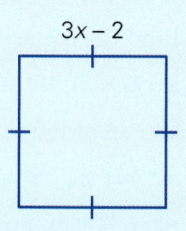

$3x - 2$

9 What is the highest common factor of $8p^2q^3$ and $12pq^2$?

10 Which of the cubes below could not have been formed from this net?

a 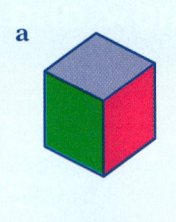   **b**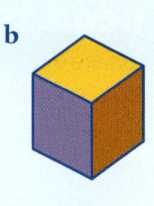

c 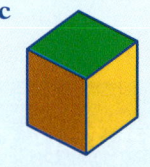   **d**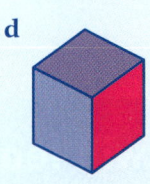

Part B—Calculator

1 Which is the better value for money: 150 g for \$4.35 or 250 g for \$7.15?

2 3500 runners entered a marathon. If 26% did not finish, how many runners completed the race?

3 This diagram shows the lengths of network cables.

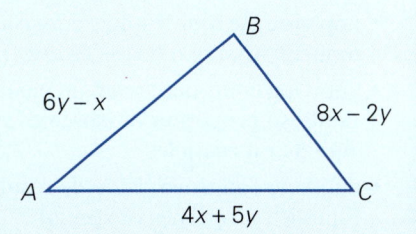

  a Find an expression for the length of cable between A and C via B.

  b How much greater is the length in **a** than the direct length from A to C?

  c What is the total length of cable used if x represents 1·2 m and y represents 1·7 m?

4 Solve for t: $1 + \dfrac{t}{2} = \dfrac{t}{3} - 2$

5 This pentagon was the symbol used by the Brotherhood, of which Pythagoras was a member. Calculate the angle at each point of the star.

1 What you need to know and revise

Outcome SGS 4.4:
Identifies similar and congruent figures stating the relevant conditions:

- identifying congruent figures by superimposing them through a combination of rotations, reflections and translations.

2 What you will learn in this chapter

Outcome SGS 5.2.2:
Develops and applies results for proving that triangles are congruent or similar:

- determining what information is needed to show that two triangles are congruent
- applying the four triangle congruency tests to justify that two triangles are congruent
- applying congruent triangle results to establish properties of isosceles and equilateral triangles
- applying congruent triangle results to establish properties of special quadrilaterals (e.g. square, rectangle, parallelogram, rhombus, kite, trapezium), including diagonal properties
- applying the four triangle congruency tests in numerical exercises to find unknown sides and angles.

Working Mathematically outcomes WMS 5.1, 5.2, 5.3
Students will be required to *question*, *apply strategies*, *communicate*, *reason* and *reflect* in the sections of this chapter.

9

Congruence

Key mathematical terms you will encounter

angle	isometric	projection	solid
congruent	net	proof	transformation
corresponding	oblique	pyramid	translation
dimension	perspective	reflection	triangle
elevation	plan	rotation	vertex
hypotenuse	prism	side	

MathsCheck
Congruent figures

Figures that are congruent are *identical* in size *and* shape.

The corresponding sides and angles of congruent figures are *equal*.

The symbol ≡ or ≅ means *is congruent to*.

Transformations

Transformations change the *size* or *position* of a figure.

A **congruence transformation** is a movement that leaves the *size* and *shape* of the figure unchanged.

The following are congruence transformations:

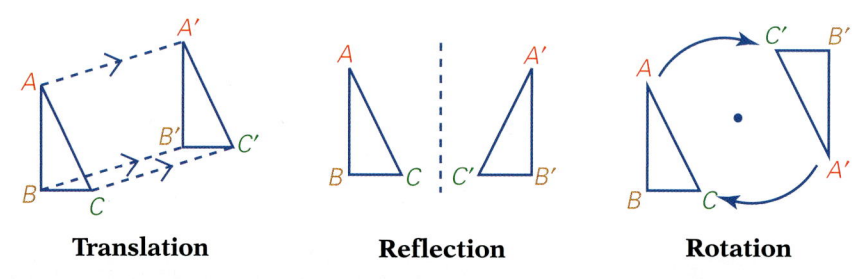

| **Translation** | **Reflection** | **Rotation** |

Note: The new figure that is produced is called the **image**, and the vertices of the image figure are labelled *A'*, *B'*, *C'*, and so on (read as '*A*-dash' etc.).

Enlargement is *not* a congruence transformation, since the size of the shape is changed.

Given these two figures, what transformations might have been performed to obtain the image figure from the original?

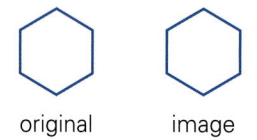

original   image

The transformation could have been:

    a translation   **or**   a rotation   **or**   a reflection

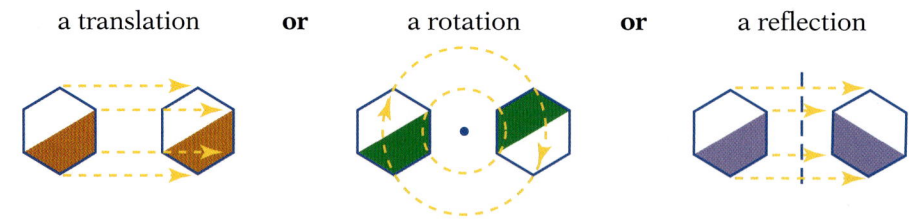

To determine which transformation has been performed, the positions of the original vertices need to be shown on the image figure.

For example, this would show that a reflection has been performed.

1 Identify all pairs of figures that are congruent:

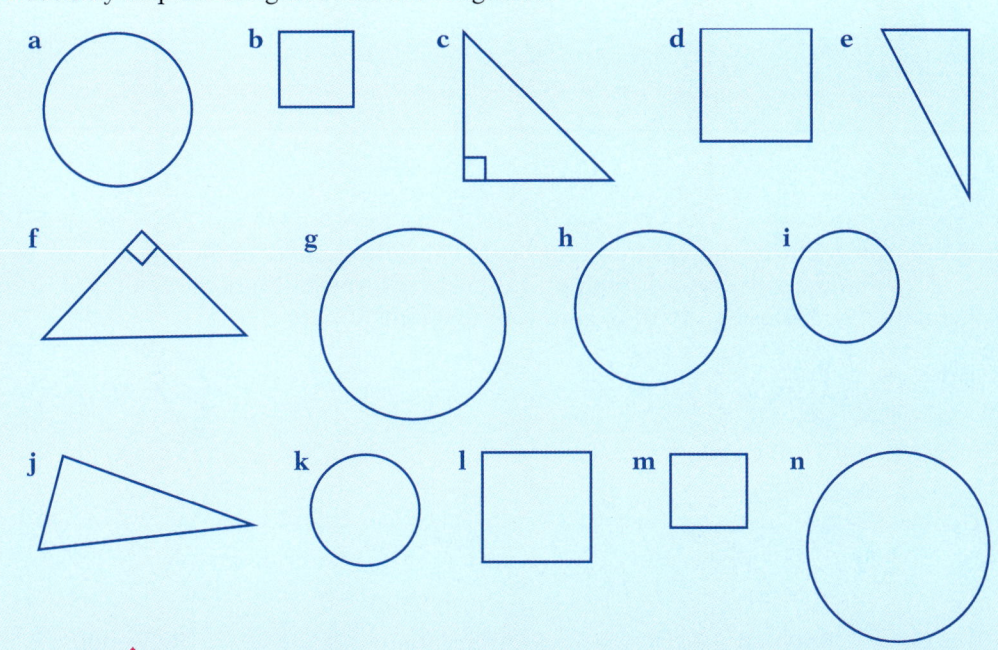

2

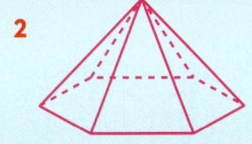 This hexagonal pyramid has its vertex directly above the centre of its base. How many congruent faces has the figure?

3 The faces of what solid are four congruent equilateral triangles?

4 Is it possible to draw two equilateral triangles that are not congruent? Explain.

5 What is the least amount of information necessary to determine whether or not two squares are congruent? Explain.

6 If two people each draw a rectangle of length 7 cm and width 5 cm, would the rectangles necessarily be congruent? Explain.

7 If two people each draw a parallelogram with one pair of sides 4 cm long and the other pair of sides 3 cm long, would the parallelograms necessarily be congruent? Explain.

8 For each of the figures shown below, determine which transformation could have been performed to obtain the image (in colour):

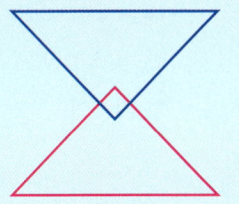 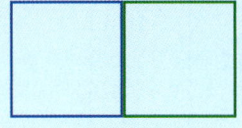 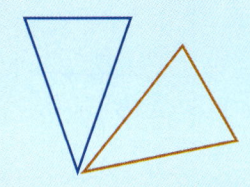

9 Copy the following figures into your book. Label the vertices of the image figure to show that the stated transformation has been performed. (Mark the centres of rotation and lines of reflection onto your diagrams.)

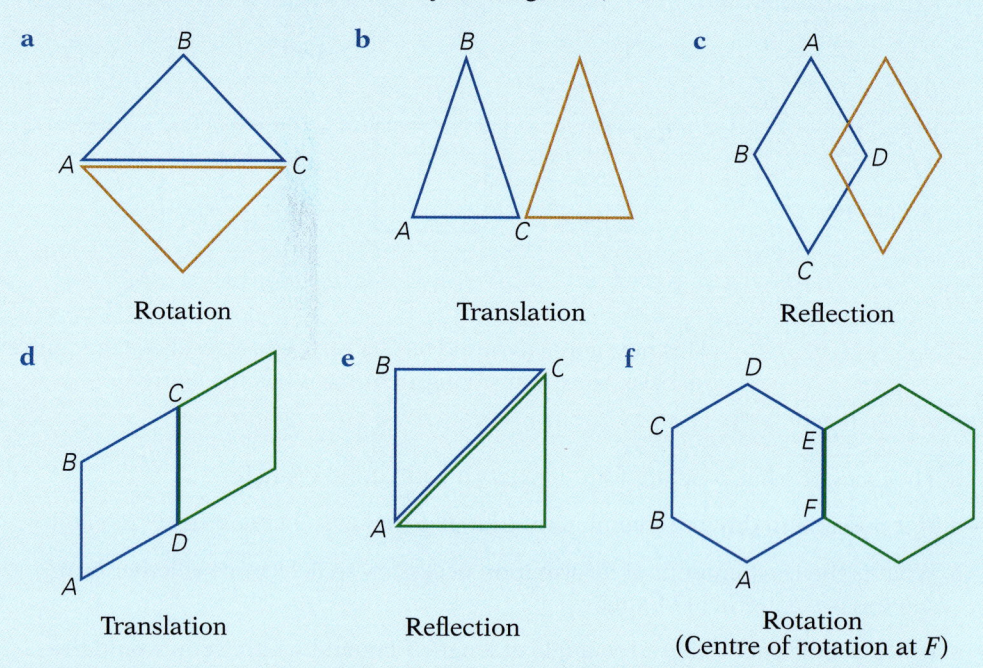

a Rotation

b Translation

c Reflection

d Translation

e Reflection

f Rotation (Centre of rotation at *F*)

10 Copy each figure into your book, and draw the image figure after performing the transformations stated. Give the coordinates *A'* after each transformation.

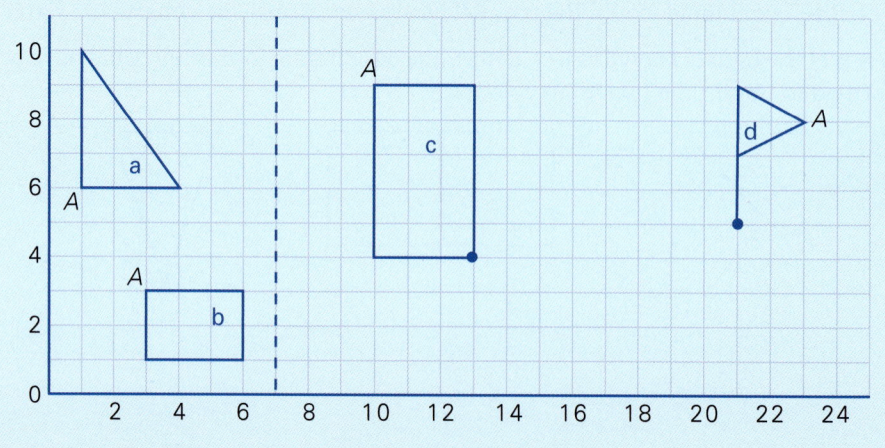

a A *translation* 3 units to the right

b A *reflection* in a vertical line (indicated)

c A 90° clockwise *rotation* about the point (13, 4)

d A 180° anticlockwise *rotation* about the point (21, 5)

11 Describe each of the following transformations *precisely* (as in the questions above):

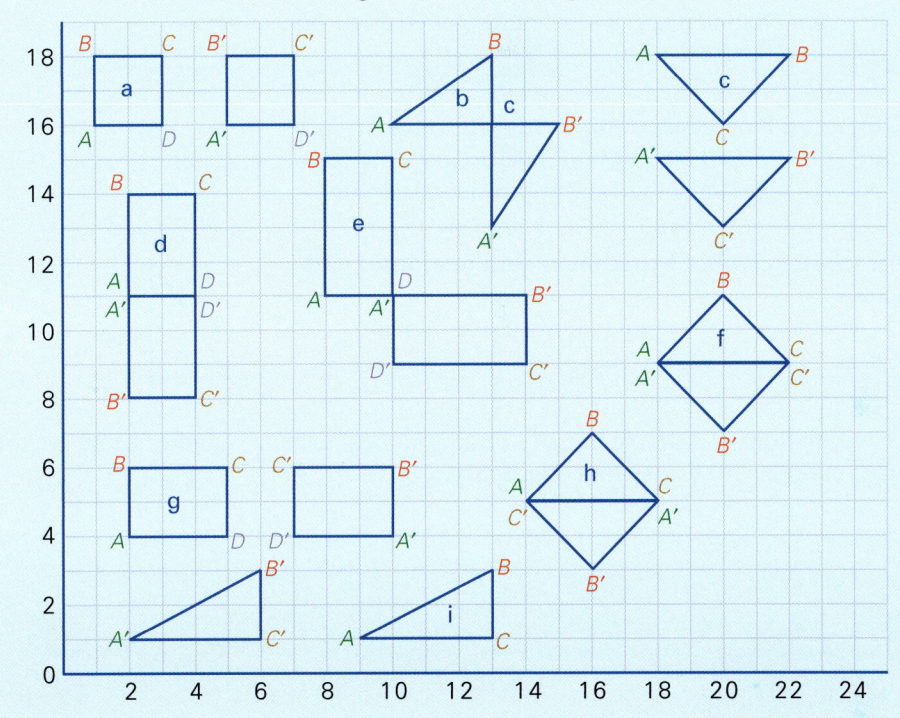

Investigation Congruent triangles

A pair of congruent triangles has six features that correspond: three sides and three angles. However it is not necessary to know that *all* six match in order to identify triangles as congruent.

Certain combinations of *three* corresponding sides and angles are sufficient. Investigate which combinations as follows.

Try drawing as many *different* triangles as possible that have:

1 three sides the same
(use sides of length 4 cm, 5 cm and 6 cm)

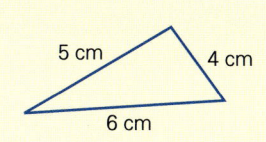

2 three angles the same
(use angles of 30°, 70° and 80°)

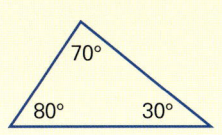

3 **two sides and their included angle the same**
(use sides of 4 cm and 5 cm with an included angle of 45°)

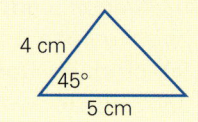

4 **two sides and a non-included angle the same**
(use sides of 4 cm and 5 cm, and a non-included angle of 40° adjacent to the 5 cm side)

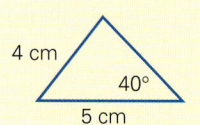

5 **two angles and a corresponding side the same**
(use angles of 40° and 60°, and the side between the 60° angle and the *other* angle (not the 40°) of length 3 cm)

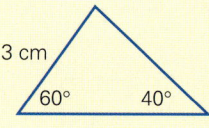

6 **a right triangle with a hypotenuse and one other side the same**
(use a hypotenuse of 5 cm and another side of 4 cm)

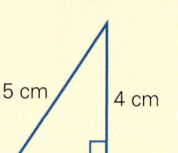

List the combinations of sides and angles that produced *just one* triangle. These are the minimum conditions necessary for congruence.

The entrance to the Louvre in Paris is constructed using triangles.

Exploring New Ideas

9.1 Congruent triangles

Congruent triangles are the same shape and size.

Three pairs of corresponding sides are equal.

Three pairs of corresponding angles are equal.

$\Delta PQR = \Delta STU$

means triangle PQR is congruent to triangle STU.

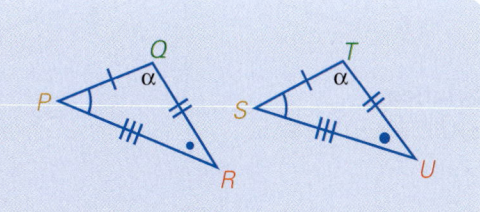

Note: The letters of the second triangle are written in order to indicate how the vertices correspond to those of the first triangle.

In the example above: $P \leftrightarrow S$ (P corresponds to S)

$Q \leftrightarrow T$ (Q corresponds to T)

$R \leftrightarrow U$ (R corresponds to U).

The following three sides and three angles also match:

$\angle PQR = \angle STU, PQ = ST$

$\angle QRP = \angle TUS, QR = TU$

$\angle QPR = \angle TSU, PR = SU$.

TESTS FOR CONGRUENCE

Two triangles are congruent if:

- the three sides of one triangle are equal   **SSS** to the three sides of the other (*side, side, side*)
- two sides and the **included** angle of   **SAS** one triangle are equal to two sides and the included angle of the other (*side, angle, side*)
- two angles and one side of one   **AAS** triangle are equal to two angles and the **corresponding** side of the other (*angle, angle, side*)
- they are right angled and the   **RHS** hypotenuse and a side of one triangle are equal to the hypotenuse and a side of the other (*right angle, hypotenuse, side*)

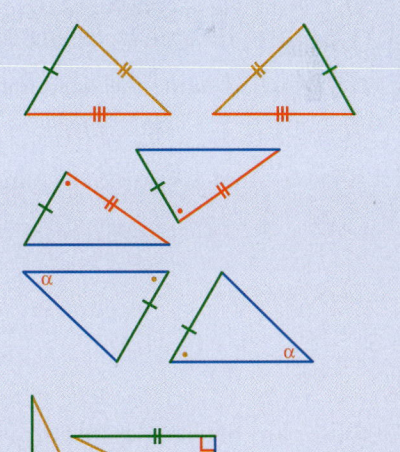

EXAMPLE

Write a congruence statement for these two triangles, and give a reason.

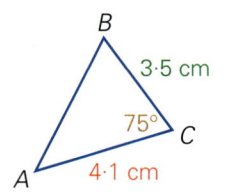 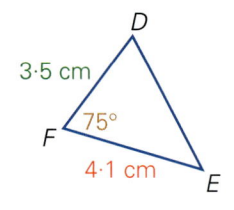

Remember: The triangles must be named with the vertices in corresponding order.

Solution

$\triangle ABC \equiv \triangle EDF$ (SAS)

EXERCISE 9A

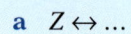

1 Given that these two triangles are congruent, copy and complete the following:

a $Z \leftrightarrow \ldots$ b $AB = \ldots$
c $A \leftrightarrow \ldots$ d $ZX = \ldots$
e $\angle ACB = \ldots$ f $\angle XYZ = \ldots$
g $\triangle ABC \equiv \ldots$ h $\triangle XYZ \equiv \ldots$

2 These two triangles are congruent:

a Describe one way of showing that the above statement is true.
b Which side is congruent to:
   i DF?   ii GH?   iii FE?
c Which triangle is congruent to:
   i $\triangle FDE$? ii $\triangle HGI$? iii $\triangle EDF$?

3 If $\triangle GFH \equiv \triangle RST$ name the side, angle or triangle that corresponds to:

a FH b $\angle FHG$ c $\triangle HFG$ d SR

4 If it is known that $\triangle XYZ \equiv \triangle JKL$, find the value of:

a $\angle YXZ$ b YZ c XZ d $\angle XZY$

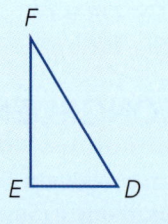 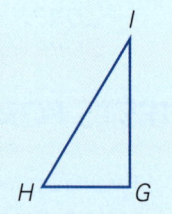 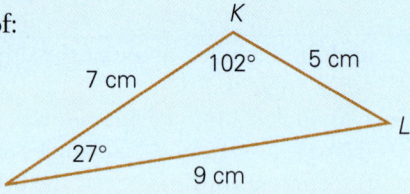

Level 2

5 For those pairs of triangles that are congruent, write a congruence statement and give a reason. For those that are not congruent, write 'not congruent'.

a 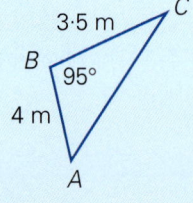 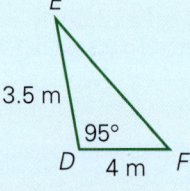   b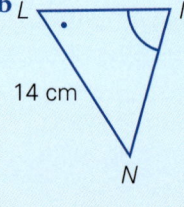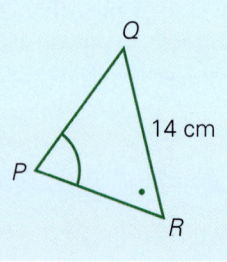

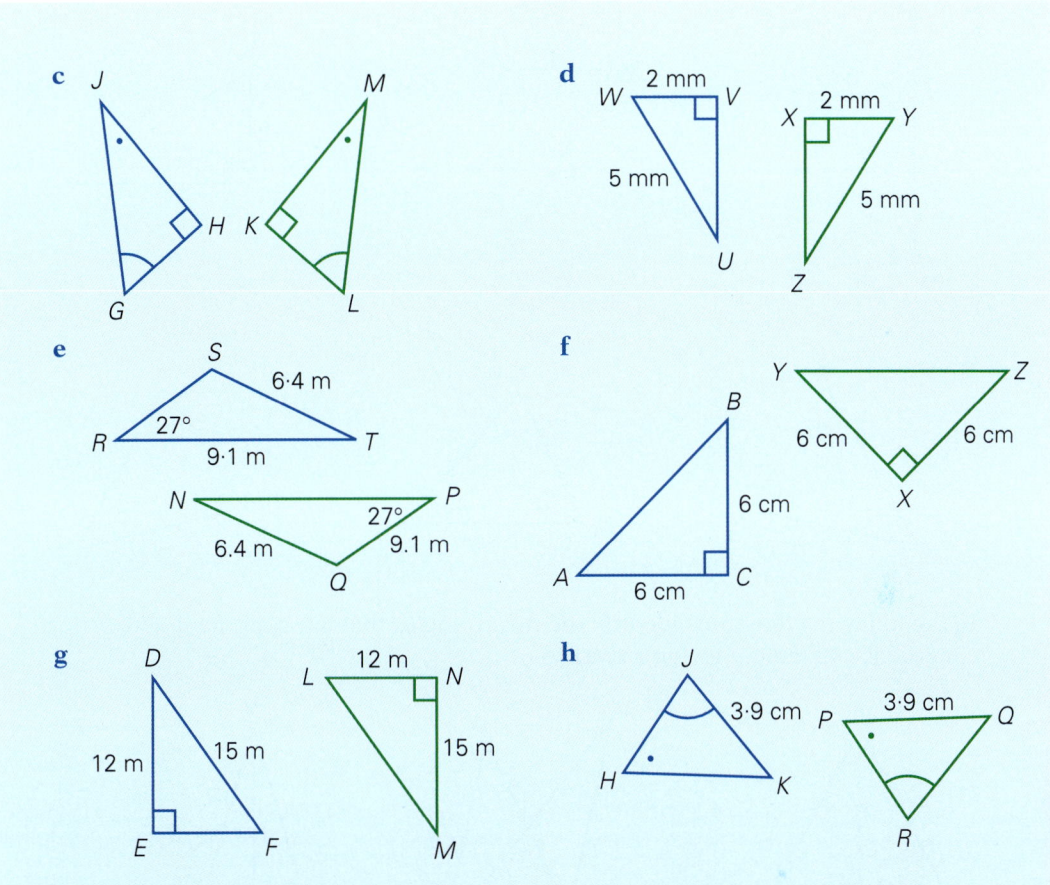

c J, M, H, K, G, L

d W — 2 mm — V, 5 mm, U, X — 2 mm — Y, 5 mm, Z

e S, 6·4 m, 27°, R, 9·1 m, T, N, 6·4 m, P, 27°, 9·1 m, Q

f B, 6 cm, A, 6 cm, C, Y, 6 cm, Z, 6 cm, X

g D, 12 m, 15 m, E, F, L, 12 m, N, 15 m, M

h J, 3·9 cm, H, K, P, 3·9 cm, Q, R

6 Decide which two triangles from the three shown are congruent and write a congruence statement, giving reasons:

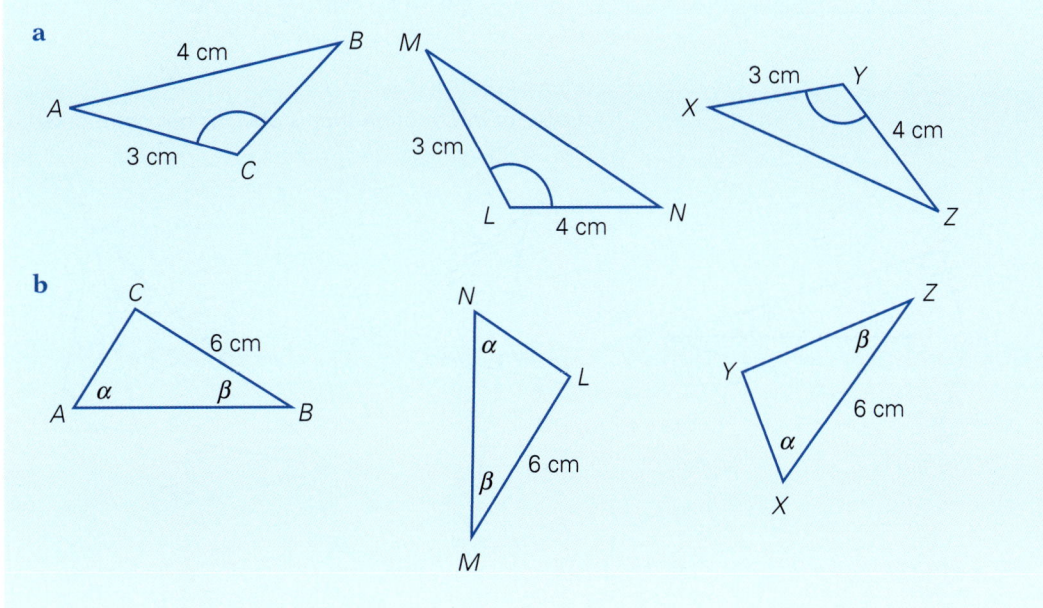

a A, 4 cm, B, 3 cm, C, M, 3 cm, L, 4 cm, N, X, 3 cm, Y, 4 cm, Z

b C, 6 cm, A, α, β, B, N, α, L, β, 6 cm, M, Y, Z, β, 6 cm, α, X

c

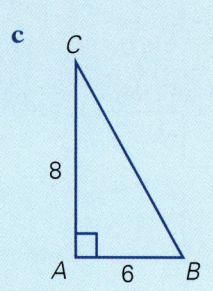 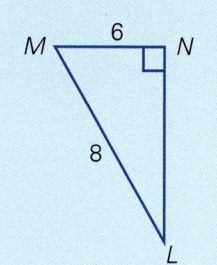 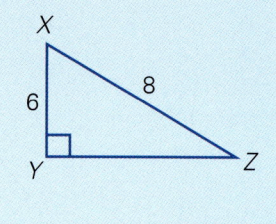

d

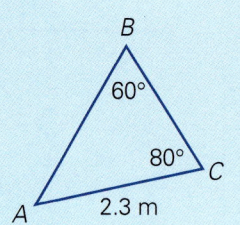 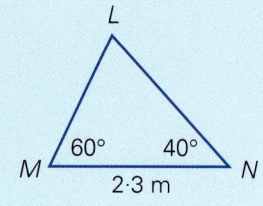 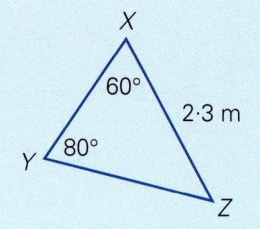

7 In the following diagrams identify the two triangles that are congruent and write a congruence statement giving a reason:

a 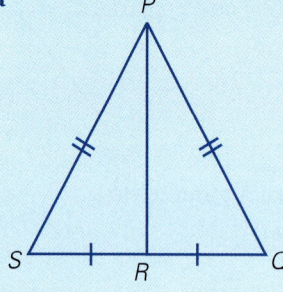 **b** 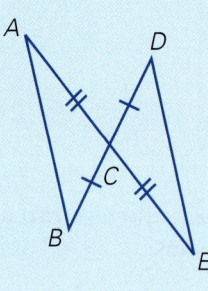 **c**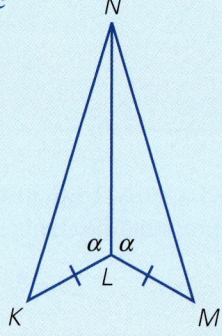

Look for information that is obvious but not marked.

d 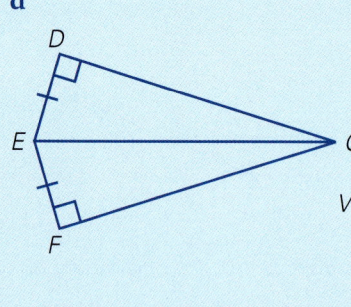 **e** 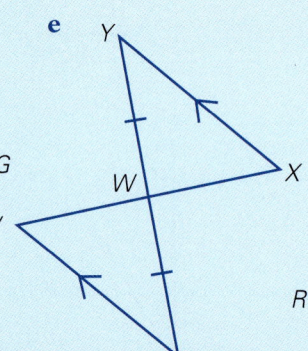 **f**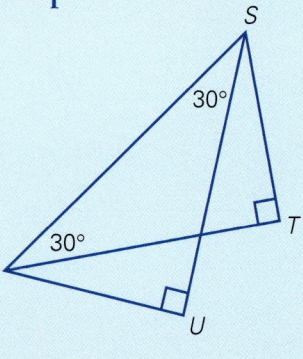

9.2 Congruence proofs

If we are asked to prove or show that two triangles are congruent, the steps should be set out in an organised manner. The conventional way to do this is shown in the examples below.

EXAMPLE 1

In the diagram, O is the centre of the circle and $PR = RQ$. Show that $\triangle OPR \equiv \triangle OQR$.

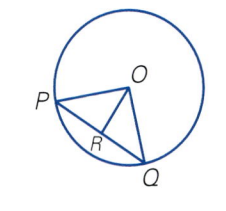

Solution

In $\triangle s$ POR and QOR
$PR = QR$ (given)
$OP = OQ$ (equal radii of circle)
OR is common
$\therefore \triangle POR \equiv \triangle QOR$ (SSS)

EXAMPLE 2

$ED \parallel AC$ and $ED = AC$. Prove that the two triangles are congruent.

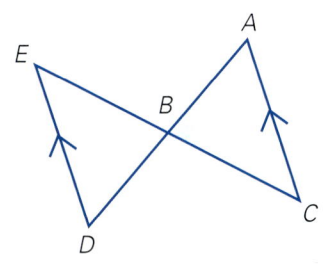

Solution

In $\triangle s$ ABC and DEB
$ED = CA$ (given)
$\angle EBD = \angle CBA$ (vertically opposite angles)
$\angle DEB = \angle ACB$ (alternate $\angle$s, $AC \parallel ED$)
$\therefore \triangle DEB \equiv \triangle ACB$ (AAS)

EXERCISE 9B

1 Copy and complete the following proofs:

a

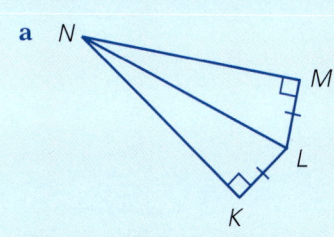

In $\triangle s$ KLN and MLN
$KL = \ldots$ (given)
$\ldots\ = \angle NML$ (given, right angle)
$\ldots$ is common
$\triangle KLN \equiv \ldots$ (RHS)

b

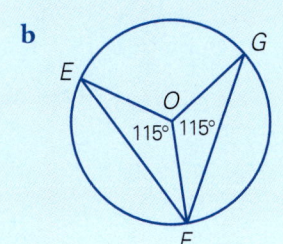

In $\triangle s$ EOF and $\ldots$
$EO = \ldots$ (equal radii of circle)
$\angle EOF = \ldots$ ($\ldots\ldots$)
$\ldots$ is common
$\triangle EOF \equiv \ldots$ (SAS)

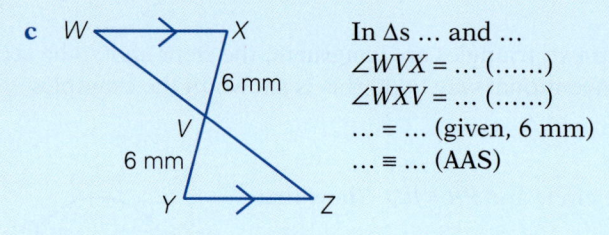

c

In Δs ... and ...
∠WVX = ... (......)
∠WXV = ... (......)
... = ... (given, 6 mm)
... ≡ ... (AAS)

2 Prove that the two triangles in each question are congruent. Set out your proofs as shown in question **1**, remembering to give a reason for each step.

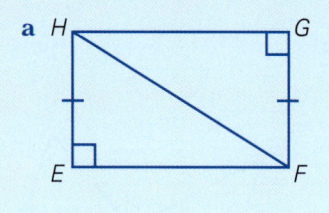

a

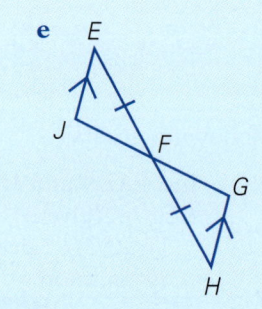

b

WXYZ is a square.

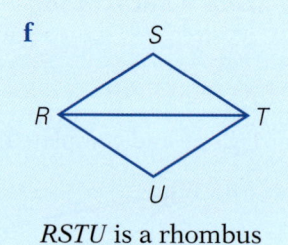

c

O is the centre of the circle.

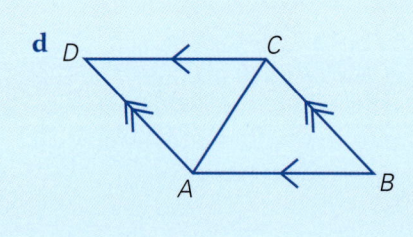

d

e

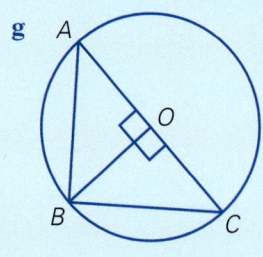

f

RSTU is a rhombus

g

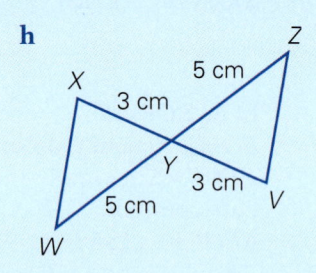

O is the centre of the circle.

h

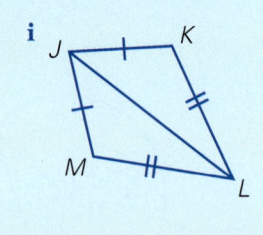

i

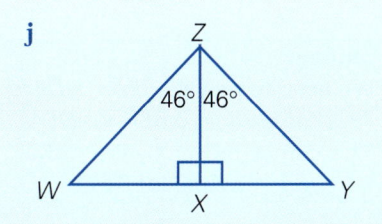

j Prove $\triangle WXZ \equiv \triangle YXZ$.

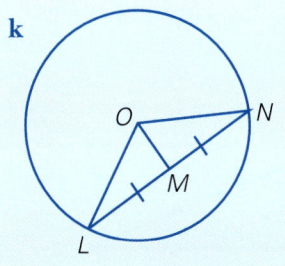

k O is the centre of the circle. Prove $\triangle OLM \equiv \triangle ONM$.

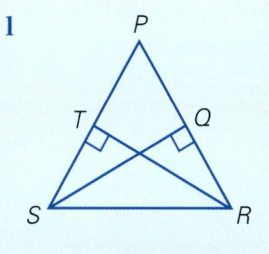

l $\angle PSR = \angle PRS$. Prove $\triangle STR \equiv \triangle RQS$.

3 PQ bisects $\angle RPS$.
Prove that $\triangle RPQ \equiv \triangle SPQ$.

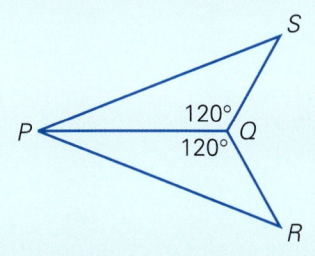

Level 3

4 In rectangle $FGHJ$ a diagonal is drawn from F to H.
Prove that $\triangle FGH \equiv \triangle HJF$.

Draw the diagram!

5 Diagonal AC is drawn in square $ABCD$. A point X is marked on AC so that $CX = CD$.
Y is marked on AD so that YX is perpendicular to AC. Prove that $\triangle CXY \equiv \triangle CDY$.

9.3 Using congruent triangles to solve problems

Once it has been proven that two triangles are congruent, it follows that *all three sides* and *all three angles* of one triangle are equal to the corresponding three sides and three angles of the other. This fact can be used to find the sizes of missing sides and angles.

EXAMPLE 1
Show that $\triangle ABE \equiv \triangle DCE$.
Hence find the length of EC.

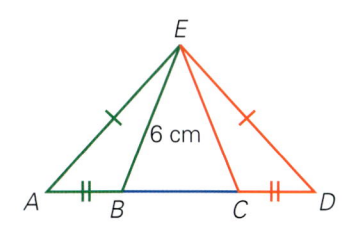

Solution

In triangles *ABE* and *DCE*:

$AE = ED$	(given)
$AB = DC$	(given)
$\angle EAB = \angle EDC$	(base angles of isosceles triangle)
$\therefore \triangle ABE = \triangle DCE$ (SAS)	
$\therefore EC = EB$	(corresponding sides of congruent triangles)
$\therefore EC = 6$ cm	

EXAMPLE 2

Prove diagonals of a kite intersect at right angles.

Solution

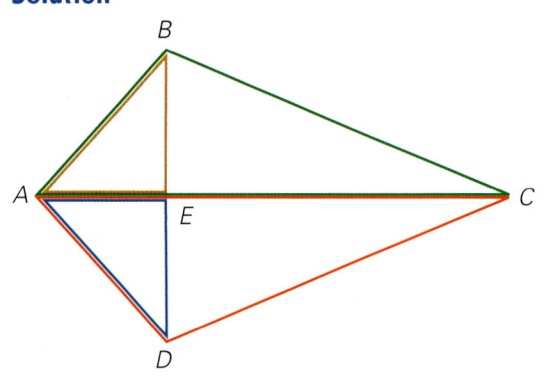

Strategy

We need to prove $\angle BEA = \angle DEA = 90°$
This comes from $\triangle BEA \equiv \triangle DEA$
This can be proven by first proving:
$$\triangle ABC \equiv \triangle ADC$$

In $\triangle$s ABC and ADC
$AB = ADC$
$AB = AD$ (adjacent sides of kite)
$BC = DC$ (adjacent sides of kite)
AC is common
$\therefore \triangle ABC = \triangle ADC$ (SSS)
  $\angle BAE = \angle DAE$ (corresponding angles of congruent triangles)
In $\triangle$s BEA and DEA
    $AB = AD$ (adjacent sides of kite)
  $\angle BAE = \angle DAE$ (proven)
AE is common
$\therefore \triangle BEA \equiv \triangle DEA$ (SAS)
$\therefore \angle BEA = \angle DEA$ (corresponding angles of congruent triangles)
But $\angle BEA + \angle DEA = 180°$ (adjacent angles in a straight line)
$\therefore \angle BEA = \angle DEA = 90°$
$\therefore$ The diagonals of the kite intersect at right angles.

EXERCISE 9C

1 Prove that the two triangles are congruent, and then find the value of the pronumeral, giving reasons:

a

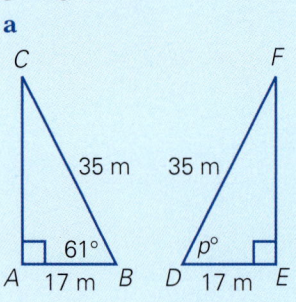

b

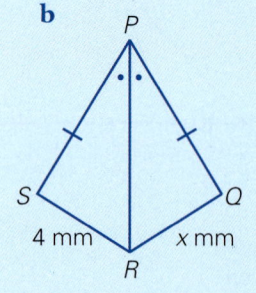

c

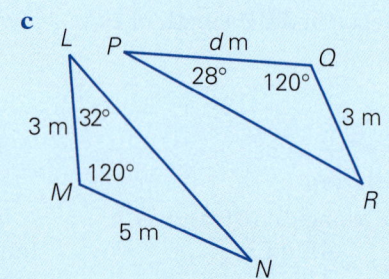

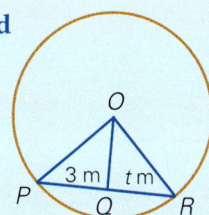
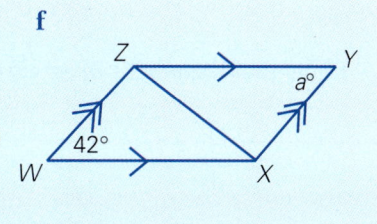

2 First prove that the two triangles are congruent, and then prove the required result:

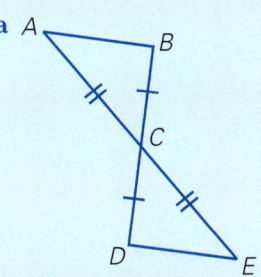

Prove that
$\angle ABC = \angle CDE$.

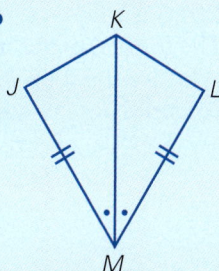

Prove that
$JK = KL$.

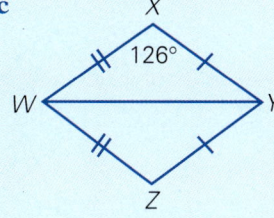

Prove that
$\angle WZY = 126°$.

Level 2

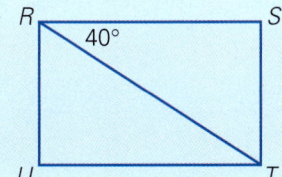

RSTU is a rectangle.
Prove that
$\angle RTU = 40°$.

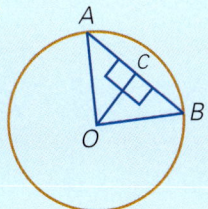

O is the centre of the
circle. Prove that
OC bisects *AB*.

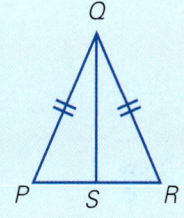

QS bisects $\angle PQR$.
Prove that
$\angle QSP = 90°$.

3 Use congruent triangles to prove the following results. Always draw a diagram first!

a *ABC* is an isosceles triangle with $AB = AC$. *M* is the mid-point of *BC*. Prove that
$\angle ABC = \angle ACB$.

b *PQRS* is a parallelogram. Prove that $\angle PQR = \angle PSR$. Join *PR*.

c *A*, *B* and *C* lie on a circle, centre *O*, with $AB = AC$. Prove that $\angle AOB = \angle AOC$.

d *WXYZ* is a parallelogram. *WY* meets *XZ* at *P*.

  i Prove that the opposite sides of a parallelogram are equal.

  ii Prove that the diagonals of a parallelogram bisect each other.

Level 3

4 Prove that equal chords are subtended by equal angles at the centre of a circle.

5 Prove that the perpendicular from the centre of a circle to a chord bisects the chord.

6 Prove that a quadrilateral with all sides equal is a parallelogram.

7 Prove that the diagonals of a rhombus bisect each other at right angles.

Try this

Prove that the angles in an equilateral triangle are 60°.

You may need to combine two separate proofs.

Try this

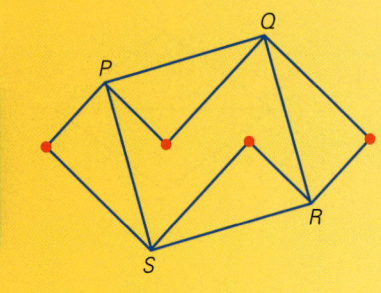

PQRS is a square.
The four triangles are right-angled.
Why are the four vertices marked with coloured dots in a straight line?

Chapter Review

Language Links

angle	isometric	projection	solid
congruent	net	proof	transformation
corresponding	oblique	pyramid	translation
dimension	perspective	reflection	triangle
elevation	plan	rotation	vertex
hypotenuse	prism	side	

Select the word from the list that matches each definition:

1 The top view of a solid.

2 Figures that are exactly the same size and shape.

3 A solid that has at most one non-triangular face.

4 Matching (as applied to sides or angles of congruent figures).

5 A way of showing depth in drawings.

6 Name the two types of projections that can be used to draw pictures of 3D shapes.

7 Name the three congruence transformations.

Give two different definitions (one mathematical, one not) for each word:

8 elevation   **9** net   **10** translation

Chapter Review Exercises

1 If $\triangle ABC \equiv \triangle FGH$, find the value of:

a BC **b** $\angle BAC$

c $\angle ACB$ **d** AB

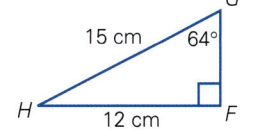

2 Select from the three triangles shown the pair of triangles that are congruent, giving reasons:

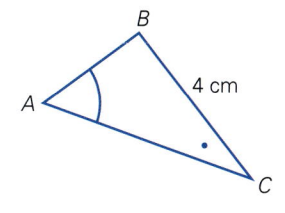 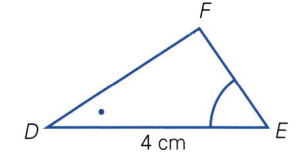 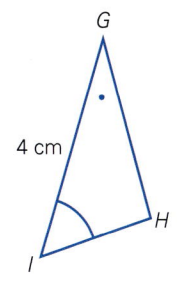

9.1

3 Prove that the two triangles shown are congruent, setting out your proof correctly, and giving reasons:

a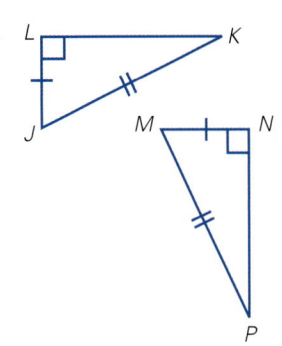

b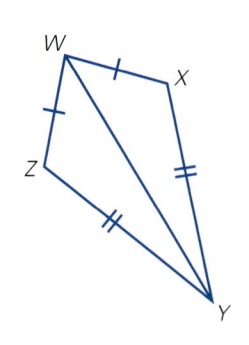

c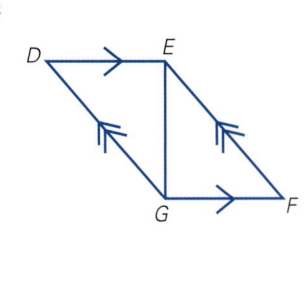

4 Identify the two triangles in this diagram that are congruent and write a congruence statement, giving a reason.

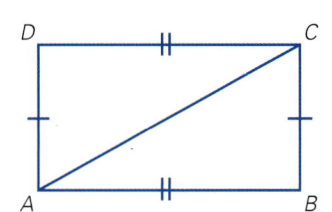

5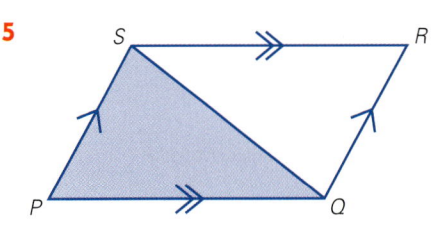

Prove that the shaded triangle is congruent to the unshaded triangle, setting out your proof with a reason for each step.

6 Select the two congruent triangles from this group of three, giving a reason:

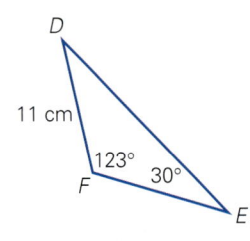

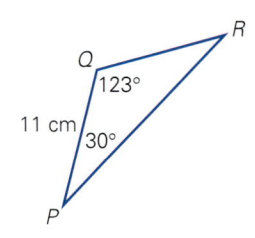

7 Explain why two triangles with three equal angles may not be congruent.

8 Prove that the two triangles in each question are congruent, setting out your proofs correctly with a reason for each step.

a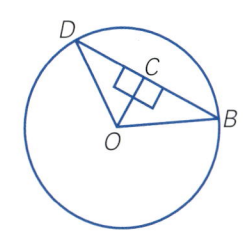

b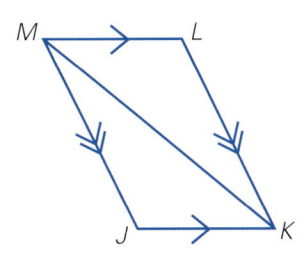

9 First prove that the two triangles are congruent, and then prove the required result:

a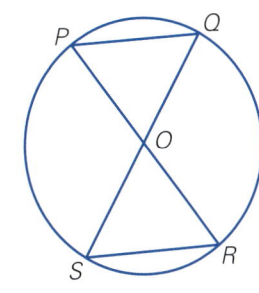

O is the centre of the circle. Prove that
PQ = *RS*.

b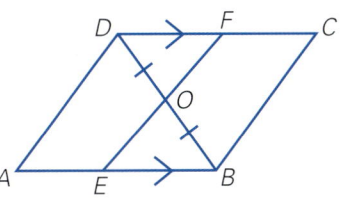

Prove that *DF* = *EB*.

c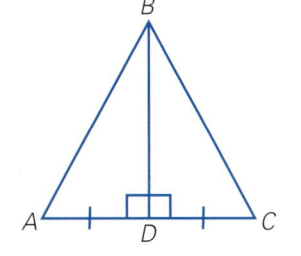

Prove that Δ*ABC* is isosceles.

Keeping Mathematically Fit

Part A—Non-calculator

1 The fraction $\dfrac{29}{*}$ has a value between 4 and 6. Give a possible whole number value for *.

2 Write the reciprocal of $1\frac{1}{2}$.

3 Six people eat in a restaurant and agree to share the $217·45 bill equally. Explain how to round off suitably and determine how much each should pay.

4 A bag of groceries weighs 3·6 kg and a box of groceries weighs 3540 g. Which is heavier, and by how much?

5 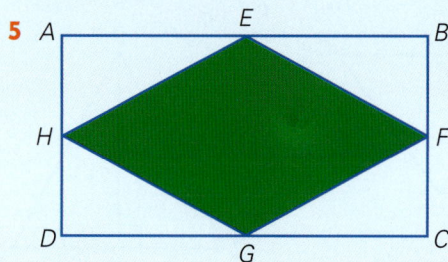 $ABCD$ is a rectangle measuring 8 cm by 6 cm. E, F, G and H are the mid-points of the sides. Find the perimeter of the shaded rhombus.

6 Five trains depart from a station at equal intervals. The first departs at 8 am and the last departs at 8:40 am. At what time does the second train depart?

7 The area of a triangle is 16 cm². The base length and height have integer values. Give one possible pair of values for the base length and height.

8 If $1014 \div 39 = 26$, what is the value of $10\,140 \div 0·26$?

9 Write a set of four scores with a range of 6 and a median of 4.

10 This sector graph shows the weight of ingredients required.
For choc chip cookies:

   a What fraction of the weight of the cookies is choc chips?
   b The cookies contain 60 g of sugar. How much flour do they contain?

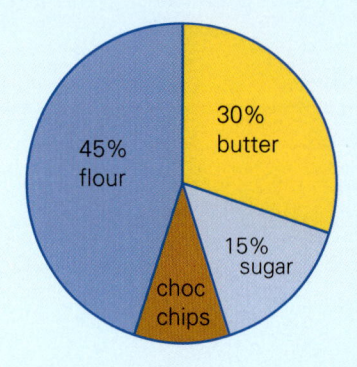

Part B—Calculator

1 Write the equation of the straight line that crosses the x-axis at ⁻2 and the y-axis at 6.

2 Teri buys $20 worth of petrol at 84·9¢ per litre. How much petrol does she get? (To the nearest tenth of a litre)

3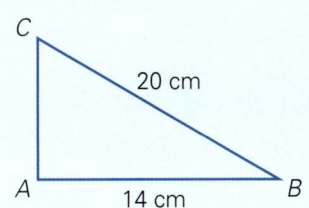

Given as much further information as possible about triangle *ABC*.

4 A recipe requires p grams of sugar for n people. How many grams would be required for q people?

A $\dfrac{p}{nq}$ **B** $\dfrac{q}{np}$ **C** $\dfrac{pq}{n}$ **D** $\dfrac{qn}{p}$

5 Three people leave apparently identical jackets in the cloakroom of a restaurant. When they check out simultaneously, the jackets are given out randomly. What are the chances that *none* of the people receives the correct jacket?

1 What you need to know and revise

Outcome NS 4.3:
Operates with fractions, decimals, percentages, rates and ratios:

- increasing and decreasing a quantity by a given percentage
- expressing profit and/or loss as a percentage of cost price or selling price
- expressing one quantity as a fraction or a percentage of another.

2 What you will learn in this chapter

Outcome NS 5.2.2:
Solves consumer arithmetic problems involving compound interest, depreciation and successive discounts:

- converting interest rates
- calculating the result of successive discounts
- compound interest and its formula
- depreciation.

Outcome NS 5.1.2:
Solves consumer arithmetic problems involving earning and spending money.

- calculating earnings for various time periods
- casual and part time rates
- calculating weekly, fortnightly, monthly and yearly incomes
- calculating net income: taxation
- simple interest
- compound interest, using repeated simple interest.

Working Mathematically outcomes WMS 5.1, 5.2, 5.3
Students will be required to *question*, *apply strategies*, *communicate*, *reason* and *reflect* in the sections of this chapter.

Consumer arithmetic

Key mathematical terms you will encounter

annual	fortnightly	overtime	simple
balance	gross	per annum	spreadsheet
bonus	income	percent	statement
borrow	increase	percentage	superannuation
casual	instalment	piecework	tax
commission	interest	principal	time
compound	invest	profit	transaction
cost	loading	purchase	wages
credit	loan	rate	withdrawal
deductions	loss	retainer	year
deposit	mark-up	salary	
discount	monthly	sales	
earning	net	savings	

MathsCheck
Percentage composition

Percentage composition means expressing each part as a percentage of the total.

- A discount is a reduction from the normal selling price.
- Depreciation is a loss in value.
- To increase an amount by 10% find 110% of the amount.
- To decrease an amount by 10% find 90% of the amount.
- Profit and loss: Profit = selling price – cost price $\text{profit \%} = \dfrac{\text{profit}}{\text{cost}} \times 100\%$

    Loss = cost price – selling price $\text{loss \%} = \dfrac{\text{loss}}{\text{cost}} \times 100\%$

1 200 vehicles pass a traffic survey point in 30 minutes. 120 are cars, 32 are trucks, 30 are vans, 12 are bikes and the rest are buses. Find the percentage of each type. Give percentage answers to the nearest 0·1%.

2 Complete each of the following tables.

a

Original price	Discount	Sale price
$90	12%	
$23·50	5%	
$176	45%	
$3·45	10%	
$8700	3%	
$97·60	$5\frac{1}{2}\%$	

b

Original price	Sale price	% discount
$34	$30	
$450	$369	
$67·95	$55	
$2350	$1350	
$2·40	$2·20	
$199·95	$179·95	

c

Original price	% mark-up	New price
$100	5%	
$1600	8%	
$3	112%	
$70	$12\frac{1}{2}\%$	
$1256	57%	
$17·93	99%	

d

Original price	Discount	Sale price
	5%	$44
	12%	$3·50
	8·5%	$126
	25%	$4200
	$1\frac{1}{2}\%$	$8·10
	$8\frac{1}{4}\%$	$99·40

Depreciation means an item decreases in size or value.

3 The expenses of owning and running a car amounted to $4600 a year. If depreciation was $2500, registration $340, insurance $496, repairs $420, and the rest petrol costs, find:

a the percentage composition of the expenses
b the amount spent on petrol.

4 A 250 mL fruit drink contains 35% fruit juice, 3·5% preservatives and colouring, and 12% sugar. The rest is water.

   a What percent is water?
   b How many millilitres of each component make up the drink?

5 A family of four has a total income of $985 per week. $310 goes in tax; $150 on food and household supplies; $280 on mortgage repayments; $120 on car payments and expenses; and $95 on telephone, insurances and electricity combined.

   a How much is left over for all other purposes?
   b Calculate the percentage composition of the family budget.

6 Shortbread is made by mixing together 300 g plain flour, 200 g butter and 100 g sugar. Calculate the percentage composition of the shortbread.

7 Calculations with percentages are common in science. A scientist may be asked to analyse a rock sample and report that it weighed 3·75 kg and contained 5% gold and 7·5% silver by weight. How many grams of gold and silver did it contain?

8 The cost price is $50 and the selling price is $65.

   a State whether a profit or loss has been made.
   b Calculate the amount of profit or loss.
   c Calculate the percentage profit or loss (to the nearest tenth of a percent).

9 Calculate the selling price of the following items if they are sold with the stated profit margin. Round off answers to the nearest 5¢ where necessary:

   a a book with a cost price of $45 and a profit margin of 45%
   b a television with a cost price of $320 and a profit margin of 72%
   c a compact disc with a cost price of $12·30 and a profit margin of 110%.

10 A surfboard marked at $560 is offered for sale at a discount of 30%. How much money would you save if you bought the board in the sale?

11 Find the whole quantity given the following parts:

   a 25% of it is 100 g   **b** 10% of it is $40
   c 30 kg is 15% of it   **d** 38% of it is $85
   e 3% of it is 4·5 m   **f** $25·80 is 60% of it
   g 150% of it is 360 mL   **h** 120% of it is $8·45
   i $12\frac{1}{2}$% of it is 250 g   **j** if 6% is 18 L, find 30%
   k 9% is 270 mm, find 45%   **l** 15% is 45 kg, find 80%
   m 45% is $360, find $2\frac{1}{2}$%

12 If 140 students in Year 9 make up 21% of the overall school population, how many attend the school?

13 Jason gets a pay rise of $38·50 a week, representing $7\frac{1}{2}$% of his previous wage. Calculate:

   a his wage before the rise
   b his new wage.

14 A discount of 23% on a CD player means a saving of $52.

   a What was the original price?
   b How much would a discount of 35% have been?

15 Jennifer is offered a pay rise from her present salary of $38 460. She can choose either (A) $20 a week more or (B) 2% pay rise.

   a How much is Jennifer's new salary if she chooses (A)?
   b How much per week does (B) earn Jennifer?
   c Which option should she choose?

16 Merryn buys a car for $24 990 and sells it 3 years later, making a loss of 60%.

   a How much did the car sell for?
   b If Merryn sold the car for 10% more than the price in **a**, what was her overall percentage loss now?
   c A car sold for $17 000 was purchased 6 years ago for 56% more than its current price. What was the cost of the car 6 years ago?

17 Savraj bought a basketball card for $6 and was able to sell it for $15.

   a What was his profit as a percentage of the *cost* price?
   b What was his profit as a percentage of the *selling* price?
   c For each of the values calculated in **a** and **b**, give an example of a situation in which Savraj might choose to state *that* percentage rather than the other one.

18 Anders buys a secondhand bicycle for $155. He spends $67 replacing some parts, and rides the bicycle for a year. He then sells it for $195 through the newspaper. The advertisement cost $14.

   a Calculate the profit or loss as a percentage of the total cost price.
   b Comment on whether or not you think Anders should be pleased with his deal.

19 Louise makes up bags of biscuits for the school fair. A 5 kg box of biscuits costs $22, each small bag costs 5¢, and the ribbon to go around the top costs 8¢ for each bag. Each made-up bag contains 200 g of biscuits, and is sold for $1·80.

   a How many bags of biscuits could Louise make?
   b How much profit is made on each bag of biscuits sold?
   c What is the percentage profit on the cost price?

20 As part of a business enterprise activity, James and Farouk are making up stationery sets that each contain 10 envelopes, 20 sheets of paper and a pen. They buy the materials in bulk, with the envelopes costing $5·50 per 100, the writing paper costing $9·50 for a ream (500 sheets) and the pens costing $45 for a pack of 20.

   a If they use a whole ream of paper, how many stationery packs can they make?
   b How much profit will they make on each stationery pack if they sell them for $4·95 each?
   c What is the percentage profit on the cost price?
   d What other costs which have not been included might there be?

21 A hotdog stall sells a hot dog in a bun with onions and tomato sauce for $1·40. The hotdogs cost $20 for a packet of 50, the bread buns cost $1·56 per dozen, the onions cost 60¢ for 1 kg (which is enough for 15 hotdogs), and the tomato sauce costs $3 per bottle (which is enough for 100 hotdogs). What percentage of the *selling* price is profit?

22 A furniture store marks up the cost price of all items by 85%, and is offering a discount of 20% on all furniture. What percentage profit will the store make on its sales?

23 A store is offering customers a choice: '10% discount or $10 off all items'. For which items would a discount of $10 be a better deal than a discount of 10%?

> 'Mark-up' is the amount added onto the cost price to get the selling price.

24 A bookstore is planning to offer a 15% discount to customers. Its standard mark-up is 35%. Consider a book that has a cost price of $20.

  a What will be the final sale price if the selling price is calculated first, and then the 15% discount is taken off?
  b What will be the final sale price if the 15% discount is taken off first, and then the 35% mark-up is added?
  c What do you notice?
  d Will this be the case for books of all prices?
  e Investigate the case where a $5 discount is to be given. Does it matter whether the 35% mark-up is calculated before or after the $5 discount is removed?

25 A manufacturer charges $300 for a DVD player and digital TV system. The wholesaler who buys it has a mark-up of 55% and sells it to the retailer. The retailer advertises the system at $1550. How much profit is made by the retailer?

26 A manufacturer producing vacuum cleaners makes a 27% profit when they are sold to the wholesaler. The wholesaler marks this cost price up 70% before selling it to the retailer. The retailer sells it for $699 to the public. If this represents a profit of 12% for the retailer, find the cost to the manufacturer of producing the cleaner.

27 As a staff member of Lucia's Boutique, you are entitled to a discount on clothing purchases—15% discount on individual items under $100, and 25% discount on individual items priced at $100 or more.
A number of items have caught your eye, and with your Christmas bonus waiting to be spent, you are having a hard time deciding what to buy.

Shopping list

Cashmere cardigan	$109·99
A 'little black number' skirt	$56·75
Trousers	$96·00
Business suit	$227·25
Pure cotton shirt	$64·99
Ramie/cotton shorts	$39·95
Black gown	$164·95

Construct a table with columns headed 'Item', 'List Price', 'Percentage Discount' and 'Discount Price'. What is the total amount you would pay?

Exploring New Ideas

10.1 Successive discounts

WEB RESEARCH

SPREADSHEET ACTIVITY

People with store discount cards often benefit from what is known as successive discounts— a further discount on an already reduced item.

EXAMPLE 1

Cara has a GB card that offers 7% discount on the final price of all items. Find the cost of a pair of shoes during a 15% off all footwear sale if the shoes are marked at $119·90.

Solution

Sale price $= 119·90 \times 0·85$

$\qquad = 101·915$

Cara's cost $= 101·915 \times 0·925$

$\qquad = 94·2713 \ldots$

Cara pays $94·27

> These are skills required in HSC subjects such as Business Studies.

> These steps can be combined:
> $119·90 \times 0·85 \times 0·925$

EXAMPLE 2

Calculate the overall percentage saved by Cara in the purchase of the shoes in example 1.

Solution

$\qquad$ Total discount $= 119·90 - 94·27$

$\qquad\qquad = 25·63$

Percentage discount $= \dfrac{25·63}{119·90} \times 100\%$

$\qquad\qquad = 21·376 \ldots$

Overall discount $= 21·4\%$ (1 dec. pl.)

> $\dfrac{\text{discount}}{\text{original amount}} \times 100\%$

> Alternative approach:
> $x \times 0·85 \times 0·925 = x \times 0·786\,25$
> $\therefore$ discount $= 1 - 0·786\,25$
> $\qquad = 21·375\%$
> $\qquad = 21·4\%$ (1 dec. pl.)

EXERCISE 10A

1 a Decrease $96 by 5%, then by a further 7%.

 b Decrease $470 by 8%, then by a further 8%.

 c Decrease $1190 by $7\frac{1}{2}$%, then by a further 10%.

 d Decrease $82·50 by 6%, then by a further 20%.

 e Decrease $97·65 by $\frac{1}{2}$%, then by a further $\frac{1}{2}$%.

> The 'holey dollar' and the 'dump' were early Australian coins. What is their history?

2 Find the overall percentage discount for each amount in question **1**.

Level 2

3 Con, a plumber, purchases supplies from a hardware store and gains a trade discount of 10%. His purchases total $249.

 a Calculate the sale price of Con's purchase.

 b If Con is given a further 8% discount for paying cash find the final amount of his bill.

 c Calculate Con's overall percentage discount.

4 Jonas receives a staff discount of 5% on the sale price of any item. Jonas purchases a DVD marked at $36·95. Find the price Jonas pays for this item.

5 If the DVD in question **4** is on sale for 15% off the marked price find:

   a the sale price of the DVD
   b the cost to Jonas for the DVD
   c the overall percentage saved by Jonas on the cost of the DVD.

6 A toy truck is offered on sale for 10% off the marked price. It is then sold for a further x% off the discounted price as the box is damaged. If the marked price was $62·90 find the value of x if the final sale price was $49.

Level 3

7 An item priced at $99·70 is to be marked down for a sale. The sales manager thought of the following alternative wording for the signs:
$10 Cash Back or 10% discount.

   a Which would result in the cheaper price?
   b Which is likely to result in more sales?

8 A jewellery store buys 9 carat gold at $26·56 a gram, 0·3 carat diamonds at $90 each and 0·3 carat rubies at $87 each. They charge customers 38% more than their purchase cost plus a further mark-up of 15%, to create the sale price of each item made.

   a Calculate the cost to the customer of each ruby and diamond purchased.
   b A customer wishes to have made a piece which requires 50 grams of gold, seven rubies and six diamonds. Find the cost to the customer for such a piece.
   c If the customer wishes to pay no more than $3000 for this piece, what discount do they need to negotiate with the jeweller?

9 The same model TV is on sale at two different stores. At the first store it is priced at $719, but a discount of 12% is offered. At the second store the TV is priced at $799, but a discount of 8% is offered, plus a further 5% off the discounted price if the TV is purchased for cash.

   a Find the cost of the TV at the first store.
   b Find the final cost for the TV at the second store if it is purchased in cash.
   c If a different model TV is $10 cheaper at store 2 than store 1 after all discounts, what is the advertised price of this TV at the first store?

10.2 Earning money: salaries and wages

People may be paid in a variety of ways for the work they do. Payment methods include:

- salaries
- wages
- casual work
- piece work
- commission
- self-employment.

An increasing number of people in Australia are self-employed and earn their income by charging a fee for service (e.g. lawnmowing), manufacturing and selling goods (orchardist), or buying and selling goods for a profit (local milkbar). The most common form of income is salary and wages.

Form of payment	Explanation	Example of occupation
Salary	An amount is paid for the year's work. (This is normally paid monthly or fortnightly.) Holiday pay, sick pay and superannuation are paid also. If additional hours are worked, no extra payment is made, but time off 'in lieu' can sometimes be taken.	Teachers
Wages	Usually based on an hourly rate for a certain number of hours per week. Employment is on a permanent basis, and holiday pay, sick pay and holiday loading are usually paid. If additional hours are worked, extra money is paid, usually at higher rates. These are typically time-and-a-half ($1\frac{1}{2}$ times the normal hourly rate) or double time (2 times the normal hourly rate).	Sales assistants

EXAMPLE 1

Janie earns $26·70 per hour as a waitress.

a Calculate Janie's weekly wage if she works 38 hours each week.

b Calculate Janie's annual wage if she works 38 hours a week for 48 weeks.

Solutions

a Wage = 26·70 × 38
= $1014·60

b $1014·60 × 48 = $48 700·80

EXAMPLE 2

Martin earns $750 per week and a total of $1052 per year in interest on his investments. How much is his total annual income?

Solution

Total income = 750 × 52 + 1052
= $40 052

Employees often choose to work extra hours each week to increase their weekly income.
Overtime is time worked in addition to normal working hours. It is usually paid at a higher rate, for example time-and-a-half or double time.

EXAMPLE 3

Jerome works as an electrician. He is paid $14·20 per hour for a standard 37-hour week, and time-and-a-half for weekday evenings and Saturday mornings.

For the Saturday afternoons and all day Sunday he is paid double time.

One week Jerome worked for 3 hours on Thursday evening, and from 10 am to 5:30 pm on Saturday, in addition to the standard hours. What would be his earnings for the week?

Solution

Normal rate = 14·20   Time-and-a-half rate = $14 \cdot 20 \times 1\frac{1}{2}$
$= 21 \cdot 30$
Double time rate = $14 \cdot 20 \times 2$
$= 28 \cdot 40$

$\therefore$ Earnings = $(37 \times 14 \cdot 20) + (5 \times 21 \cdot 30) + (5\frac{1}{2} \times 28 \cdot 40)$
$= \$788 \cdot 10$

> You can perform these calculations in one step:
> $(37 \times 14 \cdot 20) + (5 \times 1 \cdot 5 \times 14 \cdot 20) + (5 \times 2 \times 14 \cdot 20)$

EXERCISE 10B

1 Sarah earns \$72 560 p.a. as an accountant. Find her fortnightly pay.

2 Michael is employed as an actuary for a big insurance company. He earns \$1790 per week. Calculate his annual salary.

3 Allen has a weekly wage of \$976. If Allen works no overtime during the year, calculate his annual wage.

4 Allen works 38 hours a week for his wage of \$976.

   a Calculate his hourly rate of pay.
   b What would Allen earn each hour for overtime if it is calculated at time-and-a-half.
   c Calculate Allen's weekly wage if he decides to work $2\frac{1}{2}$ hours overtime on top of his 38-hour working week.

5 Wendy earns \$5·40 per hour. If she works 20 hours at normal time and 5 hours at time-and-a-half, calculate her total earnings.

6 A fruit canning company pays its workers \$11·85 per hour for a standard 35-hour week, and time-and-a-half for any additional time worked. Calculate the weekly earnings of a person who works:

   a 40 hours   b $38\frac{1}{2}$ hours   c 42 hours 45 minutes

7 Peta worked 38 hours at the normal rate of \$11·36 per hour, plus 4 hours at time-and-a-half and $3\frac{1}{2}$ hours at double time. What did she earn that week?

Level 2

8 A baker who works on Saturdays earns time-and-a-half for the first 4 hours, and double time after that. If his normal rate of pay is \$13·70 per hour, calculate his pay for working the following hours on a Saturday:

   a 3 hours   b $6\frac{1}{2}$ c 8 hours 15 minutes

9 A job is advertised as having an annual salary of \$27 800, and the conditions are to work a 37-hour week with 4 weeks annual holiday.

   a How many weeks would be worked per year?
   b How many hours would be worked per year?
   c Calculate the hourly rate of pay (to the nearest cent) for this job.
   d What would be the hourly rate of pay if the salary was changed to \$34 600?

10 A landscape gardener is paid \$10·97 per hour for a standard $37\frac{1}{2}$-hour week, time-and-a-half on evenings and Saturdays, and double time on Sundays. Calculate the total wage of the following gardeners:

  a Dan works for 7 hours on Wednesday and $4\frac{1}{2}$ hours on Friday.
  b Jolene works a standard week plus 5 hours on Saturday and 3 hours on Sunday.
  c Anthony works a standard week plus 2 hours on Tuesday evening, $3\frac{1}{2}$ hours on Saturday and 5 hours 30 minutes on Sunday.

11 Complete the table below, given the hourly rate is \$10·88.

Employee	Standard hours	Time-and-a-half	Double time	Income
Bessie	35	3	$2\frac{1}{2}$	
Rano	23	0	4	
Shane	37	$4\frac{1}{2}$	2 h 15 min	
Jez	17	7	0	

12 If the hourly rate in question **11** is increased by 10%, calculate the new incomes for each of the four employees.

Level 3

13 Bill earns a salary of \$42 150. Mary earns \$18·76 per hour and time-and-a-half for any overtime during the week.

  a Find Bill's weekly income.
  b If Mary normally works 38 hours per week, calculate her normal weekly wage.
  c How many hours would Mary need to work at her normal hourly rate to earn the same amount per week as Bill?
  d If Mary earns overtime for hours worked in excess of her 38 hours how many hours of overtime are necessary for her to equal Bill's weekly income?

14 Raymond works as a manager of a small business. During the first week of May he worked his normal 36 hours plus an extra 4 hours overtime. If his overtime is calculated at double time-and-a-half and his total earnings for the week come to \$1313·76:

  a Calculate his hourly rate of pay.
  b If Raymond's hourly rate rises by 5%, how many hours of overtime are required to keep Raymond's weekly income at \$1313·76?

15 Omar works as a waiter in a local café. During the last week in December Omar worked 30 hours at normal rates, 5 hours at time-and-a-half rates and 3 hours at double time. His total income for the week came to \$590·73. Calculate Omar's hourly rate of pay.

Investigation Who earns the most?

Employment pages

You need: the employment pages from a newspaper (the Saturday papers usually have a large section)

Employment ads often use the abbreviation K to represent one thousand. A salary of $90K is an annual income of $90 000. The abbreviation K comes from the Greek word *khilioi* which means thousand.

For each of the earning methods shown in the table on page 284, cut out from the newspaper two examples of jobs that are paid by that method. Stick the job advertisements into your book, labelling them with how much is paid, and by what method. (Some job advertisements do not give the amount, so try to find ones that do, if possible.)

Comparing methods

In groups of about four people, discuss the advantages and disadvantages of each method of payment. Write a summary of your findings, and be prepared to report your conclusions to the class.

Try these

1 Karen earns $37 560 and is given a 3% wage increase. Darren earns $35 420 and is given an increase of 3·5%.

   a Who received the larger increase?   **b** Who earns more *after* the increase?

2 In each of the following, decide which of the two advertisements has the higher rate of pay. Justify your conclusion by showing the calculations used to make the comparison.

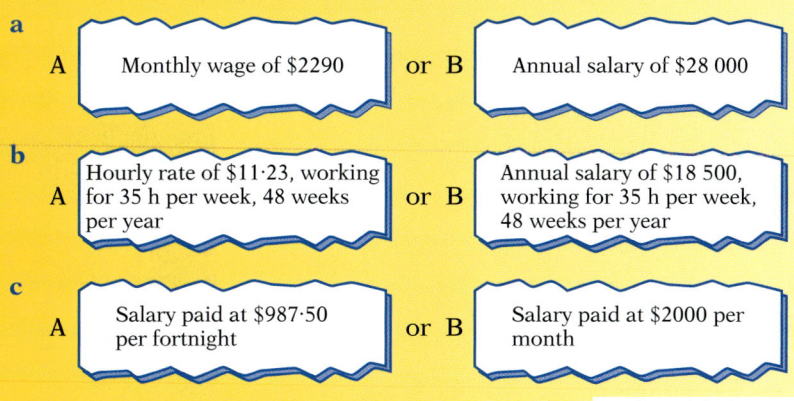

a

A | Monthly wage of $2290 | or B | Annual salary of $28 000

b

A | Hourly rate of $11·23, working for 35 h per week, 48 weeks per year | or B | Annual salary of $18 500, working for 35 h per week, 48 weeks per year

c

A | Salary paid at $987·50 per fortnight | or B | Salary paid at $2000 per month

Careful: 1 month is *not* 4 weeks.

10.3 Earning money: commission

Form of payment	Explanation	Example of occupation
Commission	The person is paid a percentage of the price of the goods sold. Sometimes a low wage (called a **retainer**) is paid in addition to the commission. Holiday pay, sick pay and superannuation may or may not be paid.	Sales representatives

EXAMPLE 1

Rose works as a sales representative for a company that sells computers. She is paid a retainer of $110 per week, plus a commission of 3% on all sales.
a How much would Rose earn if she made no sales one week?
b How much would she earn if $13 500 worth of sales were made?

Solutions

a $110

b Commission $= 3\%$ of $13 500
$\qquad\qquad = 0·03 \times \$13\ 500$
$\qquad\qquad = \$405$
Earnings $= \$110 + \$405$
$\qquad\quad = \$515$

EXAMPLE 2

Dean is a real estate agent. He charges the vendor (the person selling the property) 5% commission on the first $18 000 of a sale and $2\frac{1}{2}\%$ on the rest. How much commission would he receive on a house that sells for $187 500?

Solution

Commission on first $18 000 $= 5\%$ of $18 000
$\qquad\qquad\qquad\qquad = 0·05 \times \$18\ 000$
$\qquad\qquad\qquad\qquad = \$900$
Commission on the rest $= 2\frac{1}{2}\%$ of $(187\ 500 - 18\ 000)$
$\qquad\qquad\qquad\quad = 0·025 \times \$169\ 500$
$\qquad\qquad\qquad\quad = \$4237·50$
Total commission $= \$900 + \$4237·50$
$\qquad\qquad\qquad = \$5137·50$

EXERCISE 10C

1 Neville's company pays commission only, at a rate of 18% on all sales. What would he earn if he made sales of:

   a $520?   **b** $1600?   **c** $8700?   **d** $125?

2 Cheryl is offered a position with a fixed wage of $125 per week, plus a commission of 3% on sales.

   a What would she earn in 1 week if her sales were:
      i $1000?   **ii** $23 500?   **iii** $7800?

   b Cheryl is a confident, outgoing person. Describe how her earnings might be different from those of a quiet, shy person.

   c How might the extent of Cheryl's previous sales experience affect the amount she earns?

3 Vaughn's company pays a basic wage of $300 per month, and a commission of $4\frac{1}{2}\%$ on all sales.

   a How much would Vaughn earn if he made sales of $12 000 in a month?

   b How much would Vaughn earn if he made no sales?

   c How much would Vaughn earn if he sold goods worth $9800 during March?

Level 2

4 Yumi works as a sales representative for a pharmaceutical company. She earns a fixed wage of $500 per month, plus 7% commission on sales *in excess of* $10 000. (This means she gets no commission on the first $10 000 worth of sales, but gets 7% on anything *over* that amount.) What would be Yumi's monthly income on sales of:

   a $7600?   **b** $15 000?   **c** $23 700?   **d** $56 000?

5 Arthur's company pays a retainer of $90 per week, plus commission of 4% on all sales.

   a How much would Arthur earn if he made sales worth $2000?

   b What sales would he need to make to earn *commission* of $600?

   c What sales would Arthur need to make to earn a *total* of $510?

6 Elrica works as a real estate agent. She charges 5% of the first $18 000 of the selling price and $2\frac{1}{2}\%$ on the remainder.

   a Calculate the commission she receives on each of the following sales:

      i A two-bedroom unit for $179 000

      ii A block of land for $67 000

      iii A new office complex for $2·1 million

   b Elrica earned $6135 in commission on the sale of one house. What was the selling price of the house?

7 Percival is a used-car salesman. He is paid a retainer of $280 per week, plus 10% of the dealer's profit on the sale of each vehicle.

   a If the total profit on vehicles Percival sold in 1 week was $3260:
      i What would be his weekly wage?
      ii What was Percival's hourly rate if he worked from 8:30 am until 6 pm Monday to Saturday, with 1 hour off for lunch each day?
   b On another week Percival earned $813·60.
      i What *profit* did the company make on these sales?
      ii If profit accounts for 35% of the selling price, what was the total value of the vehicles sold by Percival? (To the nearest dollar.)

8 Hugh and Lou work for the same company. Hugh earns $100 per week plus 3·5% on sales. Lou earns commission only, at 5%.

   a How much would each earn on sales of $4000?
   b What value of sales would result in them both earning the same amount?
   c Hugh wishes to earn $64 350 this year. On average what do his weekly sales need to amount to?
   d If Lou is offered a choice of 4% commission on the first $10 000 of sales and 6% commission on the total sales in excess of $10 000, how much would he need to sell in each week to equal if not better his present 5% commission on total sales?
   e If Lou accepts this new offer, what values of sales would result in Hugh and Lou earning the same amount?

10.4 Earning money: casual work, piece work

Form of payment	Explanation	Example of occupation
Casual	A fixed hourly rate is paid. Not permanent employment, the person works when needed. There is usually no holiday pay, sick pay or superannuation. (Higher rates of pay compensate for this.)	House cleaners
Piece work	The person is paid a fixed amount for each piece of work completed. Positions are not usually permanent. No holiday pay, sick pay or superannuation are paid.	Clothes producers

EXAMPLE 1
a Ian does casual work delivering pizzas. His rate of pay is $5·85 per hour Monday to Friday, and $7·36 per hour on the weekends. Calculate his total earnings for working from 5:30 pm to 10 pm on Friday, and from 6:15 pm to 9 pm on Saturday.
b If Mark earns $1·20 per pizza he delivers, how many pizzas does he need to deliver if he hopes to earn the same as Ian?

Solution

> 5:30 pm to 10 pm is $4\frac{1}{2}$ h.

a Friday earnings $= 4\frac{1}{2}$ h @ \$5·85
$= 4\cdot5 \times 5\cdot85$
$= 26\cdot325$

Saturday earnings $= 2\frac{3}{4}$ h @ \$7·36
$= 2\cdot75 \times 7\cdot36$
$= 20\cdot24$

Total earnings $= 26\cdot325 + 20\cdot24$
$= \$46\cdot565$
$= \$46\cdot55$

> 6:15 pm to 9 pm is $2\frac{3}{4}$ h.

b Mark earns \$1·20 per pizza
$\therefore 1\cdot2 \times x = 46\cdot55$
$x = 46\cdot55 \div 1\cdot2$
$x = 38\cdot79$
$\therefore$ Mark must deliver 39 pizzas.

EXERCISE 10D

1 Dwane is a part-time attendant at a football ground. He gets paid \$7·60 per hour for mid-week games, and \$9·10 per for weekend games. Calculate his *total* earnings for the week if he worked the following hours: Wednesday $2\frac{1}{2}$ h; Saturday 6 h; Sunday $3\frac{1}{2}$ h.

Level 2

2 Calculate Dwane's *total* weekly earnings for working at the following times: Tuesday 6 pm to 9:45 pm; Friday 5:30 pm to 10:15 pm; Saturday 10:30 am to 4 pm; Sunday 1:45 pm to 4:30 pm.

3 Myron is paid 35¢ for each plate he decorates.

a How much would he be paid for producing 130 plates?
b How many plates would he need to produce to earn \$84?
c If he can decorate an average of 27 plates an hour, how much would he earn for working a 37-hour week?

4 Teresa's Temps is an organisation which provides staff for companies that need a small amount of office work done. She charges \$12 for her staff person to arrive, and then \$9·50 per hour thereafter. Barry, from Barry's Business, is considering hiring one of Teresa's staff, and wants to know what the costs would be. Draw up a table to show what the costs would be for 1–10 hours.

5 Vladimir has a casual job stapling together leaflets for a local environmental group. He is paid 74¢ per 100 leaflets completed.

a How much would Vladimir earn for stapling 2600 leaflets?
b How many leaflets would he need to staple in order to earn \$30?
c If it takes Vladimir 10 minutes to staple 200 leaflets, what would be his hourly rate of pay?

Level 3

6 Casual orange pickers are paid \$4·28 for each box of oranges picked.

a How many boxes would need to be picked for a worker to make \$50?
b If it takes Bruno $2\frac{1}{2}$ hours to fill three boxes, what is the hourly rate of pay?
c How long would it take Bruno to earn \$100 at this rate?
d How long would it take Sheralee to earn \$80 if she can fill four boxes in 3 hours?

SPREADSHEET ACTIVITY

7 Workers at a fast-food restaurant are paid $5·28 per hour for working Monday to Friday and Saturday mornings. $7·92 per hour is paid for Saturday afternoons, and $10·56 per hour for Sundays and public holidays. The time each employee starts and finishes each day is written onto a chart. Calculate the amount earned by each person.

		Mon	Tue	Wed	Thu	Fri	Sat	Sun
a	Delia	—	—	—	4:30 pm 7:15 pm	—	8:00 am 11:30 am	—
b	Marisa	—	—	6:30 pm 9:00 pm	—	4:45 pm 10:30 pm	—	10:15 am 3:30 pm
c	Nandini	10:00 am 6:30 pm	6:00 am 11:15 am	—	—	6:45 am 12:00 pm	—	—
d	Nish	—	—	9:30 am 3:15 pm	5:15 pm 10:45 pm	—	6:00 am 1:15 pm	3:30 pm 7:15 pm
e	Paul	4:45 pm 9:30 pm	3:30 pm 10:15 pm	—	—	4:30 pm 8:45 pm	11:15 am 5:30 pm	8:00 am 2:15 pm

10.5 Extra payments: bonus, holiday loading, etc.

Employees are sometimes paid extra on top of their normal wages.

Holiday loading is a bonus given to employees when they take annual leave. It is calculated as a percentage of their normal wage for the period of the holiday. The normal rate given is $17\frac{1}{2}\%$ on 4 weeks per year.

A **bonus** is given to the employees as an incentive, or as a reward for reaching certain targets, or for the successful completion of a project.

EXAMPLE 1
Shona's normal fortnightly pay is $964, and she is about to go on holiday for 4 weeks. The company she works for pays a holiday loading of $17\frac{1}{2}\%$.
a How much *extra* will she receive?
b What will be her *total* pay for the 4 weeks of her holiday?
Solutions

a Normal pay for 4 weeks = 2 × 964
$\qquad\qquad\qquad\qquad$ = $1928
$\qquad$ Holiday loading = 0·175 × 1928
$\qquad\qquad\qquad\qquad$ = 337·40
$\qquad$ Shona is paid $337·40 extra as holiday loading.

b Total pay = 1928 + 337·40
$\qquad\qquad\quad$ = $2265·40

EXAMPLE 2
Bill receives a 5% bonus due to his company reaching its projected profit. Calculate the bonus Bill received if he earns $56 100.
Solution
Bonus = 5% of $56 100
$\qquad$ = 0·05 × $56 100
$\qquad$ = $2805

EXERCISE 10E

1 Jemimah normally earns $539 per week. How much *extra* will she be paid if she receives a holiday loading of $17\frac{1}{2}\%$ for 4 weeks vacation?

2 If Sharon earns $52 510 p.a., calculate her holiday loading of $17\frac{1}{2}\%$ on her 4 weeks annual leave.

3 Company A offers a 4% bonus to all employees. What bonus is given to employees earning:

   a $45 000?   **b** $84 270?   **c** $62 500?   **d** $127 500?

4 The Commonwealth Building Society offers its employees bonuses in the way of shares. If the company makes its projected profits each section manager is awarded $1000 worth of shares in the company. If the shares are valued at $16·54 each, how many shares does each manager receive?

5 Deidre earns $387 per week. Calculate:

   a the amount of her bonus, and
   b her total pay for the week, if she receives a bonus of 22·25%.

6 Flight of Fashion has a successful year and decides to give all staff a Christmas bonus of 3% of their annual salary. Calculate the bonus received by Jay, a manager who earns $64 000 per year.

Level 2

7 Fancy Feet shoe sellers pay their workers $17\frac{1}{2}\%$ holiday loading. Calculate the amount paid to the following staff for their 4 weeks annual leave:

   a Sharman, whose weekly wage is $612
   b Petula, whose fortnightly wage is $1065.

8 Desmond is going on holiday, and his pay packet of $2876·40 includes 4 weeks pay plus a holiday loading of $17\frac{1}{2}\%$. What is his normal weekly wage?

9 Custom computers gives all staff a bonus of $1200. What percentage of annual salary would that be for:

   a Polly, the chief executive, who earns $79 000 per year?
   b Marcus, a technician, who earns $36 000 per year?
   c Write a brief statement comparing the two methods of bonus payment used by Flight of Fashion and Custom Computers. Describe the advantages and disadvantages of each and say which you think is the better way to pay the bonus.
   d How many hours of overtime at time-and-a-half would need to be worked to earn the same as 36 hours at standard rates?

     Choose any rate of pay to start with.

Level 3

10 Sally earns $45 000 per year. She is offered a choice of three bonuses:

A $2\frac{1}{2}\%$ of annual salary
B 150% of 1 week's salary
C $1000
Which bonus is the best one for Sally to choose?

11 Mary receives a wet-weather allowance of 7% of her pay for any wet day. In one month when she worked 20 days, four of which were wet, she received an allowance of $48. Calculate her total pay for the month.

12 Tom's to Mary's income is in the ratio of 2 : 3. If Mary receives a 10% bonus, calculate the ratio of Tom's income to Mary's total income.

10.6 Deductions: taxation

The amount of money earned is called **gross income**. Certain deductions are made from the gross income before the worker receives any money. These deductions include *tax* and *superannuation*. The **net income** is what is left when any deductions have been subtracted from the gross income.

> Net income = gross income − deductions

Tax is deducted from workers' gross pay before they receive their wages. It is paid to the government to fund spending on education, health services, and so on.

The amount of tax paid depends on how much is earned, with lower paid workers paying a smaller percentage of their gross earnings in tax.

The Australian Tax Office provides a table that helps people to calculate the amount of tax they should pay per year. This is in a guide called *TaxPack*, which contains instructions on how to complete a tax return.

An example of a tax table* is given below.

Taxable income	Tax on this income
0–6000	Nil
6001–20 000	17¢ for each $1 over $6000
20 001–50 000	$2380 plus 30¢ for each $1 over $20 000
50 001–60 000	$11 380 plus 42¢ for each $1 over $50 000
60 000–	$15 580 plus 47¢ for each $1 over $60 000

The above rates *do not* include the Medicare levy of 1·5%.

*You can find the most current table at www.ato.gov.au

EXAMPLE 1

Nancy's gross weekly wage is $479. She had deductions of $118·45 for tax, $19·30 for superannuation and $3·76 union fees. Calculate:

a her net pay, and

b the percentage of her gross pay that is deducted (to the nearest 1%).

Solutions

a
$$\text{Deductions} = 118·45 + 19·30 + 3·76$$
$$= 141·51$$
$$\therefore \text{net pay} = 479 - 141·51$$
$$= 337·49$$

b Percentage of gross pay $= \dfrac{141·51}{479} \times 100\%$
$$= 29·542 \ldots$$
$$\approx 30\%$$

EXAMPLE 2

Calculate the tax payable on an accountant's gross income of $58 470.

Solution

$$\text{Tax} = 11\,380 + 0·42 \times (58\,470 - 50\,000)$$
$$= 14\,937·4$$

Tax payable is $14 937·40

EXAMPLE 3

Calculate the Medicare levy due on a gross income of $62 500.

Solution

$$\text{Medicare levy} = 1·5\% \text{ of gross income}$$
$$= 0·015 \times 62\,500$$
$$= \$937·50$$

EXAMPLE 4

Michael has a gross annual income of $64 864. His employers withhold $352 per week through PAYG (pay as you go) tax system. Calculate:

a the tax due, according to the tax table, including the Medicare levy

b the refund/bill Michael will receive.

Solutions

a
$$\text{Tax due} = 15\,580 + 0·47 \times (64\,864 - 60\,000)$$
$$= 17\,866·08$$
$$\text{Medicare levy} = 64\,864 \times 0·015$$
$$= \$972·96$$
$$\text{Total tax due} = \$18\,839·04$$

b
$$\text{Tax paid by PAYG} = 52 \times 352$$
$$= 18\,304$$
$$\therefore \text{Tax bill} = \$18\,839·04 - 18\,304$$
$$= \$535·04$$

EXERCISE 10F

1 Find the take-home pay (net pay) for the following workers:

    a Gross pay is $318 per week, total deductions are $98·60.

    b Gross monthly pay is $2980, tax is $985 and other deductions are $125·46.

c Gross pay is \$1360 per fortnight, tax is \$376, superannuation is \$23·60 and union fees are \$6·77.

d Gross *annual* salary is \$23 700, and *monthly* deductions are: tax \$518·26; superannuation \$34·60; other deductions \$23·96. (Find net annual salary.)

2 Josie earns an annual salary of \$46 920. She pays 31% of her gross earnings in tax, 4% of her gross pay into a superannuation fund, \$7·56 per week towards union fees and \$12·34 per week in health insurance.

  a Calculate Josie's gross weekly pay.
  b Calculate the amount Josie pays in tax each week.
  c What is Josie's net weekly pay?

3 Find the net pay as a percentage (to the nearest 1%) of gross pay for each person:

Employee	Weekly gross pay	Tax	Other deductions
K. Costner	\$652·55	\$238·74	\$43·72
J. Foster	\$189·20	\$35·87	\$13·20
H. Ford	\$1126·90	\$519·78	\$204·37

Refer to the tax table supplied on page 294.

4 Calculate **i** the annual tax payable, and **ii** the net annual income, for workers who earn the following annual gross salaries:

  a \$17 600 **b** \$4700 **c** \$42 350 **d** \$63 400 **e** \$29 760 **f** \$6500

Level 2

5 Helen earns \$1170 gross per fortnight. Calculate:

  a her gross annual salary
  b the annual amount of tax payable, including Medicare
  c her net fortnightly pay.

6 Mike earns \$476 gross per fortnight as a casual telemarketer. He works for 46 weeks of the year.

  a How much tax does he pay over the year?
  b What is his average net fortnightly income?

7 Pedro earns \$9·80 per hour working in a café and works 15 hours per week.

  a How much tax will he need to pay per week?
  b What is the maximum number of hours he could work per week without having to pay any tax?

Level 3

8 Ngoc earns \$26 448 p.a. Calculate:

  a the tax payable on Ngoc's taxable income if Ngoc is required to pay the Medicare levy
  b the percentage of Ngoc's taxable income paid in tax.

9 Mary's taxable income was \$24 100. Her employer took out PAYG tax instalments totalling \$4810·30 from her earnings. Calculate the tax refund Mary is due.

10 Calculate the annual salaries if the following tax is paid:

  a \$7321   **b** \$5000   **c** \$1365   **d** \$11 389

- Investigate, using the Internet, the history of the Australian tax system.
- Find out about HECS and who pays it—what rates apply?
- Investigate superannuation.
- What else can you find out?

10.7 Simple interest

Simple interest is interest that is calculated on the **original amount** of money invested or borrowed. It is calculated as a **percentage** of the amount of money borrowed or invested.

For example, if the interest rate is 4% per annum (p.a.) ('per annum' means 'per year') and $500 is invested, the interest earned in 1 year is 4% of $500 = $20. The interest earned for 3 years is three times that earned in 1 year; that is, $3 \times \$20 = \$60$.

> $I = PRT$
>
> I is the **interest**
> P is the **principal** (the amount borrowed or invested)
> R is the annual **rate** of interest
> T is the **time** in years
>
> Amount repaid = principal + interest

EXAMPLE 1

Pran invests $120 for 4 years. If interest is paid at a rate of $3\frac{1}{2}\%$ per annum calculate:
a the interest earned and
b the value of the investment, at the end of 4 years.

Solutions

a $I = PRT$
$\quad = 120 \times 0.035 \times 4$
$\quad = \$16.80$

b Investment is worth $120 + \$16.80$
$\quad = \$136.80$

EXAMPLE 2

Mr and Mrs Turner borrow $35 000 from the bank to pay the deposit on a house they are buying. If the interest rate is 11·75% per annum:
a what will be the interest charges if they repay the loan after 2 months?
b what is the total amount paid?

Solutions

a $\quad I = PRT$
$\quad\quad = 35\,000 \times 0.1175 \times \dfrac{2}{12}$
Interest = $\$685.42$

b Total amount = $35\,000 + \$685.42$
$\quad\quad = \$35\,685.42$

EXAMPLE 3

Maria invested $250 at a simple interest rate of 3·5% p.a. How long must the money be invested to earn $50 interest?

Solution

$I = PRT$

$\$50 = \$250 \times 0{\cdot}035 \times T$

$\$50 = \$8{\cdot}75 \times T$

$T = 50 \div 8{\cdot}75$

$\quad = 5{\cdot}714\,28 \ldots$ years

$\quad = 5{\cdot}7$ years

$\quad = 5$ years 9 months

EXERCISE 10G

1 The table shows the amount of simple interest payable (in $, to the nearest $) on loans at a certain interest rate:

Amount ($) \ Time (years)	1 year	2 years	3 years	5 years	10 years
50	6	13	19	32	65
100	13	26	39	65	129
500	65	129	194	323	645
1000	129	258	387	645	1290
5000	645	1290	1935	3225	6450
10000	1290	2580	3870	6450	12 900
50 000	6450	12 900	19 350	32 250	64 500
100 000	12 900	25 800	38 700	64 500	129 000

a Use the table above to find the interest payable on the following loans:

   i $5000 for 1 year   **ii** $500 for 3 years   **iii** $100 for 10 years

  iv $150 for 1 year   **v** $85 500 for 5 years   **vi** $9550 for 10 years

 vii $5000 for 4 years   **viii** $50 000 for 9 years

b What rate of interest was used to create the table above?

This graph shows the annual interest earned on investments for interest rates of 4% p.a. and 6% p.a.

Use the graph to answer questions **2** to **5**.

2 Find the annual interest earned on investment of:

  a $300 at 4% p.a.
  b $520 at 6% p.a.
  c $250 at 4% p.a.

3 What investments would earn annual interest of:

  a $20 at 6% p.a.?
  b $20 at 4% p.a.?
  c $14 at 6% p.a.?

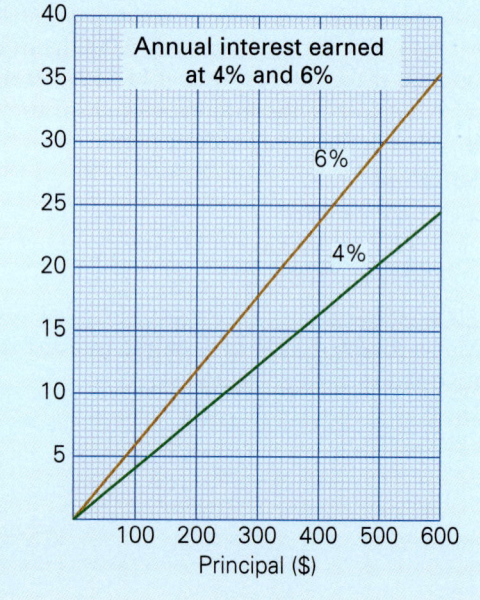

4 Calculate the interest earned on the following investments:

a $400 at 6% p.a. for 3 years   **b** $190 at 4% p.a. for 6 years

5 Calculate the *total value* of the following investments:

a $520 at 4% p.a. for 10 years   **b** $200 at 6% p.a. for 6 years
c $3000 at 4% p.a. for 1 year   **d** $50 000 at 6% p.a. for 5 years

6 Calculate:

    i the simple interest earned on the following investments
    ii the value of the investment at the end of the period.

a $250 at 3% p.a. for 1 year   **b** $800 at 4% p.a. for 6 years
c $85 at 2·5% p.a. for 9 years

Level 2

7 Calculate the simple interest on:

a $1245 for 6 months at $2\frac{3}{4}$% p.a.
b $15 500 for 3 months at 6·85% p.a.
c $7800 at 8·05% p.a. for 8 months
d $8700 for 2 years 6 months at 4·3% p.a.
e $10 850 for 3 years 5 months at $3\frac{3}{4}$% p.a.
f $450 for 4 years 10 months at 2·75% p.a.
g $15 680 at 3·95% p.a. for 1 year 4 months
h $86 400 for 2 weeks at 6·35% p.a.
i $75 for 40 weeks at $5\frac{3}{4}$% p.a.
j $12 490 for 30 days at 6·95% p.a.
k $2 million for 5 days at $6\frac{1}{4}$% p.a.

Level 3

8 The interest paid on a loan of $3500 with an interest rate of 3% was $630. What was the length of the loan?

9 How long would $350 need to be invested at an interest rate of 4·5% p.a. to earn $141·75?

10 What principal will earn $42·50 simple interest if invested at 3·5% p.a. for 5 years?

11 If the simple interest over 6 years on a loan of $12 800 is $4224, what is the rate of interest?

12 An investment of $800 is worth $814 after 6 months. What is the interest rate?

13 Debbie has seen a second-hand car she wants to buy. She organises a loan through the bank, borrowing $5600 for 3 years at 11·5% p.a. simple interest.

a What is the total amount that must be repaid?
b If the repayments are spread over equal monthly instalments, how much is each instalment?

14 Jonah borrows $34 800 for 5 years at 9·6% p.a. simple interest. If the repayments are made in equal instalments, what is the amount of each instalment?

15 Felicity has worked out that she can afford to pay up to $450 per month on loan repayments. What is the maximum amount of money she could borrow over 3 years if the simple interest rate is 12% p.a.?

10.8 Compound interest

SPREADSHEET ACTIVITY

So far in this chapter we have considered **simple interest**, where the interest is calculated on the original, unchanging principal, and calculated at the end of the time period. However, in practice, interest paid on investments or loans is usually *added to the principal*. This *increases* the principal, so the interest paid in the next period will be greater. This type of interest is called **compound interest**.

Consider $500 invested at 10% p.a.

Time	Amount	Interest	New amount
1st year	$500	$50	$550
2nd year	$550	$55	$605
3rd year	$605	$60·50	$665·50
4th year	$665·50	$66·55	$732·05

We can write:

$A = 500(1·1)$

$A = 500(1·1) \times (1·1)$
$\quad = 500(1·1)^2$

$A = 500(1·1)^2 \times (1·1)$
$\quad = 500(1·1)^3$

$A = 500(1·1)^3 \times (1·1)$
$\quad = 500(1·1)^4$

The interest each year is added to the amount invested before the interest is recalculated. As you can see the amount from which interest is calculated is continually changing.

> A formula can be written to allow us to quickly calculate the final amount when dealing with compound interest.
> $A = P(1 + R)^n$
> A = final balance
> P = initial quantity
> R = percentage interest rate per compounding period expressed as a decimal
> n = number of compounding periods

EXAMPLE 1

Joshua borrows $1000 at an interest rate of 9% p.a. Calculate the total amount owing after 3 years if the interest is compounded annually.

Solution

$A = P(1 + R)^n$ $\qquad$ $P = 1000$
$A = 1000(1 + 0·09)^3$ $\qquad$ $R = 0·09$
$\quad = 1000(1·09)^3$ $\qquad$ $n = 3$ **once a year for 3 years**
$\quad = \$1295·03$

EXAMPLE 2

Terry takes out a 3-year loan for $3500 at a rate of 13% compounded annually.

a What is the total amount he has to pay back?

b How much interest does he pay?

Solutions

a $\qquad A = P(1 + R)^n \qquad P = 3500, R = 0.13, n = 3$ **once a year for 3 years**

$\qquad\qquad = \$3500 \times (1.13)^3$

$\qquad\qquad = \$5050.1395$

Total amount $= \$5050.14$

b Interest $= \$5050.14 - \$3500$

$\qquad\qquad = \$1550.14$

EXAMPLE 3

Simone's bank pays interest into her account every 6 months, at a rate of 3·5% p.a. If she has $560 in her account, and makes no deposits or withdrawals, how much will be in her account in 2 years' time?

Solution

$A = P(1 + R)^n \qquad P = \$560, R = \dfrac{0.035}{2} = 0.0175, (3.5\% \text{ p.a.} = 1.75\%, 6 \text{ monthly})\, n = 4.$

$\quad = \$560 \times (1.0175)^4$

$\quad = \$600.241\,05 \ldots$ **twice a year for two years**

$\quad = \$600.24$

EXAMPLE 4

At what interest rate does Mary need to invest $1000 if it compounds annually and she wishes to see her investment double in 5 years?

Solution

$\qquad A = P(1 + R)^n \qquad A = 2000, P = 1000, n = 5$ **once a year for 5 years**

$2000 = 1000(1 + R)^5$

$\quad\ 2 = (1 + R)^5$

$\sqrt[5]{2} = 1 + R$

$\quad\ R = \sqrt[5]{2} - 1 = 0.1486 \ldots$

$\therefore$ A rate of 14% p.a. is needed.

EXERCISE 10H

1 By considering an investment of $400 at 12% p.a. (compounded annually), copy and complete the table below.

Time	Amount	Interest	New amount
1st year	$400		
2nd year			
3rd year			
4th year			
5th year			
6th year			

Use the compound interest formula and check that the final amount shown in the table above is the same as the answer obtained by using the formula, where $P = 400$, $R = 0.12$ and $n = 6$.

2 Calculate the value of the following investments if the interest is compounded annually:

a $2000 after 2 years at 5% p.a.
b $350 after 2 years at 3% p.a.
c $34 500 after 3 years at 6% p.a.
d $671 after 4 years at 4% p.a.
e $4860 after 2 years at 4·5% p.a.
f $1000 after 5 years at $5\frac{1}{2}$% p.a.
g $12 470 after 6 years at 11·25% p.a.
h $1 million after 4 years at $7\frac{3}{4}$% p.a.

3 Calculate the total amount owing on the following loans where the interest is compounded annually:

a $4000 for 2 years at 11% p.a.
b $580 for 5 years at 12% p.a.
c $15 000 for 3 years at 9% p.a.
d $950 for 6 years at 15% p.a.
e $25 000 for 7 years at $11\frac{1}{4}$% p.a.
f $34 500 for 4 years at 9·7% p.a.
g $3 million for 5 years at $10\frac{3}{4}$% p.a.
h $150 for 10 years at 17% p.a.

4 Diana needs a loan of $1400 to buy a new mountain bike.

a How much will she have to repay after 2 years if the 15% p.a. interest is:
  i compounded annually?
  ii calculated as simple interest?
b Which is the better option for Diana?

5 Calculate the *interest* earned on an investment of $550 if the interest rate is 4·9% p.a. compounded annually, and the money is invested for 6 years.

6 Complete the following interest rate conversions:

a 12% p.a. = _____ % per month
b 6% p.a. = _____ % per month
c 24% p.a. = _____ % per quarter
d 1% per month = _____ % p.a.
e 9% p.a. = _____ % per month
f 3% per quarter = _____ % p.a.
g 9% p.a. = _____ % 6 monthly
h 2% per month = _____ % per quarter

> You have already converted rates in chapter 2.

Level 2

7 Calculate the final amount if $2000 is invested over 5 years at 9% p.a. compounded:

a annually
b 6 monthly
c quarterly
d monthly

8 If the interest rate in question **7** doubles, recalculate the final amount of the investment.

9 If the amount invested in question **7** doubles, recalculate the final amount of the investment.

10 Calculate the interest earned on:

a $1000 invested at 6% p.a. compounded monthly for 2 years
b $250 invested at 1% per month compounded monthly for 5 years
c $4750 invested at 10% p.a. compounded semiannually for 10 years.

11 Prem has $45 000 to invest for 1 year. The bank tells him the interest rate is 6%. Calculate how much his investment is worth at the end of the year:

> A graphics calculator is a very useful tool with which to explore compound growth.

a if the interest is paid annually
b if the interest is paid every 6 months
c if the interest is paid quarterly (every 3 months).

12 a How much *interest* is earned over 4 years on $3500 invested with an interest rate of 5·5% p.a. compounded annually?

b How much *interest* must be paid on a 10-year loan of $19 000 if the interest rate is 14% p.a. compounded annually?

13 Which is the better rate of interest, 10·5% p.a. paid annually or 10% p.a. paid quarterly? Show calculations to justify your answer.

14 Bank A charges interest on its loans at a rate of 15% p.a. compounded annually. Bank B charges 1·2% per month. Explain which bank you would choose, and justify your decision.

Level 3

15 a A trout farm starts with 10 000 fish. They breed at a rate of 5% p.a. How many fish are there at the end of 3 years?

b Recalculate the number of fish left at the end of 3 years if 2500 are caught and sold at the end of each year. (Calculate the number after the fish are caught for that year.)

16 The population of a city is 1·1 million. Each year it is expected to increase by 2% on the previous year's population. What is the expected population in 10 years' time?

17 $87 000 is invested for 3 years at R% p.a. If at the end of 3 years the investment is worth $10 000, what is the applied interest rate if the investment compounds:

a annually? **b** 6 monthly? **c** monthly?

18 At what investment rate does an investment need to be invested if it is to double at the end of 5 years if it is compounding:

a annually? **b** 6 monthly? **c** monthly?

19 By estimation or use of a graphics calculator, decide on a suitable length of time for $2000 to be invested at 6% p.a. annually compounded if the value of the investment is to reach $3500.

SPREADSHEET ACTIVITY

Investigation Types of interest

Fixed interest

An investment of $75 000 earns $11 000 interest.

1 Investigate the possible **simple** interest rates and time periods that could lead to this situation. What is the relationship between time period and the interest rate?

2 Investigate the possible **compound** interest rates and time periods that could lead to the same situation, and try to establish a relationship between them.

Compounding the problem

$10 000 is invested for 2 years at an interest rate of 6% p.a. Investigate how the interest earned varies as the *interval* over which the interest is compounded varies.

Construct a *table* showing the interest earned over a range of compounding intervals, perhaps from 2 years down to 1 month. A *graph* of the results may help to show the effect of reducing the time interval. A *spreadsheet* could be used to calculate the amount of interest.

10.9 Depreciation

Depreciation is a loss of value in the original value of an item. Computers, whitegoods and cars are all examples of goods that depreciate in value.

> The compound interest formula needs to be adapted to account for items decreasing in value each year.
> $$A = P(1 - R)^n$$

EXAMPLE 1

A car originally worth \$42 900 depreciates at a rate of 12% p.a. Find its value at the end of 4 years.

Solution

$A = P(1 - R)^n$
$\quad = 42\,900(1 - 0{\cdot}12)^4$
$\quad = 42\,900(0{\cdot}88)^4$
$\quad = 25\,726{\cdot}93$

The car is worth \$25 726·93 at the end of 4 years.

EXERCISE 10I

1 If cars depreciate at a rate of 10% p.a., calculate the value of the following at the end of 5 years:

  a Ford Falcon worth \$37 400   **b** Mitsubishi Lancer coupe worth \$18 850
  c Mazda MX5 worth \$52 000.

2 Marcus's new computer cost \$2990. If it depreciates at a rate of 22% p.a., what will it be worth at the end of 3 years?

3 A microwave costs \$375. It depreciates at a rate of 4·5% p.a. Find its resale value at the end of 2 years.

Level 2

4 The Australian Taxation Department allows landlords to claim depreciation on items used by tenants. Curtains and blinds depreciate at a rate of 27% p.a.

  a Calculate the value of blinds costing \$1800 at the end of 1 year.
  b Calculate the depreciation allowed for taxation purposes.
  c After approximately how many years does the value of the blinds reach \$145?

5 Find the depreciated value of:

  a a photocopier worth \$16 000 at 12% p.a. depreciation rate calculated monthly for 4 months
  b \$4000 at 6% p.a. depreciation rate calculated monthly for 6 months
  c \$4000 at 6% p.a. depreciation rate calculated daily for 6 months (take 30 days to be a month).

Level 3

6 A car has a current value of \$7500. If it was bought 5 years ago for \$24 500, find its annual rate of depreciation.

7 A motorcycle now worth $5550 has been depreciating at a rate of 8% p.a. for the last 3 years. What was its original value 3 years ago to the nearest dollar?

8 A school's population is depreciating at a rate of $1\frac{1}{2}$% p.a. Its current population is 950 students.

   a How many students does the school expect to have enrolled in 3 years?
   b If the school is going to close when its population reaches 300 students, how many years can it remain open?

Investigation Hidden costs of mobile phones

Mobile phones are a common cause of financial problems for teenagers. Using the Web or otherwise, prepare a report on the costs of running a mobile phone for two different mobile phone providers.

10.10 Saving your money

There is now a wide selection of banks, credit unions, building societies and other places where you can open an account. Different types of accounts are available, for example:

- savings accounts
- term deposits
- statement accounts.

> Banking originated before the need for coins. In ancient Mesopotamia items of worth were stored in royal palaces and temples. In Egypt the state warehouses used for storing the harvests led to the development of a system of banking. In the Egypt of the Ptolemies (323–30 BC) the system of banking reached a new level of sophistication.

SAVINGS ACCOUNTS

One of the best ways to manage your money and help you to save is to have an account with a bank, building society or credit union. There are many different types of account to choose from. Your choice depends on various factors, including how much money you have and how you wish to withdraw your money.

For everyday use a savings account that allows you immediate access to your money is the most useful. There are several methods of accessing your money.

Passbook

A passbook contains a record of all transactions. To pay money into the account, or withdraw cash, the passbook must be taken to a branch of your bank, building society or credit union.

SPECTRUM				
DATE	DETAILS	CREDIT	DEBIT	BALANCE
2/2/03	B/d			163.89
2/2/03	Withdrawal 0219		50.00	113.89
15/2/03	Cash	65.00		178.89

ATM card

An ATM card can be used in *any* of the ATM machines that are linked to your bank, building society or credit union. They can be used to deposit or withdraw money, and may also provide other facilities such as providing a balance, or requesting a statement. Users of ATM cards are given a personal identification number (**PIN**) as a security measure in case the card is lost or stolen. (Nevertheless very good care should be taken of all cards, chequebooks, passbooks, etc.)

Cheque book

Cheque books are useful for paying bills, or when payment has to be made by mail (for example, for mail order items, or sporting event entry fees, or theatre tickets.) They also allow payments to be made when it is impossible to get to a bank. It is important that cheques are filled out correctly. Details of the cheque may be entered on the cheque book stub as your own record.

TERM DEPOSITS

With term deposits, a sum of money is invested for a fixed amount of time at a higher rate of interest than for savings accounts.

A term deposit is a good idea if you have a larger amount of money to invest (usually over $2000) and do not expect to need access to the money for an extended period of time (usually at least 3 months).

In order to obtain the higher interest rate, you cannot withdraw money from a term deposit. However, if you need the money for an emergency it can be withdrawn, and interest will then be paid at the normal rate for savings accounts.

STATEMENTS

A bank or building society **statement** shows all of the account **transactions** (money paid in or taken out) and the **balance** of the account.

Some accounts have the interest calculated on the **minimum monthly balance**. The *lowest* amount in the account during the month is used as the *principal* in the interest calculation.

Most accounts have the interest calculated **daily** on the amount of money in the account that day, which means that interest is earned on money from the *day after* it is deposited. The daily interest rate is calculated by dividing the annual interest rate by 365 (the number of days in a year).

EXAMPLE 1

Calculate the May interest paid on this account if it is paid at 2·5% p.a. of the minimum monthly balance.

Hang-Back Bank

S. Broke
7 The Avenue
Sydney
NSW 2001

HBB

Date	Details	Credit	Debit	Balance
1/4/02	Opening balance	100·00		714·56
5/4/02	Cash deposit			814·56
16/4/02	Cheque No. 301766		650·00	164·56
18/4/02	Direct credit	1289·48		1454·04
27/4/02	Programmed payment		45·67	1408·37
30/4/02	Final balance			1408·37

> Credit is money going into the account. Debit is money going out.

Solution

Minimum monthly balance = $164·56

$I = PRT$

$= \$164{\cdot}56 \times 0{\cdot}025 \times \dfrac{30}{365}$ **30 days out of 365**

$= \$0{\cdot}338\ 136 \ldots$

$= 34\cent$

EXAMPLE 2

Calculate the interest earned on this account for the month of September. The interest rate is 4·2% p.a., and is calculated daily:

Which Bank?—Republic Bank!

A. Customer
26 Memory Lane
Hopeville
NSW 2999

Date	Details	Credit	Debit	Balance	Interest
1/9/02	Opening balance			328·21	
3/9/02	Direct credit	864·57		1192·78	0·113
12/9/02	ATM withdrawal		100·00	1092·78	1·235
17/9/02	Cheque No. 000302		412·95	679·83	0·629
18/9/02	Direct credit	864·57		1544·40	0·078
24/9/02	ATM withdrawal		150·00	1394·40	1·066
30/9/02	Closing balance			1394·40	0·963
				Total	**$4·08**

Solution

Add another column to the statement to calculate the interest earned between each transaction. (Give these amounts to 3 decimal places, so final total is accurate to the nearest cent.)

Interest = PRT

To 3/9: Interest = $328 \cdot 21 \times \dfrac{0 \cdot 042}{365} \times 3$ days   **Daily rate = 4·2% ÷ 365**

$$= 0 \cdot 1132 \ldots$$
$$= \$0 \cdot 113$$

To 12/9: Interest = $1192 \cdot 78 \times \dfrac{0 \cdot 042}{365} \times 9$ days

$$= 1 \cdot 2352 \ldots$$
$$= \$1 \cdot 235$$

Interest for September = $\$4 \cdot 08$

Note: Interest may be paid into accounts each month, or every 3 or 6 months.

EXERCISE 10J

1 Calculate the interest payable on the following amounts if the interest rate is 3·75% p.a:

a $396 for 10 days   **b** $65·97 for 20 days
c $3200 for 7 days   **d** $901·65 for all of April
e $549·82 for all of December   **f** $684·73 from 6th to 11th June
g $1763·84 from 14/8 to 27/8   **h** $32·40 from 2/10 to 31/10

Level 2

2 In January Shanette had a balance of $356·75 in her account for 13 days and a balance of $468·23 for the rest of the month. Calculate the interest payable on the account for the month of January if the interest rate is 3·5% p.a. and interest is calculated daily.

3 a Complete the final column of the statement below showing:

    i the interest earned between each transaction when interest is calculated daily, and

    ii the total interest earned for the month. The interest rate is 4·3%.

In a State Bank of NSW						Interest
Date	Details	Credit	Debit	Balance		
1 March	Opening balance			125·60		
10 March	Cash deposit	50·00		175·60		
19 March	ATM withdrawal		80·00	95·60		
31 March	Closing balance			95·60		
				Total →		

b Calculate the interest if it is paid at the same rate, but calculated on the minimum monthly balance.

4 a Calculate:

    i the balance after each transaction

    ii the interest earned between transactions, and

    iii the total interest earned on this account for the month of July, if the interest rate is 5·15% p.a. and interest is calculated daily.

EFTPOS: electronic funds transfer at point of sale.

Big *Bank!*				
Date	Details	Credit	Debit	Balance
1/7/02	Opening balance			398·54
5/7/02	EFTPOS payment		119·95	
12/7/02	Cheque No. 020439		176·85	
14/7/02	Cash deposit	369·00		
23/7/02	Programmed payment		135·00	
29/7/02	Bank charges		9·85	
31/7/02	Closing balance			

    b Calculate the interest earned on the account if it is paid at the same rate, but calculated on the minimum monthly balance.

Level 3

5 Mary started off October with $185·48 in her account. On the 5th she withdrew $65, on the 13th she paid $32·67 for petrol on EFTPOS, and she wrote a cheque for $255 that was cashed on the 25th as a deposit on a lounge suite. Her fortnightly salary of $856·91 was paid into her account automatically on the 15th and 29th.

    a Make a monthly statement showing Mary's transactions.
    b Calculate the interest earned by the account if the rate is 4·85% p.a. and interest is calculated daily.
    c Calculate the interest earned at the same rate, but calculated on the minimum monthly balance.

10.11 Credit cards

Credit cards are a convenient way of making purchases, and reduce the need for consumers to carry around large quantities of cash. Purchases made with a credit card do not have to be paid for until the due date shown on the monthly statement.

Credit cards need to be used responsibly, since they allow consumers to spend money that they may not be able to afford to pay back. If a major purchase is planned, it would be cheaper to arrange a personal loan through a bank or building society rather than use a credit card, since the interest rate on credit cards is generally very high.

When the monthly statement is received, a **minimum** payment must be paid by the due date. If the balance is not paid off, then interest is charged on it. The minimum payment could be a fixed amount (say, $50) or 5% of the balance.

EXAMPLE
Aldrin's BankCard statement is shown below. How much interest will he be charged on the next statement:
a if he pays only the minimum amount?
b if he makes a payment of $200?
c if he pays the full amount?

Spectrum Bank of Australia		
Statement date: 2/5/02		
Date of purchase	**Details**	**Amount**
3/4/02	Opening balance	314·79
5/4/02	Dean's Jeans	59·95
16/4/02	Tyre Warehouse	138·50
22/4/02	Payment made—thank you	100·00
27/4/02	Cottonworth's Grocery Store	58·64
30/4/02	Interest charges	3·35
2/5/02	Closing balance	475·23
18·95% p.a.	25/5/02	23·75
Percentage rate	**Due Date**	**Min. Payment**

Solutions

a Balance owing = 475·23 − 23·75
= 451·48
Interest = $451\cdot48 \times \dfrac{0.1895}{365} \times 31$
= $7·27

b Balance owing = 475·23 − 200
= 275·33
Interest = $275\cdot23 \times \dfrac{0.1895}{365} \times 31$
= $4·43

c No interest

Note: The policy of some banks is a little different. If the entire balance is not paid, then interest is charged from the date of each purchase, calculated daily. This makes the calculations more difficult, so will not be dealt with here!

EXERCISE 10K

1 Calculate the interest charges payable on the following credit account balance, over the months stated, if the interest rate is 14·55% p.a.:

1996 is a leap year.

   a $450 for August
   c $2307 for June
   e $1709·60 for February 1997

   b $39·87 for April
   d $970·55 for January
   f $762·78 for February 1996

Level 2

2 Calculate:

   i the remaining balance and
   ii the interest charges payable

on the following credit card accounts. The interest rate is 17·65% p.a., and the period is 31 days:

a Closing balance is $392·10, amount paid is $39·21.
b Closing balance is $5612·90, amount paid is $900.
c Closing balance is $98·00, amount paid is $50.
d Closing balance is $45·67, amount paid is $45·67.
e Closing balance is $1045·63, amount paid is $845·63.
f Closing balance is $195·48, amount paid is 5% of balance.

3 This is Royston's credit card statement:

NAZ Bank		
Date	**Details**	**Amount**
1/9/02	Opening balance	214·87
4/9/02	Saltend Rd service station	29·83
15/9/02	Cheap-o Supermarket	79·38
19/9/02	Summit Restaurant	126·45
23/9/02	Payment made—thank you	120·00
30/9/02	Interest charges	...
30/9/02	Closing balance	...
	Due Date 25/10/02 **Minimum Payment**	...

    a Calculate the September remaining balance (opening balance – payment).
    b If the interest rate is 18·42% p.a., calculate the interest charges for September.
    c Calculate the closing balance of Royston's account.
    d Calculate the minimum payment if it is 5% of the closing balance.
    e What will be the October interest charges if Royston pays only the minimum amount?

Level 3

4 Tina pays 14·95% p.a. interest on her credit card account. Her opening balance for November is $129·52. She makes the following purchases during the month:

3/11 Red Edge Pizza Co. $37·90
4/11 Runaway Travel $135·60
15/11 Venus Rd service station $23·00
23/11 Runner's Shoes $138·95.

She made a payment of $100 on 16/11, which was before the due date. Make a statement for Tina, like the one shown for Royston above. Calculate the interest charge, the closing balance, and the minimum payment due in December (5% of the November closing balance).

Chapter Review

annual	fortnightly	overtime	simple
balance	gross	per annum	spreadsheet
bonus	income	percent	statement
borrow	increase	percentage	superannuation
casual	instalment	piecework	tax
commission	interest	principal	time
compound	invest	profit	transaction
cost	loading	purchase	wages
credit	loan	rate	withdrawal
deductions	loss	retainer	year
deposit	mark-up	salary	
discount	monthly	sales	
earning	net	savings	

1 Find as many words from the list as you can in the grid below. The words may be horizontal or vertical, forwards or backwards.

T	E	E	H	S	D	A	E	R	P	S
N	A	G	H	T	I	D	E	R	C	Y
E	L	A	W	A	R	D	H	T	I	W
M	S	T	H	T	N	O	M	P	N	O
L	I	N	V	E	S	T	S	N	T	R
A	M	E	E	M	I	T	E	A	E	R
T	P	C	Y	E	A	R	T	O	R	O
S	L	R	A	N	N	U	A	L	E	B
N	E	E	I	T	M	O	R	N	S	L
I	L	P	D	E	P	O	S	I	T	O
P	E	L	S	A	V	I	N	G	S	T

2 Write the definition for:

   a interest   **b** per annum   **c** compound   **d** overtime

3 Choose words from the list that best fit these descriptions:

   a A method of payment where a certain amount is paid for each item produced.
   b The difference between the cost price and selling price of an item (2 answers).
   c Possible deductions from a person's pay (2 answers).
   d A method of payment where earnings are a certain percentage of the goods sold.

4 Explain the difference between:

  a gross income and net income   **b** wages and salary.

5 The following are anagrams of words in the list above. Find each word:

  a move rite   **b** notice duds   **c** u snob

6 What is *holiday loading* and how is it calculated?

7 Explain the difference between simple interest and compound interest. Which would you prefer to earn and why?

8 What do the following acronyms represent?

  a ATM   **b** PIN   **c** EFTPOS

9 The compound interest formula is $A = P(1 + R)^n$. Write down the meaning of each pronumeral used in this formula.

Chapter Review Exercises

1 The following number of 50 g balls of wool are used to knit a jumper with a fair-isle pattern: 10 blue; 4 red; 2 white; 1 black. Find the percentage composition of the colours in the jumper, to the nearest 1%.

2 A discount of 15% on a squash racquet reduced the price by $26·40. What was the sale price?

3 Peta buys a sewing machine for $458 and later sells it for $399.

  a How much did she lose on the machine?
  b What percentage loss did she make on the cost price?

4 An electronics store has a fixed mark-up of 85%.

  a What would be the selling price of a component with a cost price of $13·20?
  b What would be the cost price of a switch that sells for $8·65?
  c How much profit would be made on a soldering kit that is sold for $317·95?
  d A guitar originally priced at $482 is discounted by 35%. What will be the sale price?

5 A leather briefcase was originally priced at $199, and is reduced to $167 in a sale. What is the percentage discount?

6 After a 6% discount a telephone bill is $56·20. What was the amount of the original bill?

7 A bike has a ticketed price of $1220. It is offered for sale for 7% off the ticket price.

  a Find the sale price of the bike.

MC

MC

MC

MC

MC

MC

10.1

b If the bike is purchased for $1120 because of a small scratch, what is the value of the further discount on the sale price as a percentage?

10.1

8 A briefcase is offered on sale at $7\frac{1}{2}$ % off the marked price. If a further 5% discount is then granted, find the original marked price of the briefcase if it sold for $199.

10.1'

9 Sven earns $6·42 per hour as a bar worker. What would he earn for working a 34-hour week?

10.2

10 Workers at Macpherson's take-away are paid a standard wage of $5·98 per hour. Overtime is paid at time-and-a-half for all time worked after 6 pm on weekdays, and all day on Saturdays. Double time is paid on Sundays. Calculate the total earnings for each person:

a Mishi: Thursday 6:30 pm to 10:30 pm and Saturday 9 am to 4:15 pm
b Arti: Tuesday 4 pm to 9 pm and Sunday 1:45 pm to 5:30 pm

10.3

11 Maurice has been offered a new job as a computer salesman, and has a choice of payment methods:

A: Commission of $12\frac{1}{2}$% on all sales
B: A retainer of $300 per month plus 6% on all sales

a What would be his monthly earnings by each method if he made the following sales:
   i $10 000?   **ii** $55 000?
b For each of the payment methods, calculate the sales he would need to make to earn an annual salary of $42 500.
c For what value of sales would he earn the *same* by *both* methods?

10.5

12 Lazarus works 38 h per week, and is paid at a rate of $15·60 per hour. His company pays him $17\frac{1}{2}$% holiday loading when he takes 3 weeks' holiday. What is his total pay for the 3 weeks?

10.2

13 Shaun earns $1430 gross per fortnight. He pays $34·94 in superannuation, $23·40 in union fees and $493·60 in tax.

a What is Shaun's net fortnightly pay?
b What percentage of his gross pay is his net pay?
c Davina needs to state her annual gross salary on a housing loan application form. She cannot remember exactly what it is, but sees on her most recent pay slip that her net pay was $998·20, with total deductions of $318·75. If she is paid fortnightly, calculate her annual gross salary.

10.3

14 Theo, a real estate agent, charges commission at a rate of 5% for the first $18 000 of a sale, and $2\frac{1}{2}$% on the rest.

a Calculate the commission received on the sale of a house worth $412 500.
b What is the value of a sale that created $5136 in commission?

10.6

15 Use the tax table on page 294 to answer the following question.
Gerald earns a salary of $3240 per month. Calculate:

a how much tax he pays per year
b his net monthly income
c the percentage of his salary that Gerald pays in tax.

16 Calculate **i** the simple interest earned and **ii** the final value, of the following investments: 10.7

  a $3000 at 4% p.a. for 2 years   **b** $268 at $5\frac{1}{2}$% p.a. for 6 years
  c $25 500 at 6% p.a. for 4 months   **d** $96 for 10 weeks at 3·75% p.a.
  e $\$\frac{1}{2}$ million for 30 days at 7% p.a.   **f** $700 at $5\frac{1}{4}$% p.a. for 11 months

17 Calculate the value of the following investments if interest is compounded annually: 10.8

  a $350 after 4 years at 10% p.a.   **b** $40 000 after 7 years at $7\frac{1}{2}$% p.a.

18 Calculate the amount owing on the following loans where the interest is compounded annually: 10.8

  a $8400 over 5 years at 12% p.a.   **b** $95 500 over 10 years at 15·1% p.a.

19 Shirley's bank pays 5·5% p.a. interest that is credited to her account every 6 months. If she has $1864 in her account now, how much will be in her account: 10.10

  a in 2 years' time?   **b** in 5 years' time?

20 If $20 000 is invested for 8 years at an interest rate of 7·5% p.a. calculate: 10.8

  a the simple interest it would earn
  b the interest it would earn if compounded annually
  c the interest it would earn if compounded every 6 months.

21 Find the value of a mountain bike worth $1450 at the end of 2 years if it depreciates at a rate of 7% p.a. 10.9

22 The simple interest over 4 years on a loan of $500 is $240. What is the interest rate? 10.7

23 Sven takes out a 5-year loan for $3000 at a simple interest rate of 12·5% p.a. If the repayments are to be paid in equal monthly instalments, how much is each instalment? 10.7

24 The following statement shows the transactions made by Mr Garran. He earns 2·7% p.a. interest on money in his account, and the interest is calculated daily. 10.11

Spectrum Bank of NSW				
Statement date: 2/10/02				
Date	**Details**	**Credit**	**Debit**	**Balance**
3/9/02	Opening balance			56·45
17/9/02	Cash withdrawal		30·00	...
20/9/02	Check deposit	120·00		...
29/9/02	ATM withdrawal		80·00	...
2/10/02	Closing balance			...

  a Calculate the amounts that would be entered in the balance column.
  b For how many days was $56·45 in the account?
  c Calculate the interest earned on this amount.
  d Calculate the interest earned between each of the other transactions.
  e What was the total interest earned by Mr Garran during September?

Keeping Mathematically Fit

Part A—Non-calculator

1 Solve $\frac{3x}{4} - 9 = {}^-12$.

2 This is the plan for a bedroom. Estimate the scale that was used to draw the plan.

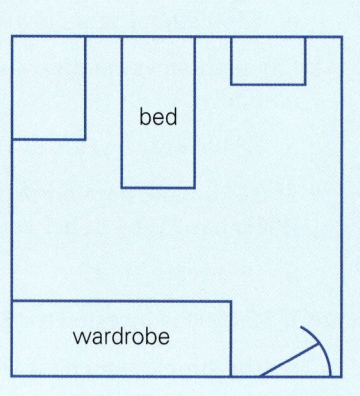

3 What is $33\frac{1}{3}\%$ of 72 kg?

4 The front view and plan of this solid are shown. Which of the following shows the left side view?

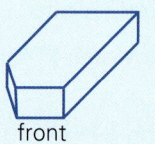 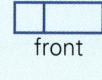 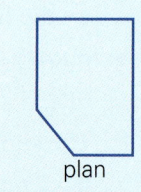

A

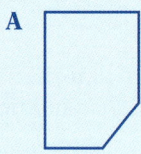

B  **C**  **D**

5 Find the value of n, giving reasons for your answer.

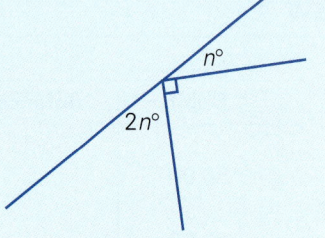

6 This graph shows newsletter printing costs.

a What is the cost of painting 200 copies?
b What is the initial set-up cost?

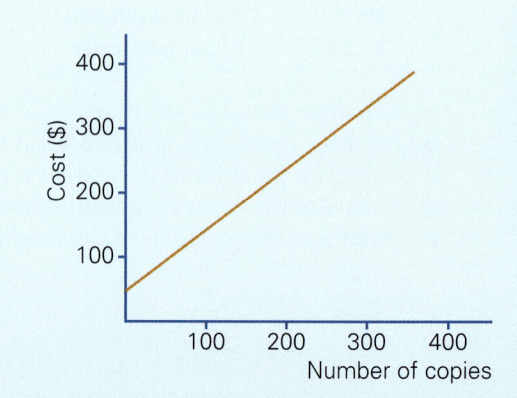

7 Prices in dollars for a particular model of scooter were surveyed in 10 shops:

67   59   75   69   59   72   65   81   70   65

   a Display the data on a stem-and-leaf plot.
   b What is the range of prices?
   c What is the median price?

8 Factorise $32t - 12t^2$.

9 Convert 1·7 ha to m^2.

10 What is the height of a rectangular prism with base 6 cm by 4 cm if its volume is 144 cm^3?

Part B—Calculator

1 Simplify $4p^0$.

2 The mid-point of A and B is $(3, {}^-2)$. If A is the point $({}^-1, 1)$, find the coordinates of B.

3 Calculate the net pay for a gross weekly wage of $946, an income tax payment of $113·65 and a superannuation contribution of 5% of the gross pay for 1 week.

4 Evaluate k: $\dfrac{2(k + 3)}{3} - \dfrac{(5k + 4)}{2} = 1$

5 Using only the digits 1, 2 and 3 and any mathematical symbols you wish, what is the largest number you can make? Each number and symbol must not be used more than once. Some possibilities might be 321, 31^2, (2·1)^3. Can you do better?

TEACHER

Cumulative Review 3

1 Expand and simplify where possible:

   a $5a + \dfrac{3}{4}(8a + 12)$ **b** $^-4r(5r^3 - 2r)$

   c $3x^2(x - 2) + x(3x + 5)$ **d** $(2t + 3)(t - 7)$

2 Factorise fully:

   a $6p + 18q$ **b** $^-12vw^2 - 30w^3$

3 Estimate the answers to the following—check your answers with a calculator.

   a $693 \times 1 \cdot 13$ **b** 52×1976 **c** 278×305

   d $\dfrac{12\ 486 - 1023}{2 \cdot 862}$ **e** $\dfrac{(77 \cdot 9 \div 19 \cdot 2)^2}{42 \cdot 3 - 11 \cdot 9}$ **f** $41 \cdot 3 \div \sqrt{34 \cdot 8}$

4 Give answers to 1 decimal place:

   a $\dfrac{132}{4 + 5^2}$ **b** $\dfrac{7 \times (20 - 14 \cdot 3)}{19 \cdot 2 - 37 \cdot 1}$ **c** $\sqrt{(9 + 7 \times 5)}$

5 Write in scientific notation:

   a   340   **b**   39 million   **c** $0 \cdot 000\ 456$

6 Write the basic numeral for:

   a $3 \cdot 5 \times 10^3$ **b** $1 \cdot 06 \times 10^5$ **c** $4 \cdot 11 \times 10^{-3}$

7 **a**   Find a formula for the nth term of this sequence: 6, 10, 14, 18, …

     b   Find the 18th term.

8 Express in index form:

   a $5 \times 5 \times 5 \times 5 \times 5 \times 5$ **b** $3t \times 3t \times 3t$

9 Simplify:

   a $16x^2y^2 \div 2xy^3$ **b** $(a^2)^3$ **c** $4t^0$

10 Evaluate:

   a $100^{\frac{1}{2}}$ **b** $(^-7)^2$ **c** 5^{-2} **d** $\left(\dfrac{1}{5}\right)^{-1}$

11 What are the limits of accuracy for a length of 1·24 m?

12 Convert the following measurements as indicated:

   a   440 g to kg   **b**   8·4 t to kg   **c**   1·4 ha to m^2

13 How high in metres would a stack of 40 of your maths textbooks be?

14 Divide 400 km in the ratio 7 : 3.

15 Alex and Simon buy a $5 lottery ticket, with Alex contributing $3·20 towards the cost. If they win $3650, how much would each of them receive if the winnings are shared in the same ratio as their contributions to the cost?

16 A map scale is given as 1 : 15 000.

    a What distance on the ground is represented by 1 cm on the map?
    b If the length of a fence is 640 m, how long is the fence line on the map?

17 Which is the better buy: 150 g of instant coffee for \$4·25 or 250 g for \$7·20?

18 If 14 gardeners can plant 220 trees in 3 days, how many gardeners would be required to plant 170 trees in 5 days?

19 Find x, correct to 1 decimal place.

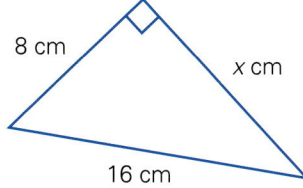

20 Find **i** perimeter, **ii** area of each figure:

a 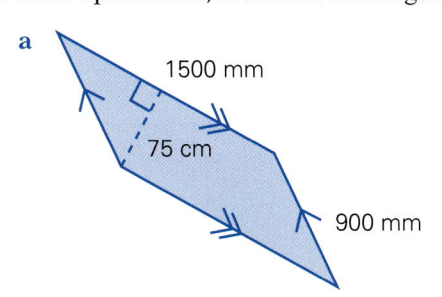   **b**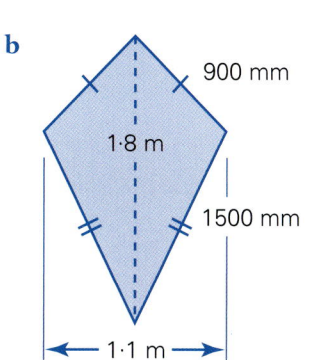

21 Solve the following equations:

    a $\dfrac{6t}{5} = 9$ **b** $3(5 - 3a) = {}^-5(a + 2) - 3$ **c** $\dfrac{2}{x} = \dfrac{3}{x - 5}$

22 Solve the following and graph the solutions on a number line:

    a $7n + 1 \geq 25{\cdot}5$ **b** $7 > 10 - 4f$

23 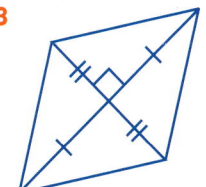 Consider the figure at left. Give a reason for each answer.

    a Is it a quadrilateral?
    b Is it a parallelogram?
    c Is it a square?
    d Is it a rhombus?

24 Give the necessary instructions for a person to make an accurate copy of this figure.

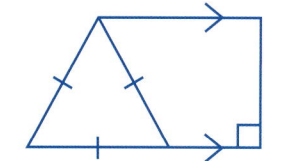

25 Use the known properties of a rhombus to find the value of each of the following:

    a $\angle ABC$ **b** $\angle DCB$ **c** $\angle AEB$
    d AB **e** DE **f** $\angle ADE$

26 Find **i** the angle sum and **ii** the size of the interior angle, of each regular polygon:

a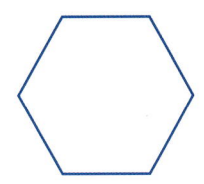

b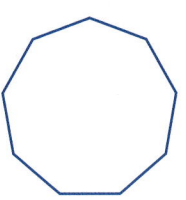

27 What size is each *exterior* angle of a regular pentagon?

28 Is every square also a rhombus? Explain.

29 Find the angle sum of any octagon.

30 Which quadrilaterals have equal diagonals?

31 Express each ratio in simplest form:

a   350 : 1400

b $2\frac{1}{4} : 3$

32 Is this triangle right-angled? Explain your answer.

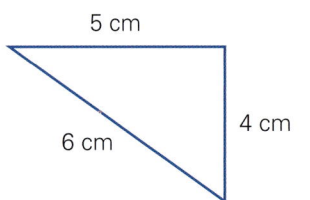

33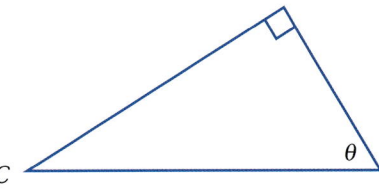

Name:

a   the hypotenuse
b   the side adjacent to θ
c   the side opposite θ

34 Calculate, correct to 3 decimal places:

a $\sin 52°$

b $\tan 10°$

c $\cos 67°$

35 Find the value of each pronumeral, correct to 2 decimal places:

a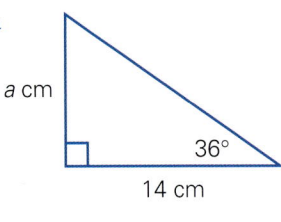

b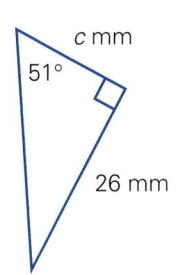

c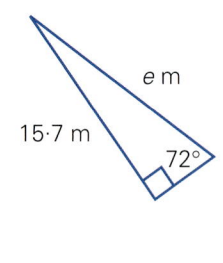

36 Find the value of θ to the nearest degree:

a

b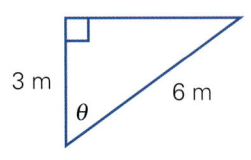

c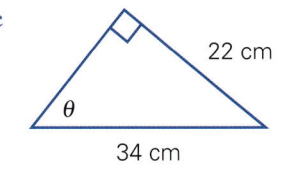

37 A mouse sees an owl on top of a 5 m lamp post, and measures the angle of elevation to be 21°. How far does the owl have to fly to reach the mouse?

38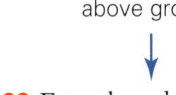

The minute hand on Muriel's kitchen clock is 9 cm long. The centre of her clock is 1·9 m above the ground.

a How high above the ground is the tip of the minute hand at 8:10 am?

b How high is it above the ground at twenty-five to seven in the evening?

1·9 m above ground

39 From her observation room 167 m above sea level, a lighthouse keeper sees a fishing boat and a passenger liner on the same bearing. If the angle of depression of the fishing boat is 22·3° and the angle of depression of the liner 7·6°, how far apart are the two boats?

40 A rectangle measures 15 cm by 23 cm. Find the sizes of the angles between the diagonals of the rectangle.

41 For the function $2y = 3x - 2$, which of the following is *not* true?

A The graph of the function is a straight line.

B The gradient of the graph is 3.

C The slope of the line is $\frac{3}{2}$.

D The graph crosses the y-axis at $(0, ^-1)$.

E The x-intercept is $\frac{2}{3}$.

42 One of the graphs shown *cannot* represent the suggested relationship. Which is it?

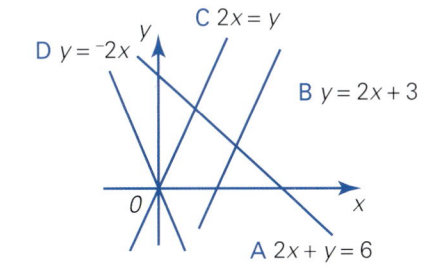

43

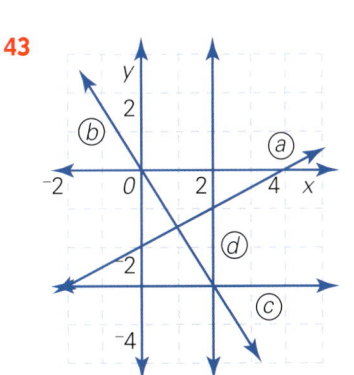

a For function ⓐ find the:
 i x-intercept **ii** y-intercept
 iii gradient **iv** equation of the line

b For function ⓑ find the:
 i x-intercept **ii** y-intercept
 iii gradient **iv** equation of the line

c Write the equation of line ⓒ.

d Write the equation of line ⓓ.

44 Give **i** the gradient and **ii** the y-intercept for each graph:

a $y = ^-3x - 4$ **b** $2y = x$ **c** $2y + 4 = 6x$ **d** $2x - 5y = 10$

45 a Find the equation of a line whose y-intercept is $^-3$ and whose gradient is $\frac{3}{5}$.

b Write the equation of a line parallel to the line in part **a** with a y-intercept of 0.

46 Sketch the line $y = \frac{1}{3}x - 2$, using gradient and y-intercept.

47 The distance between $A(2, 6)$ and $B(12, {}^-4)$ is:

   A $10\sqrt{2}$ **B** 20 **C** $\sqrt{20} \times \sqrt{10}$ **D** 100 **E** 200

48 The mid-point of the interval joining $A(n, t)$ to $B({}^-3n, 3t)$ is:

   A $(2n, {}^-t)$ **B** $({}^-n, 2t)$ **C** $({}^-2n, 4t)$ **D** $(n, {}^-2t)$

49 A triangle has vertices $({}^-2, 3)$, $(1, 1)$ and $({}^-1, {}^-2)$.

   a Find the lengths of the sides.   **b** Classify the triangle.

50 The mid-point of P and Q is $(3, {}^-4)$. If P is $(5, 1)$, find Q.

51 Write the equation of the vertical line through $({}^-3, 6)$.

52 What is the equation of the horizontal line through $(2, {}^-5)$?

53 Select the graph that represents the depth of water in this container as it is filled from a tap.

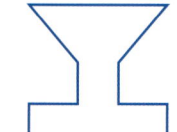

A 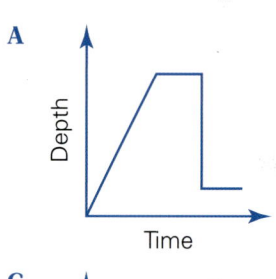   **B**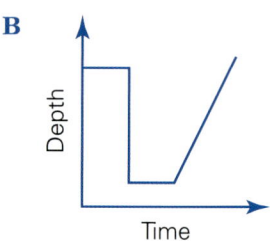

C 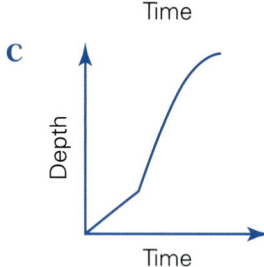   **D**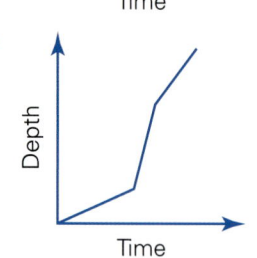

54 Show all necessary working when answering these questions:

   a Suggest two reasons why this graph may be misleading.

   b Draw a different graph that shows the same information in a fairer way.

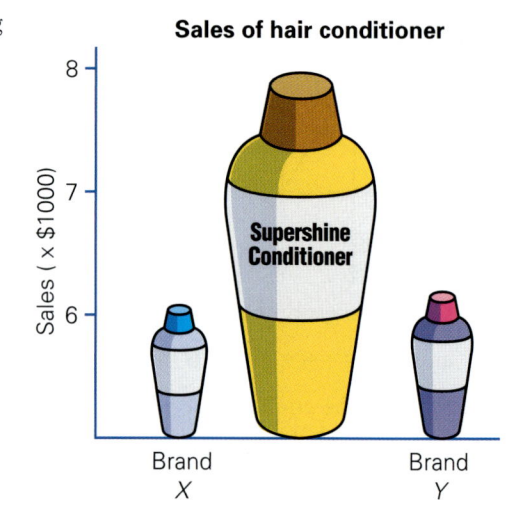

Sales of hair conditioner

55 The table shows the monthly sales figures for electric heaters sold by a large retailer:

Month	Jan.	Feb.	Mar.	Apr.	May	June	July	Aug.
Sales	5	4	6	17	47	122	145	158

  a Draw a graph to show the sales of electric heaters.
  b The sales manager suggests that the trend indicates they will be selling 200 heaters per month by Christmas. How sensible is his prediction?

56 Draw the image of $\triangle PQR$ under reflection in the mirror line m.

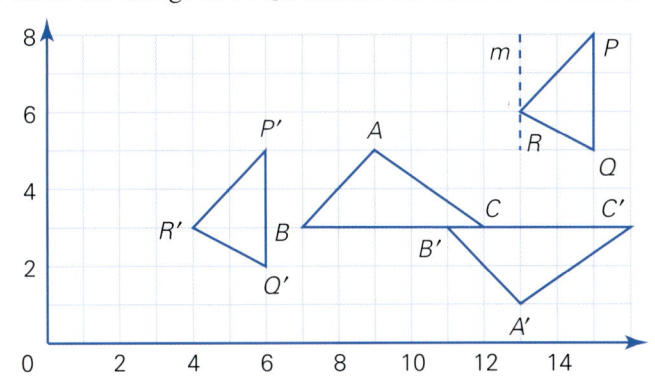

  a Give the coordinates of Q'.
  b Rotate $\triangle PQR$ 90° anti-clockwise about Q. Draw the image.
  c Give the coordinates of P'.
  d Describe the transformation of $\triangle PQR$ to $\triangle P'Q'R'$.
  e Describe the transformation of $\triangle ABC$ to $\triangle A'B'C'$.

57 If a triangle KMX is constructed so that $\triangle KMX \equiv \triangle PYD$, write the value of:
  a KX **b** $\angle KXM$ **c** XM

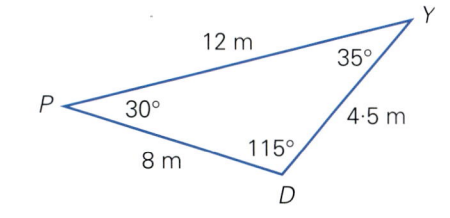

58 State whether or not the triangles on the right are definitely congruent. If they are,

  a write a congruency statement
  b give a reason for congruency.

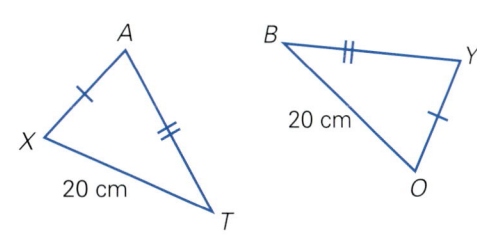

59

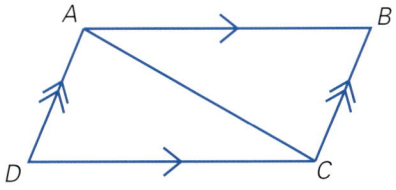

Prove that the triangles are congruent. Give a reason for each line of your proof.

60 What would be the selling price of goods listed at \$189, but subject to a 15% discount? (Round to the nearest dollar.)

61 a A real estate agency earns 5% commission on the first \$18 000 of a sale, and $2\frac{1}{2}\%$ on the balance. Calculate her earnings on sales of:
    i \$16 000   **ii** \$68 000   **iii** \$300 000
  b If a salesperson earned \$6800 in commission from the sale of a house, what was the sale price of that house?

62  This newspaper advertisement left out the sale price of the jeans. What was it?

63 What is the standard weekly wage for a $37\frac{1}{2}$ h working week at $12·78/h?

64 An annual wage of $32 468 translates into how much

    a per week?   **b** per day?   **c** per month?

65 Kali has a casual job in which she works from 5:30–9:00 pm on Thursday nights and from 12:30 to 5:00 pm on Saturdays. If her casual pay rate is $6·98/h during the week and $7·80/h on weekends, find her weekly income.

66 John's employment details are shown in the box. Calculate his gross wages for a week that he worked as shown on his time card below:

> **Hourly rate:** $11·72
> **Normal hours:** 8:30 am – 5:00 pm Mon.–Fri.
> **Lunch** (unpaid time): 1 hour/day
> **Overtime** (for periods in excess of 15 min):
> $\times 1\frac{1}{2}$ weekdays; $\times 2$ weekends.

TIME CARD
Name: John Rodes **Rate:** $11·72/h

Week ending		Mon.	Tues.	Wed.	Thu.	Fri.	Sat.	Sun.	Hours worked			
									Standard	$\times 1\frac{1}{2}$	$\times 2$	Wages
7/Feb	in	8:30	8:30	8:25	8:00	8:00	9:00	–				
	out	5:00	5:10	6:30	5:30	7:00	12:30	–				
											TOTAL	

67 The simple interest earned on $3500 at $3\frac{1}{4}$% p.a. interest over 4 years is:

    A $439·60   **B** $455   **C** $3955   **D** $45 500

68 Interest is paid at a rate of 6.5% p.a. compounded annually. The interest earned on an investment of $500 over 2 years is:

    A $65   **B** $67·11   **C** $567·11   **D** $6500

69 The following statement shows Diedre's bank transactions during November.

Bank Statement				November
Date	**Details**	**Credit**	**Debit**	**Balance**
1/11/01	Opening balance			614·75
4/11/01	ATM withdrawal		100·00	....
10/11/01	Direct credit	320·00		....
21/11/01	EFTPOS transaction		451·95	....
24/11/01	Direct credit	320·00		....
30/11/01	Closing balance			....

  a Calculate the amounts that would be shown in the balance column.
  b Deidre earns 2·8% p.a. interest calculated daily on money in her account. Calculate the total interest earned on her account for November.
  c Calculate the November interest that would be earned on Deidre's account if it was paid at 2·8% p.a. but calculated on the minimum monthly balance.

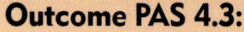

1 What you need to know and revise

Outcome PAS 4.3:
Uses the algebraic symbol system to simplify, expand and factorise simple algebraic expressions:

- expanding algebraic expression by removing grouping symbols
- factorising algebraic expressions by finding a common factor.

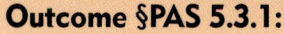

2 What you will learn in this chapter

Outcome §PAS 5.3.1:
Uses algebraic techniques to simplify expressions, expand binomial products and factorise quadratic expressions:

- factorising expressions using:
  - common factors
  - difference of two squares
  - perfect squares
  - trinomials
- grouping in pairs for four-term expressions

- using a variety of methods, including combinations of the above, to factorise expressions
- factorising and simplifying a variety of more complex algebraic expressions.

Working Mathematically outcomes WMS 5.1, 5.2, 5.3
Students will be required to *question*, *apply strategies*, *communicate*, *reason* and *reflect* in the sections of this chapter.

11

Quadratic expressions and algebraic fractions

Key mathematical terms you will encounter

algebra	constant	factorise	reciprocal
binomial	denominator	fraction	simplify
cancel	distributive	numerator	trinomial
coefficient	expand	quadratic	variable
common	expression	rational	

MathsCheck

Quadratic expressions and algebraic fractions

In so many fields of modern engineering, algebraic expressions and equations hold the key to problem solving.

Engineers, scientists, economists, computer analysts, architects, surveyors and many other specialists constantly use algebra as a basic tool.

For example, computer simulation has developed a model for monitoring the flow of blood (F) through a blood vessel in the body:

$$F = \frac{K(p_1 - p_2)R^4}{L}$$

In the early 16th century the Italian Nicolo Tartaglia was one of the first people to apply mathematics to the study of artillery. He used his knowledge of quadratics and cubics to make calculations relating to the flight of cannon balls, amongst other things.

1 Expand:

    a $6(2x + 5)$ **b** $5(4 - 3p)$ **c** $2(7t - 1)$

    d $\frac{3}{4}(8y + 12)$ **e** $^-3(2t + 7)$ **f** $^-6(4 - 3q)$

    g $2x(x - 1)$ **h** $4a(2a + 3)$ **i** $^-5p(2p - 4)$

2 Expand and simplify:

    a $2(4x + 3) - 5x$ **b** $^-8c(2 + 3c) + c^2$ **c** $3x^2(2x - 1) + 4x^3$

    d $(m + 1)(m - 5)$ **e** $(2y - 3)(3y + 1)$ **f** $(x + 2)^2$

    g $(x - 5)^2$ **h** $(2x + 9)^2$

3 Complete the factorisation patterns:

    a $3x + 6 = 3(\ldots + \ldots)$ **b** $mt - 9t = t(\ldots - \ldots)$

    c $12ab - 18ta = 6a(\ldots - \ldots)$ **d** $n^2 + n^3 = n^2(\ldots + \ldots)$

    e $12p - 8p^2 = 4p(\ldots - \ldots)$ **f** $4ac^2 + 8ac = 4ac(\ldots + \ldots)$

    g $9x + 12 = \ldots(3x + 4)$ **h** $mp - mpt = \ldots(1 - t)$

    i $24x^3 + 18x^4 = \ldots(4 + 3x)$ **j** $^-4x + 8 = ^-4(\ldots + \ldots)$

    k $^-6a + 12ab = ^-6a(\ldots + \ldots)$ **l** $^-15xt - 10xt^3 = ^-5xt(\ldots + \ldots)$

4 Complete the factorisation patterns:

    a $xy + cy + ay = y(\ldots + \ldots + \ldots)$ **b** $4x + 8x^2 + 12x^3 = 4x(\ldots + \ldots + \ldots)$

    c $x(t + p) + y(t + p) = (t + p)(\ldots + \ldots)$ **d** $x(x + 3) + 5(x + 3) = (x + 3)(\ldots + \ldots)$

    e $3p(p - 2) + 7(p - 2) = (\ldots)(3p + 7)$ **f** $(n - 4)5n - (n - 4)3 = (n - 4)(\ldots)$

TEACHER

Exploring New Ideas

11.1 Factorisation: highest common factor

To **factorise** means to change a *sum into a product*. It is the reverse of *expansion*.

$$\rightarrow \textbf{expand}$$
$$3(x + 4) = 3x + 3 \times 4$$
$$\textbf{factorise} \leftarrow$$

> $ab + ac = a(b + c)$
>
> Distributive law

The **distributive law** is the key to factorisation. Consider factorising $8x^2 + 12x$:

1 $= 2(4x^2 + 6x)$ using 2 as common factor
2 $= 4(2x^2 + 3x)$ using 4 as common factor
3 $= x(8x + 12)$ using x as common factor
4 $= 4x(2x + 3)$ using HCF $4x$.

In **1** to **3**, the expression has not been factorised *completely*, as the bracketed factors can be factorised further.

Expression **4** is completely factorised, since $(2x + 3)$ cannot be further factorised. *Always aim for complete factorisation*, unless special circumstances dictate otherwise.

We can check that the factorisation is correct by expanding the product and checking that it matches the original expression:

$$4x(2x + 3) = 4x \times 2x + 4x \times 3$$
$$= 8x + 12x$$

EXAMPLES
Factorise:

a $12a^2 - 18a$ **b** $x(x + 2) + 5(x + 2)$

Solutions

a $12a^2 - 18a$ **b** $x(x + 2) + 5(x + 2)$
   $= 6a(2a - 3)$ $= (x + 2)(x + 5)$

> $(x + 2)$ is common to both terms.

EXERCISE 11A

> You should remember these from chapter 1.

1 Factorise:

a $6x + 18$	**b** $6x - 10$	**c** $ax + xb$	**d** $x^2 - x$
e $5p - 3p^2$	**f** $27 - 18x$	**g** $mp - 9p$	**h** $7t^3 - 5t^2$
i $an^2 + a^2n$	**j** $2pt + 4px$	**k** $3kn - 6kd$	**l** $6ab - 9ta$
m $24bc - 18ac$	**n** $6n^2 + 8nt$	**o** $4x - 16x^2$	**p** $20d^3 - 15d$

2 Factorise using a negative common factor:

a $^-2x + 4$	**b** $^-3n - 6$	**c** $^-10 - 15a$	**d** $^-12t - 16$
e $^-8t + 12x$	**f** $^-x^2 + 5x$	**g** $5p - 3p^2$	**h** $^-7pt + 14t$

3 Check whether or not the following are completely factorised. If not, finish the factorisation:

a $6(2m + 5)$	**b** $4(2t + 6)$	**c** $x(4x - 8)$	**d** $9(a^2 - 5a)$
e $c(4c - 7)$	**f** $2k(6k - 9)$	**g** $3x(4xt + 12x)$	**h** $(x + 2)(5x + 15)$

4 Factorise:

a $ab + ca + 4a$ **b** $7x - 14xt + 21x^2$ **c** $6m^4 - 4m^3 + 12m^2$
d $2(a + b) + x(a + b)$ **e** $x(x + 3) + 5(x + 3)$ **f** $n(n + 2) - 3(n + 2)$
g $x(x - 4) - 7(x - 4)$ **h** $2c(c + 1) + 5(c + 1)$ **i** $7t(2t + 7) + 5(2t + 7)$
j $(2x - 1)x + (2x - 1)5$ **k** $(3b - 5)b - (3b - 5)2$ **l** $(4x - 2)4x - (4x - 2)2$
m $8(x - y) - (x - y)x$ **n** $a(a + 1) + (a + 1)$ **o** $(1 - x) - x(1 - x)$

5 Factorise where possible:

a $\pi r^2 - \pi r$ **b** $5(x + y) + x(x - y)$ **c** $\sqrt{2}\,x + \sqrt{2}\,y$

d $5\sqrt{x} + a\sqrt{x}$ **e** $\frac{1}{2}x^2 - \frac{1}{4}x$ **f** $6\pi R^2 - 9\pi R$

Level 2

6 a $3(\sin x) + t(\sin x)$ **b** $18x\sqrt{y} - 27x^2\sqrt{y}$ **c** $\frac{1}{4}(\sin \theta) + \frac{3}{4}(\sin \theta)(\cos \theta)$

    d $(x + 1)(x + 1) + 3(x + 1)$ **e** $(a + b)^2 + (a + b)$ **f** $(3 - 2x) - (3 - 2x)^2$

11.2 Factorisation: grouping in pairs

In some expressions, there is no common factor in all terms. Appropriate regrouping or pairing may allow factorisation in sections, after which a common factor may show up.

EXAMPLES

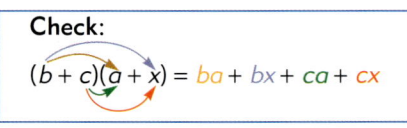

Check:

$(b + c)(a + x) = ba + bx + ca + cx$

a Factorise, if possible, $3t - ax^2 + tx^2 - 3a$.

Solution

$$3t^2 - ax^2 + tx^2 - 3a$$
$$= (3t - 3a) + (tx^2 - ax^2)$$
$$= 3(t - a) + x^2(t - a)$$
$$= (t - a)(3 + x^2)$$

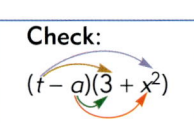

Check:

$(t - a)(3 + x^2)$

b Factorise, if possible, $x^2 + 5x - 3x - 15$.

Solution

$$x^2 + 5x - 3x - 15$$
$$= x(x + 5) - 3(x + 5)$$
$$= (x + 5)(x - 3)$$

Check:

$(x + 5)(x - 3)$

EXERCISE 11B

1 Complete each pattern:

a $3x - 6 = 3(\ldots - \ldots)$ **b** $3x - 6 = {}^-3(\ldots + \ldots)$ **c** $mn - mp = m(\ldots)$
d $mn - mp = {}^-m(\ldots)$ **e** $^-10ab + 15b = 5b(\ldots)$ **f** $^-10ab + 15b = {}^-5b(\ldots)$

2 Factorise the following expressions:

a $ax + ay + bx + by$ **b** $mp + pt + xm + tx$ **c** $x^2 + 4x + 3x + 12$
d $c^2 + 2c + 5c + 10$ **e** $tp - ts + ap - as$ **f** $10x + 20y + xc + 2yc$
g $ax + bx - ay - by$ **h** $x^2 + xb + ax + ab$ **i** $ab + b + 4a + 4$
j $x^3 + x^2 + x + 1$ **k** $xy + 5a + 5x + ay$ **l** $a^2 + nt + ta + na$
m $x^2 + 2x + 3x + 6$ **n** $y^2 + 2y + 5y + 10$ **o** $a^2 + 3a + 4a + 12$
p $a^2 - 2a + 3a - 6$ **q** $n^2 + 3n - 5n - 15$ **r** $t^2 + 3t + t + 3$

s	$x^2 - 3x - 4x + 12$	**t**	$y^2 - 4y + 7y - 28$	**u**	$d^2 - 3d - 8d + 24$
v	$f^2 - 5f + 2f - 10$	**w**	$h^2 + 8h - 10h - 80$	**x**	$k^2 - 7k - 5k + 35$

3 Factorise:

a	$ab - 2b - 5ax + 10x$	**b**	$ab^2 - ab - b + 1$	**c**	$11x + 22 - xy - 2y$
d	$2n^2 + 2n + 3n + 3$	**e**	$3x^2 + 2x + 12x + 8$	**f**	$2p^2 - 5p + 10p - 25$
g	$4a^2 - 4a + 3a - 3$	**h**	$c^2 + nc + kc + kn$	**i**	$d^2 - 2d + pd - 2p$
j	$2h^2 - 8h - 7h + 28$	**k**	$k^2 - tk - pk + pt$	**l**	$5l^2 - l + 15l - 3$

11.3 Factorising quadratic expressions

A **quadratic** expression is one in which the highest power of the variable/s is 2.

(Latin: *quadra*—square; variable is *squared*.)

$3x^2 - 4x + 6$, $x^2 - y^2$; $a^2 + 2ab + b^2$ are *quadratics*.

A quadratic expression has the general form:

$ax^2 + bx + c$ $(a \neq 0)$ a is the coefficient of x

                                   b is the coefficient of x

                                   c is the constant term

Such expressions are called **quadratic trinomials** because they have *three terms*.

It is important to match an algebraic expression with the general quadratic form **1** to see if it is a quadratic trinomial and **2** to find the replacements for a, b and c in each particular case.

A monic trinomial is one in which the coefficient of x^2 is 1, i.e. $a = 1$.

Now let us analyse how simple *quadratic trinomials* are formed by expanding a simple *binomial product*:

$$
\begin{array}{lll}
(x + 2)(x + 3) & \text{①} & (x + p)(x + k) \\
= x^2 + 3x + 2x + 2 \times 3 & \text{②} & = x^2 + kx + px + pk \\
= x^2 + (3 + 2)x + 2 \times 3 & \text{③} & = x^2 + (k + p)x + pk \\
= x^2 + 5x + 6 & \text{④} & \qquad\uparrow \qquad\quad \uparrow
\end{array}
$$

                                 sum of the constants   product of the
                           in the binomial factors   same two constants

If, then, we were given line 4, a quadratic trinomial, and told to *factorise*, our challenge would be to find a pair of numbers that multiply to 6 and add to 5.

By the quick process of guess, check and improve, we can easily track down the numbers.

Numbers	Product	Sum	
6, 1	6	7	✗
3, 2	6	5	✓

Can there only be *one* correct pair?

$$x^2 + (k + p)x + kp = (x + k)(x + p)$$

EXAMPLE 1

Determine whether or not the following are quadratic trinomials and, if so, find the replacements for a, b and c:

a $x^2 + 5x + 6$ **b** $5p - 2 - 7p^2$ **c** $5y^2 - 2$ **d** $8k^2 + k$

e $0.2n^2$ **f** $4p^3 - 3p - 2$ **g** $3n^2 - 7n - 5n^2$ **h** $x + 3^x + 2$

Solution

a Yes, $a = 1$, $b = 5$, $c = 6$ $1x^2 + 5x + 6$

b Yes, $a = {}^-7$, $b = 5$, $c = {}^-2$ ${}^-7p^2 + 5p + {}^-2$

c Yes, $a = 5$, $b = 0$, $c = {}^-2$ $5y^2 + 0y + {}^-2$

d Yes, $a = 8$, $b = 1$, $c = 0$ $8k^2 + 1k + 0$

e Yes, $a = 0.2$, $b = 0$, $c = 0$ $0.2n^2 + 0n + 0$

f No

> Variable p is cubed.

g Yes, $a = {}^-2$, $b = {}^-7$, $c = 0$ ${}^-2n^2 + {}^-7n + 0$

h No

> *Linear* expression, x^1 is highest power.

EXAMPLE 2

Factorise $x^2 + 7x + 12$.

Solution

$x^2 + 7x + 12$
$= (x + 4)(x + 3)$

> We require two numbers that multiply to 12 and add to 7; they are 4 and 3.

Number	Product	Sum	
12, 1	12	13	✗
6, 2	12	8	✗
4, 3	12	7	✓

> Check by expanding.

EXAMPLE 3

Factorise $x^2 - 12x - 45$.

Solution

$x^2 - 12x - 45$
$= (x - 15)(x + 3)$

> We require two numbers that multiply to ${}^-12$ and add to ${}^-45$.

Number	Product	Sum	
${}^-45, 1$	${}^-45$	${}^-44$	✗
$45, {}^-1$	${}^-45$	44	✗
${}^-9, 5$	${}^-45$	${}^-4$	✗
$9, {}^-5$	${}^-45$	4	✗
${}^-15, 3$	${}^-45$	${}^-12$	✓

> Check by expansion.

EXERCISE 11C

1 Which of the following are quadratic expressions?

a $8x^2 + x + 7$ **b** $7x + 3 + 5x$ **c** $6n^3 + 3n^3 + 5$ **d** $y^2 - 5y + 2$

e $n^2 - 4n$ **f** ${}^-3t^2 + 5$ **g** $3 - x - x^2$ **h** $\dfrac{a^2}{4} + 3 + \dfrac{2a}{5}$

2 In each of the following, write **i** the variable, **ii** the values of a, b and c.

a $3x^2 + 5x + 6$ **b** ${}^-2x^2 - x - 5$ **c** $x^2 + x$ **d** $k^2 - 4$

e ${}^-2n^2$ **f** $7 - 3t - t^2$ **g** $a^2 - 1.5a$ **h** $\dfrac{2}{3}d^2 - \dfrac{1}{2} - \dfrac{5d}{6}$

3 Rewrite each expression in the form $ax^2 + bx + c$:

   a $3x^2 - x + 6x^2 - 2x + 1$ **b** $5 - 8x^2 - 7x + 4 - 2x$

   c $3(2p - 5) - 4p^2$ **d** $k(k - 6) - 7k - 4k^2$

   e $2n(1 - 3n) - 5(2 - 4n^2)$ **f** $(0{\cdot}5 - 1{\cdot}5p)2p - \left(\dfrac{p}{2} + 3p^2\right)\dfrac{1}{3}$

4 Write quadratic expressions with variable x and the following values of a, b and c respectively:

   a $2, 3, 5$ **b** $4, 1, 6$ **c** $3, {}^-2, {}^-5$ **d** $1, {}^-3, 0$

   e ${}^-4, 0, 1$ **f** ${}^-5, 0, 0$ **g** $\dfrac{1}{2}, 0, {}^-3$ **h** $1, 7{\cdot}2, {}^-3{\cdot}8$

5 Find k and p, given $k \times p$ and $k + p$ respectively are:

   a $6, 5$ **b** $15, 8$ **c** $10, 7$ **d** $3, 4$ **e** $25, 10$

   f $40, 14$ **g** $12, {}^-7$ **h** $35, {}^-12$ **i** $7, 8$ **j** ${}^-6, 1$

   k ${}^-15, {}^-2$ **l** ${}^-28, 3$ **m** ${}^-10, {}^-3$ **n** $30, {}^-11$ **o** ${}^-66, {}^-5$

6 Factorise:

   a $x^2 + 5x + 6$ **b** $x^2 - 5x + 6$ **c** $x^2 - 5x - 6$ What is special about

   d $x^2 + 5x - 6$ **e** $x^2 + 8x + 15$ **f** $x^2 + 4x + 3$ parts m and n?

   g $x^2 + 14x + 40$ **h** $x^2 - 7x + 12$ **i** $x^2 - 12x + 35$ **j** $x^2 - 2x - 15$

   k $n^2 - 5n - 66$ **l** $x^2 + 7x + 10$ **m** $x^2 + 10x + 25$ **n** $x^2 + 12x + 36$

   o $x^2 + 9x + 20$ **p** $x^2 + 8x + 7$ **q** $x^2 - 11x + 24$ **r** $x^2 + x - 6$

   s $x^2 - 5x + 4$ **t** $a^2 - 2a - 15$ **u** $b^2 - 3b - 10$ **v** $c^2 - 11c + 30$

   w $d^2 - 17d - 60$ **x** $f^2 - 16f - 36$ **y** $g^2 - 17g + 42$ **z** $h^2 - 11h - 42$

7 Factorise if possible:

   a $a^2 + 10a + 4$ **b** $x^2 - 5x - 6$ **c** $y^2 + y - 6$ **d** $10 + 7n + n^2$

   e $c^2 + 8 + 9c$ **f** $t^2 - 16t + 8^2$ **g** $x^2 + 2xy + y^2$ **h** $24x + x^2 + 80$

8 Factorise each quadratic trinomial completely; first take out any common factors:

   a $l^2 - 18l + 56$ **b** $m^2 + 12m - 45$ **c** $n^2 - 22n + 72$ **d** $2x^2 + 14x + 12$

   e $3x^2 - 12x + 12$ **f** $4x^2 - 36x + 80$ **g** ${}^-36 + 12p + 3p^2$ **h** ${}^-36x - 126 + 2x^2$

11.4 Difference of two squares/perfect squares

DIFFERENCE OF TWO SQUARES

To factorise $x^2 - 9$ we need to find two numbers a and b so that $a + b = 0$, $ab = 0$ and $ab = {}^-9$. The two numbers are 3 and ${}^-3$, so $x^2 - 9 = (x + 3)(x - 3)$.

You may recall that:

$$(a + b)(a - b) = (a^2 - b^2)$$

same variables, but opposite signs — each variable squared

Note that factor order does not matter:
$$(a + b)(a - b) = (a - b)(a + b)$$

EXAMPLES

a Factorise $x^2 - 25$.

Solution

$x^2 - 25$
$= x^2 - 5^2$
$= (x - 5)(x + 5)$

b Factorise $9k^2 - 16t^2$.

Solution

$9k^2 - 16t^2$
$= (3k)^2 - (4t)^2$
$= (3k - 4t)(3k + 4t)$

c Factorise $2x^2 - 18$.

Solution

$2x^2 - 18$
$= 2(x^2 - 9)$
$= 2(x - 3)(x + 3)$

d Factorise $x^4 - 81$.

Solution

$x^4 - 81$
$= (x^2)^2 - 9^2$
$= (x^2 - 9)(x^2 + 9)$
$= (x - 3)(x + 3)(x^2 + 9)$

Note: $x^2 + 9 = x^2 + 3^2$, but the **sum** of two squares does not factorise as $(x + 3)(x + 3)$. (Check by expansion.)

$a^2 + b^2 \neq (a + b)^2$ The **sum of two squares cannot be factorised**.
$ \neq (a + b)(a - b)$

PERFECT SQUARES

To factorise $x + 6x + 9$ we want two numbers a and b so that $a + b = 6$ and $ab = 9$.

The two numbers are *both* 3, so $(x^2 + 6x + 9) = (x + 3)(x + 3)$
$$= (x + 3)^2$$

You may recall that $(x + a)^2 = x^2 + 2ax + a^2$

EXAMPLES

a Factorise $x^2 + 10x + 25$.

Solution

$$x^2 + 10x + 25$$
$$= (x + 5)^2$$

b Factorise $4x^2 + 8x + 4$.

Solution

$$4x^2 + 8x + 4$$
$$= 4(x^2 + 2x + 1)$$
$$= 4(x + 1)^2$$

EXERCISE 11D

1 Factorise each expression:

a $x^2 - 4$ **b** $x^2 - 16$ **c** $73^2 - 27^2$ **d** $a^2 - 36$
e $b^2 - 100$ **f** $x^2 - y^2$ **g** $c^2 - 81$ **h** $49 - x^2$
i $d^2 - h^2$ **j** $64 - j^2$ **k** $144 - k^2$ **l** $l^2 - 1$

m $1 - m^2$ **n** $x^2 - 0{\cdot}36$ **o** $y^2 - \dfrac{1}{4}$ **p** $n^2 - 0{\cdot}25$

q $p^2 - \dfrac{1}{16}$ **r** $q^2 - 0{\cdot}16$ **s** $r^2 - \dfrac{4}{9}$ **t** $\dfrac{9}{16} - s^2$

2 Verify the following using $a = 4$, $b = 7$ as replacements:

a $a^2 + b^2 \neq (a + b)^2$ **b** $a^2 + b^2 \neq (a + b)(a - b)$

3 Factorise:

a $x^2 + 4x + 4$ **b** $x^2 + 10x + 25$ **c** $x^2 + 2x + 1$
d $x^2 + 6x + 9$ **e** $x^2 - 6x + 9$ **f** $x^2 + 14x + 49$
g $x^2 - 14x + 49$ **h** $x^2 + 20x + 100$ **i** $x^2 - 40x + 400$

j $x^2 + 30x + 225$ **k** $x^2 - 50x + 625$ **l** $x^2 + x + \dfrac{1}{4}$

4 Express each difference as a product:

a $4x^2 - 9$ **b** $9x^2 - 16$ **c** $16x^2 - 25$ **d** $25a^2 - 36$
e $49x^2 - 1$ **f** $49x^2 - 9a^2$ **g** $81x^2 - 100y^2$ **h** $121b^2 - 196c^2$

5 Factorise completely, where possible:

a $x^2 + 16$ **b** $0{\cdot}09 - d^2$ **c** $2x^2 - 4x + 2$ **d** $\dfrac{16}{25} - f^2$

e $0{\cdot}04 + g^2$ **f** $2h^2 - 50$ **g** $3j^2 - 27$ **h** $3x^2 + 18x + 27$
i $12x^2 - 3$ **j** $m^3 - m$ **k** $54 - 24n^2$ **l** $75p - 12p^3$
m $5x^2 + 20$ **n** $n^4 - 36$ **o** $3q^4 - 243$ **p** $2x^2 - 16x + 32$
q $ax^2 - at^2$ **r** $p^2q^2 - r^2$ **s** $d^4 - d^2e^2$ **t** $d^4 - e^2f^2$

Level 2

6 What must be added to $x^2 + 6x + 5$ to make it a perfect square?

TEACHER

11.5 Non-monic, quadratic trinomials

Non–monic quadratics have coefficients of x^2 greater than 1.

In all previous cases, the coefficient of x^2 has been 1, producing *simple* quadratics. Now let us adapt our basic procedures to quadratics with coefficients of x^2 other than 1.

Consider: $(2x + 3)(x + 4)$ ①

         $= 2x^2 + 8x + 8x + 12$ ②
         $= 2x^2 + (8 + 3)x + 12$ ③
         $= 2x^2 + 11x + 12$ ④
         $\uparrow$ $\uparrow$ $\uparrow$
         $ax^2 + bx + c$

The factorisation pattern is no longer so obvious. Looking at lines ③ and ④:

$a \times c = 2 \times 12 = 24 = 8 \times 3$
    $b = 11$ $= 8 + 3$

So the key is that the split-up of bx to obtain the like terms $8x + 3x$ in ② comes from the pattern: ac (coefficient of x^2 times constant term) gives the **product** of the required two numbers;

      b (coefficient of x) gives their **sum**.

So to factorise $\dfrac{2 \times 12 = 24}{2x^2 + 11x + 12}$

We need two numbers with a product of 24 and a sum of 11.

Numbers	Product	Sum	
8, 3	24	11	✓

Split the $11x$ into $8x + 3x$.
    $2x^2 + 8x + 3x + 12$
$= 2x(x + 4) + 3(x + 4)$
$= (2x + 3)(x + 4)$

To factorise a quadratic trinomial:

1 Write the expression in the form $ax^2 + bx + c$.

2 Find two numbers that both **multiply** to ac and **add** to b.

3 Split the **middle term** bx into two *like* terms using those two numbers as coefficients.

4 Factorise by grouping the four terms into pairs.

EXAMPLE 1

Factorise $2x^2 + 13x + 18$.

We want product = 36, sum = 13.

Solution

    $2x^2 + 13x + 18$
$= 2x^2 + 4x + 9x + 18$
$= 2x(x + 2) + 9(x + 2)$
$= (x + 2)(2x + 9)$

Numbers	Product	Sum	
6, 6	36	12	✗
9, 4	36	13	✓

Check by expanding back to original form.

EXAMPLE 2

Factorise $^-11n + 7n^2 - 6$.

We want product = 42, sum = $^-11$.

Solution

$7n^2 - 11n - 6$
$= 7n^2 + {}^-14n + 3n + {}^-6$
$= 7n(n - 2) + 3(n - 2)$
$= (n - 2)(7n - 3)$

Numbers	Product	Sum	
$^-21, 2$	42	$^-19$	✗
$^-6, 7$	$^-42$	1	✗
$^-3, 14$	$^-42$	11	✗
$3, ^-14$	$^-42$	$^-11$	✓

EXERCISE 11E

1 Factorise the following quadratic trinomial expressions:

a $2x^2 + 5x + 3$ **b** $3x^2 + 8x + 5$ **c** $7x^2 + 10x + 3$

d $4x^2 + 7x + 3$ **e** $2d^2 + 5d + 2$ **f** $4n^2 + 8n + 3$

Level 2

g $3n^2 - n - 2$ **h** $3n^2 + n - 2$ **i** $3n^2 - 5n - 2$

j $3n^2 + 5n - 2$ **k** $5a^2 - 7a - 6$ **l** $5a^2 + 7a - 6$

m $5y^2 + 11y + 2$ **n** $6w^2 + 17w + 5$ **o** $6x^2 - 11x + 3$

p $2m^2 - 15m + 25$ **q** $2t^2 - 15t + 28$ **r** $9x^2 - 12x + 4$

s $4n^2 + 12n + 9$ **t** $4n^2 - 12n + 9$ **u** $1 + 2r + r^2$

2 Factorise, first taking out a common factor:

a $4p^2 + 14p + 6$ **b** $9x^2 + 15x + 6$ **c** $10t^2 + 26t + 12$

d $6x^2 + 14x + 4$ **e** $8a^2 + 4a - 24$ **f** $15c^2 - 55c - 20$

g $12x^2 + 34x + 10$ **h** $36x^2 - 33x + 6$ **i** $30x^2 - 35x - 25$

3 Factorise completely where possible:

a $10x^2 - 9x + 2$ **b** $8x^2 + 18x - 5$ **c** $20c^2 - c - 1$

d $6d^2 - 7d - 3$ **e** $8f^2 - 2f - 15$ **f** $2 + g - 10g^2$

Level 2

g $15 - 2h - 8h^2$ **h** $20 - 31k - 7k^2$ **i** $3m^2 + 10mp + 8p^2$

j $4x^2 - 8xy + 3y^2$ **k** $7a^2 - 2ab - 5b^2$ **l** $\left(\dfrac{x}{y}\right)^2 - 3\left(\dfrac{x}{y}\right) - 10$

11.6 Factorisation checklist

To ensure *complete factorisation* follow this checklist:

1 Is the expression **in simplest form**? If not, **collect like terms**.

2 Take out all **HCFs** using the distributive law.

3 Look for *known patterns*:

    a If there are *two* terms, is it a **difference of two squares**? ($a^2 - b^2$)

    b If there are *three* terms, is it a **quadratic trinomial**? ($ax^2 + bx + c$)

4 For expressions of *four* terms, try **grouping into pairs**, then factorising each pair separately.

5 If grouping already exists but factorisation cannot proceed, expand, simplify, then check through steps 2, 3 and 4.

6 Take a final look at bracketed factors to see if any common factors have been overlooked.

7 Check accuracy by expanding to recreate the original expression.

EXAMPLES

a Factorise $x^3 + 7x^2 + 12x$.

    Solution

$$x^3 = 7x^2 + 12x$$
$$= x(x^2 + 7x + 12)$$
$$= x(x + 4)(x + 3)$$

> Check: $x(x + 4) = x^2 + 4x$
>
> $(x^2 + 4x)(x + 3) = x^3 + 3x^2 + 4x^2 + 12x$
> $\qquad\qquad\qquad = x^3 + 7x^2 + 12x$, as given.

b Factorise $24x^2 - 49y^2 - 5y^2$.

    Solution

$$24x^2 - 49y^2 - 5y^2$$
$$= 24x^2 - 54y^2$$
$$= 6(4x^2 - 9y^2)$$
$$= 6[(2x)^2 - (3y)^2]$$
$$= 6(2x - 3y)(2x + 3y)$$

c Factorise $3p(p - 3) + 4(p - 7)$.

    Solution

$$3p(p - 3) + 4(p - 7)$$
$$= 3p^2 - 9p + 4p - 28$$
$$= 3p^2 - 5p - 28$$
$$= 3p^2 + {}^-12p + 7p + {}^-28$$
$$= 3p(p + {}^-4) + 7(p + {}^-4)$$
$$= (p - 4)(3p + 7)$$

> Expand first, then simplify.

EXERCISE 11F

1 Factorise each expression completely:

    a $2x^2 - 18$ **b** $n^3 + 6n^2 + 8n$ **c** $t^3 - 16t$

    d $x^2 + 8x - 9$ **e** $p^2 - 15p + 56$ **f** $4c + 12c^2$

    g $a^2 - a - 6$ **h** $2x^2 + 12x + 18$ **i** $3t^2 - 12$

j $p^3q - 9pq$	**k** $a(x + 1) - (x + 1)b$	**l** $rt + ry - 4r$
m $l - a^2b^2$	**n** $c(a - 2) + (a - 2)$	**o** $3x^2 + 2x - 3xy - 2y$
p $2p^2 + 10p + 12$	**q** $3m^2 - 9m - 30$	**r** $12a^2 - 75d^2$
s $mp^2 - mt^2$	**t** $(x + 2)^2 - 4$	**u** $(y - 5)^2 - 36$
v $8f^2 + 32$	**w** $1 - x^4$	**x** $2x^2 - 6y^2$
y $90h + h^3 + 5h^2$	**z** $12j^3 - 20j - 26j^2 - 10j$	

Level 2

2 Factorise where possible:

a $x^2 + 5x - 30$	**b** $4x^3 + 6x^2$	**c** $15x^3 + 3x^2$
d $36t^2 - 1$	**e** $p^2 + 13p - 40$	**f** $a^3 + a^2 + a$
g $2x^2 - 9x + 10$	**h** $(x + y)^2 - z^2$	**i** $5 + 6x + 6x^2$
j $2ab + 3bc + 4a + 6c$	**k** $1 + x + x^3 + x^2$	**l** $xy^2 + xyz + 3xy + 3xz$
m $2a(a - 6) + 5a - 4$	**n** $4(b^2 + 3) - b(3b - 7)$	**o** $c(c - 1) + 3(c^2 - 1)$
p $4(3x - 1) - 3x(4 - 3x)$	**q** $\dfrac{3}{81} - 48x^2$	**r** $(a + b)^2 + 3(a + b)$
s $5h - 5k + h^2 - k^2$	**t** $(2n - 1)^2 - (4 + n)^2$	**u** $(x + 3)^2 - 4(x + 3) - 12$
v $a^4 + 7a^2 + 12$	**w** $y^8 - y^6$	**x** $(x - 1)^2 - (x^2 - 1)$
y $x^4 - y^4$	**z** $2x^4 - 8x^5 + 6x^3$	

11.7 Simplifying algebraic fractions

An **algebraic fraction** has the form: $\dfrac{\text{expression}}{\text{expression}}$.

For example: $\dfrac{3x - 7}{2x(x + 3)}$

The *bar line* between numerator and denominator acts as *brackets*, and means **division**.

So the fraction shown means $(3x - 7) \div [2(x + 3)]$.

Order rules state that bracketed operations must be done first, so numerators and denominators must be *simplified before division* can properly occur.

$$\frac{8 + 12}{4} = \frac{20}{4} = \frac{5 \times \cancel{4}^{\,1}}{1 \times \cancel{4}_{\,1}} = \frac{5}{1} = 5$$

> To simplify a fraction, simplify numerator and denominator first, then **factorise** to obtain the form $\dfrac{\text{product}}{\text{product}}$ then **cancel common factors**.

Note: All of the top is divided by *all* of the bottom.

$$\frac{8 + 12}{4} \neq \frac{^2\cancel{8} + 12}{\cancel{4}_{\,1}} = 14. \text{ Also, } \frac{8 + 12}{4} \neq \frac{8 + \cancel{12}^{\,3}}{\cancel{4}_{\,1}} = 11, \text{ however tempting these options may be.}$$

Both fail to follow required *order of operations*.

With fractions, we *factorise* first, then cancel common factors.

EXAMPLES

Simplify each rational expression:

a $\dfrac{8x(x+2)}{4x(x-1)}$

b $\dfrac{2x+6}{x+3}$

c $\dfrac{x^2+5x+6}{x^2-9}$

d $\dfrac{4t^2-49}{2t^2+15t+28}$

Solutions

List questions first, 'untouched'.

a $\dfrac{\overset{2}{8x}(x+2)}{\underset{}{4x}(x-1)}$

$= \dfrac{2(x+2)}{x-1}$

b $\dfrac{2x+6}{x+3}$

$= \dfrac{2(x+3)}{x+3} = 2$

c $\dfrac{x^2+5x+6}{x^2-9}$

$= \dfrac{(x+2)(x+3)}{(x-3)(x+3)}$

$= \dfrac{x+2}{x-3}$

d $\dfrac{4t^2-49}{2t^2-15t+28}$

$= \dfrac{(2t-7)(2t+7)}{(2t-7)(t-4)}$

$= \dfrac{2t+7}{t-4}$

EXERCISE 11G

1 Simplify each fraction by first factorising where necessary:

a $\dfrac{4x}{8a}$

b $\dfrac{3m}{7m}$

c $\dfrac{12ax}{8ac}$

d $\dfrac{6n^3}{3nc}$

e $\dfrac{4(x+3)}{4}$

f $\dfrac{3(5-a)}{6}$

g $\dfrac{2(a+1)}{4}$

h $\dfrac{3(x+1)}{x+1}$

i $\dfrac{x+1}{3(x+1)}$

j $\dfrac{7(x+5)}{14(x-1)}$

k $\dfrac{5(n+a)}{1(n+a)}$

l $\dfrac{6(x-4)}{9(x-4)}$

m $\dfrac{(2a+3)(a-5)}{(a+2)(2a+3)}$

n $\dfrac{16n(n+2)}{8n(n+2)}$

Level 2

o $\dfrac{3a+3b}{6}$

p $\dfrac{12}{4x-4n}$

q $\dfrac{a+c}{5c+5a}$

r $\dfrac{3(x-2)}{2x-4}$

s $\dfrac{5x+10}{5}$

t $\dfrac{12}{3c-9}$

u $\dfrac{4x+8}{6x+12}$

v $\dfrac{4x-4}{2}$

2 Simplify:

a $\dfrac{2n+10}{n+5}$

b $\dfrac{4x+12}{2x+8}$

c $\dfrac{8a-12b}{12a-18b}$

d $\dfrac{ab-ac}{ab+ac}$

e $\dfrac{ab}{ab+a}$

f $\dfrac{x^2-x}{5x-5}$

g $\dfrac{x^2-4}{x+4}$

h $\dfrac{4n-6}{4n^2-9}$

i $\dfrac{2c^2-2}{2c-2}$

j $\dfrac{a^2+ab}{ab+b^2}$

k $\dfrac{(x+3)^2}{x^2-9}$

l $\dfrac{32-4m}{64-m^2}$

Level 3

3 Simplify each fraction where possible:

a $\dfrac{x+3}{x^2+7x+12}$ **b** $\dfrac{x^2-6x+9}{x-3}$ **c** $\dfrac{c^2-25}{c^2-10c+25}$

d $\dfrac{a^2+4a+3}{a^2+3a+2}$ **e** $\dfrac{x^2+4x-45}{x^2-6x+5}$ **f** $\dfrac{2x^2-7x+3}{6x-3}$

g $\dfrac{x^2+6x+9}{2x^2+3x-9}$ **h** $\dfrac{2s^2-s-1}{4s^2-1}$ **i** $\dfrac{a^2-n^2}{a^2+3a+an+3n}$

j $\dfrac{x^3-2x^2+13x}{4x^2-8x+52}$ **k** $\dfrac{v(v-2)-3(2v+11)}{v^2-11v}$

4 a If $a-b=c$, what is $b-a$?

b Use this result to simplify $\dfrac{a-b}{b-a}$.

5 Simplify the following:

a $\dfrac{x-y}{y-x}$ **b** $\dfrac{p-q}{2(q-p)}$ **c** $\dfrac{2(a-b)}{b-a}$ **d** $\dfrac{c-d}{2d-2c}$

e $\dfrac{3r-3t}{6t-6r}$ **f** $\dfrac{4x-2y}{y-2x}$ **g** $\dfrac{3a-9b}{6b-2a}$ **h** $\dfrac{x^2-3x+2}{1-x}$

i $\dfrac{x^2+x-20}{8-2x}$

11.8 Multiplication and division

EXAMPLE 1

Write as a single fraction:

$\dfrac{a}{b}\times 4$

Solution

$\dfrac{a}{b}\times 4$

$=\dfrac{a}{b}\times\dfrac{4}{1}$

$=\dfrac{4a}{b}$

EXAMPLE 2

Simplify $\dfrac{2m}{27}\div\dfrac{ma}{18}$.

> To divide, multiply by the reciprocal.

SPREADSHEET ACTIVITY

Solution

$$= \frac{2m}{27} \times \frac{18}{ma}$$

$$= \frac{2\overset{1}{m}}{\underset{3}{27}} \times \frac{\overset{2}{18}}{\underset{1}{ma}}$$

$$= \frac{4}{3a}$$

EXAMPLE 3

Simplify $\dfrac{3x + 6}{x + 5} \times \dfrac{x^2 - 25}{x + 2}$.

Solution

$$\frac{3x + 6}{x + 5} \times \frac{x^2 - 25}{x + 2}$$

| Factorise both numerators. |

$$= \frac{3(x + 2)^{1}}{x + 5_{1}} \times \frac{(x - 5)(x + 5)^{1}}{x + 2_{1}}$$

Cancel common factors. *Note*: $x + 5 = 1(x + 5)$
Multiply numerators, denominators.
$$\frac{3(x - 5)}{1} = 3(x - 5)$$

$$= 3(x - 5)$$

EXERCISE 11H

1 Write as a single fraction:

a $a \times \dfrac{b}{c}$ **b** $\dfrac{2p}{q} \times r$ **c** $\dfrac{e}{f} \times 3$ **d** $x \times \dfrac{3x}{y}$

e $x \times \dfrac{1}{y}$ **f** $a \times \dfrac{2}{x + y}$ **g** $\dfrac{m + n}{p} \times q$ **h** $\dfrac{x}{y} \times (a + b)$

i $\dfrac{x}{y} \times \dfrac{a}{b}$ **j** $\dfrac{4}{p} \times \dfrac{q}{5}$ **k** $\dfrac{x}{y} \times \dfrac{x}{z}$ **l** $\dfrac{3t}{r} \times \dfrac{a + b}{5}$

m $\dfrac{p}{q} \div \dfrac{a}{b}$ **n** $\dfrac{x}{4} \div \dfrac{y}{5}$ **o** $\dfrac{a}{b} \div \dfrac{c}{a}$ **p** $x \div \dfrac{x + y}{2}$

q $\dfrac{2g}{h} \div \dfrac{3h}{g}$ **r** $2a \div \dfrac{5}{c + d}$ **s** $\dfrac{a}{b} \div c$ **t** $\dfrac{x}{y^2} \div y$

2 Simplify:

Remember: $c = \dfrac{c}{1}$

a $\dfrac{x}{4} \times \dfrac{12}{x}$ **b** $\dfrac{a}{18} \times \dfrac{3}{b}$ **c** $x \times \dfrac{a}{x}$ **d** $y \times \dfrac{b}{y^2}$

e $\dfrac{a}{b} \times \dfrac{b}{2}$ **f** $\dfrac{p}{8} \div \dfrac{q}{4}$ **g** $\dfrac{x}{y^2} \div \dfrac{x^2}{z}$ **h** $\dfrac{m}{n} \div \dfrac{m^2}{n^2}$

3 Simplify where possible:

a $\dfrac{5x}{y} \div y^2$ **b** $\dfrac{4p^2}{q} \div pq^2$ **c** $\dfrac{a}{b + c} \div \dfrac{c}{a + d}$

d $\dfrac{4x^2 y}{3z + 6} \times \dfrac{6z + 12}{8xy^2}$ **e** $\dfrac{2a - 4}{3a - 9} \times \dfrac{5a - 15}{7a - 14}$ **f** $\dfrac{x^2 + x}{2x + 8} \div \dfrac{6x + 6}{4x + 6}$

g $\dfrac{n^2 - 5n}{2n - 10} \times \dfrac{2n^2 + 10n}{3n^3 + 15n^2}$ **h** $\dfrac{x^2 - 4}{x} \div \dfrac{5x - 10}{x^4}$ **i** $\dfrac{x^2 + 8x + 15}{x + 3} \times \dfrac{15 + 5x}{(x + 5)^2}$

j $\dfrac{c^2 - 49}{c^2 + 14x + 49} \times \dfrac{6c + 8}{9c^2 - 16}$

Level 2

k $\dfrac{x^2 + 5x + 6}{x^2 - 4} \div \dfrac{x^2 - 1}{x^2 - x - 2}$ **l** $\dfrac{2c^2 + 4c + 2}{4c^2 - 4} \times \dfrac{c^2 + 3c - 4}{8c + 8}$

m $\dfrac{2n^2 - 3n - 14}{3n^2 - 6n} \div \dfrac{4n^2 - 49}{n^3 - 2n^2}$ **n** $\dfrac{2y^4 + 6y^3}{2y^2 - 3y - 5} \div \dfrac{3 + y}{8y^2 - 50}$

o $\dfrac{6n^2 + 23n + 20}{25 + 4n^2} \div \dfrac{3n^2 + 5n - n}{4n^2 + 20n + 25}$ **p** $\dfrac{a^2 - b^2 + a - b}{a^2 - 2ab + b^2} \times \dfrac{5a - 5b}{5a + 5b + 5}$

4 Calculate:

a $\dfrac{\left(\dfrac{32}{8}\right)}{2}$ **b** $\dfrac{32}{\left(\dfrac{8}{2}\right)}$

5 Write as a single fraction:

a $\dfrac{\left(\dfrac{x}{y}\right)}{z}$ $\boxed{\text{This is } \dfrac{x}{y} \div z \,.}$ **b** $\dfrac{x}{\left(\dfrac{y}{z}\right)}$

6 Write as a single fraction:

a $\dfrac{\left(\dfrac{a}{2}\right)}{b}$ **b** $\dfrac{a}{\left(\dfrac{2}{b}\right)}$ **c** $\dfrac{\left(\dfrac{x}{y}\right)}{x}$ **d** $\dfrac{x}{\left(\dfrac{y}{x}\right)}$ **e** $\dfrac{\left(\dfrac{p}{q}\right)}{\left(\dfrac{q}{p}\right)}$ **f** $\dfrac{\left(\dfrac{p^2}{q}\right)}{\left(\dfrac{q^2}{p}\right)}$

11.9 Addition and subtraction

Compare the operation processes for algebraic fractions with those for common fractions:

1 $\dfrac{3}{7} + \dfrac{2}{7} = \dfrac{3 + 2}{7} = \dfrac{5}{7}$ $\boxed{\text{If (and only if) denominators are the same keep the denominator and add or subtract the numerator.}}$

$\dfrac{3}{x} + \dfrac{2}{x} = \dfrac{3 + 2}{x} = \dfrac{5}{x}$

$\dfrac{3x}{x + 2} + \dfrac{2x}{x + 2} = \dfrac{3x + 2x}{x + 2} = \dfrac{5x}{x + 2}$

2 $\dfrac{2}{3}+\dfrac{1}{5}=\dfrac{2\times 5}{3\times 5}+\dfrac{1\times 3}{5\times 3}=\dfrac{10+3}{5\times 3}$

$\dfrac{2}{x}+\dfrac{1}{y}=\dfrac{2y}{xy}+\dfrac{1x}{yx}=\dfrac{2y+x}{xy}$

$\dfrac{2}{x+3}+\dfrac{9}{x-2}=\dfrac{2(x-2)}{(x+3)(x-2)}+\dfrac{1(x+3)}{(x-2)(x+3)}$

$=\dfrac{2(x-2)+1(x+3)}{(x+3)(x-2)}$

> If the denominators are different, change both fractions to the **lowest common denominator**, then add or subtract numerators (simplify).

> Can you see how the numerator can be simplified? Denominator is left in factorised form.

EXAMPLES

Simplify:

a $\dfrac{5}{3x-2}-\dfrac{6}{2x+3}$

b $\dfrac{3}{x^2-4}+\dfrac{7}{x+2}$

Solutions

a $\dfrac{5}{3x-2}-\dfrac{6}{2x+3}$

$=\dfrac{5(2x+3)}{(3x-2)(2x+3)}-\dfrac{6(3x-2)}{(2x+3)(3x-2)}$

$=\dfrac{5(2x+3)-6(3x-2)}{(3x-2)(2x+3)}$

$=\dfrac{10x+15-18x+12}{(3x-2)(2x+3)}$

$=\dfrac{{}^-8x+27}{(3x-2)(2x+3)}$

b $\dfrac{3}{x^2-4}+\dfrac{7}{x+2}$

$=\dfrac{3}{(x-2)(x+2)}+\dfrac{7}{(x+2)}$

$=\dfrac{3}{(x-2)(x+2)}+\dfrac{7(x-2)}{(x+2)(x-2)}$

$=\dfrac{3+7(x-2)}{(x+2)(x-2)}$

$=\dfrac{7x-11}{(x-2)(x+2)}$

EXERCISE 11I

1 Simplify:

a $\dfrac{3x}{8}+\dfrac{2x}{8}$

b $\dfrac{x}{a}-\dfrac{3}{a}$

c $\dfrac{x}{2a}+\dfrac{3x}{2a}$

d $\dfrac{n}{n+1}+\dfrac{5n}{n+1}$

e $\dfrac{x+1}{2(x+3)}+\dfrac{3x+2}{2(x+3)}$

f $\dfrac{3x}{2}-\dfrac{x}{5}$

g $\dfrac{5}{1}+\dfrac{x}{4}$

h $6-\dfrac{x}{5}$

Level 2

i $1-\dfrac{3}{x}$

j $x+\dfrac{x}{3}$

k $\dfrac{1}{x}+\dfrac{1}{3}$

l $\dfrac{3}{x}-\dfrac{2}{a}$

m $\dfrac{c}{a}+\dfrac{x}{n}$

n $2+\dfrac{4}{5x}$

o $\dfrac{7x}{2}-\dfrac{8x}{4}$

p $\dfrac{3}{x}+\dfrac{7}{2x}$

q $\dfrac{5}{3x}+\dfrac{3}{4x}$

r $\dfrac{3}{x+2}-\dfrac{1}{x+2}$

s $\dfrac{4}{x+2}-\dfrac{3}{2(x+2)}$

t $\dfrac{5}{x+2}+\dfrac{6}{x}$

2 Calculate:

a $\dfrac{3}{x+1}+\dfrac{4}{x+2}$

b $\dfrac{2}{x+1}+\dfrac{3}{x-1}$

c $\dfrac{3}{n+2}-\dfrac{1}{n+3}$

d $\dfrac{2}{c+2}+\dfrac{4}{c+3}$ **e** $\dfrac{5}{m+5}-\dfrac{3}{m-2}$ **f** $\dfrac{4}{5x-2}-\dfrac{1}{4x-1}$

g $\dfrac{9}{3a+2}-\dfrac{7}{3a-2}$ **h** $\dfrac{x}{x+2}+\dfrac{5x}{x+7}$ **i** $\dfrac{c}{c+3}+\dfrac{2c}{c+2}$

j $\dfrac{x}{2x+1}-\dfrac{2x}{3x-1}$ **k** $\dfrac{7}{n}+\dfrac{8}{n(n+1)}$ **l** $\dfrac{n+1}{n+3}+\dfrac{n-2}{n+4}$

3 Simplify (denominators are already factorised):

a $\dfrac{1}{3(x+y)}+\dfrac{1}{(x+y)}$ **b** $\dfrac{2}{(x+1)x}+\dfrac{1}{x}$ **c** $\dfrac{1}{3(x+2)}+\dfrac{1}{2(x+2)}$

d $\dfrac{1}{x+5}+\dfrac{1}{x(x+5)}$ **e** $\dfrac{1}{x+4}-\dfrac{1}{(x+4)(x+1)}$ **f** $\dfrac{3}{(x+2)(x+5)}+\dfrac{4}{x+5}$

g $\dfrac{2}{(x+3)(x-3)}-\dfrac{3}{x-3}$ **h** $\dfrac{4}{(2x+1)(x+2)}+\dfrac{5}{x+2}$

i $\dfrac{3}{(x+1)(x+2)}+\dfrac{5}{(x+2)(x+3)}$

4 Simplify, factorising denominators first, where possible:

a $\dfrac{5}{3x+3}+\dfrac{1}{x+1}$ **b** $\dfrac{x}{x-3}-\dfrac{2}{3x-9}$ **c** $\dfrac{10x}{x^2-9}-\dfrac{5}{x+3}$

d $\dfrac{a}{a+5}+\dfrac{3a}{a+3}$ **e** $\dfrac{7x}{x+3}-\dfrac{1}{x-4}$ **f** $\dfrac{x}{(x-a)^2}-\dfrac{1}{x-a}$

Level 3

g $\dfrac{3}{x^2+4x-5}+\dfrac{1}{2x+10}$ **h** $\dfrac{2x}{x^2+x-6}-\dfrac{x}{x^2-4}$

i $\dfrac{2}{a^2+7a+12}+\dfrac{3}{a^2+8a+16}$ **j** $\dfrac{5}{c^2-3c-4}-\dfrac{3}{c^2-c-2}$

k $\dfrac{2}{4x^2-12x+9}-\dfrac{1}{2x^2+7x-15}$ **l** $\dfrac{x-1}{x^2-16}-\dfrac{x+1}{x^2+8x+16}$

Try this

Find the simplest form of $\dfrac{2^n-4^{2n}}{2^n}$.

Chapter Review

Language Links

algebra	constant	factorise	reciprocal
binomial	denominator	fraction	simplify
cancel	distributive	numerator	trinomial
coefficient	expand	quadratic	variable
common	expression	rational	

Select an appropriate form of a word from the list above to put in each space:

To multiply expressions containing brackets, we use the _____ law. This process is called _____. The reverse process is known as _____. Pronumerals that do not have just one fixed value are called _____. A coefficient is a _____ associated with a pronumeral.

An expression containing two terms is _____, while one with three terms is _____. A binomial product gives an expression of four terms.

To factorise an expression of four terms, group into pairs first, then apply the _____ law.

Expressions of the form $ax^2 + bx + c$ are known as _____ _____, in which a is the _____ of x^2, b is the _____ of x, and c is the _____ term. The _____ expression, $a^2 - b^2$, is called the 'difference of two squares' and its _____ are $(a + b)(a - b)$.

To _____ algebraic fraction, we _____ both numerator and _____, then cancel _____ _____.

Chapter Review Exercises

MC

1 Find the sum of $4a^2 - 3a - 7$ and $3 + 6a - 5a^2$.

2 Subtract $2x^2 + 3x - 2$ from $x^2 - 4$.

3 Expand:

a $(m + p)(q + r)$	**b** $(x + 7)(x - 6)$	**c** $(2n - 9)(7 - 6n)$
d $(x + 8)^2$	**e** $(p + 7)(p - 7)$	**f** $(11 - 5x)^2$

4 Expand and simplify where possible:

a $^-5(2x + 3) - (7 - 2x)8$ **b** $(3t - 7)(3t + 7) - (5 - 2t)^2$

11.6

5 Factorise:

a $56 - 24x$	**b** $3xt - 6tp$	**c** $15k + 20k^2$
d $x(x - 5) + 7(x - 5)$	**e** $^-14xy + 21ay$	**f** $c^2 - 64$
g $3x^2 - 27$	**h** $18x^3 - 27x^6$	**i** $2\pi r - 2\pi rh$
j $4(\sin \theta)^2 - 12 \sin \theta$	**k** $ac + da + cb + db$	**l** $(3x - 2)x - (3x - 2)5$
m $a(b + 7) + (b + 7)$	**n** $9p^2 - 36q^2$	**o** $xy + 4a + 4x + ay$

11.4

6 Calculate $26^2 - 24^2$ using the difference of two squares.

7 Which two completely factorised expressions could have been multiplied to give $^-4a^2 + 8a$?

11.3

8 True or false? Show why.

   a $(x + y)^2 = x^2 + y^2$ **b** $(x - y)^2 = x^2 - y^2$ **c** $\dfrac{3 + x}{x} = 3$

9 By relating the quadratic expression $3 - 5x - x^2$ to the general form, give the values of a, b and c.

10 Write a quadratic expression with $a = \dfrac{1}{2}$, $b = 0$ and $c = ^-1$.

11 Factorise each trinomial expression:

11.5

   a $x^2 + 9x + 20$ **b** $x^2 + 3x - 28$ **c** $a^2 - 12a + 36$

   d $25c^2 + 10c + 1$ **e** $2x^2 - 5x + 3$ **f** $6n^2 - 13n - 15$

12 Factorise if possible:

11.3

   a $x^3 - 5x^2 - 4x$ **b** $14(3 + x) + x(x - 1)$

13 Complete in as many different ways as possible: $(n\ \ldots)(n\ \ldots) = n^2 \ldots n \ldots 15$

14 Simplify the following rational expressions:

11.7

   a $\dfrac{a(a - 3)}{4a - 12}$ **b** $\dfrac{a^2 - 4}{3a^2 + 6a}$ **c** $\dfrac{10x + 15 - 5x}{x^2 - 9}$

   d $\dfrac{^-4x - 36}{3x} \times \dfrac{12x^3}{2x + 18}$ **e** $\dfrac{(x + 5)^2}{x} \div \dfrac{x^2 - 25}{4x^2}$ **f** $\dfrac{x^2 - x - 20}{x^2 - 16} \div \dfrac{x^2 - 10x + 25}{x^2 - 4x}$

11.8

   g $3 - \dfrac{4}{x + 2}$ **h** $\dfrac{2}{a + 3} + \dfrac{1}{a + 1}$ **i** $\dfrac{8}{4n + 12} - \dfrac{3}{n + 3}$

11.9

   j $\dfrac{1}{c(c + 2)} - \dfrac{2}{(c + 2)(c + 1)}$ **k** $\dfrac{7}{d^2 - 9} + \dfrac{5}{2d - 6}$ **l** $\dfrac{x + 1}{x^2 - 4x + 3} - \dfrac{x - 3}{x^2 - 1}$

15 How could you calculate 102 using the 'perfect square' expansion?

11.4

TEACHER

Keeping Mathematically Fit

Part A—Non-calculator

1 Express a length of 3·1 m using three different units.

2 An expression for the number of kilometres travelled in h hours at g km/h is:

  A $h + g$ **B** hg **C** $\dfrac{h}{g}$ **D** $\dfrac{g}{h}$

3 Is $x = {}^-3$ a solution to $4 + 5x < {}^-6$?

4 Find the value of r.

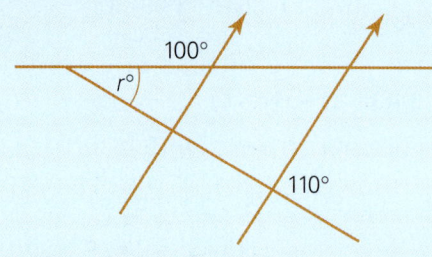

5 The mean of three numbers is 13. What number should be added to make a new mean of 14?

6 $p^0 \div p^0 =$

  A 0   **B** 1

  C undefined   **D** dependent on the value of p

7 Find x if $5 : 8 = x : 36$.

8 At what point does the line $x = 3$ cross the line $y = 4$?

9 Which of the following is closest to 0·4?

  A 0·38   **B** 0·04   **C** 0·3   **D** 0·43

10 The value of a computer depreciates at 30% per annum. If a new computer is purchased, what is its value after 2 years, as a percentage of its original value?

Part B—Calculator

1 A consultant's fee is $350 for 8 hours' work. To calculate her earnings (E) she uses the formula $E = \dfrac{350n}{8}$.

  a What does n represent?

  b How much will she earn if she works from 9 am to 5 pm for 10 days, and takes a 1-hour lunch break each day?

2 The daily traffic flow on a road in January was 61 785. This was 15% lower than in December. What was the December figure?

3 Find the diameter of a circle with centre (3, ⁻2) if the circle passes through the point (⁻1, 4). Leave your answer in exact form.

4 Draw the graph of $y = 5 - 2x$.

5 Two new houses are to be connected to an existing fibre-optic cable at the same point P. All cables follow straight lines. Where should P be located to minimise the total length of cable required?

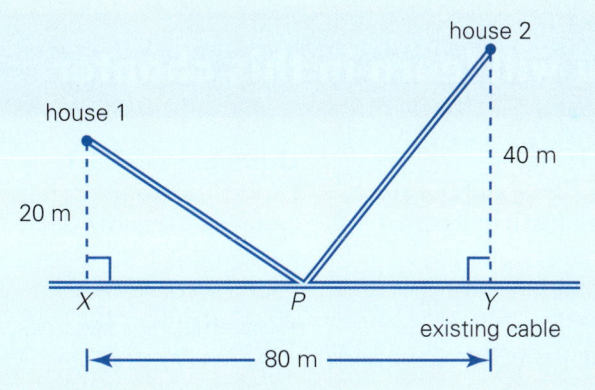

1 What you need to know and revise

Outcome DS4.1:
Constructs, reads and interprets graphs, tables, charts and statistical information:

- drawing and interpreting graphs of the following types:
  - sector graphs
  - conversion graphs
  - divided bar graphs
  - line graphs
  - step graphs
- reading and interpreting tables, charts and graphs
- organising data into a frequency distribution table (class intervals to be given for grouped data)
- drawing frequency histograms and polygons
- drawing and using dot plots
- drawing and using stem-and-leaf plots.

Outcome DS4.2:
Collects statistical data using either a census or a sample and analyses data using measures of location and range:

- finding measures of location (mean, mode and median) for small sets of data
- using a scientific or graphics calculator to determine the mean of a set of scores
- using measures of location (mean, mode, median) and the range to analyse data that are displayed in a frequency distribution table, stem-and-leaf plot, or dot plot.

2 What you will learn in this chapter

Outcome DS5.1.1:
Groups data to aid analysis and constructs frequency and cumulative frequency tables and graphs:

- constructing a cumulative frequency table for ungrouped data
- constructing a cumulative histogram and polygon (ogive)
- using a cumulative frequency polygon to find the median
- grouping data into class intervals
- constructing a frequency table for grouped data
- constructing a histogram for grouped data
- finding the mean using the class centre
- finding the modal class.

Outcome DS5.2.1:
Uses the interquartile range and standard deviation to analyse data:

- determining the upper and lower quartiles for a set of scores
- constructing a box-and-whisker plot using the median, the upper and lower quartiles and the extreme values (the five-point summary).

Working Mathematically outcomes WMS 5.1, 5.2, 5.3
Students will be required to *question*, *apply strategies*, *communicate*, *reason* and *reflect* in the sections of this chapter.

12

Statistics

MathsCheck
Statistics

1. For each of the following, say whether or not the sample chosen is biased. If it is, explain why and suggest a way to select a more representative sample.

   a. Ten Year 9 students are asked which is their favourite television program, and the results are used to predict the favourite programs of all 185 Year 9 students in the school.
   b. A school of 950 students is intending to renovate the school hall. To find out the opinion of all the students, 20 students from each year (7 to 12) are asked their opinions.
   c. A sample of 2000 people is selected from the telephone book to determine the attitudes of people in New South Wales towards forest conservation.
   d. A market researcher stands outside a supermarket from 10 am to 3 pm on a Tuesday, and asks questions about grocery purchases, to predict the grocery purchasing habits in that suburb.

2. A bookseller wants to know how many people in New South Wales read novels, so she asks a sample of people if they have read a novel in the past month.

   a. Would a representative sample be obtained if the bookseller stood outside a public library? If not, why not?
   b. Explain why the sample would not be representative if the bookseller stood outside a railway station at 6 pm and asked people.
   c. Suggest a way a representative sample could be obtained.

3. A telemarketing company telephoned people at 8 pm to find out what percentage of the population were watching television at that time. Of all the people spoken to, 83% said they were currently watching television.

   a. Could this result be used to predict that 83% of the entire population of New South Wales were watching television at that time? Explain.
   b. What further information could be recorded to increase the accuracy of the result?
   c. A postal survey required people to fill in a form and return it by post. Why would the results of this sample not be representative?

4. A survey of office workers was conducted to find out how many cups of coffee they drank each day. Their reponses are shown below:

2	0	4	2	2	1	3	1	0	5
4	0	2	3	5	3	4	2	0	3

a Copy and complete the frequency distribution table for these data:

Score	Tally	Frequency
0		
1		
2		
3		
4		
5		
Total		

b How many workers were surveyed?
c What was the most common number of cups of coffee drunk each day?
d How many people drank three or more cups of coffee per day?

5 A group of Year 9 students was surveyed to find out how many coins they had in their pocket or purse. The following results were obtained:

1	0	4	7	3	2	0	5	3	4
4	4	7	6	2	5	3	1	0	2
3	7	4	6	1	0	2	0	3	5

a Organise these data into a frequency distribution table.
b How many Year 9 students were surveyed?
c What *fraction* of the students had one coin in their pocket or purse?
d What *percentage* of students had five or more coins in their pocket or purse, to the nearest 1%?
e Is it necessarily true that the person with the most coins had the most money? Explain your answer.

6 This bar graph shows the number of cars, motorcycles, vans and trucks counted on a busy road in 1 h. From the graph find:

a the total number of vehicles
b how many more cars there were than trucks
c the percentage of the total vehicles that were vans (to the nearest whole per cent).

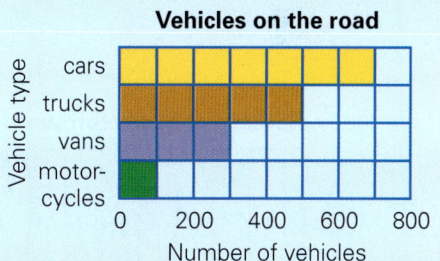

Vehicles on the road

7

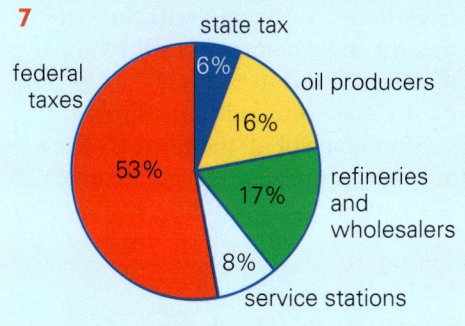

Distribution of money spent on petrol

This sector graph shows how each dollar is distributed when we buy petrol.

a i Where does most of the money we spend on petrol go?
ii How many cents does this recipient get from each dollar?
b If a motorist spends $28 on petrol, what is the service station's share of the money received?
c When neighbouring service stations compete for customers by reducing their prices, how would the percentages shown here change?

8 These charts show deaths in the world that could be prevented by immunisation.

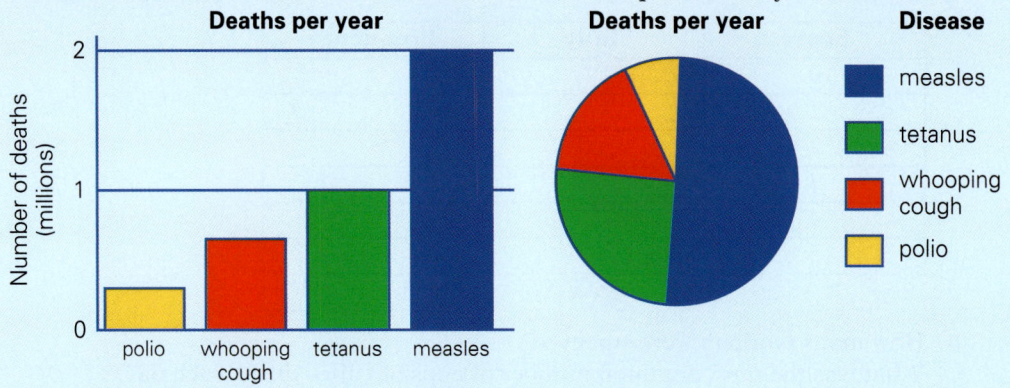

a Approximately how many deaths were caused by polio?
b What percentage of deaths were caused by measles?
c Which chart would be the better one to use to convince someone that immunisation saves lives? Why?

9 This histogram shows the number of children in the families of 35 Year 9 students.

a What is the most common number of children per family?
b What fraction of the families have less than three children?
c Why are there no families with no children?

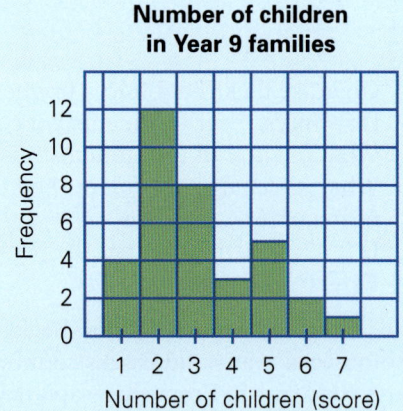

Number of children in Year 9 families

10

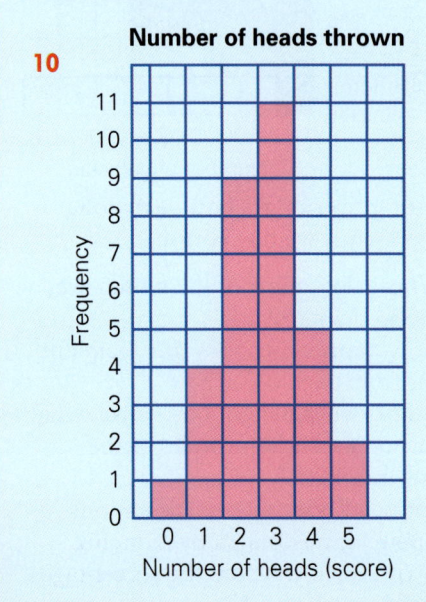

Number of heads thrown

Five coins were tossed and the number of heads recorded. This experiment was repeated 31 times, and the results are shown in this frequency histogram.

a How many times were two heads thrown?
b What was the most common result?
c What result occurred five times?
d How many times were four *tails* thrown?
e In what percentage of all the throws were *less* than three heads thrown? (To the nearest whole per cent.)

11 This frequency polygon shows the marks achieved by Year 9 students in a quiz with six questions:

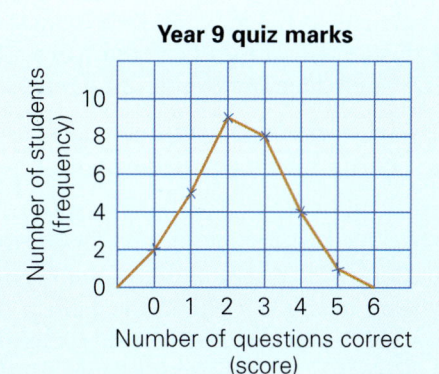

Year 9 quiz marks

a How many students got no questions correct?

b How many students got more than half of the questions correct?

c How many students did the quiz?

d Do you think the quiz was too easy, too hard or about the right level for the students? Explain.

12 This table shows the number of tries scored by the mixed touch football team in their games least season:

Number of tries	0	1	2	3	4	5
Number of games	1	3	6	7	3	2

Construct a frequency histogram for these data.

Remember to give the graph a title, and label the axes.

The first score has to start one unit in from the vertical axis.

13 Fifty families were asked how many times they ate take-away food last week. The results are shown in the table.

Draw a frequency polygon to show these data.

Number of times they had take-away food	Number of families
0	13
1	20
2	12
3	4
4	1

Remember to join the ends of the line to the horizontal axis.

14 As part of a company's 'Get Fit' campaign, employees were offered a fitness check. The first thing to be measured was the mass of each person, and the results are shown below:

65	72	54	58	67	92	74
77	83	68	73	81	70	95
56	74	85	66	93	60	78
60	82	77	76	85	59	71

a Construct a stem-and-leaf plot to show these data.

b Construct a dot plot for the data.

c What was the mass of: **i** the lightest person, and **ii** the heaviest person?

d Comment on the distribution of masses.

e Which diagram do you think represents the data most clearly? Explain why.

15 Prehna works in the city, and takes the train to and from work each day. The times of her journeys are given below to the nearest minute:

55	48	51	62	46	43	66	57	60	49
52	83	64	55	66	61	49	52	57	60

a Construct a stem-and-leaf plot to show these data.

b Construct a dot plot of the data.

c Which journey time would be classified as an *outlier*?

d Give *two* possible explanations for this time being so different from the rest.

e A friend asks Prehna 'How long does it take you to get to work?' Write a suitable reply to this question.

16 Each of the following three diagrams represent the same set of data. The reading ages of Year 9 students were tested on a special reading task, and are given in years and months. For example 14·7 means 14 years and 7 months.

Reading age of Year 9 students

11	10
12	5 7
13	0 2 7 8 8 9 11
14	0 3 3 5 6 7 7 11 11
15	1 2 2 3 5 5 6 8 10 10 11
16	0 0 0 0 0

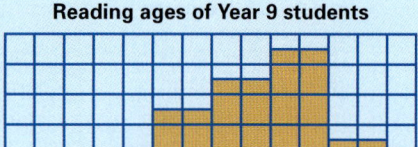

Reading ages of Year 9 students

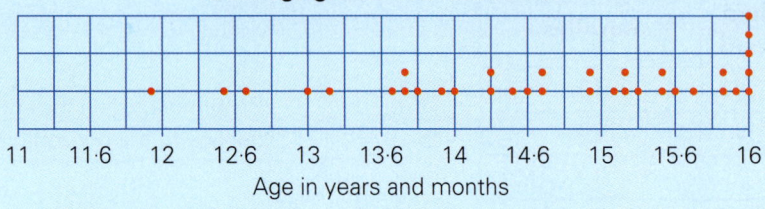

Reading ages of Year 9 students

a Suggest a possible explanation for the five ages of 16·0 and none any greater.

b For each of the following questions, suggest which of the above diagrams would be the most appropriate for that person to use, and explain why.

  i The head teacher of English when deciding which books to buy for Year 9 use.

  ii A student in Year 9 wanting to know how her reading age relates to that of other students in the class.

  iii The school librarian when choosing books for the school library.

  iv The principal wanting a quick overview of the reading ability of the class.

  v A statistician conducting research on Year 9 reading ages.

17 Scientists use tagging programs to estimate wild populations of certain animal species. For example, a scientist tags 200 wombats in a native reserve. Two weeks later 55 wombats are recaptured, 18 of which have tags. Estimate the wombat population in the reserve. What assumptions are made?

Exploring New Ideas

12.1 Summarising data

The skills and techniques covered in this chapter may be useful for analysis data in geography or science.

Sometimes it is useful to give a **single value** that represents the data. There are several possible values that can be calculated.

THE RANGE

> The range tells us how widely spread the information is.
>
> The range is the *difference* between the highest score and the lowest score.
>
> Range = highest score − lowest score.

EXAMPLE

What is the range for this set of shoe-sizes?

$7, 6\frac{1}{2}, 9, 6, 7, 6\frac{1}{2}, 6, 5, 8\frac{1}{2}$

Solution

Range = 9 − 5
   = 4

MEASURES OF CENTRALITY

> The mode is the score that occurs the *most often*.
>
> In a frequency distribution table, the mode is the score that has the **highest frequency**.

Note: There could be more than one mode for a particular set of scores, or there may not be a mode (e.g. if each score occurred only once).

EXAMPLE 1

What is the mode for this set of scores? 4, 7, 5, 6, 6, 5, 2, 3, 5, 7

Solution

The mode is 5.

> The **mean** is calculated by *adding* all of the scores, and dividing by *how many* scores there are:
>
> $$\text{Mean} = \frac{\text{sum of all the scores}}{\text{total number of scores}}$$

The mean, median and mode are all types of **average**. However, when people refer to 'the average' they are usually referring to the mean.

EXAMPLE 2

Calculate the mean of this set of data: 3, 2, 7, 5, 8, 1, 3, 5, 5, 4.

Solution

Mean =
   $= \dfrac{43}{10}$

Sum of scores is 43, and there are 10 scores.

Mean = 4·3

> The **median** is:
> - the *middle* score (for an odd number of scores)
> - the *average* of the *middle two* scores (for an even number of scores).
>
> *Note:* The scores must be placed in order to find the median.

EXAMPLE 3

Find the median of this set of scores: 7, 19, 12, 6, 11.

Solution

6, 7, (11), 12, 19

The median is 11.

EXAMPLE 4

Find the median of this set of scores: 8, 7, 3, 7, 6, 3.

Solution

3, 3, (6, 7), 7, 8

The median is $\dfrac{6 + 7}{2} = 6\cdot 5$.

EXAMPLE 5

Find the median of these scores, which have been arranged in a stem-and-leaf plot:

```
2 | 7
3 | 1 1 5
4 | 0 6 6 8
⑤ | ①1 2 3 3 5 6
6 | 3 8
```

Solution

Median score is 51.

> There are 17 scores, so the middle score is the ninth.

INTERQUARTILE RANGE

You have seen earlier in this chapter how to work out the median from a stem-and-leaf plot. Further information about the distribution of the data can be obtained by looking at the upper and lower **quartiles** and the **interquartile range**.

The *median* splits the data into *halves*; the *quartiles* split each half into *quarters*. When all scores are arranged in order:

> - The **lower quartile** in the score that is halfway between the lowest score and the median. 25% of the scores are *less* than the lower quartile.
> - The **upper quartile** is the score that is halfway between the median and the highest score. 25% of the scores are *greater* than the upper quartile.
> - The **interquartile range** is the *difference* between the *lower* quartile and the *upper* quartile.

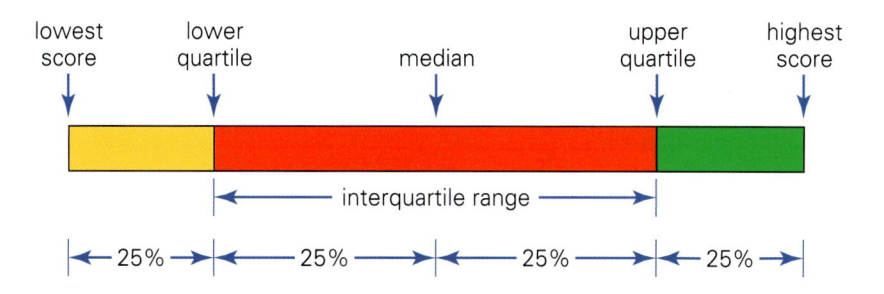

EXAMPLE 1

For these scores: 3, 3, 5, 6, 8, 11, 14, 14, 15, 18, find:
a   the median   b   the lower quartile
c   the upper quartile   d   the interquartile range.

Solutions

a   Median = $\dfrac{8 + 11}{2}$ b   Lower quartile = 5 | Middle score of lower half of the data. |

   = 9·5

c   Upper quartile = 14   d   Interquartile = 14 − 5
                                       = 9

EXAMPLE 2

Find the median, lower and upper quartiles and interquartile range for these data on heights (in centimetres):

```
14 | 8 9
15 | 2 4 6 6 8 9
16 | 0 1 1 3 6 7 8 8 9
17 | 0 2 3 3 4
```

Solution

Median = 162 cm

| There are 22 heights, so the median height is the average of the 11th and 12th height. |

Lower quartile = 156 cm

| There are 11 heights in the lower half, so the middle one of these is the 6th height. |

Upper quartile = 169 cm

| The height that is halfway between the 12th and the 22nd heights is the 17th height $\left(\dfrac{12 + 22}{2} = 17\right)$. |

Interquartile range = 169 − 156
                         = 12 cm

Note: 25% of the heights are less than 156 cm.
        25% of the heights are greater than 169 cm.
        50% of the heights are less than 162 cm.

BOX-AND-WHISKER PLOTS

A box-and-whisker plot is a diagram that shows the following features:

- the lowest and highest scores
- the lower and upper quartiles
- the median.

A box is drawn to represent the interquartile range, and lines are drawn from the sides of the box to show the bottom and top 25% of the scores. (These are the 'whiskers'.)

EXAMPLE

Draw a box-and-whisker plot to show the heights of students from the previous example.

Solution

median = 162 cm
lowest score = 148 cm
highest score = 174 cm
lower quartile = 157 cm
upper quartile = 169 cm

This is referred to as the five-point **summary**.

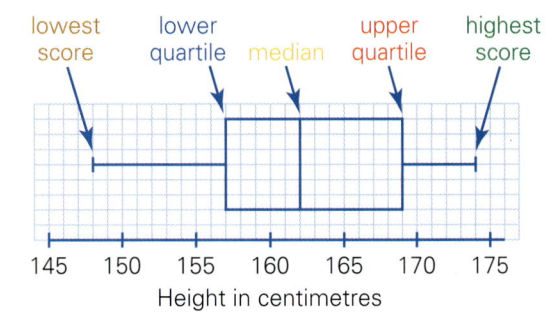

Height in centimetres

EXERCISE 12A

1 The box-and-whisker plot summarises the scores of golf players in a tournament.

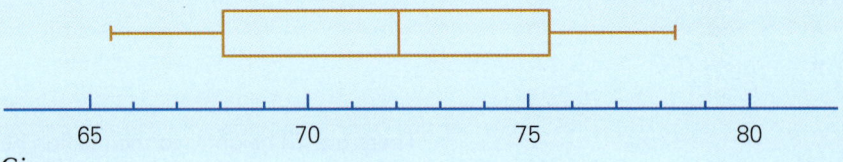

Give:
a the median   **b** the lowest score   **c** the highest score
d the lower quartile   **e** the upper quartile.

2 The number of hours worked by casual employees of a business are shown on this box-and-whisker plot. Give a five-point summary for these data.

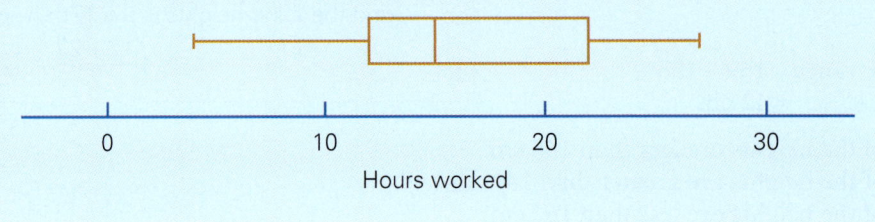

Hours worked

3 Answer parts **a** to **e** in question **1** for this box-and-whisker plot summarising exam marks.

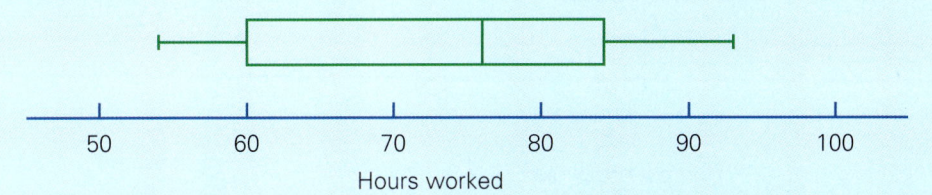

Hours worked

   f What percentage of students scored more than 84 marks?

   g What percentage of students scored between 60 and 76 marks?

4 Draw a box-and-whisker plot for the following five-point summaries:

a time in seconds:	**b** exam marks:	**c** height in cm:
median = 14	median = 62	median = 151 cm
lowest score = 3	lowest score = 25	shortest = 126 cm
highest score = 25	highest score = 86	tallest = 185 cm
lower quartile = 8	lower quartile = 41	lower quartile = 144 cm
upper quartile = 19	upper quartile = 74	upper quartile = 168 cm

5 Calculate the **i** median **ii** lower quartile **iii** upper quartile **iv** interquartile range for each set of scores.

   a 7, 7, 10, 14, 17, 18, 19, 20, 20, 23   **b** 1, 1, 1, 2, 2, 3, 3, 3, 4, 5, 5, 6

   c 21, 25, 26, 29, 35, 42, 46, 51

Level 2

6 The lengths (in millimetres) of caterpillars found in a cabbage patch were recorded on this stem-and-leaf plot.

```
1 | 4 6 8 8 9
2 | 0 0 3 4 4 7 8
3 | 1 2 5 5 7 7 7 8 9 9
4 | 0 3 6 6 8
5 | 4
```

   a What is the length of **i** the shortest caterpillar and **ii** the longest caterpillar?

   b Find the median caterpillar-length.

   c Calculate **i** the lower quartile and **ii** the upper quartile.

   d What is the interquartile range?

   e Draw a box-and-whisker plot to show the data.

   f What *fraction* of the caterpillars have lengths that lie within the interquartile range?

7 This box plot shows the number of people attending aerobics classes at Jim's Gym.

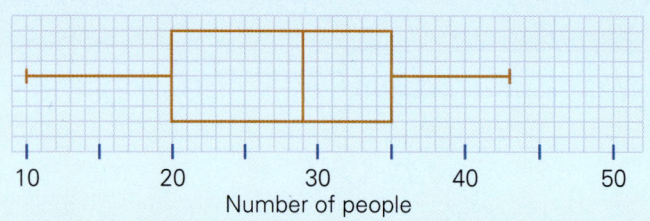

Number of people

a What was the size of the smallest class?
b What was the size of the largest class?
c What is the median class size?
d What percentage of the classes had less than 35 people?
e What percentage of the classes had between 20 and 43 people?
f What is the interquartile range of the data?
g What is the range of the data?
h Explain why it is not possible to determine the mean for the data from the box-and-whisker plot.

8 The times for students to run 200 m at the school sports carnival were recorded to the nearest second:

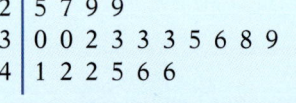

```
2 | 5 7 9 9
3 | 0 0 2 3 3 3 5 6 8 9
4 | 1 2 2 5 6 6
```

a What is the median time?
b Calculate **i** the lower quartile and **ii** the upper quartile.
c What is the interquartile range?
d Construct a box-and-whisker plot to show the data.
e Julie's time for the 200 m was 31 seconds. Describe in two or three sentences how her time compared with the times of other students.
f Is it possible to calculate the mean from a stem-and-leaf plot? Explain.

9 This box-and-whisker plot shows the driving times of 80 motorists travelling from Armidale to Sydney.

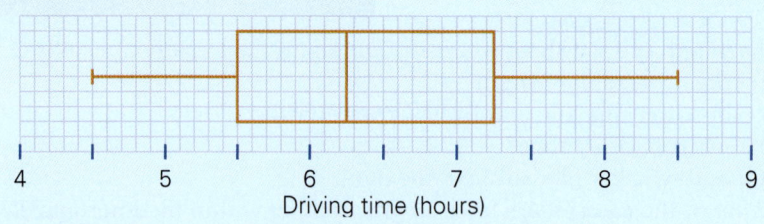

Driving time (hours)

a What is the longest time taken by any motorist?
b What is the median time taken?
c What is the interquartile range for these times?
d How many motorists took longer than $7\frac{1}{4}$ hours?
e Three more motorists have written down their times. Comment on each of the times based on the information you already have:

    i $6\frac{1}{2}$ hours   **ii** 8 hours   **iii** $3\frac{1}{2}$ hours

12.2 Using frequency distribution tables

In a frequency distribution table, scores occur more than once, so the total of the score column *does not* tell us the total of *all* the scores.

To calculate the mean we need to know the **total** of *all* the scores, so another column is added to the table that contains **frequency × score** (**fx**). These values show the **sub-totals** for each score.

Note: the conventional notation for **score** is x, and for **frequency** is f.

$\bar{x}$ (x bar) is the symbol used for the mean of x.

Σ (sigma) is the symbol used for 'the sum of'.

So the total of all scores is Σfx and the total number of scores is Σf.

$$\bar{x} = \frac{\Sigma fx}{\Sigma f}$$

You can do this on your calculator *without* the fx column. Find out how!

EXAMPLE

These data show the number of people living in each home unit in a particular block. Calculate the mean number of people per unit:

Score (x)	Frequency (f)	Freq. × score (fx)
1	4	4
2	5	10
3	4	12
4	2	8
5	1	5
Total	$\Sigma f = 16$	$\Sigma fx = 39$

Add on the fx column as shown in colour.

Estimate: Most of the scores are in the 2–3 range, so the mean is probably between 2 and 3.

Solution

Mean $= \dfrac{\Sigma fx}{\Sigma f}$

$\quad = \dfrac{39}{16}$

$\quad = 2.4375$

So the mean number of people per unit is 2·4 (to 1 decimal place).

EXERCISE 12B

1 For each set of scores find the range, mode, median and mean (correct to 1 decimal place where necessary).

    a 5, 4, 5, 6, 5
                    b 13, 10, 15, 14, 15, 11

c 3, 0, 5, 4, 2, 0, 1, 5, 2, 0, 2 **d** 2, 5, 1, 3, 8, 3, 9, 7
e 20, 50, 10, 30, 80, 30, 90, 70 **f** 12, 15, 11, 13, 18, 13, 19, 17
g Compare your results in parts **d** and **e**. Comment.
h Compare your results in parts **d** and **f**. Comment.

2 a Complete the following table and calculate **i** the range of the data, **ii** the mode, **iii** the mean, and **iv** the median, rounding off to 1 decimal place:

Score (x)	Frequency (f)	(fx)
0	3	
1	5	
2	7	
3	10	
4	6	
5	4	
6	1	
Total		

> You don't need the fx column if you know how to use a calculator.

b The scores of zero do not contribute anything to the sum of the scores, so why is it necessary to include them?

3 James is the goal kicker for his school's rugby team. This frequency distribution table shows the number of goals (x) he kicked in each game last season.

Score (x)	Frequency (f)
0	4
1	5
2	5
3	6
4	3
5	0
6	1

a Calculate the mean number of goals James scored per match.
b What number of goals is the mode?

4 Use this frequency histogram to answer the questions:

a What is the range of scores?
b What is the modal score?

> 'Modal' comes from the word 'mode'.

c Complete a frequency distribution table.
d Calculate the mean score.

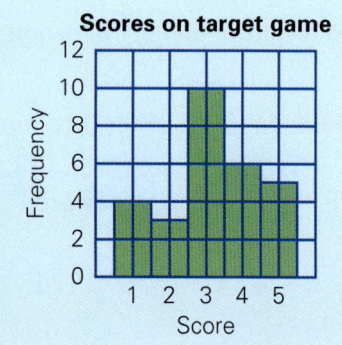

Scores on target game

5 Nicky recorded the number of goals scored by her soccer team in each game:

5	4	0	2	3	2
1	1	3	4	1	2
0	0	2	3	4	1

Organise the scores into a frequency distribution table and calculate the mean.

6 Two friends have a mean mass of 48·5 kg. If one of them has a mass of 45 kg what is the mass of the other?

7 A class of 28 students had a median mark of 49 in Science, but no-one actually scored 49 marks.

   a How many students scored more than 49?
   b Explain how it is possible that no student scored the median mark.

8 Kelly's previous two long jumps have been 4·2 m and 4·35 m. What distance does she need to jump to make the mean of her three jumps be 4·3 m?

9 The netball team had scored a mean of 18 goals per game after nine games. After the tenth game their mean was 18·7. How many goals did they score in their tenth game?

10 The mean length of five crocodiles is 2·1 m. A new arrival measures 3·3 m. What is the mean length of the six crocodiles?

11 The mean height of the 12 boys in 9A is 164 cm. The mean height of the 18 girls is 158 cm. What is the mean height of the whole class?

12 The mean of two numbers is 24.

   a Can we find the two numbers?
   b What *can* we say about the two numbers?

Level 2

13 When is the average of the averages of two sets of numbers equal to the average of all the numbers taken together?

14 Three consecutive numbers add to 57. What are they?

> Be systematic!

15 The number 246 has one digit that is the average of the other two (4 is the average of 2 and 6).

   a How many three-digit numbers have a middle digit that is the average of the other two?
   b How many three-digit numbers have any one digit that is the average of the other two?

12.3 Cumulative frequency

The **median** of a large set of data can be found from a frequency distribution table by adding the frequencies until the *middle score* is reached. This task is made simpler by adding a **cumulative frequency** column to the table, which gives a *running total* of the frequency so far.

> The **cumulative frequency** of a score is the number of scores *less than or equal to* that particular score.

It is also useful to have a way of working out the **position** of the middle score (or middle pair of scores) when there are a lot of data.

> If n is the total number of scores (i.e. the total of the frequency column), and:
> - If n is **odd**:   middle score is in position $\dfrac{n+1}{2}$
> - If n is **even**:   middle pair of scores are in positions $\dfrac{n}{2}$ and $\dfrac{n}{2}+1$

This frequency distribution table has had a *cumulative frequency* column added:

Score	Frequency	Cumulative frequency
1	3	3
2	7	10
3	12	22
4	8	30
5	2	32
6	1	33
Total	$n = 33$	

$3 + 7 = 10$ (the first 10 scores are 2 or less)

$10 + 12 = 22$ (the first 22 scores are 3 or less)

The 17th score is in here.

There are 33 scores, so the middle score is in position $\dfrac{33+1}{2} = 17$th score. So the median score is 3.

> *Note*: The final number in the cumulative frequency column is the same as the *total* of the frequency column.

EXAMPLE

Andy conducted a survey to find out how many chocolate beans there were in each of 30 packets. He recorded his findings in a frequency distribution table.

Find the median number of chocolate beans per packet.

Solution

Score	Frequency	Cumulative frequency
34	2	2
35	5	7
36	8	15
37	11	26
38	3	29
39	1	30
Total	30	

$$\text{Median} = \frac{36 + 37}{2}$$
$$= 36 \cdot 5$$

Median number of beans per packet is 36·5.

$n = 30$, median pair of scores is
$\frac{n}{2}$ and $\frac{n}{2} + 1$
= 15th and 16th scores
From cumulative frequency column,
15th score is 36 and 16th score is 37.

EXERCISE 12C

1 Copy and complete this table, and calculate the median score:

Score (x)	Frequency (f)	c.f.
0	2	
1	7	
2	10	
3	11	
4	6	
5	3	
6	1	

2

Score (x)	Tally	f	c.f.
0	IIII		
1	HHT HHT II		
2	HHT HHT III		
3	HHT II		
4	HHT III		
5	HHT I		
6	II		
7			
8	II		

Charlene surveyed members of her form to find out the number of times they had been to the movies in the past 6 months. Complete the table, and calculate the median number of visits to the movies.

3 The following marks were obtained by a Year 9 class on a Japanese vocabulary test consisting of 12 questions:

8	11	9	5	9	10	10	7	9	6
11	7	8	7	9	8	8	10	8	6
9	10	8	8	6	7	9	10	9	11

a Organise the results into a cumulative frequency distribution table, and calculate the median mark.

b How many students scored less than 50% on the test?

c What mark does a student need to score to be in the top 50% of students?

> Use the *c.f.* column.

4 The following table shows the cumulative frequencies for goals scored in a number of soccer games:

Score (x)	Frequency (f)	c.f.
0		4
1		11
2		23
3		34
4		41
5		46

a Copy the table and complete the frequency column.

b How many games were played together?

c Construct a frequency histogram.

d What is the modal number of games scored per game?

5 The school library needs to know how many books are out on loan in order to conduct the annual stock-take. A sample of students was selected, as there was not enough time to collect information from all the students in the school. The following data were collected from students in one class:

2	0	0	4	0	1	2	2	1	5
1	1	3	2	4	0	0	2	1	1
3	2	4	2	1	0	1	0	2	1

a Organise the data into a cumulative frequency distribution table.

b Calculate the median number of books that are out on loan.

c Name a different measure that could be calculated from the sample and which would be more useful to the librarian than the median. Explain your answer.

12.4 Cumulative frequency diagrams

Just as frequency histograms and polygons can be drawn from frequency distribution tables, similar graphs can be drawn showing **cumulative frequency**.

The cumulative frequency polygon, sometimes called the **ogive** (pronounced 'oh-jive'), is obtained by joining the top **right-hand** corners of the histogram columns.

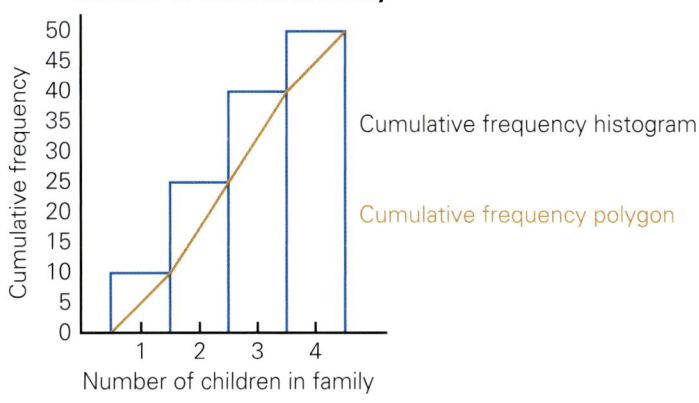

Cumulative frequency of number of children in family

MEDIAN

To find the **median** from the cumulative frequency polygon:

1 Find the point on the *vertical axis* that is **half** the total number of scores.

2 Draw a *horizontal* line to meet the polygon.

3 Draw a *vertical* from this point on the polygon to the horizontal axis. This score is the median score.

UPPER AND LOWER QUARTILES

The **lower quartile** is found by reading from the graph the score corresponding to **one-quarter** of the total frequency.

The **upper quartile** is found by reading from the graph the score corresponding to **three-quarters** of the total frequency.

The **interquartile range** is the difference between the upper and lower quartiles. This cumulative frequency histogram and polygon show the scores obtained by students in a quiz.

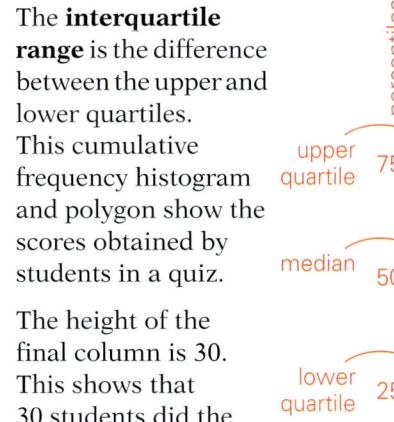

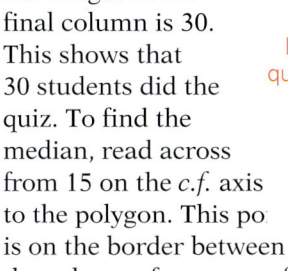

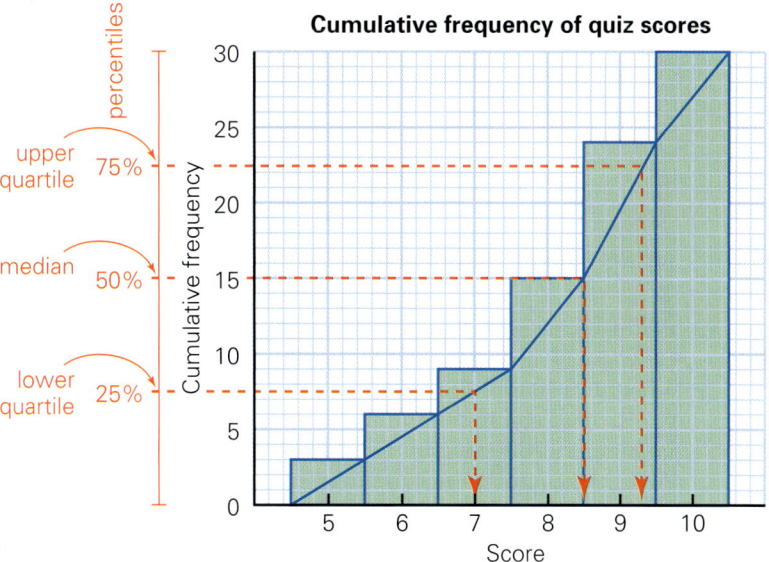

Cumulative frequency of quiz scores

The height of the final column is 30. This shows that 30 students did the quiz. To find the median, read across from 15 on the *c.f.* axis to the polygon. This po[int] is on the border between the columns for scores of 8 and 9, so the median score is 8·5.

Lower quartile cumulative frequency is $\frac{1}{4}$ of $30 = 7 \cdot 5$. Read across to the polygon and down to the score axis. Lower quartile score is 7.

Upper quartile cumulative frequency is $\frac{3}{4}$ of $30 = 22 \cdot 5$. Read across to the polygon and down to the score axis. Upper quartile score is 9. Interquartile range is upper quartile – lower quartile = $9 - 7 = 2$.

EXAMPLE

a How many scores were less than 15?
b How many scores were at least 13?
c Draw a cumulative frequency histogram and polygon for this distribution, and use the diagram to determine the median score.
d Find the lower and upper quartile scores.

Score (x)	f	c.f.
10	2	2
11	5	7
12	7	14
13	12	26
14	6	32
15	3	35
16	1	36
Total	36	

Solution

a 32 scores were less than 15.
b $36 - 14 = 22$ scores were at least 13.
c Median score is 13.
d Lower quartile: score = 12.
   Upper quartile: score = 14.

14 scores were 12 or less.

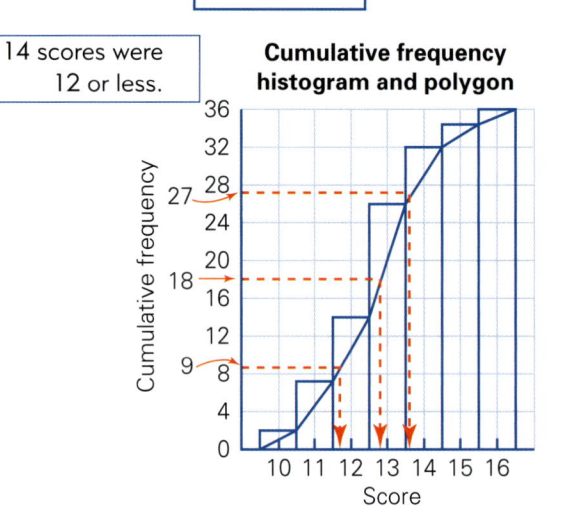

Cumulative frequency histogram and polygon

EXERCISE 12D

1 a Copy the table and complete the c.f. column.
   b Construct a cumulative frequency histogram and polygon for this distribution.
   c Use the polygon to determine the median. (Check your answer from the table.)

Score (x)	Frequency (f)	c.f.
2	1	
3	6	
4	14	
5	17	
6	2	
7	0	
8	1	

2 These cumulative frequency diagrams represent the marks scored by a Year 9 class on a quiz containing 10 questions. Use the graphs to answer the following questions:

a What was the lowest mark scored by any student?
b How many students took part in the quiz?
c What is the range of scores?
d How many students scored 8 or less on the quiz?
e How many students scores less than 7 on the quiz?
f How many students scored full marks on the quiz?
g What was the median mark scored by students?
h Find the lower and upper quartile scores.

Cumulative frequency of quiz scores

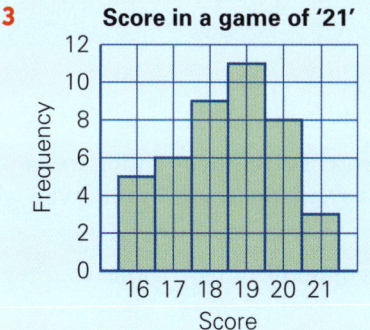

Level 2

3

Score in a game of '21'

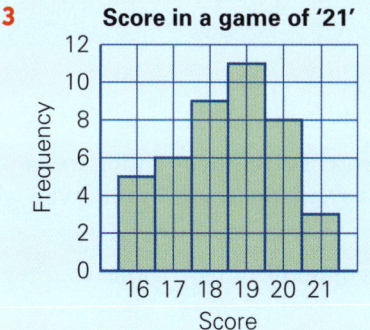

The histogram (left) shows the scores reached by players during a game of '21'.

a Construct a cumulative frequency histogram and polygon for these data.
b Calculate the median score.
c Find the lower and upper quartiles and the interquartile range.

4 Warwick and Betty were playing a game requiring two dice to be thrown, and the two numbers to be added together. They recorded the totals for each throw:

10	6	9	3	5	12	7	4	4	11
8	5	10	2	7	5	12	6	8	8
7	9	11	10	4	6	7	7	2	8
3	6	3	12	8	10	5	3	6	7
5	9	7	6	6	11	5	7	8	8
4	9	9	2	10	8	6	7	3	5

a Construct a cumulative frequency table for the data.
b How many throws scored 5 or less?
c How many throws scored more than 8?
d How many times did a score of 3 occur?
e How many times did a score of 7 occur?
f What was the median score?
g Explain the reason for the difference in the answers to parts **d** and **e**.
h Is it possible to determine how many 'doubles' were scored? Explain.

5 The cumulative frequency table shows the shoe sizes of a group of students.

Shoe size	Cumulative frequency
6	5
$6\frac{1}{2}$	13
7	29
$7\frac{1}{2}$	50
8	67
$8\frac{1}{2}$	80
9	88
$9\frac{1}{2}$	97
10	100

a How many students were surveyed?
b How many students take size 8 shoes?
c Draw a cumulative frequency histogram and polygon.
d What is the median shoe size?
e Find the interquartile range.
f Construct a frequency distribution table and calculate the mean shoe size.
g Is it possible that a column of a cumulative frequency histogram can be *shorter* than the column on its *left*? Explain.

6 Under what circumstances will the median of a set of scores be greater than the mean of the scores?

Investigation

Pulse rates

You need: one stop watch, or watch with a second hand

1 While sitting in class, measure your **resting pulse rate**. Do this by counting your pulse over a measured time period of 20 s. If you then *multiply* the result by *three* you will have your pulse rate per minute.

2 Record the results for the class on a line plot or stem-and-leaf plot. Circle your *own* pulse rate.

3 Organise the results into a frequency distribution table.

4 Calculate the mean, mode and median for the data.

5 Construct a frequency histogram and box-and-whisker plot to show the distribution.

6 Compile a brief report on the distribution of pulse rates in your class. Include the following:

- the line plot or stem-and-leaf plot
- the frequency distribution table and histogram
- the calculations of the mean, median and mode, with comments on how each represents the group
- a written description of the main features of the data
- comments on how your own pulse rates fits into the distribution.

7 Repeat this activity after running on the spot (or around the playground) for 2 min. Take your pulse immediately after you stop.

8 How did activity affect the pulse rates of the class?

9 Comment on any difference in the shape of the distribution.

10 Did the position of your own pulse rate change in relation to the rest of the class?

Conducting your own survey

Investigate one of the following:

- the number of brothers and sisters of students in your class
- the number of hours homework done last night (to the nearest 15 min)
- the number of televisions in each household
- the number of pets people have
- the time it takes people to run 100 m (to the nearest s)
- people's shoe-sizes (to the nearest whole size).

You should collect *at least* 30 results.

You may prefer to choose your own, in which case check with your teacher first to make sure it will produce suitable results.

Note: You need to collect *numerical* data. (Why?)

Use appropriate techniques to collect, organise, display and summarise the data. These could include the following:

- surveying or measuring to collect the data
- dot plot or stem-and-leaf plot and frequency distribution table to organise the data
- frequency histogram or polygon and a box-and-whisker plot to display the data
- calculation of mean, median, mode and range to summarise the data.

Write a report on your investigation, including any of the features above, with your own comments on the results. Were the results as you expected? Are the data you collected reliable and representative?

12.5 Grouped data

In all of the examples so far there have been a limited number of possible scores. Where there are a *large* number of possible scores it is more useful to group the data into **classes**.

Data can be **discrete** or **continuous**:

- **Discrete** data can take only *certain values*; for example the score in a soccer game must be a whole number, and shoe sizes can only be a whole size or half size ($5\frac{1}{2}$, $7\frac{1}{2}$, etc.). There are no values between these. Discrete data may be grouped if there are a large number of different 'scores' (more than 10 perhaps).

- **Continuous** data can take *any value*; for example when measuring heights or times, for any two measurements there can always be another one in-between. Continuous data must be grouped. (Sometimes this is done at the data collection stage, for example by measuring heights to the nearest centimetre.)

For example, if students in your school were timed to run 100 m, the data are continuous and there would be a very wide range of results. One possible way to group these heights would be using **class intervals** of, say, 2 s.

SPREADSHEET ACTIVITY

GRAPHIC CALCULATOR

It is essential that all the class intervals for a distribution are *exactly the same*.

It is usually a good idea to aim for 6 to 10 groups, as this will give a good idea of the shape of the data without requiring excessive effort.

Note: The class boundaries are chosen so that each score belongs in *only one group*. So groups of 5–9, 10–14, 15–19, and so on, might be chosen.

The horizontal axis of the frequency histogram for grouped data is labelled with the **class centres**. They are found by adding the upper and lower class boundaries, then dividing by 2.

For example, a class containing scores from 13–17 would have a class centre of $\dfrac{13 + 17}{2} = 15$ (the average or mean of the class boundaries).

The class centres are also used to calculate an estimate of the mean when data have been grouped.

EXAMPLE 1

The following data show the heights in centimetres of students in 9Y at Plum Creek High School:

160	163	154	173	169	162	175	158	161	146
159	168	155	167	163	171	154	169	158	156
170	162	158	153	166	168	157	169	178	171

Organise the data into a grouped frequency distribution table, and construct a frequency histogram to show the results.

Solution

Class	Class centre (x)	Tally	Frequency
145–149	147	I	1
150–154	152	III	3
155–159	157	IIII II	7
160–164	162	IIII I	6
165–169	167	IIII II	7
170–174	172	IIII	4
175–179	177	II	2
		Total	30

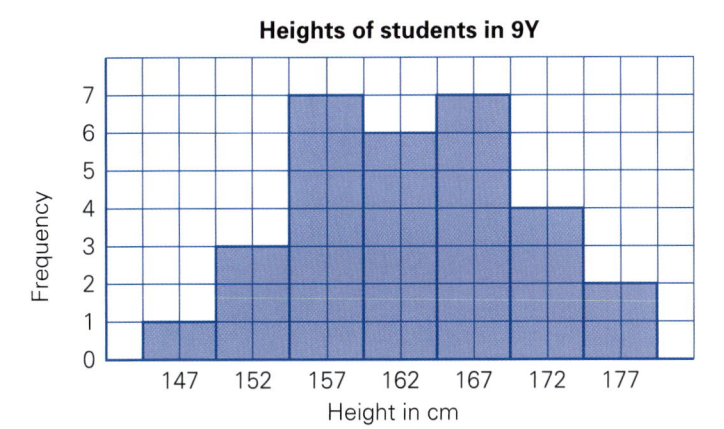

Heights of students in 9Y

Using grouped data means some changes need to be made to the way the mean, mode and median are determined and expressed.

> An **estimate** of the **mean** is calculated using the class centres.
>
> The **modal class** replaces the mode.
>
> The **median class** or an **estimate** of the **median** is calculated.

An **estimate** of the median can be obtained by reading from a cumulative frequency ogive.

Note: Where the data are **discrete**, the median should be stated as one of the possible values, or a score *halfway between* two possible values. Where the data are **continuous**, the estimate can take any value.

EXAMPLE 2

The following data show the percentages gained by students on an end-of-term test.
a Determine modal class for this distribution.
b Make an estimate of the mean.
c Give the median class and make an estimate of the median.

Class	Class centre (x)	Frequency (f)	fx	$c.f.$
31–40	35·5	7	248·5	7
41–50	45·5	9	409·5	16
51–60	55·5	10	555·0	26
61–70	65·5	11	720·5	37
71–80	75·5	7	528·5	44
81–90	85·5	4	342·0	48
91–100	95·5	2	191·0	50
Total		50	2995·0	

Solutions

a Modal class is 61–70.

b Mean = $\dfrac{\text{total of } fx}{\text{total of } f} \approx \dfrac{2995}{50}$

$\approx 59 \cdot 9$

c Median class is 51–60.
Median = 59.

Percentages on end-of-term test

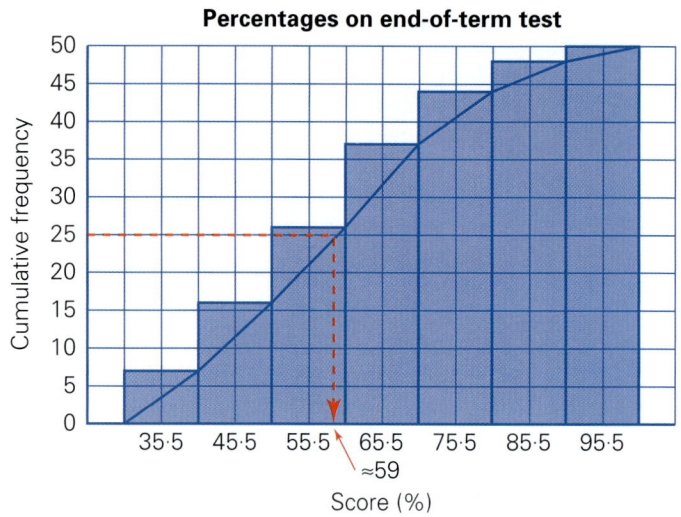

EXERCISE 12E

1 What would be the class centres for these classes?

a 12–18	**b** 5–13	**c** 43–55	**d** 6–11
e 17–50	**f** 20–49	**g** 156–172	**h** 120–145

2 The examination results of 50 students were collected as percentages:

68	67	44	66	71	64	49	48	46	55
41	31	71	80	96	86	73	61	65	57
40	57	51	59	58	69	80	67	75	93
85	60	63	76	71	56	35	47	81	89
88	41	67	60	90	72	87	53	76	61

a Complete this grouped frequency distribution table for these results:

Class	Class centre (x)	Tally	Frequency
28–36			
37–45			
46–54			
55–63			
64–72			
73–81			
82–90			
91–99			

b Which is the modal class?
c Is it possible to determine the range of marks from the table alone? Explain.
d How many students achieved a mark of *at least* 64?

e What fraction of the students gained a mark *less than* 46%?

f Draw a frequency histogram showing the distribution of examination results.

g Salim's mark in the test was 50%, so he was happy because he considers 50% to be a 'pass'. How would you interpret a mark of 50% on this examination?

Level 2

3 Using the heights of Year 9 students at Plum Creek High School (given in the example on page 375).

  a Arrange them now into a frequency distribution table with a class interval of *4 cm*.

  b Construct a new frequency histogram.

  c Compare your new histogram to the one shown in the example. What are the advantages and disadvantages of having a smaller class interval? Discuss your ideas in small groups.

4 The following speeds (in km/h) were measured by police radar:

94	102	82	92	97	112	84	106	109	97
87	111	89	106	89	109	92	119	111	109
89	82	97	96	92	109	110	107	96	111
116	110	111	89	91	110	89	88	94	91

  a Arrange these data into a grouped frequency distribution table using intervals of 80–86, 87–93, and so on. (Remember to include columns for the class centres, fx and $c.f.$)

  b How many motorists had their speed recorded?

  c How many motorists were travelling *at or below* a speed of 93 km/h?

  d What percentage of motorists were travelling at speeds *in excess of* 100 km/h?

  e Construct a cumulative frequency histogram and ogive on the same axes to display the data.

  f What was the median speed recorded?

  g What was the mean speed recorded?

5 In a golf tournament there are two preliminary rounds and a final. Only the best 50% of the players from the two preliminary rounds reach the final. The following are the combined scores for each player on the two preliminary rounds:

148	152	137	161
162	178	141	156
170	159	153	182
157	172	166	150
182	155	176	139
143	160	158	162

  a Organise the results into a grouped cumulative frequency table, using groups of 133–139, 140–146, 147–153, and so on.

  b Draw the histogram and ogive.

  c Estimate (from the ogive) the cut-off score required for players to gain a place in the final.

6 The following results are scores in an Australian mathematics competition. The top half of the participants receive a credit certificate.

68	44	121	88	73	97	50	81	103	66
84	106	91	55	82	89	76	60	49	57
56	91	76	119	102	68	82	74	71	90
67	93	74	52	87	100	94	80	107	63
56	58	95	87	114	98	51	65	72	110

a Organise the results into a grouped cumulative frequency table.
b Draw the histogram and ogive.
c Estimate the mark needed to obtain a credit certificate.
d If the top 25% of participants receive a merit certificate, estimate from the ogive the mark required to qualify for a merit certificate.

Investigation Undertaking research

1 Choose one of the following topics to research and compile a report on:

- the number of points scored by a rugby league/basketball/other potentially high-scoring sporting team over a season (not soccer, hockey, etc.)
- the times achieved by runners/swimmers at a school carnival
- the heights of your family and friends
- the cost of telephone calls made from your house
- the number of pages in the books on a bookshelf
- the exact length of time it takes you to travel to and from school each day
- or you can choose your own topic, ensuring that the data you collect are numeric, and either are continuous or have a range big enough to need to be grouped. Check with your teacher first if choosing your own topic.

2 Include the following in your report:

- a list of the 'raw data' (i.e. the numbers collected)—ensure that you collect **at least 40** pieces of information
- a cumulative frequency distribution table with the data organised into groups
- a frequency histogram and/or polygon
- a cumulative frequency histogram and polygon
- calculations of the range/mean/mode/median of the data
- a summary of your results, including comments on the distribution of the data, how it matched your expectations, and so on.

12.6 Selecting the 'best' average

For many distributions, the mean, median and mode will be similar, and will all give a representative figure for the data. (The shape of the histogram will be roughly symmetrical.)

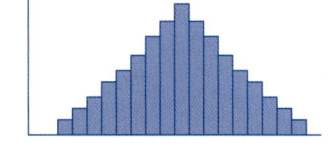

Distributions of this general shape are called 'normal' distributions.

However, if the distribution has any unusual features, or if the shape of the histogram is not very symmetrical, then the figures could be quite different.

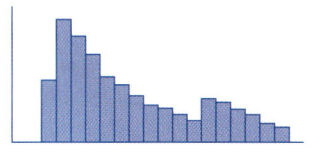

Distributions that are not symmetrical are said to be 'skewed'.

For example, imagine that the following selling prices were recorded for houses in a certain street:

$154 000 $450 000 $161 000 $142 000 $157 000

You will explore this idea in more detail next year.

Which gives a better pictures of the data, the mean or the median?

The **mean** selling price is $212 800, but this seems too high to be representative of the whole group. (Four out of five prices are way below this figure.)

The $450 000 is an **outlier**. It is far above the rest that it distorts the mean.

Put the prices in order:

$142 000 $154 000 $157 000 $161 000 $450 000

The **median** is $157 000, which gives a much better picture of the group.

Note: If we ignore the $450 000, the mean of the remaining four prices is $153 500, which would be more representative.

EXERCISE 12F

1 Every week Jonah's Maths class has a 'quick quiz' consisting of 10 questions. Jonah's results for the last 12 weeks are: 9, 10, 10, 8, 8, 10, 9, 8, 10, 8, 9, 7.

   a Calculate the **i** mode **ii** mean **iii** median.
   b Which measure do you think is the *least* appropriate? Why?

Level 2

2 This table shows the annual salaries of staff in a particular company:

24 Data entry staff	$22 000 each
4 Administrators	$27 000 each
2 Supervisors	$31 500 each
1 Accountant	$47 000
1 Manager	$68 000

   a Construct a frequency distribution table to show these salaries.
   b Calculate the mean salary to the nearest dollar.
   c Find the modal salary.
   d Calculate the median salary.
   e Draw a scale from $0 to $70 000. Mark on it the salaries earned by each staff category, and label where the mode, median and mean lie.

f Which of these three measures would be used by:

   i the manager when advertising for new staff?

   ii the staff welfare officer suggesting a pay rise?

3

Price ($)	Frequency
160 000	5
170 000	12
180 000	9
200 000	3
220 000	2
250 000	3
280 000	2

The prices of homes sold in a Sydney suburb over a 1-month period were recorded (to the nearest $10 000).

a Calculate the mean, mode and median selling price. (Round appropriately.)

b For each measure give an example of a person or group of people who might choose to use that figure. Explain why you think they would make that choice.

4 Carlos collected the following information on monthly allowances from students in his class.

Allowance ($)	Frequency
20	8
30	5
40	3
50	5
100	2

  a Carlos currently receives $30 per month. Construct an argument, backed by these statistics, to support each point of view:

    i Carlos thinks his allowance should be increased.

    ii His mother thinks it should be reduced.

    iii His father thinks it should stay the same.

  b What further information might be required to make a proper decision?

  c What factors could affect the *validity* of the information (i.e. whether the data are accurate and genuine)?

Chapter Review

average	distribution	mode	sector graph
bias	dot plot	modal	skewed
census	estimate	normal	statistics
centres	frequency	ogive	stem-and-leaf
class	groups	polygon	survey
continuous	histogram	population	table
cumulative	interval	questionnaire	tally
data	mean	range	
discrete	median	sample	

1 Select words from the table to complete these paragraphs:

The _____ (middle score) of a distribution can be found by adding a _____ _____ column to the _____ _____ table.

The median can be read directly from the cumulative frequency _____ (also called the _____).

If a survey produces a large number of _____ it is useful to organise the results into _____. The _____ _____ are found by adding the upper and lower class boundaries for each class _____.

These are used as labels for the _____ and to calculate an _____ of the mean.

With grouped data, instead of finding the mode, the _____ _____ is found.

2 From the list, select the word that most closely matches the definitions.

   a The middle score when a set of scores is arranged in order.
   b A column graph showing the number of times each score occurred.
   c A circular graph showing the composition of the whole.
   d A collection of facts, numbers, information.
   e A distribution that is not symmetrical.

3 Write a mathematical and a non-mathematical definition of these words:

   a interval   **b** ogive   **c** discrete

TEACHER

Chapter Review Exercises

1 To determine the shopping preferences of Australians, a market researcher stood outside a supermarket one Wednesday afternoon and asked 50 people where they preferred to shop.

   a Give at least three reasons why the sample chosen would be biased.

   b Suggest a better method of collecting information, which would be more representative.

2 This question was asked of 100 people: 'Should shops be allowed to open on Sundays so that the people who have to work all week have time to do their shopping?'

   a Explain why the wording of this question might affect the results of the survey.

   b Make up a question that would have the opposite effect.

   c What would be a better question to ask?

3

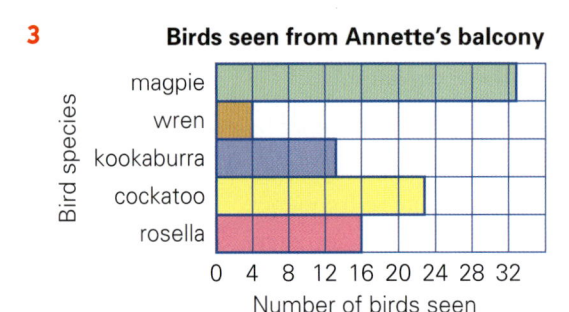

Birds seen from Annette's balcony

This bar graph shows the number of different birds seen from Annette's balcony.

   a Which species did Annette see the most of?

   b How many birds did she see altogether?

   c What percentage of the birds were magpies (to the nearest 1%)?

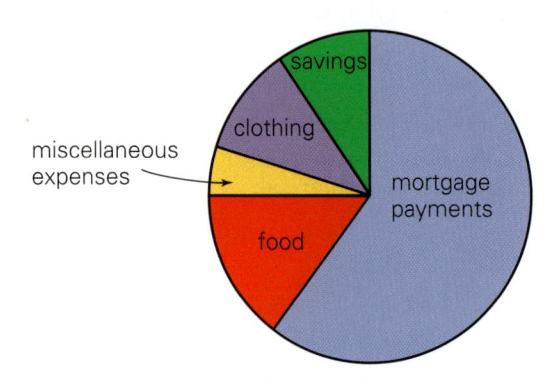

Christine's expenses

4 Christine has just moved into her own unit. This sector graph shows how she allocates her income of $1038 per fortnight:

   a Which expense takes up most of her income?

   b How much does she spent on clothing, to the nearest $10?

   c What percentage of her income does she save, to the nearest 5%?

5 These data show the number of students in each of six classroms:

12.1

15   22   18   15   12   16

  a   What is the mean number of students per classroom?
  b   What is the median?
  c   What is the mode?

6 Peter records the number of minutes running he does when training for the 'City to Surf' race.

12.4

48   57   49   62   55   48   75   35   45   52
39   46   53   58   66   54   71   45   61   59

  a   Arrange these times into a stem-and-leaf plot.
  b   What is the median running time?
  c   Calculate **i** the lower quartile and **ii** the upper quartile.
  d   What is the interquartile range?
  e   Construct a box-and-whisker plot.
  f   Comment on the distribution of Peter's running times.

7 The residents of a certain street were asked how many trees they had on their land. The results are shown below:

12.2

1   6   3   3   0   3   2   5   4   4
2   2   0   3   5   5   1   2   1   5
6   3   2   4   4   3   5   5   2   1

  a   Organise the data into a frequency distribution table.
  b   Calculate the mean number of trees per block (to 1 decimal place).
  c   What is the modal number of trees per block?
  d   What is the median number of trees per block?
  e   Construct a frequency histogram to show the distribution.

8

12.3

Score (x)	Frequency (f)
0	15
1	25
2	21
3	13
4	6
5	1
6	0
7	1

A number of students were asked how many pets their families had. The results are shown in the frequency distribution table.

  a   Copy the table into your book, adding a column for cumulative frequency.
  b   Construct a cumulative frequency histogram and ogive.
  c   How many families were surveyed?
  d   What is the median number of pets per family?

Scores in shooting section

12.4

9 The cumulative frequency histogram and ogive show the scores obtained by competitors in the shooting section of a biathlon event. Each competitor has five shots at a target.

a   How many competitors were in the event?
b   What is the median score?
c   How many competitors scores *2 or less* points?
d   How many competitors scored 5 out of 5?
e   Find the interquartile range.

12.5

10 The following data represent the number of basketball cards students had in their collection.

54	77	96	50	63
87	85	60	48	95
58	97	105	86	110
64	80	75	67	103
55	87	65	49	98
112	99	59	64	81
93	56	80	107	116
63	89	76	72	51

a   Arrange these data into a grouped frequency distribution table using intervals of 40-49, 50–59, and so on.
b   Construct a cumulative frequency histogram and ogive for the distribution.
c   What is the modal class for this distribution?
d   Determine the mean number of cards per collection.
e   Estimate the median number of cards.

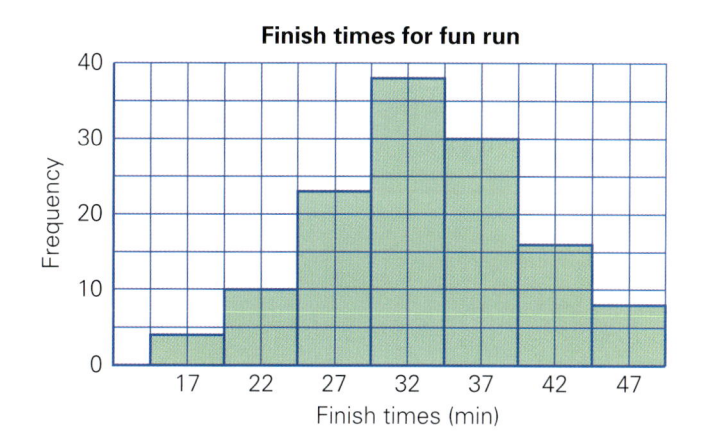

Finish times for fun run

Finish times (min)

11 This frequency histogram shows the finish times of runners in a fun run. It was constructed from grouped data.

  a How many runners took part in the fun run?
  b Construct a cumulative frequency table (include a fx column).
  c Calculate the mean time.
  d Draw the histogram and ogive.
  e If the fastest 50% of runners receive a medal, estimate the cut-off time for runners to win a medal.
  f Use the ogive to determine the upper and lower quartile times. Explain what each of these times represents with reference to the whole group of runners.

12 The following times (in minutes) were recorded for competitors at an orienteering event:

   67 72 59 68 36 70 70 38
  a Calculate:
     i the mean
    ii the median
   iii the mode
  b Which of the values in part **a**, **i–iii**, do you think is the most representative? Why?

13 The mean of the three numbers is 27. What number should be added to make the new mean 27·5?

Keeping Mathematically Fit

Part A—Non-calculator

1 Find $4\frac{1}{2}$ of \$66.

2

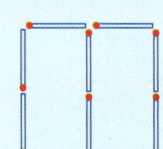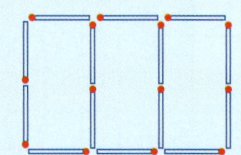

    a Write a rule relating the number of matches (m) to the number of rectangles (r).
    b How many matches are required for six rectangles?
    c How many rectangles are there in a pattern using 50 matches?

3 The circumference of a circle is x cm. Write an expression for its area.

4 $16^6 =$

    A 4^3 **B** 4^{12} **C** 8^3 **D** 8^6

5 Match the graphs to their equations.

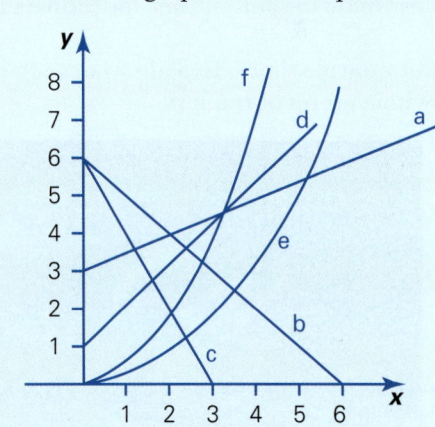

$$y = \tfrac{1}{2}x^2 \qquad x + y = 6$$

$$y = \tfrac{1}{2}x + 3 \qquad y = \tfrac{1}{4}x^2$$

$$2x + y = 6 \qquad x - y + 1 = 0$$

6 The radius (r) of a circle varies directly with the square root of the area (A). This is shown by:

    A $r^2 = \dfrac{k}{A^2}$ **B** $r = kA^2$ **C** $r = k\sqrt{A}$ **D** $r = \dfrac{k}{\sqrt{A}}$

7

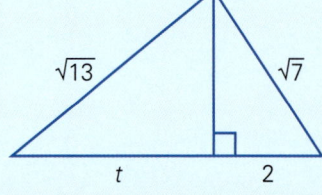

What is the value of t?

8 Which of the following is closest to $0\cdot7$?

    A 65% **B** $0\cdot07$ **C** $\dfrac{7}{9}$ **D** $0\cdot8$

9 If the sum of two-thirds of a number and three times the same number is 44, find the number.

10 Simplify $1\frac{3}{4} : 5$.

Part B—Calculator

1 Find the exact distance between $(2, {}^-2)$ and $(5, {}^-1)$.

2 Solve $3x^2 = 5(x + 3) - 2$.

3 When a certain number is added to both the numerator and denominator of the fraction, $\frac{4}{9}$ the resulting fraction is equal to $\frac{3}{4}$. What is the number?

4 What fraction of the square has been shaded?

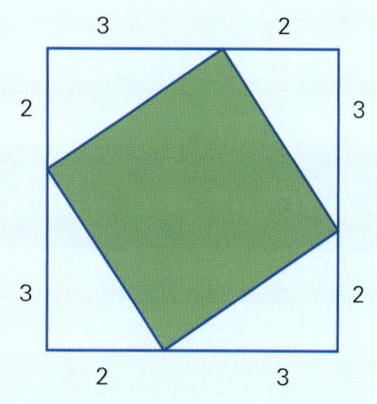

5 The seventeenth of May 1985 was special because the date creates a number pattern:

17/5/85

	17	×	5	=	85
	day	×	month	=	year

a Were there any other dates that year with a similar pattern?
b Are there any dates *this* year with that pattern?

1 What you need to know and revise

Outcome MS 4.2:
Calculates surface area of rectangular and triangular prisms and volume of right prisms and cylinders:

- using the abbreviations for cubic units, e.g. cm^3, m^3
- calculating the volume of right prisms with cross-sections that are rectangular and triangular

- finding the volume of a right prism given the area of its cross-section
- using the formula to find the volume of cylinders
  $V = \pi r^2 h$
- using the kilolitre as a unit in measuring large volumes
- converting between m^3 and kL.

2 What you will learn in this chapter

Outcome MS 5.2.2:
Applies formulas to find the surface area of right cylinders and volume of right pyramids, cones and spheres and calculates the surface area and volume of composite solids:

- recognising the relationship between the volume of a prism and a pyramid with the same base
- recognising the relationship between the volume of a cylinder and a cone with the same base
- using the formula to find the volume of right pyramids and cones
  $V = \frac{1}{3} Ah$
  where A is the base area and h is the perpendicular height

- using the formula to find the volume of spheres
  $V = \frac{4}{3} \pi r^3$
  where r is the length of the radius
- finding the volume of composite solids.

Working Mathematically outcomes WMS 5.1, 5.2, 5.3
Students will be required to *question*, *apply strategies*, *communicate*, *reason* and *reflect* in the sections of this chapter.

13

Volume and capacity

MathsCheck
Volume and capacity

Volume and capacity are related but different measurements that are often confused.

Volume is used for solids and is a measure of the amount of space a solid occupies. The most common units of measure of volume are cubic centimetres (cm^3) and cubic metres (m^3).

Capacity is the volume of fluids. We often describe the size of a container by its capacity, i.e. the quantity of fluid it will hold. The most common units of capacity are millilitre (mL) or litre (L).

$$1 \text{ mL} = 1 \text{ cm}^3$$

cc is often used for cubic centimetres.
$500 \text{ cm}^3 = 500 \text{ cc}$

Volume				Capacity		
1000 mm^3	$=$	1 cm^3	⟷	1 mL		
		1000 cm^3	⟷	1 L	$=$	1000 mL
$1\,000\,000 \text{ cm}^3$	$=$	1 m^3	⟷	1 kL	$=$	1000 L
				1 mL	$=$	$1\,000\,000$ L

Note:

- **Length** is measured in **one dimension** (a line); units are mm, cm, m …

- **Area** is measured in **two dimensions** (a flat surface); units are mm^2, cm^2, m^2 …

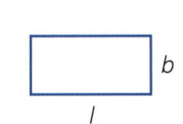

- **Volume** is measured in **three dimensions** (a solid shape); units are mm^3, cm^3, m^3 …

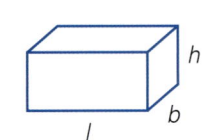

Volumes of prisms

A prism is a solid figure that has the same cross-section for its entire height. It has two congruent faces, the shape of which give the prism its name.

The distance between the two congruent faces is called the **height** of the prism.

The volume (V) of a prism is given by the formula:
$$V = Ah$$
where A is the cross-sectional area of the prism and h is the perpendicular height of the prism.

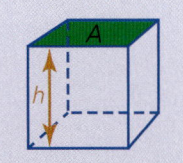

For certain prisms the formula for A can be substituted:

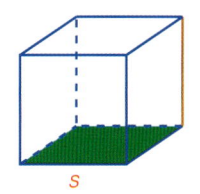

Cube

$A = s^2$
$V = Ah$
$V = s^2 \times s$
$\quad = s^3$

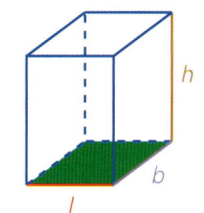

Rectangular prism

$A = lb$
$V = Ah$
$V = lbh$

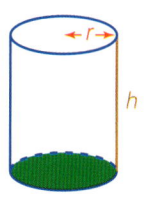

Cylinder

$A = \pi r^2$
$V = Ah$
$V = \pi r^2 h$

1 Complete the following conversions:

a   3 L = ... mL
d   645 mL = ... cm³
g $\frac{1}{2}$ L = ... mL
j   2·3 m³ = ... cm³
m   450 cm³ = ... L
p   23·6 L = ... cm³
s   0·04 kL = ... mL

b   8 kL = ... L
e   3500 mL = ... L
h   6500 mm³ = ... cm³
k $\frac{2}{5}$ L = ... mL
n   2600 L = ... kL
q   56 mL = ... L
t   3·04 L = ... mm³

c   2·5 m³ = ... kL
f   0·7 L = ... mL
i   0·5 cm³ = ... mm³
l $\frac{1}{4}$ m³ = ... L
o   2 m³ = ... L
r   0·8 kL = ... L
u   4·2 ML = ... cm³

2 Express the following as fractions of a litre:

a   200 mL
b   750 cm³
c   25 mL

3 How many 220 mL glasses could be *filled* from a 5 L carton of orange juice?

4 A red car has a 4 L engine. The engine of a blue car has six cylinders, each with a volume of 700 cc. Which car has the larger engine capacity?

5 A standard wine bottle contains 750 mL of wine. How many bottles would need to be opened to pour 34 glasses of wine if a standard measure is 125 mL?

6 Find the volume of each of these prisms, for which the area of the cross-section is given:

a

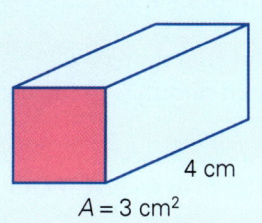

$A = 3$ cm²

4 cm

b

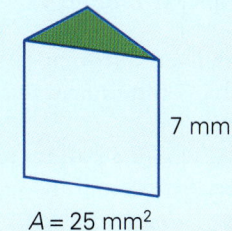

7 mm

$A = 25$ mm²

c

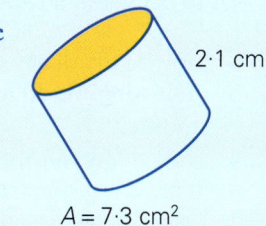

2·1 cm

$A = 7·3$ cm²

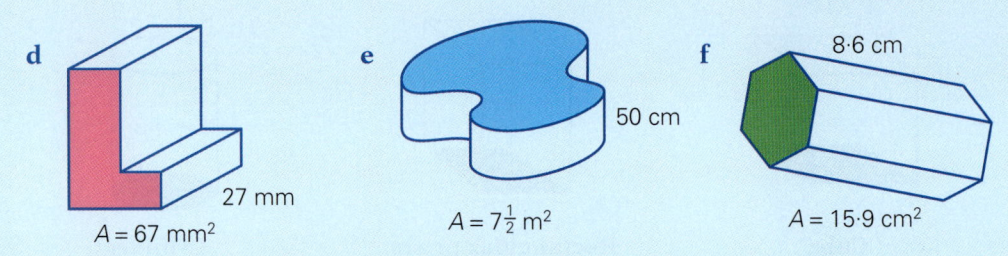

d 27 mm
$A = 67 \text{ mm}^2$

e 50 cm
$A = 7\frac{1}{2} \text{ m}^2$

f 8·6 cm
$A = 15·9 \text{ cm}^2$

7 Calculate the volume of each of these prisms:

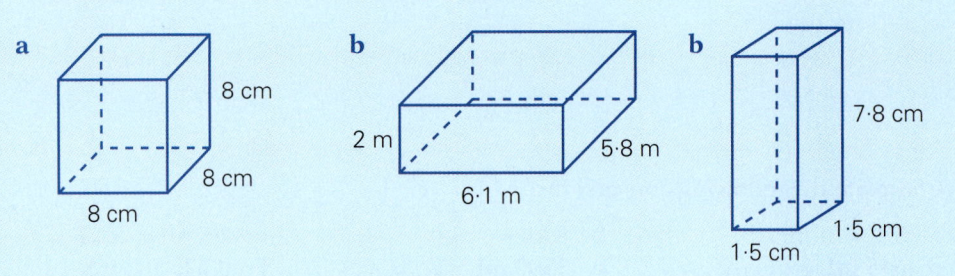

a 8 cm, 8 cm, 8 cm

b 2 m, 6·1 m, 5·8 m

b 7·8 cm, 1·5 cm, 1·5 cm

8 Find the volume of the following cylinders:

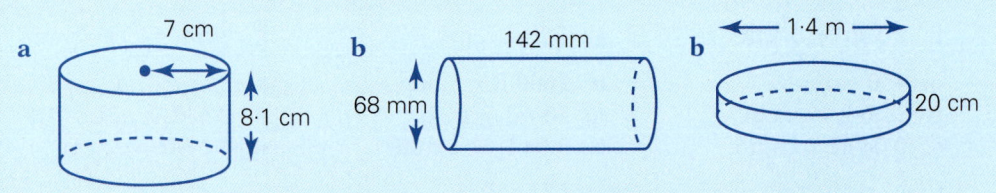

a 7 cm, 8·1 cm

b 142 mm, 68 mm

b 1·4 m, 20 cm

9 Cheryl's pool has a capacity of 26 kL. How long would it take to fill, at a rate of 85 L per minute? (Answer in h and min.)

10 Peter has 1·5 m³ of pine bark blocking his driveway. He can carry 85 L of the bark in his wheelbarrow.

    a How many trips will he need to make to move all of the bark?
    b If he piles the bark up in his wheelbarrow he can carry 15% more. How many trips would he need to make in this case?

11 An intravenous drip is used to introduce fluid into a patient's bloodstream. The drip is set to deliver at a rate of 12 drops per minute, and each drop $= \frac{1}{4}$ mL.

    a How many drops could be delivered from a bag of fluid containing 1 L?
    b How long would a 650 mL bag of fluid last, in hours and minutes, to the nearest minute?
    c How many millilitres of fluid would a patient receive in 24 hours?
    d What must the drip rate be adjusted to if the patient needs to receive 3 L in 24 hours? (Answer correct to 1 decimal place.)

Cambridge Spectrum Maths 9 5.3

Estimating volume

1 Estimate the volume of your classroom. Compare your estimate with those of other members of the class.

2 Now make the necessary measurements and calculations to find the volume of your classroom.

3 Collect a variety of other prisms (e.g. drink cartons or cans, boxes, books) and first estimate the volume of each, then make the necessary measurements to check your estimate.

Dripping taps

You need: stopwatch, measuring cylinder (or jug), access to a water tap

Taps are often left to drip when they have not been turned off properly. Investigate the amount of water wasted by dripping taps.

1 a Turn on the tap so that it is dripping fairly fast.

b Start catching the drips in the measuring cylinder as you start the stopwatch.

c Time an interval of 30 seconds, or 1 minute (or longer if necessary), so that you have enough water in the measuring cylinder to accurately measure.

d Record the amount of water in the cylinder, and the time interval over which it was collected.

e Calculate how much water would be wasted over a period of 24 hours if the tap was left dripping at this rate.

2 Repeat this activity with the tap dripping at two other rates. One should be the slowest rate possible (you may need to increase the length of time you collect for).

3 If the population of New South Wales is approximately 7 million, estimate the number of households there would be in New South Wales, and hence estimate the amount of water (in ML) which would be wasted in a year if every household left one tap dripping constantly.

4 What are the implications of water wastage, and what measures can be taken to reduce wastage?

Exploring New Ideas

13.1 Volume of prisms

To calculate the volume of a prism we use the formula $V = Ah$ where V is the volume of the prism, A is the cross-sectional area of the prism and h is the perpendicular height. It is sometimes necessary to calculate the cross-sectional area first.

EXAMPLE

Find the volume of this trapezoidal prism, correct to 3 significant figures.

Solution

$$\text{Area} = \frac{h}{2}(a + b)$$

$$= \frac{4 \cdot 2}{2}(4 \cdot 9 + 7 \cdot 6)$$

$$= 26 \cdot 25 \text{ cm}^2$$

$$\begin{aligned}\text{Volume} &= Ah\\ &= 26 \cdot 25 \times 2 \cdot 1\\ &= 55 \cdot 125 \text{ cm}^3\end{aligned}$$

Volume = $55 \cdot 1$ cm^3 (to 3 sig. figs)

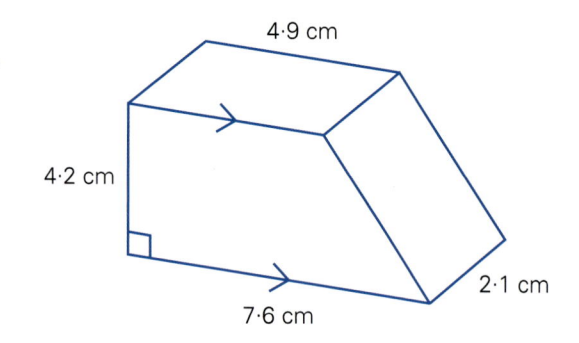

Beware! The h represents a different value in each formula.

EXERCISE 13A

Give all answers in this exercise to 3 significant figures unless otherwise stated.

1 a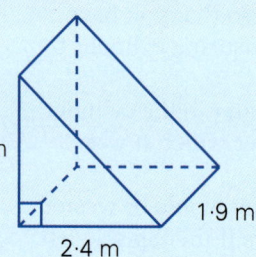

5 mm, 7 mm, 12 mm

b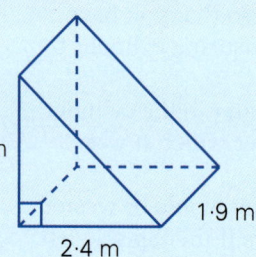

2.4 m, 1.9 m, 2.4 m

c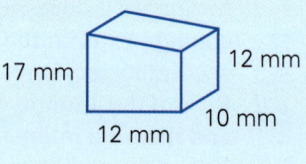

17 mm, 12 mm, 12 mm, 10 mm

d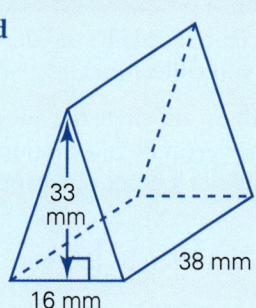

33 mm, 16 mm, 38 mm

e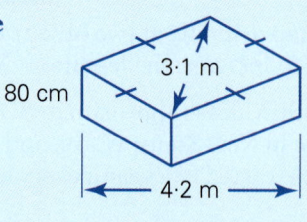

80 cm, 3.1 m, 4.2 m

f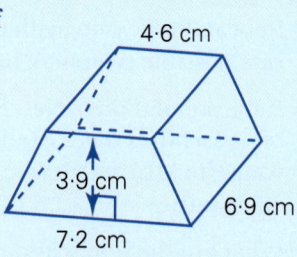

4.6 cm, 3.9 cm, 6.9 cm, 7.2 cm

2 A rectangular prism measures 6 cm by 17 cm by 23 cm. Find:

    a its volume in cubic centimetres

    b its capacity in litres.

3 A rectangular prism measures $3\frac{1}{2}$ m by 1·75 m by 2·4 m. Find:

   a its volume in cubic metres

   b its volume in litres.

4 Find the capacity of the following cylinders. Give your answer in the units stated, correct to 2 decimal places.

   a $r = 3·4$ cm, $h = 4·5$ cm. Answer in mL.

   b $d = 14$ m, $h = 2·4$ m. Answer in kL.

   c $r = 23$ cm, $h = 1·23$ m. Answer in L.

5 **a** Calculate the length market d in the diagram, correct to 2 decimal places.

   b Calculate the volume of the prism.

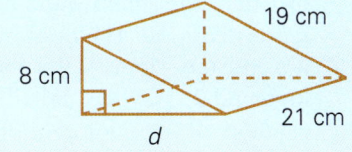

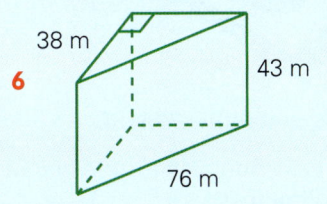

6 Calculate the volume of the prism to the nearest cubic metre.

Level 2

7 The volume of a cylinder is 45 mm³. If the end radius is 7·5 mm, what is the height of the cylinder?

8 A fish tank contains 26 L of water. If the dimensions of the base of the tank are 48 cm by 23 cm, what is the depth of the water to the nearest centimetre?

9 A new brand of orange juice is to be sold in a container that is in the shape of a cube. What size of cube would hold 1 L of orange juice?

10 Mr and Mrs Hinds are ordering pine bark for their garden. They estimated the area to be 86 m², and know that the bark should be spread to a depth of 5 cm. How many cubic metres of bark will they need?

11 A stadium is to be built in the shape of a rectangular prism. The floor dimensions are fixed at 95 m by 62 m. The building regulations state that there must be 3500 L of air space per person in buildings of this nature.

   a If the height of the building is 14 m, how many people can the building accommodate according to the regulations?

   b How high would the building need to be to accommodate 40 000 people? (Answer to the nearest cm.)

12 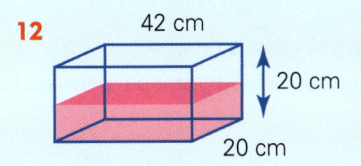 The coloured liquid in this sealed glass prism is 12 cm deep. How deep will the liquid be if the prism is stood on one of its square faces? (Answer to the nearest mm.)

13 A block of frozen pastry is in the shape of a rectangular prism measuring 32 cm by 8 cm by 6 cm. If the packet states that the pastry will cover an area of half a square metre, how thick would the pastry need to be rolled?

14 On the side of a 5 L tin of paint it states that the paint will cover an area of 23.5 m². How thick will the coat of paint be? (Answer in mm, to 1 decimal place.)

15

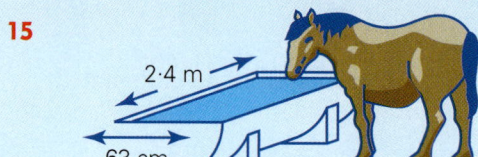

A trough with a semicircular cross-section has a width of 63 cm and a length of 2.4 m. How many litres of water does the trough hold when full?

16 A swimming pool is filled to a depth of 1 m at the shallow end and 2.1 m at the deep end. The floor of the pool is a constant slope. If the pool is 50 m long and 25 m wide, calculate the capacity of the pool in kilolitres, correct to 2 decimal places.

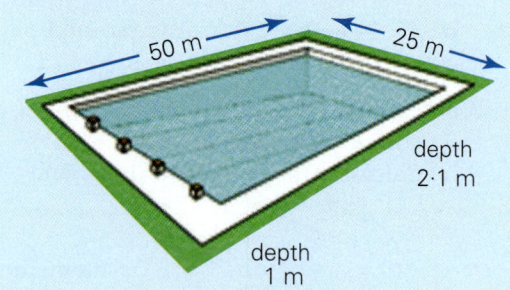

17 Mango Delight fruit drink is sold in cylindrical cans each containing 375 mL.

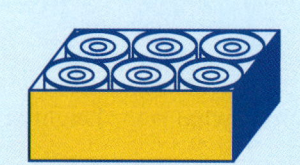

a If the diameter of each can is 65 mm, what is the height of the can to the nearest millimetre?

b Six cans of Mango Delight are to be packed into a box as shown. What are the dimensions of the box?

c What percentage of the space in the box is wasted? (Correct to 1 decimal place.)

18 An 8 cm cube of bronze is to be remodelled into a cylinder with a diameter of 10 cm. What will be the height of the cylinder? (To the nearest mm.)

Level 3

19 Blocks of butter measure 8 cm by 5 cm by 4 cm. They are to be packed into a box measuring 28 cm by 24 cm by 32 cm.

a What is the maximum number of blocks that can be packed into the box?

b Draw a diagram showing how the blocks should be arranged in the box to achieve this result.

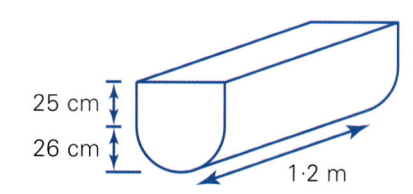

20 A and B are two cylinders of the same height. The diameter of cylinder A is twice that of cylinder B. What is the relationship of the *volume* of cylinder A to that of cylinder B?

13.2 Composite prisms

Some prisms have a cross-sectional area that is a combination of two or more simple shapes. To find the volume, this area is calculated first, then multiplied by the perpendicular height.

EXAMPLE

Calculate the capacity of this water trough in litres, correct to the nearest millilitre.

25 cm
26 cm
1.2 m

Solution

Area of cross-section = area of X + area of Y

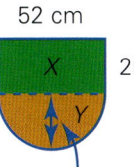 

52 cm

X 25 cm

Y

26 cm

$X = 52 \times 25$
$= 1300 \text{ cm}^2$

$Y = \frac{1}{2}\pi r^2$

$= \frac{1}{2} \times \pi \times 26^2$

$= 1061{\cdot}858\,317 \text{ cm}^2$

Area of cross-section $= 1300 + 1061{\cdot}858 \ldots$
$= 2361{\cdot}858 \ldots \text{ cm}^2$

> Keep full answer in calculator memory.

$V = Ah$
$= 2361{\cdot}858 \ldots \times 120$
$= 283\,422{\cdot}998 \text{ cm}^3$
$= 283{\cdot}422\,998 \text{ L}$
$= 283{\cdot}423 \text{ L (to the nearest mL)}$

> Convert 1·2 m to 120 cm.

EXERCISE 13B

1 Calculate the volume of the following prisms by first finding the cross-sectional area. (Answers to 1 decimal place.)

a
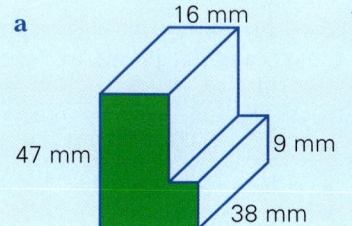
16 mm
47 mm
9 mm
38 mm
23 mm

b
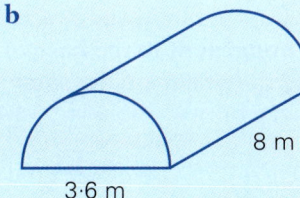
8 m
3·6 m

c
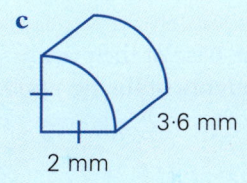
3·6 mm
2 mm

d
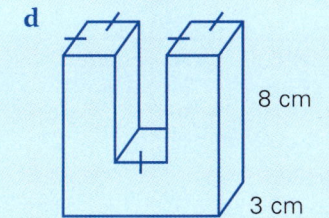
8 cm
3 cm

e
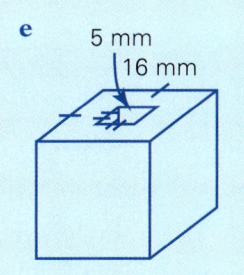
5 mm
16 mm

f
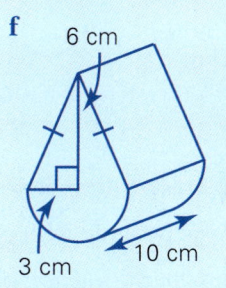
6 cm
3 cm
10 cm

Level 2

g
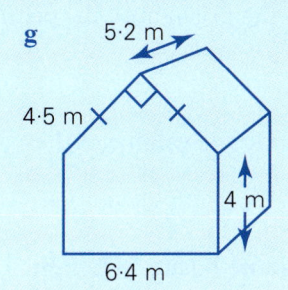
5·2 m
4·5 m
4 m
6·4 m

h
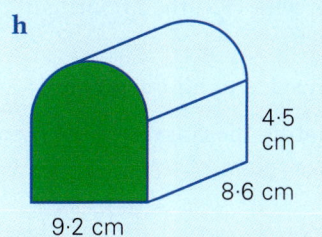
4·5 cm
8·6 cm
9·2 cm

i
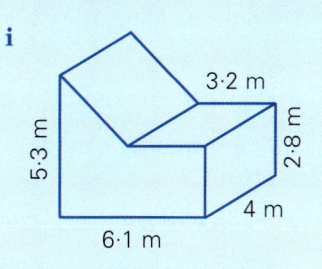
3·2 m
2·8 m
5·3 m
6·1 m
4 m

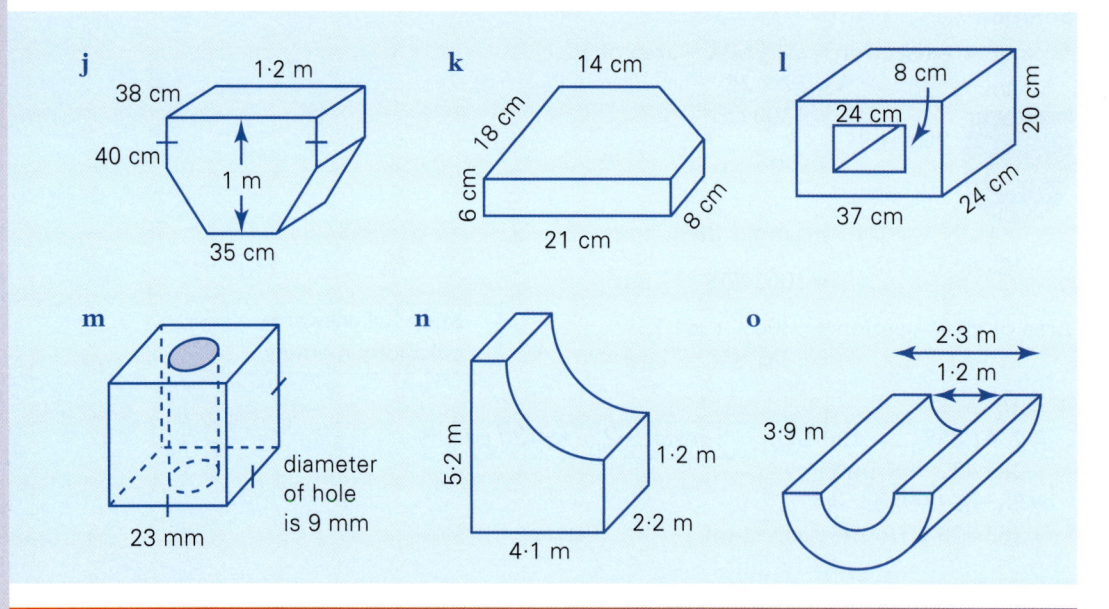

j · 38 cm · 40 cm · 1·2 m · 1 m · 35 cm

k · 14 cm · 18 cm · 6 cm · 21 cm · 8 cm

l · 8 cm · 24 cm · 37 cm · 20 cm · 24 cm

m · 23 mm · diameter of hole is 9 mm

n · 5·2 m · 1·2 m · 2·2 m · 4·1 m

o · 2·3 m · 1·2 m · 3·9 m

Investigation Pyramids and cones

You need: stiff card, scissors, sticky tape, compasses, protractor, and rice or sand

1 Accurately draw these nets for a pyramid and a rectangular prism onto card. Note that the base of the pyramid is **congruent** to the **base** of the rectangular prism, and the **heights** of the pyramid and the prism are the **same**.

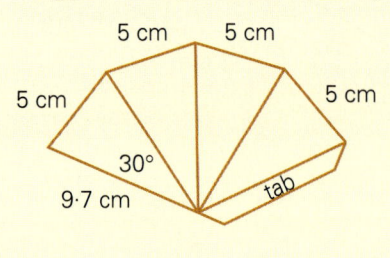

5 cm · 5 cm · 5 cm · 5 cm · 30° · 9·7 cm · tab

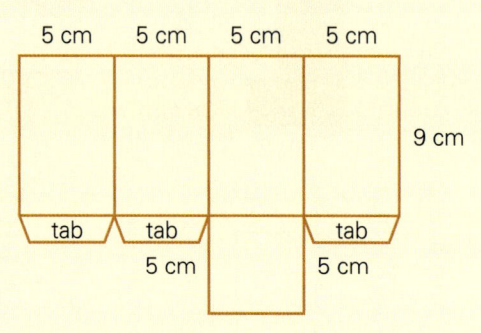

5 cm · 5 cm · 5 cm · 5 cm · 9 cm · tab · tab · tab · 5 cm · 5 cm

2 Construct both solids, ensuring that all edges are well sealed.

3 Fill the pyramid with rice. Pour the rice from the pyramid into the rectangular prism.

4 Estimate the *fraction* of the prism that is filled.

5 Continue filling the pyramid with rice, then pouring it into the prism until the prism is full.

6 How many pyramids were needed to fill the prism?

7 Complete this statement relating the volume of the pyramid to the volume of the prism:

Volume of the pyramid = ...

Note: This applies only if the pyramid and prism have the **same base** and **height**.

8 Use these nets for a cylinder and a cone to investigate the relationship between the volume of a cylinder and a cone that have the **same radius** and the **same height**. (Use the same method as shown for the pyramid and prism.)

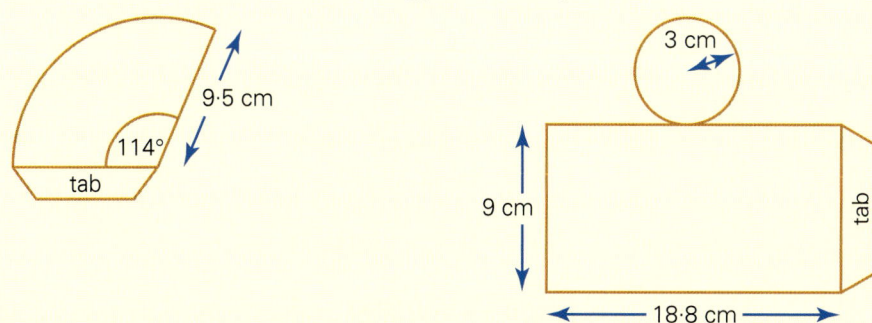

9 Write a statement that describes the relationship between the volume of a cone and a cylinder with the same radius and the same height.

13.3 Volume of pyramids

The previous investigation showed that the volume of a prism is three times the volume of a pyramid with the same base and height.

Also, the volume of a cylinder is three times the volume of a cone with the same radius and height.

> **Volume of a pyramid:** $V = \frac{1}{3}Ah$
>
> *A* is the area of the base.
> *h* is the perpendicular height.
>
>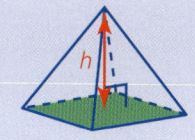
>
> The perpendicular height is also called the **altitude**.

EXAMPLE 1

Find the volume of this pyramid correct to 1 decimal place if $AB = 5 \cdot 5$ cm.

Solution

$$V = \frac{1}{3}Ah$$

$$A = 7 \times 6$$
Area $= 42$ cm²

$$V = \frac{1}{3} \times 42 \times 5 \cdot 5$$

Volume $= 77$ cm³

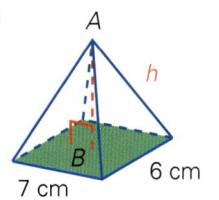

Work on developing a formula for the volume of pyramids was done in ancient China and Egypt.

EXAMPLE 2

This square pyramid has a height of 35·6 cm, and the perpendicular height of each triangular face is 46·7 cm.

a Find the dimensions of the base.
b Find the volume of the pyramid.

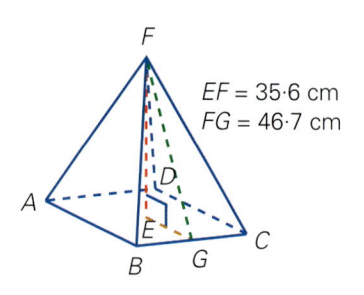

$EF = 35\cdot6$ cm
$FG = 46\cdot7$ cm

Solutions

a

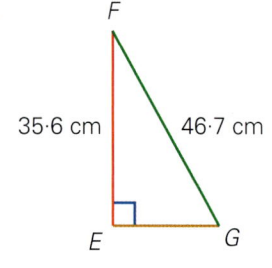

35·6 cm   46·7 cm

$$FG^2 = FE^2 + EG^2$$
$$46\cdot7^2 = 35\cdot6^2 + EG^2$$
$$EG^2 = 46\cdot7^2 - 35\cdot6^2$$
$$EG^2 = 913\cdot53$$
$$EG = 30\cdot224\,658\,81$$

$$\text{Base length} = 2 \times 30\cdot2246\ldots$$
$$= 60\cdot4 \text{ cm}$$

b $V = \frac{1}{3}Ah$

$$A = 60\cdot44932^2$$
$$= 3654\cdot12 \text{ cm}^2$$

$$V = \frac{1}{3} \times 3654\cdot12 \times 35\cdot6$$
$$= 43\,362\cdot224$$
$$= 43\,362\cdot2 \text{ cm}^3$$

> Keep full answer in calculator.

EXERCISE 13C

1 Find the volume of each pyramid, correct to 1 decimal place:

a

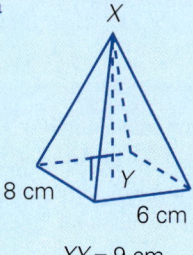

8 cm Y 6 cm

$XY = 9$ cm

b

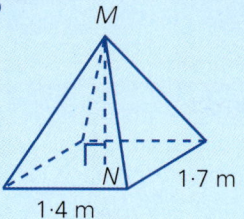

N 1·7 m   1·4 m

$MN = 1\cdot85$ cm

c

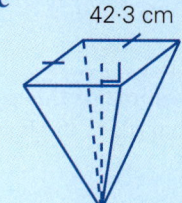

42·3 cm

Height = 39·6 cm

d

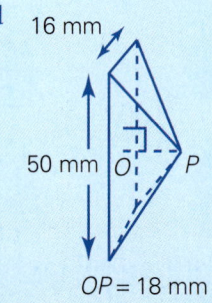

16 mm   50 mm O P

$OP = 18$ mm

e

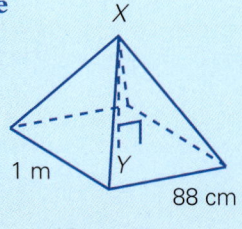

X 1 m Y 88 cm

$XY = 0\cdot95$ m

(Answer in cm³.)

f

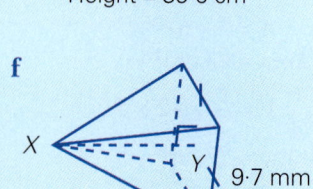

X Y 9·7 mm

$XY = 1\cdot6$ cm

(Answer in mm³.)

2 A rectangular pyramid has a base measuring 4·5 cm by 7·3 cm and a height of 5·9 cm. Calculate the volume of the pyramid, correct to 1 decimal place.

3 Calculate the volume, correct to 2 decimal places, of a square pyramid with a base edge of 12·53 m and a height of 7·22 m.

Level 2

4 A hexagonal pyramid has a base area of 46·7 cm^2. If the height of the pyramid is 3·9 cm, calculate the volume of the pyramid, correct to 1 decimal place.

5 A rectangular pyramid has a base of 120 cm by 1 m, and a height of 80 m. Calculate the volume of the pyramid in cubic metres, correct to 2 decimal places.

6 Find the volume of each pyramid, correct to 3 significant figures.

a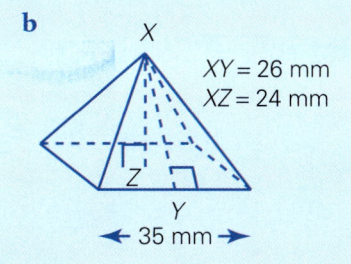

6 cm

6 cm

$PQ = 17$ cm

b

$XY = 26$ mm
$XZ = 24$ mm

35 mm

c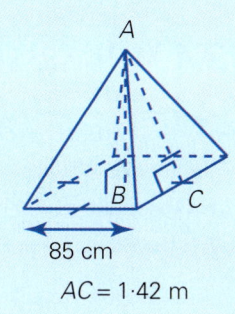

85 cm

$AC = 1·42$ m

(Answer in m^3.)

7 All the corners of a cube are joined to the *centre* of the cube as shown.

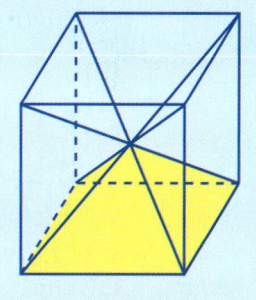

  a **i** How many identical pyramids are formed within the cube?

      ii What fraction of the volume of the cube is represented by the pyramid?

  b If each edge of the cube is 14 cm long, what is the volume of the cube?

  c Calculate the volume of the coloured pyramid, using your answers to **a** and **b**.

  d Calculate the volume of the coloured pyramid using the formula for the volume of a pyramid.

8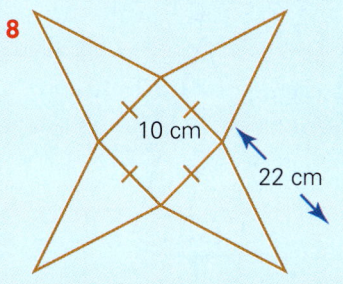

10 cm

22 cm

This diagram shows the net for a square pyramid.

  a Calculate the perpendicular height of the pyramid, correct to 1 decimal place.

  b Calculate the volume of the pyramid, correct to 1 decimal place.

9 A rectangular pyramid has a base measuring 23·5 cm by 14·7 cm. If the volume of the pyramid is 644·84 cm^3, what is the height of the pyramid?

10 A square pyramid has a volume of 9 m³. If the height of the pyramid is 2·6 m, find the side of the base, correct to 2 decimal places.

Level 3

11 A square pyramid has a 12 cm base and the **sloping edges** are each 20 cm long. Calculate the volume of the pyramid, correct to 1 decimal place.

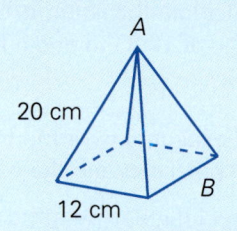

12 A square pyramid has a base area of 7·84 cm², and the area of each triangular face is 20 cm². Calculate the volume of the pyramid.

13.4 Volume of cones

> **Volume of a cone:** $V = \frac{1}{3}\pi r^2 h$
>
> r is the radius of the base.
>
> h is the perpendicular height.

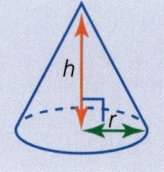

EXAMPLE 1

Find the volume of a cone with a base diameter of 15·6 mm and a height of 7·2 mm. Give your answer to the nearest cubic millimetre.

Solution

$$V = \frac{1}{3}\pi r^2 h$$

$$r = 7·8 \text{ mm}$$

$$V = \frac{1}{3} \times \pi \times 7·8^2 \times 7·2$$

$$= 458·722\ 792\ 9$$

Volume = 459 mm³

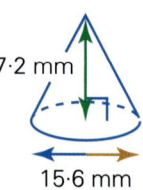

EXAMPLE 2

The slant height of a cone is 26 cm, and the radius of the base is 10 cm.

a Find the height of the cone.

b Find the volume of the cone, correct to 2 decimal places.

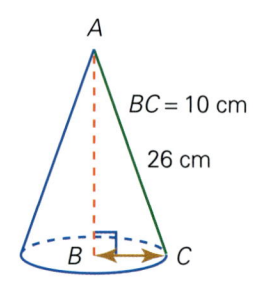

Solutions

a

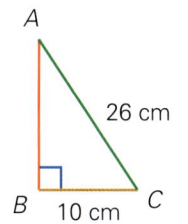

$AC^2 = AB^2 + BC^2$
$26^2 = AB^2 + 10^2$
$676 = AB^2 + 100$
$AB^2 = 576$
$AB = 24$

Height of cone = 24 cm

b

$$V = \tfrac{1}{2}\pi r^2 h$$

$$= \frac{1}{3} \times \pi \times 10^2 \times 24$$

$$= 2513{\cdot}274\ 123$$

$$= 2513{\cdot}27 \text{ cm}^3 \text{ (correct to 2 decimal places)}$$

EXERCISE 13D

1 Calculate the volume of the following cones, correct to 1 decimal place:

a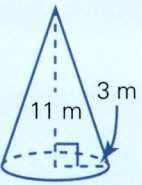

b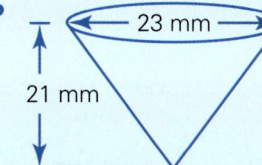

c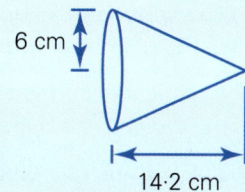

d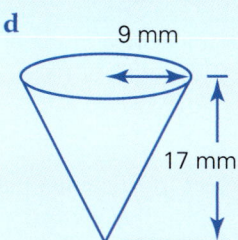

e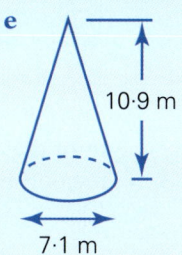

f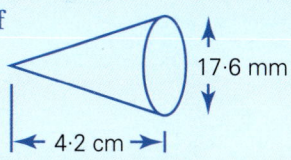

2 Calculate the volume of the following cones, correct to 1 decimal place:

a Radius = 5 cm, height = 7 cm.
b Diameter = 6·8 m, height = 7·33 m.
c Radius = 39·95 cm, height = $1\tfrac{1}{2}$ m (answer in cm³).
d Diameter = 2·3 cm, height = 8·4 mm (answer in cm³).

3 Calculate the volume of the following cones, correct to 1 decimal place:

a 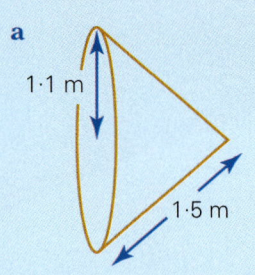 1·1 m, 1·5 m

b 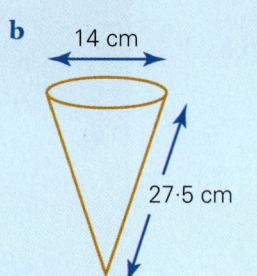 14 cm, 27·5 cm

c 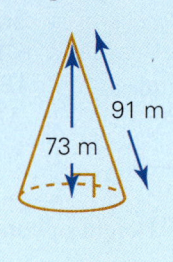 91 m, 73 m

Use Pythagoras's theorem to find ⌐ height.

4 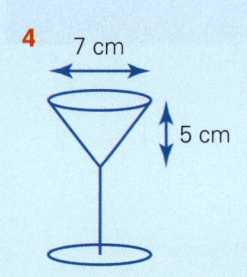 7 cm, 5 cm

How many millilitres does this cocktail glass hold?
(Assume that it is conical in shape.)

5 The volume of a cone with a radius of 1·27 m is 11·6 m³. Find the height of the cone to the nearest centimetre.

6 A conical drinking cup holds 1 L of water. If the height of the cup is 20 cm, calculate the *diameter* of the cup to the nearest millimetre.

7 The volume of a cone is 2350 m³. If the perpendicular height of the cone is 19 m, calculate the *circumference* of the base of the cone, correct to 1 decimal place.

8 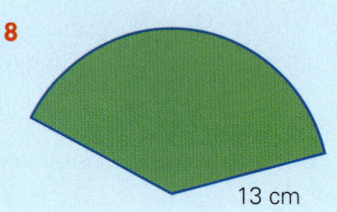 13 cm

A cone is made by cutting a sector from a circle of radius 13 cm. If the diameter of the cone is 10 cm, calculate:

a the height of the cone
b the volume of the cone, correct to 1 decimal place.

Level 2

9 A cone with a radius of 7 cm and a height of 12 cm is to be constructed from card. Calculate the radius of the sector, and the required sector angle.

10 A cone and cylinder have the same capacity and are the same height. What is the relationship of their radii?

11 a *Estimate* what percentage of this cone is filled with the liquid.
b *Calculate* the percentage of the cone that is filled. How close were you?
c How deep is the liquid if the cone contains half of its maximum capacity?

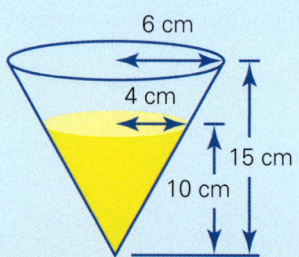 6 cm, 4 cm, 15 cm, 10 cm

12 A 200° sector is cut from a circle of card with a diameter of 14 cm. What is the volume of the open top cone formed from the sector?

13 The volume of this cone is given by $V = \frac{1}{3}\pi r^2 h$.

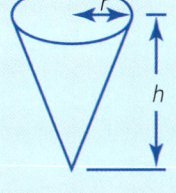

  a Another cone has the same radius but its height is twice that of the original. What is the ratio of the volume of the original cone to that of the new cone?

  b A third cone has the same height as the original cone but its radius is double that of the original. What is the ratio of the volume of this cone to that of the original?

13.5 Volume of a sphere

The formula for the volume of a sphere is difficult to prove or demonstrate.

> **Volume of a sphere:** $V = \frac{4}{3}\pi r^3$
>
> where r is the radius of the sphere.

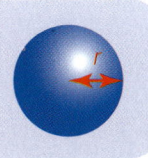

EXAMPLE
Find the volume of a tennis ball with a diameter of 6·5 cm. (Correct to the nearest cm³.)

Solution

$$V = \frac{4}{3}\pi r^3$$
$$r = 3\cdot25$$
$$v = \frac{4}{3} \times \pi \times 3\cdot25^3$$
$$= 143\cdot793\ 313\ 7$$
Volume = 144 cm³

EXERCISE 13E

Note: Assume all objects referred to in this exercise are *perfect spheres*, even though in reality they may not be.

  1 Find the volume, correct to 1 decimal place, of spheres with:

  a radius of 8 cm   **b** radius of $3\frac{1}{2}$ mm   **c** diameter of 17·5 m

  d diameter of 2·12 cm   **e** radius of $\frac{3}{4}$ m   **f** diameter of 34·9 mm

  2 Some liquid laundry detergents come with a plastic ball into which the detergent is poured before being placed in the washing machine. If the diameter of the ball is 60 mm, how many millilitres of detergent will it hold?

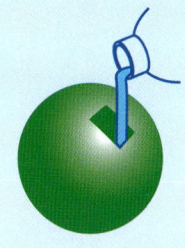

3 Calculate the volume in cubic centimetres of a sphere with a *circumference* of 1 m.

4 Calculate the volume of each of these **hemispheres**, correct to 1 decimal place.

a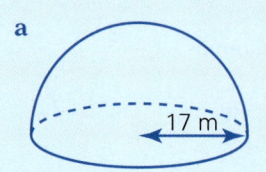

b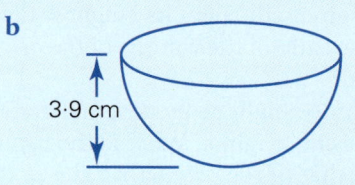

3·9 cm

c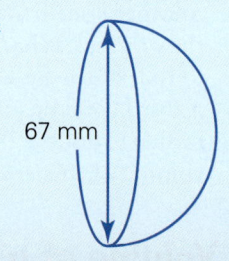

67 mm

5 The circumference of the earth at the equator is approximately 40 000 km. What is the volume of the earth? (Write the answer in standard form.)

6 A cubic box has a volume of 15 625 cm³.

  a Calculate the volume of the largest sphere that will fit into the box.

  b What percentage of the box does the sphere fill?

7 Marjory has a lump of modelling clay that is in the shape of a rectangular prism measuring 12 cm by 5 cm by 7 cm. If Marjory remodels the clay into a sphere, what will be the radius of the sphere?

8 Angus is blowing up balloons for a party. With one breath he can blow 650 cm³ of air into the balloon. How many breaths will it take to blow up the balloon to a diameter of 28 cm?

9 A chocolate orange is made from 20 identical chocolate segments stuck together to form a sphere. If 35 mL of chocolate are used to produce each segment, what is the diameter of the chocolate orange?

TEACHER

13.6 Volume of composite solids

Formulas for prisms, pyramids, cones and spheres can be combined to find the volume of other solids. Many everyday objects are composed of two or more of the basic solids for which the formulas are known.

It is sometimes the case that the objects are not exactly the same shape as the solids that have the known formulas. However, they are close enough for us to get a reasonable value for the volume.

EXAMPLE
Calculate the volume of this solid.

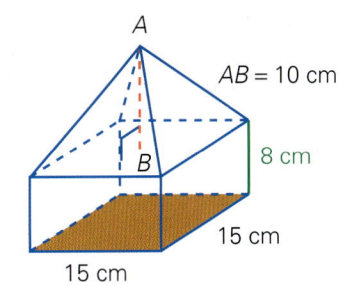

Solution

Square prism
$$V = lbh$$
$$V = 15 \times 15 \times 8$$
$$=$$

Square pyramid
$$V = \frac{1}{3}Ah$$
$$= \frac{1}{3} \times 15 \times 15 \times 10$$
$$= 750 \text{ cm}^3$$

Total volume $= 1800 \text{ cm}^3 + 750 \text{ cm}^3$
$$= 2550 \text{ cm}^3$$

EXERCISE 13F

1 Find the volume of the following solids, correct to 3 significant figures:

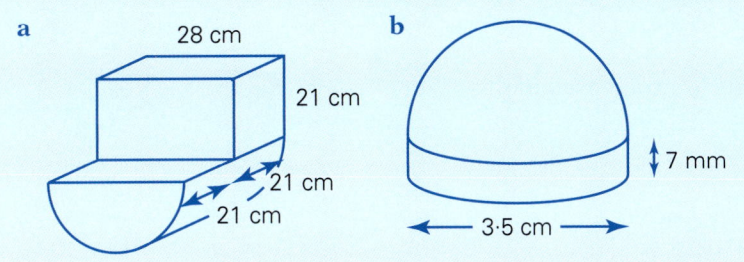

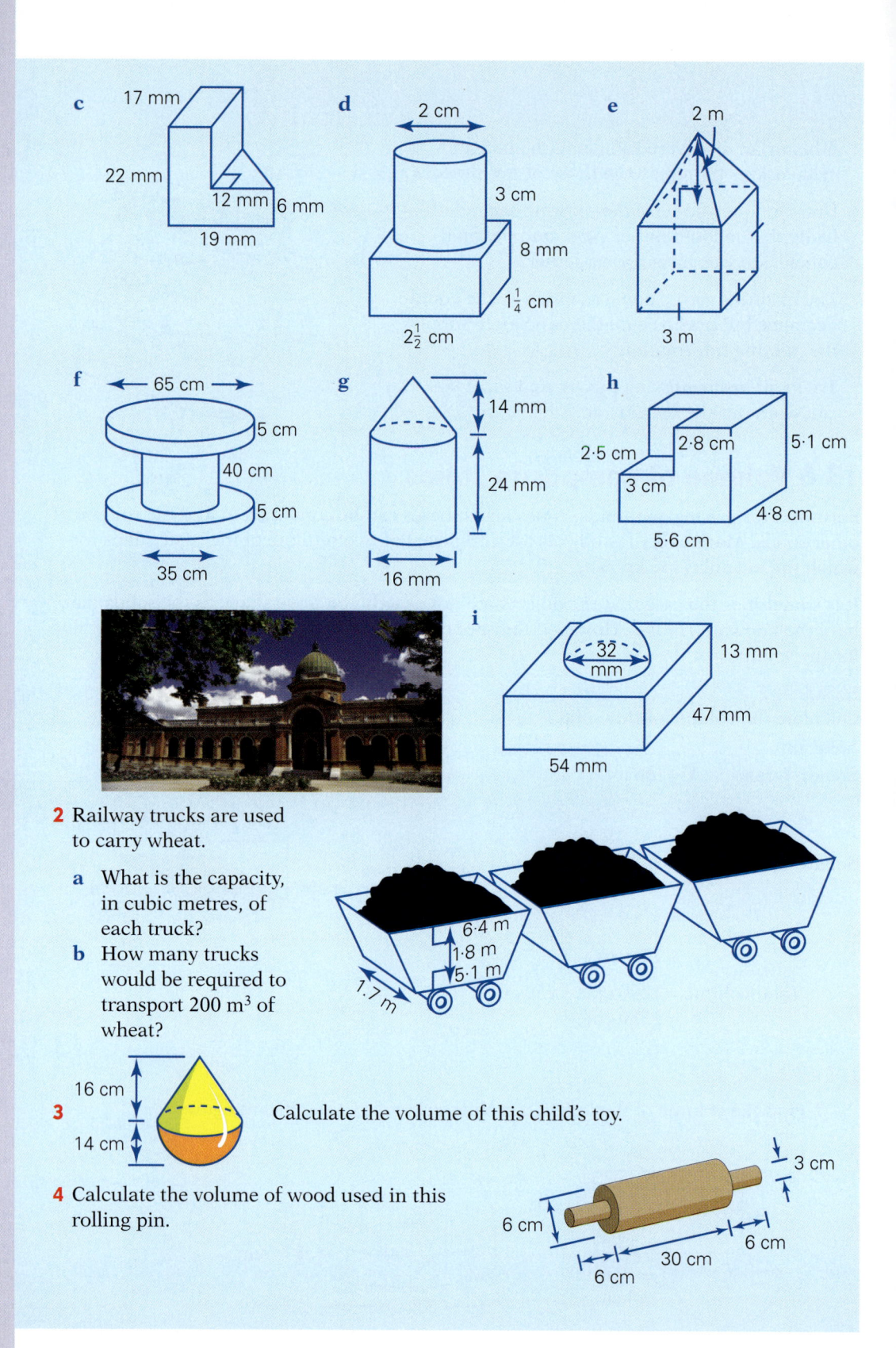

c 17 mm, 22 mm, 12 mm, 6 mm, 19 mm

d 2 cm, 3 cm, 8 mm, $1\frac{1}{4}$ cm, $2\frac{1}{2}$ cm

e 2 m, 3 m

f 65 cm, 5 cm, 40 cm, 5 cm, 35 cm

g 14 mm, 24 mm, 16 mm

h 2·5 cm, 2·8 cm, 5·1 cm, 3 cm, 4·8 cm, 5·6 cm

i 32 mm, 13 mm, 47 mm, 54 mm

2 Railway trucks are used to carry wheat.

a What is the capacity, in cubic metres, of each truck?

b How many trucks would be required to transport 200 m³ of wheat?

6·4 m, 1·8 m, 5·1 m, 1.7 m

3 Calculate the volume of this child's toy.

16 cm, 14 cm

4 Calculate the volume of wood used in this rolling pin.

3 cm, 6 cm, 30 cm, 6 cm, 6 cm

5 Calculate the volume of the solids, correct to 1 decimal place.

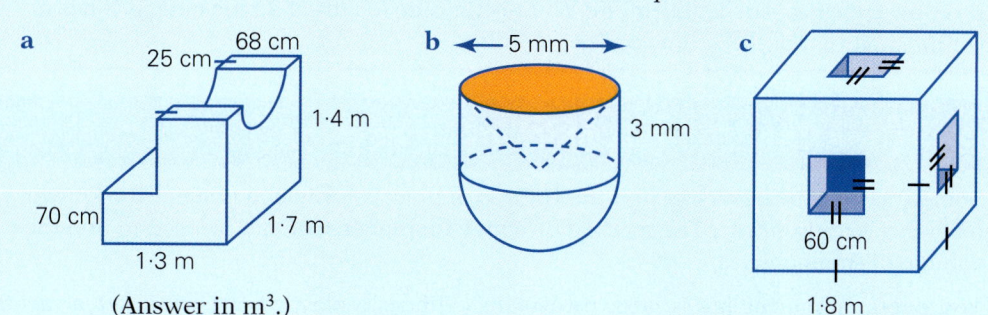

a 68 cm · 25 cm · 1·4 m · 70 cm · 1·7 m · 1·3 m (Answer in m³.)

b ← 5 mm → · 3 mm

c 60 cm · 1·8 m

6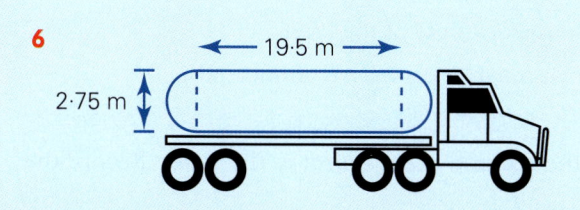

← 19·5 m → · 2·75 m

How many kilolitres of liquid nitrogen could this road tanker carry?

7 A patio sun-shade fits into a hemispherical base made out of plastic. The base may be filled with water to make the sun-shade more stable. The base has a cylindrical slot into which the sun-shade pole fits.
The radius of the base is 22 cm and diameter of the cylindrical slot is 45 mm.
How many litres of water does the base hold?

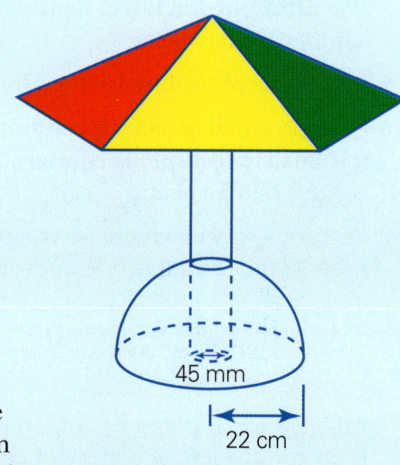

45 mm · 22 cm

8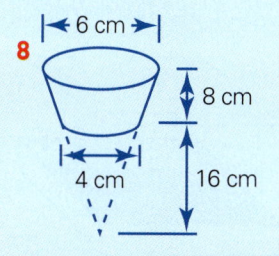

|← 6 cm →| · 8 cm · 4 cm · 16 cm

A paper cup has the shape of part of a cone, as shown in the diagram. Calculate the capacity of the cup.

9 Silicon sealer is sold in a cylindrical container with a cone-shaped nozzle.

a Calculate the volume of sealer in one tube.
b When the sealer is squeezed out it forms a very narrow 'cylinder' of diameter 8 mm. What length 'cylinder' of sealer would be squeezed out of one complete tube?

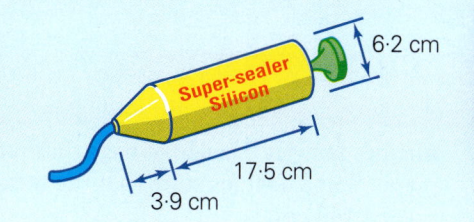

6·2 cm · Super-sealer Silicon · 17·5 cm · 3·9 cm

TEACHER

A yellow cube has side length x cm. What is the side length of a blue cube if it has a volume half that of the yellow cube?

Investigation Volume of irregular objects

Sometimes it is necessary to find the volume of objects for which none of the known formulas is appropriate. The method of **water displacement** can be used to find the volume of small objects.

You need: measuring jug or large measuring cylinder, a plastic bowl or bucket, a variety of *waterproof* objects small enough to fit into the jug or cylinder

1 About half-fill the jug with water, and make a note of the level.

2 Place one of the objects in the water (it must be *completely* immersed).

3 Note the new level of the water.

4 The **difference** in levels represents the **volume** of the object in the water. Record the volume of this object.

5 Repeat the procedure for the other objects, making a list of each object and its volume.

6 For very small objects, for example a 5¢ piece, the difference in water levels may be too small to measure accurately. Suggest a way to obtain a more accurate value for the volume of a 5¢ piece.

7 Suggest a way in which the volume of a non-waterproof object could be determined if none of the formulas was appropriate.

Investigation Making the most of a piece of card

1 An open-top box can be constructed by cutting squares from the corners of a piece of card.
What is the maximum volume for a box that is constructed from a piece of card measuring 21 cm by 29 cm?

A piece of A4 paper can be trimmed to the dimensions given, and then used to make boxes of various sizes.

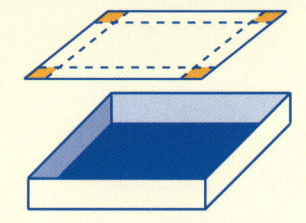

2 What would be the maximum volume for a *pyramid* cut from a piece of card with the same dimensions?

Don't worry about 'tabs' to stick it together.

Investigation Cabin baggage

Airlines restrict the size of bags that passengers can take with them into the cabin of the plane. Some airlines state that the total of length plus breadth plus height must not exceed 140 cm.

What would be the maximum volume of a bag that satisfied these requirements, assuming the bag is the shape of a rectangular prism?

Chapter Review

Language Links

capacity	dimension	length	prism
composite	fluid	litre	pyramid
cone	formula	measurement	Pythagoras
cross-section	hemisphere	mega	solid
cube	irregular	milli	sphere
cylinder	kilo	perpendicular	volume

Find a word from the list to suit each definition:

1 A solid with no plane faces.   **2** A unit that is equal to 100 cL.

3 A prefix meaning 'one thousandth'.   **4** The amount of fluid a container can hold.

4 Made from several simpler parts.

Write adjectives from these nouns:

6 cone   **7** sphere   **8** cube   **9** cylinder

Explain the meaning of these words:

10 hemisphere   **11** dimension   **12** cross-section

Chapter Review Exercises

1 A tank contains 650 L of water. Express this volume using *three* different units.

2 Seven people are sharing a 1·25 L bottle of soft drink. How many millilitres will each person get to drink? (To the nearest mL.)

3 Calculate the volume of these solids, correct to 1 decimal place:

a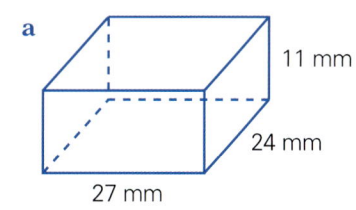
11 mm
24 mm
27 mm

b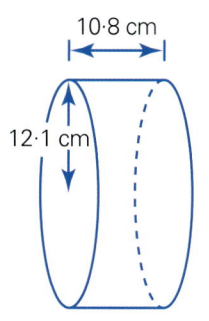
10·8 cm
12·1 cm

c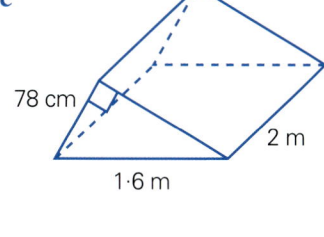
78 cm
2 m
1·6 m

4 A rectangular prism has a volume of 48 cm. What could be the dimensions of the prism?

5 A cylinder has a volume of 1 m³. If the length of the cylinder is 3·15 m, calculate the diameter of the cylinder to the nearest millimetre.

6 Find the volume of the following solids, correct to 2 decimal places:

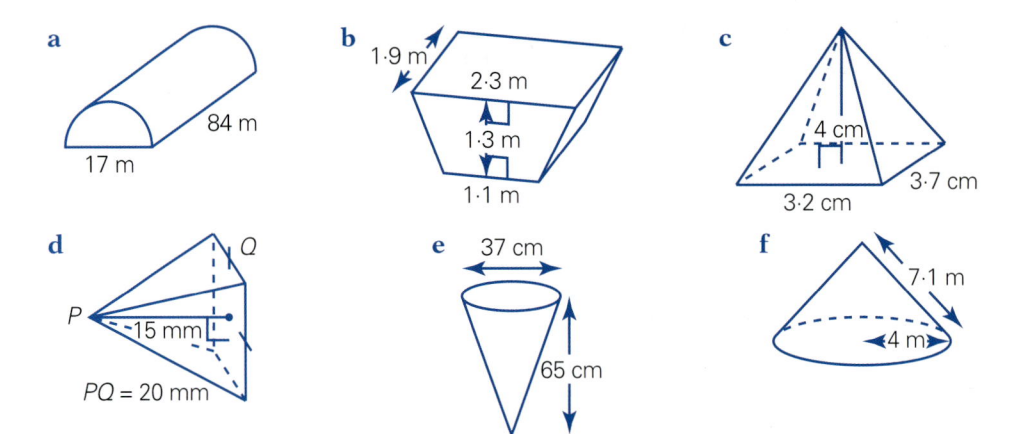

a 84 m, 17 m

b 1·9 m, 2·3 m, 1·3 m, 1·1 m

c 4 cm, 3·7 cm, 3·2 cm

d Q, P, 15 mm, PQ = 20 mm

e 37 cm, 65 cm

f 7·1 m, 4 m

13.3

7 A square pyramid has a volume of 43·9 cm³. If the height of the pyramid is 6·1 cm, find the dimensions of the base, correct to 3 significant figures.

13.6•

8 Calculate the volume of these solids, correct to 1 decimal place:

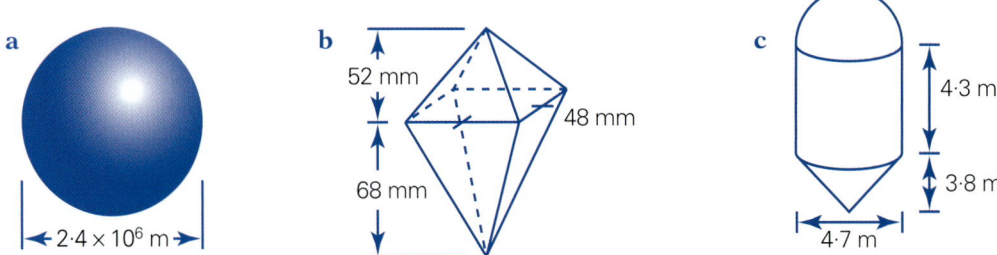

a $2·4 \times 10^6$ m

b 52 mm, 48 mm, 68 mm

c 4·3 m, 3·8 m, 4·7 m

9 A waste removal truck has the dimensions shown on the diagram.

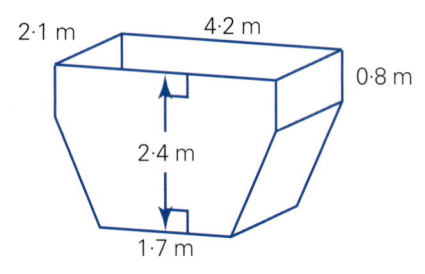

2·1 m, 4·2 m, 0·8 m, 2·4 m, 1·7 m

a What is the capacity of the truck if it is filled level with the top?

b How many trucks would be required to remove 100 m³ of rubble?

c How many cylinders each containing 75 L of soil could be emptied into each truck?

10 Claire has some marzipan that is in the shape of a cylinder. The diameter of the cylinder is 42 mm, and its length is 93 mm. The marzipan is to be rolled out to fit the top of a cake that is 20 cm in diameter. How thick should Claire roll the marzipan? (To the nearest mm.)

13.3

11 Each base edge of a square pyramid measures 8·3 cm. The sloping edges each measure 13·2 cm. Calculate the volume of the pyramid.

13.4

12 A cone is made from a sector as shown. If the radius of the cone is 6 cm and the height is 8 cm:

a what radius should the circle of paper be?

b what angle sector should be used to form the cone?

13.5

13 A spherical glass paperweight with a diameter of 52 mm is encased in a layer of polystyrene that is 45 mm thick. What volume of polystyrene is used in the casing?

TEACHER

Keeping Mathematically Fit

Part A—Non-calculator

1 $(\frac{1}{3})^{-4} =:$ **A** $\frac{1}{12}$ **B** $\frac{-1}{81}$ **C** 81   **D** 3

2 Does the point $(^-2, 5)$ lie on the line $y = 2 - 2x$?

3 A certain number is divided by 0·4, giving an answer of 18. What is the number?

4 Simplify $\frac{4x^2}{8xy}$.

5 How many square centimetres are there in 54 square metres?

6 A box contains only pink and white biscuits. Rachel knows there are 8 pink biscuits, and Matthew knows the probability of selecting a white biscuit is 0·6. How many biscuits are in the box altogether?

7 This graph shows the distance of a cyclist from home. When was the cyclist travelling the fastest?

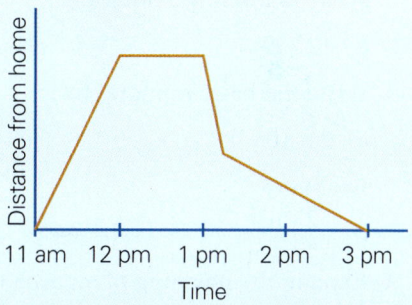

8 Simplify $\frac{3^4 \times 2^3}{6^2}$.

9 The diagram shows a rectangle and a semicircle. Find the value of x.

10 The mean of three numbers is 8, but when a fourth number is added the mean rises to 10. What is the fourth number?

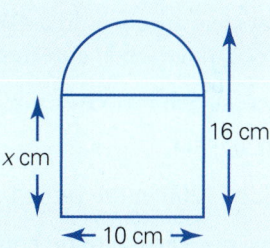

Part B—Calculator

1 A swimming pool in the shape of a rectangular prism is 8 m long and 3 m wide. If it contains 30 kL of water, what is the depth of the water?

2 The gradient of the line joining $(a, 4)$ and $(^-3, 7)$ is $^-2$. Find a.

3 On a musical scale, the frequencies of the notes doh, me, soh are in the ratio 4 : 5 : 6. If the frequency of doh is 256 hertz, find the frequencies of me and soh.

4 A lolly jar contains 3 orange, 4 lemon and 5 strawberry lollies. How many lollies would need to be taken out to be certain of getting at least 1 orange lolly?

5 A smaller rectangle has been removed from rectangle *PQRS*.

  a Calculate the shaded area in terms of x.
  b If the shaded area is equal to the area removed, form an equation and solve it to find x.

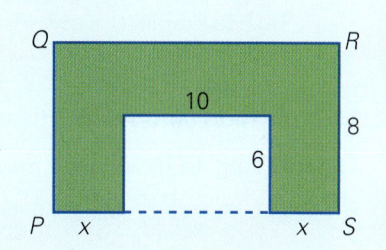

Cumulative Review 4

1 Expand and simplify where possible:

   a $5(t + 7) - 4(t + 3)$ **b** $(a + 3)(a + 5)$ **c** $(x + 4)(x + 4)$ **d** $(d - 2)(d - 9)$

2 Factorise fully:

   a $15xy^2 - 25y$ **b** $8m^2n^2 + 10mn$

3 A rounded number was given as 900. Give the range of possible values for the number if it had been rounded to the nearest:

   a 10   **b** 100

4 Write each of the following correct to 3 significant figures:

   a 3148   **b** 12 519   **c** 0·003 154 9   **d** $3·1983 \times 10^5$

5 Write in scientific notation:

   a 12 730   **b** 0·3   **c** 0·010 58

6 Write the basic numeral for:

   a 2×10^4 **b** $7·98 \times 10^{-1}$ **c** $5·002 \times 10^{-6}$

7 Evaluate:

   a $\left(\dfrac{2}{5}\right)^3$ **b** $64^{\frac{1}{2}}$ **c** $100^{-\frac{1}{2}}$ **d** $5 \times {}^-3^0$

8 Explain the meaning of an area recorded as 1·2 ha ± 0·05 ha.

9 What clearance would a 4WD that is 1·85 m high, with a storage rack 200 mm high on its roof, have when entering a garage with a door height of 213 cm?

10 Express each ratio in simplest form:

   a 0·36 : 5·4   **b** 600 g : 2 kg

11 Divide $7200 in the ratio 4 : 1 : 3.

12 If five postcards can be bought for $3·75, how much would 12 postcards cost?

13 Phuong has sketched a plan of her new bedroom, and marked on the measurements.

   a Select a suitable scale and drawn an accurate scale drawing of the room.

   b Arrange these pieces of furniture in the room:
       Bed: 2 m by 1 m
       Wardrobe: 1·4 m by 0·6 m
       Chest of drawers: 1 m by 0·5 m
       Bedside table: 0·5 m by 0·5 m

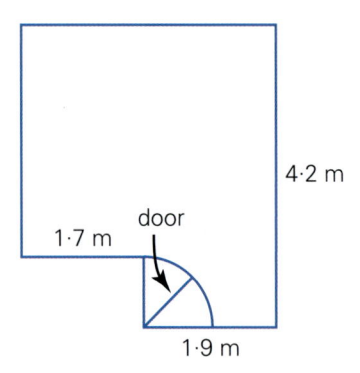

14 If the ratio t/u is greater than 1, which is larger, t or u?

15 How long, to the nearest minute, does it take to travel 345 km at 80 km/h?

16 A car uses petrol at a rate of 9 L per 100 km when travelling at a speed of 80 km/h. Calculate the rate of petrol consumption in litres per hour.

17 Find **i** perimeter and **ii** area of each figure:

a

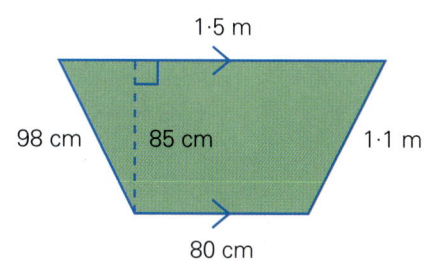

b

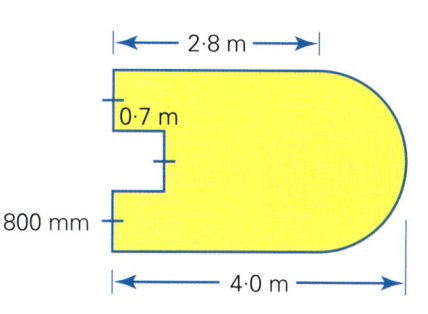

18 Solve the following equations:

a $\dfrac{5g-7}{3} = 4$

b $8(p-3) = {}^{-}10$

c $\dfrac{8}{x-3} = \dfrac{3}{x+1}$

19 Solve the following and graph the solutions on a number line:

a $-\dfrac{x}{5} < 0{\cdot}4$

b $1 > 16 + 3p$

20 Rearrange to make the letter printed in colour the subject of each formula:

a $m = \dfrac{r}{3h}$

b $y = x(4 - f) + t$

21 The length of a rectangle is 5 cm greater than the width. If the perimeter of the rectangle is 74 cm, find its area.

22 Find the value of the pronumerals in each of these diagrams, giving reasons for your answers:

a

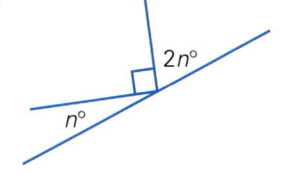

b

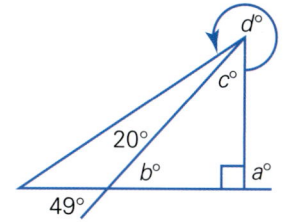

c

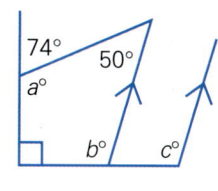

d

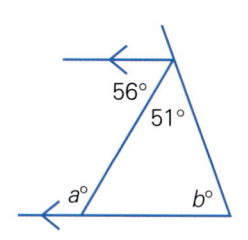

e

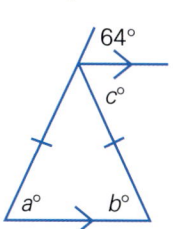

f

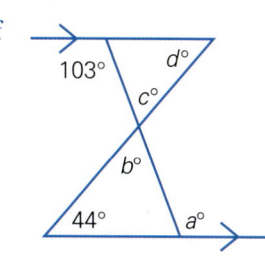

23 Which person is represented by the coloured dot:

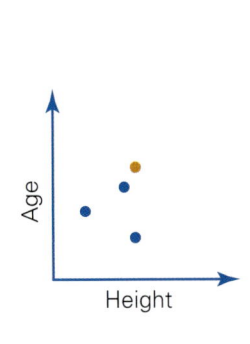 

16 yrs 15 yrs 14 yrs 17 yrs

24 The following table shows the unit costs of plants bought in various quantities by a nursery:

Quantity	Unit cost ($)
1–9	4·00
10–49	3·80
50–99	3·60
100 and over	3·40

a Construct a graph to show this information.

b What is the unit cost if 23 plants are bought?

c What is the *total* cost of:

   i 25 plants?   **ii** 75 plants?

25 Find x, correct to 1 decimal place.

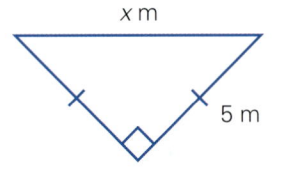

26 Is this triangle right-angled? Explain your answer.

24 cm, 26 cm, 10 cm

27 Find x to the nearest degree if:

  a $\cos x = 0\cdot4$ **b** $\sin x = 0\cdot761$ **c** $\tan x = 1\cdot55$

28 Find the value of each pronumeral, correct to 2 decimal places:

a 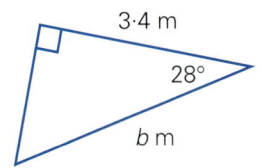   **b** 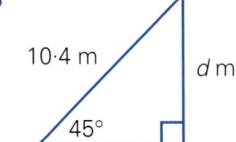   **c**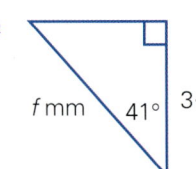

29 Find the value of θ to the nearest degree:

a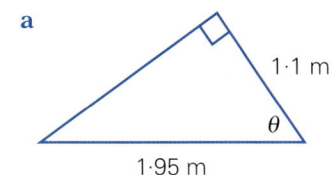

b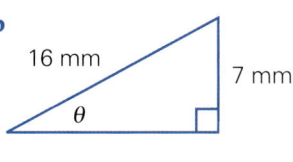

c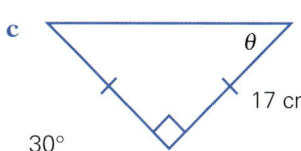

30 Calculate the length marked d in this diagram.

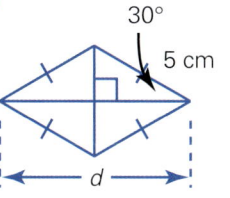

31 A boat sails from port on a bearing of 024° for a distance of 250 km. How far north of the port is the boat now?

32 ABC is an isosceles triangle with $AB = BC = 10$ cm and $AC = 6$ cm. Calculate $\angle ABC$ to the nearest degree.

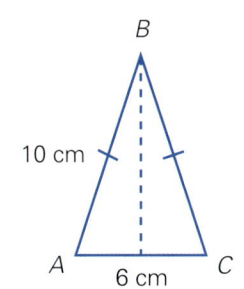

33 A regular pentagon is drawn inside a circle of radius 7 cm. Calculate the side length of the pentagon.

34 The diagonals of a rhombus are 20 cm and 17 cm long. Find:

   a each of the angles of the rhombus   **b** the side length of the rhombus

35 Refer to the diagram to answer these questions.

   a Find these distances:
      i AC **ii** CD **iii** BE

   b Find the mid-point of each interval:
      i EF **ii** CF **iii** DE

   c Find these gradients:
      i CD **ii** DB **iii** AB
      iv EF **v** BF **vi** CE

   d Name a line that is parallel to DB, stating your reason.

   e What angle does the line EA make with the positive direction of the x-axis (to the nearest degree)?

   f What is the gradient of a line that makes an angle of 30° with the positive direction of the x-axis (to 1 decimal place)?

36 $M(^-2, 7)$ is the mid-point of interval AB. If A is the point $(^-8, 10)$, find the coordinates of B.

37 A line has a y-intercept of $^-2$ and is parallel to the line $3x - y + 6 = 0$. Give the equation of the line:

   a in gradient–intercept form   **b** in general form

38 Give as much information as possible about intervals PQ and RS, given the points $P(^-5, ^-5)$, $Q(1, 7)$, $R(^-3, 4)$ and $S(3, 1)$.

39 Find the diameter of a circle with centre $(^-2, 5)$ if the circle passes through the point $(1, 3)$.

40 Find the values of d and e if $(d, 4)$ is the mid-point of $(^-4, e)$ and $(1, 12)$.

41 If the gradient of a line is $^-2$ and the line passes through $(^-3, 3)$ and $(5, a)$, find a.

42 If $\triangle TAB \equiv \triangle PSR$, copy and complete the following:

  a $TB = ...$ **b** $\angle ATB = ...$
  c $... = SP$ **d** $\angle... = \angle PRS$

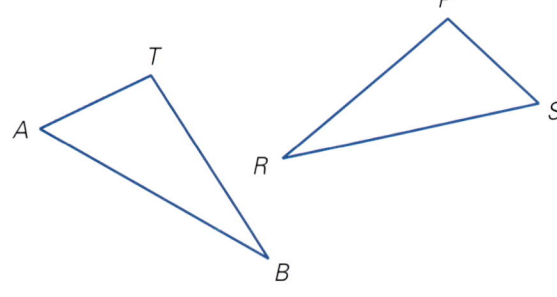

43 State whether or not the triangles in the figures below are definitely congruent. If they are, **i** write a congruence statement, **ii** give a reason for congruency.

  a 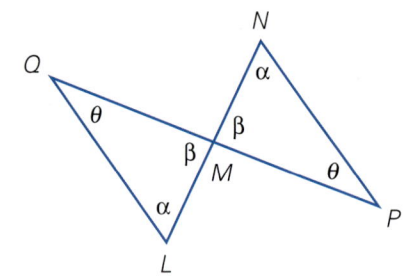   **b**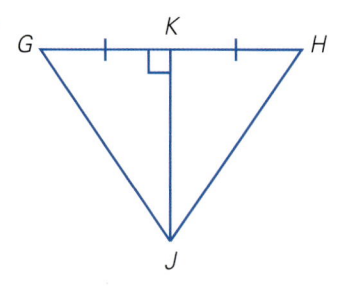

44 Prove that the triangles are congruent. Give a reason for each line of your proof.

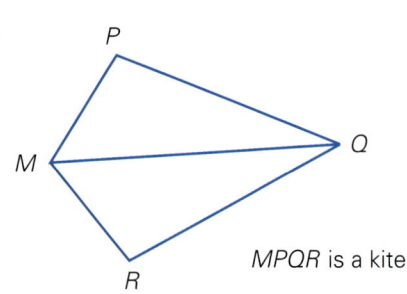

$MPQR$ is a kite

45 Brett is paid \$384·70 for a regular 38-hour week, and time-and-a-half for overtime. For Sundays or public holidays, he gets double time. What is his gross wage for a week in which he works 45 hours, 3 of which were on Anzac Day?

46 A new-car salesperson receives a retainer of \$275 per week plus 6% of the dealership's *profit* on each car she sells. She is guaranteed a minimum commission of \$50 if the profit on any deal is less than \$834. If the dealer's cost price on the particular line of vehicles she sells is \$23 468, find her gross pay for a week in which she negotiates the following selling prices: \$24 897, \$23 765, \$24 400, \$25 218.

47 Reuben bought a stereo priced at \$460 by paying 15% deposit and the balance over 15 months at a simple interest rate of 17% p.a. Find:

a the deposit
b the balance owing
c the total interest charged
d the amount of each equal monthly repayment.

48 Clarissa borrowed $14 680 from ABC Finance at $16\frac{3}{4}\%$ p.a. simple interest over 42 months.

a Find the interest charged.
b Calculate the equal monthly repayments.

49 Compare the interest earned on an investment of $5000 over 18 months at 8·2% p.a. if the interest:

a is simple interest **b** is compounded half-yearly

Write just the letter corresponding to the correct alternative for questions **51** and **52**.

50 $(2y - 3)^2$ is equal to:

A $4y^2 - 9$ **B** $4y^2 + 12y + 9$ **C** $4y^2 - 6y + 9$ **D** $4y^2 - 12y + 9$

51 $1 + \dfrac{3}{x}$ as a single fraction is:

A $\dfrac{1+3}{x}$ **B** $\dfrac{4x}{x}$ **C** $\dfrac{3+x}{x}$ **D** $x + 3$ **E** $\dfrac{13}{x}$

52 Expand the following:

a $(3 - c)^2$ **b** $(5 - 2d)(5 + 2d)$ **c** $(3 + 4t)^2$ **d** $(3n - 2)(4 - 5n)$

53 Factorise:

a $4n^2 - c^2$ **b** $3c^2 - 12c$ **c** $n^2 + 7n + 12$ **d** $x^2 - 2x - 8$
e $6 + 10p + 4p^2$ **f** $a^2 + 8ab + 16b^2$ **g** $nt + ns + pt + ps$

54 Simplify the following expressions:

a $\dfrac{8x - 4}{16}$ **b** $\dfrac{x^2 + 7x - 18}{x^2 - 4}$ **c** $\dfrac{ab}{a(x + y)}$ **d** $\dfrac{x^2}{2xy}$

e $\dfrac{t(t - 4)}{5t - 20}$ **f** $\dfrac{6x + 10}{8x^2} \times \dfrac{4x}{3x + 5}$ **g** $\dfrac{3x}{(x + 2)^2} \div \dfrac{x}{x^2 - 4}$ **h** $\dfrac{1}{8p + 12} + \dfrac{p}{2p + 3}$

55 The following marks are the percentages gained by 9M in a history test:

45	67	39	75	81	82	42	55	61	70
68	54	43	51	86	47	60	53	70	78
51	46	55	40	76	73	66	59	63	71

a Display the data on a stem-and-leaf plot.
b What is the median mark?
c Show the data on a dot plot.
d Write a sentence describing the distribution of the marks.

56 What is the median of these numbers: 10, 5, 5, 3, 7, 10, 11, 6, 6, 4, 5, 4?

A 5 **B** 5·5 **C** 6·3 **D** 10·5

57 The following data represent the ages in months of toddlers at a kindergarten:

0	8 9
1	0 5 7 7 8
2	1 1 3 5 5 6 9
3	0 3 4 4 5 7
4	2 5 6

  a How old, in years and months, is the eldest child?
  b What is the median age of the children?
  c Find the lower and upper quartiles and the interquartile range for these data.
  d Draw a box-and-whisker plot to display the data.

58 The following data show the marks out of 50 obtained by applicants for a job on a personal qualities profile test:

17	9	21	40	12	33	38	29	14	46
43	48	19	45	39	43	21	37	20	36
22	30	21	31	22	35	23	37	23	27

a Organise the data into a grouped frequency distribution table, using a class interval of 10 (starting from zero), and construct a histogram to show the results.
b Find the modal class.
c Estimate the mean.
d What mark must be scored by an applicant to obtain a second interview with that firm, if only the top 50% are accepted?

59 The weekly spending of a sample of 80 teenagers attending high school has been classified in this grouped frequency table.

a Develop the table with further columns for class centre, fx, and cumulative frequency.
b Draw the ogive.
c From the ogive, find the median class.
d Estimate the mean.
e What minimum amount is spent by those in the top half of spenders?

Amount spent ($)	Frequency
1–3	1
4–6	4
7–9	7
10–12	10
13–15	12
16–18	17
19–21	8
22–24	14
25–27	2
28–30	5

60 Calculate the volume of each of these solids correct to 1 decimal place. Show all working.

a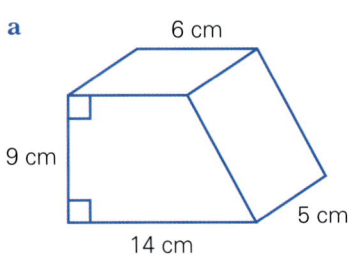

b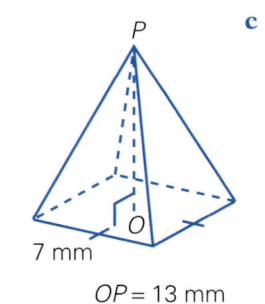

$OP = 13$ mm

c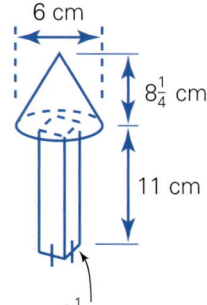

d

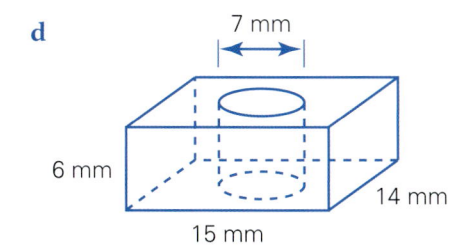

7 mm

6 mm

15 mm

14 mm

61 a 'Tee-whiz' golf balls are sold in threes, packed tightly into a square prism box. If the diamaeter of each ball is 4 cm, find:
  i the dimensions of the box
  ii the combined volume of the three balls
  iii the amount of wasted space in the box.

b Show that less space is wasted if the three golf balls are packed in a cylindrical container.

62 A plastic cube has a capacity of 2 L. What is the side length of the cube?

Glossary

A

Accuracy. How close an answer or measurement is to its true value.

Acute. An angle measuring less than a right angle.

Adjacent. Next to: adjacent sides meet at a common vertex; adjacent angles have a common vertex and arm.

Algebra. The relationship between pronumerals and numbers.

Alternate. The angles formed between two lines on the opposite sides of the transversal.

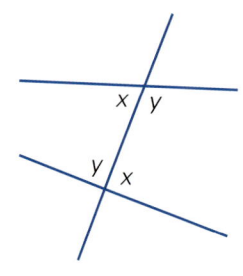

If the lines are parallel then the two pairs of alternate angles formed are equal.

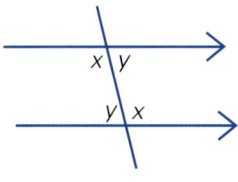

Altitude. The perpendicular distance from the vertex to the side opposite the vertex.

Angle. An angle measures the amount of turning. An angle is formed when straight intervals meet at a point.

Annual. Occurring once every year, or relating to a period of one year.

Approximation. A number that is not exact but has been rounded.

Area. The measure of the amount of space contained inside a closed two dimensional shape. Area is measured in square units.

Average. Same as mean – the number obtained by taking the total of a set of numbers and dividing it by the number of numbers in the set.

One measure of the central tendencies of a group of numbers; in other words it describes the middle.

Axis (axes). The two intersecting lines – called the x-axis and the y-axis – on a number plane. (Single form: axis; plural form: axes.)

B

Backtrack. To reverse the order of operations performed.

Balance. The amount of money you have in a bank account, or the amount of something that you have left after you have spent or used up the rest.

Base. The factor that repeats when using index notation. In 5^3 the base is 5, as $5^3 = 5 \times 5 \times 5$.

The line or surface on which a shape stands.

Bearing. An exact position.

Bias. When the data collected in a sample is not large enough or collected in such a way as to be representative of the population.

Binomial. An expression that is a sum or difference of two terms, as $3x + 2y$ and $x^2 - 4x$.

Bisect. To cut in half.

Bonus. An extra amount of money which is given to you as a present or reward in addition to the money you were expecting.

Borrow. To get or receive (something) from someone with the intention of giving it back after a period of time.

C

Cancel. To remove.

Capacity. The number of cubic units a container or solid shape can hold.

Casual. Not regular or fixed; temporary.

Census. When the entire population is surveyed.

Centre. The middle point – the point within a circle or sphere equally distant from all points of the circumference or surface, or the point within a regular polygon equally distant from the vertices.

Circle. A set of all points in a plane that are the same distance from a fixed point, known as the centre.

Circular. To be in the shape of a circle.

Circumference. The distance around a circle – its perimeter.

Class. Statistical data is often divided into groups or classes.

Coefficient. The numerical factor in an algebraic term. The coefficient of $5m$ is 5.

Co-interior. The angles formed between two lines on the same side of the transversal.

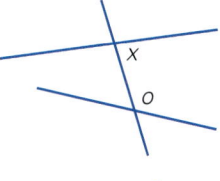

If the lines are parallel then the co-interior angles are supplementary.

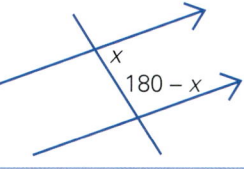

Column. A vertical line of elements. A column graph is a graph that uses columns to represent the frequency of discrete or categorical data.

Commission. Payment to someone who sells goods which is directly related to the amount of goods sold.

Common. Something that two items share. A common factor is a factor of more than one number.

Compass. An instrument used to draw circles.

Complementary. Complementary angles are two angles that add to 90 degrees.

Composite. A composite number is a number that has more than two factors. It is not a prime number.

Composite shapes are made up of more than one plane shape.

Compound. Refers to a system of paying interest in which interest is paid both on the original amount of money invested or borrowed and on any interest which that original amount has collected over a period of time.

Concentric. Circles that have the same centre but different radii.

Cone. A solid figure with a curved surface and a circular base.

Congruent. Congruent shapes are identical but in different locations.

Constant. To remain unchanged. The constant term in an algebraic expression is the term without any pronumeral factors.

Construction. Using geometrical instruments to construct or add something to a diagram.

Continuous. Without a break. Continuous data is data where all values are possible.

Conversion. To convert or change between forms.

Coordinates. An ordered pair of numbers representing the position of a point on the number plane.

Corresponding. In the same or matching positions.

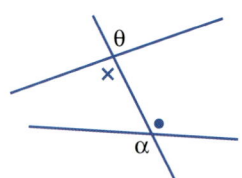

If the corresponding angles are in matching positions and the lines are parallel then the corresponding angles are equal.

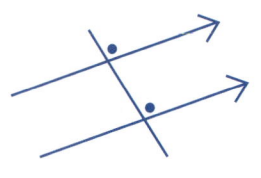

Cosine. The cosine of an angle is the ratio that compares the length of the adjacent side with the length of the hypotenuse in a right angle triangle. Cosine $= \dfrac{\text{adjacent}}{\text{hypotenuse}}$

Cost. The amount of money needed to buy, do or make something.

Credit. A method of paying for goods or services at a later time, usually paying interest as well as the original money.

Cross-section. The sections of a shape that are made perpendicular to the axis of the solid. They are parallel to the base of the solid.

Cube. A number with three identical factors. 27 is a cubic number as $3 \times 3 \times 3 = 3^3 = 27$. Cubic units are the units used when measuring volume.
A solid shape with 6 identical square faces.

Cumulative. To add as you proceed through the frequencies in a statistical table.

Cylinder. A solid with a uniform circular cross section.

D

Data. The information that has been collected.

Deductions. To take away (an amount or part) from a total.

Degree. The unit used to measure angles.

Denominator. The bottom of a fraction.

Dependent. A dependent variable is where the variable depends upon the value of one or more other variables.

Deposit. To put (something valuable, especially money) in a bank or safe; or, a sum of money you leave as part of a total payment for something.

Depression. (Also called the angle of depression.) The angle between the line from an observer or instrument to an object below either of them and a horizontal line.

Diagonals. A line joining two non-adjacent vertices of a polygon.

Diameter. A line passing through the centre of the circle. A diameter is equal to 2 radii.

Dimension. A property that refers to length, area and volume. A line has length only, so it is said to be one-dimensional; a shape with area but not volume is two-dimensional; and a shape with volume is three-dimensional.

Discrete. Discrete data is numerical data where in-between values are not possible.

Discount. A reduction in the usual price.

Distance. Length – how far apart two things are.

Distribution. In statistics, an arrangement of a set of scores.

Dot plot. A statistical graph where each score is plotted as a dot against a horizontal scale.

E

Earnings. The amount of money you are paid for the work you do.

Elevation. (Also called angle of elevation.) The angle between the line from an observer or instrument to an object above the observer or instrument and a horizontal line.

Equation. When two expressions are equal to each other, such as $2x - 9 = 8$.

Equilateral. When all sides of a triangle are equal the triangle is called equilateral.

Equivalent. Of the same value or measure. Equivalent fractions have the same decimal value.

Estimate. To make a sensible guess as to the value of something.

Evaluate. To find an answer, to work out the value of.

Expand. To make bigger, to remove brackets.

Exponent. Another word for the index. In 10^3 the exponent is 3.

Expression. A very general term used to describe or write any mathematical terms.

Exterior. On the outside. When one side of a polygon is extended it produces an angle outside the original shape.

F

Factorise. To write an expression as a product of its factors.

To insert brackets by writing the HCF out the front.

Fluid. Changing readily; shifting; not fixed, stable, or rigid.

Formula. A rule that has been written as an equation.

Fortnight. A period of two weeks.

Fraction. A numeral that represents a rational number. Fractions are formed when whole amounts are broken into equal parts.

Frequency. The number of times something has occurred.

Function. A rule that generates for each value in a set a unique value in another set.

G

Geometric. A type of pattern where one term is found by multiplying the preceding term by a number.

Gradient. The steepness of a line or interval.

Graph. A drawing that shows the relation between sets of numbers or items.

Gross. A person's gross income is the money they earn before tax is deducted from it.

Groups. Data that is put into classes.

H

Height. The altitude of a shape. The perpendicular distance from the vertex to the side opposite the vertex.

Hemisphere. Half of a sphere.

Hexagon. A polygon with 6 sides.

Histogram. A statistical column graph.

Horizontal. A line parallel, or level, with the horizon – a line with no gradient or slope.

Hypotenuse. The longest side in a right angle triangle, opposite the right angle.

I

Income. Money that is earned from doing work, or received from investments.

Increase. To become or make larger in amount or size.

Index. A short way of writing multiplication of the same factor is to express in index form. For $7^2 = 7 \times 7$ the 7 is the base and the 2 is the index or exponent. The index tells us how many times the factor has been repeated in the multiplication.

Inequality. A sentence involving greater than ($>$), greater than or equal to ($\geqslant$), less than ($<$), less than or equal to ($\leqslant$) signs.

Inequation. A statement that one quantity or expression is greater than or less than another.

Instalment. One of a number of parts into which money owed has been divided, so that each part is paid at different times until the total is reached.

Integer. A whole number ... $^{-}3, ^{-}2, ^{-}1, 0, 1, 2, 3 ...$

Intercept. To cross. The x-intercept is the point where a line crosses the x axis. The y-intercept is the point where a line crosses the y axis.

Interest. Money which is charged by a financial organisation such as a bank to people who have borrowed from it, or the profit which is made on the money invested with a financial organisation.

Interval. A section of a line. An interval is named according to its end points.

Inverse. The inverse of an operation 'undoes' the operation. The inverse operation to addition is subtraction.

Invest. To put money into something to make a profit.

Irregular. Without symmetry, even shape or formal arrangement.

Isolate. To have on its own.

Isometric. All sides being of equal measure.

Isosceles. A triangle with 2 equal sides is called an isosceles triangle.

K

Kilo. Prefix meaning one thousand. 1 kilogram = 1000 grams; 1 kilometre = 1000 metres.

Kite. A quadrilateral formed by joining two isosceles triangles. Pairs of adjacent sides are equal.

L

Label. A word or phrase indicating what quantity is represented by the scale on the axis of a graph.

Length. The measure of something from beginning to end.

Line. A continuous extent of length, straight or curved, without breadth or thickness; the trace of a moving point.

Linear. In a straight line.

Litre. A unit of measuring liquid, equal to 1000 millilitres and 1000 cubic centimetres.

Loading. A payment in addition to an award wage or salary, in acknowledgement of conditions of employment, degree of skill, etc.

Loan. A sum of money which is borrowed, often from a bank, and has to be paid back; or, the act of borrowing or lending something.

Loss. In business, a loss is when you spend more money than you earn.

M

Mark-up. To increase the price of something.

Mean. The total of all scores divided by the number of scores. One of the measures of central tendencies.

Measurement. To measure is to compare two units.

Median. The middle score when all the scores are arranged in ascending order. One of the measures of central tendencies.

Mega. The initial element in units of measure that are equal to one million of the units.

Mid-point. The point half way between two other points.

Milli. A prefix meaning 'thousandth' in the metric system.

Misrepresent. To represent incorrectly, improperly, or falsely.

Mode. The score or scores with the highest frequency. One of the measures of central tendencies.

Month. A period of about 4 weeks; one of the twelve months into which a year is divided.

N

Net. What is left after everything has been subtracted; net income is income that is left after tax has been paid.

A plane figure showing all the faces that form a solid shape when folded.

Numerator. The top of a fraction.

O

Oblique. Slanting.

Observer. Smomeone or something that observes, does not participate in an action or event.

Obtuse. An angle measuring more than 90 degrees but less than 180 degrees.

Octagon. An eight-sided polygon.

Operation. A rule or procedure for combining numbers and symbols.

Opposite. The inverse of an operation. The opposite of addition is subtraction. The opposite of multiplication is division.

In geometry opposite refers to angles that are not adjacent, usually vertically opposite angles.

Ordered. To have order.

Origin. The point with co ordinates (0, 0) where the x and y axes intersect.

Overtime. Time spent working beyond the usual time needed or expected in a job; or, being paid extra for working beyond the usual time.

P

Parallel. Two or more lines in the same plane that do not intersect.

Parallelogram. A quadrilateral with two pairs of parallel sides.

Pentagon. A polygon with 5 sides.

Per annum. Every year, abbreviated as pa.

Percent. Rated for or out of every 100; symbol %.

Percentage. A fraction or ratio with 100 understood as the denominator, for example, 0.98 equals a percentage of 98.2; or an amount, such as an allowance, duty, or commission, that varies in proportion to a larger sum, such as total sales: *work for a percentage*.

Perimeter. The total distance around the outside of a shape.

Perpendicular. Two lines that cross at 90 degrees.

Perspective. A technique of depicting 3-dimensional figures on a flat surface, i.e. aerial perspective.

Pi. The numerical value equal to the ratio of a circle's circumference to its diameter.

Piecework. Specialised work for which the amount of pay depends on the number of items completed rather than the time spent making them.

Plan. The top view of a 3-dimensional figure.

Point. A point specifies an exact location. It has position but no dimensions.

Polygon. A closed plane shape with all sides straight line intervals.

Population. The entire group about which data is being collected.

Power. Another word for index.

Principal. An amount of money which someone has invested or lent to a person or organisation so that they will receive interest on it from the bank, person or organisation.

Prism. Polyhedrons with two identical and parallel faces that are polygons, the other faces are rectangular.

Profit. Money which is earned in trade or business after paying the costs of producing and selling goods and services.

Pronumeral. A symbol, usually a letter such as x, that stands instead of a numeral.

Proof. A formal way of setting out a logical argument with a set of statements and reasons to establish the truth of an original statement.

Properties. Essential or distinctive attributes or qualities of a thing.

Purchase. To buy something.

Pyramid. Polyhedrons formed by a polygon (the base) and a number of triangular faces that meet at the apex of the solid.

Pythagoras. A Greek mathematician and philosopher who is credited with many discoveries including the relationship between sides of a right-angled triangle. Pythagoras' theorem states: *The square of the hypotenuse of a right-angled triangle is equal to the sum of the squares of the other two sides.*

Q

Quadratic power. An expression or equation where the variable is raised to the second.

Quadrilateral. A four-sided polygon.

Quantity. The measure of an amount.

Questionnaire. A list of questions, usually printed, submitted for replies that can be analysed for usable information.

R

Radius. The interval from the centre of a circle to its circumference.

Range. A statistical measure of the spread of the scores. The highest score minus the lowest score.

Rate. To compare quantities of different units in a definite order. The amount at which one quantity changes with respect to another.

Ratio. A comparison of one quantity with another of the same units in a definite order.

Rational. A number than can be written as a fraction or as an exact decimal.

Reciprocal. To invert a proper or improper fraction is to find its reciprocal.

Rectangle. A quadrilateral with opposite sides equal and all angles 90 degrees.

A parallelogram with all angles equal.

Rectangular. A solid with a rectangular cross section is said to be rectangular.

Reflection. Flipping a shape to produce its mirror image.

Reflex. A reflex angle measures more than 180 degrees but less than 360 degrees.

Replacement. To provide a substitute or equivalent in the place of.

Retainer. An amount of money which you pay to someone in advance so that they will work for you when you need them to.

Revolution. A complete turn. An angle measuring 360 degrees.

Rhombus. A parallelogram with adjacent sides equal.

Right. Formed by or with reference to a perpendicular: *a right angle*.

Rise. Vertical distance.

Rotation. Spinning a shape round a fixed point to its new position.

Rounding. To approximate a number so that it is no longer exact. Numbers are rounded to make them more easy to understand in certain situations.

Run. Horizontal distance.

S

Salary. A fixed amount of money agreed every year as pay for an employee.

Sales. The number of items sold in units or dollar terms.

Sample. A group that is chosen form the entire group (population). A subset of a population.

Savings. The money which you keep in an account in a bank or similar financial organisation; or, a reduction in expenditure or cost.

Scale. Measuring device that is a set of units, usually equally spaced.

Scalene. When no sides of a triangle are equal it is called scalene.

Scattergraph. A graph showing the relationship between two variables.

Scientific. Regulated by or conforming to the principles of exact science.

Sector. Part of a circle formed by two radii and an arc.

Sector graph. A sector graph is a graph where a circle is divided into sectors in proportion to the data collected. It has the advantage of displaying data without taking up much space. The sector angles are decided by the fraction of the whole.

Segment. The region of a circle bounded by a chord and an arc.

Sequence. A group of numbers, displayed with commas between each terms, that obey the same rule.

Side. One of the surfaces forming the outside of or bounding a thing, or one of the lines bounding a geometric figure.

Significant figures. The number of digits, starting and finishing with non-zero digits, that determine the accuracy of a number. All non-significant figures are zeros.

Similar. To have the same shape but to be of different sizes.

Simple. Simple interest is money that is paid only on an original amount of money that has been borrowed or invested, and not on the additional money that the original sum earns.

Simplify. To make smaller.

Sine. The sine of an angle is the ratio that compares the length of the opposite side with the length of the hypotenuse.

Sketch. A simply or hastily executed drawing.

Skewed. Having an oblique direction or position; slanting.

Slope. Another word often used to indicate the gradient of a line.

Solid. Shapes with three dimensions.

Solution. The answer to a question. The value that makes an equation true.

Solve. The process of finding the value of the pronumeral in an equation.

Sphere. A solid made from one surface where all points on the surface are the same distance from a fixed point, known as the centre.

Spreadsheet. A computer program that allows you to do financial calculations and plans.

Square. A regular quadrilateral.

Statement. A bank statement lists the amounts of money paid into and taken out of your bank account during a particular period of time and states the total amount that is left.

Statistics. The branch of mathematics that deals with the collection, display and analysis of information known as data.

Stem-and-leaf. A method for showing the spread of values in a set of data.

Step graph. A type of line graph that is made up of a set of lines, with definite breaks between them. The overall graph appears like a series of steps.

Substitute/Substitution. To replace one item with another. In algebra, to replace a pronumeral with a number.

Superannuation. Money taken out of or set aside from someone's pay while they are working that they will use to help pay completely or in part for their living expenses when they retire.

Supplementary. Two angles that add to 180 degrees.

Survey. To determine the exact form, boundaries, position, extent, etc., of a tract of land, section of a country, etc. by linear and angular measurements and the application of the principles of geometry and trigonometry.

A set of questions designed to collect data for statistical analysis.

Symbol. Something standing in place of a number.

T

Table. A way of displaying data in columns with headings. A frequency distribution table is used in statistics to display the scores and frequencies.

Tally. Individual marks or dashes used to indicate a score.

Tangent. A line that intersects a curve or circle at only one point.

Tax. Money paid to the government, usually a percentage of personal income or of the cost of goods or services bought.

Theorem. A rule or law, especially one expressed by an equation or formula.

Time. A particular period of seconds, minutes, hours, days, weeks, months, years etc. for which something has been happening, or which is needed for something, or which is available for something.

Title. A heading given to a graph or diagram.

Transaction. To do and complete a business activity.

Transformation. The changing of an object's position, shape or size.

The rearranging of an algebraic expression or equation.

Translate. To write in a different way.

Translation. Sliding a shape in any direction, without turning it, to its new position.

Transversal. A line intersecting two or more lines.

Trapezium. A quadrilateral with one pair of parallel sides.

Trapezoidal. A solid with a trapezium as its cross section is said to be trapezoidal.

Triad. A set of three numbers that obey Pythagoras' theorem is a Pythagorean triad.

Triangle. A three-sided polygon.

Triangular. A solid with a triangle as its cross section is said to be triangular. Numbers that can be represented by dots to form triangles, such as 1, 3, 6 and 10, are triangular numbers.

Trigonometry. Mathematics that is concerned with the measurement of triangles.

Trinomial. An expression that is a sum or difference of three terms, as $3x + 2y + z$ or $3x^3 + 2x^2 + x$.

U

Uniform. Identical or consistent.

Unknown. A symbol or pronumeral in a mathematical statement.

V

Variable. When values can change they are said to be variables.

Vertex/vertices. The point where two adjacent sides of a polygon meet.

Vertical. A line perpendicular to the horizontal.

Volume. A measure of the amount of space that a solid occupies.

W

Wages. Payment for labour or services to a worker, especially remuneration on an hourly, daily or weekly basis or by the piece.

Withdrawal. To take or move out or back, or to remove; for example, money from the bank.

Y

Year. A period of twelve months or 52 weeks or 365 days.

Answers

Chapter 1

MathsCheck

1 a quadruple no. of pentagons, add 1;
   $4n + 1$
   b 73   **c** 9
   d activity   **e** $5n + 1$
   f for polygon of x sides $T = (x - 1)n + 1$

2 a

x	$^-2$	$^-1$	0	1	2
y	0	1	2	3	4

  b

x	$^-2$	$^-1$	0	1	2
y	6	4	2	0	$^-2$

  c

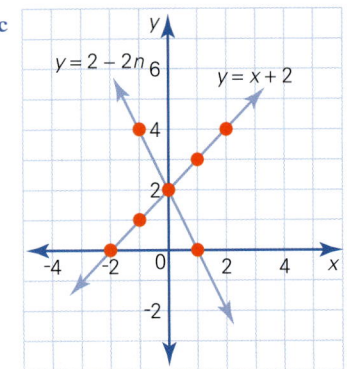

pt of int = $(0, 2)$

3 a $T = n$ **b** $T = n^2 - 1$ **c** $T = \dfrac{1}{x}$

4 a 15   **b** 224   **c** $\dfrac{1}{15}$

5 a $n + 1$ **b** $(n + 1)^2 - 1$ **c** $\dfrac{1}{n + 1}$

6 a 64   **b** $^-12$ **c** $\dfrac{1}{3}$

7 a 20   **b** $^-12$ **c** $^-1008$

8 a 50   **b** 0   **c** $^-49$

9 a 4   **b** 0   **c** 3   **d** $\dfrac{1}{2}$ **e** 0

10 a 3   **b** 1   **c** 0   **d** $\dfrac{1}{2}$ **e** 7

11 a $3x + 4ab$ **b** $6t - 2ab$ **c** $4g(a + b)$
  d $\dfrac{6ab}{2m}$

12 a $x(4 + p)$ **b** $\dfrac{8x}{2} = 4x$ **c** $(14 + x)$yr
  d $n - 3$ **e** $5t + 2$ **f** $2xy$ km
  g $10x - 4(x + 2)$ **h** $4a + 16$
  i $\dfrac{t}{2}(t + 2)$

13 a $11h + 3$ **b** $8a + 3c + 4$ **c** ^-5p
  d $^-7x^2 - 4x$

14 a $72a$ **b** a^2b **c** ^-12ab
  d $2y$ **e** 1   **f** 0
  g $\dfrac{1}{2}$ **h** 14

15 a $2pt$ **b** $24d^2t$ **c** $\dfrac{3a}{2b}$
  d $\dfrac{5}{3t}$ **e** $2d^2$ **f** $\dfrac{^-2x}{3y}$

16 a $6a$ **b** $8a + 2b$ **c** $10a + 2b$
  d $10a + 8b$

17 a $a + x^y$; 62   **b** $x^2 - 3x + a^y$; $^-4$

18 a $6xy$ **b** $9ab$ **c** $6b^2$

19 a $x^2 - y^2$ **b** $6ab$ **c** $22x^2$

20 a $ax + 5x$ **b** $3pt - t^2$ **c** $14a^2 - 35ab$
  d $^-3x - 15$ **e** $^-4x + 5a$

21 a $10 + 8x$ **b** $4x - 9$ **c** $40 - 7x$
  d $18x - 29$

22 a $6x - 6$ **b** ^-3x **c** $7 - 3x$
  d $x^2 + 3x$ **e** $2b$ **f** $^-2x + 19$

23 a $7x + 3$ **b** $x^2 + 7x + 10$ **c** $3x + 7$
  d $10 - x$ **e** $x^2 + 4x - 21$ **f** $^-x^2 - 2x - 5$

24 a $^-1$ **b** 11   **c** $^-4$ **d** $1\dfrac{1}{4}$
  e $x^2 - 4x - 1$ **f** $4p^2 + 8p - 1$

25 a 3   **b** $^-32$ **c** $4 - 9A^2$ **d** $4 - B^2$
  e $4 - A^2$

26 $3(x + h) - 4$

27 a 0   **b** 0   **c** $\dfrac{3}{4}$ **d** $p^2 - p$

28 $wn + n + 1$

29 a times

30 $3a + 6$

EXERCISE 1A

1 a m, 5, $3m$, 15   **b** x, 6, $3x$, 18, $9x$
  c a, $^-3$, $2a$, ^-3a, $^-6$, ^-a, $^-6$
  d 24   **e** x^2, $8x$, ^-6x

2 a $b^2 + 6b + 8$ **b** $d^2 + 5d + 4$
  c $ab + 5a + 3b + 15$ **d** $x^2 + 6x + 9$
  e $a^2 + 8a + 16$ **f** $c^2 + 4c - 12$
  g $x^2 + 6x - 7$ **h** $a^2 - 25$
  i $x^2 - 16$ **j** $c^2 - 36$
  k $d^2 - 6d + 8$ **l** $k^2 - 14k + 49$
  m $ab - 4a + 3b - 12$ **n** $2x^2 - x - 28$
  o $3x^2 - 13x - 30$ **p** $16t^2 - 36t + 18$
  q $8k^2 - 26k + 15$ **r** $16n^2 - 24n + 9$
  s $6 + x - x^2$ **t** $2x^2 + 2x - 4$
  u $2x^2 + 2x - 4$

3 a $x^2 - 1$ **b** $a^2 - 16$ **c** $x^2 - y^2$
  d $x^2 - 4$ **e** $4x^2 - 1$ **f** $4x^2 - y^2$
  g $x^2 - 9$ **h** $9x^2 - 16$ **i** $25 - x^2$
  j $a^2 - 16$ **k** $y^2 - 36$ **l** $25y^2 - x^2$

4 a $x^2 + 8x + 16$ **b** $x^2 - 8x + 16$
  c $4x^2 + 12x + 9$ **d** $4x^2 - 12x + 9$
  e $25 + 10x + x^2$ **f** $25 - 10x + x^2$
  g $9x^2 + 12xy + 4y^2$

5 a $7x + 12$ **b** $2x^2 - 3x - 9$
  c $2x + 1$ **d** $2x^2 + 12x + 1$
  e $x^2 - 3x - 19$ **f** $x^2 + 2x - 1$
  g $x^2 + 2x + 5$ **h** $x^3 + 3x^2 + 2x$
  i $x^3 - x$ **j** $2x^3 + 4x^2 + 2x$
  k $x^4 + x^3 + 5x^2 + 4x + 4$

l $x^4 + 2x^3 - 2x^2 + 2x - 3$
m $^-x^4 - 2x^3 + 5x^2 - 2x$ **n** $x^3 + 3x^2 - 9x - 4$

EXERCISE 1B

1 a $a^2 + 4a + 4$ **b** $a^2 - 4a + 4$
   c $x^2 + 6x + 9$ **d** $x^2 - 6x + 9$
   e $c^2 + 16c + 64$ **f** $d^2 + 20d + 100$
   g $b^2 - 8b + 16$ **h** $c^2 - 10c + 25$
   i $d^2 + 2d + 1$ **j** $x^2 - 2x + 1$
   k $4k^2 + 4k + 1$ **l** $4k^2 - 4k + 1$
   m $4n^2 + 12n + 9$ **n** $9x^2 + 24x + 16$
   o $25a^2 + 70a + 49$ **p** $25 + 30f + 9f^2$
   q $25x^2 + 40x + 16$ **r** $4a^2 + 2a + \frac{1}{4}$
   s $64 - 32p + 4p^2$ **t** $36x^2 + 9x + \frac{9}{16}$

2 a $a^2 - 16$ **b** $a^2 - 16$ **c** $x^2 - 25$
   d $c^2 - 49$ **e** $d^2 - 64$ **f** $100 - h^2$
   g $81 - t^2$ **h** $x^2 - y^2$ **i** $h^2 - k^2$
   j $4a^2 - 1$ **k** $9x^2 - 25$ **l** $25p^2 - 9$
   m $81n^2 - 64$ **n** $121 - 36k^2$ **o** $4x^2 - y^2$
   p $9a^2 - 4b^2$ **q** $16n^2 - 25p^2$ **r** $\frac{x^2}{4} - \frac{9y^2}{16}$

3 a $3^2 + 2^2 \neq (3 + 2)^2$ **b** $3^2 + 2^2 \neq (3 + 2)(3 - 2)$
4 a $(2a + 3)^2 = 4a^2 + 12a + 9$
   b $(4 + a)(4 - a) = 16 - a^2$
   c $y^2 + 12y + 36 = (y + 6)^2$
   d $w^2 - 2w + 1 = (w - 1)^2$
   e $(3x + 16)^2 = 9x^2 + 96x + 256$

5 a $x^2 - \frac{1}{x^2}$ **b** $m^4 - 1$ **c** $49 - x^4$
   d $x^2 + 2 + \frac{1}{x^2}$ **e** $x^2 - 2 + \frac{1}{x^2}$
   f $x^4 - 2x^2y^2 + y^4$ **g** $x^2y^2 + 4xy + 4$
6 a $x^2 - 8x + 12$ **b** $2x^2 - 1$
   c $^-1$ **d** $a^2 + 7a + 3$
   e $a^2 - 7a + 12$ **f** $2a^2 + 6a + 5$
   g $98 + 2a^2$ **h** ^-28a
   i $x^2 + 4x + 4$ **j** $2 - x^2$
   k $^-8x^2 - 104x - 336$ **l** $x^2 - 2x - 7$
   m $14x + 98$ **n** $6x^2 - x - 9$
7 a $A = 81, B = 9$ **b** $A = 6, B = 3$
   c any values where $ab = 1$,
     a is all real numbers and $b = \frac{1}{a}$, $a \neq 0$
   d $A = ^-3, P = 9$

EXERCISE 1C

1 a $5(x + y)$ **b** $^-2(a + b)$
   c $a(x + y)$ **d** $p(1 + q)$
   e $6k(2 + 3p)$ **f** $^-9a(2a - 3)$
2 a $8(x + y)$ **b** $a(p - t)$
   c $4(k + 2)$ **d** $x(8 - 3)$ or $5x$
   e $y(x + 4)$ **f** $3(5 + 4t)$
   g $7(b - 1)$ **h** $p(k + 1)$
   i $7d(2 - p)$
3 a $3x(1 + 4t)$ **b** $y(5 - y)$
   c $2x(3y + 4x)$ **d** $4g(4h - 9p)$
   e $^-5(x - 3)$ or $5(^-x + 3)$
   f $2p(2p - 3)$ **g** $7a(3a - 2t)$
   h $5(^-5a + 2)$ or $^-5(5a - 2)$

i $^-3(y + 4)$ **j** $^-8x(2x + 3)$
   k $7tp(4t + 2 - 3p)$ **l** $^-6xy(x + 2)$
   m $^-3a(3a + 4)$ **n** $5(x + 4y - 3)$
   o $pq(p - q + 1)$
4 a $3x + 15, 3(x + 5)$ **b** $7a + 7, 7(a + 1)$
   c $8y - 20, 4(2y - 5)$ **d** $5m + 15, 5(m + 3)$
   e $^-6x + 12, ^-6(x - 2)$ **f** $^-3a^2 + 15a, ^-3a(a - 5)$
5 a $4(x + 5) = 4x + 20$ **b** $h(2h + 3) = 2h^2 + 3h$
   c $\frac{2a}{2}(a - 2) = a^2 - 2a$
   d $\frac{1}{2} \times 8(3y - 4) = 12y - 16$
   e $\frac{\pi x^2}{4}$ **f** $\frac{3x}{2}(6x + 8) = 9x^2 + 12x$
6 a $(x + 1)(4 + x)$ **b** $(a + 7)(x - y)$
   c $\frac{x}{2}(\frac{x}{2} + 1)$ **d** $(x + y)(a + b)$
   e $\frac{x}{2}(y + x)$ **f** $A(x + 1)(1 + A)$
   g $(x + y)(a - b)$ **h** $\pi r(r + 1)$
   i $p(p - 1)$ **j** $5(x + y + 1)$
   k $(x - 2)(x - 4)$ **l** $\frac{1}{2}\pi (r^2 - R^2)$

EXERCISE 1D

1 a 7   **b** 6   **c** 11   **d** 4   **e** 3   **f** 7
2 a 3^6 **b** 5^4 **c** 8^2 **d** t **e** a^4
3 a 1   **b** 1   **c** 1   **d** 1   **e** 1   **f** 2
   g 4   **h** 1   **i** 6   **j** c **k** 1   **l** 1
   m 1   **n** 1   **o** 1
4 a 2^{11} **b** 3^7 **c** 8^{10} **d** 5^8 **e** 12^6
   f not possible   **g** m^6 **h** 10^6 **i** p^6
   j not possible   **k** x^6 **l** not possible
   m not possible   **n** $32a^5$ or $(2a)^5$
   o $\left(\frac{2}{3}\right)^7$ **p** $(0.8)^9$ **q** $6a^9$ **r** $24p^{10}$
   s $7x^7$ **t** $2a^9$ **u** $10k^4$ **v** $^-18c^6$
   w x^3y^4 **x** $^-4c^8$
5 a 0   **b** 0   **c** 0   **d** 0
6 a 1   **b** 1   **c** 3   **d** 1   **e** 1   **f** 3^4
   g 5^{10} **h** 1   **i** 0   **j** $^-5$ **k** $16p^4$ **l** 7^5
   m 2^3 **n** 3^3 **o** 8^3 **p** not possible
   q a^2 **r** c^6 **s** 10^2 **t** a^4 **u** $\left(\frac{a}{b}\right)^3$
   v x   **w** 0   **x** not possible
   y $\left(\frac{x}{y}\right)^8$ **z** $\left(\frac{1}{2}\right)^3$
7 a 6   **b** 6   **c** 16   **d** 21   **e** 81
8 a 3^{10} **b** 2^{12} **c** 5^6 **d** 4^4 **e** 3^9 **f** $(^-2)^6$
   g $\left(\frac{3}{4}\right)^8$ **h** $(2.5)^6$ **i** a^8 **j** c^{15} **k** x^{16}
   l p^{20} **m** k^{35} **n** $4x^2$ **o** $27x^6$ **p** $8a^9$
   q $16n^8$ **r** 5^5c^{25} **s** 2^6x^8 **t** $a^{15}x^{20}$
9 a $^-1$ **b** 3   **c** 10   **d** 5   **e** 5
10 a 3^3 **b** x^2 **c** 5^8 **d** a^3
   e $2a$ **f** $3a^3$ **g** $2x$ **h** a^2b
   i a^2b^4 **j** $\frac{3x^2y^2}{2}$ **k** 4^4x **l** $\frac{3 \times 4^2c}{2}$
   m abc **n** $\frac{x^2y}{3}$ **o** $\frac{4a}{3b}$ **p** y^{-1}

11 a 1　　**b** $3t^2$　　**c** $\dfrac{-2}{3}$　　**d** $^-c^2$

12 a T　　**b** F　　**c** F　　**d** F

13 a 6×10^9　　**b** 14×10^5　　**c** 6×10^7
　　d $5 \cdot 4 \times 10^6$　　**e** 2×10^2　　**f** 7×10^2
　　g 4×10^1　　**h** $\dfrac{4 \times 10^6}{3}$　　**i** 2×10^2

14 a $6x^4 - 15x^3$　　**b** $^-10a^3 - 15a^2$　　**c** $^-10n^5 + 2n^3$
　　d $^-2x^5 + \dfrac{8}{x}x^3 + 4x^2$

15 a $2a^2$　　**b** $3x^4$　　**c** $5a$　　**d** $^-8x^3y$

16 a i 162　　**ii** $^-48$　　**iii** $\dfrac{16}{9}$
　　b i 27　　**ii** 12　　**iii** $\dfrac{4}{3}$
　　c i 108　　**ii** $^-32$　　**iii** $\dfrac{32}{27}$
　　d i 81　　**ii** $^-24$　　**iii** $\dfrac{8}{9}$

17 a 8　　**b** 8　　**c** 5　　**d** 4

18 a $x = 4, y = 4$　　**b** $x = 2, y = 5$　　**c** $x = 2, y = 5$

19 a 4　　**b** 2^x　　**c** 2^x　　**d** 3^{x+1}　　**e** x^{2m}

20 a $\dfrac{6x^{11}y^3}{5}$　　**b** $\dfrac{3}{x^8 y^{15}}$　　**c** $\dfrac{x^5 y^2}{z^4}$
　　d $6a^5$　　**e** n^4　　**f** a^{12}　　**g** $2m$　　**h** $6^5 a^{10}$

21 a 1　　**b** 5^{m-1}　　**c** $3^m - 5^m$　　**d** $^-1$
　　e x^m　　**f** 10^x　　**g** x^{2m-3}　　**h** 5^m

22 a 9　　**b** $1 \cdot 5$　　**c** 6　　**d** 1　　**e** 3　　**f** $\dfrac{7}{3}$

EXERCISE 1E

1 a $^-1$　　**b** $^-2$　　**c** $^-3$　　**d** 1　　**e** 16
　　f 2　　**g** p^2　　**h** p^2　　**i** $\dfrac{1}{2}$　　**j** $^-3$

2 a $\dfrac{1}{3^4}$　　**b** $\dfrac{1}{7}$　　**c** $\dfrac{1}{4^2}$　　**d** $\dfrac{1}{2^5}$　　**e** $\dfrac{1}{x^3}$
　　f $\dfrac{1}{n^6}$　　**g** $\dfrac{1}{10^8}$　　**h** $\dfrac{8}{x^7}$　　**i** $\dfrac{3}{t^2}$　　**j** $\dfrac{1}{(2p)^3}$
　　k $\dfrac{1}{(^-9)^4}$　　**l** $\dfrac{1}{(^-3 \cdot 6)^2}$　　**m** 3^4　　**n** x^2　　**o** a^x

3 a $\dfrac{1}{25}$　　**b** $\dfrac{1}{10\,000}$　　**c** $\dfrac{1}{16}$　　**d** $\dfrac{-1}{27}$　　**e** 16

4 a T　　**b** F　　**c** T　　**d** T　　**e** F　　**g** T

5 a 3^{-1}　　**b** 10^{-1}　　**c** 2^{-3}　　**d** x^{-2}　　**e** a^{-1}
　　f $3a^{-3}$　　**g** $4x^{-2}$　　**h** $\dfrac{1}{5}p^{-1}$　　**i** $3^{-1}x^{-2}$ or $\dfrac{x^{-2}}{3}$
　　j $2 \times 5^{-1}a^{-3}$　　**k** $3xy^{-4}$　　**l** $^-7x^{-2}y^{-5}$
　　m $^-8a5^{-1}(bc)^{-6}$

6 a F　　**b** F　　**c** T　　**d** F
　　e F　　**f** T

7 a $^-2$　　**b** $^-4$　　**c** 3　　**d** $^-2$

8 3^{2^4}　　　　　　**9** -3^{2^4}

10 a $\dfrac{1}{2y^2}$ or $\dfrac{y^{-2}}{2}$　　**b** $a^2 b^{-4}$ or $\dfrac{a^2}{b^4}$
　　c $a^4 b^{-6}$ or $\dfrac{a^4}{b^6}$　　**d** x^{-m} or $\dfrac{1}{x^m}$
　　e x^{-1} or $\dfrac{1}{x}$　　**f** $4^{-3}x^{-6} = \dfrac{1}{64x^6}$

EXERCISE 1F

1 a $\dfrac{1}{2}$　　**b** $\dfrac{1}{2}$　　**c** $\dfrac{1}{3}$　　**d** $\dfrac{1}{2}$
　　e $\dfrac{1}{3}$　　**f** a　　**g** $\sqrt{a}$　　**h** 6

2 a 2　　**b** 10　　**c** 3　　**d** 5
　　e $^-6$　　**f** $^-6$　　**g** $\dfrac{1}{3}$　　**h** $0 \cdot 2$
　　i $\dfrac{2}{5}$　　**j** $\dfrac{2}{3}$　　**k** $0 \cdot 4$　　**l** 10
　　m 5　　**n** $\dfrac{1}{4}$　　**o** $\dfrac{1}{100}$　　**p** $\dfrac{2}{5}$

3 a 4　　**b** 8　　**c** $5^{\frac{5}{2}}$　　**d** $7^2 = 49$
　　e 6　　**f** a^3　　**g** $9^{\frac{1}{2}} = 3$　　**h** $10^{\frac{3}{2}}$
　　i $a^{\frac{5}{6}}$　　**j** $a^{\frac{1}{6}}$　　**k** not possible
　　l $9a^{\frac{1}{2}}$　　**m** $2a + 2a^{\frac{1}{3}}$　　**n** $3a^{\frac{1}{3}}$　　**o** $a^{\frac{4}{3}}$

4 a $\dfrac{1}{7}$　　**b** $\dfrac{1}{4}$　　**c** 6　　**d** 5
　　e $\dfrac{5}{4}$　　**f** $\dfrac{1}{10}$　　**g** $\dfrac{5}{2}$　　**h** $\dfrac{3}{2}$

5 a $\dfrac{1}{a}$　　**b** $a^{\frac{-3}{2}}$　　**c** $a^{\frac{-9}{2}}$　　**d** $a^{\frac{-1}{3}}$
　　e x　　**f** x^2　　**g** x^{-2}　　**h** x^{-2}
　　i $3a^2 b^3$

6 a 4　　**b** 16　　**c** 25　　**d** 1
　　e $\dfrac{1}{4}$　　**f** 4　　**g** $\dfrac{16}{25}$　　**h** $\dfrac{25}{16}$

7 a 8　　**b** 125　　**c** 343　　**d** 1
　　e $\dfrac{1}{64}$　　**f** $\dfrac{1}{8}$　　**g** $\dfrac{1}{125}$　　**h** $\dfrac{125}{8}$

8 a $x^{\frac{1}{2}}$　　**b** $x^{\frac{1}{3}}$　　**c** $x^{\frac{2}{3}}$　　**d** $5x^{\frac{1}{3}}$
　　e $x^{\frac{-2}{3}}$　　**f** $5w^{\frac{-2}{3}}$　　**g** $5w^{\frac{-3}{2}}$　　**h** $x^{\frac{1}{2}}y^{\frac{-1}{3}}$

EXERCISE 1G

1 a 3　　**b** 4　　**c** 3　　**d** $\dfrac{1}{5}$　　**e** x^3　　**f** x^3

2 a 65 536　　**b** 78 125　　**c** 7776　　**d** 20 736
　　e $\dfrac{1}{81}$ or 0·012 345 6　　**f** 4·768 371 6 × 10^{-7}
　　g 14　　**h** 2　　**i** $\dfrac{1}{10}$　　**j** 0·343 294 5

3 **a** $\sqrt{16}$ **b** $\sqrt[3]{8}$ **c** $\sqrt[4]{12}$ **d** $\sqrt[6]{59}$ **e** $\sqrt[6]{x}$

 f $\sqrt[7]{p}$ **g** $\sqrt[c]{10}$ **h** $\sqrt[x]{t}$ **i** $4\sqrt{9}$ **j** $\dfrac{6}{\sqrt[9]{9}}$

 k $\sqrt[7]{x^4}$ **l** $6\sqrt[5]{p^2}$

4 **a** $2^{\frac{1}{2}}$ **b** $5^{\frac{1}{3}}$ **c** $12^{\frac{1}{4}}$ **d** $28^{\frac{1}{9}}$ **e** $184^{\frac{1}{10}}$

 f $8^{\frac{1}{2}}$ **g** $10^{\frac{1}{x}}$ **h** $t^{\frac{1}{p}}$ **i** $6^{\frac{-1}{2}}$ **j** $20^{\frac{-1}{3}}$

 k $x^{\frac{-1}{6}}$ **l** $a^{\frac{-1}{n}}$

5 **a** 8 **b** 4 **c** 2 **d** 2 **e** 3

 f 5 **g** $\dfrac{1}{2}$ **h** $\dfrac{1}{7}$ **i** $\dfrac{1}{4}$ **j** 1

6 **a** 27 **b** 16 **c** 6 **d** 15 **e** 25

 f 216 **g** 49 **h** 512 **i** 625 **j** $\dfrac{1}{2}$

 k $3^{\frac{-1}{2}}$ or $\dfrac{1}{\sqrt{3}}$ **l** $\dfrac{1}{\sqrt[6]{7}}$

7 **a** $a^{\frac{2}{3}}$ **b** $x^{\frac{5}{6}}$ **c** $p^{\frac{1}{4}}$ **d** $n^{\frac{-3}{10}}$

 e $x^{\frac{1}{4}}$ **f** $5a^2$ **g** $3x^{\frac{1}{3}}y$ **h** $x^2 m^{\frac{1}{2}}$

 i $\dfrac{a^2}{x^4}$ **j** $t^{\frac{-7}{12}}$ **k** $\dfrac{m^{-2}}{x^{-4}}$ or $\dfrac{x^4}{m^2}$

8 **a** 3 **b** 27 **c** 243 **d** 59 049

 e 1 **f** 81 **g** $\dfrac{1}{81}$ **h** $\dfrac{1}{625}$

9 **a** $x^{\frac{3}{4}}$ **b** $x^{\frac{3}{4}}$ **c** $x^{\frac{1}{5}}$ **d** $x^{\frac{2}{5}}$

 e $x^{\frac{-7}{2}}$ **f** $3x^{\frac{-5}{3}}$ **g** $x^{\frac{5}{2}}y^{\frac{-3}{2}}$ **h** $x^{\frac{-3}{4}}y^{\frac{-3}{4}}$

EXERCISE 1H

1 **a** $\dfrac{1}{6}$ **b** $4x^8$ **c** -5 **d** $\dfrac{7a^5}{b^2}$

 e $\dfrac{1}{7}$ **f** a^3 **g** $\dfrac{x^6}{27}$ **h** -1

 i 8 **j** 2^{5-2p} **k** $\dfrac{25}{16}$ **l** $-24x^2y^7$

 m $\dfrac{-1}{8}$ **n** 5^{1-2p} **o** $\dfrac{125x^3}{8}$ **p** $3y$

 q x^4 **r** 2 **s** $7a^5$ **t** $81x^{28}$

2 **a** $\dfrac{1}{4}$ **b** $\dfrac{6x^2}{y^3}$ **c** 24 **d** $\dfrac{x^8}{81y^4}$

 e $\dfrac{4}{5}$ **f** $\dfrac{3}{x^7}$ **g** m^2 **h** $x^{-3}y^2$

 i m^2 **j** 1 **k** $6x^4y^2$ **l** $12x^{14}y^{11}$

 m $2x^3y$ **n** $\dfrac{y^3}{x^6}$ **o** $\dfrac{y}{x}$ **p** $x^{\frac{25}{12}}$

3 **a** $108x^9$ **b** $2x^4$ **c** $\dfrac{1}{\sqrt[3]{9}\cdot a}$ **d** $32a^{\frac{15}{4}}$

 e $20xy^2$

4 54 **5** $2n+2$ **6** $\dfrac{m-n}{2}$ **7** $3x-5$

8 $b=\dfrac{1}{4}$, $c=-4$ **9** $x=4, y=4$

10 $3x-3$

Chapter Review Exercises

1 **a** $3x$ **b** $(100P+50)$ cents
 c $T=3n+2$; $T_{15}=47$

2 **a** 3^4 **b** p^3 **c** 2^0 **d** $(-3a)^3$

3 **a** x^5 **b** 5 **c** x **d** 8

4 **a** 64 **b** 16 **c** $\dfrac{27}{125}$ **d** $0\cdot36$

 e 36 **f** 1 **g** $\dfrac{1}{10\,000}$ **h** 10

 i not possible **j** $\dfrac{1}{10}$ **k** 64

 l $\dfrac{16}{81}$ **m** -9 **n** -12 **o** $\dfrac{-1}{2}$

 p 2 **q** $\dfrac{1}{3}$ **r** $\dfrac{1}{7}$

5 **a** a^5 **b** $12p^{10}$ **c** x^3 **d** g^4f^6

 e $4c^3$ **f** a^3b **g** 7 **h** $\dfrac{-3}{2}$

 i a^{20} **j** $8^{\frac{1}{2}}x^2$ **k** $\dfrac{1}{c^3}$ **l** $\dfrac{4}{a}$

 m not possible **n** k^3+1 **o** $-7w^5$

 p 8 **q** $-2k^{\frac{1}{2}}$ **r** -12 **s** $4ab^2$ **t** $m^2t^{\frac{1}{5}}$

6 74

7 **a** $18x-24$ **b** $-6a^2+15a$ **c** $4x-\dfrac{4}{3}$
 d $-10x^4+15x^2$ **e** $5a-20$ **f** $-2c^5-6c^3$
 g $2m^2-13m+6$ **h** $9x^2-30x+25$

8 **a** $7(x-a)$ **b** $6(k+2)$
 c $(x-7)p$ **d** $-8(2x-3)$ or $8(-2x+3)$
 e $3p(2a-p)$ **f** $(x-10)(x+10)$
 g $-3a^2(2a-3x)$ or ... **h** $\dfrac{xy^2}{4}(2x^4y-1)$

9 **a** 5, 6 **b** 3, 3

10 **a** no **b** yes, $a=1$ or $a=0$

11 **a** $\dfrac{4x^5y^3}{3}$ **b** $\dfrac{3}{2}$ **c** x^m **d** w^{3m-1}

12 **a** 3 **b** -3 **c** $1625\cdot499$ (3 dp)
 d $\dfrac{-4}{3}$

13 **a** $x^{\frac{1}{2}}$ **b** $w^{\frac{1}{3}}$ **c** $p^{\frac{1}{4}}$ **d** $x^{\frac{2}{3}}$
 e $x^{\frac{1}{3}}$ **f** $a^{\frac{1}{2}}$ **g** $4x^{\frac{1}{2}}$ **h** $x^{\frac{1}{3}}y$

14 a $x^{\frac{4}{5}}$ **b** $x^{\frac{-4}{5}}$ **c** $x^{\frac{1}{2}}y^{\frac{-1}{3}}$ **d** $x^{\frac{-2}{3}}y^{\frac{-1}{3}}$

Keeping Mathematically Fit

PART A
1 0·06   **2** $\frac{2}{5}, \frac{3}{8}, \frac{4}{9}$
3 a 3 hours   **b** $4
4 6   **5** 14   **6** 8 and 9
7 11·856   **8** 24   **9** 3, ⁻3   **10** 0·$\dot3$

PART B
1 8·2%
2 a 21·2 cm   **b** 256·9 cm²
3 0 and 0·125   **4** $1\frac{11}{12}$ tspn   **5** 3·41
6 a 70 688   **b** 240

Chapter 2

MathsCheck

1

	Nearest 10	Nearest 100	Nearest 1000
a	2 640	2 600	3 000
b	7 070	7 100	7 000
c	16 440	16 400	16 000
d	8 900	8 900	9 000
e	12 310	12 300	12 000
f	10 510	10 500	11 000
g	8 010	8 000	8 000
h	7 000	7 000	7 000

2 a 0·8   **b** 2·6   **c** 0·9   **d** 7·4
3 a 0·76   **b** 0·86   **c** 6·18   **d** 9·00
4 a 0·671   **b** 0·159   **c** 8·041   **d** 4·006
5 a 17 875 910   **b** 17 875 900   **c** 17 876 000
d 17 880 000   **e** 17 900 000   **f** 18 000 000
g 20 000 000
6 a f   **b** a to c   **c** a to c
d c   **e** a or b   **f** discuss
7 a 2·5 kg   **b** 3 min   **c** 255 000 t
d 10·28 s   **e** $112.45   **f** US$0.7526
8 5, 6, 7, 8 or 9
9 a 3395 to 3404·$\dot9$ **b** 3350 to 3449·$\dot9$
10 a $\frac{3}{4}$ **b** $\frac{9}{50}$ **c** $\frac{3}{5}$ **d** $1\frac{1}{2}$

e $\frac{9}{100}$ **f** $2\frac{29}{50}$ **g** $\frac{1}{100}$ **h** $\frac{1}{25}$

i $12\frac{7}{100}$ **j** $\frac{7}{500\,000}$

11 a 0·07   **b** 0·4   **c** 0·06   **d** 1·5
e 0·8   **f** 1·75   **g** 0·$\dot4$ **h** 0·8$\dot3$
i 0·2$\dot6$ **j** 0·2$\dot8$571$\dot4$
12 a <   **b** <   **c** =
13 a 8·31, 8·302, 8·132   **b** 0·44, 0·404, 0·4

c 0·47, $\frac{3}{8}$, 0·05

14 103·61, 103·9, 258·34, 258·35, 258·41, 310·16
15 a $\frac{4}{5}$ **b** $\frac{29}{50}$ **c** $\frac{3}{20}$ **d** $\frac{2}{25}$

e $1\frac{1}{2}$ **f** $\frac{1}{50}$ **g** $2\frac{7}{20}$ **h** 3

i $\frac{7}{40}$ **j** $\frac{21}{400}$

16 a 0·27   **b** 0·45   **c** 0·06   **d** 0·09   **e** 0·13
f 1·2   **g** 2·4   **h** 1·08   **i** 0·035   **j** 0·1175
k 0·728   **l** 1·179   **m** 0·015   **n** 0·0645   **o** 3·214
17 a 7%   **b** 65%   **c** 18%   **d** 65%
e 70%   **f** 12%   **g** 150%   **h** 75%
i 60%   **j** 62·5%   **k** $66\frac{2}{3}$%   **l** $16\frac{2}{3}$%
m $5\frac{5}{9}$%   **n** 175%   **o** 280%
18 a 58%   **b** 70%   **c** 25%   **d** 9%
e 2%   **f** 140%   **g** 260%   **h** 92·5%
i 85·5%   **j** 3·5%   **k** 127·5%   **l** 18·25%
m 0·8%   **n** $66\frac{2}{3}$%   **o** $16\frac{2}{3}$%
19 a 85%   **b** 8%

c i 87·5%   **ii** 12·5%

d i 32·5%   **ii** 67·5%

20 a 8   **b** 150   **c** 100   **d** 20
e $8   **f** $60   **g** 10 m   **h** $100
i 220 kg   **j** $105   **k** 24 km   **l** 45 mL
m $100   **n** $2   **o** $60   **p** 900 g
21 a 12 cm   **b** 684 m
c 12·04 mm   **d** 2·34 t
22 a $32.50   **b** $16.90   **c** $4   **d** $6.80
23 a $15   **b** $5.63   **c** $8.56
d $20   **e** $10   **f** $201.50
g $61.92   **h** $1140
24 a $720   **b** 2300 revs   **c** $487.50
d 85·56 kg   **e** 75·15 s   **f** 786·25 m²
g 11·925 m   **h** $3643.50
25 a $62.30   **b** $20 150   **c** 506 v./d
26 a 25%   **b** $33\frac{1}{3}$%   **c** $12\frac{1}{2}$%   **d** 12%
e $11\frac{1}{9}$%   **f** 4·7%   **g** 136·1%   **h** 10·2%
27 a 25%   **b** 20%   **c** $6\frac{2}{3}$%   **d** 6·25%
e 22·5%   **f** 6·2%   **g** 25%   **h** 15·6%
28 35·2%   **29** 2·1%   **30** 20%   **31** 5·2%
32 a 1 : 2   **b** 1 : 50   **c** 3 : 7
d 2 : 1   **e** 3 : 10   **f** 15 : 4
33 a 3 : 1   **b** 3 : 1   **c** 7 : 1   **d** 1·5 : 1
34 a 1 : 1·3   **b** 1 : 3·5   **c** 1 : 3·7   **d** 1 : 1·5
35 a $20, $30   **b** $300, $500
c 240 m, 180 m   **d** 220 kg, 140 kg
e 3·2 km, 4·0 km   **f** 10 kg, 20 kg, 30 kg
36 $300 000, $400 000, $500 000
37 a 10·2 g copper, 74·8 g gold
b 12% copper, 88% gold
38 250 g chillies, 300 g garlic, 100 g nutmeg
39 a 2 : 5   **b** 7 : 10   **c** $\frac{5}{8}$ **d** $\frac{7}{8}$

e 0·4 : 5   **f** $\frac{4·8}{3·7}$ **g** $\frac{3x}{12}$ **h** $\frac{4}{m}$

40 8 : 21

41 a $1:6$ **b** $3:17$

EXERCISE 2A

1 a all except **f** and **g**

2 a $\dfrac{25}{100}$ or $\dfrac{1}{4}$ **b** $\dfrac{8}{1}$ **c** $\dfrac{-6}{1}$

d $\dfrac{13}{4}$ **e** $\dfrac{24}{10}$ or $\dfrac{12}{5}$ **f** $\dfrac{20}{100}$ or $\dfrac{1}{5}$

g $\dfrac{-4}{3}$ **h** $\dfrac{12}{1}$

3 a 1335 **b** 115 **c** 105 364
d 0·6125 **e** 31 688 **f** 11
g 309·996 **h** 1·579 473 7 **i** 0·39
j 2·28744 **k** 6·224 409 4 **l** 5·033 $\dot{6}$
m 6·99429 **n** 7·171 547 5

4 a no **b** no **c** no **d** no **e** yes

5 a nearest 1000 or 100
b nearest \$1 **c** nearest metre
d nearest metre **e** nearest mm

6 a 11 000, 10 000; 10 714
b 3000, 2000; 2447
c 15 mill., 10 mill.; 13 072 080
d 720, 560; 648·584
e 6, $4\frac{1}{2}$; 5·213 068 2
f 8·3, 8·1; 8·13303

7 a 13·2 **b** 14·1 **c** 4·2 **d** 91·4
e 6·3 **f** 25·9 **g** 18·9 **h** 11·3
i 5·3 **j** 0·9 **k** 2·3 **l** 14·8

8 discuss

9 a 19·2 m **b** 19·6 m **c** 0·4 m **d b**

EXERCISE 2B

1 a six hundred and fifty million
b seven billion, eight hundred and four million and nine hundred thousand

2 530 194 070 000 000

3 a yes **b** yes **c** no **d** no
e no **f** yes **g** yes **h** yes

4 a 10^3 **b** 1 000 000, 10^6
c 1·2, 1·2 **d** $5·08 \times 100\ 000$, 5·08

5 a $7·4 \times 10^3$ **b** $8·5 \times 10^2$
c 9×10^4 **d** $3·4 \times 10^4$
e $1·08 \times 10^5$ **f** $4·3 \times 10^6$
g $2·07 \times 10^6$ **h** $5·634 \times 10^9$
i $6·784 \times 10^2$ **j** $3·408 \times 10$
k $4·28 \times 10^0$ **l** $8·76 \times 10^7$

6 a 390 **b** 200 000 **c** 7 080 000
d 20 600 **e** 80 000 000 **f** 302 400
g 70 **h** 298·3 **i** 5076·9
j 40 **k** 680 500 000 **l** 5 070 000 000

7 a 5×10^9, 5 000 000 000
b $2·35\ 266 \times 10^{11}$, 235 266 000 000
c $1·6 \times 10^{13}$, 16 000 000 000 000

8 a $8·5 \times 10^8$ **b** 6×10^9 **c** 3×10^{16}
d 2×10^{12} **e** $6·5 \times 10^{15}$

9 a 1×10^{10} **b** $1·43 \times 10^9$ **c** $3·844 \times 10^5$

10 a 361 700 000
b 1 670 000 000 000 000 000 000
c 22 000 000

11 a 8×10^4 **b** 3×10^6 **c** 6×10^5
d $4·8 \times 10^8$ **e** $1·4 \times 10^8$ **f** $3·88 \times 10^8$

13 a $1·8 \times 10^{10}$ **b** $7·98 \times 10^{11}$ **c** $2·184 \times 10^8$
d 1000 **e** $4·7 \times 10^5$ **f** 3
g 0·284 615 3 km$^2 \approx$ 28·5 ha
h $E = m \times 9 \times 10^{16}$

EXERCISE 2C

1 a yes **b** no **c** no **d** yes
e yes **f** yes **g** no **h** no

2 a $4·7 \times 10^{-3}$ **b** 3×10^{-3} **c** 7×10^{-5}
d $1·02 \times 10^{-4}$ **e** 6×10^{-2} **f** $1·9 \times 10^{-1}$
g $8·05 \times 10^{-5}$ **h** $2·006 \times 10^{-4}$ **i** $5·09 \times 10^{-1}$
j 1×10^{-9} **k** 3×10^0 **l** $3·4 \times 10^{-3}$

3 a 0·005 2 **b** 0·000 025 4
c 0·13 **d** 0·000 604 4
e 0·000 005 **f** 0·02
g 0·000 037 07 **h** 0·1
i 0·000 000 304 5 **j** 0·000 000 080 76
k 1·02 **l** 0·0037

4 a $1·836 \times 10^{-6}$, 0·000 001 836
b $8·72 \times 10^{-7}$, 0·000 000 872
c $8·4136 \times 10^{-7}$, 0·000 000 841 36

5 a 2×10^{-3} **b** $1·2 \times 10^{-6}$ **c** $1·67 \times 10^{-21}$

6 a 0·000 08 **b** 0·000 015 **c** 0·000 001

7 a $5·2 \times 10^{-2}$, $8·33 \times 10^1$, $2·73 \times 10^7$
b $6·71 \times 10^{-7}$, $6·1 \times 10^{-1}$, $2·04 \times 10^3$
c 6×10^{-5}, $5·907 \times 10^{-3}$, $4·5 \times 10^5$
d $2·05 \times 10^{-2}$, $2·2 \times 10^{-2}$, $7·6 \times 10^3$

8 a $9·2 \times 10^{-4}$ **b** $1·9 \times 10^{-8}$
c $1·2 \times 10^{-4}$ **d** $2·4 \times 10^{-16}$
e $4·5 \times 10^{-9}$ **f** $3·6 \times 10^5$

EXERCISE 2D

1 a i $3·5 \times 10^5$ **ii** 2
b i $6·78 \times 10^6$ **ii** 3
c i $4·08 \times 10^8$ **ii** 3
d i $9·204 \times 10^{-4}$ **ii** 4
e i $7·5 \times 10^{-4}$ **ii** 2
f i $2·007 \times 10^{-3}$ **ii** 4
g i $9·0 \times 10^4$ **ii** 2 or 9×10^4; 1
h i $2·0 \times 10^{-7}$ **ii** 2 or 2×10^{-7}; 1

2 a 4 900 000 **b** 310 000
c 0·000 068 **d** 0·005 1
e 0·000 32 **f** 600 000 000
g 0·16 **h** 8·9
i 2 400 000 **j** 17
k 300 000 **l** 1000

3 a 300 **b** 300 **c** equal answers
d 1, 2, 3 or 4

4 discuss

EXERCISE 2E

1 a distance/time **b** money/time
c money/length **d** mass/time
e money/mass **f** money/area
g capacity/time **h** mass/area

2 a \$8/h **b** \$1.20/can
c 2250 revs/min **d** 1·5°/h
e 0·098 L/km **f** 9·2 m/s

g 0·05 mL/cm²   **h** 30·6 runs/wkt
i 160 km/h   **j** $152.78/m²
k 0·25 student/m³   **l** $10.98/g

3 **a** graph   **b** 2·5 mL; 17·5 mL
c 18·4 L; 11·2 L   **d** Wk = 1·25 W
4 6 709 787
5 **a** $16\frac{1}{3}$ **b** 3·7
6 150 kg/ha
7 10·5 km/L or 0·1 L/km or 9·6 L/100 km
8 **a** 90 km/h   **b** 216·7 km/h   **c** 155·6 km/h
9 **a** $\frac{3}{4}$ h   **b** $1\frac{1}{4}$ h
c 2·8 h   **d** 3·6 s
10 **a** 180 km   **b** 270 km   **c** 135 km
11 **a** 1650 m   **b** 3960 m   **c** 14·85 km
12 312·5 L/min
13 $72.78 p.a.
14 27·7 ≈ 28 min
15 **a** **i** X   **ii** 0·2 s, 2 m
b 350 g jar; more g/¢
c Jim 13·6% Jenny 14%; discuss terms
d Sale price = $6.67/m; $1.28/m cheaper
e 24.38¢/250 mL; 26.3¢/250 mL. Discuss
f 8·85 L/100 km, 10.29 L/100 km, the 1·5 L car is more economical
16 **a** B   **b** C   **c** A, steepest line
d **i** A : 16 km/h, B : 12 km/h C : 4 km/h
ii 16 000 m/h, 12 000 m/h, 4000 m/h
iii 4·44 m/s, 3·33 m/s, 1·11 m/s
17 **a** 300   **b** 1   **c** 50
d 0·57   **e** 34·20   **f** 2052
g 39·25   **h** 0·65   **i** 2000
18 **a** 1000 m/s   **b** $22\frac{2}{9}$ m/s   **c** $27\frac{7}{9}$ m/s
d 55 m/s
19 **a** 240 km/h   **b** 18 km/h   **c** 21·6 km/h
d 2·16 km/h
20 48 km/h   **21** 637·8 km/h   **22** 2400 L/h
23 **a** 0·4 mL/s   **b** 1·44 L/h   **c** 12·6 kL/year
24 **a** 2·5   **b** 5·4   **c** 1 576 800
25 **a** 60 km   **b** 540 km
c 108 000 km   **d** 1 036 800 km
26 30 min
27 $t ≈ 1·7$ h
28 **a** 1224 km/h   **b** 29 s   **c** 0·000 03 s
d 28·999 97 s   **e** discuss   **f** 0·0125 s

Chapter Review Exercises
1 **a** 4705·0   **b** 4705·04   **c** 4705·0
d 4705·04   **e** 4705·040
2 **a** 600, 490   **b** 56 − 3 × 0·2 ≈ 56 − 0·6
3 **a** $8·26 × 10^{-5}$ **b** $3·02 × 10^5$
4 **a** 7 000 000   **b** 0·000 38   **c** 514 306
5 **a** 55 100 000   **b** $5·5074 × 10^7$ **c** 55 100 000
6 **a** 4300   **b** 64 000   **c** 7·7   **d** 0·0040
7 **a** 53 300   **b** 0·000 392   **c** 44·0
d 0·800
8 2145 to 2154
9 **a** **i** 15 : 1   **ii** 7 : 10
iii 1 : 35   **iv** 1 : 20

b 0·38 : 1   **c** 6 : 7   **d** $300 : $600 : $1500
10 **a** 24   **b** 11·2
11 $5.85
12 **i** 240   **ii** $15\frac{1}{2}$ m
13 $60 000
14 **a** 72 km/h   **b** 400 g/h
15 **a** $\frac{4}{9}$ m/s   **b** 25 m/s   **c** $66\frac{2}{3}$ m/s
16 **a** 300 km/h   **b** 36 km/h   **c** 32·4 km/h
17 **a** 673·7 km/h   **b** 11·2 km/min
c 187·1 m/s
18 69·4 m
19 1 kg box; more mass per dollar
20 8 min 20 s   **21** 41 km
22 2253   **23** $63.98 more

Keeping Mathematically Fit

PART A
1 $4.50   **2** 10 000   **3** 0·6̇
4 $9   **5** (b)   **6** 17°C
7 8:22 am, 7 mins   **8** 6
9 13, 14 or 15   **10** 40 cm²

PART B
1 628 cm²   **2** 60 km/h   **3** 6·7
4 **a** family   **b** $10.67
5 **a** 343 cm²   **b** 12·12 cm

Chapter 3

MathsCheck

1 **a** value of divisions unknown, direction of scale unknown. 28 g, 29·6 g, 29·8 g, 30·2 g, 30·4 g, 32 g (others may also be correct)
b 2850 L
2 compare and discuss
3 **a** 100 000 times   **b** 70 dB
c a sound with same noise level as normal conversation
4 **a** 100 000 times   **b** $\frac{1}{100}$
5 **a** 2000 g   **b** 4500 kg   **c** 7020 g
d 60 g   **e** 7 kg   **f** 10 g
g 54·2 t   **h** 0·9 kg   **i** 2 500 000 g
j 32 000 mg   **k** 0·000 13 t   **l** 0·000 065 t
6 5·25 g   **7** 3·2 kg   **8** 444 g   **9** 7·45 kg
10 1230 g   **11** yes, combined mass is 2·95 t
12 937·5 mL **13** 73 kg
14 **a** 70 mm   **b** 600 cm   **c** 290 mm
d 5100 mm   **e** 430 m   **f** 20·6 cm
g 6·8 cm   **h** 34 km   **i** 4·5 m
j 81·2 cm   **k** 7·025 km   **l** 0·08 m
m 0·284 m   **n** 0·0605 m   **o** 0·003 m
p 500 mm   **q** 2250 m   **r** 0·052 m
15 **a** 300 000 cm   **b** 65·12 km   **c** 40 000 mm
d 0·000 673 km
16 5   **17** 5·2 km **18** Jenny by 6 cm
19 96 cm   **20** 11 pieces, 5 cm
21 16·95 km   **22** no
23 approx. 150 m, 1 200 000

24 **a** $\sqrt{145}$ **b** $\sqrt{61}$ **c** 4·78 (2 d.p.)
25 **a** 33·5 cm to 34·5 cm
 b 45·85 m to 45·95 m
 c 13·545 mm to 13·555 mm
 d 23·5° to 24·5°
 e 0·885 km to 0·895 km
26 7 cm × 8 cm, 9 cm × 6 cm, 10 cm × 5 cm, etc.
27 **a** 36 cm **b** 45·2 km **c** 5·39 cm
 d 10·73 **e** 19·2 mm **f** 27·6 cm
 g 22 cm **h** 28 cm **i** 16 cm

EXERCISE 3A
1 **a** 43·4 m **b** 3·64 km **c** 30 cm
2 **a** 28 cm **b** 0·868 m **c** 58·2 cm
 d 7·3 m **e** 17·25 mm **f** 12·9 cm
3 **a** 76·6 cm **b** 82 mm **c** 276 cm
 d 48·02 m **e** 744 m **f** 59 m
4 **a** 6·96 km **b** 12
5 115·2 m **6** 120 cm
7 18·9 cm (1 d.p.) **8** 87·3 m (1 d.p.)
9 **a** 9·5 cm to 10·5 cm **b** 38 cm to 42 cm
10 **a** 7·45 cm to 7·55 cm **b** 29·8 cm to 30·2 cm
11 20 cm

EXERCISE 3B
1 **a** 39·3 cm **b** 22·6 mm **c** 2·67 mm
 d 377 km **e** 3·14 cm **f** 547 mm
 g 1·57 m **h** 11·0 cm **i** 80·4 cm
2 78·54 cm **3** 22·0 cm
4 **a** 44·0 cm **b** 26·4 m **c** 7·33 cm
5 **a** 173 cm **b** 57·9
6 63·7 m **7** 8 **8** 33·8 cm square
9 **a** **i** 6·13 cm **ii** 10·0 cm
 b **i** 5·03 cm **ii** 9·83 cm
 c **i** 99·5 mm **ii** 137·5 mm
 d **i** 11·1 cm **ii** 44·3 cm
10 6·75 m
11 **a** 55·4 m (1 d.p.) **b** 14·3 units (1 d.p.)
 c 25·1 m (1 d.p.) **d** 68·1 m
 e 505·6 m **f** 44·8 m
12 $8\pi \doteqdot 25\cdot1$ units **13** 153·89 m
14 **a** $P = 3m$ **b** $P = \pi d$ **c** $P = \pi r + 2r$
 d $P = 6r + \pi r$ **e** $P = 8x + 2y$ **f** $P = x + y + z$
 g $P = \frac{1}{2}\pi (x + y + z)$
15 $12\pi \approx 37\cdot7$ u **16** $60\pi \approx 188\cdot5$ u
17 same distance **18** 38·9 cm

EXERCISE 3C
1 100
 10 000
 10 000
 1 000 000
 100
2 **a** 160 mm² **b** 1385·44 cm² **c** 1076 m²
3 **a** 67·92 cm² **b** 1·57 m² **c** 37·70 cm²
4 **a** 123·98 mm² **b** 971·06 m²
 c 26·86 cm² **d** 25·63 cm²
5 8292 cm² **6** 31 m²
7 **a** 13·73 u² **b** 13·73 u² **c** 1 : 1

8 107·67 cm² **9** 18·7% (1 d.p.)
10 **a** 2120·6 u² **b** 1 : 3
11 **a** 12·5 m × 12·5 m **b** 25 m × 12·5 m
12 21·99 cm to 28·27 cm
 38·48 cm² to 63·62 cm²

EXERCISE 3D
1 **a** 187 cm² **b** 3·77 cm² (1·5 cm)
 c 1·488 m² (1·1 m)
2 880 mm²
3 **a** 59·5 cm² **b** 119 cm² **c** 119 cm², yes
4 **a** 2·28 cm² **b** 1216 m² **c** 24·5 cm²
5 **a** 1·705 cm² **b** 4560 cm² **c** 12·24 cm²
6 12·2 cm²
7 **a** 29·8 m² **b** 0·210 km² **c** 180 mm²
8 26·845 m² **9** 32·4 cm² **10** 7·377 km²
11 64·6 cm² **12** 1·169 m² **13** 1·08 cm²
14 **a** 1098 mm² **b** 1116 mm²
15 260 cm² **16** 28·8 cm²
17 **a** 36 cm² **b** 60 m² **c** 106·97 m²
18 10 square units
19 15 sq. units
20 (7, 4) or (3, ⁻2) or (⁻7, 4)
21 21 sq. units
22 **a** 30 m² **b** 7·81 m **c** 3·84 m
23 **a** 14·375 cm **b** 70·16 cm
24 **a** 48 cm **b** 480 cm²
25 183·57 cm² **26** 8·8 m **27** 1350 m²
28 1128 mm² **29** 38·4 cm²
30 **a** 28·9 m² **b** 47·2 cm²
31 **a** 540 m² **b** 135 L **c** $628.02
32 43%
33 **a** use Pythagoras, **b** 26 m²
 AB = 4·6 m
 c $1170
34 189 m² **35** $\dfrac{x}{25}$
36 **a** $(36\pi + 144) x^2$ **b** cheaper

EXERCISE 3E
1 demonstrate and discuss
2 **a** approx. 2 500 000 km²
 b 7 682 000 km²
3 discuss

Chapter Review Exercises
1 **a** 275°C **b** 4·2 or 4·25 V
2 7 **3** discuss
4 **a** 3·5 m; 4.5 m **b** 23·75 min; 23·85 min
 c 5·395 kg; 5·405 kg
5 **a** 165 min **b** 8 min 15 s **c** 1 h 12 min
 d 0·195 m **e** 0·592 km **f** 60 000 mm
 g 17·65 kg
 h 0·45 t **i** 340 000 g
6 1750 kg **7** 9:53 am **8** 111
9 discuss
10 **a** 64·5 cm **b** 14·5 mm **c** 13·8 m
11 6 cm **12** 6400 km
13 **a** **i** 39·0 cm **ii** 120·8 mm²
 b **i** 25·7 m **ii** 39·3 m²
 c **i** 60 m **ii** 120 m²

d **i** 4·7 m   **ii** 0·8 m²
e **i** 35·1 cm   **ii** 76·14 cm²
f **i** 345·4 mm   **ii** 2714·9 mm²
14 approx. 14 cm²
15 **a** rhombus   **b** 313 cm²

Keeping Mathematically Fit

PART A
1 25   **2** 2b   **3** $y = 3x + 2$
4 10–12 m approx.   **5** 5 : 40

6 **a** $\frac{3}{8}$ **b** $37\frac{1}{2}$ L

7 4·07   **8** 5   **9** 0·008
10 3000 mm³

PART B
1 $3·35 \times 10^7$ **2** 10·1 m³   **3** $16\frac{2}{3}$
4 34 cm²   **5** 21·1 m

Chapter 4

Mathscheck
1 **a** 24   **b** 16   **c** 47·346
2 **a** 74   **b** 16   **c** 363
     d 3   **e** 6   **f** 5
3 **a** 8·85   **b** 2·625   **c** 1·08

4 **a** ⁻1·2   **b** $\frac{9}{775}$ **c** 2·4

5 **a** 36   **b** 618   **c** 327·969

6 **a** ⁻3   **b** $-2\frac{1}{2}$ **c** ⁻1

7 **a** ⁻3   **b** ⁻5   **c** ⁻11
8 **a** 0   **b** 1   **c** 4

9 **a** $-12\frac{2}{9}°$ **b** 32°   **c** $-17\frac{7}{9}°$

10 **a** $C = 2\pi r$ **b** $D = ST$
     c $I = PRn$ **d** $A = x^2 + \dfrac{xy}{2}$
     e $r = \sqrt{p^2 + q^2}$ **f** $P = a + b + c + \sqrt{a^2 + (c - b)^2}$
     g sum = $x + 2x + 100°$, $260° = 3x$
11 **a** $x = 5$ **b** $x = 14$ **c** $x = 6$ **d** $x = 18$
     e $n = 7$ **f** $x = ⁻4$ **g** $x = 3$
12 **a** $x = 4$ **b** $x = 14$ **c** $x = 4$ **d** $x = 7$
     e $a = 16$
13 **a** $x = 2$ **b** $x = 4$ **c** $x = 0$ **d** $x = 0$
     e $x = 2$ **f** $x = 2$ **g** $x = 8$ **h** $x = 2$
14 **a** $x = 23$ **b** $x = \dfrac{1}{3}$ **c** $x = 13\frac{1}{2}$

     d $x = \dfrac{21}{2}$ **e** $x = 17$

15 **a** $C = 850 + 156h$ **b** 7 hours
     c 8:15 pm
16 **a** hours worked   **b** 7·5 hours
17 **a** 6   **b** 3·5
18 **a** $x = 3$ **b** $n = 2$ **c** $x = ⁻3$
19 **a** $d = 6$ **b** $x = \dfrac{11}{3}$ **c** $x = 4\frac{1}{6}$ **d** $x = 0$
20 **a** and **b** only
21 **a** $x = ⁻5$ **b** $x = ⁻5$ **c** $x = ⁻1$ **d** $x = 24$
     e $x = \dfrac{⁻40}{3}$

22 discuss
23 $w = 16p$

EXERCISE 4A
1 **a** 4   **b** 4   **c** 2   **d** 5   **e** 1
     f 1   **g** 1   **h** 4   **i** ⁻1

2 **a** 2   **b** 8   **c** $\dfrac{4}{3}$ **d** $3\frac{1}{2}$

3 **a** 3   **b** 1   **c** ⁻2   **d** 17
     e 3   **f** 3
4 **a** 4   **b** 12   **c** 4   **d** ⁻1

     e 5   **f** $\dfrac{⁻9}{5}$

5 **a** $5(n + 6) = 40$; 2   **b** $3(n - 5) = 3$; 6

     c $2(n + 4) = 15$; $3\frac{1}{2}$ **d** $\dfrac{1}{3}(n + 6) = 8$; 18

     e $\dfrac{3}{4}(2n - 4) = 6$; 6   **f** discuss

6 **a** $\dfrac{⁻1}{2}$ **b** $3\frac{1}{2}$ **c** $2\frac{4}{5}$ **d** 3

     e ⁻6   **f** $\dfrac{⁻1}{3}$

EXERCISE 4B
1 **a** 28   **b** 30   **c** ⁻6   **d** 30   **e** 24
     f 30   **g** 28   **h** 77   **i** 8   **j** 6
     k 12   **l** 9   **m** $\dfrac{⁻4}{15}$ **n** 7   **o** 34
     p 1   **q** 11   **r** 3   **s** 3   **t** 2
     u 14   **v** ⁻2   **w** 15

2 **a** ① $p - \dfrac{3}{4} = \dfrac{5}{4}$ **b** ① $3s - 12 = 8$

     c ② $6 + 2k \neq 8k$ **d** ① $8 - x - 4 = ⁻7$
     e ③ $18 + 30x \neq 48x$

     f ① $\dfrac{x + \cancel{8}}{\cancel{8}}$ cancelling, possible only for x

     g ① $\dfrac{7m}{7} - 1 \times 7 = 4 \times 7$

     h ① $= 5 \times 3$ ③ $2n = 4$
     i no errors
3 **a** $p = 2$ **b** $s = 6\frac{2}{3}$ **c** $k = ⁻4$

     d $x = 11$ **e** $x = \dfrac{1}{15}$ **f** $x = 25$

     g $m = 35$ **h** $n = 7$ **i** $t = 12$
4 **a** $x = ⁻4$ **b** $x = ⁻36$ **c** $x = 14$
     d $a = 12$ **e** $w = ⁻36$ **f** $a = 6$

     g $x = 16\frac{4}{5}$ **h** $x = 12\frac{3}{5}$ **i** $a = ⁻24$

     j $n = \dfrac{⁻5}{8}$ **k** $a = ⁻1\frac{1}{11}$ **l** $x = 12$

5 **a** $a = 5\frac{5}{6}$ **b** $w = 4$ **c** $x = 5$

     d $x = \dfrac{⁻6}{7}$ **e** $x = ⁻5\frac{5}{6}$ **f** $x = ⁻\frac{1}{4}$

     g $y = 2$ **h** $k = ⁻1$

6 a $m = 5\frac{2}{7}$ **b** $x = 3$ **c** $a = \frac{1}{12}$

d $x = \frac{^-29}{5}$ **e** $x = ^-3\frac{1}{3}$ **f** $n = ^-3\frac{1}{2}$

g $x = ^-1\frac{1}{2}$ **h** $x = 4\frac{4}{5}$ **i** $x = \frac{23}{7}$

j $a = \frac{7}{16}$

7 a T **b** F, $x = ^-14$ **c** F, $a = ^-1$
d T **e** T

8 a $x = 2$ **b** $f = \frac{vu}{u + v}$

c i $r = 0$ **ii** $r = \frac{^-1}{4}$

9 discuss

EXERCISE 4C

1 a $a = 4$ **b** $w = 16$ **c** $p = 49$ **d** $x = 0$
2 a $x = 1$ **b** $p = 8$ **c** $x = 216$ **d** $a = 2 \cdot 744$
3 a $x = ^\pm 1$ **b** $x = ^\pm 10$
  c $x = ^\pm 1 \cdot 2$ **d** $x = ^\pm 0 \cdot 77$
4 a $x = 2$ **b** $x = ^-2$ **c** $x = 10$ **d** $x = 0$

5 a $x = ^\pm 5$ **b** $x = 9$ **c** $x = \frac{1}{16}$

d $x = ^\pm \sqrt{2}$ **e** $x = \pm\sqrt{50}$ **f** $x = 4$

g $x = ^-8$ **h** $x = \pm\sqrt{5}$

6 a $x = 8$ **b** $x = 10$ **c** $x = 26$ **d** $x = 12\frac{1}{2}$

e $x = \frac{25}{4}$ **f** $x = 4$. **g** $x = ^-45$ **h** $x = 90\frac{3}{4}$

7 a $x = \pm\sqrt{18}$ **b** $x = \sqrt[3]{4}$ **c** $x = ^\pm \sqrt{2}$

d $x = 2$ **e** $x = ^\pm\frac{5}{2}$ **f** $x = 1$

g $x = 4$ or $^-6$ **h** $x = 6$ or $^-4$ **i** $x = \frac{\sqrt[3]{4} - 1}{2}$

j $x = \frac{5}{3}$ or 1 **k** $x = \frac{\sqrt[3]{^-6} - 1}{4}$ **l** $x = 1$ or 9

8 a $x = ^\pm 1$ **b** $x = \sqrt[3]{^-4}$ **c** $x = 0$

EXERCISE 4D

1 a $x = 2$ **b** $x = 2$ **c** $x = 1$
  d $x = 2$ **e** $x = 2$ **f** $x = 2$

2 a $x = \frac{3}{2}$ **b** $x = \frac{4}{3}$ **c** $x = 2$

d $x = 3$ **e** $x = 2$ **f** $x = \frac{5}{2}$

3 a $x = 5$ **b** $x = \frac{5}{2}$ **c** $x = \frac{9}{2}$

d $x = \frac{1}{2}$ **e** $x = \frac{2}{3}$ **f** $x = \frac{3}{4}$

4 a $x = \frac{1}{3}$ **b** $x = \frac{1}{2}$ **c** $x = ^-3$

d $x = ^-4$ **e** $x = \frac{^-3}{2}$ **f** $x = \frac{3}{2}$

g $x = \frac{3}{2}$ **h** $x = \frac{^-3}{2}$ **i** $x = 2$

j $x = \frac{5}{12}$ **k** $x = ^-7$ **l** $x = \frac{^-4}{3}$

EXERCISE 4E

1 a $x = 1$ **b** $x = 19$ **c** $x = 2$ **d** $x = 0$
  e $x = 0$ **f** $x = 5$ **g** $k = ^\pm 4$ **h** $x = ^\pm 3$
  i $x = ^\pm 3$ **j** $x = 49$ **k** $p = ^\pm 5$ **l** $p = ^\pm 1$

m $w = 2$ **n** $a = ^\pm\frac{1}{4}$ **o** $w = 9$

2 a $x = 5$ or $^-3$ **b** $x = 3$ or $^-5$

c $x = \pm\sqrt{\frac{3}{2}}$ **d** $x = ^-1\frac{1}{5}$

e $x = ^-9$ **f** $x = \frac{1}{5}$ **g** $x = 17$

h $x = 64$ **i** $x = ^\pm\frac{2}{3}$ **j** $x = ^-2\frac{3}{4}$

k $x = 0$ **l** $x = ^-5$ **m** $x = ^-16$
n $x = 4$ **o** $x = 0$

3 a $x = \frac{1}{3}$ **b** $x = 2$ **c** $x = 3$

d $x = 1\frac{1}{2}$ **e** $x = 0$ **f** $x = ^\pm\frac{3}{2}$

g $x = \frac{1}{4}$ **h** $x = ^-1$ **i** $p = 2$

j $x = 4$ **k** $x = 0$ **l** $x = ^-2$
m $x = 0$ **n** no solution **o** no solution

EXERCISE 4F

1 $x + 6 = 25$; 19 km
2 $2x + 3 = 117$; 57 kg

3 $\frac{1}{10}x = 6$; 60kg

4 $\frac{x - 12}{5} = 14$; 82

5 $x + (x + 1) + (x + 2) = 165$; 54, 55, 56
6 $x + (x + 2) = 76$; 39
7 $180x + 350 = 1250$; 5 cars
8 $x + 16 = 3x$; 8
9 $2x + 7 = 3x + 1$; 6
10 a $2(5n + 2n) = 42$; 15 cm
   b $4(x + 3) = 52$; 13 m
   c $2(3x + 4 + 2x - 1) = 24$
11 $2(2x + x) = 72$; $l = 24$ cm, $b = 12$ cm
12 $3(5x - 2) = 219$; $x = 15$ cm
13 a 3 **b** 5 **c** $x = 12, y = \frac{64}{3}$
14 13 000
15 Emily 9
   Justine 24
16 1875 L
17 inferior $5/L
   quality $8/L
18 A: 300 L/min
   B: 450 L/min
19 $66\frac{2}{3}$ km
20 $x = 12$, $A = 384$ cm^2

1 a 13
b 45
c i 64 **ii** 3
d i 49 **ii** 0·75
e i 3 **ii** 60
f i 80 **ii** 2
g i 32 **ii** 28
h i 15·7 **ii** 100
i i 95 **ii** 0
j i 55 **ii** 28
k i 2 **ii** ⁻10·4
2 4·81 **3** 17·5
4 i 26 **ii** 0·85

5 $\dfrac{^-1}{5}$

6 a 0·11 **b** 16 **c** ⁻7·9 **d** 4·3

EXERCISE 4H

1 a $n = p - ab$ **b** $n = \dfrac{x-a}{b}$

c $n = x - L$ **d** $n = \dfrac{d}{s}$

e $n = \dfrac{a+b}{p^2}$ **f** $\dfrac{P-2l}{2}$

g $n = \dfrac{P}{2} - l$ **h** $n = \dfrac{E}{C^2}$

i $n = \dfrac{F-ac}{t}$ **j** $n = 3 - \dfrac{x}{2p}$

k $n = \dfrac{2A}{a+b}$ **l** $n = \dfrac{2A}{b} - a$

2 a $r = \dfrac{C}{2\pi}$ **b** $r = \sqrt{\dfrac{A}{\pi}}$

c $T = \dfrac{I}{PR}$ **d** $a = \dfrac{v-u}{t}$

e $m = \dfrac{y-b}{x}$ **f** $n = \dfrac{5}{4p} - 2$

g $n = \dfrac{3}{4p} + 2$ **h** $y = \dfrac{^-ax-c}{b}$

i $x = \dfrac{^-by-c}{a}$

3 a $n = \left(\dfrac{A}{p} - 1\right) \div t$ **b** $n = \dfrac{T-a}{d} + 1$

c $n = r\sqrt{\dfrac{s(t-1)}{a} + 1}$ **d** $n = \dfrac{x^2}{a}$

e $n = a - p^2$ **f** $n = \sqrt{a} - p$

g $n = \sqrt{\dfrac{x}{a}}$ **h** $n = \sqrt{m-t}$

i $n = 4\left(\dfrac{x}{3} + 1\right)$ **j** $n = ^-4t - 3u$

k $n = \dfrac{^-2p}{p-1}$ **l** $n = \sqrt{\dfrac{6m-2t}{3}}$

m $n = \dfrac{5}{6-q}$ **n** $n = \dfrac{a+b}{3t^2}$

o $n = \dfrac{p^2 - a^4}{3t}$ **p** $n = \dfrac{t^2}{t-r}$

4 a $n = \dfrac{T-a}{d} + 1$ **b** $a = \dfrac{2s}{n} - l$

c $F = \dfrac{9C}{5} + 32$ **d** $V = \sqrt{\dfrac{2E}{m}}$

e $u = \sqrt{v^2 - 2as}$ **f** $s = \dfrac{v^2 - u^2}{2a}$

g $r = \sqrt[3]{\dfrac{3V}{4\pi}}$ **h** $b = \sqrt{x^2 + 4ac}$

i $l = \dfrac{s - \pi r^2}{\pi r}$ **j** $r = \dfrac{xs}{s-x}$

5 a $x = 3A - 4$ **b** $x = \dfrac{4m}{m-3}$ **c** $x = \dfrac{4a-6n}{n+1}$

d $x = \dfrac{4}{A-1}$ **e** $x = \dfrac{b}{a-b}$ **f** $x = \dfrac{A^2+1}{2}$

g $x = \sqrt{\dfrac{9-A}{3}}$ **h** $x = 5 - A^3$

6 a 20 cm **b** 9·77 cm

7 a $r > 0, A > 0$ **b** $r = \sqrt{\dfrac{A}{4\pi}}$, positive values

8 a all values of x **b** $z \geq 0$ and $x \geq 0$

9 $t = \pm\sqrt{\dfrac{4-y}{4a^2}}$

EXERCISE 4I

1 a x equals 3
b x is less than or equal to 3
c x is greater than or equal to ⁻2
d x is greater than 0 but less than 3
e x equals ⁻3 **f** x is greater than 2
g x equals 6 and ⁻6
h x is greater than or equal to 0 and less than or equal to 3
i x is greater than 3
j x is greater than ⁻2
k x is less than 5, greater than 4
l x is less than zero, x is greater than 3

2 a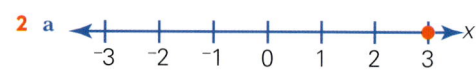

b

c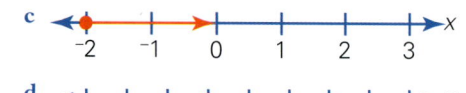

d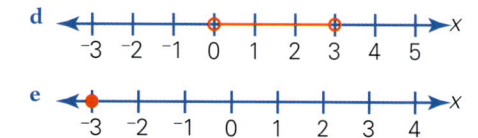

e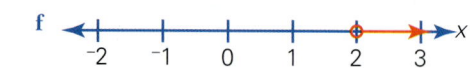

f

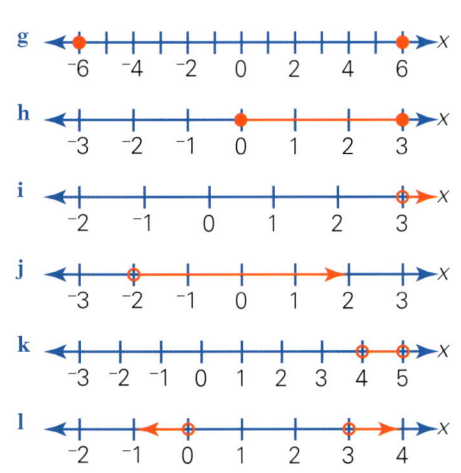

g (number line: $^-6$ to 6, filled dots at $^-6$ and 6)

h (number line: $^-3$ to 3, filled dot at 0, line to 3)

i (number line: $^-2$ to 3, open dot at 3)

j (number line: $^-3$ to 3, open dot at $^-2$, arrow right)

k (number line: $^-3$ to 5, open dots at 4 and 5)

l (number line: $^-2$ to 4, open dot at 0, open dot at 3)

3 A5, B1, C3, D4, E2

4 a $x > ^-1$ b $x \le 7$ c $x \ge ^-1$ d $x > ^-1$
   e $x < 0$ f $x \ge ^-8$ g $x > 0$ h $x < 2$
   i $x \ge ^-1$ j $x = 0, 1, 2$

5 a $x < ^-1, x > 1$ b $a \ge ^-1$
   c $w \le ^-2, w > 0$ d $0 < x \le 4$
   e $^-3 < a < 0$ f $x < 0, x \ge 1$
   g $^-2 < w < 2$ h $^-2 \le a \le 2$

6 a (number line: $^-5$ to 6, open dots at 1 and 5, arrows)

   b (number line: $^-4$ to 5, open dots at $^-1$ and 2)

   c (number line: $^-4$ to 5, filled dots at 0 and 4)

   d (number line: $^-4$ to 5, open dot at $^-1$, open circle at 4)

   e (number line: $^-4$ to 5, filled dot at $^-1$, open dot at 3)

EXERCISE 4J

1 a $n \ge 2$ (number line: $^-1$ to 2, filled dot at 2, arrow right)

   b $x < ^-7$ (number line: $^-7$ to 7, open dot at $^-7$, arrow left)

   c $p \le 1$ (number line: $^-1$ to 2, filled dot at 1, arrow left)

   d $n < 12$ (number line: 0 to 12, open dot at 12, arrow left)

   e $x \le 3$ (number line: $^-3$ to 3, filled dot at 3, arrow left)

   f $x > ^-12$ (number line: $^-12$ to 0, open dot at $^-12$, arrow right)

   g $n \le 7$ (number line: 0 to 7, filled dot at 7, arrow left)

h $x > ^-12$ (number line: $^-12$, 0, 12; open dot at $^-12$, arrow right)

i $x \le 5$ (number line: $^-5$, 0, 5; filled dot at 5, arrow left)

j $n > 12$ (number line: 0, 12; open dot at 12, arrow right)

k $x \le 0$ (number line: $^-2$, 0, 2; filled dot at 0, arrow left)

l $a < ^-7$ (number line: $^-7$, 0; open dot at $^-7$, arrow left)

m $n > ^-6$ (number line: $^-6$, 0, 6; open dot at $^-6$, arrow right)

2 a $n > 2$ b $n < 8$
   c $n < 5$ d $n \ge 12$
   e $x > 10$ f $t \le 0$ g $p \ge ^-5$ h $a > 17$
   i $h < ^-4$ j $c \ge 0$ k $y > ^-9$ l $z \le 7$
   m $n \ge 12$ n $d > ^-10$ o $x \ge 0 \cdot 8$ p $n < 2$
   q $p \ge 4$ r $t > 1$ s $c < \frac{2}{7}$ t $d \le ^-3$
   u $w > 21$ v $a \ge 20$ w $b < 4$ x $c \le 4$

3 a $y \ge 3$ b $p \le ^-4$ c $f > 6$ d $n \le \frac{1}{2}$
   e $k > \frac{^-5}{3}$ f $x > 1$ g $n > \frac{^-11}{2}$ h $n < \frac{17}{20}$

4 a $3x < 8; x < \frac{8}{3}$ b $2x + 6 > 12; x > 3$
   c $6x - 4 \le 14; x \le 3$
   d $8(x + 3) > 23 \cdot 5; x > ^-0.0625$
   e $\frac{x - 7}{4} \ge \frac{5}{8}; x \ge 9\frac{1}{2}$

5 a $1 \le 8000$ b $s \ge 1000$ c $x < 500$
   d $x \le 76$ e $x \le 4 \cdot 5$
   f $x \ge 2$ and $x \le 8$ or $2 \le x \le 8$
   g $x \le 10$ h $x \ge 85$

EXERCISE 4K

1 a $1, 2, 3$ b $^-3, ^-2, ^-1$
   c $1\frac{1}{2} < n < 5$ d $0 < n \le 2\frac{1}{2}$

2 a $^-2, ^-1, 0, 1, 2, 3, 4$
   b $^-65 < n \le ^-6, n$ is integral
   c $n < \frac{4}{9}, n$ is negative. No real solutions.

3 $^-7 < x < 0$

4 $^-3 \le n \le 675$

Chapter Review Exercises

1 a the sum of 3 and $5x$
   b the product of $^-4$ and 7 less than p
   c half the product of 3 and a plus 8
   d 6 less the product of 4 and t multiplied by $\frac{5}{7}$

2 a 3 b 112 c 327 d $^-80$ e $\frac{3}{7}$

3 a 5 b $7\frac{1}{2}$ c 10 d 3 e $4\frac{1}{2}$

4 **a** $1\frac{2}{3}$ **b** $^-1\frac{1}{8}$ **c** $\frac{5}{8}$ **d** $\frac{^-1}{3}$

e $^-4\frac{1}{2}$ **f** 1.9 **g** $\pm\sqrt{\frac{2}{3}}$ **h** $x = \pm 6$

i $x = 31$ **j** $x = 5$

5 **a** 14 **b** ± 16

6 **a** $\frac{n}{2} + 3 = 21; 36$ **b** $x + 7 = 2x; 7$

c $3x < ^-8; x < ^-2\frac{2}{3}$ **d** $42 = \frac{1}{2} \times 14h; 6$ cm

e $10 + 6x = 34; 4h$

f $500 + 7n \geq 3000; n > \$357.14$

7 $A = \frac{2P}{h} - B$

8 **a** $r = \frac{A}{2\pi h}$ **b** $r = \pm\sqrt{\frac{A}{4\pi}}$

9 $x = \frac{P}{1-P}$

10 **a** $10, 9, 8, \ldots$
  b $^-2, ^-3, ^-4, \ldots$
  c any three of: $6, 7, 8, 9, 10$

11 **a** $x > ^-1$ **b** $x \geq 0$ **c** $^-2 \leq x \leq 2$

12 **a**
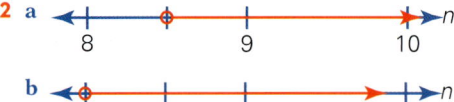

  b

  c

  d

13 **a**
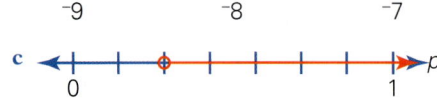

  b

Keeping Mathematically Fit

PART A
1 $^-0.001$ **2** $7:45$ pm **3** 0.4 kg
4 $1 \times 1 \times 60$
  $1 \times 2 \times 30$
  $1 \times 3 \times 20$
  $1 \times 4 \times 15$
  $1 \times 5 \times 12$
  $1 \times 6 \times 10$
  $2 \times 3 \times 10$
  $2 \times 5 \times 6$
  $3 \times 4 \times 5$

5 $\frac{2}{9}$ **6** 7 and 8

7 several possible answers
8 26.44 **9** $1\frac{1}{2}$ L

10 **a** 7 **b** $\frac{5}{12}$

PART B
1 **a** $\$12.80$ **b** 12 km
2 **a** 10.8 million **b** 30%
3 $x = 12$
4 **a** 4.1 **b** 3.5 **c** 3
5 1600 m^2

Cumulative Review 1

1 **a** $4t + 2$ **b** $5k - 2k^2$
  c $16a + 5b + 4$ **d** $-4e^2 + 11e + 8$

  e $-12v^2w$ **f** $\frac{5d}{7r}$

2 D **3** D **4** C **5** B **6** C
7 B **8** C **9** B **10** B
11 $8x^2 - 22x - 21$

12 **a** 3 **b** $\frac{1}{\sqrt[4]{f}}$ **c** $\frac{1}{6}$ **d** $\frac{1}{\sqrt[3]{t^2}}$

13 3.76 **14** $\frac{38}{10}$ **15** $760, 725.8$

16 **a** 3600 **b** 12.7 **c** 3.00 **d** $10\,400$
17 3.5×10^6
18 **a** 109 **b** $79\,000$ **c** $0.002\,314$
19 **a** 3.1×10^6 **b** $3\,100\,000$
20 B **21** A **22** D **23** C
24 **a** 13 m **b** 9 m^2
25 **a** 23.4 cm **b** 30 cm^2
26 **a** 36 cm **b** 77 cm^2
27 A **28** C **29** 150 **30** D
31 **a** $V = 31$ **b** $t = 2.9$
32 **a** $p = 3.5$ **b** $t = ^-2.5$
  c $y = ^-3$ **d** $d = 3$
  e $a = 6$ **f** $t = 4$
33 9
34 **a** $x = 12$ **b** $f = \frac{2}{3}$ **c** $n = \frac{^-2}{3}$

35 **a** $t = \frac{y}{p}$ **b** $t = \frac{v-u}{a}$ **c** $t = \frac{2A}{h} - b$

36 D

37 **a**
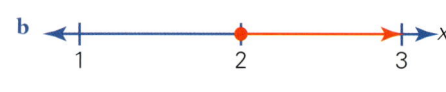

  b
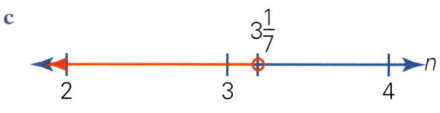

  c

Chapter 5

MathsCheck
1 **a** $75°$ **b** 5.8 cm, 3.6 cm
2, 3 constructions
4 **a** $a = 29$ **b** $b = 123$
  c $c = 47$ **d** $d = 72; e = 108$

e $g = 36; h = 80$ **f** $j = 120$
g $k = 45$ **h** $l = 57$
i $m = 140; n = 40$ **j** $p = 76$
k $q = 35; r = 145$ **l** $s = 61; t = 61$
m It is isosceles

5 a yes; $180°$ **b** no; insufficient information
c yes; $180°$ **d** yes; $180°$ **e** no; not $180°$
f no; not $180°$

6 a $t = 15$, right angle
b $x = 36$, straight line
$y = 108$, vert. opp.
c $p = 37$, straight line, $q = 148$, vert. opp.

7 a RV **b** $\angle QUW$ **c** $\angle PQU$
d $\angle SQU$ **e** $\angle TUV$ **f** $\angle QUW$
g $\angle QUT$

8 p, t, v

9 a $w = 48$ (alt. $\angle$s and $\parallel$ lines)
b $t = 55$ (corr. $\angle$s and $\parallel$ lines)
c $g = 115$ (co-int. $\angle$s and $\parallel$ lines)
d $x = 79$ (co-int. $\angle$s and $\parallel$ lines)
e $b = 52$ (alt. $\angle$s and $\parallel$ lines)
f $s = 90$ (co-int $\angle$s and $\parallel$ lines)
$t = 71$ (corr. $\angle$s and $\parallel$ lines)
g $x = 44$ (co-int. $\angle$s and $\parallel$ lines)
$y = 44$ (alt. $\angle$s and $\parallel$ lines)
h $r = 94$ (co-int. $\angle$s and $\parallel$ lines)
i $a = 47$ (corr. $\angle$s and $\parallel$ lines)
j $d = 49$ (corr. $\angle$s and $\parallel$ lines)
k $z = 124$ (vert. opp. angles and corr. $\angle$s
and $\parallel$ lines)
l $m = 50$ (co-int. $\angle$s and $\parallel$ lines)
$n = 53$ (alt. $\angle$s and $\parallel$ lines)
m $p = 76$ (corr. $\angle$s and $\parallel$)
$q = 76$ (alt. $\angle$s and $\parallel$)
n $t = 105$ (co-int. $\angle$s and $\parallel$ lines)
$u = 75$ (co-int. $\angle$s and $\parallel$ lines)
o $k = 43$ (co-int. $\angle$s and $\parallel$ lines)
p $v = 73$ (co-int. $\angle$s and $\parallel$ lines)
q $x = 90$ (alt. $\angle$s and $\parallel$ lines)
r $c = 75$ (co-int. $\angle$s and $\parallel$ lines)

10 $63°$ in p
$62°$ in q
$85°$ in r

11 a $m = 105°$ **b** $p = 156°$

12 a several possibilities, including $AD \parallel BC$ and
$\angle BDC$
b $\angle ADB$ and one other angle

13 a yes (equal angles are alternate)
b no (angles are not corresponding)
c yes (sum of co-interior angles is $180°$)

EXERCISE 5A

1 a i $43°$ **ii** $137°$
iii it equals their sum
b i $z = x + y$ **ii** check with teacher
c 6

2 a i right angle **ii** isosceles
b i obtuse **ii** scalene
c i acute **ii** equilateral

3 a $q = 28$ (angle sum of Δ)
b $e = 68$ (base $\angle$s of isos. Δ)
$f = 44$ (angle sum of Δ)
c $t = 60$ (equilateral Δ)
d $x = 45$ (base $\angle$s of isos. Δ)
e $a = 99$ (exterior angle of Δ)
f $n = 47$ (exterior angle of Δ)
g $k = 134$ (angle sum of Δ)
h $r = 120$ (exterior angle of Δ)
i $j = 32$ (exterior angle of Δ)
j $h = 132$ (exterior angle of Δ)
k $\angle CBD = 39°$ (vert. opp. angles)
$s = 58$ (exterior angle of Δ)
l $\angle ACB = 64°$ (angle sum of Δ)
$\angle ECD = 64°$ (vert. opp. angles)
$p = 76$ (angle sum of Δ)
m $\angle CBE = 55°$ (angles on a straight line)
$v = 80$ (exterior angle of Δ)
n $x = 60$ (equil. Δ)
$y = 120$ (angles on a straight line)
$z = 29$ (angle sum of Δ)
o $a = 45$ (base $\angle$s isos. Δ)
$b = 50$ ($\angle$ sum of ΔBCE)
$c = 40$ ($\angle$ sum of ΔBDE)

4 a $x = 31$ (corr. angles and $\parallel$ lines)
b $\angle CED = 56°$ (angles on a straight line)
$x = 54$ (corr. angles and $\parallel$ lines)
c $\angle CBD = 83$ (angles on a straight line)
$\angle BDC = 83$ (base $\angle$s of isos. Δ)
$x = 14$ (angle sum of Δ)
d $\angle EAB = 74$ (base $\angle$s of isos. Δ)
$x = 74$ (corr. $\angle$s and $\parallel$ lines)
e $\angle ACB = 83$ (angle sum of Δ)
$\angle BCE = 52$ (alt. angles and $\parallel$ lines)
$x = 135$ vert. (opp. angles)
f $\angle BDE = 53$ ($\angle$s in a right angle)
$x = 143$ (exterior angle of Δ)

5 6 **6** $155°$

7 $132°$, $164°$, $196°$ or $228°$

8 $\angle QRP = 42°$
$\angle PQR = 96°$

9 a constructions
b possible if the longest side is less than the
sum of the other two sides
c discuss

10 no, angle sum is $180°$, so two angles greater
than $90°$ is not permitted

11 a yes **b** yes **c** yes

12 isosceles:
a yes **b** yes **c** yes
equilateral:
a yes **b** no **b** no

EXERCISE 5B

1 a $a = 78$ ($\angle$ sum of quad.)
b $x = 98$ ($\angle$ sum of quad.)
c $t = 46$ ($\angle$ sum of quad.)
d $p = 82$ ($\angle$ sum of quad.)
e $c = 29$ ($\angle$ sum of quad.)
f $r = 88$ ($\angle$ sum of quad.)

g $d = 82$ ($\angle$ sum of quad.)

h $p = 52$ ($\angle$ sum of quad.)

i $c = 39$ ($\angle$ sum of quad.)

j $e = 21$ ($\angle$ sum of quad.)

k $a = 219$ ($\angle$s at a point)

$b = 44$ ($\angle$ sum of quad.)

l $\angle BAD = 87$ ($\angle$s on a straight line)

$\angle ABC = 83$ ($\angle$s on a straight line)

$r = 81$ ($\angle$ sum of quad.)

m $m = 90$ (co-int. $\angle$s and $\parallel$ lines)

$n = 118$ (co-int. $\angle$s and $\parallel$ lines)

n $v = 72$ (exterior angle of Δ)

$w = 105$ ($\angle$ sum of quad. *BCDE*)

o $\angle ECB = 82°$ (co-int. $\angle$s, *EA* $\parallel$ *CB*)

$c = 56°$ (co-int. $\angle$s, *EC* $\parallel$ *AB*)

$d = 124°$ (co-int. $\angle$s, *ED* $\parallel$ *AB*)

EXERCISE 5C

1 a rhombus, square

b isosceles trapezium, rectangle, square

c parallelogram, rhombus, square, rectangle

d kite, rhombus, square

e kite, trapezium

2 rhombus, parallelogram, kite, square

3 equal sides, diagonals bisect at right angles, diagonals bisect vertex angles

4 diagonals equal, all angles are right angles

5 a always   **b** sometimes   **c** sometimes

d never   **e** always   **f** always

g sometimes   **h** never

6 a yes; 1   **b** yes; 3   **c** no   **d** no

e yes; 4   **f** yes; 2

7 a no   **b** no   **c** yes; 1   **d** yes; 2

e yes; 1   **f** yes; 2

8 a $a = 55$

$b = 55$

$c = 125$

b $d = 67$

$e = 4$

c $x = 3$

$y = 4$

EXERCISE 5D

1–17 constructions

18 a all sides equal length

b kite   **c** yes

d line would not be perpendicular to *PQ*

19 a rhombus   **b** point P bisects *CD*

20 a rhombus

b equal radii form equal side lengths

c diagonals bisect each other

21 a rhombus

b diagonals bisect the angles through which they pass

c kite   **d** yes   **e** quadrilateral

f no

EXERCISE 5E

1 a $720°$ **b** $1080°$ **c** $1440°$

2 a i 540 **ii** $108°$

b i $1080°$ **ii** $135°$

c i $900°$ **ii** $128\cdot6°$

d i $1260°$ **ii** $140°$

e i $1800°$ **ii** $150°$

3 a $a = 60$ **b** $d = 40$ **c** $t = 15$

4 a $45°$ **b** $360°$

c Together the exterior angles form one complete revolution. Or show that

$$n\left[180 - \frac{(n-2)180}{n}\right] = 360\right)$$

5 a 18

b exterior angle cannot be 80° as it is not a factor of 360°

6 a $24°$ **b** $156°$

7 a $360 \div n$ **b** $180 - (360 \div n)$

c $180 - \dfrac{360}{n}$

$= \dfrac{180n}{n} - \dfrac{360}{n}$

$= \dfrac{180n - 360}{n}$

$= \dfrac{180(n-2)}{n}$

Chapter Review Exercises

1 construction

2 two sides of 4 and 4·5, total less than 9

3, 4 constructions

5 a $x = 22$ ($\angle$s in a right angle)

b $t = 75$ ($\angle$s on a straight line)

c $p = 62$ ($\angle$s at a point)

d $a = 121$ (alt. $\angle$s and $\parallel$ lines)

e $b = 109$ (co-int. $\angle$s and $\parallel$ lines)

f $c = 80$ (corr. $\angle$s and $\parallel$ lines)

g $a = 38$ ($\angle$ sum, isos. Δ)

h $p = 60$ (equil. Δ)

i $\angle CAB$ 46 ($\angle$s on a straight line)

$n = 67$ ($\angle$ sum of a Δ)

j $t = 29$ (vert. opp. $\angle$s)

$u = 61$ ($\angle$ sum of a Δ)

k $r = 126$ ($\angle$s at a point)

$s = 27$ (base $\angle$s of isos. Δ)

l $\angle BED = 95$ ($\angle$s on a straight line)

$y = 57$ ($\angle$ sum of quad.)

$x = 51$ ($\angle$ sum of Δ)

m $p = 120$ ($\angle$ sum of quad.)

n $u = 148$ (opp $\angle$s of rhombus)

$v = 32$ (co-int. $\angle$s and $\parallel$ lines)

o $g = 81$ (corr. $\angle$s and $\parallel$ lines)

$h = 99$ (co-int. $\angle$s and $\parallel$ lines)

6 isosceles trapezium

7 a both pairs of opp. sides equal

b diagonals bisect each other

c one pair of opp. sides equal and parallel

8 a square, rhombus   **b** rhombus, kite, square

9 a no   **b** yes, a square

10–13 constructions

14 **b** rhombus, all sides equal, diagonals bisect each other at right angles
15 construction
16 rectangle, square
17 rhombus, parallelogram
18 **a** 540°   **b** 2340°
19 120°   **20** 20

Keeping Mathematically Fit

PART A
1 D
2 **a** 18   **b** $2a$
3 8·6 t
4 three possibilities:
   1b, 2r, 11w
   2b, 4r, 8w
   3b, 6r, 5w
5 8·900....1 to 8·$\dot{9}$
6 1·25 m
7 1683
8 24 cm²
9 **a** 18   **b** 13
10 $1.50

PART B
1 110
2 628 cm³
3 7·2
4 140
5 150 cm²

Chapter 6

MathsCheck

1 **a**

x	0	1	2
y	1	3	5

b
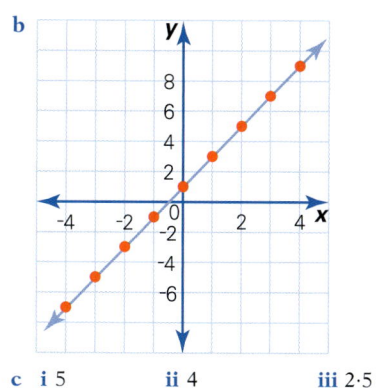

   c   **i** 5   **ii** 4   **iii** 2·5
2 **a** 20 min   **b** 15 km   **c** 70 min   **d** 30 min
   e on the way to her friend's house

3 **a** line graph
   b

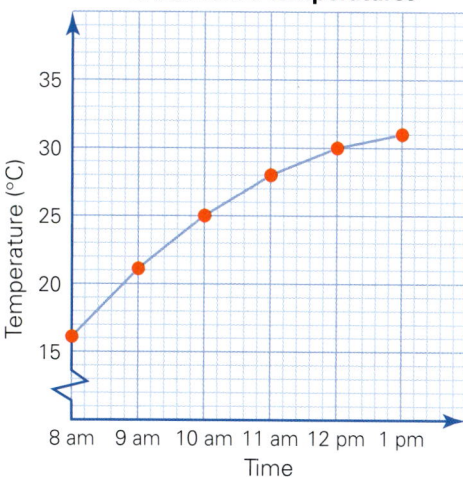

Greenhouse temperatures

   c 25·5°C   **d** 8:50 am   **e** around 31°C

4 **a**

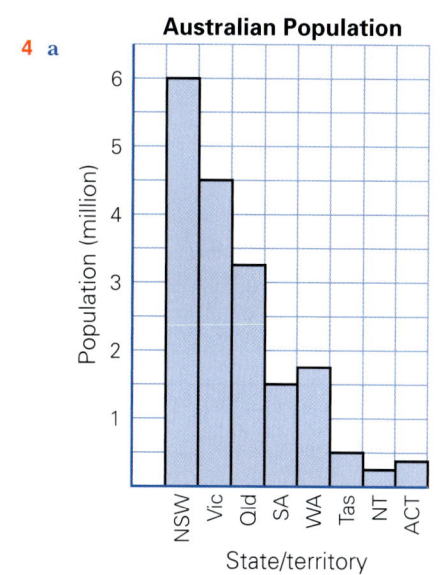

Australian Population

   b 17 893 500

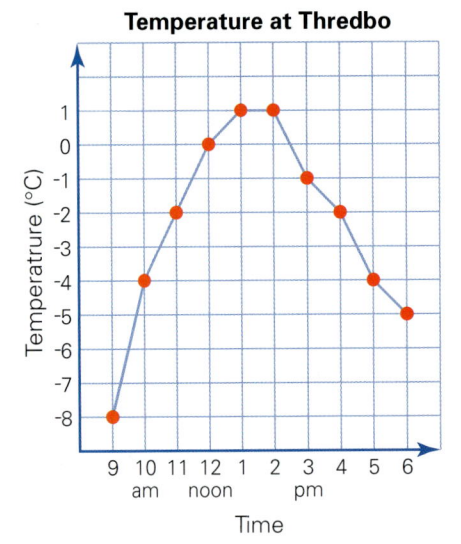

5 a

Temperature at Thredbo

b ⁻1°C   **c** 10:30 am and 4:30pm

EXERCISE 6A

1 graph

2 story based on these points:

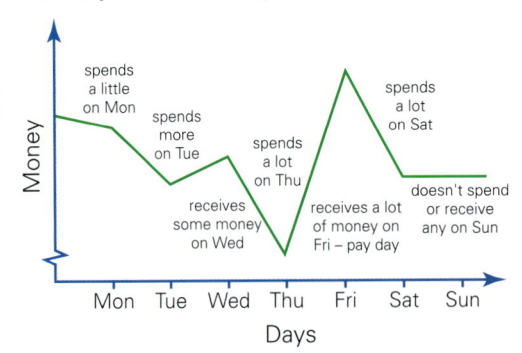

3 story based on these points:

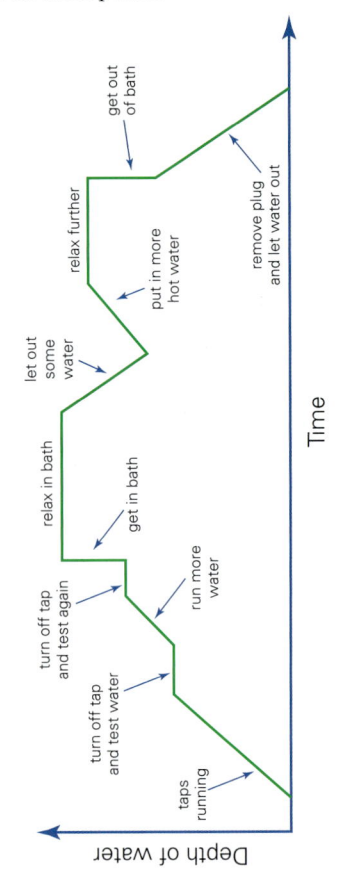

4 1 class enter room
   2 teacher asks for quiet
   3 teacher explains work
   4 class have become noisy, teacher asks for quiet
   5 class completely silent before leaving
   6 class leaving room

5 a B   **b** A   **c** C   **d** C
   e C

6 a 59 beats per min   **b** 8:25 am
   c 160 beats per min   **d** 8:57 am
   e 12 min   **f** 8 km

7 a Beryl   **b** 1 km
   c 2 km   **d** 100 m/min
   e 2 km   **f** 1 km

8 *A*: started quickly, then slowed down
   B: cycled at constant speed
   C: started slowly, then speeded up

9 a 6   **b** 8 minutes   **c** 6:32
   d A: 39·3 km/h   B: 57 km/h

10 a

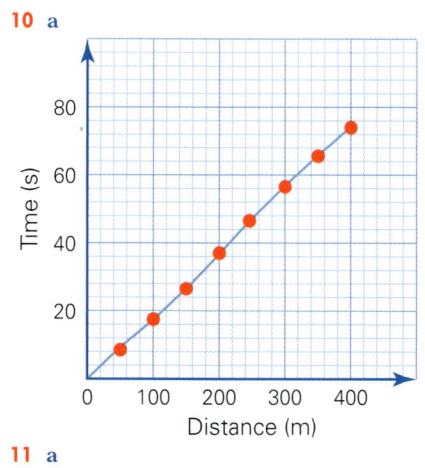

11 a

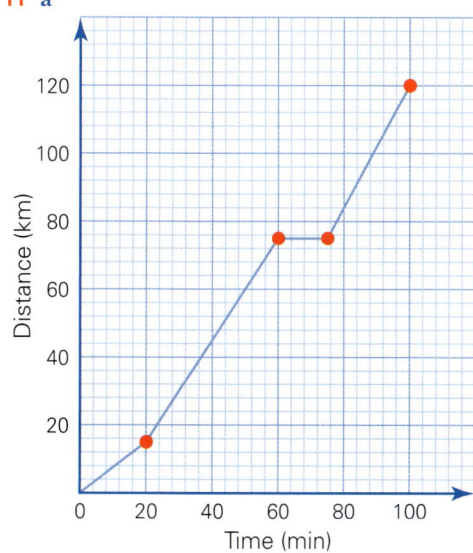

b final 25 minutes
c 108 km/h
d 72 km/h

12 a–c

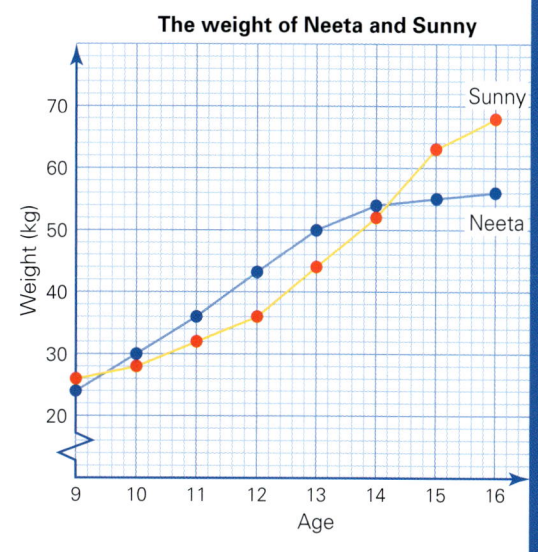

d Sunny: 14-15
  Neeta: 11-13

e $9\frac{1}{2}$ and $14\frac{1}{4}$

13 a

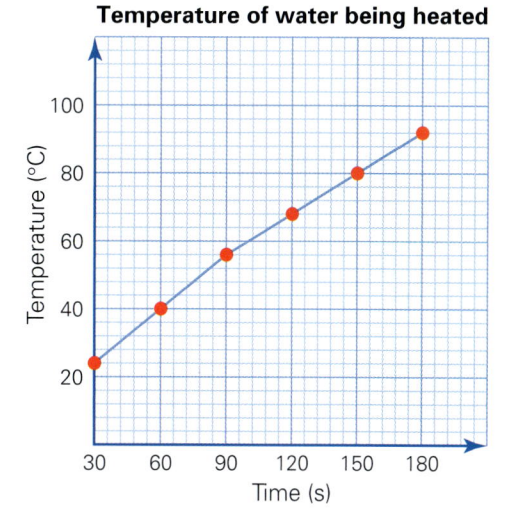

b i 31°C   **ii** 72°C
c around 210 s

14 a

Time	Temp
7 am	39·1
11 am	39·3
3 pm	39·8
7 pm	39·9
11 pm	39·4
3 am	38·1
7 am	37·6
11 am	37·0
3 pm	37·0
7 pm	37·0

b

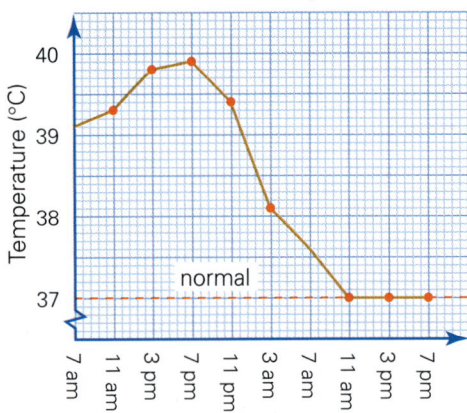

Athena's temperature

c 2·9°C **d** 39·7°C **e** 16 hours
15 a 7:47 am **b** 22 km/h **c** 8:11 am
d 1 min **e** 10 km/h **f** 52 km/h
g 31 min
16–17
compare and discuss

EXERCISE 6B
1 a $4 **b** $8 **c** $7 **d** 3 h
e $5 **f** $6, discuss
2 a $2 **b** 150 **c** $105
3 a

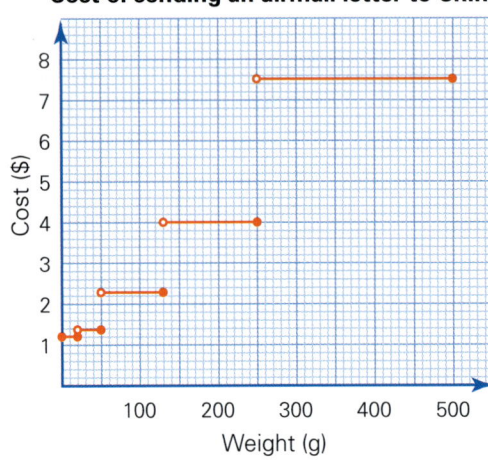

Cost of sending an airmail letter to China

b $1.20 **c** $2.30 **d** 250 g
e $1 **f** $1 **g** 70 g

4 a

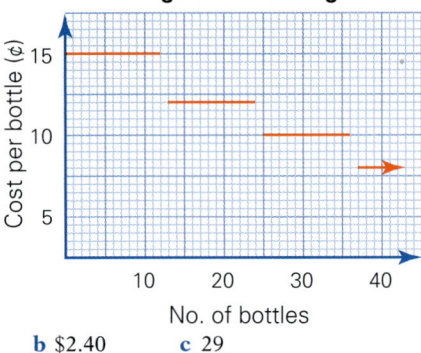

Postage and handling costs

b $2.40 **c** 29

EXERCISE 6C
1 *P*—Priscilla
Q—Jack
R—Pete
S—Jean
2 the one costing $5.99
3 cuckoo-shrike
4 *X*
5 a Bree **b** Cecil and Dorothy
6 a Car *B* cost more than car *A*
 i T **ii** F **iii** F
 iv T **v** F **vi** T
b car *A* is cheaper, older, faster, has a larger
engine, more passenger seats and is less
economical

c

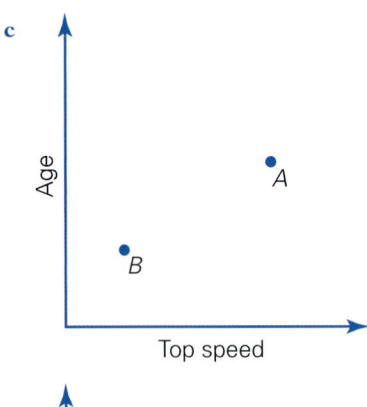

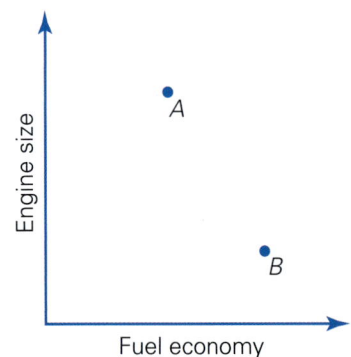

7

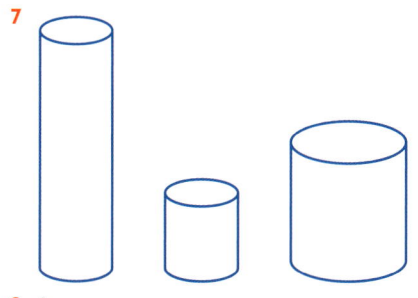

8 Ann
9 **a** *B* (short, costly)
  b *C*, *A* (low cost for any duration)
  c *D* (shorter than *C*, costs more)
  Note: *A* could also be long-distance within Australia.

10 **a**

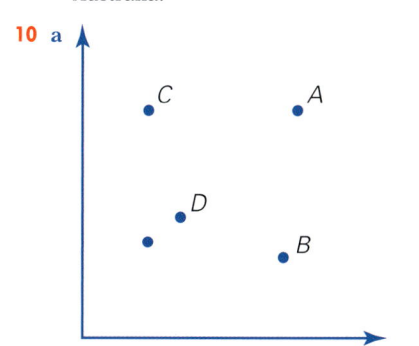

  b no, the area could not be large enough

  c

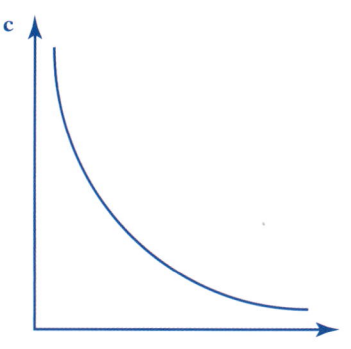

EXERCISE 6D
1 **a** part of vertical scale missing
  b spacing on horizontal axis not regular
  c use of volume instead of height
  d no scale on vertical axis
  e volumes do not represent figures

Chapter Review Exercises
1 *B*
2 **a**

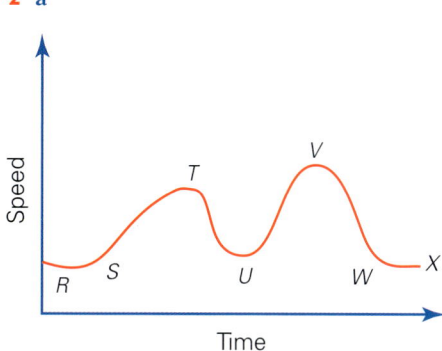

  b similar shape, but inverted
3 **a** $100 **b** $260 **c** 9 m **d** 20 cm
  e $140

4 **a**

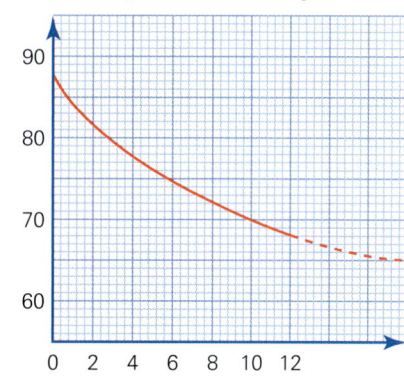

  b around 5 min **c** around 18 min
5 *A*—she oak
  B—blue gum
  C—poplar
  D—fig

6

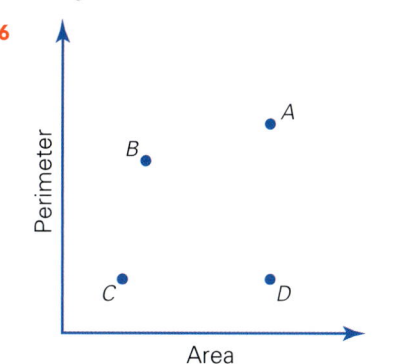

7 no label on vertical axis, horizontal scale not regular

PART A
1 30   **2** $650   **3** A   **4** 0·204   **5** $32
6 4   **7** 0·06   **8** 6:20 pm
9 Ann $48; Bettina $72; Soureya $80
10 56·5 cm^2

PART B
1 a 26·76%   b 51·36%
2 0·$\dot{6}\dot{3}$ **3** 30·$\dot{5}$ **4** 85%
5

	11	
33	4	37
	15	

Chapter 7

MathsCheck
1 a $c^2 = a^2 + b^2$ **b** $t^2 = m^2 + p^2$
   c $AB^2 = AC^2 + BC^2$
2 a 15   **b** 39   **c** 10·82
   d 5·85   **e** 8   **f** 48
   g 105   **h** 2·22   **i** 13·28
3 a yes   **b** no   **c** no
4 a yes   **b** yes   **c** no   **d** no
5 26·98 m
6 a 8·86 m   **b** 26·9 m   **c** 7·3 m
7 yes   **8** $\angle P$ **9** 2343 mm   **10** 2·69 km
11 a 4, $\sqrt{32}$ **b** $\sqrt{189}$, $\sqrt{211}$
   c 6, $\sqrt{292}$ **d** 6·6, 3·3
   e 16, 46·9   **f** 140 sq. units
12 14·5, 14·6, yes   **13** 7·984 km
14 3·5 m   **15** 1171·5 km
16 215 mm

EXERCISE 7A
1 a i AC **ii** BC **iii** AB
   b i MP **ii** QP **iii** QM
   c i YZ **ii** YX **iii** XZ
   d i DF **ii** EF **iii** ED
   e i GH **ii** GK **iii** KH
   f i BD **ii** AB **iii** AD
   g i BD **ii** BC **iii** DC
   h i BC **ii** BD **iii** DC
2 a i PR **ii** PT
   b i PT **ii** PR
3 a $\dfrac{BC}{BA}$ **b** $\dfrac{BA}{AC}$ **c** $\dfrac{BC}{AC}$
4 a $\dfrac{opp.}{hyp.}$ **b** $\dfrac{opp.}{adj.}$ **c** $\dfrac{adj.}{hyp.}$
5 a 42°30′   **b** 16°24′   **c** 243°36′
   d 6′   **e** 3°17′24″   **f** 180°48′
   g 3°15′   **h** 302°58′48″
6 a 23·5°   **b** 8·1°   **c** 8·00°
   d 90·25°   **e** 123·75°   **f** 1·02°
   g 5·27°   **h** 241·42°
7 a 13°   **b** 64°   **c** 133°
   d 4°   **e** 10°   **f** 49°
   g 3°   **h** 5°

8 a 7°14′   **b** 93°58′   **c** 136°21′
   d 2°39′   **e** 305°30′   **f** 19°43′
   g 3°3′   **h** 254° 0′
9 a i 0·42   **ii** 0·38   **iii** 0·92
   b i 0·29   **ii** 0·28   **iii** 0·96
   c i 0·53   **ii** 0·47   **iii** 0·88
10 a 75°   **b** 69°20′   **c** 37°47′
   d 50°56′

EXERCISE 7B
1 a BC/AC **b** AC/BC **c** EF/ED
   d ED/EF **e** GJ/HJ **f** GJ/JK
   g JK/GJ
2 a $\tan 30° = \dfrac{AC}{BC}$ **b** $\tan 60° = \dfrac{BC}{AC}$
   c $\tan 45° = \dfrac{MQ}{RQ}$ **d** $\tan 58° = \dfrac{PQ}{MQ}$
   e $\tan 40° = \dfrac{WZ}{ZY}$ **f** $\tan 27° = \dfrac{WZ}{ZX}$
   g $\tan x° = \dfrac{ZX}{WZ}$
3 a 2·4   **b** 3·4286   **c** 0·5333
4 a 0·0699   **b** 0·1405   **c** 0·2867
   d 0·6249   **e** 2·0503   **f** 5·6713
   g 57·29   **h** 0   **i** error; discuss
   j 1·0   **k** 0·1763   **l** 0·3640
   m 0·5774   **n** 0·8391   **o** 1·1918
5 discuss
6 a 1·0176   **b** 3·3226   **c** 0·3010
   d 1·8065   **e** 0·1441   **f** 0·5243
   g 1·2276   **h** 0·6817
7 results show $2 \tan \theta \neq \tan 2\theta$

EXERCISE 7C
1 a 27°   **b** 73°   **c** 23°   **d** 64°
   e 84°   **f** 76°   **g** 22°   **h** 2°
2 a 4°17′   **b** 27°50′   **c** 78°28′   **d** 67°23′
   e 58°0′   **f** 16°13   **g** 88°24   **h** 36°21′
3 a 45°0′   **b** 69°41′   **c** 83°0′   **d** 43°35′
4 a 45°   **b** 53°8′   **c** 28°4′   **d** 17°45′
   e $\alpha = 36°52′$ **f** $\alpha = 28°4′$
     $\beta = 53°8′$ $\beta = 61°56′$
               $\theta = 53°8′$

EXERCISE 7D
1 a 17·20   **b** 5·43   **c** 20·22   **d** 137·37
   e 16·58   **f** 1·95   **g** 137·37   **h** 144·05
   i 535·50   **j** 18·36   **k** 26·02   **l** 1·10
   m 30·49   **n** 9·98   **o** 0·08   **p** 2801·57
   q 8·40   **r** 0·01
2 a 8·1 m   **b** 5·8 km   **c** 37·1 cm   **d** 418·5 m
   e 10·9 m   **f** 72·3 cm   **g** 4·4 m   **h** 18·9 km
   i 583·0 m
3 a 274·75 m   **b** 137·49 cm   **c** 14·54 km
4 a 4·4   **b** 172·0   **c** 8·1   **d** 3·4   **e** 40·0
   f 18·4
5 a 17·4   **b** 4·36   **c** 6·68   **d** 64·2   **e** 33·4
   f 0·93

6 a 40 m   **b** 221·12 cm
  c 11·29 km   **d** 410 m
  e 21·46 m   **f** $WX = 60·17$ cm
                      $WY = 60·94$ cm

7 26·3 cm   **8** 18·66 m   **9** 29·6 cm
10 $AC = 175·97$ m
   $AB = 177·17$ m
11 7·11 m

EXERCISE 7E

1 a i BC/AB **ii** AC/AB **iii** BC/AC
  b i GH/GJ **ii** HJ/GJ **iii** GH/HJ
  c i LP/PM **ii** LM/PM **iii** LP/LM
  d i $\alpha : TE/TD, \beta : DE/TD$
    ii $\alpha : DE/TD, \beta : TE/TD$
    iii $\alpha : TE/DE, \beta : DE/TE$
  e i $\alpha : BD/AB, \beta : AD/AB, \theta : DC/BC$
    ii $\alpha : AD/AB, \beta : BD/AB, \theta : BD/BC$
    iii $\alpha : BD/AD, \beta : AD/BD, \theta : DC/BD$
  f i $\alpha : RM/RP, \beta : QM/QP$
    ii $\alpha : MP/RP, \beta : PM/QP$
    iii $\alpha : RM/MP, \beta : QM/PM$

2 a i 0·6000   **ii** 0·8000   **iii** 0·7500
  b i 0·4706   **ii** 0·8824   **iii** 0·5333
  c i 0·2195   **ii** 0·9756   **iii** 0·2250

3 a 53°8′   **b** 61°39′   **c** 62°43′
  d 60°   **e** 56°38′   **f** 56°15′
  g 11°19′   **h** 12°32′

4 α **i** $\dfrac{3}{5}$ **ii** $\dfrac{4}{5}$ **iii** $\dfrac{3}{4}$

  β **i** $\dfrac{4}{5}$ **ii** $\dfrac{3}{5}$ **iii** $\dfrac{4}{3}$

5 discuss
6 a i 0·8315   **ii** 0·5556   **iii** 1·4967
  b i 0·3846   **ii** 0·9231   **iii** 0·4167

EXERCISE 7F

1 a 30°   **b** 43°   **c** 27°   **d** 33°
  e 77°   **f** 40°   **g** 61°   **h** 57°
  i 90°   **j** 90°   **k** 54°   **l** 0°
  m 22°   **n** 29°   **o** 35°   **p** 45°
  q 48°   **r** 63°   **s** 57°   **t** 6°

2 a i 76°   **ii** 14°
  b i 16°   **ii** 74°
  c i 52°   **ii** 38°
  they are complementary angles

3 a 23°37′   **b** 73°44′   **c** 36°52′
  d 12°41′   **e** 28°4′   **f** 55°50′

4 a i 79°37′   **ii** 10°23′
  b i 53°8′   **ii** 65°13′
  c i 22°37′   **ii** 51°20′   **iii** 38°40′
  d i 38°57′   **ii** 48°59′   **iii** 10°2′

5 A: 43°, B: 47°
6 a 62°, 28°   **b** 1·7 km

EXERCISE 7G

1 a 84·80   **b** 15·43   **c** 2·45
  d 49·24   **e** 0·48   **f** 11·92
  g 11·09   **h** 36·08   **i** 25·18
  j 77·27   **k** 6·64   **l** 2·06
  m 115·91   **n** 155·98   **o** 193·25
  p 0·02
2 a 50·00   **b** 123·13   **c** 43·41
  d 15·56   **e** 70·71   **f** 7·05
3 a 17·0   **b** 754·7   **c** 8·7
  d 50·4   **e** 11·3   **f** 429·1
4 a 110·1, 136·0   **b** 171·1
  c 12·4
5 a 0·6   **b i** 0·9   **ii** 67°23′
  c 13·3 m   **d** 25 km
6 a 0·96   **b** 16°16′   **c** 73°44′

EXERCISE 7H

1 a i tan   **ii** 51·0
  b i sine   **ii** 108·4
  c i cos   **ii** 89·4
  d i tan   **ii** 8·1
  e i Pythagoras **ii** 40·0
  f i cos   **ii** 36·9°
2 a 117·6 cm   **b** 80·2 m
3 a 85°4′
  b $x = 30, y = 30\ z = 60, t = 1.7\ \Delta EGH$ equilateral
  c 5°27′
4 a 149·91 m   **b** discuss
5 a 60·1 cm, 21·9 cm   **b** 658·1 cm^2
6 70°32′, 19°28′   **7** discuss
8 a 4.7 cm   **b** 31°
9 17.7 m   **10** 8 cm^2

EXERCISE 7I

1 235 m
2 a 99·4 m   **b** 69·3 m
3 7·7 m
4 a 1°43′   **b** 18·3 m
5 a 715 m   **b** 1°26′
6 3·58 m   **7** 38·4 m   **8** 472 m
9 no, angle of elevation of sun must be 46·4°
  before window is shaded
10 a 1014 m   **b** 1130 m
11 243 m
12 a 6·605 km   **b** 5·601 km
13 a 350·6 m   **b** 5·3 km/h
  c 2·5 min

EXERCISE 7J

1 a 076°   **b** 129°   **c** 250°   **d** 304°
  e 135°   **f** 315°   **g** 239°7′   **h** 16°46′
  i 291°32′

2

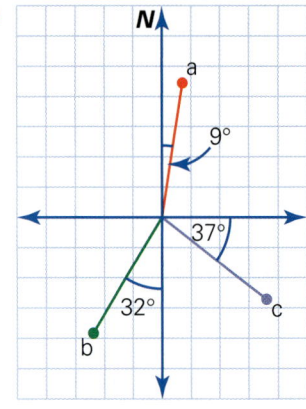

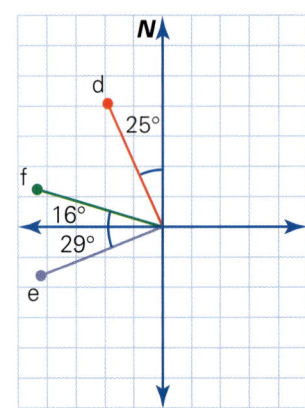

3 a 022·5° **b** 247·5° **c** 157·5°
d 292·5° **e** 067·5°
4 a 88·3 km **b** 46·9 km
5 a 5·1 km **b** 6·1 km
6 a 231° **b** 128·1 km
7 a 18·8 km **b** 315°
8 a i 324·5 km **ii** 131·1 km
b 022°
9 a 1616·8 km **b** 525·3 km
10 a 062° **b** 118° **c** 242°
11 a i 100° **ii** 280°
b i 047° **ii** 227°
c i 289° **ii** 109°
d differ by 180° **e** 030°
12 a 020° **b** 255° **c** 120°
13 a 15 km bearing 300°
18 km bearing 070°
16 km bearing 340°
b 24·1 km
c 208°
14 a 85·7 km **b** 104·6 km
15 019° **16** 255·7 m

Chapter Review Exercises
1 d
2 a yes; $37^2 = 12^2 + 35^2$
b no **c** yes

3 a $c = \sqrt{a^2 + b^2}$
b $b = \sqrt{c^2 - a^2}$
4 39
5 a 61·0 **b** 2·9
6 a 4·4 **b** 2·0
7 c
8 a AB/BC **b** BC/CA
c BC/CA **d** $AC^2 - BC^2$
9 a 0·375 **b** 0·990 **c** 0·966
10 a 49°28′ **b** 68°49′ **c** 84°52′
11 a i 0·42 **ii** 0·38 **iii** 0·38
b A **c** 23°, 67°
12 a 4·35 **b** 6·52 **c** 14·30
13 a 368·50 **b** 15·56
c $t = 9·53$
i $y = 13·82$ **ii** 50° **iii** 44°
14 33·4 m
15 a 20 cm **b** 46 cm **c** 115° **d** 295°
16 $\angle c = 50°$, $AB = 35·8$ cm, $AC = 46·7$ cm
17 9·96 m **18** 0·47 **19** 191 m
20 a 15·99 cm **b** 9·84 cm
21 \$95 405.66
22 a 18·82 km **b** 25 min
23 a 25° **b** 6·94 km
24 43°, 84° **25** 58·7 m
26 a 14 km **b** 99 km **c** 004°
27 1·44 cm
28 area = $\sqrt{3}\, x^2$ or $\approx 1·73x^2$
29 a 1159 m, 1727 m **b** 1701 m
c 1281 m **d** 311°
30 a $AC = 147·2$ **b** 35 m

Keeping Mathematically Fit

PART A
1 $y(y - 5)$ cm² **2** $^{-}1$ **3** 42, 44, 46
4 $\dfrac{3}{4}$ **5** C **6** $x = \dfrac{5y + 1}{3}$
7 12 **8** 31, 32, 33 or 34
9 $^{-}5p$ **10** 0·65 cm²

PART B
1 0·097 **2** 150 **3** 20 000 L **4** 180
5 $6 \times \$20$; $8 \times \$5$

Cumulative Review 2

1 a $\dfrac{d}{3} - 4$ **b** $p + \dfrac{q}{100}$
2 a 7^3 **b** t^5 **c** $(^{-}2b)^4$
3 a $\dfrac{4p}{q}$ **b** w^6 **c** 4
4 a $3x + 7$ **b** $4p^2 + p$ **c** $c^2 - 36$
d $9p^2 - 30p + 25$
5 a $5(x + 2)$ **b** $3t(4t - 1)$
6 a $8·1 \times 10^7$ **b** $2·9862 \times 10^4$
7 a 183·80 **b** 69·64
8 a 4500 to 5499·$\dot{9}$ **b** 4995 to 5004·$\dot{9}$
9 self-check

10 a $\frac{1}{4}$ **b** $\frac{19}{20}$ **c** $2\frac{1}{2}$ **d** $\frac{1}{50}$

11 a 74·5 cm to 75·4$\dot{9}$ cm
b 74·95 cm to 75·04$\dot{9}$ cm

12 a 2750 g **b** 2 h 35 min **c** 2·7 m

13 $6.40 **14** $4800 **15** $53\frac{1}{3}$

16 a i 6·45 km **ii** 0·84 km²
b i 5·34 km **ii** 1·69 km²

17 a 3 **b** 4 **c** 10

18 a $x < 2$ **b** $x \le {}^-2$

19 a 85 **b** 22

20 $x = \dfrac{p - y}{r}$

21 4 cm

22–24 check by measuring

25 a $a = 33°$ (straight line)
   $b = 147°$ (vertically opposite angles)
 b 51° (∠s at a point)
 c 20° (equilateral)
 d 65° (exterior angle, isosceles)
 e 114° (∠ sum of quadrilateral)
 f 120° (interior ∠, regular hexagon)
 g h = 36° (co-interior ∠s, parallel lines)
   j = 77° (∠ sum of Δ)
 h k = 42° (alt. ∠s, parallel lines)
   l = 101° (alt. ∠s, parallel lines)
   m = 37° (∠ sum of Δ)
 i 39° (co-interior and alternate ∠s, parallel lines)
 j 49° (ext. ∠ and ∠ sum of Δ)
 k r = 8 (diagonals of parallelogram bisect)
   q = 12 (opposite sides of parallelogram)
 l s = 131° (ext. ∠ and straight line)

26 square, rectangle, isosceles trapezium

27 135°

28 kite

29

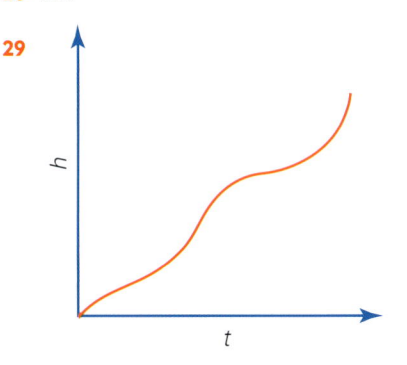

30 compare and discuss

31 a $1 min, $6 max **b** $2
 c 18 min **d** $3 **e** $1

32 a 11 kg **b** 0·92 kg
 c 2nd week, steepest down slope
 d 1st and 7th, horizontal line
 e 5th, steep upward slope
 f same rate, slopes parallel
 g during 5th week

33 a i *EF* **ii** *DF* **iii** *DE*
   iv DE
 b tan **c** complementary
 d reciprocals

34 a 0·035 **b** 1 **c** 5·671 **d** 28·636

35 a 0 **b** error (not defined)

36 a 74·88° **b** 87·74° **c** 44·57°

37 a 45 **b** 27 **c** 71

38 a 110·8 **b** 20·2 **c** 61·93

39 800 m

40 a 22°35′ **b** 13·5 km **c** 2·21 km

41 a 158 m **b** 306 m **c** 148 m
 d 418 m

42 a 5 cm **b** 2·5 cm **c** 37° **d** $\frac{4}{5}$

43 a 87·71 cm **b** 82·42 cm

44 $\frac{3}{4}$

45 a 480 km **b** 268 km

46 2·1°

47 17·2 cm

48 322 m

Chapter 8

MathsCheck

1 a (⁻3, ⁻2) **b** (⁻4, 4) **c** (4, ⁻2) **d** (0, ⁻4)

2 a 3 units **b** 2 units **c** 7 units **d** 3 units
 e 4 units **f** 4 units

3 a 5, 2 **b** 3
 c same; can find vert. dist. by subtracting y-co-ords

4 R: ⁻2, E: ⁻4
 ⁻2 − ⁻4 = 2
 same; can find horiz. dist. by subtracting x-co-ords

5 a 3 **b** 4 **c** 4 **d** 5 **e** 3 **f** 2
 g 4 **h** 3 **i** 5

6

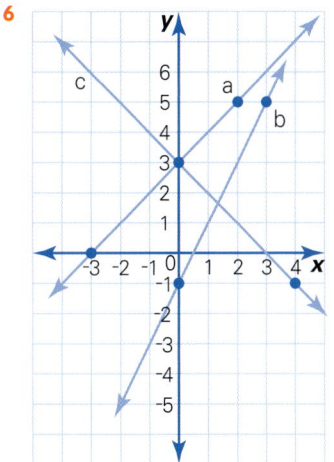

7 a ⁻2, 0, ⁻4 **b** 2, 11, ⁻1 **c** 3, 1, 5, ⁻3
 d ⁻6, 2, ⁻10 **e** ⁻2, ⁻8, 4 **f** 3, 0, ⁻4

8 a $y = 2x$ **b** $y = x - 1$ **c** $y = 6 - x$

EXERCISE 8A

1 a $\sqrt{13}$ b $\sqrt{18}$ c $\sqrt{29}$ d $\sqrt{29}$
2 a 5 units b 10 units c 13 units
 d 10 units e 5 units f 3.6 units
 g 8.1 units h 13 units i 8.1 units
 j 7.2 units k 6.5 units l 1.4 units
3 a $\sqrt{2}$ units b $\sqrt{13}$ units c $\sqrt{34}$ units
 d $\sqrt{89}$ units e $\sqrt{26}$ units f $\sqrt{10}$ units
4 $\sqrt{65}$ units 5 ($^-4$, $^-4$)
 $\sqrt{32}$ vs $\sqrt{34}$

6 both $\sqrt{10}$ away
7 a both $\sqrt{18}$ away b many answers
8 a 5 units b many answers
9 ($^-4$, 0) to (0, 3)
 = 5 units
 ($^-4$, 0) to (0, $^-3$)
 = 5 units
10 a $PQ = 5$, $PR = 10$ b 25 sq. units
 $QR = \sqrt{125}$
 $QR^2 = PQ^2 + PR^2$
11 a all $\sqrt{20}$ b $\sqrt{8}$, $\sqrt{72}$ rhombus
12 all distances from ($^-2$, 1) are $\sqrt{13}$
13 ($^-4$, $^-5$) 14 1·34
15 many answers
16 a $\sqrt{x^2 + y^2} = 4$ b $x^2 + y^2 = 16$
 c circle

EXERCISE 8B

1 a (2, 5) b (4, 8) c (3, 5) d $(2\frac{1}{2}, 4\frac{1}{2})$
 e $(6, 2\frac{1}{2})$ f $(2\frac{1}{2}, 4)$ g ($^-1$, $^-2$) h ($^-3$, $^-4$)
 i ($^-4$, $^-3$) j (1, 1) k ($^-3$, $^-4$) l (0, 0)
2 a (0, $^-2$) midpoint
 if $x = 0$, point is on y-axis
 b 2 units
3 midpoint ($^-7$, 0)
 $y = 0$, point is on x-axis
4 a $(3\frac{1}{2}, 2\frac{1}{2})$ b $(3\frac{1}{2}, 2\frac{1}{2})$ c yes
 d bisect each other
5 discuss
6 a $t = 6$ b $p = 6$ c $p = 3$, $t = 5$
 d $a = 6$, $b = 8$ e $a = 7$, $b = 4$
 f $m = ^-8\cdot5$, $t = 14$
7 a (3, 4) b $\sqrt{13}$
 c (5, 1) to (3, 4) is also $\sqrt{13}$
8 a $(^-5\frac{1}{2}, ^-3\frac{1}{2})$ b (4a, 3t)
 c (3p, 2n) d (0, 0)
 e $(\frac{5}{12}, \frac{11}{24})$ f (1·5n², ^-2p)
9 discuss
10 a $(2\frac{1}{2}, ^-4\frac{1}{2})$ b $(\frac{3}{4}, ^-2\frac{3}{4})$ c $\sqrt{\frac{49}{2}}$
11 (8, $^-4$), (12, 8), ($^-8$, 4)
12 a 1 : 1 b 1 : 2

EXERCISE 8C

1 a 1 b $\frac{^-1}{2}$ c $\frac{2}{5}$ d $^-3$
 e $^-1$ f $\frac{1}{7}$ g $\frac{1}{9}$ h $\frac{^-1}{3}$
 i $\frac{^-1}{2}$ j 2 k $\frac{^-4}{5}$ l $\frac{3}{4}$
 m 3 n $\frac{1}{2}$ o $\frac{^-2}{9}$
2 a 1 b 1 c $^-1$ d $^-1$
 e $\frac{1}{5}$ f $\frac{1}{2}$ g $\frac{^-1}{3}$ h $^-3$
 i $\frac{1}{3}$ j $\frac{1}{4}$ k $^-2$ l $\frac{^-1}{2}$
 m 0 n $\frac{1}{4}$
3 a parallel b equal
 c c and d
 j and n
4 a $\frac{1}{4}$ b $\frac{1}{4}$ c $\frac{1}{4}$ d $\frac{1}{4}$
 same gradient throughout line
5

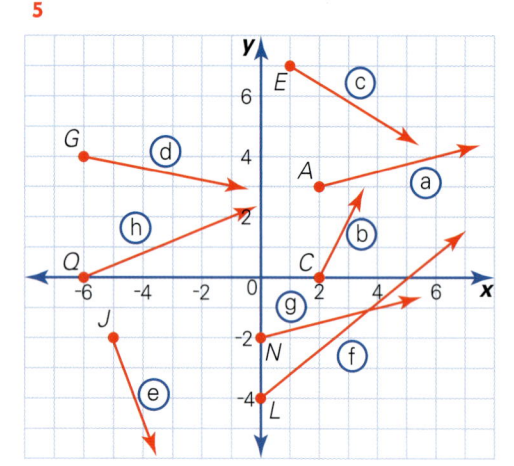

6 zero
7 a dividing by zero b not defined
8 a 3 b $\frac{^-4}{3}$ c $\frac{1}{2}$ d $\frac{1}{3}$
 e 0 f $^-3$ g 0 h $\frac{5}{18}$
9 discuss

EXERCISE 8D

1 a 2 b $\frac{1}{2}$ c $\frac{2}{3}$ d $\frac{3}{2}$
 e $\frac{3}{4}$ f $\frac{^-5}{4}$ g $\frac{1}{2}$ h $\frac{1}{3}$
 i 0 j $\frac{^-2}{3}$ k $\frac{1}{2}$ l $\frac{5}{24}$
2 $\frac{^-2}{3}$

3 **a** $\frac{-1}{2}$ **b** $\frac{-1}{2}$ **c** $\frac{-1}{2}$ **d** $\frac{-1}{2}$

e $\frac{-1}{2}$ **f** $\frac{-1}{2}$

4 **a** T **b** T **c** T

5 **a** 2 **b** $\frac{1}{3}$ **c** $\frac{-1}{2}$

6 2

7 **a** $\frac{-3}{5}$ **b** $\sqrt{34}$ units **c** $(2\frac{1}{2}, 1\frac{1}{2})$
d 2·9 units **e** $7\frac{1}{2}$

EXERCISE 8E

1 **a** yes **b** no **c** yes **d** yes **e** yes
f no **g** yes **h** yes

2 **a** 5, 8 **b** $\frac{1}{2}$, $^-3$ **c** $^-3, 0$ **d** 1, $^-4$

e $^-1, 6$ **f** $^-1, 0$ **g** $^-4, 0.9$

3 **a** **i** 2, 4, 6 **ii** 2, 0, $^-2$
b **i** $^-4, 0, 2$ **ii** 4, 3, 2
c **i** $^-7, 2\ 11$ **ii** $^-13, ^-4, 5$

4
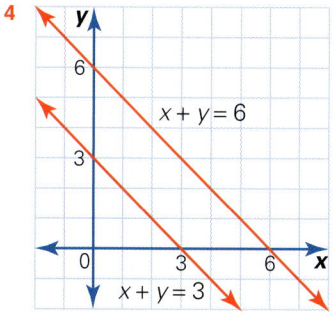

5 **a** $(0, 0); (2, 2)$ **b** $(1, 5); (^-2, ^-4)$
c $(0, ^-3); (1, ^-5); (^-1, ^-1)$

6 **a** 3 **b** $^-3$ **c** $^-4$ **d** $^-5·6$ **e** $^-6\frac{3}{4}$

7 an infinite number

8 **a** yes **b** yes **c** no **d** yes

9 no

10 **a** $y = x + 4$ **b** $y = x - 1$ **c** $y = 3x$
d $y = \frac{1}{2}x$ **e** $y = 2x + 1$ **f** $y = ^-x$

EXERCISE 8F

1 **a** **i** 2 **ii** 5 **b** **i** 3 **ii** $^-2$
c **i** 1 **ii** 1 **d** **i** 1 **ii** $^-3$
e **i** $^-2$ **ii** 4 **f** **i** $^-5$ **ii** $^-6$
g **i** 4 **ii** 0 **h** **i** 3 **ii** 0
i **i** 1 **ii** 0 **j** **i** $^-2$ **ii** 0
k **i** $\frac{1}{2}$ **ii** 4 **l** **i** $\frac{2}{3}$ **ii** 0
m **i** $\frac{-3}{5}$ **ii** 0 **n** **i** $^-1$ **ii** 0
o **i** $^-1$ **ii** $\frac{-1}{2}$ **p** **i** 1·8 **ii** $^-0·4$
q **i** $\frac{1}{5}$ **ii** $^-7$ **r** **i** $^-1$ **ii** 3

s **i** $^-3$ **ii** $\frac{1}{2}$ **t** **i** $\frac{-2}{5}$ **ii** 8
u **i** 1 **ii** 5 **v** **i** 2 **ii** 4
w **i** 0 **ii** 4 **x** **i** 2 **ii** 3

2 **a** **i** $y = 3x + 2$ **ii** $y = x + 6$
iii $y = 2x$ **iv** $y = ^-4x + 3$
v $y = \frac{1}{2}x + 4$ **vi** $y = \frac{-3}{4}x + \frac{1}{2}$
vii $y = 2$ **viii** $y = ^-3$
ix $y = 0$
b x-axis

3 **a** $y = 2x + 2$ **b** $y = x - 1$ **c** $y = \frac{1}{2}x + 2$
d $y = 3x - 3$ **e** $y = ^-2x - 2$ **f** $y = \frac{-2}{3}x + 2$
g **i** $y = \frac{1}{2}x$ **ii** $y = x$ **iii** $y = 2x$
iv $y = 6x$
h **i** $y = 4$ **ii** $y = ^-3$
i $y = \frac{-3}{4} - 1\frac{1}{2}$

4 **a** many answers **b** $x = 4$
c $x = ^-2$ **d** $x = 0$

5 gradient is not defined

EXERCISE 8G

1
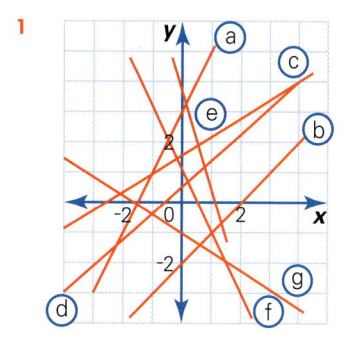

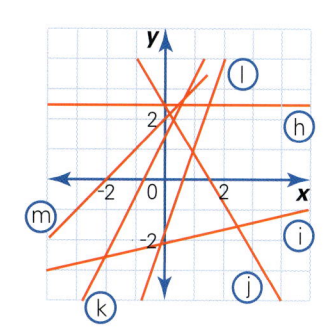

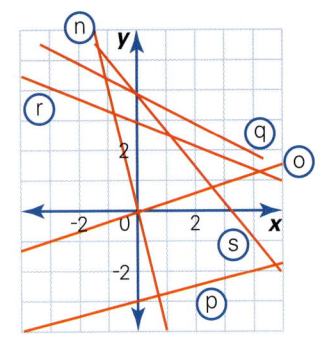

2 a i $y = 2x - 3$ **ii** 2, 3
b i $y = 4x - 2$ **ii** 4, ⁻2

c i $y = \dfrac{3x}{2}$ **ii** $\dfrac{3}{2}$, 0

d i $y = \dfrac{-3x}{2}$ **ii** $\dfrac{-3}{2}$, 0

e i $y = \dfrac{-4}{5}x + 2$ **ii** $\dfrac{-4}{5}$, 2

f i $y = 4$ **ii** 0, 4
g i $y = x - 2$ **ii** 1, ⁻2
h i $y = 2x + 3$ **ii** 2, 3
i i $y = 2x + 6$ **ii** 2, 6
j i $y = 3x - 3$ **ii** 3, -3
k i $y = 2x + 2$ **ii** 2, 2
l i $y = x - 2$ **ii** 1, -2
m i $y = 2x + 5$ **ii** 2, 5

n i $y = \dfrac{1}{2}x + 2$ **ii** $\dfrac{1}{2}$, 2

o i $y = ⁻x + 2$ **ii** ⁻1, 2
p i $y = x - 5$ **ii** 1, ⁻5

q i $y = \dfrac{-1}{3}x + 4$ **ii** $\dfrac{-1}{3}$, 4

r i $y = \dfrac{-2}{5}x + 2$ **ii** $\dfrac{-2}{5}$, 2

s i $y = \dfrac{-2}{3}x + 2$ **ii** $\dfrac{-2}{3}$, 2

t i $y = \dfrac{-1}{2}x + \dfrac{3}{2}$ **ii** $\dfrac{-1}{2}$, $1\dfrac{1}{2}$

3 a ii **b** v **c** iii **d** i
e iv **f** x-axis
4 b; d; e; f **5** discuss
6 a yes **b** no **c** no **d** no

7 a $\dfrac{3}{4}$ **b** $\dfrac{3}{4}$ **c** $m = \tan\theta$

8 a 1 **b** 0·2 **c** 4 **d** 2
e 0·6 **f** 0·9 **g** 1·6 **h** 19·1
i 0·4 **j** 0·8
9 a 27° **b** 37° **c** 63° **d** 50°
e 6° **f** 69° **g** 87° **h** 34°
i 72° **j** 56°

EXERCISE 8H

1 graph is as for $y = \dfrac{1}{2}x$

a 6 cm **b** 25 s

2 graph is as for $y = \dfrac{1}{5}x + 200$

a $600 **b** $4000
3 graph is as for $y = 10x + 40$
a 40 kg **b** 65 kg **c** $5\dfrac{1}{2}$ wk

4 a $y = \dfrac{3}{10}x + 10$ **i** $118

ii 320 km **iii** $130
b costs $10/day even if not driven at all

5 a $W = \dfrac{1}{4}t + 3\cdot2$ $\left(y = \dfrac{1}{4}x + 3\cdot2\right)$

b 5·2 kg **c** 7·2 wk **d** 12·8 wk **e** 600 g

6 a $y = \dfrac{1}{2}x - 2\dfrac{1}{2}$ **i** 5 km

ii $\approx 2\dfrac{1}{2}$ km **iii** $2\dfrac{1}{4}$ km

b intercepts tell distance from origin along compass axes

7 a $\dfrac{1}{2}$ km **b** $1\dfrac{1}{3}$ km **c** yes

Chapter Review Exercises

1 a i $\dfrac{6}{7}$ **ii** not defined **iii** 0

iv $\dfrac{-7}{4}$ **v** $\dfrac{6}{7}$ **vi** $\dfrac{-8}{7}$

b $AB \parallel DG$, same gradient, also $AC \parallel DE$
c $\sqrt{85}$ **d** (⁻1, ⁻0·5) **e** $m_{CD} = ⁻1\cdot75$
$m_{EG} = ⁻1\cdot14$
$\therefore CD$ is steeper

2 a $\dfrac{-1}{7}$ **b** 0 **c** not defined

d $m_{AB} = 2$
$m_{BC} = 2$
$\therefore$ collinear
(point in common)
3 (9, ⁻8)
4 a yes; both $\dfrac{-4}{7}$ gradients
b no; different gradients
5 a trapezium **b** no
6 a kite **b** only one bisected
c 30 sq. units

7 a 1 **b** 3 **c** $\dfrac{-3}{2}$ **d** $y = \dfrac{1}{2}x + 1$

8 a i 4 **ii** ⁻8 **b i** $\dfrac{1}{2}$ **ii** ⁻4

c i $\dfrac{3}{2}$ **ii** ⁻6

9 a $y = 0$ **b** $x = 0$

10 a $y = ⁻3x$ **b** $y = \dfrac{2}{3}x - 2$

11 a no; $m = ⁻2$ **b** yes; $m = 2$
c no; $m = ⁻2$ **d** yes; $m = 2$

12

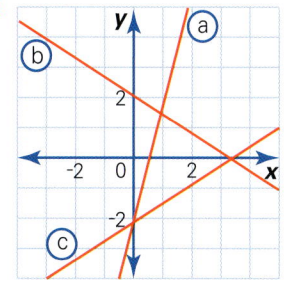

13 a $y = 3$ **b** $y = {}^-2x - 3$ **c** $x = {}^-4$

Keeping Mathematically Fit

PART A

1 $\dfrac{mn}{2}$ **2** A   **3** 200   **4** 70 km

5 D   **6** \$50   **7** 12   **8** $12x - 8$

9 $4pq^2$ **10** b

PART B

1 250 g for \$7.15   **2** 2590

3 a $7x + 4y$ **b** $3x - y$

   c 28·5 m

4 $^-18$ **5** 36°

Chapter 9

MathsCheck

1 ah, bm, cf, dl, ej, gn, ik   **2** 6

3 triangular pyramid/tetrahedron

4 yes—triangle can be any size

5 one pair of equal sides   **6** yes

7 no—angles could be different

8 a reflection, rotation

   b translation, reflection, rotation

   c reflection, rotation

   d rotation

   e translation, reflection, rotation

   f translation, reflection, rotation

9 a

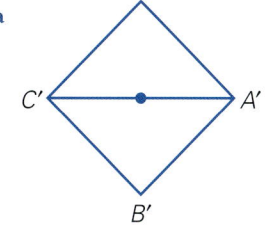

   b

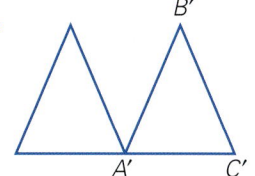

c

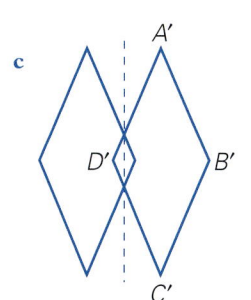

d

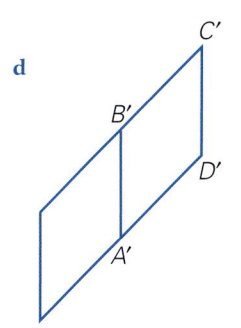

e

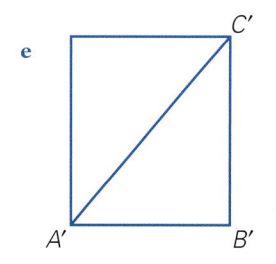

f

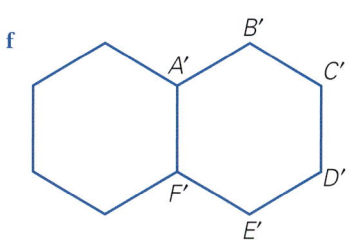

10 a $A' = (4, 6)$ **b** $A' = (11, 3)$

   c $A' = (18, 7)$ **d** $A' = (19, 2)$

11 a translation 4 units right

   b reflection in diagonal line through C

   c translation 3 units down

   d reflection in horizontal line AD

   e 90° clockwise rotation about (9, 10)

   f reflection in horizontal line AC

   g reflection in vertical line

   h rotation 180° about (16, 5)

   i translation 7 units left

EXERCISE 9A

1 a C **b** YX **c** Y **d** CB

   e $\angle YZX$ **f** $\angle BAC$ **g** $\triangle YXZ$ **h** $\triangle BAC$

2 a Measuring the sides of each triangle and checking that they match. (Discuss other methods.)

   b i HI **ii** ED **iii** IG

   c i $\triangle IHG$ **ii** $\triangle DEF$ **iii** $\triangle GHI$

3 a ST **b** $\angle STR$ **c** $\triangle TSR$ **d** FG

4 a $27°$ **b** 5 cm   **c** 9 cm   **d** $51°$

5 a $\triangle ABC \equiv \triangle FDE$ (SAS)

   b $\triangle LMN \equiv \triangle RPQ$ (AAS)

   c not necessarily congruent

   d $\triangle WVU \equiv \triangle YXZ$ (RHS)

   e not congruent   **f** $\triangle ABC \equiv \triangle YZX$ (SAS)

   g not congruent   **h** not congruent

6 a $\triangle MLN \equiv \triangle XYZ$ (SAS)

   b $\triangle ABC \equiv \triangle NML$ (AAS)

   c $\triangle NML \equiv \triangle YXZ$ (RHS) *or* (SSS)

   d $\triangle LMN \equiv \triangle YXZ$ (AAS)

7 a $\triangle PSR \equiv \triangle PQR$ (SSS)

   b $\triangle ABC \equiv \triangle EDC$ (SAS)

   c $\triangle NLK \equiv \triangle NLM$ (RHS)

   d $\triangle EDG \equiv \triangle EFG$ (RHS)

   e $\triangle ZVW \equiv \triangle YXW$ (AAS)

   f $\triangle RST \equiv \triangle SRU$ (AAS)

EXERCISE 9B

1 a In $\triangle$s KLN and MLN

   $KL = ML$ (given)

   $\angle NKL = \angle NML$

   given, right angle

   NL is common

   $\triangle KLN = \triangle MLN$ (RHS)

   b In $\triangle$s EOF and GOF

   $EO = GO$ (equal radii of circle)

   $\angle EOF = \angle GOF$ (given 115°)

   OF is common

   $\triangle EOF \equiv \triangle GOF$ (SAS)

   c In $\triangle$s WXV and ZYV

   $\angle WVX = \angle ZVY$ (vert. opp. $\angle$s)

   $\angle WXV = \angle ZYV$ (alt. $\angle$s, $WX \parallel YZ$)

   $XV = YV$ (given, 6 mm)

   $\triangle WXV \equiv \triangle ZYV$ (AAS)

2 a In $\triangle$s HEF and FGH

   $HE = FG$ (given)

   $\angle HEF = \angle FGH$ (given, 90°)

   HF is common

   $\therefore \triangle HEF = \triangle FGH$ (RHS)

   b In $\triangle$s ZWV and XYU

   $ZW = XY$ (sides of square)

   $\angle ZWV = \angle XYU$ (90°, corners of square)

   $\angle ZVW = \angle XUY$ (given, 68°)

   $\therefore \triangle ZWV = \triangle XYU$ (AAS)

   c In $\triangle$s JOK and LOM

   $JK = LM$ (given)

   $OJ = OL$ (equal radii of circle)

   $OK = OM$ (equal radii of circle)

   $\therefore \triangle JOK = \triangle LOM$ (SSS)

d In $\triangle$s ADC and CBA

   $\angle DAC = \angle BCA$ (alt. $\angle$s, $DA \parallel CB$)

   $\angle DCA = \angle BAC$ (alt. $\angle$s, $DC \parallel AB$)

   AC is common

   $\therefore \triangle ADC \equiv \triangle CBA$ (AAS)

e In $\triangle$s FEJ and FHG

   $FE = FH$ (given)

   $\angle EFJ = \angle HFG$ (vert. opp $\angle$s)

   $\angle JEF = \angle GHF$ (alt. $\angle$s, $JE \parallel HG$)

   $\therefore \triangle FEJ \equiv \triangle FHG$ (AAS) another method uses (SSS)

f In $\triangle$s RST and RUT

   $RS = RU$ (defn. of rhombus)

   $ST = UT$ (defn. of rhombus)

   RT is common

   $\therefore \triangle RST = \triangle RUT$ (SSS) (SAS could also be used)

g In $\triangle$s AOB and COB

   $AO = CO$ (equal radii of circle)

   $\angle AOB = \angle COB$ (given, 90°)

   OB is common

   $\therefore \triangle AOB \equiv \triangle COB$ (SAS)

h In $\triangle$s XYW and VYZ

   $\angle XYW = \angle VYZ$ (vert. opp. $\angle$s)

   $XY = VY$ (given, 3cm)

   WY = ZY (given, 5 cm)

   $\therefore \triangle XYW \equiv \triangle VYZ$ (SAS)

i In $\triangle$s JML and JKL

   $JM = JK$ (given)

   $ML = KL$ (given)

   JL is common

   $\therefore \triangle JML \equiv \triangle JKL$ (SSS) (alternatives possible using kite properties)

j In $\triangle$s WXZ and YXZ

   $\angle WZX = \angle YZX$ (given, 46°)

   $\angle WXZ = \angle YXZ$ (given, 90°)

   ZX is common

   $\therefore \triangle WXZ \equiv \triangle YXZ$ (AAS)

k In $\triangle$s OLM and ONM

   $LM = NM$ (given)

   $OL = ON$ (equal radii of circle)

   OM is common

   $\therefore \triangle OLM \equiv \triangle ONM$ (SSS)

l In $\triangle$s STR and RQS

   $\angle SQR = \angle RTS$ (given, 90°)

   $\angle PRS = \angle PSR$ (given)

   SR is common

   $\therefore \triangle STR \equiv \triangle RQS$ (AAS)

3 In $\triangle$s RPQ and SPQ

   $\angle PQR = \angle PQS$ (given, 120°)

   $\angle RPQ = \angle SPQ$ (PQ bisects $\angle RPS$)

   PQ is common

   $\therefore \triangle RPQ \equiv \triangle RQS$ (AAS)

4 In $\triangle$s FGH and HJF

   $FG = HJ$ (opp. sides of rectangle)

   $GH = JF$ (opp. sides of rectangle)

   FH is common

   $\therefore \triangle FGM \equiv \triangle HJF$ (SSS) (alternatives use SAS, RHS or AAS)

5 In Δs *CXY* and *CDY*
$CX = CD$ (given)
$\angle CXY = \angle CDY$ (given, and corner of square)
CY is common
$\therefore \Delta CXY \equiv \Delta CDY$ (RHS)

EXERCISE 9C

1 a $\Delta ABC \equiv \Delta EDF$ (RHS)
$p = 61$ (corresponding ∠s in congruent Δs)
b $\Delta PRS \equiv \Delta PRQ$ (SAS)
$\therefore x = 4$ (corresponding sides in congruent Δs)
c $\Delta LMN \equiv \Delta RQP$ (AAS)
$\therefore d = 5$ (corresponding sides in congruent Δs)
d $\Delta OPQ \equiv \Delta ORQ$ (RHS)
$\therefore t = 3$ (corresponding sides in congruent Δs)
e $\Delta MJK \equiv \Delta LKJ$ (AAS)
$\therefore y = 2{\cdot}5$ (corresponding sides in congruent Δs)
f $\Delta WXZ \equiv \Delta YZX$ (AAS)
$\therefore a = 42$ (corresponding ∠s in congruent Δs)

2 a In Δs *ABC* and *EDC*:
$BC = DC$ (given)
$AC = EC$ (given)
$\angle ACB = \angle ECD$ (vertically opposite ∠s)
$\therefore \Delta ABC \equiv \Delta EDC$ (SAS)
$\therefore \angle ABC \equiv \angle CDE$ (corresponding ∠s in congruent ∠s)
b In Δs *JKM* and *LKM*:
$JM = LM$ (given)
$\angle JMK = \angle LMK$
KM is common
$\therefore \Delta JKM \equiv \Delta LKM$ (SAS)
$\therefore JK = KL$ (corresponding sides in congruent Δs)
c In Δs *WXY* and *WZY*:
$WX = WZ$ (given)
$XY = ZY$ (given)
WY is common
$\therefore \Delta WXY \equiv \Delta WZY$ (SSS)
$\therefore \angle WZY = \angle WXY$ (corresponding ∠s in congruent Δs)
d In Δs *RST* and *TUR*:
$RS = TU$ (opposite sides of rectangle)
$ST = RU$ (opposite sides of rectangle)
RT is common
$\therefore \Delta RST \equiv \Delta TUR$ (SSS)
$\therefore \angle RTU = \angle TRS = 40°$ (corresponding ∠s in congruent Δs)
e In Δs *OAC* and *OBC*:
$OA = OB$ (equal radii)
$\angle OCA = \angle OCB = 90°$ (given)
OC is common
$\therefore \Delta OCA \equiv \Delta OCB$ (RHS)
$\therefore AC = BC$ (corresponding sides in congruent Δs)
$\therefore OC$ bisects *AB*

f In Δs *PQS* and *RQS*:
$PQ = RQ$ (given)
$\angle PQS = \angle RQS$ (*QS* bisects $\angle PQR$)
QS is common
$\therefore \Delta PQS \equiv \Delta RQS$ (SAS)
$\therefore \angle QSP = \angle QSR$ (corresponding ∠s in congruent Δs)
but $\angle QSP + \angle QSR = 180°$ (∠s on straight line)
$\therefore \angle QSP = 90°$

3 a

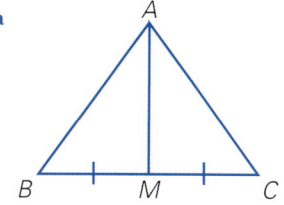

In Δs *ABM* and *ACM*:
$AB = AC$ (given)
$BM = CM$ (*M* is midpoint of *BC*)
AM is common
$\therefore \Delta ABM \equiv \Delta ACM$ (SSS)
$\therefore \angle ABM = \angle ACM$ (corresponding ∠s in congruent Δs)

b

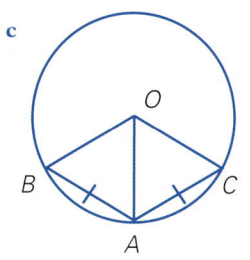

In Δs *PQR* and *RSP*:
$\angle RPQ = \angle PRS$ (alternate ∠s, $PQ \parallel SR$)
$\angle QRP = \angle SPR$ (alternate ∠s, $PS \parallel QR$)
PR is common.
$\therefore \Delta PQR \equiv \Delta RSP$ (AAS)
$\therefore \angle PQR = \angle RSP$ (corresponding ∠s in congruent Δs)

c

In Δs *AOB* and *AOC*:
$OB = OC$ (equal radii)
$AB = AC$ (given)
OA is common.
$\therefore \Delta AOB \equiv \Delta AOC$ (SSS)
$\therefore \angle AOB = \angle AOC$ (corresponding ∠s in congruent Δs)

d

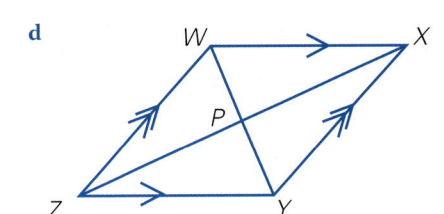

i In △s *WXZ* and *YZX*:
∠*WXZ* = ∠*YZX* (alternate ∠s, *WX* ∥ *ZY*)
∠*WZX* = ∠*YXZ* (alternate ∠s, *WZ* ∥ *XY*)
ZX is common.
∴ △*WXZ* ≡ △*YZX* (AAS)
∴ *WX* = *YZ* (corresponding sides in congruent △s)
and *WZ* = *XY* (corresponding sides in congruent △s)
∴ opposite sides of parallelgram are equal.

ii In △s *WXP* and *YZP*:
WX = *YZ* (proven in **i**)
∠*WPX* = ∠*YPZ* (vertically opposite ∠s)
∠*PXW* + ∠*PZY* (alternate ∠s, *WZ* ∥ *ZY*)
∴ △*WXP* ≡ △*YZP* (AAS)
∴ *XP* = *ZP* (corresponding sides in congruent △s)
and *WP* = *YP* (corresponding sides in congruent △s)
∴ diagonals bisect each other.

4

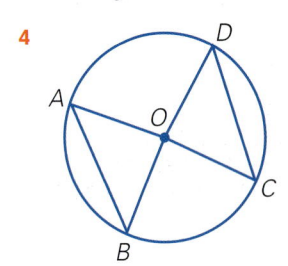

In △s *AOB* and *DOC*:
AO = *DO* (equal radii)
OB = *OC* (equal radii)
∴ ∠*AOB* = ∠*DOC* given
∴ △*AOB* ≡ △*DOC* (SAS)
∴ *AB* = *DC* (corresponding sides in congruent △s)

Chapter Review Exercises

1 a 15 cm   **b** 90°   **c** 26°   **d** 9 cm
2 △*DEF* ≡ △*GIH* (AAS)
3 a In △s *JLK* and *MNP*
   JK = *MP* (given)
   LJ = *NM* (given)
   ∠*JLK* = ∠*MNP* (given, 90°)
   ∴ △*JLK* ≡ △*MNP* (RHS)
b In △s *WZY* and *WXY*
   WZ = *WX* (given)
   ZY = *XY* (given)
   WY is common
   ∴ △*WZY* ≡ △*WXY* (SSS)

c In △s *EDG* and *GFE*
   ∠*DEG* = ∠*FGE* (alt. ∠s, *DE* ∥ *GF*)
   ∠*DGE* = ∠*FEG* (alt. ∠s, *DG* ∥ *EF*)
   EG is common
   ∴ △*EDG* ≡ △*GFE* (AAS)
4 △*ABC* ≡ △*CDA* (SSS)
5 In △s *PSQ* and *RQS*
   ∠*PQS* = ∠*RSQ* (alternate ∠s, *SR* ∥ *PQ*)
   ∠*PSQ* = ∠*RQS* (alternate ∠s, *PS* ∥ *QR*)
   SQ is common
   ∴ △*PSQ* ≡ △*RQS* (AAS)
6 △*LMN* ≡ △*QRP* (AAS)
7 One may be an enlargement of the other.
8 a In △s *DOC* and *BOC*:
   OD = *OB* (equal radii)
   ∠*OCD* = ∠*OCB* = 90° (given)
   OC is common
   ∴ △*DOC* ≡ △*BOC* (RHS)
b In △s *MLK* and *KJM*:
   ∠*LMK* = ∠*JKM* (alternate ∠s, *ML* ∥ *JK*)
   ∠*JMK* = ∠*LKM* (alternate ∠s, *JM* ∥ *LK*)
   MK is common
   ∴ △*MLK* ≡ △*KJM* (AAS)
9 a In △s *OPQ* and *ORS*:
   OP = *OR* (equal radii)
   OQ = *OS* (equal radii)
   ∠*POQ* = ∠*ROS* (vertically opposite ∠s)
   ∴ △*OPQ* ≡ △*ORS* (SAS)
   ∴ *PQ* = *RS* (corresponding sides in congruent △s)
b In △s *DOF* and *BOE*:
   DO = *BO* (given)
   ∠*DOF* = ∠*BOE* (vertically opposite ∠s)
   ∠*ODF* = ∠*OBE* (alternate ∠s, *DF* ∥ *EB*)
   ∴ △*DOF* ≡ △*BOE* (AAS)
   ∴ *DF* = *EB* (corresponding sides in congruent △s)
c In △s *ABD* and *CBD*:
   AD = *CD* (given)
   ∠*ADB* = ∠*CDB* = 90° (given)
   BD is common
   ∴ △*ABD* ≡ △*CBD* (SAS)
   ∴ *AB* = *BC* (corresponding sides in congruent △s)
   [or ∠*BAD* = ∠*BCD* (corresponding ∠s in congruent △s)
   ∴ △*ABC* is isosceles

Keeping Mathematically Fit

PART A

1 5, 6 or 7   **2** $\frac{2}{3}$
3 $219: $36.50 each
   or $222: $37 each
   or $240: $40 each
4 bag; 60 g
5 20 cm   **6** 8:10 am
7 16 cm, 2 cm or 8 cm, 4 cm
8 39 000   **9** several possibilities

10 **a** $\frac{1}{10}$ **b** 180 g

PART B
1 $y = 3x + 6$ **2** 23·6 L
3 $AC = 14·3$ cm   **4** C
  $\angle ACB = 44°26'$
  $\angle ABC = 45°34'$
5 $\frac{2}{3}$

Chapter 10

MathsCheck
1 cars 60%
  trucks 16%
  vans 15%
  bikes 6%
  buses 3%
2 **a** $79.20 **b** 12% **c** $105 **d** $46.30
    $22.35   18% $1728 $4
    $96.80   19% $6.36 $137.70
    $3.10   42.5% $78.75 $5600
    $8439   8·5% $1971.92 $8.20
    $92.25   10% $35.68 $108.35
3 **a** depreciation 54·3% **b** $844
    registration 7·4%
    insurance 10·8%
    repairs 9·1%
    petrol 18·3%
4 **a** 49·5%   **b** 88 mL fruit juice
                 9 mL preservative
                 30 mL sugar
                 124 mL water
5 **a** $30   **b** tax: 31·5%
                 food: 15·2%
                 mortgage: 28·4%
                 car: 12·2 %
                 telephone etc: 9·6%
                 other: 3·0%
6 flour 50%
  butter 33·3%
  sugar 16·7%
7 gold = 187·5 g, silver = 281·25 g
8 **a** profit   **b** $15   **c** 30%
9 **a** $62.25   **b** $550.40   **c** $25.85
10 $168
11 **a** 400 g   **b** $400   **c** 200 kg
   d $223.68   **e** 150 m   **f** $43
   g 240 mL   **h** $7.04   **i** 2 kg
   j 90 L   **k** 1350 mm   **l** 240 kg
   m $20
12 667
13 **a** $513.33   **b** $551.83
14 **a** $226.09   **b** $79.13
15 **a** $39 500   **b** $754.41   **c** A
16 **a** $14 994   **b** 34%   **c** $26 520
17 **a** 150%   **b** 60%   **c** discuss
18 **a** 17% loss   **b** discuss

19 **a** 25   **b** 79¢   **c** 78·2%
20 **a** 25   **b** $1.77   **c** 55·7%
   d packaging, marketing costs
21 57·1%   **22** 48%
23 anything less than $100
24 **a** $22.95   **b** $22.95   **c** same price
   d yes   **e** yes
25 $233\frac{1}{3}$%   **26** $289.07   **27** $595.68

EXERCISE 10A
1 **a** $84.82   **b** $397.81   **c** $990.68
   d $62.04   **e** $96.68
2 **a** 11·65%   **b** 15·36%   **c** 16·75%
   d 24·8%   **e** 0·9967%
3 **a** $224.10   **b** $206.17   **c** 17·2%
4 $35.10
5 **a** $31.41   **b** $29.84   **c** 19·25%
6 $x = 13·4$
7 **a** $10 off   **b** discuss
8 **a** gold $42.15, rubies $138.07, diamonds
    $142.83
   b $3930.97
   c 23·68%
9 **a** $632.72   **b** $698.33   **c** $1666.67

EXERCISE 10B
1 $2790.77   **2** $93 080   **3** $50 752
4 **a** $25.68   **b** $38.53   **c** $1072.32
5 $148.50
6 **a** $503.63   **b** $476.96   **c** $552.51
7 $579.36
8 **a** $61.65   **b** $150.70   **c** $198.65
9 **a** 48   **b** 1776   **c** $15.65   **d** $19.48
10 **a** $126.16   **b** $559.47   **c** $622.55
11 $484.16, $337.28, $524.96, $299.20
12 $532.58, $371.01, $577.46, $329.12
13 **a** $810.58 **b** $712.88 **c** 43 h   **d** 3·5 h
14 **a** $28.56   **b** 3·12 h
15 $13.58

EXERCISE 10C
1 **a** $93.60 **b** $288   **c** $1566   **d** $22.50
2 **a** **i** $155   **ii** $830   **iii** $359
   b discuss **c** discuss
3 **a** $840   **b** $300   **c** $741
4 **a** $500   **b** $850   **c** $1459   **d** $3720
5 **a** $170   **b** $15 000   **c** $10 500
6 **a** **i** $4925   **ii** $2125   **iii** $52 950
   b $227 400
7 **a** **i** $606   **ii** $11.88
   b **i** $5336   **ii** $15 246
8 **a** Hugh: $240   **b** $6667
    Lou: $200
   c $1 690 000   **d** $20 000   **e** $12 000

EXERCISE 10D
1 $105.45   **2** $139.68
3 **a** $45.50   **b** 240   **c** $349.65

4	Hours	Costs($)	Hours	Cost ($)
	1	21.50	6	69.00
	2	31.00	7	78.50
	3	40.50	8	88.00
	4	50.00	9	97.50
	5	59.50	10	107.00

5 **a** $19.24   **b** 4054   **c** $8.88
6 **a** 12 boxes   **b** $5.14   **c** 19·5 hours
   d 14 hours
7 **a** $33   **b** $99   **c** $100.32
   d $140.58   **e** $196.68

EXERCISE 10E
1 $377.30   **2** $706.87
3 **a** $1800   **b** $3370.80   **c** $2500
   d $5100
4 60 shares
5 **a** $86.11   **b** $473.11
6 $1920
7 **a** $2876.40   **b** $2502.75
8 $612
9 **a** 1·5%   **b** 3·3%   **c** discuss   **d** 24 h
10 B   **11** $3476.57   **12** 20 : 33

EXERCISE 10F
1 **a** $219.40   **b** $1869.54   **c** $953.63
   d $16778.16
2 **a** $902.31   **b** $279.72   **c** $566.60
3 **a** 57%   **b** 74%   **c** 36%
4 **a** $1972   **b** 0   **c** $8877
   d $16 560   **e** $5100   **f** $85
5 **a** $30 420   **b** $5754.30   **c** $948.68
6 **a** $841.16   **b** $439.43
7 **a** $5.37   **b** 11·8 h
8 **a** $4503.12   **b** 17%
9 $1408.30
10 **a** $37 163.33   **b** $29 426.67
   c $14 029.41   **d** $50 723.33

EXERCISE 10G
1 **a** **i** $645   **ii** $194   **iii** $129
     iv $19   **v** $54 825   **vi** $12 320
     vii $2580   **viii** $58 050
   Note: questions **vii** and **viii** may vary slightly
   depending on which rows in the table were
   used.
   b 13%
2 **a** $12   **b** $31   **c** $10
3 **a** $330   **b** $500   **c** $230
4 **a** $72   **b** $45.60
5 **a** $728   **b** $272   **c** $3120
   d $65 000
6 **a** **i** $7.50   **ii** $257.50
   b **i** $192   **ii** $992
   c **i** $19.13   **ii** $104.13
7 **a** $17.12   **b** $265.44   **c** $418.60
   d $935.25   **e** $1390.16   **f** $59.81
   g $825.81   **h** $211.02   **i** $3.32
   j $71.35   **k** $1712.33
8 6 years   **9** 9 years   **10** $242.86

11 5·5%   **12** 3·5%
13 **a** $7532   **b** $209.22
14 $858.40   **15** $11 911.76

EXERCISE 10H
1 final amount = $789.53
2 **a** $2205   **b** $371.32   **c** $41 090.05
   d $784.98   **e** $5307.24   **f** $1306.96
   g $23 641.04   **h** $1 347 935.51
3 **a** $4928.40   **b** $1022.16   **c** $19 425.44
   d $2197.41   **e** $52 727.86   **f** $49 962.67
   g $4 998 502.68   **h** $721.02
4 **a** **i** $1851.50   **ii** $1820
   b simple interest
5 $182.85
6 **a** 1   **b** $\frac{1}{2}$ **c** 6
   d 12   **e** $\frac{3}{4}$ **f** 12
   g 4·5   **h** 6
7 **a** $3077.25   **b** $3105.94   **c** $3121.02
   d $3131.36
8 **a** $4575.52   **b** $4734.73   **c** $4823.43
   d $4886.44
9 **a** $6154.50   **b** $6211.88   **c** $6242.04
   d $6262.72
10 **a** $127.16   **b** $204.17   **c** $7853.16
11 **a** $47 700   **b** $47 740.50   **c** $47 761.36
12 **a** $835.89   **b** $51 437.20
13 10·5% p.a. (10% p.a. paid quarterly is
   equivalent to 10·38% p.a. paid annually)
14 15% p.a. is a lower rate (1·2% per month is
   equivalent to 15·39% p.a.) so choose
   bank A—lower interest rate.
15 **a** 11 576 fish   **b** 3695
16 1·34 million
17 **a** 7·7% p.a.   **b** 7·59% p.a.   **c** 7·46% p.a.
18 **a** 14·9%   **b** 14·4% p.a.   **c** 13·9% p.a.
19 10 years ($3581.70)

EXERCISE 10I
1 **a** $22 084   **b** $11 131   **c** $30 705
2 $1418.91   **3** $342
4 **a** $1314   **b** $486
   c approx. 8 years
5 **a** $15 369.54   **b** $3881.49   **c** $3883.37
6 21% p.a.   **7** $7127.37
8 **a** 908 students   **b** 76 years

EXERCISE 10J
1 **a** $0.41   **b** $0.14   **c** $2.30   **d** $2.78
   e $1.75   **f** $0.35   **g** $2.36   **h** $0.10
2 $1.25

3 **a** **i**

Interest
$0.148
$0.186
$0.135
$0.47

ii $0.939

   b $0.35

4 a

Date	Balance	Interest
5/7/02	278.59	$0.281
12/7/02	101.74	$0.275
14/7/02	470.74	$0.029
23/7/02	335.74	$0.598
29/7/02	325.89	$0.284
31/7/02	325.89	$0.092
		$1.56

b $0.45

5 a

Date	Details	Credit	Debit	Balance	Interest
1/10	Opening balance			185.48	
5/10	Cash withdrawal		65.00	120.48	$0.123
13/10	EFTPOS payment		32.67	87.81	$0.128
15/10	Automatic credit	856.91		944.72	$0.023
25/10	Cheque		255.00	689.72	$1.255
29/10	Automatic credit	856.91		1546.63	$0.367
31/10	Closing balance			1546.63	$0.411

b $2.31   **c** $0.36

EXERCISE 10K

1 a $5.56   **b** $0.48   **c** $27.59   **d** $11.99
  e $19.08   **f** $8.82
2 a i $352.89   **ii** $5.29
  b i $4712.90   **ii** $70.65
  c i $48   **ii** $0.72
  d i nil   **ii** nil
  e i $200   **ii** $3.00
  f i $185.71   **ii** $2.78
3 a $94.87   **b** $1.43   **c** $331.96
  d $16.60   **e** $4.93

4

Date	Details	Amount
1/11	Opening balance	129.52
3/11	Red Edge Pizza Co	37.90
4/11	Runaway Travel	135.60
15/11	Venus Rd Service	23.00
16/11	Payment — thank you	100.00–
23/11	Runner's shoes	138.95
30/11	Interest charges	0.36
	Closing balance	365.33
	Minimum payment:	18.27

Chapter Review Exercises

1 blue: 59%
  red: 24%
  white: 12%
  black: 6%
2 $176
3 a $59   **b** 12·9%
4 a $24.42   **b** $4.68   **c** $146.09
  d $313.30
5 16·1%   **6** $59.79
7 a $1134.60   **b** 1·3%
8 $226.46   **9** $218.28
10 a $100.91   **b** $83.72
11 a i A: $1250 B: $900
   ii A: $6875 B: $3600

b A: $340 000 B: $648 333
c $4615.38
12 $2089.62
13 a $878.06   **b** 61·4%   **c** $34 240.70
14 a $10 762.50   **b** $187 440
15 a $7836   **b** $2587   **c** 20·1%
16 a i $240   **ii** 3240
  b i $88.44   **ii** $356.44
  c i $510   **ii** $26 010
  d i $0.69   **ii** $96.69
  e i $2876.71   **ii** $502 876.71
  f i $33.69   **ii** 733.69
17 a $512.44   **b** $66 361.97
18 a $14 803.67   **b** $389 723.51
19 a $2077.65   **b** $2444.92
20 a $12 000   **b** $15 669.56   **c** $16 044.56
21 $1254.11   **22** 12%   **23** $81.25

24 a

Balance
56.45
26.45
146.45
66.45
66.45

b 15 days   **c** $0.06
d i $0.006   **ii** $0.097   **iii** $0.015
e $0.18

Keeping Mathematically Fit

PART A

1 ⁻4   **2** 1 : 100   **3** 24 kg
4 C   **5** 30°
6 a $240   **b** $50
7 a

80	1
70	0 2 5
60	5 5 7 9
50	9 9

  b 22   **c** 65
8 $4t(8 - 3t)$ **9** 17 000 m²
10 6 cm

PART B

1 4   **2** (7, −5)   **3** $785.05
4 $\dfrac{-6}{11}$ **5** 3^{21}

Cumulative Review 3

1 a $11a + 9$ **b** $^{-}20r^4 + 8r^2$
  c $3x^3 - 3x^2 + 5x$ **d** $2t^2 - 11t - 21$
2 a $6(2p + 3q)$ **b** $^{-}6w^2(2v + 5w)$
3 a 770   **b** 100 000 **c** 90 000   **d** 4000
  e $\dfrac{1}{2}$ **f** 7
4 a 4·6   **b** ⁻2·2   **c** 6·6
5 a 3.4×10^2 **b** 3.9×10^7 **c** 4.5×10^{-4}
6 a 3500   **b** 106 000   **c** 0·004 11
7 a $2(n + 2)$ **b** 40
8 a 5^6 **b** $(3t)^3$
9 a $\dfrac{8x}{y}$ **b** a^6 **c** 4

10 a 10 **b** 49 **c** $\frac{1}{25}$ **d** 5
11 1·24m ± 0·005 m
12 a 0·44 kg **b** 8400 kg **c** 14 000 m²
13 discuss **14** 280 km and 120 km
15 Alex $2336, Simon $1314
16 a 150 m **b** 4·3 cm
17 150 g **18** 7 **19** 13·9
20 a i 4800 mm **ii** 11 250 cm²
 b i 4·8 m **ii** 0·99 m²
21 a $t = 7·5$ **b** $a = 7$ **c** $x = ^-10$
22 a $n \geq 3·5$ **b** $f > \frac{3}{4}$
23 a yes; 4 sides
 b yes; diagonals bisect each other
 c no; diagonals not equal
 d yes; diagonals bisect at right angles
24 discuss
25 a 110° **b** 70° **c** 90° **d** 36 mm
 e 24 mm **f** 55°
26 a i 720° **ii** 120°
 b i 1260° **ii** 140°
27 72°
28 yes; satisfies all conditions
29 1080°
30 square, rectangle, (isosceles, trapezium)
31 a 1 : 4 **b** 3 : 4
32 no; $c^2 \neq a^2 + b^2$
33 a CB **b** AB **c** AC
34 a 0·788 **b** 0·176 **c** 0·391
35 a 10·17 **b** 21·05 **c** 16·51
36 a 36° **b** 60° **c** 40°
37 14 m
38 a 1·945 m **b** 1·822 m
39 844 m
40 66° and 114° **41** B **42** B

43 a i 4 **ii** $^-2$ **iii** $\frac{1}{2}$ **iv** $y = \frac{1}{2}x - 2$

 b i 0 **ii** 0 **iii** $\frac{^-3}{2}$ **iv** $y = \frac{^-3}{2}x$

 c $y = ^-3$ **d** $x = 2$

44 a i $^-3$ **ii** $^-4$ **b i** $\frac{1}{2}$ **ii** 0

 c i 3 **ii** $^-2$ **d i** $\frac{2}{5}$ **ii** $^-2$

45 a $y = \frac{3}{5}x - 3$ **b** $y = \frac{3}{5}x$

46
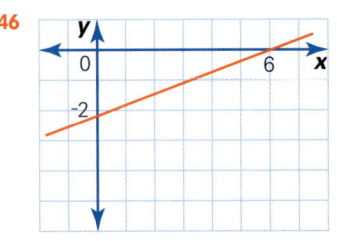

47 A **48** B

49 a $\sqrt{13}$; $\sqrt{13}$; $\sqrt{26}$
 b isosceles, right-angled at (1, 1)
50 $Q = (1, ^-9)$ **51** $x = ^-3$ **52** $y = ^-5$
53 C
54 a Vertical scale does not start from zero. Use of 3D objects magnifies the effect of the height difference.

 b

Sales of hair conditioner

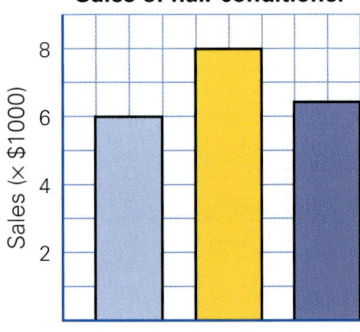

55 a

Heater sales

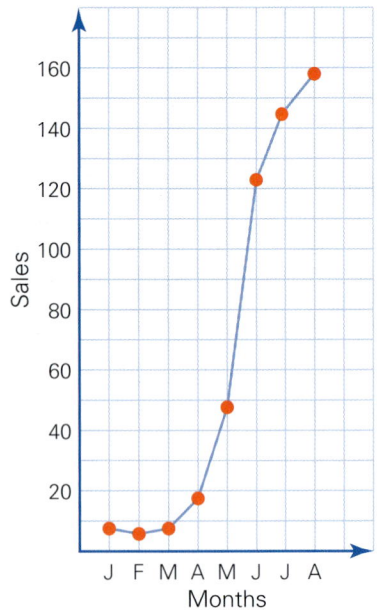

 b Poor prediction; sales are seasonal and will start to reduce towards the end of winter. (The graph shows the sales are growing less quickly by the end of August.)
56 a (11, 5) **c** (12, 5)
 d translation, back 9 down 3
 e translation, right 4 then reflect in $y = 3$
57 a 8 m **b** 115° **c** 4·5 m
58 a $\Delta XAT \equiv \Delta OYB$ **b** SSS

59 In △s ABC and CBA
$\angle DAC = \angle BCA$ (alt. $\angle$s $\parallel$ lines)
$\angle ACD = \angle CAB$ (alt. $\angle$s $\parallel$ lines)
AC is common
$\therefore \triangle ADC \equiv \triangle CBA$ (AAS)
60 \$131
61 **a i** \$800 **ii** \$2150 **iii** \$7950
b \$254 000
62 \$44.33   63   \$479.25
64 **a** \$624.38 **b** \$88.95   c \$2705.67
65 \$59.53   66 \$610.91   67 B
68 B

69 **a**

Balance
\$614.75
\$514.75
\$834.75
\$382.80
\$702.80
\$702.80

b \$1.54   **c** \$0.88

Chapter 11

MathsCheck

1 a $12x + 30$ **b** $20 - 15p$ **c** $14t - 2$
d $6y + 9$ **e** $^-6t - 21$ **f** $^-24 + 18q$
g $2x^2 - 2x$ **h** $8a^2 + 12a$ **i** $^-10p^2 + 20p$
2 a $3x + 6$ **b** $^-23c^2 - 16c$
c $10x^3 - 3x^2$ **d** $m^2 - 4m - 5$
e $6y^2 - 7y - 3$ **f** $x^2 + 4x + 4$
g $x^2 - 10x + 25$ **h** $4x^2 + 36x + 81$
3 a $(x + 2)$ **b** $(m - 9)$ **c** $(2b - 3t)$
d $(1 + n)$ **e** $(3 - 2p)$ **f** $(c + 2)$
g 3 **h** mp **i** $6x^3$
j $(x + ^-2)$ **k** $(1 + ^-2b)$ **l** $(3 + 2t^2)$
4 a $(x + c + a)$ **b** $(1 + 2x + 3x^2)$
c $(x + y)$ **d** $(x + 5)$
e $(p - 2)$ **f** $(5n - 3)$

EXERCISE 11A

1 a $6(x + 3)$ **b** $2(3x - 5)$ **c** $x(a + b)$
d $x(x - 1)$ **e** $p(5 - 3p)$ **f** $9(3 - 2x)$
g $p(m - 9)$ **h** $t^2(7t - 5)$ **i** $an(n + a)$
j $2p(t + 2x)$ **k** $3k(n - 2d)$ **l** $3a(2b - 3t)$
m $6c(4b - 3a)$ **n** $2n(3n + 4t)$ **o** $4x(1 - 4x)$
p $5d(4d^2 - 3)$
2 a $^-2(x - 2)$ **b** $^-3(n + 2)$ **c** $^-5(2 + 3a)$
d $^-4(3t + 4)$ **e** $^-4(2t - 3x)$ **f** $^-x(x - 5)$
g $^-p(^-5 + 3p)$ **h** $^-7t(p - 2)$
3 a yes   **b** $8(t + 3)$ **c** $4x(x - 2)$
d $9a(a - 5)$ **e** yes   **f** $6k(2k - 3)$
g $12x^2(t + 3)$ **h** $5(x + 2)(x + 3)$
4 a $a(b + c + 4)$ **b** $7x(1 - 2t + 3x)$
c $2m^2(3m^2 - 2m + 6)$ **d** $(a + b)(2 + x)$
e $(x + 3)(x + 5)$ **f** $(n + 2)(n - 3)$
g $(x - 4)(x - 7)$ **h** $(c + 1)(2c + 5)$
i $(2t + 7)(7t + 5)$ **j** $(2x - 1)(x + 5)$

k $(3b - 5)(b - 2)$ **l** $(4x - 2)(4x - 2)$
m $(x - y)(8 - x)$ **n** $(a + 1)(a + 1)$
o $(1 - x)(1 - x)$
5 a $\pi r(r - 1)$ **b** not possible
c $\sqrt{2}(x + y)$ **d** $\sqrt{x}\,(5 + a)$
e $\frac{1}{2}x\,(x - \frac{1}{2})$ **f** $3\pi R(2R - 3)$
6 a $\sin x(3 + t)$ **b** $9x\sqrt{y}\,(2 - 3x)$
c $\frac{1}{4}\sin\theta(1 + 3\cos\theta)$ **d** $(x + 1)(x + 4)$
e $(a + b)(a + b + 1)$ **f** $2(3 - 2x)(x - 1)$

EXERCISE 11B

1 a $(x - 2)$ **b** $(^-x + 2)$ **c** $(n - p)$
d $(^-n + p)$ **e** $(^-2a + 3)$ **f** $(2a - 3)$
2 a $(x + y)(a + b)$ **b** $(m + t)(p + x)$
c $(x + 4)(x + 3)$ **d** $(c + 2)(c + 5)$
e $(p - s)(t + a)$ **f** $(x + 2y)(10 + c)$
g $(a + b)(x - y)$ **h** $(x + b)(x + a)$
i $(a + 1)(b + 4)$ **j** $(x + 1)(x^2 + 1)$
k $(a + x)(y + 5)$ **l** $(a + t)(a + n)$
m $(x + 2)(x + 3)$ **n** $(y + 2)(y + 5)$
o $(a + 3)(a + 4)$ **p** $(a - 2)(a + 3)$
q $(n + 3)(n - 5)$ **r** $(t + 3)((t + 1)$
s $(x - 3)(x - 4)$ **t** $(y - 4)(y + 7)$
u $(d - 3)(d - 8)$ **v** $(f - 5)(f + 2)$
w $(h + 8)(h - 10)$ **x** $(k - 7)(k - 5)$
3 a $(a - 2)(b - 5x)$ **b** $(b - 1)(ab - 1)$
c $(x + 2)(11 - y)$ **d** $(n + 1)(2n + 3)$
e $(3x + 2)(x + 4)$ **f** $(2p - 5)(p + 5)$
g $(a - 1)(4a + 3)$ **h** $(c + n)(c + k)$
i $(d - 2)(d + p)$ **j** $(h - 4)(2h - 7)$
k $(k - t)(k - p)$ **l** $(5l - 1)(l + 3)$

EXERCISE 11C

1 a yes   **b** no   **c** no   **d** yes
e yes   **f** yes   **g** yes   **h** yes
2 a i x **ii** $3, 5, 6$
b i x **ii** $^-2, ^-1, ^-5$
c i x **ii** $1, 1, 0$
d i k **ii** $1, 0, ^-4$
e i n **ii** $^-2, 0, 0$
f i t **ii** $^-1, ^-3, 7$
g i a **ii** $1, ^-1·5, 0$
h i d **ii** $\frac{2}{3}, \frac{^-5}{6}, \frac{^-1}{2}$
3 a $9x^2 - 3x + 1$ **b** $^-8x^2 + ^-9x + 9$
c $^-4p^2 + 6p + ^-15$ **d** $^-3k^2 + ^-13k + 0$
e $14n^2 + 2n + ^-10$ **f** $^-4p^2 + \frac{5}{6}p + 0$
4 a $2x^2 + 3x + 5$ **b** $4x^2 + x + 6$
c $3x^2 + ^-2x + ^-5$ **d** $x^2 - 3x$
e $^-4x^2 + 1$ **f** $^-5x^2$
g $\frac{1}{2}x^2 - 3$ **h** $x^2 + 7·2x - 3·8$
5 a $3, 2$ **b** $5, 3$ **c** $5, 2$ **d** $3, 1$
e $5, 5$ **f** $10, 4$ **g** $^-4, ^-3$ **h** $^-7, ^-5$
i $7, 1$ **j** $3, ^-2$ **k** $^-5, 3$ **l** $7, ^-4$
m $^-5, 2$ **n** $^-6, ^-5$ **o** $^-11, 6$

6 a $(x+3)(x+2)$ **b** $(x-3)(x-2)$
c $(x-6)(x+1)$ **d** $(x+6)(x-1)$
e $(x+5)(x+3)$ **f** $(x+3)(x+1)$
g $(x+4)(x+10)$ **h** $(x-4)(x-3)$
i $(x-7)(x-5)$ **j** $(x-5)(x+3)$
k $(n-11)(n+6)$ **l** $(x+5)(x+2)$
m $(x+5)(x+5)$ **n** $(x+6)(x+6)$
o $(x+4)(x+5)$ **p** $(x+7)(x+1)$
q $(x-8)(x-3)$ **r** $(x+3)(x-2)$
s $(x-4)(x-1)$ **t** $(a-5)(a+3)$
u $(b-5)(b+2)$ **v** $(c-6)(c-5)$
w $(d-20)(d+3)$ **x** $(f-18)(f+2)$
y $(g-3)(g-14)$ **z** $(h-14)(h+3)$
7 a not possible   **b** $(x-6)(x+1)$
c $(y+3)(y-2)$ **d** $(5+n)(2+n)$
e $(c+8)(c+1)$ **f** $(t-8)^2$
g $(x+y)^2$ **h** $(x+4)(x+20)$
8 a $(l-4)(l-14)$ **b** $(m+15)(m-3)$
c $(n-4)(n-18)$ **d** $2(x+6)(x+1)$
e $3(x-2)^2$ **f** $4(x-5)(x-4)$
g $3(p+6)(p-2)$ **h** $2(x-21)(x+3)$

EXERCISE 11D

1 a $(x-2)(x+2)$ **b** $(x-4)(x+4)$
c $(73-27)(73+27)$
   $= 46 \times 100$ **d** $(a-6)(a+6)$
e $(b-10)(b+10)$ **f** $(x-y)(x+y)$
g $(c-9)(c+9)$ **h** $(7-x)(7+x)$
i $(d-h)(d+h)$ **j** $(8-j)(8+j)$
k $(12-k)(12+k)$ **l** $(l-1)(l+1)$
m $(1-m)(1+m)$ **n** $(x-0.6)(x+0.6)$
o $(y-\frac{1}{2})(y+\frac{1}{2})$ **p** $(n-0.5)(n+0.5)$
q $(p-\frac{1}{4})(p+\frac{1}{4})$ **r** $(q-0.4)(q+0.4)$
s $(r-\frac{2}{3})(r+\frac{2}{3})$ **t** $(\frac{3}{4}-s)(\frac{3}{4}+s)$
2 a $7^2+4^2 = 49+16$ **b** $4^2+7^2 = 65$
   $= 65$ $(4+7)(4-7)$
   $(7+4)^2 = 11^2 = 121$ $= 11 \times {}^-3$
          $= {}^-33$
3 a $(x+2)^2$ **b** $(x+5)^2$ **c** $(x+1)^2$
d $(x+3)^2$ **e** $(x-3)^2$ **f** $(x+7)^2$
g $(x-7)^2$ **h** $(x+10)^2$ **i** $(x-20)^2$
j $(x+15)^2$ **k** $(x-25)^2$ **l** $(x+\frac{1}{2})^2$
4 a $(2x-3)(2x+3)$ **b** $(3x-4)((3x+3)$
c $(4x-5)(4x+5)$ **d** $(5a-6)(5a+6)$
e $(7x-1)(7x+1)$ **f** $(7x-3a)(7x+3a)$
g $(9x-10y)(9x+10y)$
h $(11b-14c)(11b+14c)$
5 a not possible   **b** $(0.3-d)(0.3+d)$
c $2(x-1)^2$ **d** $(\frac{4}{5}-f)(\frac{4}{5}+f)$
e not possible   **f** $2(h-5)(h+5)$
g $3(j-3)(j+3)$ **h** $3(x+3)^2$
i $3(2x-1)(2x+1)$ **j** $m(m-1)(m+1)$
k $6(3-2n)(3+2n)$ **l** $3p(5-2p)(5+2p)$
m $5(x^2+4)$ **n** $(n^2-6)(n^2+6)$

o $3(q^2-9)(q^2+9)$ **p** $2(x-4)^2$
q $a(x+t)(x-t)$ **r** $(pq+r)(pq-r)$
s $d^2(d+e)(d-e)$ **t** $(d^2+ef)(d^2-ef)$
6 4

EXERCISE 11E

1 a $(2x+3)(x+1)$ **b** $(3x+5)(x+1)$
c $(7x+3)(x+1)$ **d** $(4x+3)(x+1)$
e $(2d+1)(d+2)$ **f** $(2n+1)(2n+3)$
g $(3n+2)(n-1)$ **h** $(3n-2)(n+1)$
i $(3n+1)(n-2)$ **j** $(3n-1)(n+2)$
k $(5a+3)(a-2)$ **l** $(5a-3)(a+2)$
m $(5y+1)(y+2)$ **n** $(3w+1)(2w+5)$
o $(3x-1)(2x-3)$ **p** $(2m-5)(m-5)$
q $(t-4)(2t-7)$ **r** $(3x-2)^2$
s $(2n+3)^2$ **t** $(2n-3)^2$
u $(1+r)^2$
2 a $2(2p+1)(p+3)$ **b** $3(3x+2)(x+1)$
c $2(5t+3)(t+2)$ **d** $2(3x+1)(x+2)$
e $4(2a-3)(a+2)$ **f** $5(3c+1)(c-4)$
g $2(3x+1)(2x+5)$ **h** $3(4x-1)(3x-2)$
i $5(2x+1)(3x-5)$
3 a $(5x-2)(2x-1)$ **b** $(2x+5)(4x-1)$
c $(4c-1)(5c+1)$ **d** $(3d+1)(2d-3)$
e $(4f+5)(2f-3)$ **f** $(2g-1)({}^-5g-2)$
g $(2h+3)({}^-4h+5)$ **h** $(k+5)(4-7k)$
i $(m+2p)(3m+4p)$ **j** $(2x-3y)(2x-y)$
k $(7a+5b)(a-b)$ **l** $(\frac{x}{y}+2)(\frac{x}{y}-5)$

EXERCISE 11F

1 a $2(x-3)(x+3)$ **b** $n(n+4)(n+2)$
c $t(t-4)(t+4)$ **d** $(x+9)(x-1)$
e $(p-7)(p-8)$ **f** $4c(1+3c)$
g $(a-3)(a+2)$ **h** $2(x+3)^2$
i $3(t-2)(t+2)$ **j** $pq(p+3)(p-3)$
k $(a-b)(x+1)$ **l** $r(t+y-4)$
m $(l+ab)(l-ab)$ **n** $(c+1)(a-2)$
o $(x-y)(3x+2)$ **p** $2(p+3)(p+2)$
q $3(m-5)(m+2)$ **r** $3(2a-5d)(2a+5d)$
s $m(p-t)(p+t)$ **t** $x(x+4)$
u $(y-11)(y+1)$ **v** $8(f^2+4)$
w $(1-x)(1+x)(1+x^2)$ **x** $2(x^2-3y^2)$
y $h(h^2+5h+90)$ **z** $2j(6j+5)(j-3)$
2 a not possible   **b** $2x^2(2x+3)$
c $3x^2(5x+1)$ **d** $(6t+1)(6t-1)$
e not possible   **f** $a(a^2+a+1)$
g $(2x-5)(x-2)$ **h** $(x+y+z)(x+y-z)$
i not possible   **j** $(b+2)(2a+3c)$
k $(x^2+1)(x+1)$ **l** $x(y+z)(y+3)$
m $(2a+1)(a-4)$ **n** $(b+4)(b+3)$
o $(4c+3)(c-1)$ **p** $(3x-2)(3x+2)$
q $3(\frac{1}{9}-4x)(\frac{1}{9}+4x)$ **r** $(a+b)(a+b+3)$
s $(5+h+k)(h-k)$ **t** $3(n-5)(n+1)$
u $(x-3)(x+5)$ **v** $(a^2+4)(a^2+3)$
w $y^6(y-1)(y+1)$ **x** ${}^-2(x-1)$
y $(x-y)(x-y)(x^2+y^2)$
z $2x^3({}^-4x-3)(x-1)$

1 a $\dfrac{x}{2a}$ b $\dfrac{3}{7}$ c $\dfrac{3x}{2c}$ d $\dfrac{2n^2}{c}$

e $x+3$ f $\dfrac{5-a}{2}$ g $\dfrac{a+1}{2}$ h 3

i $\dfrac{1}{3}$ j $\dfrac{x+5}{2(x-1)}$ k 5 l $\dfrac{2}{3}$

m $\dfrac{a-5}{a+2}$ n 2 o $\dfrac{a+b}{2}$ p $\dfrac{3}{x-n}$

q $\dfrac{1}{5}$ r $\dfrac{3}{2}$ s $x+2$ t $\dfrac{4}{c-3}$

u $\dfrac{2}{3}$ v $2(x-1)$

2 a 2 b $\dfrac{2(x+3)}{x+4}$ c $\dfrac{2}{3}$ d $\dfrac{b-c}{b+c}$

e $\dfrac{b}{b+1}$ f $\dfrac{x}{5}$ g $x-2$ h $\dfrac{2}{2n+3}$

i $c+1$ j $\dfrac{a}{b}$ k $\dfrac{x+3}{x-3}$ l $\dfrac{4}{8+m}$

3 a $\dfrac{1}{x+4}$ b $x-3$ c $\dfrac{c+5}{c-5}$ d $\dfrac{a+3}{a+2}$

e $\dfrac{x+9}{x-1}$ f $\dfrac{x-3}{3}$ g $\dfrac{x+3}{2x-3}$ h $\dfrac{s-1}{2s-1}$

i $\dfrac{a-n}{a+3}$ j $\dfrac{x}{4}$ k $\dfrac{v+3}{v}$

4 a ^-c b $^-1$

5 a $^-1$ b $\dfrac{^-1}{2}$ c $^-2$ d $\dfrac{^-1}{2}$ e $\dfrac{^-1}{2}$

f $^-2$ g $\dfrac{^-3}{2}$ h $2-x$ i $\dfrac{^-(x+5)}{2}$

1 a $\dfrac{ab}{c}$ b $\dfrac{2pr}{q}$ c $\dfrac{3e}{f}$ d $\dfrac{3x^2}{y}$ e $\dfrac{x}{y}$

f $\dfrac{2a}{x+y}$ g $\dfrac{q(m+n)}{p}$ h $\dfrac{x(a+b)}{y}$ i $\dfrac{ax}{by}$

j $\dfrac{4q}{5p}$ k $\dfrac{x^2}{yz}$ l $\dfrac{3t(a+b)}{5r}$ m $\dfrac{bp}{aq}$

n $\dfrac{5x}{4y}$ o $\dfrac{a^2}{bc}$ p $\dfrac{2x}{x+y}$ q $\dfrac{2g^2}{3h^2}$

r $\dfrac{2a(c+d)}{5}$ s $\dfrac{a}{bc}$ t $\dfrac{x}{y^3}$

2 a 3 b $\dfrac{a}{6b}$ c a d $\dfrac{b}{y}$

e $\dfrac{a}{2}$ f $\dfrac{p}{2q}$ g $\dfrac{z}{xy^2}$ h $\dfrac{n}{m}$

3 a $\dfrac{5x}{y^3}$ b $\dfrac{4p}{q^3}$ c $\dfrac{a(a+d)}{c(b+c)}$ d $\dfrac{x}{y}$

e $\dfrac{10}{21}$ f $\dfrac{x(2x+3)}{6(x+4)}$ g $\dfrac{1}{3}$ h $\dfrac{x^3(x+2)}{5}$

i $\dfrac{5(x+3)}{x+5}$ j $\dfrac{2(c-7)}{(c+7)(3c-4)}$ k $\dfrac{x+3}{x-1}$

l $\dfrac{c+4}{16}$ m $\dfrac{n(n+2)}{3(2n+7)}$ n $\dfrac{4y^3(2y+5)}{y+1}$

o $\dfrac{(2n+5)^3}{n(4n^2+25)}$ p 1

4 a 2 b 8

5 a $\dfrac{x}{yz}$ b $\dfrac{xz}{y}$

6 a $\dfrac{a}{2b}$ b $\dfrac{ab}{2}$ c $\dfrac{1}{y}$ d $\dfrac{x^2}{y}$

e $\dfrac{p^2}{q^2}$ f $\dfrac{p^3}{q^3}$

1 a $\dfrac{5x}{8}$ b $\dfrac{x-3}{a}$ c $\dfrac{2x}{a}$ d $\dfrac{6n}{n+1}$

e $\dfrac{4x+3}{2(x+3)}$ f $\dfrac{13x}{10}$ g $\dfrac{20+x}{4}$ h $\dfrac{30-x}{5}$

i $\dfrac{x-3}{x}$ j $\dfrac{4x}{3}$ k $\dfrac{3+x}{3x}$ l $\dfrac{3a-2x}{ax}$

m $\dfrac{cn+ax}{an}$ n $\dfrac{10x+4}{5x}$ o $\dfrac{3x}{2}$ p $\dfrac{13}{2x}$

q $\dfrac{29}{12x}$ r $\dfrac{2}{x+2}$ s $\dfrac{5}{2(x+2)}$ t $\dfrac{11x+12}{x(x+2)}$

2 a $\dfrac{7x+10}{(x+1)(x+2)}$ b $\dfrac{5x+1}{(x+1)(x-1)}$

c $\dfrac{2n+7}{(n+2)(n+3)}$ d $\dfrac{6c+14}{(c+2)(c+3)}$

e $\dfrac{2m-25}{(m+5)(m-2)}$ f $\dfrac{11x-2}{(5x-2)(4x-1)}$

g $\dfrac{6a-32}{(3a+2)(3a-2)}$ h $\dfrac{6x^2+17x}{(x+2)(x+7)}$

i $\dfrac{3c^2+8c}{(c+3)(c+2)}$ j $\dfrac{-x^2-3x}{(2x+1)(3x-1)}$

k $\dfrac{7n+15}{n(n+1)}$ l $\dfrac{2n^2+6n-2}{(n+3)(n+4)}$

3 a $\dfrac{4}{3(x+y)}$ b $\dfrac{x+3}{x(x+1)}$

c $\dfrac{5}{6(x+2)}$ d $\dfrac{x+1}{x(x+5)}$

e $\dfrac{x}{(x+4)(x+1)}$ f $\dfrac{4x+11}{(x+2)(x+5)}$

g $\dfrac{-3x-7}{(x+3)(x-3)}$ h $\dfrac{10x+9}{(2x+1)(x+2)}$

i $\dfrac{8x+14}{(x+1)(x+2)(x+3)}$

4 a $\dfrac{8}{3(x+1)}$ b $\dfrac{3x-2}{3(x-3)}$

c $\dfrac{5}{x-3}$ d $\dfrac{2a(2a+9)}{(a+5)(a+3)}$

e $\dfrac{7x^2 - 29x - 3}{(x+3)(x-4)}$ f $\dfrac{a}{(x-a)^2}$

g $\dfrac{1}{2(x-1)}$ h $\dfrac{x(x+1)}{(x+3)(x+2)(x-2)}$

i $\dfrac{5a+17}{(a+4)(a+4)(a+3)}$ j $\dfrac{2}{(c-4)(c-2)}$

k $\dfrac{13}{(2x-3)^2(x+5)}$ l $\dfrac{6x}{(x-4)(x+4)^2}$

Chapter Review Exercises

1 $^-a^2 + 3a - 4$ 2 $^-x^2 - 3x - 2$

3 a $mq + mr + pq + pr$ b $x^2 + x - 42$
  c $^-12n^2 + 68n - 63$ d $x^2 + 16x + 64$
  e $p^2 - 49$ f $121 - 110x + 25x^2$

4 a $6x - 71$ b $5t^2 + 20t - 74$

5 a $8(7 - 3x)$ b $3t(x - 2p)$
  c $5k(3 + 4k)$ d $(x - 5)(x + 7)$
  e $7y(^-2x + 3a)$ or $^-7y(2x - 3a)$
  f $(c - 8)(c + 8)$ g $3(x - 3)(x + 3)$
  h $9x^3(2 - 3x^3)$ i $2\pi r(1 - h)$
  j $4\sin\theta(\sin\theta - 3)$ k $(a + b)(c + d)$
  l $(3x - 2)(x - 5)$ m $(b + 7)(a + 1)$
  n $9(p - 2q)(p + 2q)$ o $(a + x)(y + 4)$

6 100 7 $^-4a(a - 2)$

8 a F b F c F

9 $^-1, ^-5, 3$ 10 $\dfrac{1}{2}x^2 - 1$

11 a $(x + 5)(x + 4)$ b $(x + 7)(x - 4)$
  c $(a - 6)^2$ d $(5c + 1)^2$
  e $(2x - 3)(x - 1)$ f $(6n + 5)(n - 3)$

12 a $x(x^2 - 5x - 4)$ b $(x + 7)(x + 6)$

13 $(n + 1)(n + 15) = n^2 + 16n + 15$
  $(n - 1)(n + 15) = n^2 + 14n - 15$
  $(n + 1)(n - 15) = n^2 - 14n - 15$
  $(n - 1)(n - 15) = n^2 - 16n + 15$
  $(n + 3)(n + 5) = n^2 + 8n + 15$
  $(n - 3)(n + 5) = n^2 + 2n - 15$
  $(n + 3)(n - 5) = n^2 + 2n - 15$
  $(n - 3)(n - 5) = n^2 - 8n + 15$

14 a $\dfrac{a}{4}$ b $\dfrac{a-2}{3a}$

  c $\dfrac{5}{x-3}$ d $8x^2$

  e $\dfrac{4x(x+5)}{x-5}$ f $\dfrac{x}{x-5}$

  g $\dfrac{3x+2}{x+2}$ h $\dfrac{3a+5}{(a+3)(a+1)}$

  i $\dfrac{-1}{n+3}$ j $\dfrac{1-c}{c(c+2)(c+2)}$

  k $\dfrac{5d+29}{2(d+3)(d-3)}$ l $\dfrac{8}{(x+1)(x-3)}$

15 $(100 + 2)^2$
  $= 100^2 + 2 \times 200 + 2^2$
  $= 10\ 404$

Keeping Mathematically Fit

PART A

1 310 cm, 3100 mm, 0·0031 km
2 b 3 yes 4 30° 5 17
6 B 7 22·5 8 (3, 4) 9 A
10 49%

PART B

1 a number of hours worked
  b $3062.50
2 72 688 3 $\sqrt{208}$

4

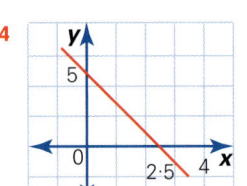

5 27 m from X

Chapter 12

MathsCheck

1–3 discuss answers

4 a

Score	Tally	Freq.
0	IIII	4
1	II	2
2	ĦI	5
3	IIII	4
4	III	3
5	II	2
	Total	20

  b 20 c 2 d 9

5 a

Score	Tally	Freq.
0	ĦI	5
1	III	3
2	IIII	4
3	ĦI	5
4	ĦI	5
5	III	3
6	II	2
7	III	3
	Total	30

  b 30 c $\dfrac{1}{10}$ d 27%

  e No, one $2 coin is worth more than nineteen 10 cent coins
6 a 1600 b 200 c 19%
7 a i federal taxes ii 53 cents
  b $2.24 c discuss
8 a around 300 000 b around 53%
  c the column graph, since it shows the actual numbers
9 a 2 b $\dfrac{16}{35}$

c Since the results are from children in Year 9, there must be at least one child in each family.

10 a 9   **b** 3 heads   **c** 4 heads
   d 4   **e** 45%

11 a 2   **b** 5   **c** 29   **d** discuss

12
Touch football results

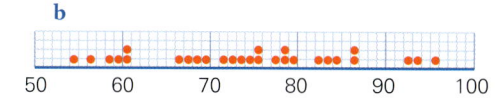

Histogram: No. of games (y-axis, 0–8) vs No. of tries (x-axis, 0–5)

13
Take-away food habit

Line graph: No. of families (y-axis, 0–20) vs No. of times (x-axis, 0–4)

14 a
```
5 | 4 6 8 9
6 | 0 0 5 6 7 8
7 | 0 1 2 3 4 4 6 7 7 8
8 | 1 2 3 5 5
9 | 2 3 5
```

b

Dot plot from 50 to 100

c i 54 kg   **ii** 95 kg
d most between 65 and 85 kg
e discuss

15 a
```
4 | 3 6 8 9 9
5 | 1 2 2 5 5 7 7
6 | 0 0 1 2 4 6 6
7 |
8 | 3
```

b

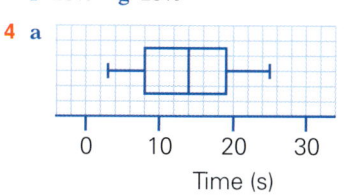

Dot plot from 40 to 80

c 83 min
d train cancellation, missed train, didn't go directly to work etc
e discuss

16 a The scale only goes up to 16.
   b discuss

17 65; discuss assumptions

1 a 72   **b** 65·5   **c** 78   **d** 68   **e** 75

2 median = 15
   lowest score = 4
   highest score = 27
   lower quartile = 12
   upper quartile = 22

3 a 76   **b** 54   **c** 93   **d** 60   **e** 84
   f 25%   **g** 25%

4 a

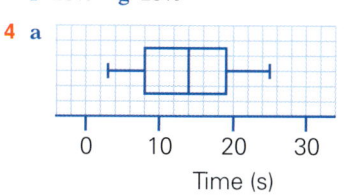

Box plot: Time (s), scale 0–30

b

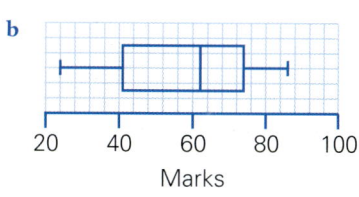

Box plot: Marks, scale 20–100

c

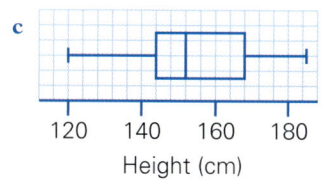

Box plot: Height (cm), scale 120–180

5 a i 17·5   **b i** 3   **c i** 32
   ii 10   **ii** 1·5   **ii** 25·5
   iii 20   **iii** 5   **iii** 44
   iv 10   **iv** 3·5   **iv** 18·5

6 a i 1·4 cm   **ii** 5·4 cm   **b** 3·35 cm
   c i 2·15 cm   **ii** 3·9 cm   **d** 1·75 cm
   e

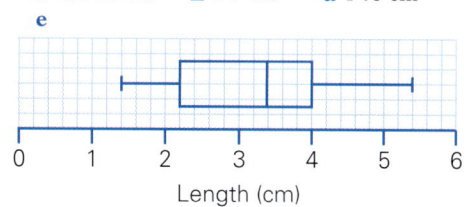

Box plot: Length (cm), scale 0–6

   f $\frac{1}{2}$

7 a 10   **b** 43   **c** 29   **d** 75%   **e** 75%   **f** 15
   g 33   **h** all individual scores not given

8 a 34 s   **b i** 30 s   **ii** 41·5 s   **c** 11·5 s
   d

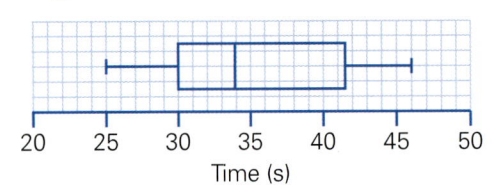

Time (s)

   e discuss   **f** yes, you know all of the scores

9 a 8 h 30 min   **b** 6 h 15 min
   c 1 h 45 min   **d** 20
   e i slightly longer than the median journey
      time
    ii one of the longest times
   iii very unlikely!

EXERCISE 12B

1

	range	mode	median	mean
a	2	5	5	5
b	5	15	13·5	13
c	5	0, 2	2	2·2
d	8	3	4	4·75
e	80	30	40	47·5
f	8	13	14	14·75

   g all multiplied by 10
   h all except range are increased by 10

2 a

Score	Frequency	fx
0	3	0
1	5	5
2	7	14
3	10	30
4	6	24
5	4	20
6	1	6
Total	36	99

    i range = 6
   ii mode = 3
  iii mean = 2·8
   iv median = 3
  b they contribute to the *frequency*; they still
    represent a score

3 a 2·1   **b** 3

4 a 4   **b** 3

   c

Score	Frequency	fx
1	4	4
2	3	6
3	10	30
4	6	24
5	5	25
Total	28	89

   d 3·2 (to 1 decimal place)

5

Score	Frequency	fx
0	3	0
1	4	4
2	4	8
3	3	9
4	3	12
5	1	5
Total	18	38

   mean = 2·1̇

6 52 kg

7 a 14
  b The median is calculated as the mean of the
    central two values if there is an even number
    of scores. To get a mean of 49, the two values
    need not be 49.

8 4·35 m   **9** 25   **10** 2·3 m   **11** 160·4 cm

12 a no   **b** their sum is 48

13 when there are the same number of scores in
   each set, or when the means of the two sets are
   equal

14 18, 19, 20

15 discuss

EXERCISE 12C

1

c.f.
2
9
19
30
36
39
40

   median = 3

2

f	c.f.
4	4
12	16
13	29
7	36
8	44
6	50
2	52
0	52
2	54

   median = 2

3 a

x	f	c.f.
5	1	1
6	3	4
7	4	8
8	7	15
9	7	22
10	5	27
11	3	30

   median = 8·5
  b 1   **c** 9

4 a

Score	Frequency
0	4
1	7
2	12
3	11
4	7
5	5

b 46

c

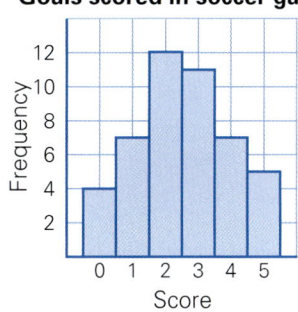

Goals scored in soccer games

d 2 goals

5 a

x	f	c.f.
0	7	7
1	9	16
2	8	24
3	2	26
4	3	29
5	1	30

b 1   **c** mean or mode—discuss

EXERCISE 12D

1 a

c.f.
1
7
21
38
40
40
41

b

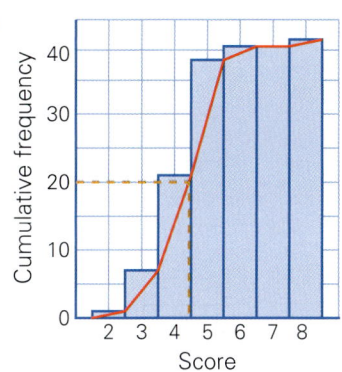

c 4

2 a 4   **b** 29   **c** 6   **d** 22
   e 9   **f** 2   **g** 7   **h** 6, 8

3 a

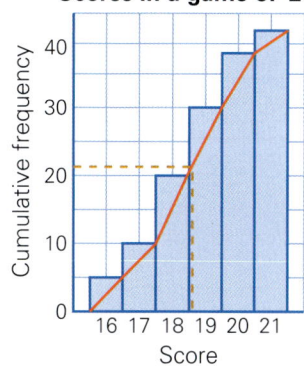

Scores in a game of '21'

b 19   **c** 17, 20, IQR = 3

4 a

x	f	c.f.
2	3	3
3	5	8
4	4	12
5	7	19
6	8	27
7	9	36
8	8	44
9	5	49
10	5	54
11	3	57
12	3	60

b 19   **c** 16   **d** 5   **e** 9   **f** 7

g there are more combinations that give 7 than give 3

h no, only the *sum* was recorded

5 a 100   **b** 17

c

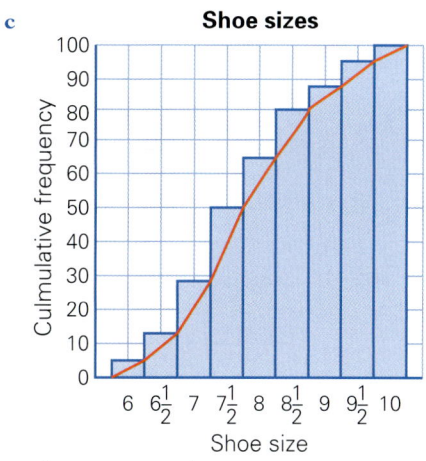

Shoe sizes

d $7\frac{3}{4}$ **e** $1\frac{1}{2}$

f

x	f	fx
6	5	30
$6\frac{1}{2}$	8	52
7	16	112
$7\frac{1}{2}$	21	1575
8	17	136
$8\frac{1}{2}$	13	110·5
9	8	72
9	9	85·5
10	3	30
	Total	785·5

mean = 7·855

g no, since frequencies are always being added on

6 discuss

EXERCISE 12E

1 a 15   **b** 9   **c** 49   **d** 8·5
   e 33·5   **f** 34·5   **g** 164   **h** 132·5

2 a

Class	C.c.	Tally	Freq.
28–36	32	II	2
37–45	41	IIII	4
46–54	50	IIII I	6
55–63	59	IIII IIII I	11
64–72	68	IIII IIII II	12
73–81	77	IIII II	7
82–90	86	IIII I	6
91–99	95	II	2

b 64–72

c no, highest and lowest scores cannot be determined from the table

d 27   **e** $\frac{3}{25}$

f

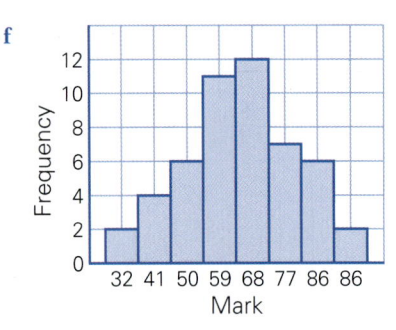

g discuss

3 a

Class	Class centre	f
145–148	146·5	1
149–152	150·5	0
153–156	154·5	5
157–160	158·5	6
161–164	162·5	5
165–168	166·5	4
169–172	170·5	6
173–176	174·5	2
177–180	178·5	1
	Total	30

b

Heights of Year 9 students

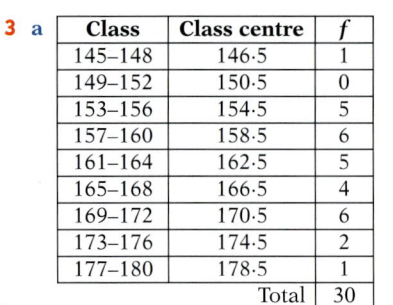

c represents data more accurately, but involves more work

4 a

Class	C.c. (x)	f	fx	c.f.
80–86	83	3	249	3
87–93	90	12	1080	15
94–100	97	7	679	22
101–107	104	4	416	26
108–114	111	12	1332	38
115–121	118	2	236	40
	Total	40	3992	

b 40   **c** 15   **d** 45%

e

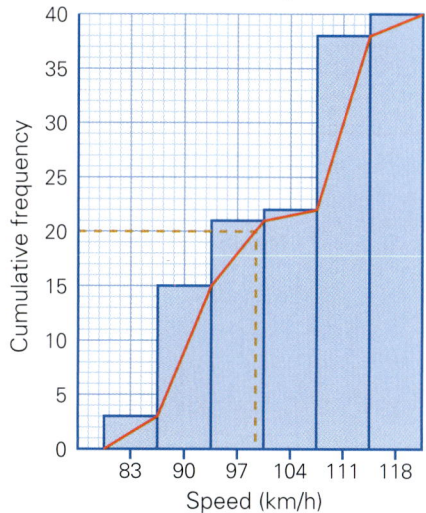

Motorists' speeds

(Cumulative frequency vs Speed (km/h): x-axis 83, 90, 97, 104, 111, 118)

f 99 km/h   **g** 99·8 km/h

5 a

Class	C.c. (x)	f	c.f.
133–139	136	2	2
140–146	143	2	4
147–153	150	4	8
154–160	157	6	14
161–167	164	4	18
168–174	171	2	20
175–181	178	2	22
182–188	185	2	24
	Total	24	

b

Golf scores

(Cumulative frequency vs Scores: x-axis 136, 143, 150, 157, 164, 171, 178, 185)

c 158

6 a Note: the table may vary depending on the classes chosen.

Class	C.c. (x)	f	c.f.
40–49	44·5	2	2
50–59	54·5	8	10
60-69	64·5	7	17
70–79	74·5	7	24
80–89	84·5	9	33
90–99	94·5	8	41
100–109	104·5	5	46
110–119	114·5	3	49
120–129	124·5	1	50

b

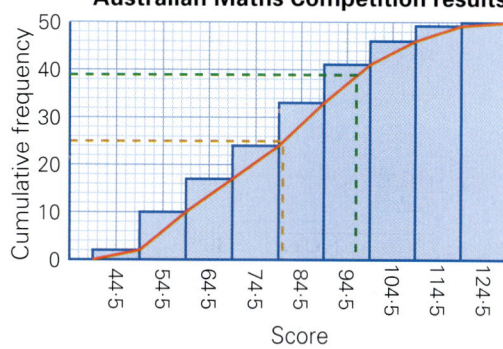

Australian Maths Competition results

(Cumulative frequency vs Score: x-axis 44·5, 54·5, 64·5, 74·5, 84·5, 94·5, 104·5, 114·5, 124·5)

c around 80   **d** 94

EXERCISE 12F

1 a i 8, 10   **ii** 8·8 (to 1 decimal place)
   iii 9
   b discuss

2 a

Score	Frequency	fx
$22 000	24	528 000
$27 000	4	108 000
$31 500	2	63 000
$47 000	1	47 000
$68 000	1	68 000
Total	32	814 000

b $25 438   **c** $22 000   **d** $22 000

e

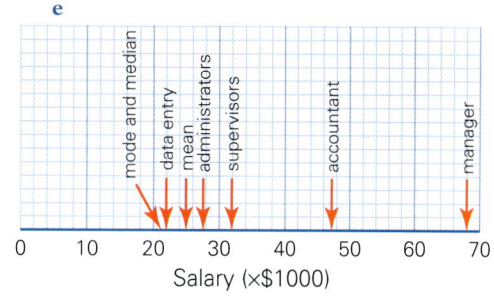

(Salary (×$1000): x-axis 0, 10, 20, 30, 40, 50, 60, 70; labelled mode and median, data entry, mean, administrators, supervisors, accountant, manager)

f i mean (highest value)
   ii median or mode (lowest value)

3 a mean = $189 167   **b** discuss
   mode = $170 000
   median = $180 000

4 a i use mean ($38) **c** discuss
  ii use mode ($20)
  iii use median ($30)
 b discuss

Chapter Review Exercises
1, 2 discuss
 3 a magpie **b** 89
  c 37% (to the nearest percent)
 4 a mortgage payment **b** $110 or $120
  c 10%
 5 a 16·3 **b** 15·5 **c** 15

 6 a
```
3 | 5 9
4 | 5 5 6 8 8 9
5 | 2 3 4 5 7 8 9
6 | 1 2 6
7 | 1 5
```
 b 53·5 min
 c i 47 **ii** 60 **d** 13
 e

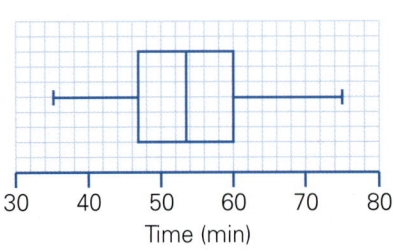

Time (min)

 f Clustered between 45 and 62. Others are outliers.

7 a

Score	Frequency	fx
0	2	0
1	4	4
2	6	12
3	6	18
4	4	16
5	6	30
6	2	12
Total	30	92

 b 3·1 **c** 2, 3 and 5 **d** 3
 e

Number of trees per block

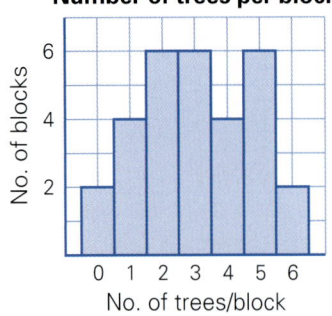

No. of trees/block

8 a

x	f	$c.f.$
0	15	15
1	25	40
2	21	61
3	13	74
4	6	80
5	1	81
6	0	81
7	1	82

 b

Number of pets in family

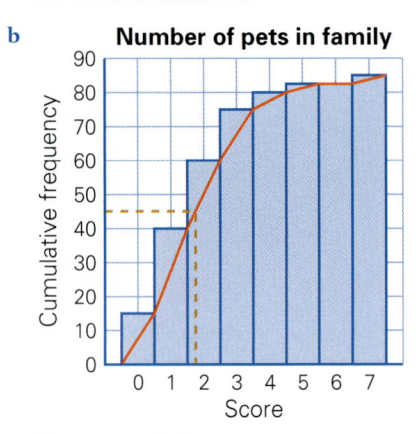

Score

 c 82 **d** 2
9 a 18 **b** 3 **c** 5 **d** 2 **e** 2
10 a

Class	$C.c\ (x)$	f	fx	$c.f.$
40-49	44·5	2	89·0	2
50-59	54·5	7	381·5	9
60-69	64·5	7	451·5	16
70-79	74·5	4	298·0	20
80-89	84·5	8	676·0	28
90-99	94·5	6	567·0	34
100-109	104·5	3	313·5	37
110-119	114·5	3	343·5	40
Total		40	3120	

 b

Number of basketball cards

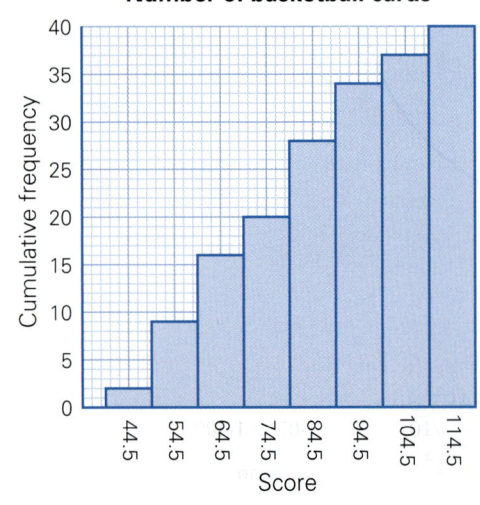

Score

c 80–89   **d** 78   **e** 79·5
11 a 129

b

x	f	fx	$c.f.$
17	4	68	4
22	10	220	14
27	23	621	37
32	38	1216	75
37	30	1110	105
42	16	672	121
47	8	376	129
Total	129	4283	

c 33·2 min

d

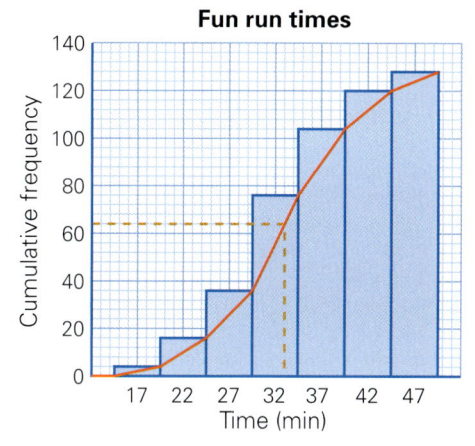

Fun run times

e 33 min
f Lower: 29 min, 25% of the runners were
slower than this. Upper: 38 min, 25% of the
runners were faster than this.
12 a i 60   **ii** 67·5   **iii** 70
b the median; outliers distort mean, mode
has low frequency
13 29

Keeping Mathematically Fit

PART A
1 $2.97
2 a $m = 4r + 2$ **b** 26   **c** 12
3 area $= \dfrac{x^2}{4\pi}$ **4** B
5 a $\frac{1}{2}x + 3$ **b** $x + y = 6$
c $2x + y = 6$ **d** $x - y + 1 = 0$
e $y = \frac{1}{4}x^2$ **f** $y = \frac{1}{2}x^2$
6 C   **7** $\sqrt{10}$ **8** A   **9** 12
10 7 : 20

PART B
1 $\sqrt{10}$ **2** 3·075, ⁻1·409   **3** 11
4 $\dfrac{13}{25}$ **5 a** no   **b** discuss

Chapter 13

MathsCheck
1 a 3000 mL   **b** 8000 L   **c** 2·5 kL
d 645 cm³   **e** 3·5 L   **f** 700 mL
g 500 mL   **h** 6·5 cm³   **i** 500 mm³
j 2 300 000 cm³   **k** 400 mL
l 250 L   **m** 0·45 L   **n** 2·6 kL
o 2000 L   **p** 23 600 cm³   **q** 0·056 L
r 800 L   **s** 40 000 mL
t 3 040 000 mm³   **u** 4·2 × 10⁹ cm³
2 a $\frac{1}{5}$ L   **b** $\frac{3}{4}$ L   **c** $\frac{1}{40}$ L
3 22   **4** blue 4·2 L   **5** 6
6 a 12 cm³   **b** 175 mm³   **c** 15·3 cm³
d 1809 mm³   **e** 3·75 m³   **f** 137 cm³
7 a 512 cm³   **b** 70·8 m³   **c** 17·6 cm³
8 a 1250 cm³   **b** 516 000 mm³
c 0·308 m³
9 5 h 6 min
10 a 18   **b** 16
11 a 4000 drops   **b** 3 h 37 min   **c** 4320 mL
d 8·3 drops per min

EXERCISE 13A
1 a 210 mm³   **b** 5·47 m³   **c** 1740 mm³
d 10 000 mm³   **e** 5·21 m³   **f** 158·8 cm³
2 a 2346 cm³   **b** 2·346 L
3 a 14·7 m³   **b** 14 700 L
4 a 163 mL   **b** 369 kL   **c** 204 L
5 a 17·23 cm   **b** 1450 cm
6 53 773 m³   **7** 0·25 mm
8 24 cm   **9** 10 cm   **10** 4·3 m³
11 a 23 560   **b** 23·77 m
12 25·2 cm   **13** 3·07 mm³   **14** 0·2 mm
15 374 L   **16** 1937·5 kL
17 a 11·3 cm   **b** 19·5 cm by 13 cm by 11·3 cm
c 21·5%
18 6·5 cm
19 a 126
b 4 cm along 28 cm edge,
5 cm along 32 cm edge
20 4 times

EXERCISE 13B
1 a 30 970 mm³   **b** 40·7 m³
c 11·3 mm³   **d** 171 cm³
e 3696 mm³   **f** 321·4 cm³
g 185·8 m³   **h** 641·9 cm³
i 82·8 m³   **j** 359 100 cm³
k 2058 cm³   **l** 13 152 cm³
m 10 703·8 mm³   **n** 19·3 m³
o 5·9 m³

EXERCISE 13C
1 a 144 cm³   **b** 1·5 m³
c 23 618·6 cm³   **d** 4800 mm³
e 278 666·7 cm³   **f** 501·8 mm³
2 64·6 cm³   **3** 377·85 m³
4 60·7 cm³   **5** 0·32 m³

6 a 204 cm³ **b** 5600 mm³ **c** 0·342 m³

7 a i 6 **ii** $\frac{1}{6}$ **b** 2744 cm³

  c 457·3 cm³ **d** 457·3 cm³
8 a 21·4 cm **b** 714·1 cm³
9 5·6 cm **10** 3·22 m
11 869·3 cm³ **12** 37·2 cm³

EXERCISE 13D
1 a 103·7 m³ **b** 2908·3 mm³
  c 535·3 cm³ **d** 1442·0 mm³
  e 143·9 m³ **f** 340·6 mm³
2 a 183·3 cm³ **b** 88·7 m³
  c 250 699·5 cm³ **d** 1·2 cm³
3 a 1·3 m³ **b** 1364·6 cm³
  c 225 666·9 m³
4 64 mL **5** 7 cm **6** 13·8 cm **7** 68·3 m
8 a 12 cm **b** 314·2 cm³
9 13·9 cm, 181·4°
10 radius of cone is $\sqrt{3}$ times radius of cylinder
11 a your estimate **b** 29·6%
  c 11·9 cm
12 92·2 cm³
13 a 1 : 2 **b** 4 : 1

EXERCISE 13E
1 a 2144·7 cm³ **b** 179·6 mm³
  c 2806·2 m³ **d** 5·0 cm³
  e 1·8 m³ **f** 22 257·4 mm³
2 113.1 mL **3** 16 886·9 cm³
4 a 10 289·8 m³ **b** 124·2 cm³
  c 78 739·6
5 1·08 × 10¹² km³
6 a 8181·2 cm³ **b** 52·4%
7 4·6 cm **8** 18 **9** 11 cm

EXERCISE 13F
1 a 25 300 cm³ **b** 18·0 cm³ **c** 3230 mm³
  d 11·9 cm³ **e** 33·0 m³ **f** 71 700 cm³
  g 5760 mm³ **h** 116 cm³ **i** 41 600 mm³
2 a 17·6 m³ **b** 12
3 9031 cm³ **4** 933·1 cm³
5 a 1·97 m³ **b** 72·0 mm³ **c** 4·32 m³
6 126·7 kL **7** 22 litres **8** 159·2 mL
9 a 567·6 cm³ **b** 11·29 m

Chapter Review Exercises
1 any 3 of these:
  650 000 mL
  650 000 cm³, 0·65 kL
  0·65 m³
2 179 mL
3 a 7128 mm³ **b** 4967·6 cm³ **c** 1·1 m³
4 several possibilities **5** 0·636 m
6 a 9533·16 m³ **b** 4·20 m³
  c 15·79 cm³ **d** 3500 mm³
  e 23 296·22 cm³ **f** 98·29 m³
7 4·65 cm
8 a 7·2 × 10¹⁸ m³ **b** 92 160 mm³
  c 123·8 m³

9 a 17 m³ **b** 6 trucks **c** 226
10 4 mm **11** 271·5 cm³
12 a 10 cm **b** 216°
13 1 425 592 mm³
  = 1425·6 cm³

Keeping Mathematically Fit

PART A
1 C **2** no **3** 7·2 **4** $\frac{x}{2y}$
5 540 000 cm² **6** 20
7 1 pm to 1:15 pm **8** 18
9 11 cm **10** 16

PART B
1 1·25 m **2** ⁻1·5
3 me: 320; soh: 384 **4** 10
5 a 16x + 20 sq. units **b** 2·5

Cumulative Review 4
1 a t + 23 **b** a² + 8a + 15
  c x² + 8x + 16 **d** d² − 11d + 18
2 a 5y(3xy − 5) **b** 2mn(4mn + 5)
3 a 895 to 904·9 **b** 850 to 949·9
4 a 3150 **b** 12 500 **c** 0·003 15
  d 3·20 × 10⁵
5 a 1·273 × 104 **b** 3 × 10⁻¹
  c 1·058 × 10⁻²
6 a 20 000 **b** 0·798
  c 0·000 005 002
7 a $\frac{8}{125}$ **b** 8 **c** $\frac{1}{10}$ **d** 5
8 any area from 1·15 ha to 1·24 ha
9 8 cm
10 a 2 : 30 **b** 3 : 10
11 $3600, $900, 2700 **12** $9
13 check with teacher **14** t
15 4 h 19 min **16** 7·2 L/h
17 a i 4·38 m **ii** 0·9775 m²
  b i 13·17 m **ii** 8·42 m²
18 a g = 3·8 **b** p = 1·75 **c** x = ⁻3·4
19 a x > ⁻2 **b** p < ⁻5

20 a $h = \frac{r}{3m}$ **b** $f = \dfrac{4 - \left[\frac{y-t}{x}\right]}{g}$

21 336 cm²
22 a n = 30° (∠s on a straight line)
  b a = 90° (∠s on a straight line)
  b = 49° (vert. opp. ∠s)
  c = 41° (∠ sum of Δ)
  d = 299° (∠s at a point)
  c a = 106° (∠s on a straight line)
  b = 114° (∠ sum of a quad)
  c = 114° (corresp. ∠s on ∥ lines)
  d a = 124° (coint. ∠s on ∥ lines)
  b = 73° (coint. ∠s on ∥ lines)
  e a = 64° (corresp. ∠s on ∥ lines)
  b = 64° (base ∠s of isosceles Δ)
  c = 64° (alt. ∠s on ∥ lines)

f $a = 103°$ (alt. ∠s on ∥ lines)
  $b = 59°$ (ext. ∠s of Δ)
  $c = 59°$ (vert. opposite ∠s)
  $d = 44°$ (alt. ∠s on ∥ lines)

23 D

24 a

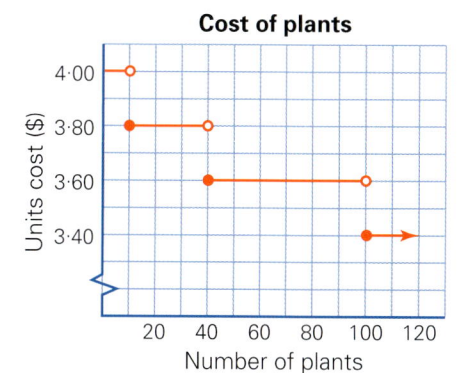

Cost of plants

b $3.80   **c i** $95   **ii** $270
25 7·1   **26** yes, $c^2 = a^2 + b^2$
27 a 66°   **b** 50°   **c** 57°
28 a 3·85   **b** 7·35   **c** 5·17
29 a 56°   **b** 26°   **c** 45°
30 8·7 m   **31** 228 km
32 35°   **33** 8·2 cm
34 a 81° and 99°   **b** 13·1 cm
35 a i 8   **ii** $\sqrt{13}$ **iii** $\sqrt{34}$
  b i $(0, ^-2)$ **ii** $(^-1, 1)$ **iii** $(^-1.5, -1)$
  c i $\frac{^-2}{3}$ **ii** $\frac{1}{2}$ **iii** $\frac{1}{3}$
  iv $\frac{1}{2}$ **v** $^-3$ **vi** $^-3$
  d EF same gradient   **e** 45°
  f 0·6
36 $(4, 4)$
37 a $y = 3x - 2$ **b** $3x - y - 2 = 0$
38 PQ gradient = 2, length = $\sqrt{180}$
  RS gradient = $^-\frac{1}{2}$, length = $\sqrt{45}$
39 7·2 cm   **40** $d = ^-1.5, e = ^-4$
41 $^-13$
42 a PR **b** $∠SPR$ **c** AT **d** TBA
43 a not necessarily congruent
  b i $\Delta GKJ ≡ \Delta HKJ$ **ii** RHS
44 In Δs MPQ and MRQ
  $MP = MR$ (adjacent sides of kite)
  $PQ = RQ$ (adjacent sides of kite)
  MQ is common
  $\therefore \Delta MPQ ≡ \Delta MRQ$ (SSS)
45 $506.18   **46** $571.66
47 a $69   **b** $391   **c** $83.09   **d** $31.61
48 a $8606.15   **b** $554.43
49 a $615
  b $640.56
  $25.56 extra by compounding

50 D   **51** C
52 a $9 - 6c + c^2$ **b** $25 - 4d^2$
  c $9 + 24t + 16t^2$ **d** $^-15n^2 + 22n - 8$
53 a $(2n + c)(2n - c)$ **b** $3c(c - 4)$
  c $(n + 3)(n + 4)$ **d** $(x - 4)(x + 2)$
  e $2(2p + 3)(p + 1)$ **f** $(a + 4b)^2$
  g $(n + p)(t + s)$
54 a $\frac{2x - 1}{4}$ **b** $\frac{x + 9}{x + 2}$ **c** $\frac{b}{x + y}$
  d $\frac{x}{2y}$ **e** $\frac{t}{5}$ **f** $\frac{1}{x}$
  g $\frac{3(x - 2)}{x + 2}$ **h** $\frac{4p + 1}{4(2p + 3)}$

55 a
```
3 | 9
4 | 0 2 3 5 6 7
5 | 1 1 3 4 5 5 9
6 | 0 1 3 6 7 8
7 | 0 0 1 3 5 6 8
8 | 1 2 6
```
  b median = 60·5
  c

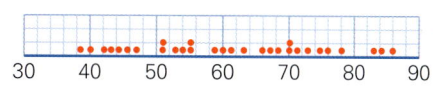

  d Fairly evenly spread between 39 and 86.
  No outliers.

56 B
57 a 3 years 10 months   **b** 25 months
  c 17 months, 34 months
  d

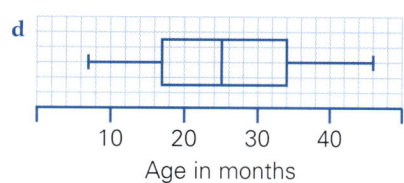

Age in months

58 a

Group	Class centre (x)	Frequency (f)	fx
0–9	4.5	1	4.5
10–19	14.5	4	58
20–29	24.5	10	245
30–39	34.5	9	310
40–49	44.5	6	267
		30	885

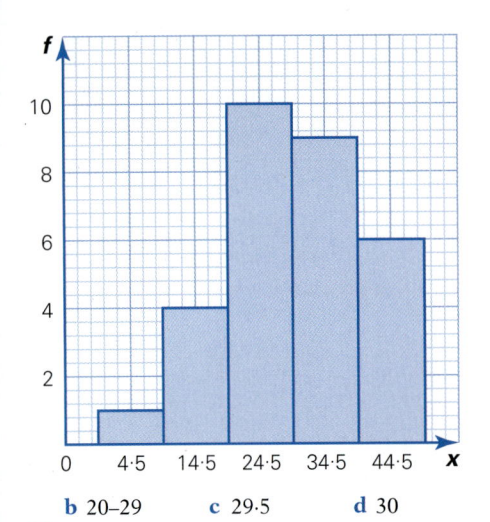

b 20–29   **c** 29·5   **d** 30

59 a

Group	Class centre (x)	Frequency (f)	fx	cf
1–3	2	1	2	1
4–6	5	4	20	5
7–9	8	7	56	12
10–12	11	10	110	22
13–15	14	12	168	34
16–18	17	17	289	51
19–21	20	8	160	59
22–24	23	14	322	73
25–27	26	2	52	75
28–30	29	5	145	80
		80	1324	

b

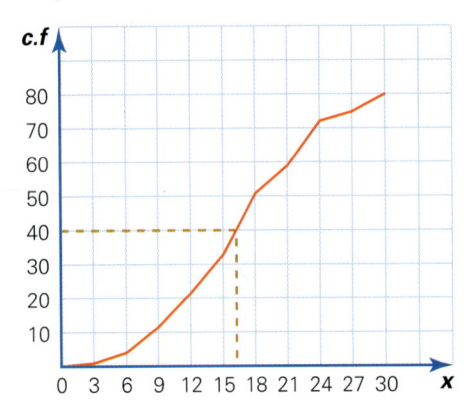

    c 16–18   **d** $16.60   **e** $16

60 a 450 cm^2 **b** 212·3 mm^2 **c** 146·5 cm^2
    d 1029·1 mm^2

61 a i 12 cm × 4 cm × 4 cm
      ii 100·5 cm^3 **iii** 91·5 cm^3
    b 50·3 cm^3

62 12·6 cm